Nicholas Patrick Wiseman

Lectures on the principal doctrines and practices of the Catholic Church

Delivered at St. Mary's Moorfields during the Lent of 1836. Vol. 1

Nicholas Patrick Wiseman

Lectures on the principal doctrines and practices of the Catholic Church
Delivered at St. Mary's Moorfields during the Lent of 1836. Vol. 1

ISBN/EAN: 9783337259884

Printed in Europe, USA, Canada, Australia, Japan

Cover: Foto ©Lupo / pixelio.de

More available books at **www.hansebooks.com**

LECTURES

ON THE

Principal Doctrines and Practices

OF THE

CATHOLIC CHURCH;

DELIVERED AT ST. MARY'S, MOORFIELDS, DURING THE LENT OF 1836.

By CARDINAL WISEMAN.

TWO VOLUMES IN ONE.

VOL. 1.

*Sixth American, from the last London Edition.
Revised and Corrected.*

BALTIMORE·
KELLY, PIET AND COMPANY,
No. 174 BALTIMORE STREET,
1870.

CARDINAL WISEMAN'S
LECTURES
ON THE
PRINCIPAL DOCTRINES AND PRACTICES
OF THE
CATHOLIC CHURCH.

PREFACE

TO THE

THIRD AMERICAN EDITION.

AMONG the numerous and learned productions of Dr. (now Cardinal) Wiseman, his "Lectures on the Principal Doctrines and Practices of the Catholic Church" hold a distinguished place, and may be ranked in general among the most valuable specimens of doctrinal and polemical writing of which Catholic literature can boast.

Though important changes have taken place in the religious views and feelings of a large portion of the Christian world since the first edition of these Lectures was presented to the public, they still form a series of discourses admirably adapted to the present state of controversy between the Catholic Church and the various sects of Protestantism. The Tractarian movement in England and in this country has given a new phase to religious polemics, but it has not changed substantially the state of the question. The main points which it involves are developed and settled by Dr. Wiseman with a force of reasoning, a felicity of illustration, and a conciliatory spirit, which are unsurpassed, if equalled, in any other English work of a similar character. The Scriptural argument on the matters treated, is more fully and logically pursued than in most other works of this description. Hence, it will always be a standard reference on these subjects, useful alike to the members of the true church and to her adversaries. The former will find it an armory, where they will always be readily supplied with the most effective means of defending the Catholic cause; while the latter will be enlightened by its forcible and luminous reasoning, and convinced of the lamentable errors introduced by the pretended Reformation. With these remarks, the publishers offer it with confidence to the American community, and trust that it will receive the patronage which it so eminently merits.

PREFACE TO THE FIRST EDITION.

In the advent of 1835, I delivered a course of evening lectures in the Royal Sardinian Chapel, Lincoln's-Inn-Fields, upon controversial subjects. It was comprised in seven lectures, and was honored by a very numerous attendance. At the approach of Lent, this year, I was desired by the venerable prelate, whom the London district has just lost, to undertake another course in the more spacious church of St. Mary's, Moorfields, upon the same subjects. It was proposed to confine it to a few lectures upon one topic; so that no disappointment might ensue, in case my health, or occupations, or a want of interest on the part of the public, should render it expedient to discontinue it. The subject selected was the rule of faith, or the authority of the Church, which occupies the first volume of this publication. But, through God's blessing, I found myself able to persevere in my undertaking; though, in the preceding Lent, I had been unequal to reading, in a room, two lectures of half an hour's duration, in a week:[*] and, at the same time, I had the consolation of witnessing the patient and edifying attention of a crowded audience, many of whom stood for more than two hours, without betraying any symptoms of impatience. This endurance, which could only be attributed to the interest felt in the truths of our holy religion, encouraged me to proceed with the less connected subjects, comprised in my second volume.

The lectures were taken down in short-hand: and it was understood that, upon my return to Rome, they should be prepared for publication. In the mean time, however, before the course was completed, an unauthorized edition began to appear, partly inaccurate, partly imperfect, and devoid of many references and illustra

---

[*] The "Lectures on the Connection between Science and Revealed Religion," just published.

PREFACE TO THE FIRST EDITION.

In the advent of 1835, I delivered a course of evening lectures in the Royal Sardinian Chapel, Lincoln's-Inn-Fields, upon controversial subjects. It was comprised in seven lectures, and was honored by a very numerous attendance. At the approach of Lent, this year, I was desired by the venerable prelate, whom the London district has just lost, to undertake another course in the more spacious church of St. Mary's, Moorfields, upon the same subjects. It was proposed to confine it to a few lectures upon one topic; so that no disappointment might ensue, in case my health, or occupations, or a want of interest on the part of the public, should render it expedient to discontinue it. The subject selected was the rule of faith, or the authority of the Church, which occupies the first volume of this publication. But, through God's blessing, I found myself able to persevere in my undertaking; though, in the preceding Lent, I had been unequal to reading, in a room, two lectures of half an hour's duration, in a week:* and, at the same time, I had the consolation of witnessing the patient and edifying attention of a crowded audience, many of whom stood for more than two hours, without betraying any symptoms of impatience. This endurance, which could only be attributed to the interest felt in the truths of our holy religion, encouraged me to proceed with the less connected subjects, comprised in my second volume.

The lectures were taken down in short-hand: and it was understood that, upon my return to Rome, they should be prepared for publication. In the mean time, however, before the course was completed, an unauthorized edition began to appear, partly inaccurate, partly imperfect, and devoid of many references and illustra

---

* The "Lectures on the Connection between Science and Revealed Religion," just published.

tions, which could not be well given in an extemporaneous delivery. I was urged, as the only effectual means to prevent injury to myself or to my cause, to commence an edition sanctioned by myself.

This I undertook, though still engaged with a more laborious publication, which has caused considerable interruption in the regular issue of the numbers. I have added many notes and details, which I originally intended to reserve for my revision at Rome; and this has been a further cause of delay.

Those who attended the delivery of the lectures will observe many changes and additions, which are attributable to different causes. First, to the imperfect state of the short-hand writer's notes, which made it often less laborious for me to write a considerable portion of a lecture over again, than to correct the copy before me. Secondly, to the necessity, under which I often was in the delivery, of abridging or condensing, or omitting remarks and authorities, from want of time, which, in my publication, I have deemed it right to place at full. Thirdly, to my having occasionally turned back in a lecture to matter belonging to a preceding one, in consequence of difficulties communicated to me in the interval, or of an afterthought on my part; and such additions I have now transferred to their appropriate places. Fourthly, to my having omitted, in my second course, many views and passages which had appeared to make a sensible impression in my former one. This was done, partly from a desire to preserve a terser and more argumentative manner, partly from the fear of fatiguing an audience, partly composed of the same persons, by repetition. But these passages have been now inserted.

In spite of these changes or intended improvements, much of the crudeness of unwritten discourses must still pervade these volumes, and many expressions will not present that accuracy which a well meditated and carefully revised composition would have possessed. Had I come to England prepared for such an undertaking, I flatter myself that, with God's grace, much more justice would have been done to the holy and beautiful cause.

I need not say, that in this publication, as in every other that proceeds from my pen, I completely subject myself to the judgment of the Church, and mean to preserve the strictest adherence to every thing that she teaches.

CONTENTS OF VOLUME I.

LECTURE I.
The Object and Method of the Lectures on the Rule of Faith... 13

LECTURE II.
On the Protestant Rule of Faith.. 33

LECTURE III.
Exposition of the Catholic Rule of Faith................................. 60

LECTURE IV.
The Catholic Rule of Faith proved.. 80

LECTURE V.
The Catholic Rule of Faith further proved............................. 108

LECTURE VI.
On the practical Success of the Protestant Rule of Faith in converting Heathen Nations.. 144

LECTURE VII.
On the practical Success of the Catholic Rule of Faith in converting Heathen Nations.. 181

LECTURE VIII.
On the Supremacy of the Pope.. 225

LECTURE IX.
Recapitulation of the Lectures on the Church..................... 255

Before closing these preliminary remarks, I must acknowledge my obligations to two works, which have been of particular use to me, as they must be to any one treating upon controversial subjects. The first is the Symbolik of my learned friend, Prof. Möhler, the most profound work, if I may coin a phrase, on the Philosophy of Divinity, which our time has produced; the other, better known in this country, is the useful compilation of Messrs. Kirk and Berington, from which I have in general drawn my quotations of the Fathers.

And now, having nothing further to premise, I commend this little book to the favor and protection of the Almighty, begging his blessing upon both writer and reader; and I commit it to the candid and unbiased judgment of all who shall take it into their hands; entreating them to lay aside, while they peruse it, all preconceived opinions regarding our faith, if they profess it not, and by no means to be offended with any contradiction which they shall therein find, of their manner of thinking. For, whatever they shall read hath been written with a kind intent, and hath proceeded from a charitable spirit, and wishes to be received and pondered in hearts that love Christian meekness, and long after unity and peace.

London,
On the Feast of our Lord's Transfiguration, 1836.

ADVERTISEMENT TO THE SECOND EDITION.

Since the first edition of these lectures appeared, important changes have taken place in the religious state and feelings of this country. Upon being called on to prepare a second edition, I hesitated whether or no I should so far alter them as to adapt them better to the present order of things. I soon found that the labor would be that of a new work. But, further, I considered that I was desired to republish lectures once actually delivered; and that it would be a departure from historical accuracy, were I to give as spoken in 1836, that which could only have been true in 1843. I have, therefore, determined to publish the lectures in their original form, with such verbal or other trifling alterations and improvements as would not essentially alter their character; leaving it to later publications to represent the intermediate and present condition of religious opinions in England.

S. Mary's College,
First Sunday of Advent, 1843.

LECTURE THE FIRST.

THE OBJECT AND METHOD OF THE LECTURES ON THE RULE OF FAITH.

2 CORINTHIANS vi. 1.

"Brethren, we exhort you that ye receive not the grace of God in vain."

It is difficult to say, my brethren, whether the Church of God, in proposing to the meditation of the faithful the epistle read in the liturgy of this day, from which these words are taken, had you principally in view, or us, to whom is committed the ministry of His word. For, on the one hand, *you* are exhorted, not only that *ye receive not the grace of God in vain*, but farther, that *you* give offence to no man, lest thereby *our* ministry should be blamed. But while these words seem intended to exhort you, especially at this holy season, to attend to those instructions which are delivered for your edification, it must be owned, that the greater portion of the epistle is mainly directed to teach us, what are the qualities whereby the word of God should be recommended, and our ministry distinguished.

And, in the first place, we are commanded *to show ourselves worthy ministers of Christ in the word of truth, in the power of God, by the armour of justice, on the right hand and on the left;* that is to say, that clothing ourselves, as in mail of proof, with our conviction of the truth of all those doctrines which we deliver, we should stand forth, ready to encounter any opposition which they may meet; that we should urge, with all our strength, and with that energy which the word of God must always inspire, those truths which it has committed to our charge. But, while we are commanded thus to preach with power, it is expressly enjoined us, also, to preach in *sweetness, and in long-suffering, and in the Holy Ghost;* that is, to avoid any thing, in what we deliver, which could, in any wise, hurt the interests of virtues dearest to the Son of God. Whatever may be the strength and energy with which we endeavor to deliver our doctrines, they should be so tempered with meekness and gentleness, as to wound and hurt the individual feelings of no man. But there is yet a third quality in our ministry, prescribed by the Apostle, which seems most particularly adapted to the circumstances of these times; and it is, that we should preach our doctrines *through good report, and through evil report, through honor and dishonor; as deceivers, and yet true; as unknown, and yet known.* That is to say, we must expect, that while some, indeed, will listen to us in the spirit of sincerity, and kindness, we must expect from others only an evil report of that which we shall deliver. With many, our preaching will gain for us rather dishonor than credit: for, however conscientious we may be in delivering doctrines, of whose truth we are firmly convinced, we must expect to be treated by many, perhaps even by those that hear us, as merely practised and cunning deceivers. It is thus prepared, therefore, and having fully before me these consequences, which the apostle of God has enumerated, and thereby has forewarned us of, that I open, this evening, a course of instruction whereunto what I am now delivering may serve as a general introduction.

I have, for the present, undertaken to address myself to one point only; to the examining, in a series of evening lectures, the fundamental principles of the Catholic and Protestant religions; in other words, the essential ground of separation between our Church, and those friends and fellow-countrymen whom we would gladly see cemented with us in religious unity. For this purpose, I will explain, in the simplest manner possible, the grounds whereupon we ground our faith, on which we build the doctrines which we profess; I will examine, in other words, whether we are justified in admitting, as the groundwork of all that we believe, an authority, a living authority, established by Christ in his Church, with his security against error—in contradistinction to that principle which admits of no supreme, infallible authority in doctrine, save the written word of God.

Now it is merely to this course—which may occupy, perhaps, six or seven lectures—that I wish, this evening, to preface some remarks, upon the object which it will have in view, and the method in which they will be conducted.

First, as to the object which I propose to discuss. If you ask any of our brethren who are separated from us, why it is that they are not Catholics, undoubtedly you will receive a multiplicity of answers, according to the peculiar character of each one whom you interrogate. But I have no doubt that the essence and substance of each reply would be this—that the Catholic Church is infected with innumerable errors, having engrafted upon the revelations of Christ many doctrines untaught by Him, which are, consequently, but the invention of man; that she has adopted many principles of morals and practice, directly at variance with those which He and his apostles inculcated; so that, however truly she may have been once joined to the true and universal Church of Christ, she has allowed herself to be separated from it, by allowing such errors gradually to creep into her creed, and then sanctioning them, with her usurped authority, as divine.

But if you were to press the inquiry still closer, I am sure you would find the whole of these various grounds gradually reduced to one. You would be told, that the great besetting sin of the Catholic Church is, having rejected God's written word in his Scriptures as the only rule and authority of faith; so much so, that the different corruptions, so often laid to her charge, have only been produced by the admission of the false principle, as it is called, of human authority; and that, consequently, all other accusations are but minor points, which merge entirely in this one.

It is evident, therefore, that the question between us and Protestants, divides itself into two; the one being a question of fact, the other of right. For, whether each of the various instances, commonly produced, is to be considered a corruption, an invention of man, or contradictory to the true revealed word of Christ, whether any Catholic dogma or practice, as transubstantiation, or confession, or purgatory, is to be pronounced a deviation from that which our Saviour instituted; such questions form matters of separate consideration, involving distinct facts, each whereof may rest upon its own peculiar proofs. But, if you proceed to examine the ground whereon these are upheld, and find that Catholics maintain them all exclusively by the same principle, of their being taught by an infallible authority, vested in the Church; it is evident, that all these various independent questions of fact are united, and concentrated in one: that is, in the inquiry, whether there be any authority which could sanction them, and upon which we are justified in believing them.

This is an important consideration: because it must be manifest, that, if we establish that right whereon, alone, we base all particular doctrines; if, in other words, we can prove that, besides the written word of God, an infallible authority exists, and always has existed, in the Church—which, being under the guidance of God, cannot be deceived in sanctioning any thing as having been revealed by Him—assuredly, we likewise make good all those different points, on which we are charged with having fallen into error, but which thus will be proved to have their foundation on an authority derived from God. And therefore, however, for the sake of entirely convincing the minds of those who doubt, and of more easily satisfying their peculiar difficulties, we may be induced to treat singly such points as I have instanced, it is evident, that they are all virtually and essentially demonstrated, if this one leading fundamental proposition can be proved: and, thus, all the questions of fact are absorbed in the one touching the divine right possessed by the Church to decide, without danger of error, in all matters regarding faith.

Now, my brethren, I may observe that this line of argument is completely opposite to that pursued, if I may use the expression, on the other side; for, not considering the manner in which these questions hang together, nothing is more common than to hear, or read, of preachers who represent the fundamental question as only one on a level with the others; and, instead of at once closing with the main point, *what is the rule of faith*, treat the withholding of the Bible from the faithful, as it is called, or the doctrine of tradition, as *one* among what are to be considered the corruptions of the Church of Rome.

But, in this process of reasoning, there is, besides, a manifest logical error. For, whether or no it be a corruption to admit tradition, or to pronounce the Bible ill-calculated for a rule of faith to each individual, depends upon, or rather is identical with, the question, whether God intended the Scriptures to be the only rule of faith. This the Protestant asserts, and the Catholic denies. But, therefore, when it is pretended to disprove the truth of the Catholic religion, by taxing it with additions to God's word, or with restraining the people from its use, it is manifest that the identical question is assumed as certain on one side: namely, that Scripture *is* the only rule of faith. For, if this be not true, and if tradition be equally a rule of faith, the Catholic Church is not guilty of the alleged corruption. But this, as I before observed, is the whole kernel of the controversy between the two religions. So that, first, the very point in dispute is taken for granted, and then an argument is based upon it. Assuredly, it cannot be difficult to prove Catholics in the wrong, when the Protestant principle of faith is taken as a lemma.

Thus much may suffice as to the grounds which would be given, were we to interrogate any one who is separated from the Catholic Church, Why he is not a Catholic?

But, supposing now that we proceeded farther with the scru-

INTRODUCTION.

tiny, and asked him, Why he is a Protestant? the answer must, certainly, be different; for no religion can stand upon mere negative grounds. You cannot believe one doctrine rather than another, simply because that other, which is proposed by some men, is false. Each religion must have grounds of demonstration essentially in itself, and independent of the existence of any other sect. We should have been able to prove the divinity of Christ, although Arianism and Socinianism had never arisen: and even now, if any one asked us for a demonstration of that doctrine, it would be no reply, to say that Arianism has been confuted, or that Socinianism has been proved false; but the dogma, and the system, of religion, which takes it for a foundation, must have their own essential reasons, independent of the rejection of another doctrine. Hence it is, that each one, if asked, not simply, why he is not a Catholic? but, why moreover he is a Protestant? must have positive reasons to give, wherefore he is a member of this communion.

It follows, necessarily, that, by this principle, a very common ground for being a Protestant is, at once, excluded. For preachers will too often imagine, and their hearers will follow them in the idea, that when they have held up to hatred, or rejected as impious and absurd, the tenets of Catholicity, they have thereby established the cause of Protestantism. How many works have been published "against the errors of the Church of Rome," or in confutation of Popery: how few systematic attempts are made to establish Protestant principles upon positive demonstration. Hence it is, that many consider religious belief only as based on a choice between the two religions, in which, the rejection of the one sufficiently demonstrates the other.

To such as are Protestants, on this ground, I would say—suppose that you lived in a country, or in any part of this country, where there was not within your reach a single Catholic; where, consequently, it had not been necessary to hold up our doctrines to your execration,—indeed, where there would have been no opportunity given you even of hearing them. It is evident, that you could not have been a Protestant upon this ground: but, that some positive reasons or motives, must have been proposed to you to satisfy you, that Protestantism is the true and normal state of the Christian religion; its rule of faith would have been propounded to you, based upon a series of positions and arguments, not relative or negative, but direct and positive.

But, my brethren, for the better understanding of this point, I wish to draw your attention to a very important distinction, and one which, I fear, is often not sufficiently observed; it is *the distinction between the grounds of adhesion to, or communion with, any Church;* and *the grounds of conviction of its truth.* I am sure, that, if those who have been educated Protestants would ask their own minds, why they profess that religion, many would receive such an answer as would appear a justification to themselves for remaining in that communion, but yet does not involve the acceptance of the fundamental grounds of their religion. They would say, for instance—and I am sure that many, if they search their own breasts, will find it a reason of great weight—they would say, that they were born and educated in that religion; that it is the religion of their country; and that they think it shameful to abandon the faith of their forefathers. These are so many reasons, therefore, why they are Protestants; but they are precisely the same grounds which might be given for a thousand ordinary opinions; they are the very reasons by which you might account why you are attached to your country; but they do not include, in themselves, the essential, the radical reasons, upon which Protestant doctrines are based. They are motives which justify the individual, in his own idea, for remaining in a communion; but, certainly, they contain no pledge of having adopted the principle of any. Others will tell you, that they are of that persuasion, because they take it for granted that their religion is demonstrated; they have been accustomed to hear it spoken of as a thing satisfactorily settled, and they have not thought it necessary to trouble their minds by inquiring farther; learned men have done it for them; and the principles of the Reformation have been too firmly established, and too surely demonstrated, to need reconsideration or private study.

You must perceive—and a minute examination would only serve to demonstrate it—that, whoever gives you such reasons as these, for being a Protestant, only gives you such *motives* as influence him to continue in the profession of his creed, but they are not *reasons* which touch the grounds whereon Protestantism justifies its original separation from our Church; for the fundamental principle of Protestantism is this, that THE WRITTEN WORD OF GOD ALONE IS THE TRUE STANDARD AND RULE OF FAITH. But, to arrive at this, there is required a long course of complicated and severe inquiry. You must, step by step, have satisfied yourselves, not merely of the existence of a revelation; but, that such revelation is really confided to man in these very books; that they have been transmitted to you in such a state, that is, that the originals have been so preserved, and the translations so made, as to make you confident, that in reading them you are reading the words which the Spirit of God dictated to the prophets and apostles; and, still more, that you have acquired, or that you possess, the lights necessary to understand them. You must not only be satisfied that the Bible has been given as the word of God; but you must be ready to meet the innumerable and complicated difficulties which are alleged against the inspiration of particular books, or individual passages; so that you may be able to say, that from your own knowledge and experience, you are internally convinced, that you have in that book the inspired word of God, in the first place; and, in the second, that you are not only authorized, but competent, to understand it. How few, my brethren, are there who can say, that they have gone through this important course! and, yet, it is the essential ground of Protestantism, that each one is to be considered responsible to God for every particular doctrine which he professes—that each one must have studied the word of God, and must have drawn from it the faith which he holds. Unless he does all this, he has not complied with those conditions which his religion imposes upon him; and, whatever reasons or motives he may feel or quote, for being a Protestant, it is manifest that they noways lead him essentially to the practical adoption of the groundwork of his religion.

You may, perhaps, be tempted to think that I have overstrained my assertions, for the sake of an argument. You may say, that it is nowise contrary to the principles of Protestantism, to accept religious truth on the teaching received in education; so that the long and painful process I have described is by no means required from each individual. I will, therefore, justify what I have asserted, by the authority of one considered eminently orthodox among the divines of the Church of England. Dr. Beveridge, in his "Private Thoughts," has recorded most exactly the train of reasoning he pursued, regarding the necessity of individual examination in matters of religion; and you will see that he goes much farther than I have ventured to do, in his statement of what Protestantism exacts. In the sixteenth page of that work he writes as follows, concerning the self-examination which he instituted into the grounds and motives of his belief.

"The reason of this my inquiry, is, not that I am, in the least, dissatisfied with that religion I have already embraced, but because it is natural for all men to have an overbearing opinion and esteem for that particular religion they are born and bred up in. That, therefore, I may not seem biassed by the prejudices of education, I am resolved to prove and examine them all, and hold fast to that which is best, for though I do not, in the least, question but upon that inquiry, I shall find the true Christian religion to be the only true religion in the world, *yet I cannot say it, unless I find it upon good grounds to be so indeed.* For to profess myself a Christian, and believe that Christians only are right because my forefathers were so, is no more than the heathens and Mahomedans have to say for themselves.—*To be a Christian only upon the grounds of birth and education, is all one as if I was a Turk or a heathen, for if I had been born amongst them, I should have had the same reason for their religion as now I have for my own.* The premises are the same, though the conclusions be never so different. 'Tis still upon the same grounds, that I profess religion, though it be another religion." Here, then, according to this learned bishop, not only is the Protestant bound, as I said, to satisfy his mind individually on the ground of his creed, but he is no better than a heathen or Turk, if he be *a Christian* at all upon other grounds. But, then, he bears me out still further in my assertions, by owning that the great body of Protestants are only such, upon the unjustifiable grounds which he rejects, and which I above enumerated. For he says in continuation: "I can see but little difference betwixt being a Turk by profession, and a Christian only by education, *which commonly is the means and occasion, but ought by no means to be the ground, of any religion.*" In which words is found the very distinction I before laid down between the motives of adherence, and the principle of conviction. But at our next meeting I shall have better occasion to quote other and stronger authorities, for all I have asserted.

From what I have said, it is evident, that those motives of adherence, do not necessarily and essentially, lead to that principle; that is to say, that a person may be all his life a member of a Protestant Church, without once taking the pains to examine, by the serious and minute, and difficult method which is required, all the doctrines which he believes; he may possess, therefore, those reasons which keep him in communion with that Church, without his ever being led by them to the adoption of that course which it requires, as fundamental to his religion. Not only so; but I will say, that these motives are contradictory to that principle. For, if any man tells me, that he remains a Protestant simply because he has been so born and educated; that from what he has heard in sermons, or read in books, he is satisfied that no other sect of Christianity has any grounds to support it—I reply to him, at once, that he is acting in direct contradiction to the principle whereby alone his religion allows him to be convinced; for conviction, according to that, must be based upon individual research, and individual satisfaction; and not merely, therefore, upon having been born in it, or having been educated in it by others; nor on having heard certain doctrines delivered from pulpits by men as fallible as himself; and certainly, still less on having heard the doctrines of others represented in a manner which I have no hesitation in saying, is almost always incorrect, and perhaps often such as to deserve a harsher name.

Now, on the other hand, let us examine the grounds upon which Catholics stand, viewing them precisely with the same distinction. And, I will own, that the grounds upon which Catholics adhere to their religion, or the motives by which they are brought to it, if they have not been therein educated, are not only as various and as numerous as those which I have mentioned, when speaking of Protestants, but, infinitely more so: and hence, it may be, that Catholics, if interrogated, will give the most various reasons why they are Catholics. But, now, observe the difference between the consequences in the two religions.

That the grounds upon which men may be brought to the true religion of Christ are various, is evident, both from the conduct of those whom the word of God has proposed to us as examples, and from what we have witnessed in all ages, even unto our own. For, there can be doubt, that in the preaching of the apostles, Christianity was not proposed upon one inflexible, unvarying system; but the announcers of God's word drew their evidences from any just grounds, which they knew must make the greatest impression upon those whom they addressed. It is, in fact, the beauty and the perfection of truth, that it should stand the action of the most varied tests. That is only an impure ore which, while it perhaps resists the action of one or two reagents, will in the end, yield before the energy of a third; for the pure metal will defy the action of every successive test. Truth may be compared to a gem without a flaw, which may be viewed in different lights; which, though held up to the eye on any side, and without artificial assistance, shall always present the same beauty and purity. But it is the characteristic of error, that it may, by the assistance of an artful setting, and by a certain play of light thrown upon it, produce the appearance of being without fault; but, if it be slightly turned, or shown under another angle, it instantly discovers its imperfections. It was evidently, with this feeling, that the apostles acted, and thus, by them, was Christianity preached. It was considered by them as a system, intended to meet the wants of all mankind, so that its true evidence resided in the mind of every individual, as well as in the general feelings and cravings of the entire human race. They felt that, whatever characteristic of truth their hearers might have adopted, whether the counterpart of a previous revelation, or the certain conclusions of profound philosophy, whether drawn from the yearnings of human nature after perfection, or from individual consciousness of misery and ignorance, whether consisting in the harmonious beauty of all the parts of a system, or in strong evidence in favour of special propositions, any would equally lead to the verification of Christianity. Thus, consequently, when they preached to the Jews—who possessed the volume of the old law, and in it types, prophecies, and other foreshadowings of the dispensation that was to come—the task was simply, to assume what these already believed, and show them its counterpart and fulfilment in the truths of Christianity, and in the character of our Saviour; and thus they generally won their way to conviction, through principles already held.* When Philip met the eunuch of the queen of Ethiopia on the highway, he found him reading a certain passage in the prophet Isaiah; and, from that passage alone, he convinced him of the truth of Christianity, and admitted him to baptism. He was searching for something that would correspond to the description there given: Philip merely proposes to him what a simple comparison led him to see, must be the counterpart to what he had read; and he, instantly, yielded himself a captive to faith, and adopted all the scheme of Christianity, implied in the baptismal rite.† But when St. Paul goes among the Gentiles, and stands before the learned Athenians, he does not appeal to prophecies, wherein they believed not, and which they knew not; for he does not consider it necessary, that they must, in a manner, first become Jews, before they be brought to Christianity. He has recourse to a totally different character of evidence; he preaches to them —men of a philosophical and studious mind—a sublimer morality than they had been accustomed to hear; he presents to them the striking doctrine of the resurrection; he shows them the futility and absurdity of their idolatry; he quotes to them the words of their own poets, to prove how necessary a purer

---

* Acts ii. iii.   † Acts viii.

belief in God, such as he preached, was to the human soul; he intimates, that, already among them was discernible a dissatisfaction with their present religion, and a certain longing after a better faith, from their having erected an altar " to the unknown God." He lays hold of those threads, which he found already prepared in the minds of his hearers, he attaches to them the evidences of Christianity, and thus insures the introduction of its doctrines within their breasts.*

When we come down to a later period, we find the same practice in the church—for in the first century, and in the second and in the third, we see totally different classes of motives, whereupon religion was preached, and received by men. We find, for instance, that in the first century, it was the courage of the martyrs, the seeing how flesh and blood could endure tortures and death in support of a religion, which brought the greater portion of converts to the truth. In the following centuries, a new system of evidences was introduced. The study of philosophy, which, under the patronage of the Antonines in the west, and through the impulse of the great Platonist schools in the east, was become very prevalent, led to the examination of Christianity in connexion with the philosophical systems of ancient Greece. It was soon seen that in all these there were problems innumerable, regarding the nature of God, the human soul, the origin and end of man, which all the acuteness and meditation of sages had not been able to solve, and whose solution, however interesting and necessary, they even acknowledge to be out of reason's power. But when Christianity was examined, it was discovered to present a full and consistent answer to every query, a satisfactory solution of every doubt, and a perfect code of ethics and mental philosophy. And this was considered by the Justins, the Clements, the Origens, and other philosophical minds, a sufficient evidence of its truth. For, as we should not require other proof that a key was made for a certain lock, than finding that it at once insinuates itself through all its complicated wards, and fits in them, and moves among them without grating or resistance, and easily turns the bolts which they kept drawn, so did the 'rue religion then, and so does it now, require no better demonstration of its being truly made for the mind and soul of man, and of its having come from the same all-wise Artist's hands as created them,—than the simple discovery of how admirably it winds into all their recesses,

---

* Acts xvii.

and fits into all their intricate mazes, turning at will the bars, and opening the entrance, of all the secret mysteries of self-knowledge.

Now, coming down to our own times, the same variety of motives is perceptible in the writings of those who have, within these late years, joined the Catholic faith. I do not allude so much to what has occurred in this country; because, however great may have been the spread of the Catholic religion since the commencement of this century amongst us, however frequent the conversions which we hear of, and see—all this is, in one respect, as nothing to what goes forward elsewhere. For while with us the work of conversion, with several brilliant exceptions, has been chiefly confined to persons of a less literary class, on the Continent—and I speak particularly of Germany—there is hardly a year, and there has not been for some time back, in which some individuals have not embraced the Catholic religion, who were previously distinguished in their own country, as men of first-rate abilities, and deep learning; often holding important situations, and particularly, employed as professors in Protestant universities. Now, many of these have published the motives which brought them to the Catholic religion. Those who peruse their accounts will find them often written in a profound reflective manner, and their arguments conducted with a terseness and closeness which, in this country, could be hardly popular. But, what I wish principally to note, their motives are as varied as the different pursuits in which each of the writers was engaged. You will find one who has made history the study of his life, and who has taught that branch of learning in one of the most celebrated universities, announce to you, that he has become a Catholic, simply by applying the sound principles of his science to the facts recorded in the annals of Europe.* You may hear another draw his arguments from motives connected with the philosophy of the human mind—from his discovering, that only in the Catholic religion can he find a system of it adapted to the wants of man; and another, whose enthusiasm has first been kindled by observing that the principle of all that is beautiful in art and in nature is nowhere to be found, except in the Catholic religion.† You will read a political economist, who tells you, that having made a deep study of that science, he was forced to admit, that only in Catholic morality could he

---

* Prof. Phillips, late of Berlin, now of Munich.
† Stolberg, Schlegel, Veith, Moliter, Beautain, &c.

discover the principles whereon it could be honestly conducted, and so was led to the practical adoption of the Catholic creed.* Another, by watching that very event which some have considered a proof of the demoralizing power of the Catholic religion, by attentive study of the dreadful tragedies of the French revolution, became a Catholic; and has since produced learned works treating of social rights.†

These are but a few out of many instances which I could quote; but, now, mark the difference between all these motives and those which I before described. I said, that the motives assigned by Protestants for their adhesion to their religion, did not lead to their true principle of conviction—to the adoption of the only grounds on which Protestantism is based. A man may be a Protestant for those reasons which are ordinarily given, without his being brought by that circumstance to the personal examination of each doctrine, or to that deep study of God's written word, upon which alone his religion allows him to be a Protestant. But, in every one of the cases to which I have referred,—no matter whence the conviction came, no matter what was the first impulse, or the line of argument which brought the individual into communion with the Catholic Church,—the grounds of connection or adhesion necessarily ended in the Catholic principle of conviction. For none of these men became Catholics by discovering the true principles of political economy, or of history, or of the fine arts, or of philosophy, in the Catholic religion. These various motives produced admiration and esteem for it; but, however learned or distinguished, we should not, and could not, have called any of them ours, though they had persevered in these sentiments, unless they had specifically adopted the Catholic principle of Church authority, and submitted their understanding and mind implicitly to its teaching. Here, then, we have a characteristic difference between the groundwork of the two religions. For, on the one hand, there is no security given in the profession of Protestantism, that its fundamental principle of individual examination has been *practically* adopted: while, on the other, no man can be for one instant a Catholic, without the vital principle of catholicity being actually embraced; nay, no man can become a Catholic save through, and by its reception. The Catholic Church is thus as a city to which avenues lead from every side, towards which men may travel

---

* See De Coux's First Lecture on Political Economy.
† Adam Müller.

from any quarter, by the most diversified roads,—by the thorny and rugged ways of strict investigation,—by the more flowery paths of sentiment and feeling; but, arrived at its precincts, all find that there is but one gate whereby they may enter, but one door to the sheepfold, narrow and low, perhaps, and causing flesh and blood to stoop as it passes in. They may wander about its outskirts, they may admire the goodliness of its edifices and of its bulwarks, but they cannot be its denizens and children, if they enter not by that one gate, of absolute, unconditional submission to the teaching of the Church.

Assuredly, there is something here beautifully contrasted, to the eye of the philosopher, with the manifest imperfections of the other system. There is a natural and obvious beauty in the simplicity of this basis, which at once gives stability and unity to conviction, which makes the terms whereon men are received into the pale of a religion, equal to all, whether learned or illiterate, quick or dull of apprehension, and which obliges all to divest themselves of their peculiar prejudices and opinions, if they clash with the doctrines taught.

But the beauty of this system ends not here: for, after each one has thus embraced the religion, upon a principle one and indivisible, his affections and tastes are allowed their fullest play; they may devote themselves to the adorning and commending of his religion, from the various storehouses of topics which their pursuits may afford them; and he will in it find a fitting and a perfect theme to repay all his zeal and love. The motives which led him to the adoption of the faith will still continue within him as links of attachment to its profession; but the ground of his belief will be unchanged for ever.

And this leads me to another reflection of no mean importance. It is extremely common, to ask an untutored Catholic on what grounds he became, or is, a Catholic; and it will often appear, that the answer which he gives is not logical, or satisfactory. It probably is not to you; but, mark! while he answers the question, he is not giving you *the grounds* on which he believes the doctrine of the Catholic Church: he is only giving you the motives which brought him, or bind him to it; and these grounds are as different, as diverse, as the affections, as the pursuits, and as the characters of individuals. You have not in your mind the key necessary to understand the force of those motives which influenced him. But it is not on their strength that he believes in transubstantiation; it is not on that ground—whatever it be—that he believes in auricular confession, or that he practises it. He is not giving you, therefore, the grounds of his belief; he is giving you the reasons by which he was led to satisfactory inquiries regarding the grounds of faith. And this is certainly remarkable, that in every one who has embraced the Catholic religion, whatever was his difficulty in first receiving it, whatever may have been the first obstacles to his complete conviction, when once he has embraced and received it, it takes as strong a hold upon his affections and thoughts, as it could have done if he had been educated in it from his infancy. It is, if I may illustrate it by a comparison, like a shoot or slip, which is forced into the ground, and requires a certain degree of violence for the purpose. It must be by a sharp and wounding point that it is made to penetrate the hard surface of the earth; but no sooner has it once been there placed, than it sends forth shoots, to go and suck the nourishment on every side; and the earth that has so received it, closes and entwines itself around it, and becomes kindly and attached to it; so, that if you should wish, after a short time, to root it up, you must rend and tear that earth in pieces, into which originally it seemed to be driven against its will.

But now, allow me to contrast with the examples of conversion which I have just given you, others of a different class.

I have told you, that in perusing the works of men who have within these few years become members of the Catholic Church —men of talent and erudition—we shall hardly find two of them agree upon the grounds which they record, as having induced them to embrace the Catholic religion. But you may also read similar works on the other side, purporting to give the grounds upon which individuals have abandoned the Catholic Church, and become members of some Protestant communion. It is, indeed, very seldom, that men of any considerable ability, or at all known to the public for their learning, have written such treatises; but still, such as they are, they have been, in general, widely disseminated. It has been thought useful to throw them, in a cheap form, among the public, and particularly among the lower orders, that they may see examples of conversion from the Catholic religion. Now, I have read such of these as have fallen in my way, and have noted, that, instead of the rich variety of motives which have brought learned men to the Catholic Church, there is a sad meagreness of reasoning in them; indeed, that they all, without exception, give me but one argument. The history, in every case, is simply this: that the individual— by some chance or other, probably through the ministry of some pious person—became possessed of the word of God, of the Bible; that he perused this book; that he could not find in it transubstantiation or auricular confession, that he could not discover in it one word of purgatory, or of venerating images. He perhaps goes to the priest, and tells him that he cannot find these doctrines in the Bible; his priest argues with him, and endeavors to convince him that he should shut up the book which is leading him astray; he perseveres, he abandons the communion of the Church of Rome—or, as it is commonly expressed, the *errors* of that Church—and becomes a Protestant. Now, through all this process, the man was a Protestant; from the beginning he started with the principle, that whatsoever is not in that book, cannot be true in religion, or an article of faith—and that is the principle of Protestantism. He took Protestantism, therefore, for granted, before he began to examine the Catholic doctrine. He set out with the supposition, that whatever is not in the Bible, is no part of God's truth; *he* does not find certain things in the Bible; and he concludes that *therefore* the religion that holds these, is not the true religion of Christ. The work was done before; it is not an instance of conversion; it is only a case of one, who has lately, perhaps unconsciously, had his breast filled with Protestant principles, coming openly to declare them. The ground on which the inquiry should have been conducted was, manifestly, not to assume, in the first instance, that there is no truth but what is expressly contained in the Bible; but to examine whether that is the only rule of faith, or whether there are not other means also of arriving at a knowledge of God's revelation.

From all that I have said, you will easily deduce, that the object which I shall have in view, through my first course of lectures, will be to examine the relative value of the two RULES OF FAITH; to see whether the Catholic is not fully justified in the admission of this principle, that God has appointed His Church, the infallible and unfailing depository of all truth.

I now come to say a few words on the manner in which the inquiry shall be conducted. You will naturally at once suppose, that these will be what are commonly called *controversial* lectures. I own that I have a great dislike—almost an antipathy—to the name; for it supposes that we consider ourselves in a state of warfare with others; that we adopt the principle which I reprobated at the commencement of my discourse—of establishing our doctrines by overthrowing those of others. Now, my brethren, it is not so. We hold, that the demonstration of our belief, and of its grounds, may be conducted without the slightest reference to the existence of any other system. I might prove the doctrines of the Catholic Church to you, precisely as I should if addressing an eastern audience, who had never, perhaps, heard even the name of Protestantism. I could expound the grounds on which we believe, without ever adverting to the existence of any opposing system. We do not wish to think that we have adversaries or enemies to attack; for we are willing to consider all who are separated from us, as in a state of error indeed, but of *involuntary* error. We hope that, having been educated in certain principles and opinions, and not having taken leisure to examine sufficiently into the grounds of their faith, or having had their first impressions so far strengthened by the subsequent efforts of their instructors, that it is almost impossible for any contrary impression to be made, they are rather separated from us than armed against us—rather wanderers from the city of God, than enemies to its peace. Hence, it is not in the way of controversy, it is not as attacking others, or even as wishing to gain a victory, or to have a triumph, that I intend to address you. In stating and explaining our own doctrines, I will avoid, as much as possible, the examination of others' opinions; because I am satisfied that the course of argument to be pursued, is such as, in establishing our doctrines, will prove them not merely true, but *exclusively* true. The method, therefore, which I shall follow, I would rather call *demonstrative* than controversial. It will consist in laying before you the grounds of our doctrines, rather than in endeavoring to overthrow those professed by others. It will likewise be essentially *inductive*—that is to say, I will not take any one single principle for granted, which will possibly bear a dispute. I will begin with the simplest elements, and they shall, as they go on, develop themselves, by their own power. It shall be my endeavor to conduct the inquiry precisely as one would do who has no prejudice on either side; but who, using such measure of sagacity or inductive skill, in tracing out proofs, as he may possess, should proceed to search out what is right and true. We will open the word of God; we will examine it by such principles as all must admit; we will discover what are the only consequences that can be drawn from it; and for whom the consequence shall be, his doctrine we will embrace. This is the simple method which I intend to follow; and this will certainly exclude what I fear has been too common elsewhere, and that, not merely because the method itself will not allow it to enter, but because I trust, that whatever method were pursued in this holy place, it would not admit it:—I mean, the system of misrepresentation of the doctrines of others, which is, alas! too common in this city. I have no hesitation in saying, that never yet has an attempt been made to expound Catholic doctrines, in any other place of worship but our own, without those doctrines being most strangely misrepresented—without their being, in the first place, themselves made totally different from what they are; and then, supposed to rest on grounds which we absolutely reject.

Now, as I said before, I shall scarcely have to touch on the opinions of others; I do not intend to involve myself in questions regarding what any sect or section of Christians believes; I will lay before you, what the Catholic doctrine is, and endeavor to explain the proofs of that doctrine; and if I have to answer objections—which will be extremely seldom—or to comment upon the principles of others—I will always make it a point, as much as possible, to give my statement in the words of some accredited defender and supporter of the Protestant cause.

The last quality and characteristic which I shall be anxious to infuse into this course of instruction, will be that which the epistle I have quoted to you, is particular in inculcating—that is, a spirit of mildness and of gentleness, the avoiding of any expression which can possibly wound the feeling of any individual, the refraining from any term of reproach, and from the use of any name which is reprobated and disliked by those of whom we speak. It shall be my endeavor to keep clear, as much as possible, of individuals, except when obliged to quote their words, in justification of expressions I may use. This is the practice, and always has been, amongst us. It has been our rule, in treating of the differences between us and many of our fellow-countrymen, to speak of them, as much as we can, with charity and compassion. We are accused, indeed, of an eager spirit of proselytism, of going from door to door to gain converts; and were there any bitterness in our heart, were there any feeling of dislike, of antipathy to others, were there any thing but the true spirit of kindness and charity, and love of our neighbors in God, in the motives of our ministry, assuredly we should not take the trouble and pains for which we are reproved.

But, my brethren, this has been the fate of the Catholic religion at all times, though never so much as now, that it has to be preached less in honor than in dishonor—in evil repute rather than in good repute. In whatever way we may propose our doctrines, it is impossible for them not to be reprobated, and misrepresented too. We may say, as did our Saviour to the Jews, "Unto whom shall I liken the men of this generation, and to what are they like? They are like unto children sitting in the market-place, and speaking one to another, and saying, We have piped unto you, and ye have not danced; we have mourned, and ye have not wept. For John the Baptist came neither eating bread nor drinking wine; and ye say, He hath a devil. The Son of man is come eating and drinking; and ye say, Behold a glutton and drinker of wine, a friend of publicans and sinners! And wisdom is justified by all her children!"* If the Catholic Church enjoin the doctrine of severe mortification and penance, she is immediately traduced as opposed to the word of God, by substituting the efficacy of man for the merits of Christ. If, at other times, she seem to relax that severity which others would desire, and allow innocent mirth to mingle with the close of that day which God has dedicated to his service, then is she, on the contrary, represented as being lax in her morals, and as encouraging the profanation of God's holy seasons. If her anchorites gird themselves with sackcloth, and retire for prayer and meditation from the haunts of men, it is a gloomy and unholy superstition; if her priests minister at the altar, clad in costly raiment, it is pronounced mere vanity, and a worldly spirit. And thus, whatever we do, whatever doctrine we teach, whatever practice we inculcate, it is sure to be found reprehensible; and some ground or other is easily discovered, whereon it must be condemned.

But then, let us fulfil the other portion of this text, and justify the divine wisdom of our religion in our conduct. You, who well know this wisdom, and the principles inculcated by your teachers and guides, have often heard how, even in this respect, it was meet for your religion to resemble its divine founder; how, as He was ever calumniated, and persecuted, and ill-treated by men, so must you likewise expect that—whether in prosperity or in adversity—your doctrines, and opinions, and institutions, should be held up to the hatred and the scorn of the world. But remember, that while your Redeemer submitted in every other respect to the will of his persecutors, while he allowed himself to be bound, and scourged, and crowned with thorns, and mocked, and scoffed, and even crucified for your sins, there was one thing only, in the course of his passion, wherein he refused to yield to the designs of his enemies; one point in which he

* Luke vii. 31.

would not submit to their inflictions; and that was, when they attempted to force gall and vinegar upon his lips; for, *when he had tasted he would not drink.** And in this respect, therefore, do you likewise refuse to submit to that whereunto others may wish to drive you. Allow nothing which they may say—allow no excesses on their part—to lead you to the utterance of one word of bitterness or acrimony. Let them not ever gain the triumph over you of making you, in this respect, like themselves, by extorting from you reviling and scoffing words, instead of sound and solid argument, urged in the mildest phrase.

In conclusion, my brethren, allow me to say, that it is only the grace of God which can give us mutual strength to go through the task which I have proposed; that all our efforts will fail, that your attendance will be without profit, and my ministry without fruit, unless God send his blessing upon us; unless he give force and efficacy to my unworthy lips, and put a candid and teachable spirit in your hearts; that so ye may be moved to come hither, not by idle curiosity, or a desire to hear something new, but from a real anxiety every day to learn more and more, and to improve yourselves, not merely in the knowledge of your faith, but in the practice of all that it inculcates and teaches; that so you may be not only hearers of the word, but also doers—a blessing which I pray God to grant you evermore. Amen.

---

* Matt. xxvii. 34.

LECTURE THE SECOND.

ON THE PROTESTANT RULE OF FAITH.

1 THESSALONIANS v. 21.

"*Try all things, and hold fast that which is good.*"

I own, my brethren, that I feel considerably rejoiced and comforted, at seeing the good-will with which you have commenced your attendance upon this course of lectures; and still more, at seeing such a full attendance here this evening. For, I must acknowledge, that I have feared lest the necessarily abstract nature of the subject which I treated in my opening discourse, added to the circumstance that, from previous fatigue, I had not, in my estimation, done justice to the interesting view which I wished to propose, might, perhaps, have deterred many from continuing their attendance upon what promised such comparatively slight interest. Nothing, indeed, my brethren, is easier than to throw considerable interest over any subject, by condensing its facts into a small space, and crowding together the most striking aspects that it will bear. But, although upon another occasion I may have been compelled to follow that course, it is always an unsatisfactory one; because, by it, injustice is done to two important parties—the cause in hand, and those who are anxious to hear its demonstration. To the cause, for this simple reason, that, although, in every question, there must be some more leading and more important points, yet are the connecting links likewise of essential importance; and though, by sweeping away that intermediate matter, you may place the object in a more striking and moving point of view; yet you essentially weaken it, by depriving it of that support and consistency which the connection between it and other parts of the system, through those less important elements, alone can give. And injustice is, likewise, done to those who come to learn: for, it may perchance be that their difficulties, if they differ from us, do not so much lie in the leading and important features of the case, as in some comparatively insignificant circumstance, some trifling objection, which, from their particular cast of mind, has much greater force with them than we can understand; and so they may depart with the impression, that we have only acted the part of skilful advocates, putting forward some few favorable points, while we pass over the weaker portions of our case. And hence it is that I shall have, more than once, to claim your indulgence—but I feel that, on simply asking it, the boon is granted—for entering into more minute particulars, and comparatively secondary matter, than may appear to some of sufficient value to occupy attention. Even this evening, it will be impossible for me to grapple so closely with the subject in hand as I intend, hereafter; and if, upon seeing me place in the way so many preliminary observations, and remove, to a certain distance, the closer examination of the important points which I have proposed for discussion, any one should be tempted to think that it is my wish to escape from them, I only entreat of him to continue his attendance; and I will promise him, that, in due time, after such introductory observations as I consider requisite for the full understanding of the question, he shall see every point met in the fairest, the fullest, and the most impartial manner. Now, therefore, to connect what I have to say this evening, with what I have already premised, I shall take the liberty of giving you, in a few sentences, what I said at our last meeting. I there endeavored to establish a very important distinction between the grounds on which a man justifies himself to his conscience and conviction, in his adherence to any particular religion, and the essential foundation whereupon rests its creed—the principle, if I may so say, of its very existence. I observed, that many professed the Protestant religion, merely because they were born in it; because they have always heard it spoken of as certain and true, or because they are accustomed to hear every other religion rejected and condemned, as absolutely untenable; and I pointed out the clear distinction, between this reasoning and the grounds, on which that religion must justify itself. I observed that a person might be a Protestant on most of these motives—and the great majority of Protestants are so on some one of them—and that yet, not one of these touched upon, or led to, the fundamental principle which Protestantism proposes as its basis—the individual examination, and discovery of its doctrines in the Word of God; whereas, on the contrary, it was impossible for any man to be brought to the Catholic religion, or to adhere to it, upon any principle whatever, without, in the act of entering it, embracing, and identifying with his conscience and conviction, the fundamental principle of Catholicity. For no one is, or can be a Catholic, but by his entire submission to the authority of his Church.

The consequence which I wished to draw from these reflections was of an important character: namely, that, in all discussions upon this solemn topic, we have nothing to do with the motives which many give, why they are attached to, and love, their religion; but only with the grounds whereupon they believe, whereupon they found their faith, and justify their particular profession; and this leads us to the examination of what is the vital, fundamental principle of the Protestant, and what of the Catholic, religion. The discussion of these two points will form the subject of the course on which I have entered. This evening, I will confine myself exclusively to the treating of that principle which is held by Protestants, as the essential and fundamental principle of their faith. And having, thus, occasion to speak so largely of the Word of God, and wishing to complete that section of my subject, I will explain what is the doctrine of Catholics regarding it. But I will proceed no farther with their belief, reserving to myself to expound it more largely and satisfactorily at a future meeting.

There is nothing easier than to give the popular statement of the difference between Catholics and those who dissent from them, regarding THE RULE OF FAITH. It is very easy to say that Catholics admit the authority of the Church; and that Protestants allow of no rule but the written Word of God. Such a statement appears, at first sight simple; but, if any one will take the pains to analyze it, he will find it fraught with considerable difficulties.

For instance, what is the meaning of the Word of God, or the Scriptures, being "the only rule of faith?" Does it mean, that it is to be the rule for the Church, or for its individual members? Does it mean, that public declarations or the symbols of faith are based upon the Word of God? or, to borrow the language of some ancient philosophers who used to say that each man is a microcosm or a little world—shall we consider him likewise, as a little Church, with power of examining and deciding upon matters of religion? Does it mean, that there is an individual light promised, or granted, by God, so that each one is under the guidance and infallible authority of the Holy Ghost; or that, abandoned to those lights which he may possess, from his own learning or acquirements, his peculiar measure of mind and understanding is to be his rule and guide in drawing his faith from the Word of God? But to show that these difficulties are not

LECTURE II.

imaginary, let us examine the Articles of the Church of England, in which its rule of faith is laid down; articles which all the clergy must subscribe to, and teach as their belief.* In the Sixth Article it is said, that "Holy Scripture containeth all things necessary to salvation; so that whatever is not read therein, nor may be proved thereby, is not to be required of any man that it should be believed as an article of faith, or be thought requisite or necessary to salvation." In this passage there is not one word about the individual right of any one to judge for himself—it only teaches that no one is to be charged with the belief of any doctrine, no one can be required to give his adhesion to any article, which is not contained in the Word of God. But it is here evident, that the application of the rule is placed in other hands; that it is intended to prevent some one, not named, from exacting belief beyond a certain point; it is a limitation of the power to *require* submission to the teaching of some authority. That this authority is the Church, there can be no doubt, if we compare the Twentieth Article. There it is said, that "The Church hath power to ordain rites and ceremonies, and authority in controversies of faith; and yet it is not lawful for the Church to ordain any thing contrary to God's Word written; neither may it so expound any passage of Scripture, as to be repugnant to another."†

---

* I have been censured for including the Church of England among those Protestants who hold private judgment, and arguing against it on this ground. I am ready to acknowledge that there is a large and respectable body in the Anglican Church, to whose principles the reasoning of this and other lectures will not apply; and this is even more true now than when the lectures were delivered. But I should greatly doubt whether among the great numbers who attended them there were any, or at least sufficient, to warrant my departure from the discussion of *popular* Protestantism, whether in or out of the Church. To such, therefore, must the published lectures be considered as addressed. The peculiar views of a certain portion of the English Church, represented by the Oxford Divines, belong to a totally different sphere of controversy.

† The reader will observe, that I overlook the important inquiry, whether this article, as far as "and yet," is genuine or not. Dr. Burnet acknowledges that it is not found in the original manuscripts containing the subscriptions; and it is absent from the copy of the articles approved by Parliament. The bishop supposes it to have been added between the subscription and the engrossing; and fancies the engrossed copy to have perished at Lambeth. (Exposition of the Thirty-nine Articles, Lond. 1695, p. 10.) But this conjecture, as well as other arguments in favor of the clause, are ably confuted by Collins, in his "Priestcraft in Perfection." Lond. 1710. To his arguments we may add, that, in the "Articles of Religion agreed upon by the Archbishops and Bishops of Ireland, in 1615," Lond. 1629, the clause on authority in controversies of faith is omitted, though the articles are verbatim the same, with additions. In the "Copie of the proceedings of some worthy and learned Divines, appointed by the Lords, to meet at the Bishop of Lincolne's, in Westminster, touching innovations in the doctrines and discipline of the Church of England,"

LECTURE II.

This Article seems further to increase the complexity and confusion of the rule of faith, as laid down by the Established Church. It says, in the first place, that the Church has authority, in matters of faith; and then, that the Church cannot prescribe any thing contrary to Scripture. But, if it be determined, in these solemn terms, that the Church shall not enforce doctrines nor define systems contrary to the Word of God, the very proposition recognises the necessity of a superior authority, to control its decisions. For, if we should say, that, in this country, the judges of the land have authority in matters of law, but yet shall not be allowed to decree any thing contrary to the statutes; I ask you, is it not necessarily implied in the very enunciation of that proposition, that an authority somewhere exists, capable of judging whether those magistrates have contravened that rule, and of preventing their continuing so to act. When, therefore, it is, in like manner, affirmed that the Church has authority in matters of faith, yet a rule is given whereby the justice of its decisions is to be determined, and no exemption from error is allowed to it, it is no less implied that, besides the Church, there is some superior authority to prevent its acting contrary to the code that has been put into its hands. Now, what authority is this, and where does it reside? Is it that each one has to judge for himself, whether the Church be contradicting the express doctrines of Scripture, and, consequently, is each person thus constituted judge over the decisions of his Church? If so, this is the most anomalous form of society that ever was imagined. For, if each individual, singly in himself, has greater authority than the whole collectively—for the Church is a congregation formed of its members—the authority vested in that whole is void and nugatory.

Wherever there is limitation of jurisdiction, there must be superior control: and if *the Church* is not to be obeyed when it teaches any thing contrary to Scripture, there are only two alternatives,—either that limitation supposes an impossibility of its so doing, or it implies the possible case of the Church being lawfully disobeyed. The first would be the Catholic doctrine, and at open variance with the grounds whereon the Protestant Churches justify their original separation. The Catholic, too, will say that the Church *cannot* require any thing to be believed that is contrary to God's written word; but then the word which

---

Lond. 1641, we read, p. 1, "Innovations in Doctrine, 'quære, Whether, in the Twentieth Article, these words are not inserted, Habet Ecclesia authoritatem in controversiis fidei.'"

I pronounce emphatically is taken by him literally; the Church *cannot* teach any such doctrine, because God's word is pledged that she shall not. The superior control exists in the guidance of the Holy Spirit. But if the Church, not being infallible, may teach things contrary to Scripture, who shall judge it, and decide between it and those whose obedience it exacts? "If the salt lose its savor, with what shall *it* be salted?" In other words, if there be a tribunal of appeal from this fallible Church, where does it exist; in whose persons is its representation vested? Surely these are simple and obvious inquiries, resulting from this ill-conceived theory of Church authority.

But if I mention them, I cannot be expected to answer them; nor is this my duty. I propose them merely to show some of the many difficulties which arise against the ordinary and popular way of propounding the Protestant rule of faith. Well, then, we will take the rule with all its difficulties—we will take it on the terms on which it is commonly understood, namely, that it is the prerogative, the unalienable privilege, of every Christian, to establish for himself the truth of his doctrines from that Book which God has delivered to man; nay more, that, (according to Doctor Beveridge's rule, which you will see confirmed by other and later authors,) each individual is bound to look to the proofs of what he specifically believes, and obliged to be a member of his Christian Church, on grounds which he has himself verified. I will first take the principle in this general and broad view, and see how far it is possible to apply it as the basis of faith: to simplify the examination, I will look at it under three different aspects. First, I will discuss the ground or authority for this rule; secondly, its application; and thirdly, its end.

I. I must suppose that the moment human authority is alluded to, in connection with the doctrines of Christianity, there will be the greatest jealousy and reserve about allowing it, in any way, to interfere in the scale or range of argument whereby the principle that excludes all authority has to be established. I must suppose that every Protestant, in examining the grounds of his religion, is most careful not to allow a single ingredient to mingle which might seem to give the authority of man any weight among the grounds on which he believes. I am willing to suppose that he must have a method independent of this dreaded principle, whereby he can satisfy himself individually of the divine authority of the Book in which he exclusively believes: and there must be some train of reasoning, whereby he can assure himself that the written record, in which he professes to put his whole trust, and which he holds as the only rule of faith, is really a volume of divine revelation. If it be the duty of every one to take the word of God as his only and sufficient rule, that rule thereby becomes universal in its application, being the rule of every individual member of the Christian Church. The grounds, therefore, on which it rests must be equally universal, and within the reach of all. If every man, even the most illiterate, have a right to study the word of God,—if it be not only his right, but his duty to do so, and thence to draw his belief,—it is no less his duty to satisfy himself that it is the word of God: and the process of reasoning by which to arrive at that conclusion must be naturally so simple, that none who is obliged to use it can be debarred from its construction.

The investigation whereby he can reach the conclusion that the sacred volume put into his hand is really the Word of God, is of a twofold character. In the first place, before any Protestant can even commence the examination of that rule, which his religion proposes to him, he must have satisfied himself, that all the books or writings collected together in that volume, are really the genuine works of those whose names they bear; and that no such genuine work has been excluded; so that the rule be perfect and entire. Then, in the second place, he must satisfy himself, by his own individual examination, that this book is inspired by God.

Now, my brethren, allow me to ask you, how many of those who profess the Protestant religion have made these examinations? How many can say, that they have satisfied themselves, in the first place, that the canon of Scripture put into their hands, or that collection of sacred treatises which we call the Bible, really consists of the genuine, authentic works of their supposed writers, and excludes none that have a claim to equal authenticity? I do not intend to show you the difficulties of this process, on my own authority; I do not maintain that it is not followed by Protestants, on my own assertion; nor do I intend to demonstrate, that it is the duty of every Protestant to search and satisfy himself, by my bare word,—but, I will quote to you the authority of two divines, who are generally considered learned and well-informed in this department of sacred literature.

The first whom I will quote, is the Reverend Jeremiah Jones, a celebrated Nonconformist divine, at the commencement of the last century; as he died in 1724. He published a very learned and careful, and even difficult treatise, entitled, "A new and full method of settling the canonical authority of the New Testament."

The Reformation had already lasted a great many years, and yet, it was only then that he found out a *new* and *full* way of establishing the New Testament in canonical authority. To the first volume he prefixes a long dissertation on the importance and difficulties of his subject. I will content myself with reading to you the heads of the sections or essays which compose it, as summed up at its commencement. I quote the edition published at Oxford, in 1827; in the first page of which we have the following heads: " First, that the right settling of the canonical authority of the books of the New Testament *is attended with very many and great difficulties.* Second, that it is a matter of the greatest consequence and importance. Third, *that a great number of Christians are destitute of any good arguments for their belief of the canonical authority of the books of the New Testament.* Fourth, *that very little has been done on this subject."*

After this, we have an enumeration of the reasons why it is exceedingly difficult to prove the authenticity of all the books which compose the New Testament. The first is, the immense number of works, professing to be written by apostles and evangelists, which are to be excluded from the canon; for Toland, in his Amyntor, enumerates eighteen such, which have been condemned, and, consequently, are not now received; and Mr. Jones remarks that the list is very far from being complete. Then there are other works, acknowledged to be written by disciples of the apostles, by persons in the same situation as St. Luke and St. Mark. Such are Barnabas and Hermas; whose writings, accordingly, some divines of the last century thought should be received as portions of the canon of Scripture. For Pearson, Grabe, and others, consider them genuine productions of disciples; and therefore good reasons should be given why they are not to be received, as well as the writings of St. Luke or St. Mark. These, our author observes, are matters of serious difficulty, and require immense reflection and trouble to be satisfactorily explained. In fact, he occupies three closely printed volumes in examining and discussing them. Yet, all this is only preliminary to the inquiry, whether the Scripture be the Word of God.

The second head is, " that this is a matter of the greatest consequence and importance," and here this writer has remarked, precisely what I have, that it is the duty of every member of the Reformed Church to satisfy himself, individually, of the grounds on which he receives the Bible. In the third section, he states, "that a great number of Christians are destitute of any good arguments for their belief of the canonical authority of these Books;" and this is completed by the last section, wherein he proves, "that nothing at all had been done by the Church of England, or the foreign Reformed Churches, to prove that these were the Scriptures!" I will now quote you his own words, to put his sentiments beyond doubt, and to justify all that I have said. In page 12, he speaks thus: "He who has but the least occasion to acquaint himself with the religious state of mankind, cannot but with surprising concern have observed, how slender and uncertain the principles are, upon which men receive the Scriptures as the word of God. The truth is, though a very painful one, that many persons commence religious at once, they don't know why, and so with a blind zeal persist in a religion which is they don't know what; and, *by the chance of education, and the force of custom, they receive these Scriptures as the Word of God, without making any serious inquiries, and consequently, without being able to give any solid reasons why they believe them to be such.*" The greater portion of Protestants, then, according to this divine, believe in the Scriptures, without having any foundation for doing so—they receive it gratuitously as the Word of God, without being able to prove it, or ever having heard the reasons on which it can be proved.

Yet this is not so strong as what I will now read, from another divine, of nearly the same period; I mean the celebrated Richard Baxter, who, in his well-known and popular work, "The Saints' Everlasting Rest," speaks very feelingly on the subject, and puts a very strong argument into our mouths. In page 197, he says, "Are the more exercised, understanding sort of Christians able by sound arguments to make good the verity of Scripture? Nay, are the meaner sort of ministers able to do this? Let them that have tried, judge." Not only, then, according to him, the better exercised and understanding class of Protestants, but even the lower order of ministers or teachers, are not able to prove the truth of Scripture. In page 201, we have the following still more remarkable passage:—"It is strange to consider how we all abhor that piece of Popery, as most injurious to God of all the rest, which resolves our faith into the authority of the Church; and yet that we do, for the generality of professors, content ourselves with the same kind of faith, only with this difference,— the Papists believe Scripture to be the Word of God, because their Church saith so, and we, *because our Church or our leaders say so*. Yea, and many ministers never yet gave their people better grounds, but tell them that it is damnable to deny it, *but help*

F 4*

them not to the antecedents of faith." Again, in the following page:—"It is to be understood, that *many thousands do profess Christianity*, and zealously hate the enemies thereof upon the same grounds, to the same end, and from the same inward corrupt principles, as the Jews did hate and kill Christ. It is the religion of the country, and every man is reproached that believes otherwise; they were born and brought up in this belief, and it hath increased in them upon the like occasions. Had they been born and bred in the religion of Mohammed, they would have been as zealous for him. The difference between him and the Mohammedan is more that he lives where better laws and religion dwell, than that he hath more knowledge or soundness of apprehension."

I need not, perhaps, remind you, that the last of these divines was, subsequently to the Restoration, chaplain to the king, and that, consequently, he may reasonably be supposed to have known, not merely the doctrines of his Church, but the state of its members.

I am sure, that the extracts from these two authors will abundantly demonstrate, and justify every assertion I have made. They bear strong testimony to what I advanced last evening, and proved from Dr. Beveridge: first, that it is the duty of each Protestant to satisfy himself of the grounds on which he receives and holds his faith: secondly, that the process whereby the first antecedents of faith are to be demonstrated is extremely difficult; that the attainment of the first step in the graduated reasoning necessary for establishing the Protestant rule, the fixing of its first link, is a complicated and uneasy operation: thirdly, that the majority of Protestants do live and remain Protestants without ever having gone through that course of conviction which their religion requires as absolutely necessary; in other words, are not brought, by the profession of their religion, to the embracing, practically, of the vital principle of their creed; nay, that many of them, as Dr. Beveridge has likewise observed, have no better grounds for being Christians than a Turk has for being a Mohammedan: fourthly, that the Protestant Church, for two hundred years, had done little or nothing towards establishing the first elementary principles of its belief upon any logical foundation.

Yet is all this inquiry but secondary or preliminary, when compared with the great investigation into the inspiration of the Scriptures. These Scriptures are inspired—that is the general, and, doubtless, the true belief. But, on what grounds does it rest? Is it a matter of very simple demonstration, or one which proves itself almost intuitively? If you wish to satisfy yourselves on this point, take up the writings of authors who have treated of their inspiration, and you will be astonished, I am sure, to find how exceedingly difficult it is to bring such arguments as will satisfy an unbeliever. I will venture to say, that, having perused, with great attention, all that has fallen in my way, from Protestant writers, on this subject, I have hardly found one single argument advanced by them, that is not logically incorrect; so, that, if I had not higher grounds on which to rest my belief, they could not have led me to adopt it.

There are two classes of proofs generally advanced in favor of inspiration: internal arguments, drawn from the books themselves, and external ones, from the testimony of others. Now, regarding the first; it is not fair to consider the Sacred Volume, when under this examination, as forming an individual whole. Many of its books stand, necessarily, on different grounds from the rest. For instance, learned Protestant divines, especially on the Continent, have excluded from inspiration the writings of St. Luke and St. Mark, for this reason, that according to them, the only argument for inspiration in the New Testament, is, the promise of divine assistance given to the apostles. But these were not apostles, they were not present at the promise, and if you extend that privilege beyond those who were present, and to whom the promise was personally addressed, the rule will have no farther limit. If you admit disciples to have partaken of the privelege, on what ground is Barnabas excluded, and why is not his epistle held canonical? Therefore, if argument is drawn from the character of those who wrote, it is evident that they do not all rest upon the same proof.

Further, in examining the inspiration of the two Testaments, we stand upon different ground. For the Old, as having been received as inspired by our Saviour and his apostles, we have all the evidence which we require. But the New must be proved upon evidence, other than that of persons themselves inspired. For nowhere does our Saviour tell his apostles, that whatever they may write shall enjoy this privilege, nor do they anywhere claim it. We are, therefore, driven to the inquiry, was all that an apostle wrote necessarily inspired, or were only those books which we possess? If the former be the case, then we have surely lost many inspired works; for no one, I should think, can doubt, but that St. Paul wrote many more epistles or letters than have been preserved. If the latter, I would ask what internal mark of inspiration can we discover in the third epistle of St. John, to show that the inspiration, *sometimes* accorded, must have been granted here? Is there any thing in that epistle which a good and virtuous pastor of the primitive ages might not have written? any thing superior in sentiment or doctrine, to what an Ignatius or a Polycarp might have indited?

It is unfair, then, in the extreme, as I before intimated, to consider the New Testament, and still more the entire Bible, as a whole; and to use *internal* arguments from one book to another; to assume, for instance, that the Song of Solomon has internal evidence of inspiration, because the book of Jeremiah, which is in the same volume, contains true prophecies; or that the Epistle to Philemon is necessarily inspired, because the Apocalypse by its side is a revelation. Yet, such is a common way of arguing. If internal evidence have to decide the question, show it me for each book in that sacred collection.

A popular opponent of the Catholic belief, on a late public occasion, summing up the arguments for the inspiration of Scripture, reduces the internal evidences to such heads as these: the *exalted character given to God, the description of human nature, the provision revealed in it to man* after his fall, *its morality, and its impartiality.** Now I would appeal to any man of unbiassed

---

* Rev. Mr. Tottenham, Downside Discussion, p. 144.—He divides the evidences into three classes,—the historical, of which something will be said in the text, the internal, and the experimental. This consists in the effects produced by *the Bible* in *changing the character of men.* Here is an error; for the Bible, as a book, has not that effect; but only the doctrines it contains. These, if preached, will be often more effectual in changing the lives of sinners, than if read. And as such conversions do not prove the preacher's sermon to be inspired, but only the doctrines which he teaches to be good, and, if you please, divine; so neither can a similar fact prove the Bible inspired, but merely its doctrines to be holy and salutary. The "Imitation of Christ" may be thus proved to be an inspired work. Mr. Tottenham quotes a passage from Abbot, to show that, as a boy would know phosphorus, from his learning from good authority where it was bought, from its looking like phosphorus, and from its burning, so may we know the Scriptures to be inspired from similar arguments, but principally from the last. Here is the error repeated. A boy may have seen phosphorus a thousand times already; he has a term of comparison. We have no other Bible or inspired work, of which to say, our Bible is inspired, because it has the qualities of inspiration known to exist in that. But Protestants first, from the very book under examination, *assume* the characteristics of inspiration, and then apply them as evidence or tests to itself. What is meant by the "universal and irresistible power of the Bible, in changing the character and saving from suffering and sin," I do not understand. *Grace,* I should imagine, is the effectual agent in these acts; and how the Bible is proved to be *inspired,* by being a channel and instrument of grace, any more than an effectual sermon which brings the sinner to repentance, is not very clear. For I cannot for one moment suppose, that "power" is supposed by these writers to reside in the material book, or its letters; though there is some reason to fear that such image-worship is far from uncommon in this country.

judgment, whether these considerations would amount to a convincing argument, in the mind of one who had yet to believe the great, supernatural fact of a divine inspiration? For, observe, the entire mass of proofs consists in an assumption of the disputed point. For, whether the morality of the Bible, and its doctrines regarding God and the soul, are proofs of inspiration, must depend upon our previous conviction that the systems of these things, there taught, are true. We have learnt from the Bible that man fell, we have imbibed from it the idea that the best and only remedy for his state was an atonement; and then we conclude that the Book must be inspired which gives so consistent a remedy, of whose aptitude or even possibility we never should or could have thought, but for the very book whose inspiration we are establishing.

But these proofs will be as nothing to the unbeliever, whom you wish to gain to a belief in this groundwork of the Protestant faith, and who knows or believes not that man is fallen, and needed a provision; or that the character of human nature is so much more correct in the Bible, as to have necessarily been dictated by God. The Hindoo brings every one of the same heads of evidence for his Vedas;* and the Mohammedan for his Koran.

But two classes of arguments this writer throws among the historical ones, which prove still further the weakness of his reasoning. The first is "*miracles*, which were wrought in attestation of their *doctrine*, by the writers of the books of Scripture." —Yes, in favor of the truth of *their doctrines*, but not of the inspirations of their writings: for the facts are perfectly distinct. Barnabas, too, wrought miracles in proof of the Christian *doctrine;* but not, therefore, has his epistle been considered canonical, even by those who think it genuine. Tertullian, Eusebius, and others, speak of miracles wrought by early Christians, to prove their faith; yet not, therefore, were their writings inspired.

His second proof is the prophecies recorded in Scripture. These may, indeed, prove any book to be inspired which is composed of them, but not, surely, any wherein they are merely recorded.

But no one, perhaps, has more completely betrayed the impossibility of proving the inspiration of Scripture upon mere

---

* See the Rev. A. Duff's "Church of Scotland's India Mission;" Edinburgh, 1835, p. 4.

Protestant grounds, than one who has been most laborious in the task. The Rev. Hartwell Horne has devoted a very long chapter of his "Introduction to the Critical Study of the Holy Scriptures," to the proofs of inspiration. Now mark the very heading of this chapter, or rather of its leading section. "The miracles *related* in the Old and New Testaments, are proofs that the Scriptures were given by inspiration of God." And the substance of the chapter corresponds with its title, for it is taken up with proving that the miracles *recorded* in the Gospel are true miracles.* True miracles! Yes, certainly, but there are true miracles related in the writings of Josephus, and in ecclesiastical history, yet are not they proved thereby to be inspired. The argument is treated by Horne, under a complicated variety of heads, so that it is not easy to discover the line of argument that conducts him through it; but the result amounts to this, that the Scripture is inspired, because true miracles are *recorded* in it.

I leave it to you to judge whether this reasoning be sound. Such recorded miracles might satisfy me, that those who wrote the records of them would tell the truth, if they should ever say that they were inspired; because God's working miracles to support their assertions would give the sanction of His authority to what they wrote. But show me where St. Matthew or St. Mark say that they have written their books under the inspiration of the Holy Ghost; or by the command of God, or for any other than human purposes? Unless you can show this, any miraculous evidence of their character will prove that whatever they wrote is true; but not that it was written under the guidance of the Holy Ghost.

Precisely of a similar form is his argument drawn from prophecy; it is never attempted to be shown how the prophecies *recorded* in the New Testament, were intended to prove the inspiration of the books which contain them; how, for instance, the truth of our blessed Redeemer's prophecy, touching the destruction of Jerusalem, can demonstrate that the Gospel of St. Matthew must be inspired, because it relates it.†

If these methods of proving the inspiration fail, you must have recourse to outward authority—that is to say, to the testimony of man. But how is this to be obtained? Here again, considerable difficulties are introduced by writers on this subject. For there is a great difference between testimony to

---

* Vol. I. p. 204, 7th ed.   † Ibid. p. 272.

external and that to internal facts. We require a very different chain of evidence to connect the last link with the conviction of our minds, in the one and in the other. I will explain my meaning. That St. Matthew, St. Mark, or St. John wrote the gospels which bear their names, is a public fact; one to which many persons might be qualified to speak, who either saw them engaged on them, or received them from them, or knew from public and uncontradicted belief, in or near their times, that they composed and published them. This historical evidence is considered sufficient for attesting the genuineness of any other author's writings; and I must consequently admit it here. Nay, were you to deny the genuineness of the sacred writings, because there is not evidence of them for twenty or thirty years after they were written, you must reject many ancient works, which were not published for many years after their authors' deaths; of which, yet, nobody doubts the genuineness.

But when you come to speak to me of what passed in the minds of the authors when they wrote these books, I must have some more immediate connecting link—I must have the earliest relater of the circumstance. Let us take a similar case: if I am told by history that such an architect erected a building among the ruins of Rome, and I find it recorded on the edifice, I do not doubt the fact: but if you tell me that he built it in consequence of a particular dream, which suggested the idea of its peculiar parts; in order to satisfy myself of the truth of this circumstance, I surely require a different character of testimony than will convince me of the overt, visible and notorious fact, that he merely raised it. I must trace it to some one who had it directly from him; for he alone can give testimony of the covert and inward fact. Thus, similarly, you may believe who wrote and published those books, upon the simple attestation of history; but when you come to establish their inspiration— the internal, secret, mysterious communication that passed between the innermost soul of the writer and the Holy Ghost, of which none other could be conscious, or have evidence save from them, you require the last link of evidence which completes the chain, and which can alone establish the fact.

The authority then, of history, or of ecclesiastical tradition, independently of the divine force allowed it by the Catholic, can prove no more than the genuineness or truth of the Scripture narrative; but, to be available as a proof of inspiration, it must carry us directly to the attestation of the only witnesses capable of certifying the circumstance. It may be true that the Church, or body of Christians, in succeeding times, believed the books of the New Testament to be inspired. But if that Church and its traditions be not infallible, that belief goes no farther than a mere human or historical testimony: it can verify, therefore, no more than such testimony ever can; that is, outward and visible facts; such as the publication, and, consequently, the legitimacy of a work. The only way in which it can attest the interior acts which accompanied its compilation, is by preserving the assurances of those who, besides God, could alone be witnesses to them. Now, ecclesiastical history has not preserved to us this important testimony; for nowhere have we it recorded of any of these writers, that he asserted his own inspiration. And thus, by rejecting tradition as an infallible authority, is the only basis for the inspiration of Scripture cut away.

Hitherto, my brethren, of what have I been treating? Why, of nothing more than the preliminaries requisite to commence the study of the Protestant rule of faith. I have merely shown that the obstacles and difficulties to receiving the Bible as the word of God, are numerous and complicated; and yet, if it is the duty of every Protestant to believe all that he professes, *because* he has sought and discovered it in the word of God; if, consequently, it is his duty to be satisfied only on his own evidence, as the divines of his Church have stated; if, to attain this conviction, it is necessary for him to go through a long and painful course of learned disquisitions; and if, after all these have been encountered, he cannot come to a satisfactory demonstration of the most important point of inspiration,—I ask you, can the rule, in the very approach to which you must pass through such a labyrinth of difficulties, be that which God has given as a guide to the poorest, the most illiterate, and simplest of his creatures?

II. Such, then, is merely the difficulty of obtaining possession of the rule; but when it has been obtained—(I come now to speak of the application)—is it not surrounded with equal, or even greater difficulties than these? We are to suppose that God gave his Holy Word to be the only rule of faith to all men. It must be a rule, therefore, easy to be procured, and to be held. God himself must have made the necessary provision, that all men should have it, and be able to apply it. What then does he do? He gives us a large volume written in two languages; the chief portion in one known to a small and limited country of the world. He allows that speech to become a dead language, so that countless difficulties and obscurities should spring up re-

LECTURE II.

garding the meaning of innumerable passages. The other portion he gives in a language spoken by a larger body of mankind, but still by a very small proportion, considering the extent of those to whom the blessings of Christianity were intended to be communicated; and we are to suppose that he gives this book as a satisfactory and sufficient rule of faith.

In the first place, then, we must naturally understand that it is to be translated into every language, that so all men may have access to it: in the second place, it must be so distributed, that all may have possession of it; and, in the third place, it must be so easy, that all men may use it. Are these the characteristics of this rule?

1. Suppose it to be the only rule of all who believe in Christ, are you aware of the difficulty of undertaking a translation of it? Whenever the attempt has been made in modern times, in the first instance, it has generally failed; and even after many repeated attempts, it has proved unsatisfactory. Had I time, or were it necessary, I could show you, from various Reports of the Bible Society, and from the acknowledgment of its members, that many versions, after having been diffused among the natives of countries to be converted, have been necessarily withdrawn, on account of the absurdities, impieties, and innumerable errors which they contained. And this is the rule that has been put into the hands of men! But look to the history of even more celebrated translations, such as are put forth by authority. I speak not of those early versions which were made when the knowledge of the facts and circumstances was fresh, and when those who wrote, better understood the original languages. But look at any modern version, such as that authorized in these realms. Read the account of how often it was corrected; what combinations of able and learned men it required to bring it to a tolerable degree of accuracy. Its worth, after all, as a rule, must depend upon the skill and fitness of individuals for the task of translating; and can we reasonably suppose that the providence of God would stake the whole usefulness and value of His rule upon the private or particular abilities of man?

2. Secondly, what are the difficulties attending its diffusion? Oh, my brethren! could you look at this matter in another age from the present, you might better understand it. You fancy, possibly, that because Bibles are now multiplied by thousands, and by millions, their application as a rule is obvious and easy; that because there is one nation on the globe possessed of immense wealth, and mighty empire, and having ships that fre-

quent the farthest bounds of earth—that because there are men willing to devote their time, and wealth, and zeal to the publication and diffusion of these books—that because, in this country, and at the present time, a combination of political, commercial, and literary circumstances facilitates this distribution, therefore the rule is sufficiently accessible to all mankind. But God does not plan the rule of his faith in accordance with the possible literary or commercial prosperity of any country; nor so construct the groundwork of his truth as to depend upon the mechanical inventions of man. The Gospel's being the rule of faith, can have no connection with the circumstance, that the press, by the aid of the strongest mechanical power applied to it, has now produced the Bible in measureless abundance. God could not mean, that, for 1,400 years, man should be without a religious guide; or that he should have to wait until human genius had given efficacy to one by its discoveries and inventions. Such cannot be the qualities or conditions of the rule. We must look for it as one for all times, and for all places; as something coming into operation so soon as delivered, and destined to last until the end of time. We cannot therefore admit, as the only necessary rule of faith, that which depends for its adoption on the accidental instrumentality of man, and requires, essentially, his unprescribed co-operation.

For I think that, on reflection, any unprejudiced mind will rather wonder how, in the Word of God, there should have been no provision made for this important condition. Why do we never find any precept given to the apostles to disseminate the Scriptures, after having them translated into all languages? How comes it, that no intimation is ever given therein of the duty of ministers to provide copies of the sacred volume for those whom they are bound to instruct? If this dissemination of the written word was and is an essential part of Christianity, and if in scripture alone is to be found the rule and criterion of all that is essential, how comes this important provision to be there omitted? Nay, as our acquaintance with history proves to us the utter impossibility of the Bible's being extensively circulated without the aid of the press, why was not its invention provided for, as the necessary instrument for arriving at the rule and groundwork of faith? Surely the Bible Society is no part of the economy and machinery of Christianity; and yet, without it, the Scriptures could not have been diffused, to the extent which we have witnessed in modern times.

3. This difficulty of disseminating the supposed rule of faith,

is much exceeded by that of understanding it. For to be the rule of faith, it cannot be sufficient that men should possess and read it; but they must surely be able to comprehend it. In fact, who ever heard of the propriety or wisdom of placing in men's hands a code, or rule, which it was impossible for the greater portion of them to comprehend?

As I perceive that I have already detained you much beyond what the proportion of my subject already discussed might seem to warrant, I shall be obliged to condense, considerably, what remains of my discourse; and I cannot dwell at length upon the consideration of much that is important; such as the examination of those serious difficulties which prevent ordinary readers from understanding even the easier parts of Scripture. For I will not speak of sublimer passages; of those divine Psalms, which are acknowledged to be lyric poetry of the highest order—a class of writing difficult to most readers in their own language, often almost unintelligible in the profane authors of antiquity, and still more so in the Scriptures, from the greater boldness of the figures, and the greater conciseness of the speech. I will not dwell upon the mysterious imagery of the prophets' visions, and the obscure language in which it is recorded. But I might select ordinary passages of Scripture, and show you the difficulties that exist in the way of arriving at a proper conception, or any understanding, thereof. And this might still be farther confirmed, by stating the elaborate commentaries, and the immense mass of conflicting opinions of Protestant expositors, when attempting to clear up the obscurity of passages, which many of my hearers have, perhaps, read again and again, without perceiving that they contained a difficulty. And this has happened, not because there was no difficulty, but because they looked with a superficial eye on the words of the text, so as best to accommodate them to preconceived opinions, or else because they wanted acuteness sufficient even to discover a real difficulty where it exists. But this is a subject on which I need not touch. It is sufficient to look over the collections of commentators, to count the number of their volumes, and measure the bulk of matter written on almost every verse of Scripture, to satisfy yourselves that it is not so easy a book.

Such, therefore, are the difficulties regarding the application of this rule: a difficulty of procuring and preserving the proper sense of the original by correct translations; a difficulty of bringing this translation within the reach of all; a difficulty, not to say an impossibility, of enabling all to understand it.

III. I have thus treated of the grounds of the rule, and of its application. I shall now say a few words regarding its end. What is the end to be attained by the use of any rule? Uniformity of thought and action, in those matters which it regulates. What is the end of any law, but that all men should know what their conduct ought to be in any given case, and what will be the result and consequence, good or evil, of a different course? Of what use is a code of regulations drawn up by any body or society, but that all its members should act in the same manner, and so procure that union which is the necessary basis and bond of every society? And if God has given us a rule, or code of principles, is it not that all should be brought to know the same duties, and to practise the same virtues? Is it not that all should be brought to entertain the same faith?

And has this rule of faith proved equal to that only end? Most avowedly not. It is not necessary to go far from the ground on which I am standing, to see many places of worship maintaining conflicting doctrines, and all professing to be taught on the authority of that one book. Here one man will denounce, as contrary to the Christian faith, the doctrines of Calvinism; there, another, with equal zeal, upholds them as the most essential groundwork of Christianity. In one, you will hear the divinity of the Son of God, and the sublime mystery of the Trinity, decried as a human device; and in another, you will hear a creed recited, wherein all those who deny those doctrines are condemned to eternal loss. And yet all hold the same book in their hands, and quote almost the same passages, while they profess an almost endless variety of conflicting and contradictory doctrines.

And is not this result, this solution of the problem, a satisfactory evidence of the insufficiency of the proposed rule? Suppose that a law were passed, and that, as we have often seen within the last few years in these realms, it were found, that, in one part of the country, the magistrates, with it in their hands, were led to one course of proceeding, and, in another, to an opposite line, so that contradictions should arise, and men know not how to act upon it; would it not be considered inadequate for its purposes; and would not a new one be brought in to correct and amend that which had been found deficient? And why? Because a law is, in every system of jurisprudence, considered inadequate to its end, if it do not bring men to uniformity of action. And this, by analogy, being the end of a rule of faith, to bring men to a uniformity of faith, that rule must be insufficient that does not answer such a purpose.

Thus much may suffice regarding the Protestant grounds of faith, considered merely in themselves. I have endeavored to show you the necessity of every Protestant satisfying himself, not only of the truth of his doctrine, but of the very rule on which he bases it; and I have exposed to you not only the difficulty, but the impossibility, on his principles, of arriving at a clear definition of this rule; then, the difficulty which accompanies its application, and its insufficiency for its end.

As I have spoken so much of the Word of God, and as I fear that some present, misled, perhaps, by feelings infused into them by education, may have been tempted to think that we, universally, and myself in particular, speak with unbecoming disparagement thereof, I wish, before closing this portion of my subject, to state what is the practice and belief of Catholics regarding the Scriptures.

We are told that the Catholic loves not the Scriptures; that his Church esteems not the Word of God; that it wishes to suppress it, to put the light of God under a bushel, and so extinguish it. The Catholic Church not love and esteem the word of God! Is there any other Church that places a heavier stake on the authority of the Scriptures, than the Catholic? Is there any other Church that pretends to base so much of rule over men on the words of that book? Is there any one, consequently, that has a greater interest in maintaining, preserving, and exhibiting that Word? For those who have been educated in that religion know, that when the Church claims authority, it is on the Holy Scriptures that she grounds it; and is not this giving it a weighty importance beyond what any other Church will attempt? And not only has she ever loved and cherished it, but she has been jealous of its honor and preservation, so as no other religion can pretend to boast. Will you say that a mother hath not loved her child, who has warmed and nursed it in her bosom for years, when nothing else would have saved it from perishing—who has spent her blood and her strength in defending and rescuing it from the attempts of foes and rivals on its life; who has doated on it till scoffed at by others; lavished treasures on its embellishment, and done whatever her means would allow to make it seem beautiful, and lovely, and estimable in the eyes of men? For, if you would say this, then may you also say, that the Church hath not cherished and esteemed the Word of God.

For, first, she caught up its different fragments and portions, as they proceeded from the inspired writers, and united them together. To those who pretend that the Catholic Church extended not so far back, I will say, that it was the Catholic principle of unity which, alone, could have enabled Churches to communicate to one another the respective books and letters addressed to them by the apostles; and it was only on the communication of the authority which their testimony gave, that the canon of Scripture was framed. Did she not afterwards keep men by hundreds, and thousands, employed in nothing else than in transcribing the Holy Word of God; ay, in letters of gold, and upon parchment of purple, to show her respect and veneration for it? Has she not commanded it to be studied in every religious house, in every university, in every ecclesiastical college, and expounded to the faithful in every place, and at all times? Has she not produced, in every age, learned and holy men, who have dedicated themselves to its illustration by erudite commentaries, and popular expositions? Were there not, in what are called the darkest ages, men like Alcuin and Lanfranc, who devoted much of their lives to the detection of such errors as had crept into it by accident? And is it not to all this fostering care that we are indebted that the Word of God now exists? And while we have copies of it so splendid as to attest the immense labor devoted to their production, we have others in the cheapest and most portable form that could be procured from the pen, to show that they were in the hands of all who could possibly, under such circumstances, be able to obtain them. But every copy was the work of the penman, and could not be so easily produced, nor so widely circulated.

But I say, that the Catholic Church has been always foremost, not only in the task of translating the Scriptures, but also in placing it in the hands of the faithful. It is but a few months since I was, I may not say shocked, but truly and deeply grieved, to see the whole country roused, by the trumpet of bigotry, to celebrate what was called the Jubilee of the Reformation! and that was dated from what was announced as the first complete translation of the Bible into English.* I was grieved, I say, to see, in the first instance, that any Church could be so deluded as to consider a duration of three hundred years a motive for triumph—that any establishment purporting to be based upon the Rock of Ages, and to exist by the unalterable decrees of Divine

---

* This alludes to the tercentenary commemoration of the Reformation, celebrated on the 4th of October, 1835.

LECTURE II.

Providence, professing to hold the purest and most enduring doctrines, should think three hundred years worthy to be made a date of universal rejoicing, while we can count hundreds upon hundreds; nay, the two-thousandth year shall come without our signalizing it in any manner, save by the discharge of our duty to give daily praise and thanks to the Almighty. In the second place, I was grieved to think, that all this excitement should have been created—I will not say, by falsehood, but by misapprehension; that an attempt should have been made to bring crowds together, to commemmorate an event as giving commencement to a certain period, which yet had no connection with it.

For it is well known, or ought to have been known, to those who raised this cry, that long before any Protestant version existed in any language in Europe, there were, not one, or two, or five, or ten, but almost innumerable translations, not only in manuscript, but in print, for the use of the faithful, in the short interval between the invention of printing and the rise of Protestantism. And as I know that a different opinion prevails, even among some Catholics, on this point, I will give a few particulars, that so you may be on your guard against similar misconceptions.

Let us take Germany as an instance. A clergyman, who was among the most active promoters of the late tercentenary festival, speaks of Luther's version as the first published in Germany. He simply says, that "so early as the year 1466, a German translation from the Latin Vulgate, was printed, the author of which is unknown. Scarcely, however, had the Reformation commenced, when Luther meditated a new version."* And a little later, he observes, "that besides the versions made by Protestants, there are also translations made by Romish divines, some of which appeared *almost* as early as that of Luther."† Now, how accurate all this is, you shall see, from the enumeration which I will give you of the Catholic translations, and their editions made before that of Luther, which was begun in 1523, but not completed until eleven years afterwards.

In the first place, there is a copy yet extant of a printed version so old as to have no date; for the first printed books had

---

* Horne, vol. ii., Appendix, p. 88.
† P. 91, Mr. Horne adds, that "the Romanists, in Germany have evinced an ardent desire for the Scriptures, notwithstanding the fulminations of the Papal See against them." The inaccuracy of this writer, in all that concerns Catholics, is truly astonishing. Why did he not tell us when these fulminations were pronounced?

neither a date nor name of place. In the second place, a Catholic version was printed by Fust, in 1472, nearly sixty years before the completion of Luther's version. Another had appeared as early as 1467; a fourth was published in 1472; and a fifth in 1473. At Nuremberg, there was a version published in 1477, and republished *three times more*, before Luther's appeared. There appeared, at Augsburg, another in the same year, which went through eight editions before that of Luther. At Nuremberg, one was published, by Koburg, in 1483, and in 1488; and at Augsburg, one appeared in 1518, which was republished in 1524, about the same time that Luther was going on with his; and down to the present time, the editions of this version have been almost countless.

In Spain, a version appeared, in 1478, before Luther was thought of, and almost before he was born. In Italy, the country most peculiarly under the sway of Papal dominion, the Scriptures were translated into Italian, by Malermi, at Venice, in 1471; and this version was republished seventeen times before the conclusion of that century, and twenty-three years before that of Luther appeared. A second version of parts of Scripture was published in 1472; a third at Rome, in 1471; a fourth by Bruccioli, at Venice, in 1532; and a corrected edition, by Marmochini, in 1538, two years after Luther had completed his. And every one of these came out, not only with the approbation of the ordinary authorities, but with that of the Inquisition, which approved of their being published, distributed, and promulgated.*

In France, a translation was published, in 1478; another, by Menand, in 1484; another, by Guiars de Moulins, in 1487; which may rather be called a History of the Bible; and, finally, another, by Jacques le Fevre, in 1512, often reprinted.

In the Belgian language, a version was published at Cologne, in 1475, which, before 1488, had been republished three times. A second appeared in 1518.

There was also a Bohemian translation, published in 1488, thrice reprinted before Luther's; not to speak of the Polish and Oriental versions. In our own country it is well known that there were versions long before that of Tyndal or of Wickliffe.

---

* I remember, some years ago, reading in an English Review that my learned and amiable relative, Don Tomas Gonzales de Carvajal, had met with difficulties from the Inquisition about the publication of his metrical version of the poetical books of Scripture. I believe the Inquisition did not exist at that time; but at any rate, the entire statement was without foundation.

LECTURE II.

Sir Thomas More has observed, that "the hole Byble, was, long before his (Wickliffe's) dayes, by vertuous and wel lerned men, translated into the English tong, and by good and godly people, with devotion and soberness, wel and reverently red."* And if it be said that the Scriptures were not disseminated, it was because the want of printing and of a general literary education prevented this.

I have mentioned these facts, to show how unjust is the assertion, that the spread of the Reformation gave rise to Scriptural translations,—how unjust it is to say that the Church has withheld the Bible from the people. But mark the change. The Scriptures had been diffused among the faithful, and would have so continued, had not dangerous doctrines sprung up, which taught that men should throw aside all authority, and each one judge for himself in religion; a system which we have seen fraught with such dreadful difficulties, that it is no wonder that it should have been made matter of discipline, to check, for a time, its perilous diffusion. Sir Thomas More truly observes, that, if we look at the act of Parliament on this subject, we shall find, that it was not any Church authority, but the civil government which first interfered. Because it was when the Scriptures had begun more to be read, from the times of the Waldenses and Wickliffe, that the doctrine was broached that the civil magistrate lost all his authority when he committed crime, and that no man had a right to possess jurisdiction, civil or ecclesiastical, if he was in a state of sin. When these doctrines had raised the arm of fanatics against social order, the civil authority called in the aid of the Church; although, in the first instance, the Church did not prohibit the diffusion of the Scriptures.

Those, therefore, who say that the Reformers were the first to communicate the Scriptures, are evidently in error; for they had previously been spread in the Catholic Church, which, subject to the supervision of its pastors, permitted almost, I might say quite, their indiscriminate perusal.

Thus much may suffice for the present. I have only as yet kept you amidst the outworks.—I have not yet brought you within the precincts, of the inquiry. In treating of the Protestant rule of faith, I have refrained from alluding to the decision of Scripture itself. As yet, I have handled it merely as a question of moral and philosophical discussion. I have simply deduced, from the nature of the rule itself, how far it can be considered

---

* A "dialogue concernynge heresyes." B. iii. c. 14, p. 232.

satisfactory. I have arrayed its difficulties before you, and I have shown that it requires a strong shelter under divine warrant and sanction to justify the institution of so complicated and difficult a rule. Now, whether there be that divine authority, I have not yet examined; for I have not touched upon the passages adduced, to prove that the Scripture is a satisfactory rule of faith. That I reserve for future discourses; when I hope I shall be able to meet, before you, all the arguments that are to be drawn from the Word of God. Next Friday, I will pass to the positive portion of my theme. Having first excluded, or partially removed, the system of others, I will proceed to what I consider the true and legitimate mode of argument on this subject; that is to say, to proving what we believe; and when you can compare the two systems together, you will judge between them which is the institution of God.

You may, perhaps, consider that system which I have already described, (and upon which, more has yet to be said,) as at first sight appearing regular, orderly, and beautiful. It may be compared to a handsome, modern edifice, which strikes you when passing along the high-road, and which, only judging of it, as you hasten on, by the measure of its outward proportions, by the artful scale on which it has been constructed, and the apparent uniformity of all its parts, has seemed to you to possess within, a proportionable fitness and beauty and convenience; but which, when you have entered in, as I have partly led you this day, you discover to be composed of dark and tortuous passages, and of strait and inharmonious, and ill-contrived apartments, which give no joy or comfort to those who therein dwell. Now from this, I will lead you to a far more beautiful fabric, of which the other will seem to be but a mean copy, as though its architect had seen the exterior of ours, but had not been allowed the privilege of entering. It will appear at first to you, as if upon it there were time-stains, and other traces of the course of centuries over its surface; but, on a nearer approach, even these will be respected, as venerable signs of sacred antiquity. But, when you have looked within, you will see, through the whole of the edifice, beauty, and symmetry, and just proportion, and grandeur, in every part; where all the members of the goodly building are harmoniously composed into one beautiful whole, and all its chambers adorned with whatever can rejoice the heart of man and gladden his existence. Then, I am sure, you will acknowledge, that if that which you have just seen was but the work of man, this, which you will have thoroughly examined, was the erection of God. And I trust that you will not so content yourselves with looking in—that you will not be satisfied with taking a cursory glance at all the beauties and perfections of the edifice; but that, using the lights which it is given to fallen man to have, you will, under my humble guidance, enter therein: that so, many, who now stand without, may come therein, to abide with the children of Christ, and to sit around that banquet of heavenly gifts which there only is to be enjoyed on earth, as an earnest of what God has prepared in heaven.

LECTURE THE THIRD.

EXPOSITION OF THE CATHOLIC RULE OF FAITH.

1 PETER, iii. 15.

"*Sanctify the Lord Jesus Christ in your hearts; being ready always to satisfy any one that asketh you the reason of the hope that is in you.*"

IN my last discourse, I was principally occupied with the less pleasing task of examining and confuting the opinions of others I endeavored, with the utmost impartiality, to analyze the principle of belief adopted by those religions which have rejected ours; and, without any reference to express authority, by simply tracing it to its simple elements, I attempted to show you that it was fraught with so many difficulties, as absolutely to render it in practice inapplicable, and void of fruit. For, while it supposes, on the one hand, the obligation of each individual to examine for himself the word of God, and draw thence the doctrines which he believes, as therein contained; it, on the other hand, necessarily supposes a train of difficult, learned, and often abtruse inquiry, to which very few, comparatively, can be equal.

I come now to the more agreeable duty of explaining to you the faith which we hold: and I shall endeavor to proceed precisely in the same manner as I did at our last meeting. I will at present content myself with giving you the outline of our belief; showing, as I proceed, how simple and obvious is the whole process of our reasoning,—such, indeed, as must at once satisfy the most accurate and logical inquirer; and yet, at the same time, be within the reach of the most illiterate capacity. I will endeavor, also, to point out the beautiful harmony of all its parts, and the striking way in which the adoption of such a rule must influence, not only the whole basis and nature of the demonstration, but also the construction of perfect Christianity.

We are told, in the 31st chapter of Deuteronomy, how, when Moses had completed the law of God, and had written it in a book, he gave it to the Levites who bare the Ark of the Lord, and commanded that it should be placed beside the Ark of the Covenant, within the Tabernacle, as a testimony against Israel.

LECTURE III.   61

But that was not the only precious thing which received so distinguished an honor. For we read how, on a certain occasion,* when many would have disputed the supreme priesthood of Aaron's line, and, jealous of the authority vested in him as the priest appointed of God, would have claimed a share in his dignity, the Almighty commanded Moses to give a rod unto each of the tribes, whereon the name of its head was written; and all were placed in the presence of the Lord; and on the next morning, it was found that the rod of Aaron had blossomed, and brought forth fruit. And then God commanded this rod, which was the emblem of authority, and a witness that he had confided the spiritual rule and the teaching of the people to one line, to be also deposited and kept in the same place, as a testimony in like manner to the people of Israel. And even so, on another occasion, Moses commanded Aaron to take a certain portion of the manna, of the holy and spiritual food sent down from the clouds to feed the people of Israel; and having put it into a vessel, he treated it likewise with the same distinction, and placed it to stand in the Sanctuary, before the Mercy-seat of God.†

Now, my brethren, all these are perfectly symbolical of the elements, which the Catholic supposes to enter into the composition of the groundwork of his faith. For, first, above all, he reveres and values the Sacred Volume revealed by God, which he places as the foundation-stone of his faith, in the holiest of His temple. But beside, it is also the rod of the children of Aaron, the sceptre of power and authority, the badge of dignity and command which God hath given to the rulers and pastors of the Church; and in this also he recognises the honorable right to claim a place beside the other in the Sanctuary, although with such distinctions as I shall just now explain. Then, in the third place, he believes also, that a necessary and important ingredient in the formation of individual faith, is the strengthening and life-giving grace which God sends down into the soul, which infuses faith as a virtue into the heart, ready to be exercised the moment its object is properly placed before it. And such is the threefold composition of the provision made by God for the acceptance of his holy religion: a divine revelation, having its essential basis in his written word; an unfailing authority to preserve, propose, and explain it; and an inward aid to receive and embrace it. And the emblems of these, as was done

---

* Numb. xvii.   † Exod. xvi. 33

of old, we carefully cherish in the tabernacle of God with men, which is his Church.

What, then, my brethren, is the rule of faith which our Church admits? The Word of God—the Word of God alone and exclusively; but here comes the great trenching difference between ourselves and others, in the inquiry, what is the extent of God's Holy Word? The Churches which separated from us at the time of the Reformation, separated from us, I may say, upon this principle,—that the Catholic Church had introduced another ground, beside the Word of God, into the principle of its religion; that it admitted the traditions of man, and had given to them the title, the name, and dignity of God's word. It is, therefore, necessary for me to propose a few simple explanatory distinctions. You often hear of Catholics admitting *tradition*—sometimes of their receiving what they call the *unwritten word of God*. Perhaps you have not a clear apprehension of these two terms. Then, besides them, you will sometimes hear of the *power* of the Church to *make decrees* of dogma, or of the *authority* of General Councils, or of the Universal Church, or of the Pope, to *define matters of faith*, with a number of other terms, often vaguely, and sometimes equivocally used. The meaning of all these phrases, to the reasonable and instructed Catholic, is sufficiently obvious; but they should be used with great caution, and accurately defined, when we explain our doctrines to persons not equally competent to understand them. In the first place, then, as it has pleased God to order things, the Catholic has no need of any other groundwork of his faith beyond the written word of God. For it has pleased Him (though he might have otherwise ordered it) to give us in his Holy Scriptures sufficient evidence of that authority which he has bestowed upon his Church. This reasoning may be thus illustrated, as we do not allow of any doctrine which is not contained and rooted in Christ Jesus incarnate, the Word of God, and Eternal Wisdom of the Father, and yet we admit other doctrines, only remotely connected with him, based only on him, and less directly referable to him,—for no doctrine can have any force except inasmuch as it rests on his authority; so likewise if the Church claims authority to define articles of faith, and to instruct her children what they must believe, you must not for one moment think that authority, and the sanction for that power, she conceives herself to derive from the clear, express, and explicit words of Scripture. Thus, it may be truly said, that whatever is believed by the Catholic, although not positively expressed in the *written* word of God, is believed, because the principle adopted by him is there expressly revealed.

By the *unwritten* word of God, we mean a body of doctrines, which, in consequence of express declarations in the *written* word, we believe not to have been committed in the first instance to writing, but delivered by Christ to his apostles, and by the apostles to their successors. We believe that no new doctrine can be introduced into the Church, but that every doctrine which we hold, has existed, and been taught in it ever since the time of the apostles; having been handed down by them to their successors, under the only guarantee on which we receive doctrines from the Church, that is, Christ's promises to abide with it for ever, to assist, direct, and instruct it, and always teach in and through it. So that, while giving our implicit credit, and trusting our judgment to it, we are believing, and trusting to the express teaching and sanction of Christ himself.

Tradition, therefore, my brethren, or the doctrines delivered down, and the *unwritten word* of God, are one and the same thing. But it must not be thought, that Catholics conceive there is a certain mass of vague and floating opinions, which may, at the option of the Pope, or of a General Council, or of the whole Church, be turned into Articles of Faith. Neither is it implied by the term *unwritten word*, that these Articles of Faith or traditions are nowhere recorded. Because, on the contrary, suppose a difficulty to arise regarding any doctrine—so that men should differ, and not know what precisely to believe, and that the Church thought it prudent or necessary to define what is to be held; the method pursued would be to examine most accurately the writings of the Fathers of the Church, to ascertain what, in different countries and in different ages, was by them held; and then, collecting the suffrages of all the world and of all times—not indeed to create a new Article of Faith—but to define what has always been the Faith of the Catholic Church. It is conducted, in every instance, as a matter of historical inquiry, and all human prudence is used to arrive at a judicious decision. But when the Church is assembled for this solemn purpose, in consequence of those promises of Christ, which I shall develop at full length hereafter, we believe it impossible that the decrees which she issues can be false or incorrect; because Christ's promises would fail and be made void, should the Church be allowed to fall into error.

Thus, then, we allow of no authority but the Word of God, written or unwritten; and maintain that the control so necessary over the latter, exists in its depository,—that is, in the Church of Christ, which has been appointed by God to take charge of, and keep safe those doctrines committed to her from the beginning, to be taught, at all times, to all nations. Now, therefore, proceeding on the same plan which I followed in analyzing and testing the first principle or rule of Faith professed by others, I will briefly explain what is the ground of ours, what its application, and what its end; and you will, I trust, see the consistency of the whole reasoning from its beginning to its close, and its adaptation for the purpose for which any rule must be given.

1. In the first place, as to the *ground* of this rule. By this term I do not mean the arguments whereby it is supported; because, these must form the subject of two or three probably lengthy discourses. At present I mean to speak of the train of reasoning, by which we arrive at the individual possession of this principle. Let us therefore, suppose that, not content with the more compendious method whereby God brought us, through baptism and our early instruction, into the possession of the Faith, we are disposed to investigate the authority on which it rests; we begin naturally with Scripture—we take up the Gospels, and submit them to examination. We abstract, for a moment, from our belief in their inspiration and divine authority—we look at them simply as historical works, intended for our information, writings from which we are anxious to gather truths useful for our instruction. We find, in the first place, that to these works, whether considered in their substance or their form, are attached all those motives of human credibility which we can possibly require;—that there is, throughout them, an absence of every element which could suggest the suspicion that there has been either a desire to deceive, or a possibility of having been mistaken. For, we find a body of external testimony sufficient to satisfy us that these are documents produced at the time when they profess to have been written, and that those persons were their authors whose names they bear. And as these were eye-witnesses of what they relate, and give us, in their lives and characters, the strongest security of their veracity, we conclude all that they have recorded to be certain and true. We thus arrive at the discovery, that besides their mere narrative, they unfold to us a system of religion, preached by One who wrought the most stupendous miracles to establish and confirm the divinity of his mission. In other words, we are led by the simple principle of human investigation to an acknow-

ledgment of the authority of Christ to teach, as one who came from God: and we are thus led to the necessity of yielding implicit credence to whatever we find Him to have taught. So far, the investigation, being one of outward and visible facts, cannot require any thing more than simple historical or human evidence.

Having once thus established the divine authority of Christ, we naturally inquire, what is it that Christ taught? and we find that he was not contented merely with teaching certain general principles of morality; that he was not satisfied with unfolding to mankind doctrines such as none before him had attempted to teach, and thereby making man acquainted with his own fallen nature, and with his future destiny; but that, moreover, he took means to preserve those doctrinal communications to mankind. We find it, obviously, his intention, that the system which he established should be beneficial, not only to those who lived in his own days, and heard his words, but to the entire world, until the end of time; that he intended his religion to be something permanent, something commensurate with the existence of those wants of humanity which he came to relieve: and, consequently, we naturally ask, in what way the obligations which he came to enforce, and the truths which he suffered to seal, were to be preserved, and what the place wherein they were to be deposited? If they were to be perpetual, proper provision must have been made for their perpetuation.

Now, the Catholic falls in with a number of very strong passages in which our blessed Saviour, not content with promising a continuance of his doctrines, that is to say, the continued obligation of faith upon men, also pledges himself for their actual preservation among them. He selects a certain body of men: he invests them, not merely with great authority, but with power equal to his own; he makes them a promise of remaining with them, and teaching among them, even to the end of time; and thus, once again, the inquirer naturally concludes, that there must for ever have existed, and that there must actually exist, a corresponding institution for the preservation of those doctrines, and the perpetuation of those blessings which our Saviour thus communicated.

Proceeding thus by mere historical reasoning, such as would guide an infidel to believe in Christ's superior mission, he comes, from the word of Christ, whom those historical motives oblige him to believe, to acknowledge the existence of a body, depository of doctrines which he came to establish among men. This succession and body of persons constituted to preserve those doctrines of faith, appointed as the successors of the apostles, having the guarantee of Christ teaching among them for ever—is what he calls the Church. He is in possession, from that moment, of an assurance of divine authority, and, in the whole remaining part of the investigation, has no need to turn back by calling in once more the evidence of man. For, from the moment he is satisfied that Christ has appointed a succession of men whose province it is, by aid of a supernatural assistance, to preserve, inviolable, those doctrines which God has delivered—from that moment, whatever these men teach is invested with that divine authority which he had found in Christ, through the evidence of his miracles. This body, so constituted, immediately takes on itself the office of teaching, and informs him that the sacred volume, which he had been hitherto treating as a mere history—that the document which he had been perusing solely with a deep and solemn interest, is a book which commands a much greater degree of respect and attention than any human motives could possibly bestow. For now the Church stands forth with that authority wherewith she is invested by Christ—and proclaims: "Under that guarantee of divine assistance which the words of Christ, in whom you believe, have given me, I pronounce that this book contains the revealed word of God, and is inspired by the Holy Spirit, and that it contains all that has a right to enter into the sacred collection." And thus the Catholic at length arrives, on the authority of the Church, at these two important doctrines of the canon and the inspiration of Scripture, which I endeavored to show, at our last meeting, it was almost, if not quite, impossible, to reach by any course of ordinary human investigation.

But some, perhaps, will say, "these are natural, and, consequently, insufficient testimonies; you believe that the Scripture first teaches you the Church, and then that the Church teaches you the Scripture."

To this I might reply, that there is a fallacy in the very reasoning. When an ambassador presents himself before a sovereign, he is asked, where are his credentials? He presents them, and on the strength of them is acknowledged as an ambassador; so that he himself first presents that document, whereby alone his mission and authority are subsequently established. Again, on whose authority do you receive the laws of your country? On that of the legislature, which sanctions and presents them to you. And whence does that legislature derive its jurisdiction and power to make those laws? Why, from that very code, from those very statutes which it sanctions. In either of

LECTURE III. 67

thes) cases there is no fallacy of reasoning, no vicious circle, as it is called. How, then, can Catholics be charged, as they are, by Burnet and others, with this defect in their similar reasoning?

But, in fact, the argument is falsely stated. We do not believe the Church on the authority of Scripture, properly so called; we believe it on the authority of *Christ;* and if his commands in her regard, were recorded in any other book which we felt ourselves bound to believe, although uninspired, we should receive them, and, consequently, the authority of the Church, equally as now. We consider the Scriptures, therefore, in the first instance, as a book manifesting to us One furnished with divine authority to lay down the law; we take it in this view, and examine what he tells us; and we discover that, supported by all the evidence of his divine mission, he has appointed this authority to teach; and then, that authority not merely advises, but obliges us, by that power which Christ has invested in it, to receive this sacred book as his inspired word.

Some may, perhaps, think, that a similar line of reasoning would, with a slight variation, be applicable to the demonstration of the other rule of faith. To a certain point we may both go, step by step, through the same process. We both take up this sacred volume, on human and historical testimony, and we receive all that Christ has in it taught us. So far we march together, and then we diverge. *We* take for our guide those texts which appoint the Church to teach; the others take the proposition, that the Bible is to be the rule of faith.

Now, my brethren, I beg your impartial attention while I explain to you the difference between the two courses. In the first place, when we have received the Scriptures, according to the Catholic doctrine, we not only receive the one class of passages, but also the other, to its fullest extent; because, whatever argument will prove that the Scripture must be absolutely taken as the rule of faith, that argument the Catholic will receive, and receive with gratitude. For, while he admits the authority of the Church to define what is undoubtedly the written word of God, he receives this as his rule, and is as anxious to uphold it as the follower of any other religion can be. But, on the other hand, while he willingly admits the texts which prove the Scriptures to be the rule of faith, he has passages which give authority to a living power to teach; and all these must be rejected, or otherwise explained by those who maintain the exclusiveness of Scripture as a rule. In their view, the two classes of passages are not compatible; with us, they harmonize perfectly together; and,

LECTURE III.

consequently, while we have no difficulty in admitting whatever arguments they can bring in favor of the Bible, they find themselves obliged to answer strong and powerful documents in our favor.

But, in the second place, while the authority of Scripture, as a rule of faith, is thus perfectly compatible with the existence of an authority to teach, the existence of an authority to teach *excludes*, not, indeed, the Scripture, but the *all-sufficiency* of Scripture. For, where there is a supreme authority given, and man is commanded to obey it, from that command there is, assuredly, no retreat. And therefore the Scripture must needs be received, so as to be reconciled with the existence of a supreme authority in matters of faith existing in the Church.

In the third place, there must be texts, at least equally strong, brought against us, as what we adduce for our system; not merely such as say that the Scripture is useful, good, and profitable, but such as positively assert that the Scripture is *sufficient;* not such as tell us to search the Scriptures for particular objects, but such as command us to seek *all things* therein. There must be texts, the words of Christ or his apostles, to command us to make use of no rule but the written word; for observe, that in sanctioning any rule or principle whereby man is to be guided, it is necessary that the principle be somewhere laid down and explicitly defined, so that he should know what is to be the rule of his life, and the law whereby he must direct and regulate his conduct. And thus we, on our side, are not content with vague allusions to the authority of the Church, as a voucher for the doctrines therein taught; but believe that we have an express definition, that its authority is the rule of faith, and that all must obey and follow its guidance.

But there is another and more important distinction, which you can hardly fail to observe; that the moment the Catholic, in his train of argument, has taken his first step from profane to holy ground—the moment he has come to the conclusion, that the teaching of our blessed Saviour was divinely authorized, from that moment he returns not back again to human testimony; he has the divine sanction at every subsequent step, till he arrives at his last conclusion. Our Saviour gives a divine authority to the Church. The Church, with that authority, sanctions the book of Scripture. But analyze the other course of reasoning; suppose that you have arrived at the knowledge of Christ's divinity, and the authority of the apostles; you then take those passages which seem to you to say that the Scripture is the rule of faith.

LECTURE III.

Be it so—you have reached a vague authorization, that whatever writings are entitled to that name, are to be received as a guide in religion. Your next step must be to determine what writings have a claim to be considered inspired. But if the Church have no divine authority, you must go back to the ground you have left—of human testimony: you return from the authority of our Saviour and his apostles, in favor of studying the Scripture, back to another historical investigation, to discover what Scripture is, before you can resume the thread of the argument. This is an essential and vital flaw in the reasoning proposed as parallel to ours, and as sufficient to prove the efficacy of Scripture, as a rule of faith.

Such, therefore, is the course of argument which the Catholic Church pursues, and such is the course which any instructed Catholic would pursue, whenever he should think it necessary to refresh his mind as to the grounds of his belief; and by it he arrives at a perfectly logical and connected consequence, upon the authority of the Holy Scriptures. But before leaving this portion of my subject,—though I shall have to enlarge on this important consideration hereafter,—allow me to observe that the comparison between the old and new law, regarding the rule of faith, gives us very great and most useful lights, tending essentially to confirm the view which we have taken. For, we find, that to the Jews was given, indeed, a written law, but that there was a most express *command* to write it—that Moses was ordered to register all those precepts which God had given, even to the most minute particulars; and that this law was to be read to the people in the most solemn manner, every seventh year, at the Feast of Tabernacles.* Besides this, the law was purposely so interwoven with the daily actions and domestic concerns of the Jewish people, as to require that it should be ever before their eyes, that they should all possess a minute acquaintance with its provisions, so as to understand, at every turn, how to regulate their conduct. This, I conceive, we must consider characteristic of a written law, that it should not be merely formed of documents collected together, as it were, accidentally; but that provision should be taken for the rule's being drawn up, and then its being communicated to those whom it has to guide.

One would, therefore, naturally expect, that if our Saviour had intended to direct us to a knowledge of our duties by some writ-

* Deut. xxxi. 10.

ten code of faith or morality, he would have expressly said to his apostles: "All the things which you hear from me, or which you see me perform, take care and register carefully; and preserve their records from all danger and risk, by multiplying and diffusing them among the faithful, for their future guidance. For, that which you write will form a code by which their conduct may be regulated, and by which they will be one day judged." But you do not meet, in the new law, with any thing of this sort; there is not a hint or intimation that our Saviour ever intended one word to be written down.

We find, moreover, on examining the history of these compositions, that they were, every one of them, the offspring of casual circumstances, and written for some local or personal purpose, which seemed to call them forth; that, if errors or abuses had not arisen so early in the Church, you would probably have been deprived of the most beautiful writings in the New Testament; that, if the blessed apostle St. John had not been preserved to a preternatural existence, after having suffered, what to others would have been fatal, the torments of martyrdom, he would not have been spared to complete the sacred volume. We find that St. Luke and St. Matthew wrote for a specific class of readers, for one particular country, or for even separate individuals; that the epistles of St. Paul were manifestly directed to different churches, and were intended merely to silence doubts, or answer difficulties, proposed by them, and also to correct and amend some accidental, or local corruptions; and if we examine them carefully, we shall find that the greater portion of our most important dogmas, instead of St. Paul's defining and explaining them, are only occasionally, parenthetically, and as illustrations introduced.

Now all this seems the reverse of a settled plan for the delivery of a code of laws; and the contrast is unquestionably greater when placed beside the Mosaic dispensation, in which there was an explicit injunction to record, and write down, and preserve with the greatest care, both by monuments, and by the depositing of the archetype in the sanctuary, those laws which had been dictated by divine command. But this necessarily is not the whole of the difficulty; for it is singular to observe in the Mosaic law, how, although we have in it the characteristics of a written code, and an express injunction to note down whatever was taught, yet by far the most important doctrines were not committed to writing: so that among the Jews there was a train of sacred tradition, containing within itself more vital dogmas than are written in the inspired volume. I could lay before you the arguments of a very learned living author, who has, within these few years, published a very elaborate treatise upon this subject; and who might have formed one of those instances, to which I alluded in my opening discourse, of persons brought to the Catholic religion, by the most diversified trains of argument. Here is one who, educated in the Jewish religion, had made himself perfect master of all the writings of the Jews, and who, it is evident from the whole line of argument that pervades his work, was brought to the Catholic religion, and is now one of its defenders, simply from finding that among the Jews there was a series of traditions, which received its development only in Catholic Christianity, and a sacred system of mystical theology, which has been manifestly preserved and continued, in our Church. The author to whom I allude, is the learned Molitor, of Francfort, author of two volumes replete with deep research, entitled, "The Philosophy of History, or on Tradition."

Those who will take the requisite pains to trace the doctrine of the Jews in this regard, either by their own research, or in the pages of this estimable writer, will find that, from the very beginning, from the delivery of the law to Moses, there was a great mass of precepts, not written, but committed to the keeping of the priesthood, and by them gradually communicated or diffused among the people, but yet hardly alluded to in the writings of the sacred book. A little consideration and examination will convince any one of this important fact; for it is certain, that when our Saviour came, the Jews were in possession of many doctrines exceedingly difficult to trace in Scripture, and yet doctrines of vital importance. Many of you are doubtless aware that a divine of the Established Church (Warburton) wrote to prove the divine legation of Moses, on the extraordinary ground, that he was able to achieve the great work of organizing a republic, and constituting a law to bind the people, without the sanction of a future state. He maintains, with great show of plausibility, that you cannot discover in the writings of Moses, or of the earlier Jews, one single positive text in proof of the future existence of the soul, or of a place of rewards and punishments in another life. And I am sure that any of you who is well versed in Scripture, if he will only run through his own recollections on the subject—if he will only try to gather for himself such a body of argument in Scripture as would convince any one, or teach a people those important truths, will find it extremely difficult so to construct it, as to bear the test of accurate examination. But yet did the Jews believe in them? Did they possess them? Undoubtedly they did. For it is manifest, from many passages of the New Testament, and from their own works, that the doctrines of a future state, and a resurrection, were fully believed and taught. Here, then, is an important dogma, not of natural, but of revealed religion, and one which is expressly received, repeated, and confirmed, by additional sanctions, in the New Law, which must have been handed down by secret teaching and tradition. So true is this, that the Sadducees, followed in later times by the Karaites, formed a sect among the Jews, who rejected traditional doctrines, and consequently the resurrection of the dead, and the existence of a spiritual soul in men.* And thus we find St. Paul join himself to the Pharisees, who held the two, not as to a sect, but as to the true orthodox portion of the Jewish Church. "I am a Pharisee, the son of Pharisees: concerning the hope and resurrection of the dead I am called in question. For the Sadducees say that there is no resurrection, nor angel, nor spirit; but the Pharisees confess both."† And as such our Saviour acknowledges them: although he clearly distinguishes between their authority in teaching dogma, and their corruptions in matters of practical morality, and bases the former on their descent, as teachers, from the legislator Moses.‡

When our Saviour deduces the sublime doctrine of a future resurrection, from the Almighty's being styled the God of Abraham and of Jacob—the God, not of the dead, but of the living; it is, perhaps, difficult to discover the link between these two members of the argument. For how can the resurrection be proved from God's calling himself the God of Abraham? But by knowing the Jewish forms of reasoning, and the manner in which they connect the two dogmas of the soul's survival, and the body's resurrection, we understand how his hearers were satisfied by the argument.§

In the same way, our Saviour tells us that Moses bore testimony of him; and in conversing with his two disciples on the road to Emmaus, quoted the authority of Moses for the necessity of his suffering, and so entering into glory;‖ and yet you will in vain search the books of Moses to discover this important dogma, of the necessity of the Messiah's dying to redeem his people. Where, then, had these points been preserved, save in

---

* See Molitor, tom. 1. cap. 3.
† Acts xxiii. 5—8; xxvi. 5. Comp. Matt. xxii. 23.
‡ Matt. xxiii. 3.   § Matt. xxii. 32.   ‖ Luke xxiv. 26.

LECTURE III.

the traditions of the Jews, as may be proved from their later works?

Another example may be drawn from the New Testament. When our Saviour proposed to Nicodemus the doctrine of a spiritual birth, or regeneration, and he truly or affectedly understood it not, he reproved him in these words: "Art thou a master in Israel, and knowest not these things?"* What does this rebuke imply, but that a teacher among the Jews ought to have been acquainted with this important doctrine, from his very office as a teacher? Yet tell me where it is ever taught in the old law, or whence could he have possessed it, except from the traditional lore preserved among the priests and learned?

In the later writings of the Jews, we observe clear manifestations of their belief in the Trinity, and in the mystery of the Incarnation, and this couched in the very terms made use of by St. John. For in the earliest uninspired writings of the Jews, we have the *Word of God* spoken of as something co-equal and co-existing with Him,† and yet scarcely a trace of such doctrines is to be found in the written law, although they belong not to natural but to revealed religion. They must therefore have been delivered as a deposit into the hands of the priesthood, and by them preserved inviolate to the time of Christ. I need hardly add, that the Jews themselves acknowledge this delivery by tradition, of a secret and more important doctrine. The learned author to whom I refer puts this quite out of doubt: and I will content myself with saying, that in the first page of one of their most esteemed and most ancient treatises, which, at least in Italy, is put into the hands of Jewish children for elementary education, it is expressly stated that Moses received on Sinai, besides the written, an oral and traditional revelation, which he delivered to the priests.‡

I have brought these instances by way of illustration, to show what a strong class of arguments it must require to prove that rule of faith which excludes traditional teaching; because we see that, even when the written law is expressly enjoined, it is far from excluding the existence of an unwritten law; yea, and of one to which is committed the exclusive preservation of most important doctrines. In like manner, therefore, when we come

---

* John iii. 11.
† In the Targumim, or Chaldee paraphrases, wherever God is said to speak within himself, this is rendered by "God said to his Word."
‡ Pirke Aboth.

to examine authorities, we shall find that it requires reasons exceedingly strong to prove, not merely that the Scripture is the rule of faith, but that it is an *all-sufficient—the exclusive* rule: and however strong the terms may otherwise be, we cannot easily admit them to be exclusive of that other traditional teaching, even though backed by a formal command to have a written code.

II. Such, my brethren, is the simple and usual train of argument whereby we arrive at the possession of the Holy Scriptures, and of its entire canon and inspiration. But you will say, What have we gained, and in what is our condition better than that of others? Even here is a train of argument requiring considerable investigation; by it we are equally left to inquire into the authenticity of the sacred books, and the faith we should put in the circumstances they relate; because we have first to learn what Christ taught regarding his Church. Another explanation must therefore be made, of the manner in which our rule is applicable; and here the doctrine of the Catholic Church is such as obviously to remove these difficulties, and make the rule one of the simplest acceptance, and yet able to bear the investigation of the most learned. For the Catholic Church teaches and believes—(I beg to observe that I am not *proving* our doctrines, but only stating them, that you may understand what I shall hereafter by argument establish)—that faith is not the production of man's ingenuity, not the result of his study or investigation, but a virtue essentially infused by God in baptism; and such must be, more or less, the belief of every Church that adopts the practice of infant baptism. True, the article of the Church of England regarding this sacrament, which says that by baptism "faith is confirmed and grace increased," would seem to suppose that faith exists in the soul before baptism is administered; but however that anomaly has to be explained, it is certain that the very idea of infant baptism, as a sacrament, supposes a living and vivifying principle communicated in it—that is, a communication to the person so baptized of the faith of the Church into which he is admitted. And therefore, assuming faith to be a principle infused by God, it follows that in a soul purged of sin, and adorned by him with the graces given in baptism, that virtue becomes an active and living principle, and ready, on the presentation of its proper object, to come into complete and perfect action. The moment, therefore, that the doctrines of religion are proposed, and the understanding, now able to apprehend the truths revealed by God, is presented with them, no matter in what order, or by what means, provided the doctrines are true, there is a proper object presented to the action of that virtue; the two necessary elements are brought together—the actual truth and the faculty or virtue which God has given us for its apprehension: and the consequence is, that truth is believed on substantial grounds, and under the influence of a living and heavenly principle. Whereas, if we admit the supposition that no man has a right to believe any thing but that which he has himself investigated, and of whose truth he is personally satisfied, we must presume that, before the first act of faith, there existed an interval of infidelity positive or negative, during which fundamental truth, not having been discovered, was consequently not believed. This simple process allows the child and the most illiterate to perform an act of faith grounded on proper motives. We are subsequently led by the Church to the full knowledge of the grounds and motives of our belief; we are encouraged to exercise our abilities, research, and learning, in demonstrating and confirming, in every way we can, the doctrines which it teaches, and which that preliminary instruction had brought us to believe. And thus, as I before remarked, while by its simplicity it is adapted to the weakest and lowest, it leaves room for the exercise of the faculties of the most able and learned men.

III. This may suffice as to the simplicity of the principle in its application; a few words more will prove its adequacy to its natural ends. I observed, when we last met, that the end of every rule and law, and consequently of every rule of faith, was to bring men into a unity of principle and action. I showed you that the rule proposed by others is proved by experience to lead to exactly opposite results; in other words, that it removes men farther from that union towards which it must be intended to bring them; for it leads them to the most contradictory opinions, professing to be supported and proved by precisely the same principle of faith. But now, if you will only examine, in its action, the principle which the Catholic Church admits, you will see that it is fully equal to those objects for which the rule was given: inasmuch as its necessary tendency is to bring all the opinions and understandings of men into the most perfect unity, and to the adoption of one only creed. For, the moment any Catholic doubts, not alone the principle of his faith, but any one of those doctrines which are thereon based—the moment he allows himself to call in question any of the dogmas which the Catholic Church teaches as having been handed down within

LECTURE III.

her—that moment the Church conceives him to have virtually abandoned all connection with her. For she exacts such implicit obedience, that if any member, however valuable, however he may have devoted his early talents to the illustration of her doctrines, fall away from his belief in any one point, he is cut off without reserve; and we have, in our own times, seen striking and awful instances of this fact.

But, my brethren, does not this seem tyrannical?—Is it not an iron yoke and a band of brass, to the subjugation of men?— a bowing down involuntarily of those powers and faculties which the Almighty left free, to be exercised by each individual? If any of you should think thus, he understands not the principle of Catholic Unity. I know that it is often represented as like that tyrannical sway which the conqueror exercises over vanquished vassals; as though the zeal which the Church has for seeing men in distant quarters of the globe subject to her laws, were no other feeling but what swells the emperor's pride, as he receives tribute from natives of a distant land, a feeling of triumph over the liberties of men, an exultation to see their souls bowed down in homage before her throne. But those who know the feelings with which this submission is united, are well aware how fallacious such a representation is.

Nothing can be more beautiful, in the conception of a Christian Church, than a perfect unity of belief. Such an idea is beautiful to the imagination, because it is the consecration of the first and most essential principles whereon society is based. For the social union tends to merge the feelings of each individual in the general mass, and leads him to embrace mankind, rather than individual men. And in like manner does the principle of religious unity tend to excite your love towards them, no longer as brethren in the flesh, but as connected with you by a holier and diviner bond, and assists towards inspiring every member of the community with all that can be reciprocally felt, in the nearest ties and connections of our nature. And if the very idea of a republic or government in which men were united by such real or ideal bonds, as that they fought side by side, or contributed towards the common weal, did seem to them of old so beautiful and heavenly, that the very conception of such a state, embodied under outward symbols, should have been deified and worshipped, what shall we say of that sacred union which holds men together, not merely as constituents of a community, but as members of one mystical body; not cemented together by the sense of mutual want, or strung one unto another by the ties of the flesh, or the interests of the world, but firmly united by the headship of One in whom the sublimest flight of thought reposes, as in its proper sphere; and inly communicating through the circulation of vital influences passing from one unto the other; not contributing to the common stock, the gifts or qualities of earth, but the fairest virtues, the most precious ornaments of our nature; not directed, in their views, towards a worldly aggrandizement or a passing glory, nor linked in battle-field by a bond of hatred against a human foe, but looking upwards for their trophies and rewards to the peaceful smile of heaven, after they shall have contended together in the gentle strife of mutual and universal love? Then add the reflection, how this influence stretches beyond the reach of any other known sentiment among mankind; for, outstripping all the motives of sympathy among men of different countries, it flies over mountains, and seas, and oceans, and puts into the mouths of nations, the most remote and the most dissimilar, one canticle of praise, and into their minds one symbol of belief, and into their hearts one sentiment of charity. And thus professing alike, they kneel in countless multitude before one altar, and from the soul of each proceeds the golden chain which joins them unto it, which God joins unto the rest, which he holdeth in his hand, for in Him is the centre towards which the faith of all converges, and in His truth it is blended into uniformity and oneness of thought. Surely this is the idea which you would wish to conceive, of the efficiency and of the effects of that rule which has been given by God to produce unity of belief; and such you will find it existing and acting in the Catholic Church.

This idea too is beautiful to the mind of the Catholic, from its obvious tendency to equalize and level the minds and understandings of men, when brought before the searching eye of God. Not to him is religion a deep well, to which comes each one, furnished with his own vessel, and draws and carries away a different proportion, according to its capacity or his strength; but it is a living and ever-gushing fountain, springing up unto eternal life, where all may drink to equal refreshment, who put their mouths to its quickening stream. Not with him is that distinction granted in the inward, which St. James condemns in the outward man; that of a higher place being allotted to him that hath the ring upon his finger, and the costly robe upon his shoulders, while the poor in intellect sitteth at his footstool. But he, on the contrary, sees all minds attuned to the same feelings, and all understandings brought down to the same simplicity of belief, till the intellectual and the rude, the wise and the foolish, stand on an equal ground. Brought down, did I say? Rather are both caught up and borne on the wings of the same sacred truth, to a conception so lofty above all human wisdom, as that the distance between the two, when standing here below, shall seem but an infinitesimal element in the height.

But this idea of religious unity does not merely by its beauty satisfy the imagination of the Catholic; it meets all the notions which his reason could suggest of the character of truth. For this, in its own nature, must seem to be one and indivisible, the reflection of that knowledge which exists in the Godhead, communicated through the one Mediator, the incarnate Word and Wisdom of the Father. And thus, by the idea of only one faith, secured by an unerring authority, he establishes the existence in religion of real *objective* truth, instead of the *subjective* in each one's mind;—he conceives the eye to be fixed on the correct prototype, rather than on its image, broken, and refracted, and distorted, through the imperfect medium of individual examination.

And the consideration of this aptness and conformity of such a system to the idea of truth, will be further enhanced to the Catholic's reason, when he considers wherefore it has been given. For assuredly they who are to be guided are one in nature and feelings, have the same passions to conquer, the same perfection to attain, and the same crown to win. And therefore should it seem no less reasonable that the road whereon they travel should be equal, and the food and remedy supplied should be the same, and the guide that conducts them be only one.

But then also is this unity of faith subservient to another great end, to the evidence of our blessed Saviour's true religion. For he was pleased to declare, that the unity observable among his followers should be among the strongest evidence of his heavenly mission. "And not for them only," he exclaimed, "do I pray, but for them also who, through their word, shall believe in me: that they all may be one, as the Father in me and I in thee, *that they also may be one in us, that the world may believe that thou hast sent me.*"* And that this unity is not merely of the heart through love, but also of the mind in faith, his blessed apostle hath abundantly declared. For, according to him, if we wish to walk worthy of the vocation wherein we have been called, it must be not only by "humility, and mildness, and patience, supporting one another

---

* John xvii. 20, 21.

in charity," but we must be "careful to keep the unity of the Spirit in the bond of peace," so as to be "one body," as well as "one Spirit," and to have "one faith," as much as "one Lord and one baptism."* Not surely that charity, the beautiful and the perfect, steps not beyond the circumscribing line of religious unity, or that her genial influences, like a flower's sweet odor, spread not abroad far beyond the plant which first produces it; but universal as must be our love of men, this will be ever its noblest exercise, to wish and to strive that all be brought to that closer union and unity, which is in, and through faith. Our charity should ever lead us to labor with others, that they may see, like ourselves, how complete and perfect unity can only be based upon this profession of a common faith: and that no rule, no principle, can attain this great object, save that which the Catholic Church holds, and proposes, the institution whereof by God's authority, shall form, under the divine blessing, the subject of our next disquisition.

"And the grace of our Lord Jesus Christ be with your spirit, brethren. Amen."†

---

* Ephes. iv. 2, 4.   † Gal. vi. 18.

LECTURE THE FOURTH.

THE CATHOLIC RULE OF FAITH PROVED.

MATTHEW, xvii. 1.

"*And after six days, Jesus taketh unto him Peter, and James, and John his brother, and bringeth them up into a high mountain apart, and he was transfigured before them.*"

THE incident of our Saviour's life, which is recorded in this day's Gospel, must be a subject of consolation to every Christian. To see our blessed Lord,—whose instructions were indeed listened to with avidity by crowds, and whose miracles filled the world with wonder and curiosity, but yet, whose doctrines were so little followed, and whose cause was espoused by so few,—retired, on this occasion, though but for a moment, into the happy society of those who really loved and honored him,—to see him receive the willing homage of his chosen ones on earth, and of the spirits of the just made perfect in heaven,—to see him, moreover, obtain that glory from the Father which his sublime dignity deserved, is assuredly some consolation to our feelings, and some compensation for that bitter sympathy which we must feel towards him through his neglected career.

But yet, my brethren, there is a circumstance of much greater importance than such feelings, connected with this cheering and consolatory narrative. For, you will observe, on the one hand, who are chosen to be the witnesses of this glorious scene. They are the most favored of his apostles, the representatives, in a manner, and deputies of those who had to preach his doctrines with most especial authority, and give to their commission the strongest sanctions of its truth: James, who was destined to be the first of the twelve to seal his doctrine with his blood; John, who was intended to prolong the age of the apostles almost beyond its natural duration by his protracted life, and thus, as it were, to dovetail their authority and evidence into the teaching of those that succeeded them; and, above all, Peter, who was expressly appointed, after his fall and conversion, to confirm his brethren, to open the gates of salvation to Jews and Gentiles, and be the solid foundation of the entire Church.

LECTURE IV.

We may, therefore, easily imagine with what awful strength and power the testimony must have been presented to their minds which was given on this solemn occasion; and we find that by the apostles themselves, it was considered as giving the most formal sanction to the teaching of their divine Master. For St. Peter expressly says, "We have not followed cunningly devised fables, when we made known to you the power and presence of our Lord Jesus Christ, but having been made eye-witnesses of his majesty. For he received from God the Father honor and glory, this voice coming down to him from the excellent glory: 'This is my beloved Son in whom I have pleased myself; hear ye him.' And this voice we heard brought from heaven, when we were with him in the holy mount."*

It is to the testimonies, then, given at this time, that St. Peter appeals, as some of the strong groundwork on which he builds his authority to preach. And what were the testimonies here given? They were, manifestly, of a twofold character. For, in the first place, there appeared, beside our Saviour, Moses and Elias, the two most eminent and divinely gifted men of the olden time,—bearing homage and giving testimony unto Him, resigning all the privileges and pledges of the law into His hands, who was come to perfect and complete it. For, my brethren, not merely by the words of the law are we taught; but we all understand, that whatever happened unto the Fathers was done to them in figure; so that not in their writings only, but in their persons and actions, we may find a certain allusion and prophetic reference to that which later was fulfilled. But besides theirs, was another and incomparably mightier testimony here given unto Christ, that of the eternal Father, commanding the apostles to lend implicit credence to whatever they should hear from His mouth. "This is my beloved Son in whom I have well pleased myself, hear ye him." Judge, therefore, how solemnly the authority of our divine Saviour must have been impressed on the minds of these apostles; and when, afterwards, they heard Him transfer to them that authority which here He received—when afterwards they heard Him say, that, "as the Father had sent Him so did He also send them,"—that "all who heard them heard also Him—that whosoever despised them despised not only Him, but Him also who sent Him;" consider what a strong warrant and security this must have been to them; how, recurring to the strong assurances given in *His* favor on mount Thabor,

---

* 2 Peter i. 16, 19.

they must have felt themselves invested with mighty power, when they went forth to teach; yea, with the same authority, precisely, as they had heard given on this occasion to His words.

Now, it is to these two classes of testimonies in favor of this authority to teach, not only as granted to the apostles, but as perpetuated in the Church, that I wish to call your attention this evening. First, we will consider the testimony of Moses and Elias, or of the old law, in its constitution and prophecies, to the form, character, and qualities of the Church of God: and, Secondly, we will hear the voice of God in the express words and injunctions of our blessed Saviour, seeing what they would lead us to conceive regarding the rule and principle of faith, which I endeavored to explain to you at our last meeting, namely, the guidance of his church as the infallible depository of His truth.

The plan which I have followed in these discourses, that is, the simple inductive form of argument, which I have preferred, as leaving less ground for cavil, renders it necessary that one discourse should be closely linked with the foregoing, so as to have an unbroken idea of the entire argument, to see the influence which the antecedents have upon what follows, and also the strong confirmation, which they, in their turn, receive from that which succeeds them. It is, therefore, perhaps, at the risk of being tedious, that I take the liberty of detaining you a few moments, while I recapitulate one or two points, on which I dwelt at full length in my last discourse. Two things I particularly beg to be remembered; in the first place, the explanation which I gave regarding the foundation of Church authority. You may remember that I did not enter on any arguments, but contented myself with laying before you the whole Catholic system—showing the connection of one part with another; and I endeavored to account to you for every step in the process of reasoning, which might be necessary to arrive at its full demonstration. I observed, therefore, that in the Church of Christ was a body of rulers and teachers, selected in the first instance, by our blessed Saviour Himself, from among the most fervent of His followers, to whom he confided certain doctrines and laws, coupled with sure pledges, that those who succeeded them should be the depositaries, and inheritors of whatsoever He had conferred on them; and, consequently, of the promises expressly given, that He would himself teach through that body in the Church, and be himself the director of all its counsels until the end of time. Hence, the Catholic believes, that the Church of Christ consists

LECTURE IV.

of the body of the faithful united with its pastors, among whom Christ resides, and through whom He teaches; so that it is impossible for the Church to fall into error.* And as we admit, at the same time, that no new revelation of doctrines can be made, so do we believe, that the power of the Church consists in nothing more than defining that which was believed from all times, and in all her dominion. Such is the authority of the Church, according to Catholic principles.

The second point to which I beg to recall your attention, although it was only incidentally mentioned, is an important link of connection with what I am going to explain this evening; I mean the fact of the Old Law having been expressly a written law; while, at the same time, most essential doctrines existing among the Jews at the time of our Saviour, and often assumed by Him as the very basis of His preaching to them, had not been delivered in the law, nay, were scarcely clearly recorded in the prophets, and must, therefore, have been handed down by secret and unwritten tradition.

I proceed now to the first portion of my task, which forms the completion and development of that idea, by explaining the strong arguments of analogy which the Old Law gives us, for constructing the Church to be by Christ established. And you will bear with me if I first propose some preliminary observations.

St. Paul has described the glorious triad of virtues whereby man is brought into union with God, when he says: "now there remaineth *faith, hope, charity*, these are three."† And if you will reasonably consider this matter, you will, methinks, hardly fail to observe that threefold, according to the number of virtues here rehearsed, are the stages whereby it hath pleased Divine Providence to accomplish its designs in behalf of man, and to bring him to that sum of perfection whereof he is capable.

The first state was that of hope, in the dispensation given to the fathers; wherein, as divided into its three eras of promise, of prophecy, and of silent expectation, all was referred to the future, and every other virtue was in some way embraced and comprehended in this one. For if they believed, their faith should seem to have been a disposition and readiness to believe one day the teacher whom God had promised, and, in the fulness of time, should give unto his people, after whose manifestation their just did pant as the hart after the water-springs, rather than a clear

---

* Lect. iii. p. 65.   † 1 Cor. xiii. 13.

apprehension of what we justly consider the great mysteries of salvation. And hence it is, that St. Paul, speaking of the peculiar faith of some among them, and how difficult it was, doth tell us in express words, that "against hope they believed in hope." And so likewise in hope may they be said to have loved, inasmuch as their love, or charity, was but a wistfulness and longing after God's coming to them in the flesh, that so they might stand in His blessed presence, a treasuring up and deep-embosoming, as it were, of the affections for a future outburst of the same, when the sum of His mercies should be cast up in their behalf; and not a clear and distinct sense of His beauty and loveliness, or any anxious yearnings after union with Him, whose light, inaccessible, had hitherto rather dazzled and oppressed, than invited and cheered them. Thus it came to pass, that all the doctrines and rites proposed to them wore their looks, in a manner, towards the dawn and day-spring of a brighter season, that their teaching was all in prophecy, their history all in types, their worship all in symbols, and, by a just analogy, their righteousness all in hope.

Next came the ministration of faith, wherein it is our happiness to live, in which much of what then was future now is past, and most of what was then but hoped for, is now believed; and every other good gift and virtue is, somehow, exercised through this one, which, to us, is the root and nourisher of them all. For, if a great part of former hope hath been swallowed up in us by faith, that which remaineth unto us of this virtue consists no longer in dark adumbrations and mysterious images, but in objects proposed to us definitely, though dimly, by faith and in faith, with clear and express conditions, and subject to no farther varieties or distincter revelations.

And charity too, in our regard, reaches us in the same manner. For, if the glorious things of God are seen by us, as St. Paul saith, but darkly in the glass of faith, yet hath this glass a concentrating power which makes their rays converge into one point, and play upon our innermost soul, with a warming, as well as a brightening influence; and the difference between us and those of the older dispensation, is briefly this: that the revelation of a final state, wherein God should be the soul's full possession, shone to them as a distant light in a dark place, *towards* which, indeed, they might direct their course, but *by* which they could hardly guide their steps; whereas to us it is a lamp, as

---

* Rom. iv. 18.

LECTURE IV.

well as a beacon, the cheerer, as well as the aim, of our toilsome pilgrimage.

And then at last will come that final state of blessedness, when faith and hope will be entirely swallowed up in boundless and endless charity; when the "light intellectual full of love" shall reabsorb and quench, in its peerless brightness, the scattered beams it had before suffered to wander upon earth; when every other good and holy thing shall melt and be transmuted in that one assimilating, unifying essence; and, like dewdrops which have refreshed us in the morning, and then have been caught up by some heaving swell of the ocean-tide, though small and imperfect, shall become the elements of the unlimited and eternal.

We, thus, are placed in a middle state, between one past and one that is yet to come, a state necessarily intended as the completion of the former, and as a preparation for the latter; whereof the type is shawdowed forth in that which hath preceded, while itself is the emblem and fair image of that which shall follow. Now, this position must give rise to many interesting analogies; forasmuch, as all things being thus in unbroken progress from the beginning to the end of God's dispensations, without violent shocks or sudden changes, we must expect to find, in the present order or state, such qualities and dispositions as may suit this its twofold character, that is to say, perfective of a former, and initiatory of a future state. And even as a skilful geometer shall, by the accurate measurement of a shadow, under certain conditions, tell you exactly the height and proportions of the object which projects it, and, again, from the survey of this, shall define what the other should at any time be, so may we, by a diligent study of those two other dispensations as well as of our own, the one whereof we are the fulfilment, the other whereof we are the figure, arrive at much important knowledge regarding the condition of our present estate. For the present, my theme confines me to the evidences of the past; how the present dispensation may be the image of the future state, I may yet find a fitting occasion to declare.

A promise of redemption was the first good word spoken to man by God, after his original sentence of punishment; and this word of hope fell as a seed upon a soil that craved it, and it grew therein and brought forth fruits, the only ones which could remind the exile of his lost paradise, fruits of holy knowledge and restored life, to be one day tasted without further danger. And as the different families of the human race did separate from their first dwelling place after the flood, and disperse into distant lands, each took with it some graft or seedling of this precious plant, as a memorial of its lost, and of its hoped-for destinies, and bequeathed it to its descendants as a sacred and priceless trust. In fact, there is no mythology so dark as not to promise the restoration of some forfeited golden age; and a heathen fable has recorded to us the belief, that of all the treasures which heaven bestowed upon him at his formation, hope was alone left to forlorn man, when he lost them by his folly. But how soon were all these divine promises disfigured and corrupted; how soon was their true purport clean forgotten; how completely did they degenerate into the fond inventions of men, and fall into the wicked subserviency of all their worst desires! And, hence, whatever were the benefits intended by God's goodness in giving this entailed blessing to the human race, all those benefits would have been inevitably lost, the goodness which designed them would have been thrown away, and the blessing itself would have been but as a prodigal's gift, if God's infinite wisdom had not provided an expedient against such a sad misfortune.

For this purpose, He chose, out of all the nations of the earth, one people whom He made the keeper of His great deposit; He separated them from among the rest, He made them the sacerdotal caste of the human race, He surrounded them with badges of His protection, and of His special watchfulness over them, He gave into their hands documents of their authority to teach; and then, placing the rest of mankind, no matter how learned or how polished, in the rank of untaught scholars, He left them to receive from those alone, all accurate knowledge of what concerned holier truths and purer revelations. Then, as all those organs in animate or inanimate nature, which have to perform notable functions, are themselves composite, being made up of smaller organs like themselves, and these again involving within them an ever decreasing compound series, so here also, out of this people he chose one tribe, and out of that tribe one family, and from that family one man and his line; that each should respectively stand towards the class whence chosen in the same superior relationship: and so the connecting band should be drawn spirally round from mankind to the sanctuary, and the saving influences which blessed God's promises past, through still widening channels, upon the world.

From this it would appear, that the means taken by God's wisdom for preserving those doctrines of hope which He had communicated unto mankind, was to institute a visible and compact society, within which, He virtually guaranteed their perseerance, and over which He watched with tender solicitude: and we see that His action upon this body was not detailed upon each individual, but was through a more select order of men, constituting a graduated hierarchy, whose duty it was to edify by example, to purify by sacrifice, to instruct by explanations of the law, to stand, in fine, between God and His people, ministering unto both, as His chosen servants, and their appointed teachers. The objects of this internal organization could only be the preservation of essential unity of worship and of heart. Reuben was obliged yearly to come from beyond the Jordan, and Zabulon from over the mountains, and both to worship with their brethren, at one altar, in Jerusalem; lest new opinions or rites should creep in among them, and that communion which is the essence of religion, be even slightly broken.

Now, looking for the application of this beautiful constitution to the dispensation whereof it was a shadow, the first thing that must strike us is, how completely the New Testament links the one unto the other, by applying to the new state all the imagery and phraseology employed in prophecy, as descriptive of the peculiar characteristics of the old. The Church, or dispensation of faith, is now the kingdom which was to be restored with its worship by the Son of David; there is a priesthood and an altar, there is authority and subordination, there is union and unity all as before: and, indeed, in the later prophecies of the old law, the Church is never otherwise described than as a revival, extension, and perfection of the former state. Now, this is all explained only by two reflections. First, that the former constitution was not abolished, but exchanged, and by that change perfected; and in this manner did Jesus say, that he came not to abolish, but to complete or accomplish: secondly, that the former was a type and merged into its reality, not so much dying as passing into a second existence, where a true sacrifice covered a typical oblation, where redemption given, passed before redemption expected, where uncertainty had ripened into knowledge, and hope yielded its kingdom to faith. To illustrate the noble by the base, the former state was, as that living but creeping sheath wherein lie infolded for a time the corresponding parts of a more splendid and gorgeous insect, which in due time takes upon itself the vital functions, till then, by the other exercised, —and rises towards heaven, the same yet different,—a transmigration rather than an offspring.

It is evident, then, that there must be counterparts in the two dispensations, analogies and resemblances, clearly showing ours to be the perfecting and filling up of the other's outline; that all forms or institutions, framed to ennoble the former before the nations of earth, to draw their respect and attention towards it, to invite them to learn the truths intrusted to it, must be found here in greater perfection; that to it must be granted a stronger guarantee and security of God's constant love, protection, and support; that in it must reign, far beyond the other, that beautiful co-ordination of parts, sympathy of feeling, and harmony of design, which God did in its prototype ordain. If you admit not all these, not only do you destroy all necessary resemblance, but you lower infinitely the present beyond the former dispensasation: you invert the order of God's working, you destroy that fair progressive course of development, which is the characteristic of all His works, wherein are no breaks or violent passages, but all succeeds by a most sweetly-guiding ordinance.

And are the truths and blessings now communicated to mankind less precious than those former ones, that they should require smaller securities, and less jealous precautions for their preservation, than of old? Should there be less dignity, less authority conferred upon their depositaries? Or have men so changed, that what before was necessary to keep them from fatal error and corruption, is now no longer needed? On the contrary, my brethren, hope, the great deposit of the elder dispensation, is that feeling which is the first to be conceived, and the last to be thrown off, a feeling rather dangerous from its tendency to increase, than from any fear of its extinction; while faith is ever a sterner and drier quality; something which we adopt with effort and pain, and lose more easily; and which requires consequently still stronger defences. Then again, there is a still greater difference; for hope may in its forms be various as the divers imaginings of men, borrowing its scenery and lively shapes from whatever to each seems most desirable; but faith is the impress—the coinage of God's own truth upon the soul, and God's own truth can be but one.

In all this, methinks, we have a key to explaining much in what Christ was pleased to ordain. For, if I see him appoint teachers to his people, shepherds to his flock, and established thus an order of subordination in doctrine and faith; then, promising His uninterrupted guidance till the end of time to those whom He has appointed to rule and instruct, thereby secure unreserved assurance to all that follow their doctrine: if then I take all these arrangements and ordinances in their plain and simple meaning, and construct therewith, in my mind, a great religious community, professing entire unity of doctrines under teachers directed by God; I see there so complete, so just a reality to the shadow of the previous dispensation, so true a correspondence of parts, so nice a fitness of them to similar ends—and all this so improved, so ennobled, so perfected into a purer and more spiritual character, from the nature of its objects, of its doctrines, of its diviner sanctions, that I cannot for a moment hesitate to believe, that, hereby alone, *could* accomplishment be given to the foreshowings of the former state, and that consequently no other conception of its fulfilment can be correct.

But now resolve, on the other hand, religion into a mere aggregate of individuals, each having his own peculiar measure of faith; bound up only together, as in one bundle, by external ties, not inly communicating by vital influences, like branches of one tree; deprive them collectively as individually of all security against fatal error, of all promise of permanent support; deny in it existence of any one universal aggregation towards which all men, no matter what their color or country, shall turn in full assurance that it can give them life; strip it of all the venerable rights which authority and a divine sanction alone can give, and assuredly you shall have produced something so curiously different from all whereunto God had so long prepared the world, that they who look therein for the accomplishment of past types, and the completion of the former state, must perforce acknowledge that the order of God's designs hath suffered strange perturbations.

But you will perchance say: With all the precautions which His providence took to secure the safe transmission of his promises, see how fearfully they of old did fall from Him, and forget all that He had taught them; and shall He then be supposed to have retained the same imperfect institutions now, which failed so sadly then? Now, far from there being any objection in this to what I have hitherto said, it seems to me to afford rather a confirmation thereof. Much falling off there often was—a total loss never. It was necessary that the hopes of the people should be often tried, and this was done in the way best suited to put them to the keenest test. First, they were left to wander forty years in the wilderness, that they might long for their promised land; then they were from time to time given over to enemies, that they might wish for deliverers from God, that so the desire for redemption might ever be before their eyes. And this period may all well correspond to the early days of persecution in Christianity, wherein rest and ease from tyrannical oppression were its most earnest prayer. Then came, in both, the time of religious dissension, of schism and heresy. For in the old times, men must have been severely tried, after the division in the kingdom took place, and later when in Samaria the true God was worshipped in a separate national communion, by hardly knowing how to reconcile domestic feelings and social customs with that unity which called them to God's appointed temple in a foreign land; and many doubtless thereby fell, and kept themselves separated from it through these worldly considerations. And, even, as then, this sort of trial was allowed by God to prove the fidelity of his people, so does St. Paul assure us that "now there must needs be also heresies, that they also that are approved may be made manifest among us."* But never formerly did the greatest of those defections destroy the deposit of hope given unto God's children; seeing that in the main it was found entire in their hands when Jesus Christ came to demand it; and that, whenever they had seemed most grievously fallen away, it needed no new reformings or great study of matters, to restore the knowledge of all that had once been taught.

And here we come to the last and great fulfilment of former types. The Jewish dispensation was necessarily imperfect; otherwise it never need have been superseded. It was subject, therefore, to constant disturbances and failings; and a remedy was supplied for these in the establishment of prophecy—of a series, that is, of godly men—extraordinary messengers sent by God, whenever any particular derangement or error had crept into His inheritance. Now since prophecy, considered as an ordinance, was necessarily to cease with fulfilment, some provision was requisite to take its place in the new state, and counteract the tendency towards error of the human mind. And see how beautifully this part of the figure was accomplished, and that in two ways. First, the prophets were the types of Jesus Christ; and, we shall see Jesus Christ himself come and take their place, assuming here also their ministry, promising to remain with His new kingdom, teaching therein always, to the consummation of the world. Secondly, the prophets were the tongues of the Holy Ghost; and the Holy Ghost himself comes down upon His Church to guide it into all truth. And thus is an institution for the removal or correction of error, changed, by a twofold fulfilment of the most beautiful and perfect character, into a provision for the entire and perpetual prevention of the same.

---

* 1 Cor. xi. 19.

LECTURE IV.   91

But, my brethren, I have thus far rather appealed to your own recollections, than laid before you any specific proof either of the connection which I have described as existing between the old and new Testaments, or of the correspondence of institutions between the two, especially in reference to the preservation of the Church from error. I could, indeed, have occupied your attention much longer, by entering into a detailed examination of the prophecies of the old law; I could have shown you how, from the very beginning till the end, there is a most beautiful series of manifestations, which go on gradually unfolding new qualities of the kingdom of Christ, until at length the picture is not only as complete as I have attempted to sketch it, but goes beyond my representation in clearness and strength, as much as the word of God is superior to that of man.

But yet, that I may not appear to be building upon a frail foundation, I will read to you one prophecy, and a very small portion of another, which seem to contain within themselves all that I have laid down, and give us much more than is required, to secure the train of argument which we shall afterwards pursue. Both are from the prophet Isaias; and all interpreters, who admit the existence of prophecy, allow them to be descriptive of the Church of the Messiah. The first is comprised in the fifty-fourth chapter.

"Enlarge the place of thy tent and stretch out the skins of thy tabernacles; spare not, lengthen thy cords, and strengthen thy stakes. For thou shalt pass on to the right hand and to the left, and *thy seed shall inherit the Gentiles*, and shall inhabit the desolate cities. Fear not, for thou shalt not be confounded nor blush, for thou shalt not be put to shame; because thou shalt forget the shame of thy youth, and shalt remember no more the reproaches of thy widowhood. *For He that made thee shall rule over thee, the Lord of Hosts is His name, and thy Redeemer, the Holy One of Israel, shall be called the God of all the earth.* For the Lord hath called thee as a woman forsaken, and mourning in spirit, and as a wife cast off from her youth, said thy God. For a small moment have I forsaken thee, but with great mercies will I gather thee. In a moment of indignation have I hid my face from thee, but *with everlasting kindness have I had mercy on thee, saith the Lord, thy Redeemer*. This thing is to me as in the days of Noah, to whom I swore that I would no more bring the waters of Noah upon the earth; so have I sworn not to be angry with thee, and not to rebuke thee. For the mountains shall be moved, and the hills shall tremble; *but my mercy shall*

LECTURE IV.

not depart from thee, and the covenant of my peace shall not be moved, said the Lord, that hath mercy on thee. Oh, poor little one, tossed with tempest, without all comfort, behold I will lay thy stones in order, and will lay thy foundation with sapphires.— *All thy children shall be taught of God, and great shall be the peace of thy children.* And thou shalt be founded in justice; depart far from oppression, for thou shalt not fear: and from terror, for it shall not come near thee. Behold, *an inhabitant shall come who was not with me; he that was a stranger to thee before, shall be joined to thee.** *No weapon that is formed against thee shall prosper; and every tongue that resisteth thee in judgment thou shalt condemn.* This is the inheritance of the servants of the Lord, and their justice with me."

To this striking passage I will add the concluding verse of the fifty-ninth chapter. "*This is my covenant with thee, saith the Lord. My spirit which is in thee, and the words that I have put in thy mouth, shall not depart out of thy mouth, nor out of the mouth of thy seed, nor out of the mouth of thy seed's seed, saith the Lord, from henceforth and for ever.*"

Surely, my brethren, the drift of these two passages cannot be mistaken. In them we are told that the Church of God, identified with the Jewish Church then existing—for this is addressed—should not continue much longer in a state of abasement; but that God should raise it up and extend its boundaries, so as to embrace all the kingdoms of the world, and the nations from the east unto the west; that it should be authorized to condemn every one that might rise up against it in judgment; that its teaching should be such as though the very words were put into its mouth by God; that there shall not depart from its seed, that is, its latest posterity, to the end of time; that God Almighty, the Lord of Hosts, the God of heaven and earth, should Himself teach in it, and that this divine teacher should be the Redeemer of His people, in such a way, that all its children should be called "taught of God." This covenant is everlasting, and can no more fail than God's covenant made with Noah, that the waters of the deluge shall no more return to cover the earth; and, hence His protection is pledged to prevent any attempt from prospering, which shall be designed or directed against its existence or success.

---

* This verse is obscure in the original Hebrew, and is translated in the version authorized in the English Church, so as to accord with the succeeding verses; but even so, the general sense of the prophecy is not weakened. It may be right to state that the title of the chapter in this version, applies it to the Church of the Gentiles.

LECTURE IV.

Now, my brethren, all this I am confident, is more than sufficient to prove, first, the exact connection between the old and the new dispensation, inasmuch as the latter was but the continuation and prolongation of the former; and, secondly, that a supreme advantage belongs to the religion which Christ came to establish, in its being taught and instructed by the Almighty himself, the Redeemer of His people. If, therefore, the principles which I have laid down are correct, on looking into the New Testament, we must necessarily expect to find such an institution as will exactly comprise within itself all the terms of this prediction, corresponding accurately to the means provided in the old law to teach mankind, and preserve from destruction the doctrines by God delivered. And I think, that if we diligently study the several passages of the New Testament, wherein our blessed Lord directs and describes the constitution of His Church or kingdom, we shall easily discover precisely such a continuation and such a provident scheme. Thus we are brought to the second portion of my theme, the direct testimony of God to the teaching of His Church.

Where can we better expect to find such a testimony, than in the very words wherein Christ conveys to His apostles and their successors His own supreme authority? For we read in the last verses of St. Matthew's Gospel, how, before He ascended into heaven, He called them all together, and addressed them in most solemn language, giving them His last and most special charge; and introduced this by a preamble wherein He should seem to allude to that testimony, which at the beginning of this discourse I described, that of His eternal Father, who commanded all to hear Him, as one in whom He was ever well pleased. Listen, I pray you, to this charge.

"All power is given to me in heaven and on earth.—Go ye, therefore, and teach all nations, baptizing them in the name of the Father, and of the Son, and of the Holy Ghost—teaching them to observe all things whatsoever I have commanded you. And behold! I am with you all days, even unto the end of the world."

"I am with you, all days, even unto the end of the world!" What, my brethren, is the meaning of these expressions? There are two ways of reading the word of God. Nothing is easier than, upon perusing a passage, to attach to it that sense which best accords with our preconceived system, and seems best suited to confirm the doctrines which we have embraced. Now, in this way, according as we, or those who differ from us, read these words, it is evident that there will be different meanings attached to them. For, the Catholic will say, that here a promise is clearly given by our blessed Redeemer, that He will assist his Church even to the end of time, so as to prevent the possibility of her falling into error, or of her allowing any mixture thereof with the truths committed to her charge. While we draw this important conclusion, others will say that the words imply nothing more than a mere protection and superintendence, a sort of security that the general system of doctrines and belief comprehended in Christianity shall never be lost upon earth. Others will perhaps conceive a promise to be here given to each individual member of the Church, that our Saviour will assist him in the formation of his system of faith.

Now it is evident that these different interpretations cannot be all correct, except so far as one may include the other. For that which we hold, does indeed comprehend that which the others propose, inasmuch as we believe that it secures that providential care and watchfulness which is the amount of their deduction, but with the addition of something more important, which their interpretation excludes. For these reject the truth of our explanation, otherwise they must needs adopt our doctrine. It is plain that there must be a certain criterion—a sure way to arrive at a correct knowledge of our Saviour's meaning; and I know not what rule can be better proposed, than the obvious one on every other occasion; that is, to analyze and weigh the signification of each portion of the sentence, so as to arrive at the meaning of the words which compose it; and then, by reconstructing the sentence, with the intelligence of all its parts, see what is the meaning intended by Him who spoke. And, for this purpose, we can have no better guide than the Holy Scriptures themselves. For, if we discover what is the meaning of words, by the various passages in which they so occur, as to be applicable to the interpretation of the one under examination, every one will agree that we have chosen the most satisfactory and plainly true method of settling the sense intended by our Lord.

We have a two-fold investigation to make; first, with the aid of other passages, to ascertain the exact meaning of the phrases in themselves; and then to see, in what relation they stand together, or, in other words, what is the extent of the commission which they imply.

1. In the first place, our Saviour says, that He "*will be with His disciples,* all days even unto the consummation or end of the

word." Now, what is the meaning in Scripture of "God's being with any person?" It signifies a more especial providence in regard of that individual than is manifested towards others—a particular watchfulness on the part of God over his interests, in such a way, that what he undertakes shall infallibly succeed. This is the signification which this phrase always bears in Scripture. For instance, (Genesis xxi. 22,) Abimelech says to Abraham, " *God is with thee* in all that thou doest." It is manifest, that here was meant that the patriarch had special assistance and succor from God. In the 26th chapter, (*v.* 3,) God said to Isaac, "Sojourn in the land, and *I will be with thee,* and will bless thee." And in the 24th verse, the same assurance is repeated, "Fear not, *I am with thee.*" Later, we hear the Almighty address Jacob in the same words—"Return into the land of thy fathers, and to thy kindred, and *I will be with thee;*" (xxxi. 3;) and Jacob expresses himself in the very same terms—"The God of my father *hath been with me;*" (*v.* 5;) words which he himself explains of a special protection and defence, two verses later,— "God hath not suffered him (Laban) to hurt me." The peculiar providential care, which watched over the innocent Joseph, and made him ever successful, is recorded in the same phrase, with a sufficient explanation. Thus, (Genesis xxxix. 33,) we read,— " And *the Lord was with him*, and he was a prosperous man in all things, and he dwelt in his master's house, who saw that *the Lord was with him*, and made all that he did to prosper in his hand." And in the 23d verse, we read again, " *The Lord was with him*, and made all that he did to prosper." In the New Testament, the phrase is used in the same sense. "Master," says Nicodemus to our Saviour, "we know that thou art come a teacher from God; for no man can do these signs which though doest, unless *God be with him.*"*

To most of these texts, we have a paraphrase or explanation attached, which clearly defines the sense of the phrase to be, that any one with whom God was, He blessed and made to prosper in all things. Such, then, in the first place, is the definite meaning of that phrase in our text. In the ancient and authoritative Greek version of the Old Testament, commonly called the Septuagint, precisely the same words are used in rendering all the passages which I have quoted, as occur in the original text, in the place under consideration, of St. Matthew.

2. Christ then was to watch over His apostles, and use towards

---

* John iii. 2.

them an especial providence, "all days to the consummation, or end, of the world." Here, again, a controversy arises regarding the meaning of the expression. The word translated "world"* has also another signification; it may mean the term of a person's natural life. Why not, therefore, adopt this meaning; and then the text will signify that Christ would be with His apostles so long as they remained upon earth? This suggestion must be judged precisely by the same rule as I laid down just now; and what will be the result? Why, that the word has sometimes the proposed meaning, but only in profane authors, and not in any single passage of the New Testament; for wherever it occurs, in this, it can be translated in no other way than "the world."

The only passage that can be brought to give plausibility to the other meaning, is Matt. xii. 32; where our Saviour, speaking of the sin against the Holy Ghost, says, "It shall not be forgiven him, neither in this world nor in the next." Here it might be said, that "this world" means the term of a person's natural life, during which his sin might be forgiven him under ordinary circumstances; and therefore, the same meaning may be attached to the same word in the text under discussion. But a slight reflection will satisfy you that even in that passage the word has not the supposed meaning. For, as the sentence is antithetic, having yet that same substantive for both members, this must have the same meaning in both. Now, the "next world" cannot signify the term or duration of a natural life, but clearly signifies a future order or state of things. And therefore, "this world," which is opposed to it, must mean the present or existing order.

But, even this reasoning is unnecessary; for, allowing that in the alleged passage it had that meaning, it could not, by any analogy, have it in Christ's promise. For, it is acknowledged by the best commentators, that in every instance where the word is used in conjunction with the word "consummation,"† it unquestionably and invariably means "the world;" that is, the duration of the present state of things. In this sense it occurs, Heb. i. 2, and ii. 5; also 1 Tim. i. 17. In Matthew xiii. 39, 40, and 49 verses, we have it used in the compound form to which I have just alluded, so as to leave no alternative in determining its meaning. "The harvest is *the end of the world*. So shall it be *at the end of the world:* the angels shall go out, and shall separate the wicked from among the just." The same expression is used by the disciples when they ask their Master, what should

---

* Αἰών. † Συντέλεια.

be the sign of his coming, "and of the end of the world."*
For, according to a Jewish notion, they confounded the destruction of the Temple, which it was supposed the Messiah would render imperishable, with the end of all things.

3. We have thus gained the meaning, and the only meaning, as given in Scripture, of another of our expressions. But it may be asked, is not this signification necessarily modified, and restricted to the apostles, by the use of the pronoun "you?" Can we suppose this pronoun to be addressed to the successors of the persons then present? Most undoubtedly; and first, because similar expressions occur in other parts of the New Testament. For example, when St. Paul speaks of those Christians who were to live at the end of the world, he uses the pronoun of the first person, which in extent of application, corresponds to the second. In the first Epistle to the Corinthians, chap. xv. v. 52, he writes, "*We* shall be changed." And so again, writing to the Thessalonians, (l. iv. 16,) he says, "Then *we* who are alive, who are left, shall be caught up, together with them in the clouds." The pronoun here is applied to those Christians who shall be living after the lapse of many ages; and consequently, there is no reason why it should not be in our text, nor why it should restrict that only meaning which the phrase just now discussed—"the end of the world"—has throughout the Holy Scriptures.

But you must be aware, that in the giving of all commissions, a similar form of expression is necessarily used:—only the person present is invested with the authority, which has to descend to his successors; so that, if we admit the limitation in this instance, it will apply to every authority, jurisdiction, command, or power, assumed by any Church. For, on the dispensation, or orders, given in the Gospel to the apostles, their successors, whether real or not, in every Church, ground their claim to authority; much of it perhaps upon the terms of this very text. The Church of England demands obedience to her bishops, on the strength of passages clearly addressed to the apostles; those societies which dedicate themselves to the preaching of the Gospel, in distant parts of the world, pretend to rest their right and commission upon the very words, "Go teach all nations." It is consequently evident, that every class of Christians agrees with us, that the pronoun cannot form any limitation to this or any other similar passage.

* Matt. xxiv. 3.

Putting now together the various significations thus discovered for the phrases composing the text under investigation, we have the following plain interpretation of it: that Christ promised to watch with peculiar care and solicitude over, and exert his most especial providence in favor of His apostles; and that this care and providence would not be limited to the lives of those whom He immediately addressed, but should be unfailingly continued, through all successive ages to the end of time, in the persons of those who should succeed them.

But, you may perhaps ask, what have we hereby gained in favor of the infallibility claimed by the Church? For so far we have done nothing towards ascertaining what is the object and extent of this peculiar watchfulness and assistance. This important point remains to be discovered; and we will now endeavor, with the divine blessing, to reach it, by the same tests of truth.

On examining the practice of Scripture, we find that, when God gives a commission of peculiar difficulty, one which to those that receive it must appear almost, nay entirely, beyond man's power, He assures them that it can and will be fulfilled, by adding, at the end of the commission, "*I will be with you.*" As if he would thereby say—"The success of your commission is quite secure, because I will give my special assistance for its perfect fulfilment." A few passages will make this position quite clear.

In the 40th chapter of Genesis, 3d and 4th verses, God says to Jacob, "I am God, the God of thy father; fear not to go down into Egypt, for I will make thee a great people. *I will go down with thee* into Egypt." That is, "I will accompany thee, *I will be with thee;* therefore fear not." This assurance is added as a special guarantee for the truth of the promise, that the descendants of Jacob should be a great people. They were to become, by fulfilling the command given them, subjects of another state; their chances of becoming a mighty nation seemed greatly lessened, or rather quite at an end; yet God pledged his word that He would so protect them, as that the promise *should* be fulfilled; and this He does by adding the assurance, "I will go down with thee." But this application of the clause is still clearer in the book of Exodus, where the Almighty commands Moses to go to Pharaoh and free his people. He executes this commission! he who had been obliged to flee from Egypt under a capital accusation,—who was now not only devoid of interest at court, but was identified with that very proscribed and persecuted race,

LECTURE IV.

whose extermination Pharaoh had vowed,—who, should he come forward, could only insure his own destruction, and the more certain frustration of the hopes which God had given to His captive people! How, then, does God assure him, that, in spite of all these apparent impossibilities, he shall be successful? "And Moses said unto God, Who am I that I should go to Pharaoh, and that I should bring forth the children of Israel out of Egypt? And He said unto him, *I will be with thee.*"* The fulfilment is secure, no other assurance is given; Moses has the strongest guarantee which God can propose to him, that he will be successful. Again, when Jeremiah is sent to preach to his people, and considers himself unfit for the commission, God promises him success in the same terms, and with the very introductory phrase used in the commission given to the apostles, "and behold!" and with other no less extraordinary coincidences. In the first chapter of that prophet (*v.* 17, 19,) we thus read; "Gird up thy loins, and arise and *speak unto them all that I command thee; and behold!* I have made thee this day a walled city. . . . And they shall fight against thee, but they shall not prevail, *for I am with thee,* saith the Lord." Here is a command given, precisely such as we have seen delivered to the apostles, to tell the people *all that God had commanded;* and to it is appended the very same form of assurance as is addressed to them.

It will not surely be rash to conclude, that we have thus a clear rule or axiom,—not arbitrarily assumed, but deduced from the examination of similar forms of speech in other parts of Scripture,—that, whenever a commission is given by God to accomplish what appears impossible by human means, he guarantees its complete success and perfect execution, by adding the words, "I am with thee." And if so, we have a right to conclude, that, in the text under examination, Christ, by the same words, promised to His apostles, and to their successors till the end of the world, such care, such a scheme of especial providence, as might be necessary and sufficient, to secure the full accomplishment of the commission given them. Nothing therefore remains, save to see what that commission is, and the case is closed.

"Go teach all nations;" such is the first part of the commission intrusted to the apostles. It comprises universality of teaching and governing, an authority and an influence beyond that

---
* Exodus iii. 11, 12.

LECTURE IV.

of the Roman Empire. How far above the reach of twelve poor Jewish fishermen! And further, what are the things to be taught? *"To observe all things whatsoever I have commanded you!"* How can they, dull, illiterate men; how, still less can their successors in remote countries and ages, hope to retain with accuracy or to teach with unfailing authority, *all and every thing* which our Lord has taught? This twofold commission is surely far beyond the power of man. Yet still it has to be fulfilled and will be, for Jesus Christ Himself has added to it these words of certain sanction: "BEHOLD I AM WITH YOU." Therefore the Church has ever been, is, and will continue till the end of time to be the universal instructor of all nations. Therefore her teaching will ever include "all things whatsoever" her Lord and Founder "commanded" to be taught, to the seclusion of whatever would confuse and vitiate the sum of His truth, or shake her authority.

I ask you, is not this a commission exactly comprising all that I have said we might be prepared to expect? Does it not institute an order of men to whom Christ has given security, that they shall be faithful depositaries of His truths? Does it not constitute His kingdom, whereunto all nations have to come? Does it not establish therein His own permanent teaching, in lieu of prophecy, so as to prevent all error from entering in? and is not this kingdom of His Church to last till the end of time? Now, here is all that the Catholic Church teaches, all that she claims and holds, as the basis and foundation whereupon to build her rule of faith. The successors of the apostles in the Church of Christ have received the security of His own words and his promise of "a perpetual teaching," so that they shall not be allowed to fall into error. It is this promise which assures her that she is the depositary of all truth, and is gifted with an exemption from all liability to err, and has authority to claim from all men, and from all nations, submission to her guidance and instruction.

Such is the first ground of the system which I endeavored to lay before you at our last meeting; but although I fear I have already trespassed too long on your attention, I am anxious, not indeed, to close the argument, but to finish the counterpart of what I represented to you in the first portion of my discourse, and for that purpose to refer to one or two other texts. I said then, that, even as, to fulfil the ends of prophecy, we might have expected to find Him whom the prophets typified, not only removing, but preventing error in the more perfect law; so might

LECTURE IV.

we hope to find the Holy Ghost, who was the inspirer of the prophets, who moved their tongues and directed their teaching, in like manner substituting for them, His own infallible and unquestionable instruction. Now, we do find several texts of Scripture, connecting themselves clearly with what I have already said; and obviously pointing out an institution for this very purpose. For, in the 14th chapter of St. John, (v. 16, 26,) we hear our Saviour say, "I will ask the Father, and He shall give you another Paraclete, that He may abide with you for ever; the Spirit of truth, whom the world cannot receive, because it seeth Him not, nor knoweth him: but you shall know Him, because He shall abide with you, and shall be in you." "But, the Paraclete, the Holy Ghost, whom the Father shall send in my name, He will teach you all things." And again, in the 16th chapter, (v. 13,) "But when He, the Spirit of truth is come, He shall teach you all truth."

Here again are words addressed to the apostles. I know there are some who consider them as spoken individually, to all the faithful, and suppose them to contain a promise of inspiration to all. But we must be consistent; if you allow that these words contain a promise not confined to the apostles, but to be extended not merely to later ages, but to every individual, then you must not limit the other promise made to the apostles to the compass of their lives alone. It must be extended in the same degree, and be considered as given for the benefit of every future age. I just now remarked, that the two passages are clearly related one to another, for the object of both is the same—to provide for the teaching of truth. Not only so, but these words are addressed, in a peculiar manner, to the apostles; because it is said, that the Holy Spirit is to be the supplementary teacher to the Son of God, and will complete what He had begun; so that this guidance is clearly for those who had been already appointed and instructed by the Saviour himself.

Now, certainly, no one will say that the commission before discussed extended to all the faithful; for if so, all would be commanded to preach and teach, and then, whose duty would it be to listen and learn? It is manifest that it establishes two orders—one of superiors, of directors, of governors, of instructors; the other of subjects, of scholars, and of followers. The texts, too, now more immediately under consideration, taken in their context, lead to the same conclusion. For, in the same discourse, our Redeemer clearly distinguishes between the teachers of His doctrines, and those who, through their means, are to learn them.* Thus do the two promises, joined together, afford the strongest proof of a constant security against error given to the Church of Christ, until the end of time, through the authoritative teaching of the successors of the Apostles, with the guarantee and sure co-operation of Jesus Christ and of the Holy Spirit.

There remains another passage, containing words of our Saviour, which would deserve to be commented on at some length; I mean that interesting promise wherein, after basing His Church on a certain foundation, He says, that "the gates of hell shall not prevail against it."† But I shall have occasion, some evenings later, to dwell more fully upon this text, because it is connected with the important doctrine of the authority of the Holy See; and I will therefore reserve it for my discourse on that subject.

But, having thus spoken of those promises and pledges which Jesus Christ gave to his Church, of unfailing protection and direction, may I not be met by other texts of a character apparently contradictory, such as must, if not destroy, at least neutralize, those which I have alleged? Are there not a series of strong passages in which, so far is the stability of the Church from being secured, that its total defection is foretold? Is there not to be a universal and awful apostasy from the truth as taught by our blessed Redeemer? Nay, still more, have not grave and learned divines placed these prophecies among the strongest evidences of Christ's divine mission, proved, as it is, in their fulfilment?‡

My brethren, in replying to this species of objection, I must be on my guard. I must avoid touching upon that view of it, however popular it may be, which pretends to see in the Catholic Church the foul characteristics attributed to the enemies of Christ in the Apocalypse, and other writings of the New Testament; and I must follow this course for several reasons. First, because, I would not profane the holiness of this place with the blasphemous calumnies which I should have to repeat, nor stoop to notice accusations, whereof it would degrade me in mind to think that they could be ever made but through a pitiful ignorance, or a lamentable prepossession. Secondly, because my plan does not allow me to seek out adversaries, but leads me to pro-

---

* John xvii. 20.   † Matt. xvi. 18.
‡ See Horne's Introduction, vol. i. p. 328. "We shall add but two more instances in illustration of the evidence from prophecy. The first is the long apostasy and general corruption of the professors of Christianity, so plainly foretold."

LECTURE IV.

ceed by an onward line of positive demonstration. Thirdly, because I cannot persuade myself that any of you who have so kindly continued to attend these lectures, listen to me with the impression that you are hearing the upholder of idolatry, or the advocate of antichrist.

Leaving aside, therefore, that class of applications, let us simply take and try the position, that a general defection from the truth is foretold in the New Testament; and that this prediction is even to be reckoned among the evidences of Christianity. Good God! and is it possible that any believer in the divinity of our Lord can assert so monstrous a proposition, as that He could have ever given such a proof as this of His heavenly mission and authority! I will present the case familiarly to you, in the form of a parable.—A certain king lived at a great distance from his children, whom he tenderly loved. They dwelt in a tabernacle, frail and perishable, which he had long and often promised should be replaced by a solid and magnificent abode, worthy of his greatness, and of his affection towards them. And after many days, there came unto them one who said, he was sent by him to raise this goodly building. And they asked him, "What evidence or proof dost thou give us that the King our father hath sent you, as fully qualified and able to build us such a house as shall worthily replace the other, and be our future dwelling?" And he answered and said: "I will raise a costly building, spacious and beautiful; its walls shall be of marble, and its roofs of cedar, and its ornaments of gold and precious stones; and I will labor and toil to make it worthy of him that sent me, and of me its architect, even so that my very life shall be laid out on the good work. And this shall be an evidence of my mission to the work, and of my approved fitness for undertaking it: that, scarcely shall it be completed but the lustre of its precious stones shall be dimmed, and the brightness of its gold shall tarnish, and its ornaments shall be defiled with foul spots, and then its walls shall be rent with many cracks and crannies in every part, and then it shall crumble and fall; and a few generations shall see the whole in ruins, and overspread with howling desolation!" And what would they reply unto him? "Go to," they would say, "for a fool, or one who taketh us for such: are these the proofs thou givest us of thy fitness to build a house for our abode?"

And if so, my brethren, must we not call it almost impious and blasphemous, to suppose that our Saviur can have given, as evidence of His divine commission to establish a religion and a church, that His work should not stand; but, after a few years, become disfigured with error and crime, and in a few centuries perish; or, what is worse, relapse into idolatry and corruption?* For, let those who say that the whole Church fell away into idolatry, remember, that it was to overcome this foul usurpation of the devil, that Jesus Christ taught and preached, and suffered and died? and shall we dare to say that He conquered not? Shall we presume to assert that, after having wrestled with the monster, even unto the shedding of His priceless blood, and having crushed its head, and left it apparently lifeless, yet it did too soon revive, to assail and lay waste His inheritance, and tear up the vineyard which His hands had planted? Why, the weak and material prototype of His truth and law had more power of old! For, when the Ark of His Covenant was placed, even by the hands of His enemies, in the temple of Dagon, it not only overthrew the idol, but it broke off its feet, so that it might no more be replaced upon its pedestal. Even the false prophet of the East shall have proved more successful! For, so powerful is the dogma of God's Unity, that wherever the doctrines of Islamism have been proclaimed, idolatry has been banished, so as never more to have returned. And shall Christianity have proved feebler than they? shall it alone have been compelled to yield to the power of Satan? shall Jesus Christ alone have been baffled by His enemy, and unable to establish what he came to teach? Away from us such impious and ungodly thoughts!

But if these prophecies exist,—every one of which I unhesitatingly and solemnly deny,—have we not a right to expect some intimation of the glorious event which was to remedy the said defection? When God foretold, through his prophets, the captivity of His people, He always presented the balm with the wound, and cheered them with the prospect and certainty of redemption. And is it possible that such an event should be omitted in the annals of prophecy, as that return of the Church from universal idolatry, by its favored portion in the islands of the West,† which, at last, should give efficacy to what Christ and

---

* " So that clergy and laity, learned and unlearned, all ages, sects, and degrees of men, women, and children, *of whole Christendom*, (a horrible and dreadful thing to think,) *have been at once drowned in abominable idolatry*, of all other vices most detested of God, and most damnable to man, and that by the space of eight hundred years and more,—*to the destruction and subversion of all good religion universally*."—Book of Homilies, (*Hom*. 8, p. 261, ed. of Soc. for Propagating Christian Knowledge,) pronounced, in the 35th of the Thirty-nine Articles, "to contain godly and wholesome doctrine, and necessary for these times."

† Anastasius, speaking of Pope Celestine's liberation of our island from Pelagian-

LECTURE IV. 105

His apostles had in vain attempted to achieve? Then, with His spouse, the Church, how different is His conduct from His dealings with His stiff-necked people! She is left in total and cheerless darkness; she is only to be assured that she shall be degraded and defiled, without a word of hope that mercy will be ever again shown unto her! But no, my brethren; let us not be so inconsistent as to imagine such things, after the clear, incontrovertible proofs which we have seen, both in the prophecy of the old law, and in the promise of the new; for, never will she be abandoned by God, any more than the earth shall be again desolated by a deluge;—and so far from the gates of hell thus prevailing against her, Jesus Christ and His Holy Spirit of truth will teach in her, and abide with her, till the end of time.

And now, in conclusion, allow me to remark that, if any one will dispassionately look at the constitution of the Church, such as I endeavored to describe it at our last meeting, and have partially, although I trust so far satisfactorily, proved it to-night, it must seem to be precisely what, in the nature of things, we should expect to find it. For we cannot fail to observe, that the system pursued by the Almighty in every other case where it is His intention to mould or form men for any certain condition of mutual relation—where He intends to prepare their minds for any state requiring uniformity of purpose and of action, is to bring them into it through the principle of authority. On what principle has he grounded the domestic society, but on that of subjection and obedience? Is it not an instinctive feeling inherent in our nature, that the child who has to learn, could not do so unless a scheme of rule and of submission existed in the little republic of each family? And if he be not so placed under the instruction and direction of his parents, or other masters, and by them formed and trained to those domestic virtues which it is the intention primarily of domestic order to instil and perfect, does not experience prove that the mind will be untutored and wild, devoid of the best affections, and open to the occupation of every passion, and the dominion of every vice? And as the domestic virtues are the stock, whereon are ingrafted our social qualities, never could we expect that by any other system the youth of any country could be brought to the adoption of the same moral and social feelings and pursuits, than by the natural course of youthful discipline and restraint, whereby the mind

---

ism, thus expresses himself:—" Quosdam inimicos gratiæ, solum suæ originis occupantes, etiam ab illo secreto exclusit oceani."
O

gains that self-command and love of principle which can alone well direct it.

And is it not so, likewise, in the course followed by Almighty Providence for the preservation of social order? Who ever heard of a society held together but by the principle and tie of authority and lawful jurisdiction? Can we conceive men enjoying the benefits of the social state, acting towards one another on certain fixed rules and principles, united for the great purposes of public co-operation—be it for peace or for war, or for their mutual support in private life, or the great and more general wants of human nature—otherwise than when united upon a system of proper authority and control? And not only so, but must they not have among them a *living* authority, fully competent to prevent every infraction of the law, and to secure the state against the corruption which results from the private opinions of men?

And, although it may appear perhaps somewhat foreign to the subject, yet I cannot help making a remark connected with this observation: that such is peculiarly the nature of our own constitution. It is singular, that we have a letter addressed by one of the oldest popes to a sovereign of this kingdom, which, even if it be not allowed all the antiquity attributed to it, must yet be considered anterior to the conquest; in which he expressly says, that the constitution and government of all the other nations of Europe are necessarily less perfect than that of England, because they are based on the Theodosian, or an originally heathen code, while the constitution of England has drawn its forms and provisions from Christianity, and received its principles from the Church. It is remarkable that, perhaps, no other country has such a steady administration of the laws, in consequence of the admission into it of that very principle which corresponds to the unwritten or traditional code of the Church. For, besides the statute law of the kingdom, we have also the common law, that law of traditional usage now recorded in the decisions of courts, and in other proper and legitimate documents, precisely in the same manner as the Church of Christ possesses a series of traditional laws, handed down from age to age, written, indeed, now, in the works of those who have illustrated her constitution and precepts and demonstrated every part of her system, but still differing from the Scripture much in the same way as the unwritten differs from the written law. This may be sufficient to show how far from unreasonable our system is, and how

LECTURE IV.

far remote from any tyranny, or oppression, or unjust restraint of men's minds, wherewith it is so often charged.

I trust, my brethren, that I have now shown you how consistent with sound reason, and how strongly confirmed in Holy Writ is the rule of faith which the Catholic holds, in the authority of the Church. I trust, too, that you will have seen how beautifully it harmonzies through all its parts, from one extreme to the other, so as to be worthy of being considered the work of God's hand. When you behold a majestic tree standing in the field, which has darted its roots far and deep into the earth, and spreads its branches wide around it, and produces, year after year, its store of leaves, and flowers, and fruit; you might as well imagine *it* to be the fashioning of man's hands, an ingenious device and artifice of his, which he feeds and nourishes, as suppose the same of the system I have described; which, as you have seen, entwines its roots through all the shadowy institutions of the elder dispensation, and, standing tall and erect in the midst of the new, defies the whirlwind and the lightning, the drought and scorching sun, burgeoning widely, and, like the prophet's vine, spreading its branches to the uttermost parts of the earth, and gathering all mankind underneath its shade, and feeding them with the sweetest fruits of holiness. For I have yet to show you much of its fairest graces and mightiest influences. Yes, and of it we may well exclaim, with Peter, in this day's gospel, "Lord, it is good for us to be here." Under its branches we have done well to make unto ourselves a tabernacle, where, with Moses and Elias, as the bearers of evidence from the old law, and with Jesus and his chosen apostles, as our vouchers in the new, we repose in peace and unity, in joy and gladness, in the security of faith, in the assurance of hope, and in the firm bond of charity.

LECTURE THE FIFTH.

THE CATHOLIC RULE OF FAITH FURTHER PROVED.

1 TIMOTHY, iii. 15.

"*Know how thou oughtest to behave thyself in the House of God, which is the Church of the living God, the pillar and the ground of Truth.*"

HAD you, my brethren, seen the exact and finished design for some sumptuous building, such as it proceeded from the hands of one, all whose works are necessarily most perfect, and who has the power to accomplish whatever he designeth, and did you know that it had been put by him into the hands of zealous, and willing, and competent workmen, by whom it might, under his superintendence, be brought into execution, I am sure you would consider it superfluous to inquire whether the command had been fulfilled, and whether that which was so beautiful in its design was not confessedly more so, and endowed with tenfold perfection, when in work accomplished. Now, such, precisely, is the position wherein we stand with regard to the present inquiry. I have endeavored, by the simplest course possible, to trace out from the beginning the plan by Divine Providence manifestly laid down for the communication of truths to mankind, and for their inviolable preservation among them.

After having, in my preliminary discourses, explained to you the different systems adopted, by us and by others, regarding the rule of faith; after having shown you the complicated difficulties which arise incessantly in the one, and the beautiful simplicity and harmony which reign throughout the other; I endeavored, commencing with the very first and less perfect system adopted by God in His communications with man, to show you what would be naturally and necessarily required, to give at once consistency and perfect beauty to the course which He had commenced, and what would be necessary to give solidity and reality to the typical and symbolical method pursued of old. I essayed, also, with the clear and explicit words of prophecy, to construct, in a manner even before its appearance,

LECTURE V.

that fabric of religion which the Son of God came down from heaven to establish; and then, unfolding before you the Sacred Volume, I endeavored, to the best of my power, to discover the exact tally and correspondence between the two, to show how that which was most beautifully foreshown, was much more beautifully fulfilled; so that we might conclude it impossible to construct any other system, but that which the Catholic Church maintains and teaches, competent to fulfil either the prophecies of the Old Testament, or the institutions of the New.

And having thus, therefrom deduced what was the work placed in the apostles' hands, what the commission intrusted to their care, what the ground-plan on which they were to erect God's Church, it must, I am sure, appear an almost needless search, to ascertain how far these faithful followers and dutiful disciples carried into execution the plan committed to them for these purposes. But still, my brethren, it must be interesting, and useful, too, to follow the same course as I have begun, and, ever going simply forward in the form of historical investigation, see the full and final completion of that which had been foretold and instituted, and trace, in the conduct of the apostles and their first successors, clear evidences of the impossibility of any other rule of faith having then been adopted, save that which the Catholic Church maintains at present. And such is the simple inquiry through which I am anxious to conduct you this evening. The investigation will merely consist in the statement of a few historical facts; and I shall be careful to support it by what must be considered incontestable authority; indeed, to base it on such admitted grounds, as, I trust, will leave no room for cavil or objection.

Christ, then, in completion of the work which He had begun, gave a commission to His apostles to go forth and preach His gospel to all nations, with the injunction to teach them all things whatever He had commanded, and with a promise that He himself should assist them, and all those who succeeded them in their ministry, to the consummation of the world. Such a promise, as we saw by comparing those words of the New Testament with other passages of Scripture, leaves no room to doubt, that thereby was guaranteed the preservation of God's entire and complete truth in the Church of Christ, to the end of time.

In explaining the grounds of the Catholic rule of faith, I dwelt chiefly on those passages which expressly argued the supernatural assistance of God towards preserving His Church from error:

but I felt then, and I feel as yet, that I was far from doing ample justice to my subject. Nor can I even now, from the course which I have marked out for myself, and must necessarily pursue, supply my deficiency; but I must unwillingly pass over a great deal of strong confirmatory matter that should justly have come in to complete the views which I gave in my last discourse. I should, for instance, have dwelt upon those different commissions which our blessed Saviour gave to his apostles; where He appointed them the governors of His flock; and where, under different symbols of authority and power, such as giving them the keys of His kingdom, commanding them at discretion to bind and to loose, He bestowed upon them, as on another occasion you will see, great jurisdiction and authority over men. I might have led you to consider, how this principle of authority not only forms the basis and groundwork of faith in the Christian Church, but pervades its minor departments, in a descending, consistent scale of gradations, even into its inferior orders:—how, when any member of it becomes refractory, he was to be subject to an authority vested even in its smaller divisions;* and, above all, I should have dwelt at full length, on those important passages, wherein supreme jurisdiction is given to one; and so the very substruction and foundation-stone of Church authority is laid. But this will form hereafter the subject of a particular discourse.

I have rehearsed these examples, to show how argument upon argument might have been piled up before you; but, at present, I will content myself with recalling to your mind one or two texts, before only hinted at, and request your attention to them only for a moment. I allude to those passages in which Christ manifestly transferred His authority to His apostles—where He tells them that, even "as the Father had sent Him, so also does He send them,"†—where He says, "He that heareth you, heareth me, and he that despiseth you, despiseth me, and he that despiseth me, despiseth Him that sent me."‡ No doubt, the apostles well knew, and fully understood, the authority and sanction which He had from God to teach and enforce His doctrines; the sanction, not only of His Father, but of His own divine nature; and, therefore, when we find Him constituting them His vicegerents on earth, with the full deposit of truths come down from heaven in their hands, when we see them sent forth in such terms to preach and instruct, we cannot but understand how

---

* Matt. xviii. 17-19. † John xx. 21. ‡ Luke x. 16.

LECTURE V. 111

they must have felt themselves possessed of authority to teach, and to decide, and to exact homage from man's individual reason to their superior and divinely authorized instruction.

How, then, did the apostles go forth? what was the principle on which they conducted their instruction? In the first place, we do not observe that they on any occasion suggested the necessity of individual examination of the doctrines of Christianity. We find that they endeavored to narrow their proofs as much as possible; that they reduced them to one single point—their testimony to some principal evidence of their truth. Thus, for instance, the doctrines of Christianity were made to rest on the truth of Christ's resurrection; and we find that they were content with bearing witness to their having themselves seen Christ after he rose from the dead.* And although you may say that the miracles which they wrought were a motive which induced men to believe their testimony, yet is it no less true that the grounds on which they were believers was really the authority with which by miracles they proved themselves empowered to teach. It is necessary for you to retain a distinct idea of some observations which I made in my first, or opening discourse, on this important subject; for although, no doubt, a great many of the first believers were brought to give credence to the preaching of the apostles, in consequence of the miracles they wrought, it is nevertheless certain that their faith was not to be built on their miracles, but on the truth of the doctrines proposed to them by Christianity. After these motives had brought them to embrace it, there must have been a security given them that all the doctrines which would be proposed must be true. The very fact of its evidences being placed and accepted on so narrow a point as the demonstration of the resurrection, shows that a principle existed among them which secured the assent of the convert to all that should be taught him. This could only be implicit reliance on the teaching of his instructors—in other words, the Catholic principle of an infallible authority to teach.

We find not, in the second place, when they preached, the slightest intimation given by them that there was a certain book, which all Christians must study and examine, and thereon ground their faith. We hear them appeal to the Old Testament whenever they address the Jewish people, because therein were

---
* Acts ii. 32; iii. 15; v. 30, 32; xiii. 30; xvii. 31, &c.

truths contained which they clearly admitted, and which necessarily referred to the gospel for their completion, so as to serve for an easy guide and introduction to the demonstration of Christianity. But we never find the slightest intimation that the history of our Saviour's life, or the doctrines which they taught, were to be necessarily committed to writing, and thus proposed to the individual examination of the faithful.

Instead of this, we discover another much more important principle—and it is, that, wherever they went, they appointed persons to teach the flocks or congregations they had formed. Nothing can be more evident than that these persons had authority and power placed in their hands, as the means whereby they were to teach and govern. They are told not to allow any one to despise them on account of their youth; they are empowered to receive accusations, even against priests; and so early as this, the very conditions and forms of the judicature are established.* These things, primarily, indeed, appertain to discipline; but they show how, from the very beginning, the entire system of the Church was essentially based on the principle of authority and authoritative direction. Not so content, we find that the apostles gave the most minute instruction to those individuals, and to their Churches—not, indeed, to read the forthcoming word of God in the New Testament, when written, for it is not even hinted that it was ever to be so recorded —but to be careful in preserving the doctrines given into their hands.

St. Paul thus addresses his favorite disciple Timothy: "O Timothy, keep that which is committed to thy charge, avoiding the profane novelties of words, and oppositions of knowledge falsely so called; which some promising have erred concerning the faith."† That is to say, remember those doctrines which I have given you, lest they be perverted even in their words; take care to retain even correctness of expression in the teaching of what I have delivered to you, lest, by the oppositions of false knowledge, it be corrupted; in which words, St. Paul alludes to Gnosticism, or the earliest errors that crept into the Church. Now, had his idea been that the doctrines of religion were to be recorded in a book, and that the words of that book were to be the only text on which religion should be grounded; nay more, had he felt that in the very epistle which he was inditing, he was actually writing a portion of that new code, and consequently

---

* 1 Tim. iv. 12; v. 19.   † 1 Tim. vi. 20

LECTURE V.   113

had it in his power to prevent the danger of perversion, assuredly it would not have been necessary to inculcate with such care the preservation of even the words delivered. Moreover, observe, that he does not commit his doctrines to each individual in the Church, nor to its entire congregation collectively, but to one individual, whom he had clearly appointed to preside over it, as having to render an account to God for the souls of his flock.

Still further, he thus addresses him, "Hold the form of sound words, which thou hast heard of me in faith, and in the love which is in Christ Jesus. Keep the good thing committed to thy trust by the Holy Ghost who dwelleth in us."* Here we have a beautiful recognition in practice of the teaching of the Holy Spirit of God, and the assistance of our Saviour, through the pastors of his Church; and the consequence is, that the immediate disciple and successor of the apostle is exhorted to keep exactly the very form of words in which this teaching is couched. Some have said, that the form of words here alluded to is the creed or symbol of the apostles. But, in the first place, we should have proof of this; secondly, the preservation of this could not require to be so energetically inculcated to a bishop then, any more than now; since the more it was taught, and the more it was made the property of the flock, the less chance there was of its being lost or altered. Here, then, we have the first step in a system of traditionary teaching—the delivery of the doctrine in words, by one sent primarily to preach them, to one whom he delegates to continue his work. Let us now see the next link in the chain. Timothy, after a few verses, is thus further exhorted:—"The things which thou hast heard of me by many witnesses, commend to faithful men, who shall be fit to teach others."† Once more, St. Paul does not say, "Treasure up this my epistle as a part of God's holy word, and give copies of it to those whom you have to instruct;" which surely might have appeared the safest way of preserving the doctrines delivered in it; but he tells Timothy to choose faithful or trustworthy men, and to confide the truths he had received into their hands, that they, in their turn, might communicate them to others. Is not this clearly assuming oral teaching as the method to be established and pursued by the Church of Christ?

Before quitting the epistles of St. Paul to his chosen disciples, I cannot refrain from calling your attention to one or two more texts, as appearing strongly confirmatory of the Catholic rule.

---

* 2 Tim. i. 13, 14.   † Ib. ii. 2.

First, he says to Timothy: "I desired thee to remain at Ephesus when I went into Macedonia, that thou mightest *charge some not to teach otherwise;* nor to give heed to fables and genealogies without end, *which minister questions* rather than the edification of God, which is in faith."* No dissent therefore is allowed, nothing which leads to questions, and diverts the mind from building up within itself the simple faith of God; and to prevent this was the principal object intended by St. Paul, when he appointed Timothy to preside over the Church at Ephesus. Now, suppose this to be the commission of all bishops, and that consequently proper means are placed by God in their hands to secure these objects, a simple test of experience would show us, which of the principles now adopted was the one to be used by Timothy. For surely experience must have shown, that if thus appointed to hinder dissent, with no other principles and no more power than even Episcopal Churches among "the reformed" admit, his means must have been sadly unequal to their purpose.† Whereas, similar observation will show that the bishops of the Catholic Church are effectually able to preserve unity among their flocks, by their authoritative teaching. In vain would the former *charge* their clergy or laity "not to teach otherwise," or to avoid topics "which minister questions," while the latter are secure that the danger is remote from their fold, and rule it without disturbance or dissension. Thus may we plausibly conjecture what was the rule which Timothy had to follow.

To Titus, the language of St. Paul is still more remarkable. "A man," he writes, "that is a heretic, after the first and second admonition, avoid, knowing that he, who is such a one, is subverted, and sinneth, being condemned by his own judgment."‡ I am not going to dwell upon the first portion of this text, so to justify the conduct of the Catholic Church towards those who broach error, and corrupt the purity of faith by innovations of doctrines; the argument to be drawn from this sternness of command against changes of doctrines, I leave you to your own reflections. It is the latter portion of the text which I consider for our present purpose most important. St. Paul, at that early age, when hardly any one could have been born and brought up

---

* 1 Tim. i. 3, 4.

† The dissensions which have burst out so flagrantly before the public in the Wesleyan Methodists' body would afford a ground for many interesting observations on the necessity of rule and authority in religion.

‡ Tit. iii. 10, 11.

LECTURE V.

in heresy or error, necessarily means by the word, *heretic*, one who, having professed the true religion, turns away from it to embrace new opinions, without relapsing into idolatry; for one who did this he would have called an apostate, and not a heretic. Now, of such a person, he tells us that he necessarily "sinneth, being condemned *by his own judgment*." But in our days, if a person changes from one Protestant community to another, so far from its being considered sinful, or involving a necessary self-condemnation, it is thought that a man may be, and is generally therein *approved* "by his own judgment." For this judgment, it is considered, is, and ought to be, his guide in matters of religion. The principle of Protestantism consequently is quite at variance with this awful doctrine of the apostle. For he supposes the existence of some internal principle, which necessarily condemns, in his own judgment, the man who abandons the truth. But this can only be a principle giving certain assurance that you possess the truth, a principle which convinces you that all you hold is correct; for only by abandoning such a principle, could you stand self-convicted by the change. The doctrine of St. Paul, in this regard, is precisely that of the Catholic Church. Putting aside the case of unwilling ignorance, no Catholic, who really possesses within him the principle and rule of faith, whereby he is united to his Church, can offend heretically against any of his doctrines, without his own judgment condemning him as a violator of those essential principles, and convicting him of a grievous sin.

From the instructions given by the apostle of the Gentiles to the rulers whom he appointed over his infant churches, let us turn to hear the exhortations which he directs to these. To the Thessalonians he thus writes; "Therefore, brethren, stand fast; and hold the traditions which you have learned, whether by word, or by our epistle."* Here, again, we have mentioned the two species of doctrines, some written, but others unwritten; while both are placed exactly on an equal footing, so that both should be received by the Church with equal respect, and both be committed to the successors of the apostles. Upon perusing these testimonials, and seeing the principle of an oral teaching, with authority, thus prescribed, and at the same time observing the total silence on any thing like a written code of Christianity to be produced and substituted for it, can you hesitate for a moment as to the course pursued by the apostles, and the grounds

---

* 2 Thes. ii. 14.

on which they built their Church? Must we not conclude that an authority to teach was communicated to them, and by them to their successors, together with an unwritten code, so that what was afterwards written by them was but a fixing and recording of part of that which was already in possession of the Church?

But let us go a little farther into this consideration. I have said that we discover in the New Testament no hint or intimation whatever, that the Christian code was to be committed to writing; but, on the other hand, we see the apostles preaching the gospel, teaching Christianity to many foreign nations; and, according to ecclesiastical history, not only over all Europe, but to the furthermost bounds of the east. St. Thomas, for instance, is said to have preached in the peninsula of India; St. Bartholemew carried the faith into parts of Scythia; St. Thaddeus into Mesopotamia; and other apostles into the interior of Africa. We have had learned treatises written, among them one by the present Bishop of Salisbury, to prove that St. Paul preached in this island, and converted the Britons.

It must be interesting to discover the principle on which they proceeded in converting and teaching those distant nations. Doubtless they based their doctrines on the true rule of faith, and took the proper means for these being well learnt and securely preserved in their respective Churches. Was the Scripture, then, the written word, this rule and foundation, and means of security? If so, we surely must have translations of this sacred book in the different languages of those nations. We have in some of them, as the Indian, works extant, written before the time of our Saviour; and is it credible that the first task of the apostles would not be to translate the Scriptures into them? the more as they had the gift of tongues, and could have done it without difficulty or error? If the presentation of the Bible to all men, and to each individual, be the first step to Christianity and its most vital principle, and if the only ground of faith be the personal examination of each article of belief, surely the only means for securing these requisites would not be neglected? Yet, the only versions of the New Testament that have come down to us are, the Latin one used in the west, called the *Vulgate*, and the Syriac translation.* Now, of the Latin Vulgate we do not know the origin. Probably it was written in the first

---

* I omit the Coptic or Sahidic version, as less important, and probably not so old as the other two.

or second century, but we have the strongest reasons to believe that, for the first two centuries, it was confined exclusively to Africa;* so that Italy, and Gaul, and Spain, countries whose language was Latin, used no Scripture, except the original Greek of the New Testament, and the Greek version of the Old; not a text in the vernacular tongue, such as the poor could understand—not that which could alone be read by the great mass of Christians. The Syriac version, in like manner, was known only to a small portion of the apostles' early conquests. Even of its existence we have no evidence previous to the third century, so that we have, perhaps, two centuries passing over without the Bible, or even the New Testament being in the hands of the eastern Christians.

But, what shall we say of our own country, which was in a manner separated from the rest of the world? We are told that, from the beginning, the Church of this country, so far from being in communion with the See of Rome, would receive nothing from it; that she always stood in fierce defiance and opposition to its mandates; that the British Church was apostolic, pure, and free from every error and corruption, which later times had introduced into that of Rome. Where, then, did it gain this knowledge of the pure doctrines of Christianity? There was no version of the Scriptures into the British language; none which the people could possibly read: and we must therefore conclude that all these pure doctrines, which are supposed to have existed in the early church of this island, must have been handed down by tradition. But this very circumstance excludes the idea of considering the Scriptures as the sole foundation on which the apostles built the Church.

Before leaving this early period of our investigation, let us see in what way one of the most ancient fathers of the Church confirms what I have said. I allude to St. Irenæus, the illustrious bishop and martyr of Lyons, who lived in the third century. Speaking of the necessity, or non-necessity of the Bible as the rule of faith, he thus expresses himself: " And had these apostles left us nothing in writing, must we not in that case have followed the rule of doctrine which they delivered to those to whom they intrusted their Churches? To this rule many barbarous nations submit, who, deprived of the aid of letters, have the words of salvation written on their hearts, and carefully

---

† See "Two letters on some parts of the Controversy concerning 1 John v. 7, by N. Wiseman, D. D." Rome, 1835. Let. 2, pp. 45–66.

guard the doctrine which has been delivered."* Even in the third century, then, according to this venerable authority, there were many Churches, which believed all the doctrines of the apostles, without having had the word of God presented to them in any written form which they could understand.

We must not conclude this portion of our theme, without, for a moment, examining what can have been the principle on which the apostles received converts into the religion of Christ. We read, in the Acts, of three or five thousand souls being converted in one day, and admitted into the Church, through baptism?† Does this fact possibly allow us to imagine that they were all instructed in detail in the mysteries of religion? By baptism, it was understood that they were received into perfect community with the faithful; and can we therefore suppose that all those whom the apostles at once baptised, had time to go through the minute examination of all the doctrines presented to their belief? The very words of Scripture itself are at variance with such a supposition, because it speaks of these conversions as having been instantaneous. But there must have been some compendious principle—some ground on which they were received into Christianity, which involved their acceptance, when taught, of whatever would be explained by those who had converted them; there must have been a summary and complete confession of faith exacted from them, which guaranteed their subsequent adhesion to every doctrine that should be taught; otherwise it would have been but a profanation of the solemn rite and sacrament of baptism, to admit men within the pale of the Christian Church, and yet leave them the option of retiring again from it, should they not be able to satisfy themselves that each of its doctrines was true. Now, imagine what you please, make what hypothesis you like, you can give no adequate solution, short of supposing implicit reliance on the teaching of the pastors of the Church,‡ which, in matters of religion, amounts to a belief in the infallibility of the teaching power; you must conclude it was understood, that whatever doctrines should afterwards be placed before them by their instructors, they were willing to re-

---

* Adv. Hæres. lib. iii. c. iv. p. 205.
† Acts ii. 41; iv. 4.
‡ This method was followed not merely by the divinely commissioned apostles, but by those no less who only had a delegated mission from them, and partook not of the high prerogatives and peculiar powers of the apostleship; as by Philip, (Acts viii. 12,) who was only a deacon. This observation is important, as it shows the method to have been founded on a system, not merely on a reliance on the personal infallibility of the apostles.

ceive. And, in fact, we do find this to have been the case in practice: because, when the apostles subsequently made decrees, and published laws regarding the practice of the Church, when they came to a decision on matters of belief and discipline, all the faithful submitted to those decrees; all the faithful reverenced them, not only as teachers, but as superiors, to whose authority they were obliged to bow. This admission explains at once the difficulty, and shows the principle on which the early converts were admitted into the Church. It was upon the understanding, and upon a sufficient pledge given, that they were ready to embrace the doctrines of Christianity, not because they had minutely and individually examined them; but because, satisfied of their first step being right, the belief in an authority vested in the apostles, they were willing, and obliged, to receive implicitly whatever might afterwards come from their mouths.

Apply this to the two rules of faith. Suppose a missionary arriving in a foreign country, where the name of Christ was not known, and advancing as his fundamental rule, that it was necessary for all men to read the Bible, and for each one to satisfy his own mind on all that he should believe. I ask you, not if you think it possible that thousands could be ever, properly speaking, said to be converted by one discourse, under such a principle, but whether, if the missionary conscientiously believed and taught this principle, he could, in one day, admit those thousands, by the baptismal rite, into the religion of Christ? Would he be satisfied that he had made true converts, who would not go back from the faith once received? I am sure any one conversant with the practice of modern missions will be satisfied that no missionary, except one from the Catholic Church, would receive persons so slightly instructed into its bosom, or be satisfied that they would persevere in the religion they had adopted. But *they* can do it at this day, and they have done it in every age; for St. Francis Xavier, like the apostles, converted and baptized his thousands in one day, who remained steadfast in the faith and law of Christ. And all may be so admitted at once into the Catholic religion, who give up belief on their own individual judgment, and adopt the principle that whatever the Catholic Church shall teach them must be true.

While, therefore, so far as from history and their own writings we can ascertain the conduct of the apostles, we find not the slightest proof that the Scripture, the New Testament, was to be the rule of faith, we see the course pursued by them necessarily supposing the Catholic principle of authority, and of infallible teaching in the Church of God. We will now descend to a later period, and see how far the Church continued, in her earliest and best days, to act on the same principle. I am not now going to startle you by bringing forward the authority of tradition itself, in favor of the system which I have endeavored to explain and prove. I am not going to quote authorities for what I have said; but, by looking at the question only historically, and supposing that those who were the immediate successors of the apostles would naturally persevere in the methods enjoined by them, that they learned their way of instructing the Church of Christ from the same persons from whom they learned their faith itself, we may have in their conduct a confirmation of what I have advanced; and may further determine another important point in our examination; how far, that is, the methods followed by the apostles depended upon their peculiar privileges and personal authority, or were the result of a principle permanently instituted in the Church. For, if we find that the very same homage to authority in teaching was exacted by the successors of the apostles, and willingly paid by the faithful, we surely must conclude that this system was an integral part of Christianity, and the principle of faith which we have proposed, not a temporary one resting upon the apostolic character, but the essential groundwork of all belief.

Let us study the second and third centuries of the Church, the ages of martyrs and confessors, for then surely she was marked by no one spot or taint, nor can any imputation be cast on the purity of her morals or the integrity of her doctrines.

If, looking at those ages, we examine the method pursued in private instruction, or their belief regarding the evidences of Scripture, or, finally, their sentiments respecting the authority of the Church, we shall find precisely the same ideas, precisely the same method.

I. To begin, therefore, with the first; it is a well-ascertained fact, that, during the first four centuries of the Church, it was not customary to instruct converts in the doctrines of Christianity before their baptism. There was a certain discipline, popularly known by the name of the *discipline of the secret*, by virtue of which the most important doctrines of Christianity were reserved for the baptized. Persons who applied for admission into the Christian Church were kept, generally at least two years, in a state of probation. During that time they were allowed to attend in the Church for a certain portion of the service; but the moment the more important parts of the liturgy approached, they were obliged to leave it, and remain without. In this way, until actually baptized, they were kept in ignorance of the most important dogmas of Christianity. There is indeed some controversy regarding the extent to which that reserve was carried; many suppose that the doctrines of the Trinity and Incarnation were communicated before baptism; others maintain that even these were jealously withheld from the converts until they had actually entered into the Church by baptism; so that nothing more than an implicit belief in Christianity was previously exacted from them. I do not mean to say, that this is my opinion; but I will show you, by and by, that it is the opinion of learned Protestant divines.

Let us now consider what were the motives which led to this discipline. It is supposed to have been grounded on several passages of Scripture, such as that where our Saviour warns his apostles "not to throw pearls before swine,"—not to communicate the precious mysteries of religion to those who were unworthy of them. Several hints, too, of such a system are thrown out in the Epistles of St. Paul, where he speaks of some doctrines as being food for the strong, while others are compared to milk, which may be communicated to infants in faith; and the unbaptized were, in the early language of the Church, called children, or infants, in comparison with the adult, or perfect faithful. It was deemed, therefore, expedient, and almost necessary, to conceal the real doctrines of Christianity from heathenish persecutors—not, indeed, from a dread of being treated with greater severity, but rather through fear of the mysteries being profaned and subjected to indecent ridicule or wanton curiosity.

Now, this being the object to be attained, upon what principle can the system have been carried into effect? Suppose, for a moment, that the principle of faith among these early Christians had been the examination of the doctrines proposed by their teachers in the written Word of God; and that the examination had to be carried on by each individual, with responsibility for himself, that he believed nothing but what he could satisfy himself was so proved. Suppose this to have been the principle of faith, how can it be reconciled with the ends of that system? The object of this was, to prevent exposure of the sacred mysteries, by betrayal from those who had been instructed in them. But if we suppose the principle just mentioned to have been followed by the Church, she exposed herself, uselessly, to a dreadful risk. Instead of at once proposing her doctrines to the examination of the candidate for baptism, and, if he were not satisfied, allowing him to withdraw, we are to suppose that she preferred receiving such actually into her communion, leaving them, of course, the option of then retiring from it—not only the option, but the necessity of doing so, if they could not afterwards satisfy themselves of every doctrine proposed to them. This would have been defeating the very object in view; because, in this case, apostates, if ever there were any, would have been, necessarily, actual members of the Church, and practically acquainted with all its rites and sacraments; and the guilt of profanation would, in every instance, have been added to their treachery and apostasy. Unless, therefore, a sure pledge had been possessed after baptism there could be no danger, or moral possibility, humanly speaking, of dissatisfaction with any of the doctrines communicated, and, consequently, of any wish to draw back from Christianity: this discipline would have defeated its own object. Not only so, but it would have been an act of the greatest injustice; it would have been inveigling men into an unknown system, and, at the first step, exacting from them what every moralist must consider, under ordinary circumstances, essentially wrong—adhesion to doctrines or practices not explained to them, and of the correctness whereof they were not allowed to judge. Unless, therefore, there was some principle embraced by the catechumens, as they were called, before they were baptized, which gave a guarantee to the Church that it would be impossible for them to go back, no matter what doctrine, what discipline, or what practices should be subsequently imposed upon them—however sublime or incomprehensible the dogmas, or however severe the sacrifice they required of their feelings and opinions—unless there was a security to this extent before baptism—it would have been unjust in the highest degree—it would have been immoral, to admit them to it. Nay, more—it would have been sacrilegious; it would have been a conniving at the possibility of the sacrament being bestowed upon persons who had not, even virtually, the entire measure of faith, but had yet, on the contrary, the momentous duty to discharge, of studying their belief, and making up their minds whether or no they would accept those doctrines as scriptural, which the baptizing Church held and would propose to them.

There is only one principle which could justify and explain this discipline—the conviction of those subject to it that they would be guided by such authority as could not lead them astray; that in giving their future belief into the hands of those

LECTURE V.

that taught them, they were giving it into the hands of God; so as to be previously satisfied of a supreme and divine sanction to all the mysteries of religion that might afterwards be taught them. On this principle alone could security have been given, that, after being baptized, the new Christians would not turn back from the faith; and consequently, only by the admission of this principle as the groundwork of Christian truth, can we suppose the ancient discipline to have been preserved in the Church, or the practice of admitting persons so uninstructed to baptism, warranted or justified.

I will read to you one authority in support of all that I have said. It shall be a very modern one, and one which, in the Church of England, should be considered essentially orthodox. It is from a work published by Mr. Newman, of Oxford, only two years ago, entitled, "The Arians of the Fourth Century;" a work which has been, to my knowledge, highly commended and admired by many, who are considered well acquainted with the doctrines of that Church. The passage is more important, because it would bear me out farther than I have gone, and confirms what I before stated, that the great and essential doctrines of Christianity, were not, according to some, at first revealed to catechumens. In page 49, he says, speaking of them: "Even to the last, they were granted nothing beyond a formal and general account of the articles of the Christian faith; the exact and fully developed doctrines of the Trinity and the Incarnation, and, still more, the doctrine of the Atonement, as once made upon the Cross, and commemorated and appropriated in the Eucharist, being the exclusive possession of the serious and practised Christian. On the other hand, the chief subjects of cathechisings, as we learn from Cyril, were the doctrines of repentance and pardon, *of the necessity of good works*, of the nature and use of baptism, and the immortality of the soul, as the apostles had determined them." The only doctrines, according to this authority, taught before baptism, were the immortality of the soul, the necessity of good works, the use of baptism, and of repentance and pardon. No more than a general idea of Christianity was given; the important doctrines—I might say, the most important doctrines, for, by Christians of any denomination, these must be so considered—of the Trinity, and the Incarnation, and above all, that dogma which now-a-days particularly is considered the most vital of all, the Atonement on the Cross, were not communicated to the new Christian before he was baptized. But here comes an objection to this statement, and you shall hear its answer.

LECTURE V.

"Now, first it may be asked, how was any secresy practicable, seeing that the Scriptures were open to every one who chose to consult them?" That is, if the Bible was in the hands of the Faithful, and they were supposed or recommended to read it, thence to satisfy their conviction; how was it possible to preserve these doctrines from observation? Hear now the answer. "It may startle those who are but acquainted with the popular writings of this day; yet I believe the most accurate consideration of the subject will lead us to acquiesce in the statement, as a general truth, that the doctrines in question have never been learned merely from Scripture. Surely the Sacred Volume was never intended and was not adopted to *teach* us our creed; however certain it is that we can *prove* our creed from it, when it has once been taught us, and in spite of individual producible exceptions to the general rule. From the very first, the rule has been, as a matter of fact, for the Church to teach the truth, and then appeal to the Scripture in vindication of its own teaching. And, from the first, it has been the error of heretics to neglect the information provided for them, and to attempt of themselves a work to which *they* are unequal, the eliciting a systematic doctrine from the scattered notices of the truth which Scripture contains. Such men act, in the solemn concerns of religion, the part of the self-sufficient natural philosopher, who should obstinately reject Newton's theory of gravitation, and endeavor, with talents inadequate to the task, to strike out some theory of motion by himself. The insufficiency of the mere private study of Holy Scripture for arriving at the entire truth which it really contains, is shown by the fact, that creeds and teachers have ever been divinely provided, and by the discordance of opinions which exist whenever those aids are thrown aside; as well as by the very structure of the Bible itself. And if this be so, it follows, that when inquirers and neophytes used the inspired writings for the purposes of morals, and for instruction in the rudiments of the faith, they still might need the teaching of the Church, as a key to the collection of passages which related to the mysteries of the Gospel—passages which are obscure from the necessity of combining and receiving them all."

Here, then, my brethren, we have an acknowledgment made, within these last two years, by a learned divine of the Established Church, that the Christians in early times were not instructed in the important dogmas of religion, until baptized; and he answers the objection that the Scriptures were then the rule of faith, by asserting that they were indeed employed by the Church to *confirm* the faith which it taught, but were never considered as the only ground upon which faith was to be built. This is more than sufficient for my purpose;—it not only admits the premises which I have laid down, but goes as far as I can wish in the consequences it draws.

II. Thus much may suffice as to the method of instruction in the three first centuries; it was conducted on precisely the same principle as I explained in my last discourse. The next inquiry is, on what grounds the Christians of these centuries received the word of God. Did they consider the Scripture as the sole groundwork of faith, or, with us, as a book to be received and explained on the authority of the Church? You shall judge from the very few passages which I will read to you from their works; because it would detain you a great deal too long, if I entered fully into this portion of the argument. There is a remarkable saying on this subject of the great St. Augustine; for he is speaking of the method by which he was brought to the knowledge of Christianity. Disputing with a Manichee, one of a class of heretics with whom in early life he had associated himself, he says expressly, as it should be rendered, from the peculiarity of the style: "I should not have believed the Gospel, if the authority of the Catholic Church had not led or moved me."* This little sentence declares at once the principle on which he believed. This greatest light of the century in which he lived, declares that he could not have received the Scripture, except on the authority of the Catholic Church!

See now the way in which St. Irenæus, the same father whom I before quoted, speaks on this point: "To him that believeth that there is one God, and holds to the head, which is Christ, to this man all things will be plain, if he read diligently the Scripture, with the aid of those who are the priests in the Church, and in whose hands, as we have shown, rests the doctrine of the apostles."† That is to say, the Scripture may be read, and will be simple and easy to him who reads it, with the assistance of those to whom the apostles delivered the unwritten code, as the key to its true explanation.

Still clearer are the words of another writer of the same cen-

---

* Contra epist. Fundamenti op. to. vi. p. 46, ed. Par. 1614, "Evangelio non crederem, nisi me Catholicæ ecclesiæ commoveret auctoritas." Heraldus observes, that an Africanism here exists in the text, and *crederem* is for *credidissem*.—See Desiderii Heraldi animadv. ad Arnobium. Lib. 4, p. 54, or "Two Letters," as above, p. 66.

† Ibid, l. iv. c. 52, p. 355.

tury: but I will first premise a few words regarding the peculiar nature of his work. I allude to Tertullian, the first writer in the Latin language on the subject of Christianity; and the father, consequently, who gives us the very earliest account of the methods pursued, in matters of faith and discipline, in the western Church. He has written a very instructive work, when considered at the present time, entitled " On the prescription of Heretics," that is, on the method whereby those are to be judged and convicted, who depart from the universal Church. The whole drift of his argument is to show, that they have no right whatever to appeal to Scripture, because this has no authority as an inspired book, save that which it receives from the sanction of the infallible Church; and that, consequently, they are to be checked in this first step, and not allowed to proceed any farther in the argument. They have no claim to the word; it is not theirs; they have no right to appeal to its authority, if they reject that of the Church, on which alone it can be proved; and if they admit the authority of the Church, they must at once believe whatsoever else she teaches. Go, he tells them, and consult the apostolic Churches at Corinth, or Ephesus; or, if you are in the west, Rome is very near, "an authority to which we can readily appeal," and receive from them the knowledge of what you are to believe.

I will quote to you one passage; and I might read you the entire work, and you would not find one doctrine differing from that which I have laid down on this subject. "What will you gain," he asks, "by recurring to Scripture, when one denies what the other asserts? Learn rather who it is that possesses the faith of Christ; to whom the Scriptures belong; from whom, by whom, and when, that faith was delivered by which we are made Christians. For where shall be found the true faith, there will be the genuine Scriptures; there the true interpretation of them; and *there all Christian traditions*. Christ chose his apostles, whom he sent to preach to all nations. They delivered his doctrines and founded Churches, from which Churches others drew the seeds of the same doctrine, as new ones daily continue to do. Thus these, as the offspring of the apostolic Churches, are themselves deemed apostolical. Now to know what the apostles taught, that is, what Christ revealed to them, recourse must be had to the Churches which they founded, and which they instructed by word of mouth, and by their epistles. For it is plain that all doctrine which is conformable to the faith of these mother Churches, is true; being that which they received

LECTURE V.

from the apostles, the apostles from Christ, Christ from God; and that all other opinions must be novel and false."*

Is not this, my brethren, precisely the very rule which the doctrine of the Catholic Church proposes at the present day? Does it not comprise every one of those principles which I have been striving for several successive evenings to explain? The doctrine of Tertullian is nowise at variance with that of other fathers; for, subsequently to him, we have plenty of writers, in both the Latin and in the Greek Church, who show that the grounds on which they proceeded were precisely the same. I will content myself with quoting two passages, one from each of these Churches.

The first is from Origen, one of the most learned men in the early ages of Christianity, a man of philosophical mind, and fully able to detect any flaw of reasoning, had it existed, in the train of argument advanced in demonstration of Christianity. "As there are many," he writes, "who think they believe what Christ taught, and some of these differ from others, it becomes necessary that all should profess that doctrine which came down from the apostles, and now continues *in the Church*. That alone is truth, which in nothing differs from ecclesiastical and apostolical tradition."† Again: "Let him look to it, who, arrogantly puffed up, contemns the apostolic words. To me it is good to adhere to apostolic men, as to God, and his Christ, and to draw intelligence from the Scriptures, *according to the sense that has been delivered by them*. If we follow the mere letter of the Scriptures, and take the interpretation of the law, as the Jews commonly explain it, I shall blush to confess, that the Lord should have given such laws.—But if the law of God be understood as the Church teaches, then truly does it transcend all human laws, and is worthy of him that gave it."‡

And in another place: "As often as heretics produce the canonical Scriptures, in which every Christian agrees, and believes, they seem to say, Lo! with us is the word of truth. But to them (the heretics) we cannot give credit, nor depart from the first and ecclesiastical tradition: we can believe only, *as the succeeding Churches of God have delivered*."§

One short passage more, from St. Cyprian, and I will close this portion of my argument. In his treatise on the unity of the

---

* De præscrip. hæretic. p. 334, ed. 1662.
† Præf. Lib. 1. Periarchon, T. 1. p. 47, Edit. PP. S. Mauri, Paris, 1733.
‡ Hom. vii. in Levit. T. 11. pp. 224-226.
§ Tract. xxix. in Mat. T. iii. p. 864.

Church—a treatise entirely directed to prove that unity, or oneness of faith, is the essential characteristic of the Church, and, that unity of faith, unity of government, and unity of communion, are to be preserved by unity of rule—he thus writes: "Men are exposed to error, because they turn not their eyes to the fountain of truth; nor is the head sought for, nor the doctrine of the heavenly Father upheld. Which things would any one seriously ponder, no longer inquiry would be necessary. The proof is easy. Christ addresses Peter: *I say to thee, that thou art Peter, and upon this rock I will build my church, and the gates of hell shall not prevail against it.* ..... He that does not hold this unity of the Church, can he think that he holds the faith? He that opposes and withstands the Church, *can he trust that he is in the Church?*"* The Church here alluded to is that which is in communion with St. Peter, that is, as appears from many passages in his writings, that Church which is in communion with the See of Rome.

So far, therefore, the principle followed both in private instruction, and in the more universal teaching through the Church, at least when she discussed or explained the grounds of her belief in Scripture, was, evidently, the same which we receive, that is, the infallible authority of the Church, assisted by God.

III. There is another point, closely connected with the foregoing, and more directly belonging to the public teaching of the Church: and that is, the method pursued by it when united together, to define any doctrine of faith. Now, nothing can be more certain than that, when opinions, deemed erroneous, arose in the Church, the only method followed was, to collect the authorities of preceding centuries, and ground thereon a definition or decree of faith; and that the adversaries of the dogma, without being allowed to define, to argue, or to defend their opinions, were called on to subscribe some formula of faith, contradictory of their errors.—The first and most signal example of this was, the first general council after the apostles, that which was convened against the doctrines of Arius. It is extremely remarkable, that when the council is enacting canons or rules of discipline, it prefaces them by saying, "it has appeared to us proper to decree as follows." But, the moment it comes to state the decree or doctrines of faith, it says—"The Church of God teaches this" —not the word of God, not the Scriptures, but the Church of God teaches this doctrine; and because the Church of God

---

* De Unit. Eccl. pp. 194–195.

teaches it, all who are present, and all the bishops over the world, must subscribe to it.

No one, I should conceive, could possibly persuade himself that this council of the entire Church met with any other idea, than that it had a power of uttering a binding and final decision. We cannot, for a moment, imagine that three hundred and eighteen bishops from the east and west, among whom were aged men, who had drunk of the Lord's chalice, by undergoing, in by-gone days, the torments of persecution, would have met together, at much cost and with much trouble, for no other purpose, than to give an opinion, subject afterwards to the judgment of every private individual; or that they believed themselves convened for no object but such as every member of the Church was equally competent to effect; or for any work which he would still be obliged to do. Yet to such inconsistent assertions as these, divines are driven who deny the infallibility of the Church, but maintain the responsibility of each individual's judgment; whereby they constitute each member of the Church the judge over all its collective decisions. This has actually been done; and, as a specimen of this reasoning, I will quote the Protestant Church historian, Milner. After giving an account of this general council of Nicea, he thus comments: "It behoves every one, who is desirous of knowing simply the mind of God from his own word, *to determine for himself how far their interpretation of Scripture was true.*"* So that every person had to judge whether the council was right or wrong, by doing what he could have done just as well if the council had never met, by discovering, that is, through his own study of Scripture, whether he should adopt or reject the doctrines of Arius! Surely, such a theory would sound strange, if broached of the supreme legislative council of any state!

The principle followed on this occasion was continued in every subsequent council of which we have any notice in ecclesiastical history; and that principle and method, again, suppose the same ground as all the preceding examination has exposed. They assume, that the moment the explanation of the different Churches was found to agree on any point of faith, that must necessarily be true, and no appeal was to be allowed—no argument admitted, that might seem directed to set aside that ground of authority.

And, undoubtedly, we find very few of those who, in the first

---

* History of the Church of Christ, vol. ii. p. 59, ed. 1810.

R

centuries, ventured to wander from the universal Church, who did not attempt to show that they had tradition in their favor, and that the fathers of the preceding centuries thought with them. In the fourth and fifth centuries, the great era of ecclesiastical literature, we see the fathers taking pains to ascertain, collect, and preserve the opinions of those who had gone before them.

From these writers, innumerable passages might be brought to prove the universal admission of this our rule. Such, for instance, are the words of St. John Chrysostom, when commenting on the words of St. Paul to the Thessalonians: "Hence," he writes, "it is plain that all things were not delivered in writing, but many otherwise, and are equally to be believed. Wherefore let us hold fast the traditions of the Church. It is tradition: let this suffice."* Or those of St. Epiphanius, when he says: "Our boundaries are fixed, and the foundation, and the structure of faith. We have the traditions of the apostles, and the Holy Scriptures, and the succession of doctrine and truth diffused all around."† But passing over detached passages, and omitting to dwell even upon the triumphantly Catholic writings of Vincent of Lerins upon this express subject, I will only call your attention to a principle laid down by St. Augustine, and other fathers, which can leave no doubt regarding *their* belief. It is this: that, so far from considering it necessary to be able to trace back every point to the time of the apostles, if any doctrine is found existing now, and in times past, through the Church, the origin of which cannot be discovered, it must be deemed to have come from the apostles. Thus writes St. Augustine: "What the whole Church observes, what was not decreed by councils, but always retained, is justly believed to be of apostolic origin."‡ Such a principle surely implies a conviction that the Church can never fall into error.

It would therefore appear that, coming downwards from the time of the apostles, we find no other principle acted upon in the Church, either in private, as regarded individuals, or publicly, in proposing the Scriptures, and in the definition of doctrines, except that which we admit—an infallible authority in the Church of Christ.

After this, we come to another, and a very remarkable period, generally considered as one of darkness, error, and supersti

---

* Hom. iv. in 2 Thessal.   † Hær. lv. Tom. i. p. 471.
‡ De Baptismo cont. Donat. lib. iv. c. xxiv.

tion—the time when many fancy that all the doctrines of Christianity had been already corrupted, and that the Church could no longer pretend to claim any part in the promises of our blessed Redeemer to his apostles. But it is remarkable as the great age of conversion; for any one conversant with ecclesiastical history will be aware, that between the seventh and thirteenth centuries, the greater part of northern Europe, and considerable tracts of Asia, were converted to the faith; and every one of these countries, with hardly any exception, was converted by missionaries sent from Rome.

Here we may expect to find a very interesting and accurate test of the rule of faith, by seeing where Christ's commission to teach all nations has been fulfilled; in other words, where the blessing of God has rested, in regard of one important portion of the work confided to the Apostles. For I think we should have reason to conclude, that in that Church hath the promise of God's presence and of a true teaching been best preserved, in which the command to teach all nations has best and most effectually been fulfilled. For, as one individual blessing, and one promise, is given to both charges, and neither could be executed without it, when one part can be proved to have it, the other may be safely assumed likewise to possess it. But I consider this inquiry of such importance, and think that it will admit of so many interesting details, that I will pass over it for the present, and reserve, until Friday and Sunday evenings, a minute examination of the methods followed in converting, by the two Churches; that is, by the Catholic Church, and by the collection of different sects, collectively known by the name of Protestant, and of the success which has attended each.

I proceed, therefore, at once, to what I consider necessary for the full development and explanation of the matter in hand this evening. So far, I have treated of the methods pursued in the early Church for instructing her children and preserving the faith. But an important question may rise in the minds of some—Were not these methods totally unsuccessful? The Church may, indeed, have professed from the beginning to follow our principle; and it may be that, during the first ages, it mattered but little whether it was correct or not; since the seeds of Christianity cast by the Apostles had still sufficient vigor to produce fruit, in spite of corrupt principles; but has not the consequence been, that, in course of time, the grossest errors have been introduced into the Church of Christ? Is it not true, that the Church of Rome, in particular, has fallen away from the truth into a state of frightful apostasy, and has disgraced Christianity by many absurd and impious doctrines?—Such is the view presented, with many varieties, in popular works.

I was careful, in my opening discourse, to caution you against such a line of argument as this. I endeavored to point out the necessity of discussing principles and not facts, which, after all, must be referred to principles; I showed you that it was an assumption of the question in hand, to maintain what are commonly considered abuses to be such on the grounds whereon they are so represented. And here allow me, first, to observe, that nothing is more open to misrepresentation than this portion of the inquiry. For an important distinction is generally overlooked, by those who thus speak and write, between doctrine and discipline. Many practices which the Church may have introduced at any time, and which she could alter to-morrow if she pleased, are treated by them as points of faith; it is assumed that they are defended, not as matters of expediency, but as coming from the apostles, or from divine tradition. This distinction should be borne in mind, whenever you hear of the pretended corruptions of the Catholic Church. If such things are mentioned, insist at once upon proof that these are *doctrines of faith* in the Catholic Church—insist upon proof that the Church teaches you them on the same ground as she teaches the doctrines of the Trinity, the Divinity of Christ, or the Incarnation; and if you cannot find express proofs brought to that extent, you must not allow an argument to be brought from them to show that she has lost any portion of that deposit of faith which was originally given to her.

In the second place, as I formerly remarked, there is, generally, in such cases, an assumption of the point in dispute. For example, what is the method very often pursued in attacking the doctrine of auricular confession? It is not found in Scripture; therefore the Church has erred, by adopting a doctrine contrary to faith. Are you not here assuming as the very basis of the reasoning, the very question under discussion? You are endeavoring to prove that tradition is not a sufficient rule, because, by its use, errors have crept into the Church. You are asked to specify some such error, and you give that example; and when called upon to prove, what is essential to your argument, that it *is* an error, you prove it on the ground that it has no authority but tradition! Can any reasoning be more vicious than this? The fact is, that all questions of difference between us and any other Church must rest on this one point, must turn on this one pivot

—has Christ instituted in his Church an authority to teach, and has he guaranteed the preservation of truth in this authority, to the end of time? If that be made good, we must believe that whatever that Church, following it down the stream of time, has taught, must be received as truth; and consequently no ground can be given on which a separation from her communion could be justified. If, on the other hand, you shall find the other rule as explicit and clear as that which I have proved, and the texts for excluding church authority, and making the Scripture the sole rule of faith, as strong and as well explained in Scripture as those which I have quoted, then you may suppose that we are corrupt in every article which is not clearly defined in the written word. But upon this point alone must all controversy turn; if we prove our foundation true, whoever differs from us, however extraordinary the doctrines we teach, in rejecting them, rejects the authority of Christ.

Let us probe this matter still deeper. The Church of Rome, it is said, fell into grievous corruption; and it was necessary to reform it, or perhaps even to separate from it. Now, here comes a very important consideration. It would seem, that in Christianity, due provision should have been made for its most essential wants. You saw how, in the old law, there was an order of prophets established from the days of Moses; for God expressly foretold that, from time to time, he should send prophets to correct errors, and to give his people rules by which they should be guided. He thus made provision against the prevalence of error, and for the reformation of any fatal or serious abuse that might gradually creep into His kingdom. But, if you deny the principle of an infallible authority in the Church of Christ, if, in other words, you reject that course of reasoning which I have pursued to prove how the Catholic principle of Christ's teaching in his Church exactly corresponds to the institution of prophecy, and if you do not admit any other provision for the removal of error, you necessarily place Christianity on a lower scale of perfection than the ancient law; you leave it unfurnished with what was necessary of old, and what must be equally necessary at present. Can you conceive the Almighty establishing a religion as the sole and final revelation which man was to receive till the end of time, and yet appointing no means and making no provision for the removal of error, if it should ever insinuate itself among his truths? Can you conceive that, in the judgments of His providence, the whole system of Christianity was doomed to fall into a state of absolute corruption, and yet that He never should have pointed out a way whereby that corruption was to be cured, or whereby individual man was to be prevented from falling into it? Yet, if you look into the whole of the New Testament, can you tell me where there is a provision for this important object? And if the Church was to be so long in the state of degradation and moral corruption described by so many writers, can you conceive it possible that there was not some resource reserved for her, some indication given of a method to be pursued in this last extremity, to recover her from that frightful condition? There is not a word, not the obscurest hint of such a remedy—the case is not contemplated as possible—so that we must imagine the wisest provision to have been made in the old law, which, though doubly necessary, was totally overlooked in the constitution of the new.

But if you will still say that the Church fell into grievous errors in faith and morals, at some time or other, I will ask you to determine the date when this occurred. There are only two opinions, on this point, that have in them any semblance of consistency or reason. The first is one which I have heard sometimes advanced, that it was precisely at that very Council of Nicea, in which the divinity of Christ was defined, that the Church first erred from the faith. And this hypothesis was maintained on consistent grounds; namely, that the dogmas of faith were then defined on the authority of tradition, whereby a different rule of faith than Scripture was introduced into the Church. So that we are to suppose that, within three hundred years after Christ, the Church sank into a state of absolute error and fatal corruption, and remained in that condition twelve or thirteen centuries, before Luther and Calvin undid the evils of the three hundred and eighteen Fathers of that venerable synod, and the Reformation restored the real rule of faith! Is it possible to believe such a hypothesis as this? Will any one persuade himself that the very moment God crowned His Church with glory, and gave her rest, after three hundred years of persecution,—her return was, to abandon His law, and follow, instead, the corruptions of men?—that the very first time she assembled to vindicate the honor of His Son, and proclaim His divinity, she by the very act forsook and denied Him, and corrupted her vital and fundamental truths?

Others place this epoch at the other extremity of the chain; and say, that they cannot consistently fix the corruption or apostasy of the Church of Rome at an earlier period than the Council of Trent; in other words, after the Reformation had

LECTURE V.

already commenced: so that, whatever her errors or corruptions previously were, she was still the true Church of Christ until that moment. Now, all, however opposed they may be to our dogmas, must acknowledge that no new doctrines were introduced into the Church between the twelfth and fifteenth centuries: so that, for at least three or four centuries, the Church must have been in a state of absolute and fatal error, and in her was no energy or power to raise herself from that state. Then, if that power came three centuries later, on what was it founded? Was it on any new development of the principle of faith by our Saviour given, with efficacy to shake off the errors and corruptions of man? If there was that power and inward virtue in the Church to restore herself to purity, how comes it that three or four centuries were suffered to pass over without her being able to exert it? Was it that Divine Providence did not let loose the spring which was to give tone and action to that virtue? But if the sum of corruption had reached its accumulating height already, why was not this energy called into activity? Necessarily, there cannot have been any latent virtue in the Church, if it so long remained dormant when so much needed. There must surely then have been some extraordinary grant of power at that particular moment: and when you come to say, that any thing of this sort, not mentioned in the Bible, was essential to the Church, I ask you for another order of proofs. For, when men are sent out of the ordinary line of Providence, it has ever given them a means to show that they were so sent; and if there was a peculiar authority given to some men at that period, I wish to know on what that authority was based.

Thus you see how the two opinions mutually throw the whole argument into our hands. For, on the one hand, some assert that the first general council after the time of the apostles, was the first to corrupt or abandon the rule and standard of faith. These say, therefore, to the others: "If you do not agree with us in placing the defection at the first general council, if you do not allow the first step in the assumption of authority here taken to have been fatal, where will you stop? If you admit the authority of the Church to define articles of faith in the first council, can you refuse it to the second or to the third? and thus, the Catholics may go on from one to another, till the Council of Trent; which, having been convoked in an exactly similar way with the others, can on no just or consistent reason be condemned or rejected."

Then the others reply, that it is too frightful an admission to be made, that the spouse of Christ should have been so soon divorced from him, that the succeeding ages, the times of the Augustines, the Jeromes, the Chrysostoms, the Basils, should be ages of sinfulness and error, that the visible Church should so soon have ceased to exist, and the blessings of salvation have been so soon withdrawn from the earth; yea, at the very moment when God seemed to have ordered the ways of his Providence for their greater diffusion. Yet, finding no intermediate space whereon to rest, they determine that the Church in communion with Rome was the true one, in spite of error and corruption, till at Trent she sanctioned her doctrines.

But, before leaving this opinion, I must make one more observation. It has become a very fashionable theory of late, to abandon the plan of denouncing the Catholic Church as corrupt and antichristian for so many ages, and to allow it to have been the true Church, till the sanction of the last council fixed and consecrated the supposed errors, which, till then, had merely floated in her; and thus it is said, that they who adhered to the council, separated themselves from the Church, and became schismatical.* But they who make this argument, forget that the dogmas which they consider to have been fatally defined at Trent, had most of them been already decreed and sanctioned in other councils; that the books which they reckon among the Apocrypha, the seven sacraments, and many other such points, had been clearly defined at Florence, in 1439; confession, at the council of Lateran; the corporal presence of Christ in the Eucharist, in the synods against Berengarius; and other doctrines, in the celebrated epistle of Pope Nicholas I. to the Bulgarians, which the Church had received. So that, if the definition of these doctrines constitutes the pretended schism of the Catholic Church from those who accepted not her definition, that is to say, from a small remnant in the north of Europe, it follows that the entire Church had apostatized at the previous decisions,—and had left none standing in her place, for all assented to the decrees; and thus the Church had completely failed, which is the

---

* See the conclusion of Newman's "Arians of the Fourth Century." The Rev. M. O'Sullivan, a few evenings ago, delivered an anti-catholic sermon, in the church of St. Clement's Danes, the entire drift of which was to show that *Popery*, or the *Romish religion*, was only introduced by the creed of Pius IV. This doctrine must appear very consoling and edifying to Protestants of the present day, when they consider how they have been stunned with outcries about the total corruption of the Church for ages before, and the Pope's being antichrist; or when they compare it with the assertions of the Book of Homilies.—See above, p. 104.

LECTURE V.

difficulty whereof the asserters of the hypothesis wish to keep clear.

Thus, whatever step you take, in either supposition, you are involved in difficulties which are irreconcilable with the truth. The fact is, there is only one consistent view, and that is, to believe that the very principle adopted by the apostles has continued for ever in the Church, down to the present day—that in her lives and reigns the Holy Spirit of Truth, and the teaching of Christ, through their successors, which will not allow her to fall into any fatal error.

I can hardly believe that a Christian of any persuasion, if desired by one yet unconvinced to give a historical sketch of Christianity, that so he might ascertain whether an all-wise God had kept guard over it, as a thing dear to Him, and worthy of His wisdom and power, would induce himself to give such a poor and miserable picture of its lot as the system opposed to ours must conceive. He might, indeed, without shame, describe the life of its divine founder; how, in infancy, He suffered cold and poverty and every privation, and was obliged to fly when his life was sought; how He led a life of obscurity, sorrow, and wretchedness; how He was in the end mocked, and scoffed, and tortured, and crucified; for all these sufferings were amply compensated by the glories of His resurrection, and the majesty of His ascension, and the brightness of His present state; and through them all He proved himself the holy and the just One, and for them all the Lord God hath made Him see a long generation and a fruitful inheritance. But surely he would not dare to attempt a parallel with the history of his spouse, the Church, and say how she, indeed, like Him, was at first little, and poor, and persecuted, and neglected, and how princes did thirst for her blood, and in part spilt it; and how, too, prophets bore her in their arms, and saints sighed after her full manifestation: but that, as she grew up, she plunged into every excess of wickedness, and harlotry, and blood, and clothed herself with all the abominations that ever disgraced idolatrous nations; and that, at last, after ages of such filthiness and abominations, she rose, not indeed like her author, every limb clothed with new suppleness, and vigor, and beauty, and her head crowned with fresh, unfading glories, and her youth, as the eagle's, renewed, but rather like the spurious vegetation said to sprout from the decayed mangroves on the rivers of Africa, as though a few branches had revived with a different life, while the trunk has remained as yet a mass of corruption and decay. Or, rather, he would not describe it like one of those very rivers, appearing first as a broad, majestic stream, issuing from a pure, untainted source; sweeping along in increasing strength, bearing down, by the calm power of its steady course, the petty obstacles which nature and man raised in its way; carrying on its waters the arts of peace and happiness from people to people, and establishing a communication between many countries unknown to each other, save through its means; then suddenly swallowed up by the thirsty desert, and changed, for a long space, into brackish marshes and noisome pools, till from these issues again a small, puny stream, which pretends to mark its continuation, by its insignificant current, over some confined tracts of the habitable globe.

No, rather he would love to represent it as a noble edifice, richly adorned as befits God's temple, the lustre of whose golden ornaments may have been sometime dimmed by neglect, whose decorations may have suffered from mildew and rust, but whose foundations are based on the eternal hills, and may not be shaken by the earthquake or the storm.

And such have we regarded it in all ages, as the great universal Church, towering above all other objects; even so, as in this country, you may see the splendid cathedrals of antiquity majestic among the petty edifices, sacred or profane, which have been built and rebuilt, and have again crumbled into dust around them; while they look down unaltered and unchanged, as they did of old, forming a striking and beautiful feature wherever they are placed.

And, surely, if we have recourse to the results of experience, we shall easily ascertain which system of faith is more conformable to God's institution; that wherein man is left to his own erring judgment without a guide, or the one where the doctrines of Christ are supposed to be preserved in a durable and consistent scheme, by being embodied with outward forms, in the safe keeping of an unfailing and living body. For, if you wish to preserve some precious odour, you expose it not abroad in its pure ethereal essence, knowing that thus it would soon evaporate and waste away; but you do rather knead it up with something of more earthly mould, which may be unto it, as it were, a body, whence it may long breathe its perfume to all that approach. And just so must it be with a religious constitution; for hath not experience taught *us*, at least, how the attempt to spiritualize it to the extreme, depriving it of outward circum

LECTURE V.

stance, and abandoning the principle of authority, must end in its gradual enfeebling and final decay?

Do we not all know a Church possessed of every material engine of power, that hath in its hands most glorious temples, marvellously designed to be the theatres of boundless influence over countless multitudes? And such were they once; while now they are all day so empty and waste as to seem rather the mighty tombs of a departed, than the temples of a living worship. And how else hath this sad change been wrought? The religion which built them, in ages past, was one of many sisters, obedient and subject to a common mother. For centuries she had ruled by authority, spiritual and ecclesiastical, and her reign had been peaceful and splendid. But a froward spirit arose within her, and, in the pride of her heart, she exclaimed: "I need not, that men may honor, and court, and obey me, these badges of authority and rule, which, at the same time, mark my dependence too. For my own comeliness will I be worshipped. I will none of those touching memorials around me, the tombs of martyrs, or the rival beauty of saintly images; for what are they to me? or what have I to do with the memory of past days? I scorn the bravery of sumptuous raiment, and the dazzling procession of ministers, and the clouding of their incense, and the brightness of their tapers; I will sit me down alone in the midst of my naked dwelling-place, as a white-robed virgin; and men shall love, and serve, and worship me for my own sake." And for a season it was done—so long as those lived who remembered the days of her glory, and loved her as a remnant and memorial of what once she was.

But after these, came a generation that knew not those days—men with arms upfolded on their bosoms, and brows bent in perpetual frownings; and when they came before her, she found that they had learned rebellion from her example, and from her lips had caught up the words of scorn and infamy wherewith she had disgraced her mother. And they cast her down, and trampled her in the dust, and did make her eat her very heart for sorrow. Then, indeed, by the arm of power, she was once more set up, but only to undergo a crueller and more lingering doom; to see, year after year, her worshippers slinking away, and her temples less frequented, and her many rivals' power exalted, as well as their numbers ever more increased. And even now, are not men dicing over her spoils, and quarrelling how they had best be divided? Do they not speak irreverently of her, and weigh her utility in iron scales, and value in silver pieces the souls whom she serves? Is she not treated with contumely by those that call themselves her children? Is not her very existence reduced by them to a question of worldly and temporal expediency?

And, when we see the cathedral service shrunk into the choir originally destined for the private daily worship of God's special ministers, or when we find the entire congregation scattered over a small portion of the repaired chancel, while the rest of the edifice is a majestic ruin, as I but lately witnessed, surely any one must be more prone to weep than to exult at the change which has taken place since these stately fabrics were erected. Who can visit that beautiful church beyond the river, so lately restored,* and dwell on the exquisite screen which overshadows the altar, with its numerous niches and delicate traceries, and not feel that the great object to which all these were accessories hath been removed; that men would not have labored so, and given their time and ability, only to prepare a standing-place for that ordinary table, on which all turn their backs who worship there; but that *there* was once an altar which men loved and revered, and which it was deemed most honorable to honor. Who can witness the worship as performed in a cathedral, and see so many points yet recalling ancient practices, so much effect curtailed of its power by the destruction of the feeling and motive which gave it rise, such a wish, but so manifestly baffled, to fill with religious majesty the mighty edifice, more by the organ's voice, than by the emblems of God's presence, or by any accord of feeling thrilling through the hearts of a multitude; and not weep to think how a nation can have been cheated out of the most beautiful and moving parts of its religion, and glory in retaining but its shreds and fragments?

Assuredly, when I see these things, and still more, when I hear men admiring the English liturgy as a matchless and sublime composition, and not reflecting how it is all taken from ours, which they abolished—only that what they have retained, and what forms the essential part of their service, is with us but a part inferior and preparatory to a more solemn rite—that their sublime collects, with the epistle and gospel, are among us but as an introduction and preface to a sublimer action; when I see this Church thus treasuring up and preserving from destruction the accessories of our worship, so highly prizing the very frame in which *our* liturgy is but enclosed, I cannot but look upon her

---

* St. Mary's Overbury, or St. Saviour's.

as I would on one whom God's hand hath touched, in whom the light of reason is darkened, though the feelings of the heart have not been seared; who presses to her bosom, and cherishes there, the empty locket which once contained the image of all she loved on earth, and continues to rock the cradle of her departed child!

But if, from this scene of inconstancy, mutability, and decay, we turn to look for a contrast, I cannot have much difficulty in finding one. Oh that I could bear you, on the wings of my affections, to that holy city, where all that is Christian and Catholic bears the stamp of unfading immortality! Thither must the Catholic look to find the surest proof of how effectual, and how universal, is the one principle of faith which animates and directs his religion. There I could show you to demonstration, how tenacious the Catholic Church has always been of every doctrine; since she has taken such pains and care to preserve the meanest edifice or monument that might recall to her mind past times, or which has recorded on it a doctrine or a discipline, the remnant of a dearer and a happier age. I could show you many churches yet standing, not, indeed, like the ancient, lofty, and magnificent piles which we see in this country, but humble and poor, though entire and untouched, scattered over tracts once, perhaps, the most populous upon earth, and adorned with the most sumptuous buildings, but now become dreary wastes and heaps of ruins; standing alone, and appearing great by their solitude—the early temples of Christianity. And you would ask me, perhaps, wherefore are still preserved these churches of the early Christians, in places where now there are no congregations to frequent them? For soon would you see that the religious edifices which you meet in the most populous and crowded parts of this city, are not nearer one to the other, than those of the now uninhabited tracts of Rome. And you might ask me, too, what it was that saved them from the ruin which hath made cities desolate, hath emptied the palaces of kings, and crushed into dust the monuments of empires? For you would marvel how these, although built of the most costly and durable materials, grasping, as it were, with their foundations, the very rocks below, and banded and covered with brass and iron, should now be fallen; while those, on the other hand, which were formed of frail and perishable materials, have withstood the shock. And I would reply to you, that religion hath embalmed them with the sweet savour of her holiness, so that neither rust nor moth could assail them; and that, when the barbarian ravaged and raged around, she marked their door-posts with the blood of martyrs, and the destroyer bowed his head and passed them by, and left them as a refuge for the desolate, in the wildest times of riot and bloodshed.

And you would find that from that time all care has been taken to preserve them in the most perfect integrity; that all those arrangements in these venerable Churches, which supposed a state and order of discipline varying from what we now follow, may there be yet observed; you would see the place where the catechumens stood in the porches, and where the penitents of the different orders waited, imploring the prayers of the faithful, and the pulpits wherein the gospel was read by saints, and the very episcopal chair wherein the holy Doctor St. Gregory was wont to preach, and the entire church standing now, even as it did of old, with a calm and majestic solemnity about it, which bears us back to the feelings of peace and unity in which these edifices were originally planned. And what is the principle which these places record? Not merely do they tell events of older times—not only do they keep alive in our hearts and minds those feelings of attachment which connect us with happier and better days; but they are a pledge and a security that the same spirit which has kept them entire, would preserve still more the doctrines therein originally taught, and imbodied in their very plan and constitution.

And then note, with this enduring power, what an elasticity and vigor for recovery this same principle has ever communicated. You have seen the Church of this country, already exhibiting symptons of sad decay, and yielding to the undermining power of its own disuniting, enfeebling principle. Now, then, look upon that country and city to which in mind I have transported you; and remember, that twenty years have scarce elapsed since the rule of the scoffer and the plunderer came to an end, of those who stripped religion of all its splendor, and bound her rulers in bonds of iron. But she had before taken too frequent experience of such scenes, to fear their consequences. In days past, for ages, periodical invasion from barbarous foes had been her lot, and she had always found them, like the Nile's inundations, renovators of her fertility, where the very slime they left behind them became a chosen soil for the seed of her doctrine. See how soon the plundered shrines have been replaced, the disfigured monuments repaired, the half-ruined Churches almost rebuilt! See how, from morning till night, her many splendid temples are open, and without price, to great and small, and her daily services are attended by crowds, as if nothing had passed in their generation to disturb their faith, or deprive them of its instruments! And whence is this difference? Why, simply herein, that their religion, while it exercises absolute control over their judgments and belief, speaks to their senses, to their feelings, to their hearts. For that, my brethren, is a city long accustomed to rule, but to rule through the affections. Believing herself, and, I confidently say it, justly believing herself, invested by God's promises with authority to teach all nations, she hath used this authority to keep all in the unity of faith, giving the same creed with the same gospel to the Americans and the Chinese, as she had given to the African and the Briton. But while she swayed her sceptre with uncompromising equality, she feared not to adorn it with jewels. She knew that the gold and the silver, and the precious spices were the Lord's, and by his hand had been given to his house; and she lavished them on his service, and she cherished all the arts of life, and she compassed herself with every splendor, and clothed herself with all beauty; and she hath made herself beloved by the lowly, and respected by the great; and, secure upon the rock of an eternal promise, she fears no earthly changes, nor infernal violence; from the one secure by accomplishing, in her outward constitution, the typical forms of the older, less spiritual, dispensation of hope: from the other, safe, as the symbol and image of the blessed kingdom of eternal love.

LECTURE THE SIXTH.

ON THE PRACTICAL SUCCESS OF THE PROTESTANT RULE OF FAITH IN CONVERTING HEATHEN NATIONS.

MARK xvi. 15.

"*Go ye unto the whole world, and preach the Gospel to every creature.*"

This, my brethren, was an important commission delivered by our Saviour to the apostles. It stands in close connection with His other command on which I have already expatiated at great length; to *teach all nations, teaching them to observe all things whatever He had commanded them*, with His promise to be with them all days, even unto the end of the world. On that occasion, I endeavored to show you, by the construction of the very text, that there was annexed a promise of success to the commission given: so that what was therein enjoined to the apostles and their successors, in the Church of Christ, He himself would for ever enable them to put in execution. It must therefore be an important criterion of the true religion of Christ, or, in other words, of that foundation whereon He intended His faith to be built, to see where that blessing, that promise of success from His assistance, hath rested, and where, by its actually taking effect, it can be shown to have been perpetuated, according to the words of our blessed Redeemer.

For we cannot doubt that the apostles, in virtue of that promise, went forth, and not only preached to nations, but actually converted them. It was in virtue of this same commission, that their successors in the Church continued to discharge the same duty of announcing Christ, and Him crucified, to nations who had never heard His name; and there can be no doubt, that their success was due to their being in possession of the promise with it given; and, consequently, to their having built the Gospel on that foundation to which the promise was annexed. In other words, it must be a very important criterion of the true rule of faith, delivered by our blessed Redeemer to His Church, to see whether the preaching according to any given rule has been

LECTURE VI.

attended with that blessing which was promised, and which secures the enjoyment of His support; or, whether its total failure proves it not to have satisfied the conditions He required.

Such, my brethren, is the subject on which I am going to enter. I wish to lay before you, in this and my next discourse, a view of the success which has attended the preaching of the gospel, according to the two different rules of faith which I have endeavored to explain. I will begin, in the first place, and it will occupy me this evening, with examining the history of the different institutions formed in this and other Protestant countries, for the purpose of diffusing truth among the nations who sit in darkness and in the shadow of death. For this purpose, it is my intention to make use, as much as possible, of authorities which no one will impugn,—I intend, perhaps with one or two exceptions, not to quote any Catholic witnesses; indeed, I will endeavor, as much as I can, to confine myself to the testimony of such as are actually engaged on these missions, or to the reports of the societies which direct and support their efforts.

The progress of conversion had gone forward from age to age, ever since the time of the apostles; and not a century, particularly among those commonly designated as dark and superstitious times, not a half century had passed in which some nation or other was not converted to the faith of Christ. By conversion, I do not simply mean their being kept in the missionary state, under the direction and tutelage of persons sent from another country, but their being so established, in the course of a very few years, as to be able to exist independently of foreign aid. They, of course, always remained in connection and communion with the mother Church, whence their faith had originally come; but yet so as to have their own native hierarchy, governing many congregations and churches regularly organized; and to be so well and solidly established, that where once this had taken place, the errors which had been removed no more sprang up and resumed their influence. This is the only idea which we can justly form of *complete* conversion; this alone was meant by conversion during the ages to which I have alluded. And so far was this spirit of conversion from failing in later times, that, on the contrary, it is remarkable how, just at the moment of the Reformation, a new field was opened, and was cultivated with success, among the natives of America, and in the peninsula of India.

Now, when the new religion took possession of this and some

continental countries, it soon struck those who embraced it, that it was incumbent on them to show themselves inheritors of the promise made by Jesus Christ; and, moreover, to diffuse the new light which they imagined themselves to have received, among those nations who did not enjoy the same happiness. Hence it was, that so early as the year 1536, the Church of Geneva instituted a mission for the conversion of heathens, who had not received Christianity in any form. Of the history of the mission, I can say nothing: but it is acknowledged, on all hands, that it proved abortive, and was very soon discontinued, in consequence of its ill success. We may, therefore, date the missionary labors of Protestantism from the beginning of the last century. In the year 1706, Frederic IV., king of Denmark, established a mission, which still enjoys considerable celebrity, and of which I shall later give you some details. It flourished chiefly, after the middle of the last century, under the direction of Ziegenbelg, Schultze, and Schwartz: and this seems to have been the first mission attended with any appearance of success.

In this country, in the year 1701, the first missionary society was formed, and incorporated by royal charter,—that is, the "Society for the Diffusion of Christian Knowledge;" and, about the same period, the "Society for the Propagation of the Gospel in Foreign Parts" was also completely organized, and in activity From that time, until towards the end of the last century, nothing particularly striking was done in this department. It was in 1792, that the Baptist Missionary Society, since become so celebrated by its many versions of the Scripture into the eastern languages, made at its head-quarters at Serampore, was first instituted and consolidated; and in 1795, the "London Missionary Society," which belongs to the Independent Congregation, was also formed; followed, in the next year, by the "Scotch Missionary Society." In 1800, the "Church Missionary Society" came into operation. Since that time, a great number of secondary associations have sprung up; many of them formed by members of different religions in this country, as the Wesleyans, and others, whom it is not necessary to enumerate. Besides these societies in our own country, there are similar ones in America, in Germany, and in France, which have directed their labors to the same important purpose. In other words, I may say, that the most wealthy and most enlightened nations of the earth, according to the flesh, have devoted themselves, with extraordinary zeal and diligence, to compass this important end, of bringing heathens to a knowledge of Christianity.

LECTURE VI. 147

Next we may inquire, what are the means which they have in their hands? They are such as never, from the time of the apostles, have been brought to bear, I will not say upon the work of conversion, but on the attainment of any great moral object. I have not always had the convenience of consulting documents down to the very latest period, and I have consequently been obliged to content myself with such as have come within my reach. I mention this as a precaution, that if I do not always quote the notices received within this and the last year, it may not be supposed that I have been ruled by a wish to avoid what might appear adverse to my assertions. With the greatest pleasure I would have examined the history of every mission down to the present day, if my other avocations had permitted me, or if it were possible to have access to the necessary documents. It has been in my power, however, to obtain those of two or three years ago in a pretty complete form; and this is why I shall seem to choose my specimens from that period. The statements I shall be able to make will be sufficiently accurate, to direct your attention to the working of a principle,—to the discovery of how the method pursued has been found to act; for this will be accomplished whether we take the average of a smaller, or a greater number of years. For if we shall discover that the failure of these attempts has been in consequence, not of a want of time, but of a want of power in the means employed, we can arrive at a proper estimate of the correctness of their principle.

We find, from authentic documents published in the "Chistian Register," for 1830, that five of those societies, from among which some of the most opulent are deducted,* amassed funds, in this country alone, to the amount of 198,151*l*.; and if the other societies received in the same proportion, the sum must have been, perhaps, nearly double that amount.† In addition

---

* The Society for Promoting Christian Knowledge, and the Scotch Missionary Society, are omitted.
† The following are the specific details:

Wesleyan Missions	£55,565
Church Missionary	47,328
London Independent Mission	48,226
Baptist	17,185
Society for the Propagation of the Gospel	29,847
Total	£198,151
There are omitted, the Society for Promoting Christian Knowledge, which we may moderately reckon at	50,000
And the Scotch Missionary Society, say	45,000
Total	£293,151

to this, however, we must not omit the co-operation of foreign societies, especially those of America, the contributions of which have also been very considerable.

There is another way of making a calculation. In the year 1824 it was boasted that 1000*l.* a-day were expended upon the work of conversion, which would give us an estimate of 365,000*l. per annum*, devoted to this great task.* And you will see, presently, that even this falls below the truth at the present day.

But, in addition, it would be unjust to overlook the immense assistance afforded to these societies by that which is generally considered the most important and most interesting in this country—the Bible Society. For, a great portion of its funds go indirectly to these societies, by furnishing them with copies of the Scripture—the essential instrument, in their idea, for the accomplishment of their object. The thirty-first annual report, the last published, gives the net receipts for the year ending March 1, 1835, at 125,721*l.* 14*s.*† And from the same report we learn, that the expenditure of the Society, during the thirty-one years of its existence, amounts to 2,121,640*l.* 18*s.* 11*d.*‡ It appears, moreover, that this society alone has printed *nine millions, one hundred and ninety-two thousand, nine hundred and fifty* Bibles or New Testaments: to which, if we add the issues from other societies in Europe and America, amounting to 6,140,378, we have the enormous aggregate of *fifteen millions, three hundred and thirty-three thousand, three hundred and thirty-eight copies* of Scripture.§ This statement, in any other age, would have appeared incredible; and if the true way of working conversion be the dispersion of the written word, surely an abundant harvest might, by this time, have been expected; for the seed has not been avariciously scattered abroad.

But, after we have added the income of this society to that of the missionary associations which I have rehearsed, we shall not have reached the sum total of their resources: in consequence, doubtless, of omissions in the list which I have given you. For the Missionary Register exhibits a table of the progressive increase of income enjoyed by religious Protestant societies, from

---

* Quarterly Review, June, 1825, p. 29.
† Thirty-first Report, London, 1835, p. 156.
‡ Ib. p. 142.
§ Pp. 145, 142. I do not know whether the copies purchased abroad for the Society, and counted in their nine millions, should not be deducted from the foreign issues.

LECTURE VI. 149

1823 to 1835, in which we see a steady advance from 367,373*l.* to 778,035*l. per annum*,* the income of last year.

In this great sum are not included grants from the government, whether general or local. In India, for instance, is a well-appointed church establishment of bishops, archdeacons, and chaplains, not left to depend on contingencies, but amply provided for, and able to devote their time and attention to the work of conversion. In New South Wales, the local government, on orders from this country, grants 500*l.* a-year to two missionaries appointed by the Church Missionary Society, to undertake the conversion of the natives.† Similar grants are, I believe, made in other colonies, as in Canada; and to the African missions, for the liberated slaves, some support of a similar character is, I understand, afforded. So that as far as the power goes, which almost unlimited means can give towards this object, I may say, that these societies possess it.

These funds are naturally directed to the support of persons who undertake the work of the ministry; these are, therefore, sent forth in every direction; but the estimates which I have been able to see of the number employed are so contradictory, that it is not easy positively to state it. I know that a scientific journal, a few years ago, reckoned them at five thousand.‡ There is here, perhaps, some exaggeration. Still, if we may judge by the proportion of income possessed and devoted, doubtless, to these purposes, the number must be considerable. As early as 1824, the Church Missionary Society, alone, had 419 agents, and the Wesleyan was reported to have 623.§ Thus two associations would give us 1,042 missionaries. If we take a ratio from these, and apply it to the income of the others, it would give us upwards of 3,000, exclusive of the American and other foreign missionaries, who are very numerous. Be this, however, as it

---

* Quoted by the Rev. E. Bickersteth, is his "Remarks on the Progress of Popery," p. 66.

† Parliamentary Papers on Aboriginal Tribes, ordered by the House of Commons to be printed 14th Aug. 1834, p. 148. The instructions given by this Society to *one* of the missionaries, sounds very unapostolical to Catholic ears. It begins thus:—"Instructions of the Committee of the Church Missionary Society to the Rev. W. Watson, *and Mrs. Watson*, on *their* proceeding to New South Wales, *on a mission* to the aborigines of New Holland. Dearly beloved in the Lord! The Committee address you, *Mr. and Mrs. Watson*, with a *paternal* solicitude." (p. 151.) Has the society episcopal, or other jurisdiction, that it has parental rights over ordained ministers of the Gospel? or are these missionaries *sent* by the society?

‡ Nouveau Journal Asiatique, 1828, vol. ii. p. 32.
§ Quarterly Review, *ut sup.*, p. 29.

may, I have no hesitation in saying, that they are three or four times the number which the Catholic Church employs.

These men are sent forth provided with every thing necessary for the work; there is no danger of their being left destitute; they have not merely sufficient to secure their subsistence, but enough to give them that station in the places where the mission lies, which insures them a certain character and weight, so far as station can procure them. The allowance given to the different missionaries varies with the places to which they are sent. To some, as to the American missionaries, there is an allowance made of 100*l.* a year; in other countries, particularly in Asia, this goes as high as 240*l.*, with 40*l.* additional if the missionary be married, and 20*l.* more for each of his children. The clergyman at the Cape of Good Hope has 300*l.*; and in the Australian mission, of which I spoke just now, there are two missionaries, with an allowance of 500*l.* a year. It is plain, that here can be no thought or anxiety for the cares of the day; but that it is in the power of the missionary to devote himself exclusively to the important work which he has taken in hand. I may just note, casually, (because I shall enter more fully upon the subject next time,) that the missionaries sent out by the See of Rome, or by the congregation devoted to that object, receive not more than from 25*l.* to 30*l. per annum.*

Here, then, we have all the human elements that can be required to produce great effects; and all that can be done by education, by abundant means, and by efficient support, ought certainly to be here expected.

By way of confirmation, I will give you the remarks of Dr. Buchanan regarding India, one of the most important theatres of Missionary labours at the present day. He had resided many years in that country, and to his active and energetic representations, the establishment of an episcopal see in India is mainly owing. "No Christian nation," he observes, "ever possessed such an *extensive* field for the propagation of the Christian faith, as that afforded to us by our influence over the hundred million natives of Hindoostan. No other nation ever possessed such facilities for the extension of its faith, as we now have in the government of a passive people, who yield, submissively, to our mild sway, reverence our principles, and acknowledge our dominion to be a blessing."* So that the modern missionary is not like an apostle going forth into a barbarous and unconquered

---

* Memoir on the Expediency of an Ecclesiastical Establishment in British India, 2d ed. p. 48.

country, plunging at once among wild and savage natives, as a lamb in the midst of wolves, without any defence save his own innocence and confidence in God, and preaching a gospel exactly opposed to all their feelings, interests, and habits; but, in most instances, he goes forth with all possible protection, and with every facility for undertaking his work.

Now let us proceed to examine the results of these immense preparations. I must take, necessarily, the subject in detail; and I will begin with India, and thence pass, successively, to other countries which appear to merit any particular observation. I regret being obliged to leave aside what I think would have been an interesting view of the subject. I had collected a number of passages from different reports of the Missionary Societies through several years, to show how, by a singular coincidence, in every case they speak of hopes, of promises, of expectations, of what is going to be done, and what may be looked for after a few years; but never of what has been done, of conversions. made, of persons who have been induced to embrace the faith of Christ. This investigation would have led us over almost all the field of missionary cultivation, and would have afforded everywhere the same results. I am obliged, however, to pass it over, on account of the extensive range we have still to traverse.

In India, there are several societies or religious bodies which dedicate themselves to the propagation of the Christian Faith and the conversion of heathen natives. That which naturally first merits attention, is the church connected with the Establishment of this country; the one which has all the support that a wealthy, or, at least, a well-provided Episcopal Establishment can possibly give. Now, to ascertain what has been done by its mission, we need not go beyond the reports given us by the active and zealous bishop of Calcutta, Dr. Heber. He made a visitation of a great portion of India, to examine into the state of religion, and the prospects held out to the labours of conversion. He does, indeed, every now and then, mention converts, members of the Established Church, whom he found in different places. For instance, at Benares, which contains a population of 582,000 souls, he confirmed 14; and the number of Christians, according to his calculation, was one hundred. Now, one would be induced to suppose, at first sight, that these were converts, properly speaking, made from the natives, in consequence of sermons, or other instructions of the missionaries, in which the doctrines of Christianity were expounded to them. His own account very soon undeceives us in this respect. For, speaking of Chumar, he says,—"The labors of the missionaries have, after all, been chiefly confined *to the wives of the British soldiers, who have already lost caste by their marriage*, or to such Mussulmans or Hindoos as, of their own accord, prompted by curiosity, or a better motive, have come to their schools or churches." Nor must we suppose, that by these he means actual converts: for thus he writes of them:—" The number of these *inquirers after truth, is*, I understand, even now, *not inconsiderable*, and increasing daily. But, *I must say, that of actual converts except soldiers' wives, I have met with very few, and these, I think, have been all made by the Archdeacon*," (Corrie.)* So that, in a very large district of populous towns, the converts have been only at the rate of 100 out of 582,000 natives; and these are almost, without exception, individuals who had already lost caste by having married Europeans, and who have been naturally drawn to embrace the religion of their husbands, by this circumstance, rather than by the exertions of the missionaries.

In another place, the Bishop says:—" These native Christians, who are members of the Church of England, in the Presidency, (Bengal,) do not exceed in number, at most, 500 adults, who are chiefly at the stations of Benares, Chumar, Buxar, Meerut, and Agra, *a large proportion being the wives of European soldiers*."† Now, this is a very important confession; for here we have the number of native Christians, out of the immense population of several millions, comprised in that Presidency, reduced to five hundred adults; and most of these belonging to the class I have described. Not that I mean to cast any imputation on them, for they surely are not the worse for having lost caste among their heathen countrymen, or for being united in marriage with Europeans; not but that I consider the soul of the meanest and poorest in the lowest caste equal, in the estimation of God, to that of the Rajpoot, or the most distinguished Brahman of the land;—but, when we are speaking of the efficacy of a system, we are bound to estimate it by the influence which *it* possesses; and it is evident that the Bishop does not attribute the conversions made to the doctrines preached by the missionaries, so much as to the circumstance of these native women having married Europeans, and being cast off by their own people.

I have taken some pains to collect the scattered notices of

---

* "Narrative of a Journey through the Upper Provinces of India," 2d ed. vol. I p 395.

† Vol. iii. p. 338.

LECTURE VI. 153

conversions mentioned in his tour; and have found both points fully confirmed,—the small number of the converts, and their being persons already rejected from their own religion. Thus, at Buxar, mention is made of *one* convert of Mr. Corrie, *widow of a sergeant*, and another of Mr. Palmer's, of the same character.* Again, at Agra, we have a small congregation, consisting of about twenty individuals, also formed by the Archdeacon:† but a few pages after, we find all the native Christians of that district described as *descendants of Europeans*.‡ At one place, he speaks of *two* converts;§ in another, he says, "this is the *third* or *fourth* Christian of whom I have heard, as dispersed through the hilly provinces."‖

But it is not difficult to collect sufficient acknowledgments from this writer and eye-witness, of a total failure in the Indian Church missions. In one place, he writes to Sir W. Horton, that "instances of actual conversion to Christianity are very rare."¶ Again, in a letter to Mrs. Douglas, he says, that "certainly very few have as yet embraced Christianity;"** and, on another occasion, he admits that barely sufficient Indians and Mussulmans have become Christians, to show conversion possible.††

But it has been remarked, that Bishop Heber looked towards the south, as the great seat of Protestantism in India; and was wont to say, as his chaplain relates: "There is the strength of the Protestant cause."‡‡ So confirmed was he in this idea before he visited the country, as to send regarding it, what must be called exceedingly exaggerated accounts, over to England. For instance, he thus writes:—"You are all aware of the considerable number (I believe about 40,000) of Protestant Christians in different part of the Presidency, the spiritual children of Schwartz and his successors."§§ Now, hear a passage, from a letter written *eleven days later:*—"The number is gradually increasing, and there are now in the south of India about two hundred Protestant congregations, the numbers of which have been sometimes vaguely stated at 40,000. I doubt whether they reach 15,000; but even this, all things considered, is certainly a great number."‖‖

And certainly it is a great number, and, I have no hesitation in saying, very much too great; as I shall at once proceed to

---

* Vol. ii. p. 334	† Ib. p. 339.	‡ Ib. p. 342.	§ Ib. p. 16.
‖ Ib. p. 257.	¶ Vol. iii. p. 253.	** Ib. p. 261.	†† Ib. p. 284
‡‡ Report of P. C. K. Soc., 1827, p. 25.		§§ Vol. iii. p. 444.	‖‖ Ib. p. 460.

U

show you. Those missions were established in 1706, consequently had been in existence a hundred years; but dating them only from the time of Schwartz, they had been at least fifty-six years in what may be considered their most flourishing state. Schwartz enjoyed very peculiar advantages; he became a favorite of the reigning prince, the Rajah of Tanjore, whose nephew and successor, the present Maha Rajah Sambogi, he instructed, although the prince never embraced Christianity; he was often his mediator with the British government, twice he saved Tanjore, and, on several occasions, levied the tribute of rebellious provinces; and, being a man of excellent character and exemplary life, the prince used to tell him, that he wished him to make Christians of all his subjects, so as to reform them, if possible, from their wicked practices.* These were very great advantages, and they are acknowledged as such by the Bishop, who says that Schwartz did more than any other person who has been in India. And what was his success? He is said to have converted seven thousand natives;† and as I think you will see that these missions have been in a state of decay, rather than of improvement, since his death, you will perceive what a further diminution must be made of the 15,000 Christians.

The Bishop, towards the close of his life, for he died during the visitation, went to that part of India, and has given us an exact report of what Christians he there found. He came, therefore, to Tanjore, the head-quarters of Schwartz, where no Bishop had ever been before, and confirmed all those who were ready for that rite. The number of these was *fifty*, and the number of communicants in the whole congregation was *fifty-seven*.‡ Thence he proceeded to Trichinopoli, another most important mission, and the number for confirmation was *eleven!*§ Instead, then of the 40,000—instead of the 15,000, to which that number was subsequently reduced—in two of the most populous places where Schwartz labored in person, and was succeeded by the heads of the mission, were found eleven, and fifty Christians to be confirmed! Now, make any estimate of the population you please,—make any proportion for the number of Christians in other places, and it will be difficult to suppose that they were any thing like 15,000. The Bishop himself acknowledges, that so far from these missions being in progress—so far from the

---
* Buchanan, p. 77.   Memoir of the Rev. H. Martyn, 1825, p. 327.
† Heber, ibid.
‡ Letter by Kohloff, the missionary, ib. vol. iii. p. 495.
§ P. 499.   The chaplain reckons them at fifteen.   "Report," *ut sup.* p. 24.

LECTURE VI.   155

number of Christians daily increasing—so far from considering it the spot whither to look for the prospects of the Protestant religion—they are in a state of dilapidation and decay. "The missions, however," he thus writes, "are in a state which requires much help and restoration; their funds, which were considerable, have been much dilapidated since the time of Schwartz, by the pious men (but quite ignorant of the world) who have succeeded him; and though I find great piety and good will, I could wish a little more energy in their proceedings at present."*

But we have another very important document on this head, which is the report of a formal visitation, sent to examine into the state of those missions. The report is signed by Kohloff and Sperschneider, who were at the head of the mission in the years from 1820 to 1823. The report states that there are twelve native congregations, and that each of these congregations consists of from five to twelve villages; so that we have the state of religion in 111 villages. Now, what do you think is the number of Christians in these hundred and eleven villages? Why, in 1823, they are given as 1388! So that, the number first stated at forty thousand, then at fifteen thousand, is, by the report of the missionaries themselves, reduced to thirteen hundred and eighty-eight! And these missions, observe, were founded between 1730 and 1744. But it appears from these reports, that between 1820 and 1823, there was an increase of 83, so that some improvement, at least, had taken place. But, by comparing the returns of baptisms with those of deaths, within that period, we find an excess of 74 births over the deaths, and, consequently, the number of persons who joined the congregation in four years, was 9; and, in fact, the same report, in another place, speaks of nine adult baptisms in that interval.† Here, then, is a mission, considered by the Bishop as the strongest

---

* Vol. iii. p. 455.
† "Report of P. C. K. Soc.," *Lond.* 1825, p. 110. The number of Christians is stated—

In 1820 1305
1825 1388

Increase in four years 83
Children baptized in that period 223
Deaths 149

Excess of births............................. 74

The *nine* converts are thus distributed:—In 1820, *three;* 1821, *one;* 1822, *one;* 1823, *four.* The number of baptisms thus given, would, according to the ordinary rules of calculation, give nearly the same result as to the numbers of the congregation—that is, about 1650.

part of the Protestant force in. India, which had been founded more than a hundred years, and had flourished fifty or sixty from the time of the man who had done marvels worthy of the apostolic age; and the result of all, at the end of this period, is a congregation of little more than 1300 Christians, in a population of one hundred and eleven villages, with an excess of births over deaths of 74 in four years; while the augmentation by conversion from heathenism is at the rate of nine in four years, or an average of two in every year! I ask you if this is a flattering picture of the prospects or rather progress of the Gospel, preached as it has been there?

But I must not conclude the account of this mission without observing, that the visitors, at the same time, expressed their regret, that the mission should be in such a dreadful state of decay. They acknowledge, that the number of converts in these four years was indeed small, but that, considering the difficulties and disadvantages to which the Christians of that country are exposed, the increase is worthy of notice.* They complain, too, of serious abuses; observing that, at Vatistergoody, the children are badly instructed, to such an extent, that all hopes of having worthy Christians must cease, till an improvement takes place; and that some Christians yet live in a state of bigamy; that at Ser fajeerasahpooram they practise heathenish customs; that at Manickramam they are in the lowest state of religious ignorance; that at Tarasaram, and Kawastalam, neglect of religion is so scandalous, that it has been found necessary to excommunicate several families.† I could bring much to confirm this view of the sad decay in these missions; but I beg simply to refer you to the 20th Report of the Missionary Register, in which we read of bitter disappointments. One missionary, at Tranquebar, expresses a wish that he could communicate any instance of conversion wrought by God's grace, and a regret at "the slow progress, which till now has appeared, in the *ancient and venerable* missions on the Coromandel coast."‡ And another complains from Travancore, that the real efficacy of the missionaries in the preceding year had been but small.§

But even here I must modify the returns I have given still further: because I find it asserted, by an authority of great weight,

---

* Ib. p. 103.
† Ib. p. 4–8. Bishop Heber likewise complains of the dissensions between the pastors and their flocks, and of the tyrannical and fanatical conduct of the former, to. iii. p. 444.
‡ P. 153. § P. 165.

LECTURE VI. 157

and I have reason to think, that these conversions of Schwartz and his followers, were chiefly among the half-castes, or descendants of Europeans. Martyn, the same missionary whom I alluded to before, a man for whose character every one must feel the greatest esteem, and who always speaks with such liberality of others, and so simply and unaffectedly of his own failures, that we must consider him an authority above suspicion, thus writes in his private journal. "Schwartz and Kohloff, and Jönecke, kept a school for half-caste children, about a mile and a half from Tanjore, but went every night to the Tanjore Church to meet about sixty or seventy of the King's regiment, who used to assemble for devotional purposes; afterwards he officiated to their wives and children in Portuguese."* Such is the account of his labors; how different from the one sent over at first! I do not say that it was intended to deceive; but it is evident that, in some way or other, the most exaggerated picture of the success of these missions in India, and elsewhere, have been pubblished in England.

But Bishop Heber has some very striking passages regarding their prospect of success, and what is to be expected in the present condition of India; and even those who may not acknowledge his views to be well grounded, must admit them to have been based on what he himself had seen.—When he speaks of conversion in India as next to impossible, he must have had the experience of the past to warrant him in such a conclusion. He thus speaks of a Mohammedan impostor who was travelling about the country:—"But how long a time must elapse before any Christian teacher in India can hope to be thus loved and honored! Yet, surely, there is some encouragement to patient labor, which a Christian minister may derive from the success of such men as these in India—inasmuch as where others can succeed in obtaining a favorable hearing, *the time may surely be expected, through God's blessing, when our endeavors also may receive their fruit, and our hitherto barren Church* may 'keep house, and be a joyful mother of children.'"† Again, in another passage, "With regard to the conversion of the natives, a beginning has been made, and though it is a beginning only, I think it a very promising one."

This, surely, will show us sufficiently, what his feelings were regarding the barrenness and fertility of the Church which he represented. But with regard to the missions of the Church of

---
* P. 354. † Tom. iii. p. 337.

England in India, we have also several striking documents in the reports of different years. For instance, in the year 1827, in the report of the Society for the Propagation of the Gospel, there is an extract of a letter from Professor Craven, in which he states, that in regard to conversion, they have as yet done nothing to satisfy the unbounded zeal, which, intent on its object, does not calculate the obstacles opposed to it: this would not surprise the Society which he had the honor to serve, but all that it was possible to do, with the divine blessing, was *attempted* at present, by Mr. Christian, one of the Society's missionaries.* In the following year, we have another report; and at p. 49, the same gentleman speaks of a mission opened by Mr. Christian, among the inhabitants of the mountains, which seemed to be particularly promising, from the circumstance of the natives not being under the prejudices of caste; "a prejudice," he writes, "which has hitherto been found insuperable by all the efforts of the most jealous and most exemplary missionaries." We have here the admission of an obstacle which has been found insuperable, by the most zealous and gifted missionaries of the Church of England.

Bishop Heber remarks, "Except in Calcutta itself, and its neighborhood, there is actually no sect worth naming except the Church of England."† Of course he is speaking of the Protestants; for I shall show you at our next meeting that there are very considerable congregations of native Catholics in some districts, and I hope you will see that there are more Catholics in some towns, than there are Protestants acknowledged to be in the whole Presidency itself, by missionaries who are necessarily interested, at least in not diminishing the number of conversions. But there is another class of Protestants exceedingly active and zealous, I mean the Baptists, of whose establishment I before spoke, and who have particularly distinguished themselves in making and disseminating translations of the Holy Scriptures. Now, a few years back, the Abbé Dubois, who had been for thirty years in India, had publicly stated that not a single convert had been made by the Protestant missionaries. He was answered, and particularly by missionaries who had themselves been there; and I will first quote one, who has been very much distinguished as a zealous upholder of the missionary establishments there, Mr. Hough, speaking of the Anglican missions. Here was an opportunity naturally and necessarily of bringing forward any examples of conversion, and thus confuting this bold asser-

---

* P. 144.   † Tom. III. p. 377.

tion. Listen therefore how he, in the first place, meets it. "But while I thus explain the *means* which Protestant missionaries employ for the conversion of the natives of Hindoostan, and maintain, in opposition to the Abbé Dubois's assertion to the contrary, that they are more likely to accomplish that end than any which the Jesuits have used, I nevertheless beg to state, that, without God's blessing, they do not *depend* upon *any* means of success. Truly do I concur with him in opinion, as he restates his position, that, under existing circumstances, there is no human possibility of converting the Hindoos." Here, then, is the express acknowledgment of a missionary who has been among them, that, under existing circumstances, there is no human possibility of converting the Hindoos. Had conversions taken place, could he have said this? would he not have stated them, when professedly answering to such a decided denial? Mr. Townley replied, on behalf of the Baptists, and what I am going to read from his answer is interesting, because in it he speaks of what has been effected by other missionary societies: "My object is not so much to count the number of converts upon whose sincerity we may rely, as to show from my own experience that the work of conversion is actually begun in India." Actually *begun* in India! and he is speaking of the years 1823 and 1824, and consequently of more than thirty years after the society had begun its labors! He does not then even pretend to mention actual converts, but only to show that the work has begun, which he thus demonstrates: "I have given *three* cases at least of native converts who have come under my personal observation, and of whose real conversion I can speak with some confidence. When I left Bengal, in the month of November, 1822, there was *one* Hindoo, concerning whom the missionaries in Calcutta had hopes that he was really, from upright motives, seeking admission into the Christian Church; these hopes have been subsequently strengthened, and he has been actually baptized. Herein there has been a similarity between the first fruit of missionary exertions reaped by the London Society, and that gathered by the Baptist missionaries. The first Hindoo convert effected by the instrumentality of the missionaries of the Baptist denomination, was won to the cross of Christ after the society had commenced its operations in India about seven years; the London Society in Calcutta have obtained their first convert after about the same lapse of time. It may be added, that the Church Society reaped their first fruits at Burdwan also, after having the faith and patience of their missionaries put to the test during a period of about the same duration."*

Here, then, we have an admission that *three* societies had been for seven years laboring before they obtained a single convert; and the writer does not pretend to say, that from this beginning any great increase subsequently followed; for, on the contrary, the first passage just read by me is completely at variance with this supposition. Now a periodical particularly attached to the interests of the Established Church, takes notice of these observations, and expresses its astonishment that such acknowledgment should be made by the very individuals who make tours from time to time, to describe the fruits and success of their missionary labors, as most satisfactory, and lead their hearers to suppose that the Indians are becoming Christians by hundreds and thousands. "Mr. Hough and Mr. Townley," the critic says, "reply that, to the best of their belief, ten or twelve real conversions have taken place. Is this the language of Mr. Townley in the sermons which he delights to preach in all the market-towns in the kingdom? Is this the language of Mr. Parsons, who has harangued so many Church missionary meetings in the course of the last summer? We can only say, that we never met with one of their hearers who viewed the business in this light."†

And I think that any one who recollects the statements popularly put forth, will agree that it was not the impression made on his mind, that the work of conversion had succeeded so very ill as this; that, by the acknowledgment of the missionaries themselves, they had been disappointed of their hopes; that, after so many years since these societies have been established, their success is now questioned; and that, after seven years' labor, they only obtained one convert each, at such immense expense, with such great trouble, and with such an expenditure of personal labor.

In the year 1823, a letter was addressed by a Mr. Ware, at Cambridge, to a celebrated Brahman, who some years after became better known in this country, Ram Mahoun Roy, who is often spoken of as a convert to Christianity; although there are strong reasons to suppose that he never was completely weaned from his affection for the religion of his own country. One question put to him, among others, was, "What is the true success of the great efforts which have been made for the conversion of the native Indians to Christianity?" His answer is dated the 2d of

---

* British Crit. Jan. 1835. † Ibid.

LECTURE VI. 161

February, 1824, and was published at Calcutta, by the Rev. Mr. Adams, in the same year. I am not now going to speak my own words, but to quote those of another person; and as they have been published by a missionary, or minister of the Established Church, I trust I am bringing such authority, to make good my point, as those who might be inclined not to take my assertion without proof, will not consistently reject. "It is a very delicate matter," he says, "to answer this question; because the Baptist missionaries at Serampore have determined formally to contradict whoever dares to express the slightest doubt regarding the success of their labors; and have on different occasions given the public to understand that their proselytes are not only numerous, but well conducted. But the young Baptist missionaries at Calcutta, although they are second to no other class of missionaries in abilities and learning, or in zeal for the cause of Chrristianity, have had the sincerity publicly to confess that the number of proselytes, after six years of grievous labor, does not exceed *four*. The Independent missionaries, also, of this city, who have even greater means at command than the Baptists, allow with sincerity that their labors, after a missionary career of seven years, have not produced above *one* proselyte."*

Such, then, appears to be the result of the labors of another of the most important societies engaged in the conversion of India; and that I may not have to return again to it, I will briefly mention the mission which it endeavored to establish in the Burmese empire, by means of Mr. Judson and his lady. They resided there a number of years, and published their own journal. The result of their mission, from their own confession, was, that, after seven years, they have not made a single convert; that, after the seventh year, they received one, and that he afterwards brought another, so that in the end they had four proselytes; when, in consequence of the war breaking out, the mission was broken up.† Here, then, we have the same mystical number of seven years, which seems to mark the period of barren and fruitless exertions of every society, again spent in the task of conversion; at the end of which the Church consisted of only one convert, and, in two or three subsequent years, was further increased to four. We have, described in the journal of these simple persons, how they attempted the work of conversion. We find that it was by presenting the natives with the Bible, and

---

* Nouveau Journal Asiatique, to. ii. p. 38.
† See their Journal, or its review in the Quarterly, Dec. 1825, p. 53.
V   14*

desiring them to read it, fancying that, in this way, they might be brought to embrace the doctrines of Christianity.

There is another society whose labors are directed to heathen India, but of whose success I have yet said nothing. I allude to the Scotch Missionary Society, founded in 1794. The pamphlet which I hold in my hand contains an eloquent and sensible address, made to the society in May of last year, by the Scotch Assembly's first missionary to India, Mr. Duff. He details, in an interesting manner, the defects of the system hitherto followed, and dwells on the difficulties to which the missionary is subjected when he attempts to preach the gospel. He is perplexed whence to draw his evidences, or to what authority he should appeal. If he speak of the internal evidence of the Scriptures, the Brahman immediately meets him with the Vedas, and attempts to show as strong grounds for their divine authority. If the Christian appeal to the Scripture miracles, the Indian has an abundant store to place in opposition. Thus, every argument fails; and if you succeed in driving them from their own convictions, the consequence too often is, according to the author's expression, that they leap over Christianity, from Paganism into Atheism. The Scotch Missionary Society has, consequently, adopted a new plan; that of educating the natives, from childhood, for missionary purposes. Whether this will prove a more successful method, time alone can show. But the departure from the system pursued by all other societies, and by this one itself at first, proves that experience has shown it to be ineffectual. Indeed the entire statement of the missionary supposes, and is directed to prove, that it has been unattended by any fruit.

Coming now to a general conclusion, with regard to the whole of India, we find again a number of confessions that, considering it altogether, without reference to one religion or society rather than another, there have been little or no good results. In a work, published at Edinburgh in 1822, entitled, "Reflections on the State of British India," the author gives us the result of his experience on the subject of Indian conversion. "The extraordinary conversions," he writes, "announced in the *Quarterly Review*, may have taken place, but in the East they are unknown. The individuals who have embraced the Christian religion are mostly considered as persons driven from their castes in consequence of their crimes, and attracted to a new religion by a less severe morality."* Here, again, we have the circumstance

---

* P. 42.—Not having access to the work, this passage has rather the substance than the very words of the author.

repeated, that all the converts had previously lost caste; but we have this very severe remark in addition, that they were led to embrace the religion preached to them, because it proposed a laxer code of morals than their heathenish law!

Another work, also, of about the same period, which certainly does not seem hostile to the cause of missionary societies, expresses itself in this manner. "It is a fact that may be unpalatable to those who are sanguinely looking for the conversion of Hindoostan; but it ought not to be dissembled, that up to this day, Christianity has made little or no real progress among that people. Thirty years have passed since the missionaries commenced their labors, and it may be confidently asserted, that more than 300 converts have not been made in this long space of time; among whom, it may be doubted, if any Brahmin or Rajahpoot can be named."*

There is another authority, which I will quote, before leaving these missions. "The London Asiatic Journal" for 1825 observes, that in the actual state of the Hindoos, the difficulties opposed to the progress of Christianity are altogether insuperable; and that there is not the slightest reason to believe that the sweet and mild truths of Christianity will make them renounce their errors. This Journal, which possesses considerable sources of information, again declares, that, so far as its experience goes, there is no reason to think it possible to convert the Indians—and that hitherto, obstacles which are considered insurmountable have been found in the way.†

So much for the propagation of Christianity in India. You have seen how it has been acknowledged, by persons of every class interested in the success of these missions,—by persons who have all the means of arriving at correct information regarding them,—and I have not quoted one Catholic writer,—that, hitherto, nothing has been done that can be considered demonstrative of the divine blessing on their labors who have undertaken them. The fact is, that they must be pronounced completely unsuccessful; for, after all, one, or two, or even five hundred conversions, would not be wonderful in any case; because there are always local or individual interests, by which

---

* Monthly Review, vol. xcix. p. 223.

† P. 158.—It is evident from later writers, that little or no improvement has taken place in the Indian mission since the date of the documents which I have quoted. Consult, for instance, Hoole's "Personal Narrative of a Tour in the South of India," from which we may draw both negative and positive proof of the total failure of any thing like conversion among the Hindoos.

some may be led to embrace any system of religion, out of such an immense population. This is not the success which Christ intended His Church to have; nor is it what she ever before understood by the conversion of heathen nations.

If we go to North America, we have circumstances of another character, but still of a very interesting nature. It is necessary carefully to distinguish the work of conversion, where undertaken alone, upon its own merits, from it when connected with the work of civilization. In India, the case is such as to admit of a very fair test—the natives there were in possession of the arts of life, sufficient to make them satisfied with their own condition, and, perhaps, look down on European civilization as of a lower character than their own. They were in possession of a literature, of sacred books, and other documents, which they considered to rest on grounds sufficiently demonstrable: and, consequently, they were not to be easily led by any thing but the presentation of truth itself; that is, of truth manifestly preferable to the opinions in which they had been brought up. But when you go among savage tribes, and offer them, not merely religion, but, through it, the arts of life; when the missionary bears, in one hand, the Bible, but with the other presents to them the plough; when he communicates advantages which put them on a level with surrounding populations, which they are obliged to acknowledge superior to themselves; there are excited feelings of such a complex character, (the result of totally different inducements,) that it is difficult to decide whether the doctrines presented on the one hand, or the results of these doctrines, as producing an improvement of their outward condition, on the other, are the influencing motive. If to this we add the consideration, that the people so addressed are actually reduced to a small and insignificant number; that they see themselves completely surrounded, and, against their will, absolutely incorporated with nations of a different character, and of different habits, who through those very differences have been able to subdue them and become their masters; can we be surprised if, seeing that very civilization, which makes others so superior, proffered to them, and embodying among its principal elements a new religion, they give way, after struggling for years against this influence, and yield up their former habits, and with them their religious feelings and opinions? These reflections are of considerable importance towards making a proper estimate of the only two countries in which it can be said that the Protestant

LECTURE VI. 165

missions have at all succeeded; and if you will follow my slight historical sketch of them, you will acknowledge their truth.

No sooner was the Society for the Propagation of the Gospel founded in this country, than it was determined to establish a mission among the natives of North America. The first attempt was made among the Yammosses of North Carolina, and completely failed. It was renewed a few years afterwards, and Archbishop Tennison, by command of Queen Anne, undertook the commencement of the work, by sending out missionaries. One, of the name of Moore, went out in 1704; but, after a very short time, finding all his efforts unsuccessful, he embarked for England, but was lost at sea. This failure is attributed to the influence of the Catholic missionaries, who, as the "Christian Remembrancer" complains, had won the confidence of the Indians.*

In 1709 the missionary Andrews was employed, who was well calculated for the task, because he could speak the language of the natives; and, to aid him in his labors, he had a translation of the New Testament, made by Mr. Freeman, Dutch clergyman at Schenectady, and fully competent to the task. This mission was founded in 1709, and in 1719 was again given up; and the reason assigned was, that the society could no longer maintain so expensive a mission. Yet it had been undertaken at the request of four chiefs, who had come to England to ratify a treaty. Some years later it was renewed, and after that time seemed attended with some success. But it may be necessary to state some circumstances connected with the history of these tribes.

The missionaries of whom I have spoken were sent to the tribe of the Mohawks, then living in the neighborhood of New York, and forming a portion of the Six Nations, known, also, by the name of Iroquois. During the American war, this confederation, with the exception of two of the tribes, took part with England; and in 1770 suffered a bloody defeat from the troops of the United States. The consequence was that the confederacy was destroyed; and the Mohawks, with a portion of another tribe, emigrated, in 1776, from the territory of New York, under the guidance of Sir John Johnson; and George III. gave them a tract of land, one hundred miles in length, on the Ouse, or Grand River. This outline is given, to show how the missions, now carried on for this settlement, are lineally in succession to those first established in the neighborhood of New York; so that they

---

* Vol. iii. p. 302. London, 1825.

have continued in operation more or less for one hundred years ; and, as a link between the two missions, it may be sufficient to notice, that the Mohawks still preserve the church-plate sent to them by Queen Anne, when living in their former settlement. Here, then, is an old-established mission among these native Indians.

The first authority which I will quote respecting it is that of Brown, author of a history of the missions among the American Indians; and, in order not to give my own impressions of the results of his work, I will give it in the words of another Protestant writer. " This history is the record of a series of failures, the less to be expected because some circumstances seem to point out these nations as peculiarly prepared for the reception of the gospel. They generally believe in the unity and spirituality of the Divine Being; they are not idolaters; their religion is free from those obscene and bloody rites which are the usual attendants of superstition; and amid all the vices which ignorance and uncontrolled passions produce, they are characterized by a grave good sense and a correct moral feeling which might make more civilized nations feel remorse for the neglect of their own advantages. To such a people, it might have been expected that Christianity would have been a welcome guest: and, indeed, missionaries have, in almost all cases, been kindly received among them, and heard with respect and attention; so that in many places, first appearances promised a permanent establishment of Christianity—without a single exception, however, these appearances have proved fallacious."*

Such is the result of Brown's history of these missions up to the earlier part of the present century. Let us, however, enter into a few details. In 1826, a letter was published in the Report of the Society for the Propagation of the Gospel, from Mr. Leeming, who was then resident missionary among the Mohawks, on the Grand River, in which he says, that " he feels great pleasure in stating that they are very attentive during the time of divine service; that he has *twenty-two* communicants, and baptized fifty children a-year; that the schoolmaster, Hess, is an excellent man, and makes himself very useful, and has seldom less than *twenty-five* scholars."† This is the result of the labor of the missionaries for so many years—*twenty-two* communicants and *twenty-five* scholars!

---

* Monthly Review, vol. lxxxiv. p. 143
† Report, 1826, p. 131.

LECTURE VI. 167

Again, in the same year, the Rev. Mr. Stewart, since appointed to the see of Quebec, went there on a species of visitation, and stated that he had found a new village, occupied by English inhabitants, and that on the 5th of June he had baptized twelve children, and administered the sacrament to twenty-four communicants, which are within two of the number before stated.* In another village, inhabited by the Tuscarora tribe, a portion of whom, as I before hinted, emigrated with the Mohawks, he baptized five adults and eight children. He then goes on to state, that this tribe was going with retrograde steps in the knowledge and exercise of Christian principles, although, after the Mohawks, they were formerly the most attentive of all the tribes in their public worship, the use of the liturgy, and the instruction of their children; whereas now the light of the gospel was becoming more dim, though it was not entirely extinguished; and he hopes that, with necessary assistance, it will be so revived as to shine brilliantly before the neighboring nations.† Thus, again, the oldest missions are going into decay, and falling away from Christianity, till in them the light of the gospel is almost extinguished.

In 1827, we have another report from Mr. Hough, dated Mohawk Village, 27th Sept.; who, speaking of some of the villages in which he had resided several months, says, "that in these places he paid great attention to the character of the Indians who profess Christianity; that he hoped many of them were really Christians, but he was sorry to say that he feared too many of them were unworthy of the very name; being given to drunkenness, which was their great besetting sin, and some of them being reduced, by it, to a most miserable state."‡ Such is the report of the state of these missions, the oldest attempted by societies established in England, among the American tribes. With regard to those tribes which did not emigrate, but remained in the United States, and whose religious instruction has been continued by the New York Missionary Society, I will content myself with an account of them, given in a work published in that country, by the Rev. Dr. Morse. He says, "that for a hundred years the matrimonial rite has not been used among them, and, consequently, they are living more like wild beasts than civilized men."§

Now, I am willing to acknowledge that, within these four or five years, there has been, to all appearance, a most important change in this part of the missionary district; in consequence

---
* Ib. p. 23.   † Ib. p. 124.   ‡ Report for 1828, p. 174.
§ The American Universal Geography. Boston, 1812. Vol. i. p. 367.

of the work having been undertaken among some of the tribes, by half-natives, who have had the benefit of European education, while they possessed the confidence of their fellow-countrymen. Among these is the Wesleyan missionary Jones; and it is certain that he has succeeded in bringing a considerable number to the profession of Christianity; probably the first instance in which the labors of any Protestant missionary have been successful. Still, it is right to observe how the poor savages are situated, in the midst of Europeans, their hunting grounds almost completely taken from them, and they, consequently, necessarily obliged to settle down in the only form of life suited to their new position, and followed by all around them. What has been done, therefore, is not merely presenting them with Christianity, but giving them examples of civilization, and furnishing them with the means of establishing themselves in a comfortable and respectable manner. The government has built houses for them, supplied them with the necessary implements of agriculture, and given them the means of properly cultivating their grounds. They have thus adopted Christianity as a part and portion of civilization. I mean not to say that all this is not right and beneficial; but I must contend that it is not a fair experiment of the principles proposed, when they are backed, not merely by sensible advantages, but almost by the force of unavoidable circumstances, which leave men no alternative between receiving Christianity and refusing civilization.

Yet even here I must not omit the observation of experienced persons, that what is now doing is only what has been done before, and will come to as little good. A late traveller in America, very zealously attached to the Protestant religion, went to visit those settlements, and expresses what he terms his satisfaction at what he has seen; but yet he regrets to find that experienced persons, and those who perfectly understand the Indian character, did not go with him to the extent of his satisfaction; because the same effects had been witnessed before, through the agency and influence of particular individuals, but were afterwards lost, and the Indians fell back into their former state, as soon as the hand that guided them had been withdrawn.* Consequently, all this may be considered as a sort of experiment; and we have as yet to see how far these converts will hold to the religion they have received, and continue in the profession of Christianity,

---

* Travels in North America, in 1827 and 1828, by Capt. B. Hall. Edin. 1829. Vol. I. p. 260.

after the individuals, whose influence has made them Christians, shall have been removed.*

There are a number of secondary missions, but of small interest to us, and the history of all which is the same. In the year 1765, a mission was founded among the Kalmucks of the Wolga, at Sarepta, under the auspices and protection of the Empress Catherine, of Russia, by the Moravians. Mr. Henderson, an English missionary, who visited them in 1821, states that, after having been established fifty-six years, they have not succeeded in making one convert. All that they can boast of is a few girls, who gave encouraging hopes of the work of the Holy Spirit in their souls; but among the grown natives there has not been one conversion.† I might say the same of many other of their missions; which are rather agricultural and manufacturing colonies than apostolic missions. The Moravians established many missions in the last century; in Saxony, in 1735; on the coast of Guinea, 1737; in Georgia, 1738; at Algiers, 1739; in Ceylon, 1740; in Persia, 1747; and in Egypt, 1750; of which not the slightest trace exists at the present day.

Before leaving the missions of the Moravians, I may mention the observations of several travellers, and, among others, of Klaproth, that the settlement at Sarepta, and, indeed all their other missions, end in becoming mere commercial establishments,‡ and the Chevalier Gamba, resident French Consul at Astracan, gives a singular instance of supposed degeneracy in Moravian settlements, which have apparently become only industrious villages, without any traces of religious principles.§

In 1802, Messrs. Brunton and Paterson opened a mission among the Tartars at Karass, under an escort of Cossacks, and that also is stated by Henderson to have failed,‖ as well as one attempted for the conversion of the same people by Mr. Blythe. The late Emperor Alexander put an end to this and other missions, and forbade their prosecution; but, even before that, they were acknowledged not to have produced any fruit.

It would be easy to collect acknowledgments of a more general character, that prove the failure of missionary attempts, conducted by these numerous societies, over all the world. Thus,

---

* I regret being obliged, from fear of becoming tiresome, to omit the history of attempted conversion in the West Indies, where the series of failures is as remarkable as in the other parts of the world of which I have treated.
† Biblical Researches and Travels in Russia. Lond. 1826, p. 411.
‡ Voyage au Mont Caucase et en Georgie. Par. 1823, tom. i. p. 261.
§ Voyage dans la Russie méridionale. Par. 1826, tom. ii. p. 370.
‖ Ubi sup. p. 420.

the Rev. Mr. Bickersteth, secretary of the Church Missionary Society, publicly declared, in a speech, at York, in May, 1823, that, "in the course of the first *ten years*, the society never heard of *a single individual* who passed from idolatry to Christianity."* The Missionary Register, after twenty years' labor, acknowledges, that "*a present and visible success* is not the criterion that their labors have been accepted by God." The Church Missionary Society confess, after the same period of attempt, that they have no proof of success to bring forward, and that small success has yet appeared in the actual conversion of the heathen. A missionary, in the same journal, speaking of a youth, who had shown symptoms of conviction, but, without being converted, apologizes for his delight at such a trifle, compares himself to a poor wretch, wandering in darkness, who leaps with joy at the distant appearance of light; and hails this first example of approximation, as an augury that *our children's children* will, perhaps, see the result of these labors !† I will close these acknowledgments with the words of a periodical to which I have before referred. "We should lay aside this history of the propagation of Christianity among the heathen, with some mortification and despondency, if our hopes of the diffusion of our religion depended on the success of such undertakings as the present volumes record;"‡ that is to say, the attempts made to propagate Christianity among the Indians of America.

There is still another mission, which may appear, at first sight, to have been attended with considerable success; that I mean, to the Islands of the Pacific, undertaken with the same or greater advantages than I have described when speaking of the native tribes of America. It is a very singular fact, that this is almost the only instance on record of a nation having been the first to desire Christianity, and, consequently, of its having been willing to receive it under whatever form it should first come. It is a known fact, that the natives of those islands, from seeing the superiority of the traders from other nations, and principally of those from America, were led to ask for missionaries to propagate Christianity among them. This at once forbids our considering the establishment of Christianity there as the result of any principle of faith, presented to the acceptance of the individuals. They conceived that Christianity was a better system than their own, because they had seen it give men a superiority

---
* York Herald, May 31, 1823.
† Quoted in the Catholic Miscellany, Jan. 1823.
‡ Monthly Review, Vol. 84, p. 152.

LECTURE VI. 171

of mind and character; and, with exceeding good sense, no doubt, they determined on embracing it. But it cannot be considered as a fair specimen of the success which Protestant doctrines can have, when preached to heathen and uncivilized nations. I should be sorry to enter on a history of this mission on another account. Having conceded to it all that can be called outward success, that is to say, having granted that great numbers of the natives have embraced Christianity; and having excluded it from the object which I have in view, which is to try the comparative strength and power of the different systems preached, I should be sorry to enter into a history of it, because it seems to present one of the most lamentable effects of misguided zeal that probably could be conceived. I have with me extracts from writers, describing the state of these islands after they had been, not converted, but subjugated, by the missionaries: who, after having made themselves masters of the whole temporal dominion of the islands, after having made the king and his people their slaves, after having stript the natives of that simplicity of character for which they were before remarkable—and I am sure you would hardly believe it possible that men, under the shelter of the word of God, and professing to teach the doctrines of Christianity, could have so acted,—have reduced the country to a state of such wretchedness, that persons who have since visited it, declare, that, instead of a blessing, the new religion has been its utter ruin. They say, that the system of Christianity enforced on the natives has been such as totally to change them for the worse; that, instead of an active open-hearted race, it has rendered them crafty, indolent, and treacherous: so that, immense tracts of country, which were formerly seen covered with the most beautiful crops, are now totally barren; and the cultivation of that important plant, the bread-fruit tree, has been so neglected, that it is in danger of becoming extinct in the island;—that feuds, quarrels, and disputes have been so general, that a prince, one of the most intelligent persons in the country, and the first to embrace Christianity, on the arrival of the missionaries, had fitted out an expedition, to emigrate from his own country, because he could not bear the severity of their yoke. These are facts which have been published in this country;* but I shall perhaps have occasion to return to them, and say something

---

* Consult the "Voyage of H. M. S. Blonde to the Sandwich Islands." Lond. 1827. "The Quarterly Review," vol. xxxv. p. 400, and lxx. p. 609. Kotzebue's "Second Voyage round the world," and Augustus Toole's "Account of nine months' residence in New Zealand."

more of these islands, when I come to treat of the missions established in them by the Catholics within these few years.

Such seems to be the result of the missionary system, as hitherto tried, in every case; and I am not conscious of having concealed any thing, or of having overlooked any testimony that could go against me. I have carefully drawn my extracts from the original reports; but I have not given you one half the store of materials which I had brought together in examining the subject. The result, however, is satisfactory beyond any thing, that hitherto the attempts made to preach the Gospel to the heathen on the Protestant principle, that the Bible alone is sufficient—that there is no other sanction or authority in religion—has almost, without exception, everywhere failed. There is yet another point to be examined. In spite of what I have said, we meet constantly, in the reports of the societies, an account of many persons being converted. Now, I have not been able to help noting certain criterions of great importance, in estimating the character of the conversions so stated.

In the first place, you must not allow yourselves to be led away by those reports, which speak of the immense number of copies of the Bible and the New Testament distributed among the natives of heathen countries,—you must not suppose that this gives any evidence of conversion,—nor that, because missionaries ask for innumerable quantities of Bibles, any thing like a proportionate number of conversions are made. For these Bibles are sent out in cargoes, and accumulated in warehouses abroad, or distributed to persons who make no use of them at all, or make them serve any purpose, as you will see by a few examples, which I will give you just now. General Hislop, in his "History of the Campaign against the Mahrattas and Pindarris," says, that "these missionaries think that this distribution of the Gospels in Chinese, Sanscrit, &c., is sufficient to obtain their purpose; and as they send out these books to English agents and magistrates, in different places, so they reckon the number of their converts, and the success of their labors, in proportion to the copies distributed." He says that he knew several residences, where no vessel ever arrived without a case or bale of Bibles for distribution. The residents send them in every direction, by hundreds at a time. The Chinese look at them, and say that they have more beautiful histories in their own literature, and have not the least idea whether they are intended for amusement or instruction, and, after having read them, throw them aside; so that the resident could not possibly distribute any more: but the ardent zeal of the Malacca missionary continued to supply them, by ship after ship, in such quantities that they were obliged to be placed in a warehouse! He adds that "this is the missionary who had written to the Bible Society that they might send him out a million of Bibles; and in this way it would have been easy to dispose of them."*

I have also seen a letter, and will quote it, although it is from a Catholic authority, written a few years ago, by the Vicar Apostolic of Siam, who relates precisely the same circumstance,— "That two English emissaries had arrived, and were distributing Bibles in every direction; the people used them to wrap up their merchandise in the shops; some of them, however, brought them to the Catholic clergy as of no use." He then remarks: "In this way, reports are sent over, and the number of converts are reckoned by the number of Bibles distributed. I know that not a single conversion has been made by them."†

In the French "Asiatic Journal," we are assured, on the authority of a letter from Macao, that copies of Dr. Morrison's Bible, which had been introduced into China, were afterwards sold by auction; and that the greater part of them were bought by manufacturers for different purposes, but principally by the makers of slippers, who used them to make linings with them. It is painful, and humiliating, and almost unbecoming the solemnity of this place, to mention such circumstances; but they are important towards undeceiving those who think that all these Bibles are put to a useful purpose, instead of this degrading and disrespectful use being made of the word of God.‡

But the fact is, that the Bibles so sent are easily and willingly received by the natives, under peculiar circumstances; and I will read you, in illustration, an extract from Martyn's Diary.

---

* See the Month. Rev. No. 94, p. 369.

† The letter is dated 20th June, 1829, and was communicated to me by the Cardinal Cappellari, to whom it was addressed, now worthily raised to a higher dignity. I will give the good Bishop's own words, as they contain other curious facts. "Duo emissarii societatis biblistarum huc venerunt a decem circiter mensibus: immensos libros Bibliorum lingua sinica scriptos sparserunt inter Sinenses. Alii illis utuntur ad fumandum tabacum, alii ad involvenda dulciaria quæ vendunt, alii denique tradiderunt nostris, qui ad me detulerunt tanquam inutiles. *Numerant isti biblistæ libros sparsos, et postea scribunt in Europam, dicentes, tot esse gentiles factos christianos quot sunt libri sparsi: at ego, qui sum testis ocularis, dico, ne unum quidem factum christianum.* Voluit ab initio rex Siam expellere eos, significatum est illis nomine regis ut abirent, petierunt ut simul expellerentur missionarii apostolici. Respendit Barcalo, primus regni minister, sacerdotes gallos habere confidentiam regis ab initio etc. Videtur mihi rex timuisse ne nationem illorum offenderet, et mediante pecunia, ut puto, usque modo remanent."

‡ Nouveau Journal Asiatique, 1828, to. ii. p. 40.

He says: "Early this morning they set me ashore, to see a hot spring. A great number of Brahmans and Fakirs were there. Not being able to understand them, I gave away tracts. Many followed me to the budgerow, where I gave away more tracts, and some Testaments. Arrived at Monghir about noon. In the evening, some came to me for books, and among them those who had travelled from the spring, having heard that I was giving away *copies of the Ramayuna.* They would not believe me when I told them it was not the Ramayuna. I gave them six or eight more."* Ramayuna signifies the adventures of the god Ramah, which these poor creatures supposed the Bible to contain. How easily might missionaries, who did not know the language, have stated, that they were so anxious for the Bible as to have followed them miles to obtain a copy! Again:—"A man followed the budgerow along the walls of the fort, and, finding an opportunity, got on board with another, begging for a book, not believing but that it was the Ramayuna."† In another place, he tells us that he sent a copy of the Bible to one of the native princesses; and you may see how little good it was likely to do here, and what a small chance of conversion there was by such a process The Ranee of Daudnagar, to whom he had sent it through the Pundit, returned her compliments, and begged to know what was to be done to obtain benefit from the book; whether she had to say a prayer, or was she to make a salaam, or bow, to it?‡ All the idea she had of the book was, that some superstitious homage should be paid to it. To these examples I could add many more, of a similar character. The Abbé Dubois has related an amusing anecdote, concerning the Telinga version of St. Matthew's Gospel, which a deputation of native Catholics laid, in grave silence, at his feet. It had been received from a Protestant missionary, and had proved the utter perplexity of several villages, the readers of which, assembled in council, had not been able to comprehend a syllable of it. They had at length taken it to an eminent astrologer in the neighborhood, who, having studied it to no purpose, and wishing to conceal his ignorance, seriously assured them that the work was a complete treatise on magic, and must be destroyed, lest some calamity might befall them. And they had now accordingly brought it in a bag to their priest, to know how they might best dispose of it."§

Again, we are assured, upon good authority, that a version of

---

* Ubi sup. p. 260. † Ib. ‡ Ib. p. 240.
§ "Annales de la Propagation de la Foi," tom. i. p. 159, 1829.

the Bible was sent among the Tartars of the Caucasus, *supposed* to be in their own language; but it was so written that they did not understand a word of it; and the consequence was, that the books were torn in pieces, and made use of as wadding for their guns. The Chevalier Gamba observes that, at Astracan, a great number of Bibles were sent out to convert the natives, but as the greater part of them could not read, of course they could not make the slightest use of them: so that the present was completely thrown away.* These are a few out of many examples, to show you how very fallacious it is to judge of the extent of conversion, or of the propagation of Christianity, by the returns of the distribution of Bibles among the natives of heathen countries.

Another fallacious rule is the number of scholars and schools. Missionaries constantly write that all their congregation consists of their schools. But, with regard to this part of missionary labors, there are two important remarks to be made. The first is, that many heathens, especially among the Hindoos, have no objection to frequent these schools, and to send their children to them; but yet are not thereby led to embrace Christianity. Mr. Lushington, in a work published at Calcutta, in 1824, enters at full into this subject. He says, "that it is now proved that, to a certain extent, they are not withheld by the circumstance of this learning being communicated through our religious books; but that their thus consenting to read the New Testament must not be taken in proof of any abatement in their prejudices against Christianity. However numerous the scholars may be who frequent these schools, their attendance lasts no longer than is necessary to learn to read, write, and cast accounts, so as to be able to gain a living by joining the numerous fraternity of accountants or *sircars*. He argues that, in the present state of their minds, no better results are to be expected; but if any transient impression is made upon their minds by the books used in the schools, it must soon be effaced from want of being renewed."†

Dr. Heber confirms this assertion. For he tells us, that a Baptist mission had established at Decca twenty-six schools, frequented by upwards of a hundred boys, who all read the New Testament, without any one opposing it. "It is true," he adds, "that of these, few will be converted."‡ The same concession,

---

* "Journal Asiat." ibid.
† "The History, Design, and Present State of the Religious, Benevolent, and Charitable Institutions, founded by the British in Calcutta and its vicinity," p. 217.
‡ Narrative, vol. iii. p. 299.

that this education does not lead to conversion, is made by the American missionary, Gordon Hall.* An agent of the Church Missionary Society writes, that "the children have been found ready to say their lessons whenever he had it in his power to give them a mouthful of food."†

But there is another still more important consideration; and it is, that Christianity is most carefully excluded from the teaching of these schools. We have a proof of this in Bishop Heber's work, where he tells us, that at Benares there was a school frequented by 140 Hindoos, and that when, after visiting it, he went to see one of the most celebrated pagodas in the neighborhood, he found one of the boys, who had seemed the most clever there, wearing the Brahman string, and ready to show him through every part, with as manifest an eagerness and interest, as the most scrupulous Hindoo could have exhibited, who had never frequented a Christian school. All this struck the Bishop forcibly, and he thus comments upon it: "The remarks of the boy opened my eyes more fully to a danger which had before struck me as possible—that some of the boys brought up in our schools might grow up accomplished hypocrites, playing the part of Christians with us, and with their own people of zealous followers of Brahma; or else that they would settle down into a sort of compromise between the two creeds, allowing that Christianity was the best for us, but that idolatry was necessary and commendable in persons of their own nation. I talked with Mr. Frazer and Mr. Morris on this subject in the course of the morning; they answered, that the same danger had been foreseen by Mr. Macleod, and that in consequence of his representations, they had left off teaching the boys the creed and the ten commandments, choosing rather that the light should break on them by degrees, and when they were better able to bear it."‡ Thus, according to this system, the attendance at the schools may be very general; yet Christianity will not be learnt, because it is not taught in them.

Another false criterion is, to suppose that because large congregations assemble to hear sermons, they are become Christians Several missionaries state that they have extensive congregations and audiences amounting to many hundreds, but do not feel that they have made a single convert. Martyn acknowledges

---

* Memoir of the Rev. Gordon Hall, Andover, U. S., 1826, p. 256. He calculates the number of missionaries necessary to convert India alone at 30,000. This plan er idea of "arguing in platoons" is not surely that followed by the apostles!
† Cath. miscell. *ut sup.*   ‡ Tom. L p. 379.

LECTURE VI. 177

that he had a considerable audience, but yet the fruit of all his time, and of all his missionary labors in India, was the making of one or two converts on whose sincerity he depended. Indeed, it is impossible not to be struck with the feeling of mortification and disappointment manifest in his journal upon this subject. "The service in Hisdoostanee," he writes, "was at two o'clock. The number of the women not above one hundred. I expounded chapter iii. of St. Matthew. Notwithstanding the great apathy with which they seemed to receive every thing, there were two or three who, I was sure, understood and felt something. But not a single creature beside them, European or native, was present."*

This was at Dinapoor; but he wrote immediately after to Archdeacon Corrie, that they all abandoned him, upon his reproving one of them for unbecoming behaviour at worship.†

In another place, he states that his congregation was tolerable, but that, having preached against the errors of popery, hardly any one of them came again; and, "I suppose," he adds, "that after another Sunday I shall not have even one."‡

Nor are these remarks to be confined to India. The missionary at Kissey, in Africa, writes, that he has a congregation of more than 300, but, that up to that moment, not one of them has ears to hear, or heart to understand. He then explains the mystery, by informing us that he has under his inspection 500 individuals, who depend entirely upon a daily allowance from government, and that, thus, having the people more at command, he humbly *hopes* that the Lord will bless his word, although he probably shall not see the fruit he so much desires.§ "My sermons," writes the one of Digah, "have been well frequented, and that very attentively; but there is *not one* of whom I can say, behold he prayeth."‖

---

* P. 253.

† P. 278.—As no one, among modern Protestant missionaries, has exerted himself more than Martyn, or won more personal esteem, I will here give the history of his success. After a long time, *one* woman, wishing to be married, applied to him for baptism; but, not finding her disposed, he refused to admit her.—(p. 255.) That was the only approach to conversion which he witnessed at Dinapoor. Another who always attended, and was even moved to tears at his sermons, refused to confer with him.—(p. 279.) From that station he proceeded to Cawnpoor, where his biographer tells us that, in spite of his delicacy, he baptized one old Hindoo woman, who, though very ignorant, was very humble.—(p. 314.) In fine, *one* other conversion is all that his panegyrist pretends to attribute to him during his mission in Persia and India.—(p. 483.)

‡ P. 387. § Quoted in Miscell. *ut sup.*

‖ Missionary Register, 20th Rep. p. 56.

X

LECTURE VI.

I must now hasten to a conclusion.

You will observe that I have hardly quoted any authorities that can be considered hostile to the missionary societies. I have scarcely referred to any Catholic writer; and in general have chosen such witnesses as cannot be considered opposed to the scheme of proselytism. I have endeavored to choose my authorities from the missionaries themselves, from their reports, or from their acknowledged advocates; and the results, if balanced against the means employed, the immense resources at command, both material and moral, the wealth, and still more, the superior attainments of those who have devoted themselves to the work, are such as justify what I said at the commencement of my discourse. Allow me, therefore, to repeat, that if we look here for the blessing promised by God to the method of propagating the faith which He appointed, and if this blessing is to be manifested by their success who undertake the work; if, moreover, the promise of His aid was given to those who should succeed the apostles, as in their ministry and in their doctrines, so likewise in the methods which He prescribed; we have every evidence that it is not on the system here exhibited that the blessing was pronounced, nor those promises bestowed.

If the distribution of the Bible in a language intelligible to the people be His appointed way of conversion, and if the principle, which leads to that distribution, be the ground of faith which He inculcated, surely it is time to see *some* good results, after fifteen millions of copies have been scattered abroad. Time and quantity are, it is true, as nothing in His estimation; but surely, looking at the simple form and obvious methods which He chose for the infancy of His Church, we can hardly explain such an enormous want of ratio between the instrument and the effects which Himself had chosen. Who can imagine that the command to teach all nations, not only involved the command to print the Bible, but to print it by millions, before it should yield fruit? Surely then, if we ever are allowed to argue from the failure, to the inadequacy of the means, we must confess, that, after millions of Bibles have been distributed to so little purpose, their distribution is not the means appointed by God for conversion; and, consequently, that His blessing is not upon the work, nor His approbation upon its principle—the all-sufficiency of the written word. It is true that, "the husbandman waiteth for the precious fruit of the earth, patiently bearing till he receive the early and the latter *rain*."* But if he shall, year after year, have scattered his seed in vain; if, after having used every means which skill and perseverance can supply, he still receive, in return, but deceitful blossoms, or a fruit which "sets his teeth on edge," he will surely conclude that his seed is defective, or that he understands not the cultivation of the land.

And this mortifying conclusion must become doubly unavoidable, if he shall see others around him, who, pursuing a rival process, reap yearly, from the same soil, a rich harvest of enduring fruit. And how this is exemplified in the present case, will be seen when next you favor me with your attendance.

You will perceive that I have carefully abstained from whatever might tend to decry or vilify the system followed; I have not said one word derogatory to the character of the missionaries employed. I have not, as has often been done, even in official documents, alluded to any of them being uneducated, or ignorant, or not qualified by their attainments or information for the task which they have to perform. I have not cast the slightest aspersion on their moral character, nor on the motives which have moved or directed them. I have not hinted that any thing like personal interest influences those who are concerned in the management of these societies. I have abstained from every thing of this nature, and have simply used the facts laid before us by themselves; for I have considered throughout, that the English establishment, or any other religious body, must naturally best understand what means are calculated to effect its own purposes.

Indeed, I will farther say, that it is impossible for any person to peruse the documents which I have quoted, and make himself familiar with their detail, and (far from conceiving any feeling of contempt for those engaged in this work) not be brought to acknowledge, what a fund of beautiful religious spirit this country possesses, were it only directed in those channels which God has appointed, that they may be effectual! We have it here shown, that there exist, to this moment, amongst us, some remains of that spirit, which led so many of our countrymen, in former ages, into foreign lands, to be, in the hand of Providence, merciful instruments for bringing many great nations to the profession of Christianity.

Let but the same principle, which they bore with them to the task, return again, as a general blessing to our country; let the

* James v. 7.

mantle of the Bonifaces and Willibrords, with their twofold spirit of Catholic faith and Catholic love, be caught up by this nation, and it shall divide the rivers, and open the seas before its missionaries, and shall make them the inheritors of their grace, and render this island once more, what formerly it was, a gushing well-spring of Christianity and salvation to the nations of the earth.

LECTURE THE SEVENTH.

ON THE PRACTICAL SUCCESS OF THE CATHOLIC RULE OF FAITH, IN CONVERTING HEATHEN NATIONS.

LUKE xi. 20.

"But if I, in the finger of God, cast out devils, undoubtedly the kingdom of God is come upon you."

In the Gospel which the Church has selected for your edification in the service of this day, it is related how our Blessed Saviour cast out the devil from one that was blind, and deaf, and dumb. In the words of my text, He concludes, from this circumstance, that, seeing how this wonderful power could not be attributed to any human or earthly agency, but must have come from God, His hearers were bound to acknowledge, that the kingdom of God was really, in His person, brought among them. Now, as the venerable Bede observes, in his commentary on this passage, what on this occasion was done in the body is daily performed in spirit, in the Church of God, by the conversion of men unto the faith; inasmuch as, the devil being from them expelled, their eyes are first opened to see the light of God's truth, and afterwards their tongues being loosed, they are allowed to join in His praise. And as this efficacy and power was assumed by our blessed Saviour for a proof that the kingdom of God was indeed with Him, and through Him was presented to the acceptance of the Jews; so may we say, that in the parallel power of the Church is to be found a similar demonstration, that where it at present exists, there also is Christ's kingdom.

Such, my brethren, is the topic on which I wish to occupy your attention this evening; it is but a completion of the task which I commenced at our last meeting; when, having laid before you the touchstone of the rule of faith, which exists in the power of effecting conversion among such as know not Christ, I entered upon the application of this proof to that principle of religion, to that groundwork of faith, which is held to be essential by those who differ from us on this head. Exclusively making

LECTURE VII.

use, with the exception of one or two immaterial confirmatory instances, of documents put forth by persons who have a natural interest in their respective establishments for propagating Christianity among the heathen, I showed you how it was acknowledged, that hitherto no success had attended their labors; but that, in every country, in the east and the west, the preaching of Christianity, with that sanction, and upon that basis, which their religion required, had proved abortive. I then promised to go into the other side of the question; and, from the progress and the actual state of similar efforts made, and daily making, by Catholic missionaries, to prove that the divine blessing does appear to rest on their labors, and that they have succeeded in the very field where the others acknowledge themselves to have failed; yea, and that they have succeeded, according to the confession of their very rivals.

This, then, is the task on which I am now about to enter. It was originally my intention, as I believe I hinted in the first instance,* to begin my narrative from rather a remote period; I wished to commence the history of Catholic conversion from those centuries in which it is universally acknowledged that the peculiar doctrines of the Church of Rome, as they are called, were sufficiently established to prove the identity of that Church which then sent forth missionaries, with the present Roman Catholic Church. I should have commenced probably from the seventh or eighth century; but I soon found that it was quite impossible to condense, even into a lengthened discourse, the facts which this plan would oblige me to bring before your consideration; and besides, however my case may, in some respects, appear to suffer by laying aside what I consider a very powerful support, I think that you will naturally take more interest in those circumstances and occurrences which are nearer your own time, and which can be put more fairly in contrast with what I exposed at our last meeting. For there might be differences of circumstances in former times; there might be causes in operation which cannot now be discovered; and consequently the success which attended the early missionaries sent out by the Church, or rather by the See of Rome, to convert nations, as in the north of Europe, may be supposed to have depended on peculiar circumstances, which now no longer act.

It is for these reasons, therefore, that I shall confine myself to later times. But I cannot pass over one event, and that is, the

---

* See p. 130.

conversion of this country—I mean its last conversion, after the Saxon occupation, to the Christian religion. It is a very interesting and important inquiry, for any person endowed with a truly candid and reflecting mind, and at the same time possessing the patience to look minutely into the circumstances of the case, to see what were the causes that produced that almost instantaneous, yet lasting and universal effect, which the preaching of the first missionaries sent by St. Gregory into this country did produce. Now it was generally thought at the time when this conversion was made, and by the individuals themselves who wrought it, that no power could have effected it, and that no power did effect it, except the gift of miracles, which they believed to have been granted for that purpose by God. In discussing the subject of the continuance of miracles in the Church of Christ, the late Professor of Divinity in the University of Oxford says, that "when, in later periods, persons sent to preach the gospel were placed in circumstances similar to those of the apostles, there can be no difficulty in acknowledging that God may have furnished them with the same means as were granted in the first instance, and may have given them the power of working such signs and wonders as would effect the conversion of a people."* And, in fact, there can be no material or valid objection to that power having been granted for ends precisely similar to those for which it was given to the apostles. Nor can I believe that any one acquainted with the life, the writings, and the character of the great Pontiff—justly called "The Great"—who sent those missionaries into our country, will hesitate to pronounce him a person infinitely above all suspicion of craftiness, or an attempt to deceive mankind. And I believe, too, that whoever considers the circumstances under which those who first landed with Christianity on our shores came to the task—the dangers which they encountered—the advantages which they renounced—their feeble prospect, humanly speaking, of producing any effect in a country whose language to them was strange, and whose natives must have looked on them with jealousy—will hardly for a moment imagine that any thing but the purest and best of motives could have instigated them to undertake so toilsome and so thankless a work.

And yet we find that St. Augustine writes to the holy Pontiff, that he himself believed God to have performed, through his hands, such signs and wonders as led these islanders to embrace

---

* Lectures on the Ecclesiastical History of the Second and Third Centuries.

the faith of Christ; and we have the answer of the holy Pontiff, in which he exhorts him not to allow himself to be puffed up and made vain by the communication of this supernatural gift; and so convinced was he of its reality, that we have another letter of his, wherein he communicates the intelligence to the bishops of the East, as a new proof of the assistance afforded by Christ to His Church, in her office of conversion. There is surely here every appearance of sincerity on both sides; there can be no reason to think that there could have been any motive for fiction or deceit; for, as the work of conversion was effectually performed, that was a merit and a matter of consolation sufficient to enable them to dispense with such false and disingenuous acts, if under any circumstances they had been possible. This reasoning is so obvious, that even writers exceedingly opposed to the Catholic doctrine of miracles have acknowledged that they must attribute the conversion of this country to their influence. And, in justification of what I have said, I will quote a few lines from Fuller:—"This admonition of Gregory is, with me, and ought to be with all unprejudiced persons, an argument beyond exception, that though no discreet man will believe all Augustine's miracles in the latitude of monkish relations, he is ignorantly and uncharitably peevish and morose who utterly denies some miracles to have been wrought by him."

If I have dwelt thus at length upon this case, my object has been to prove to you, how they, who formerly undertook the labor of conversion, were firmly convinced of God's assistance so being with them, as to show His finger working through them, and so convince the nations of the earth that the kingdom of God was come among them. And it would be difficult to find any ground on which, coming down to later times, as to the case of St. Francis Xavier, the great converter of India and other countries of the East, we should not allow the exercise of similar powers. I do not mean to enter specifically into this question, nor to do more than merely suggest the parallelism between the two cases, and the unreasonableness of denying later miracles in conversion, if the older ones are admitted. And as the conversions of that modern apostle have not been rivalled in later times, and as you will see that they have been as permanent, and have produced as stable and as lasting fruit as those of Augustine in England, or of the apostles in the provinces allotted to their preaching, there can be no reason to suppose that God might not exercise His power in the later as in the older case. But there is another curious reflection to be made connected

LECTURE VII.

with this subject, and it is, that, while we thus have the acknowledgment of Protestant divines, that miracles were wrought by the apostles of our island, others maintain that they preached the doctrines of the Church of Rome. For treatises have been written by many, and, among others, by a prelate of the present day, to show that the British Church was not in communion with the Roman See till they came. And to bring these remarks to a close, I will only observe, that, Hacluyt, Tavernier, and Baldeus, three Protestant writers not very remote from that time, acknowledged, from their own observation, that it was firmly believed by all the natives of southern India, that St. Francis Xavier wrought such miracles as induced them to become members of the Church of Christ.

All this, however, is merely preliminary to our more important task. Let us now see what is the actual state of the missions established in different parts of the world, under the direction and authority of the Holy See; and as, on a former occasion, I laid before you a slight account of the instruments employed, and the resources and means brought into action, in this noble work, I will premise a few observations on the same subject with regard to our missions.

In the first place, then, there is a board or congregation at Rome, consisting of the first dignitaries of the Church, which devotes itself expressly to the superintendence of Catholic missions, and is well known by the name of the Congregation of the Propaganda. It has a large establishment for the conduct of its affairs, with a college, in which are generally about 100 individuals, from almost every nation under the sun. It has another college for Chinese at Naples; and has dependent upon it other establishments belonging to religious orders, whence the principal number of its missionaries is drawn. The number yearly sent out must be limited; and I am sure does not exceed four or six a year. However, the Propaganda receives into its service persons willing to become missionaries in foreign parts, whether seculars or members of religious congregations. But still, even with this addition, (and I can speak from personal knowledge,) the number of missionaries sent forth do not amount to ten in the year.

In France, there is an association of private individuals for the purpose of contributing to the support of foreign missions, and, at Paris, there is a college exclusively for the preparation of persons who feel called to this holy work. The society to which I have alluded is divided into two districts; the one communicating with a council at Lyons, the other with one established at Paris. By a simple and beautiful system, subscriptions are received from every part, with very little expense; most of them being but of a *sous* a week, collected by unpaid agents, who have each a hundred subscribers under their care. I understand, too, that the great merit of this work is due to a lady, who, crippled and confined to her chamber, has dedicated herself to the organization of this association. The sum raised in France, and its colonies, during 1834, amounted only to 404,727 francs, or about 16,189*l.*; less by 1000*l.* than the poorest of the many English missionary societies raised several years ago. This association was first established at Lyons, in 1822.* It requires no public meetings—no itinerant preaching—to nourish it and keep it alive; the Catholic principle of unity and subordination supplies sufficient instruments for the quiet and noiseless co-operation of charitable spirits.

The congregation of Propaganda is often considered wealthy to an enormous degree, and reports are often spread of its contributing large sums towards the support of the Catholic religion in all parts of the world. But it is poor, if compared to the vast sums collected by any one of the societies in England. I will venture to say, that, although three illustrious Cardinals have, within these few years, bequeathed to it all their property,† its annual income does not reach 30,000*l.* And out of this sum, it must be remembered, that the expense of educating more than a hundred individuals has to be defrayed.‡

But the best proof of our comparatively limited means, may be taken from the provision for individuals employed on these missions. In his examination before a committee of the House of Commons, 23d June, 1832, the Abbé Dubois, who had been thirty years a missionary in India, complained of the want of provision for the Catholic missionaries at the head of extensive congregations in India, and proposed that the Government should give them such succor as would make them respectable to their flocks. Now, the scale which he proposed was as follows:—To every Bishop, 60*l.* per annum; to every European Pastor, with

---

* "Situation comparée de l'œuvre de la propagation de la foi pendant l'année 1834." *Lyons*, p. 1.

† The Cardinals De Pietro, Della Somaglia, and the great statesman Consalvi.

‡ I say nothing of the Leopoldine Institute at Vienna, the annual contributions of which, I am happy to see, have gone on gradually increasing; because the object of its charitable assistance is not so much the conversion of pagans, as the succor of the poor dioceses of North America.

a congregation of 3000, 30*l*., to every native priest, with a similar congregation of 3000, 20*l*.; and to catechists and schoolmasters, from 5*l*. to 7*l*.; and this, he thought, would be a large provision, considering the destitute state in which they are at present!* I remember reading an account of a visit paid by a traveller to the French Vicar Apostolic and Bishop residing in Mesopotamia, whom he describes as living in a miserable hut, not sheltered from the weather,—unable to afford himself shoes or stockings, —and wearing the shreds of a tattered cassock, as his only garment.

Such is the difference in the provision made for individuals; but we have different returns to show the comparative footing on which the two religions stand. On the 6th of August, 1833, a return of what was allowed by the Government of India to the clergy and places of worship, of different denominations, was ordered by Parliament to be printed. What follows is the proportion in the three Presidencies,—the calculation being made in rupees, equal to about 2*s*. 6*d*.:—

    To the Episcopal Established Church, - 811,430
    To the Scottish Church, - - - - - - 53,077
    And to the Catholic, - - - - - - - 10,163

So that the provision made for the Established Church, which I showed you at our last meeting, has but comparatively little to do, is 811,000 rupees, while the Catholics, amounting to several hundred thousand, have only 10,000 as a provision for them.

There are some other preliminary remarks to which I wish to draw your attention. The first is the peculiar misfortunes which have befallen our missions. They do not, like those supported by this country, draw their resources from a nation in a state of continued prosperity; but it must be recollected, that the missions in the East, with the exception of what is done by the native priests, (of which I could give you sufficient examples,) have been supplied exclusively by individuals sent from France, Spain, or Italy, generally members of different religious orders, and that their funds were drawn from their respective countries. Now when it is recollected that at the French Revolution the religious orders of that country were totally suppressed, it must be evident that their establishments for foreign missions were also extinguished. Thus, since the last ten years of the nine-

---

* See "The British Catholic Colonial Quarterly Intelligencer," No. II. p. 151. *Lond*. 1834.

teenth century, till 1822, the funds and individuals required were prevented from being sent from that country to the work. A few years later, at the invasion of Italy, the Propaganda was suppressed, and all its funds seized by the French usurpation; the religious orders were also suppressed, and their supplies ceased to be any longer transmitted. I shall be able to show you instances, lamentable indeed, of congregations suffering under the privation of spiritual direction, in consequence of this circumstance.

Another—and without entering into the justice or injustice, the propriety or impropriety of the measure, but looking at it simply in reference to these missions—another serious blow was the suppression of the order of Jesuits. I know that the mention of this name may call up to the minds of some individuals a feeling of suspicion and aversion: they may have associated with it the idea of double-dealing, hypocrisy, and many other worse vices. But I will say that it is impossible for any one to consider and read what they have endured for the propagation of the faith—it is impossible to see in what manner hundreds have laid down their lives, within the last three hundred years, after undergoing the fiercest tortures, rather than renounce it, or even to see with what alacrity, and with what success, they have undertaken to convert infidel nations to the knowledge of Christ Jesus, and not be satisfied that truly they have been chosen instruments in the hands of Divine Providence for the greatest ends. And, although there may have been among them defects, and members unworthy of their character, (for it would not be a human institution if it was not imperfect,) it must be admitted that there has been maintained among them a degree of fervor and purest zeal for the conversion of heathens, which no other body has ever shown. So that it is not wonderful if, immediately after the horrors of the French Revolution, the celebrated Lalande should have said of them that they were an "institution such as no other human establishment had ever resembled—the object of his eternal admiration, gratitude, and regret."* But, as I may often have to allude to the mission of these zealous religious men, I wish to remove any prejudice against them, by reading the opinion of one who writes expressly to prove that the method pursued by the Protestant missionaries is decidedly superior to that which ours follow. "The success of the Jesuit missionaries," he says, "is chiefly to be ascribed to the example

---

* In the "Bien Informé, 3d Feb., 1800.

LECTURE VII.   189

they displayed of Christian charity in its most heroic degree."* The author goes on to relate an interesting anecdote: how the emperor of Japan called to him Father Necker, who was at the head of the mission, and said to him, "Tell me in confidence, and I promise not to betray you to any man, do you really believe in the doctrines which you preach? I have called my Bonzas (priests) and desired them to tell me sincerely what they thought of their own doctrines; and they have candidly confessed, that what they teach the people is only a tissue of absurdity and falsehood, in which they do not themselves put the slightest credence." The missionary pointed to a terrestrial globe in the chamber, and desired the emperor to measure the breadth of ocean which he had crossed to come to him, and then see what he had gained, or could hope to gain, by the course he was pursuing. "Your Bonzas," he added, "are rich, happy, and respected, and have every earthly good they can desire. I have abandoned every thing to come and preach these doctrines to you; and tell me, is it possible that I would have undergone so much, if I were not satisfied of their truth, and of their necessity for you?" Such an answer, surely, was worthy of any minister of Christ's Gospel. But let us proceed.

That circumstance, to which I have alluded, of the interruption of supplies, from our funds having been involved in the destruction of the bodies which furnished them, must necessarily have been greatly felt; and it is impossible not to be sensible that, from these effects, many missions have not yet recovered, and will not for some time to come. And their loss was not merely pecuniary, but their supply of pastors was also cut off by the calamities which befell southern Europe: so that they are now slowly recovering and regaining the state in which they were previously. Nor have the religious orders themselves yet recovered the shock, which an interruption of thirty years had occasioned in their bodies.

A few words now regarding the reports of our missions. The Propaganda publishes no report whatever—no appeal is ever made by it to the public; the congregation meets privately, and although persons who take pains may procure information, there is nothing like an official document put forth, to bring what is done by its missionaries before the world. On the contrary, I, for one, have earnestly urged, again and again, the propriety of publishing the beautiful and interesting accounts received; but

---

* Quarterly Review, No. lxiii. p. 3.

the answer has always been, "We have no desire to make any display of these things; we are satisfied that the good is done, and that is all we can desire." The fact is, that the Catholic Church does not fancy herself to be doing more than her ordinary and indispensable duty when she preaches the faith to heathen nations; neither does she believe that her success is more than a part of that enduring and inherent blessing which was coupled with the command to preach it. Hence no clamor or boast is heard within her: but she perseveres in the calm fulfilment of her eternal destiny, as unconscious of any extraordinary effort, as are the celestial bodies in wheeling round their endless orbits and scattering rays of brilliant light through the unmeasurable distances of space. She leaves it to those who find the very attempt at conversion a new thing—who, in their very statements speak of it as a fresh calling, and of an experimental effort—to blazon forth every new attempt, to hoard up, in their annual reports, every gleaning of hope, and employ the orator's skill, and the democratic arts of public appeals, to keep alive the apostolic vocation.

The French association does indeed publish reports, but of a very different form from their's. They do not consist of a yearly collection of heterogeneous materials, but appear monthly, as edifying tracts, composed almost exclusively of letters from the missionaries, generally written in a strain of simple, cheerful piety, which makes us feel, in perusing them, that they who wrote them are the successors in spirit, as in their ministry, of the ancient converters of nations. There is an absence in them of all affected phrase, and of all reliance on particular dogmas, to the exclusion of others no less important, which we too often find in the jarring narratives of other religions. These reports, too, if we ought so to call them,* do not embrace any thing like the whole of our missions, but only comprise those which are supported by the French association.

The materials, therefore, which I shall use, I have been obliged to glean from such documents as have fallen in my way, or as I have

---

* They appear under the title of "Annales de l'Association pour la Propagation de la Foi." *Paris* and *Lyons*. It is a pity that this beautiful and cheap publication is not more known in England, or rather that it is not regularly translated and republished here. It would do much to open the eyes of many to the superior spirit which animates our missionaries. But what is no less important, it would present a fund of consolation and encouragement to clergy and laity amidst their respective trials, and show them how the grace of the apostleship, and the prowess of the martyrs yet reside in the Church of God [The wish here expressed has since been complied with.]

LECTURE VII. 191

been able, with some pains, to procure. One great source, however, of information I particularly value. In my last address to you, when treating of the success of Protestant missions, you will recollect that I made use exclusively of Protestant authorities, and chiefly of the acknowledgments of missionary reports themselves. Now, therefore, in fairness, I may be allowed to use Catholic testimonials, in speaking of Catholic missions. But I wish to renounce this advantage as much as possible, and give you the account of them, from Protestant authorities, and even from the confessions of those who allow their own failure in the same territory. This, at any rate, will place my assertions above suspicion, and will give weight and credit to the statements of our own missionaries when I quote them. But for some countries, into which they alone have penetrated,—that is, for all countries where persecution rages, and where the striving for the faith is unto blood,—we *must* be content with their testimony; yet even for these, I hope to gather confirmatory evidence from those who, there at least, have never entered into rivalry with them.

We will begin, as I did when speaking of the Protestant missions, with India; and the first authority whom I will bring, is Bishop Heber. You remember, perhaps, that I quoted a passage from him, wherein he said, that in the south of India was the strength of the Christian cause, and that there congregations were to be found containing 40,000, or at least 15,000 souls; but that, upon examination, these were nowhere to be found. Now, Bishop Heber acknowledges, that even in these districts, the Catholics are much more numerous than the Protestants. "The Roman Catholics," he writes, "are considerably more numerous, but belong to a lower caste of Indians; for even these Christians retain many prejudices of caste, and, in point of knowledge and morality, *are said* to be extremely inferior. The inferiority, as injuring the general character of the religion, *is alleged* to have occasioned the very unfavourable eye with which all native Christians have been regarded in the Madras government."* Here are two or three assertions on which I shall just now make a few observations; in the first place, that the native Catholics belong to a lower caste, and are inferior in morality to the Protestant Christians in India; secondly, that, in consequence of this bad character of the Catholics in the south of India, the law, of which I shall say something by and by, was enacted, which does,

* Vol. iii. p. 460.

or did, not allow any convert to hold office under the government. But, at present, it is sufficient to take his testimony to this fact, that, in the south of India, where the greatest congregations of Protestants were supposed to exist, the Catholics are "considerably more numerous."

In another place he says, speaking of the north of India, "the native Christians of the Catholic persuasion amount, I am told, to several thousands."* Now, he could not find one hundred native Protestants in the same district, in which he says that the Catholics amount to many thousands. Again, speaking of the town of Tannah, he writes: "It is principally inhabited by Catholic Christians, *either converted natives* or Portuguese."†

Here, then, we have an acknowledgment of the success of Catholic conversion; but there are authentic returns, which give us something like specific numbers. For instance, a parliamentary document, laid before the House of Commons a few years back, gave the number of Catholics, in one diocese of Malabar, as 35,000; while another diocese is said, in the same return, to contain 127,000 Catholic natives. In one of the reports of the Church of England, a missionary writes, that in the single town of Tinevelli there are 30,000 Roman Catholics; and mentions another village, the inhabitants of which have been converted to the Catholic religion.‡

Another eyewitness, and one whose word cannot be well called in question, the Missionary Martyn, thus writes:—"Colonel N., who is writing an account of the Portuguese in this settlement, told me that the population of the Portuguese territory was 260,000, of which 200,000, he did not doubt, were Christians"— and of course Catholics; and if we allow even half of them to be the descendants of Portuguese, we have at least the other half converted Indians. "Begged the governor of Bombay to interest himself, and procure us all the information he could about the native Christians; this he promised to do. At Bombay there are 20,000 Christians; at Salsette, 21,000, and at this place there are 41,000, *using the Mahratta language*,"§ consequently natives, and every one of them Catholics. So far, therefore, we have the acknowledgments of those interested in Protestant missions, and taking a part in them, of the fact of there being many *converts* in India to the Catholic faith, and of their amounting to 20, 30, and 40,000 in single towns.

---

* Page 338. † Page 89.
‡ Quoted in Cath. Miscell. vol. iii. p. 278. § Page 330.

LECTURE VII.

This is assuredly a very strong contrast to what the same writers allow, where I quoted them at our last meeting; and it will be strengthened greatly just now.

Having produced these acknowledgments and returns, in favor of Catholic success, I have now a right to make use of our own authorities, which, while they coincide with the former, give us something more positive in their statements.

The Abbé Dubois, the same missionary whom I mentioned as having resided thirty years in the country, and who is always represented as more inclined to depreciate than to exaggerate the number of Catholics and their converts,—for it is well known that he had a particular theory on this subject, which he endeavored to maintain,—says, in his examination before the committee of the House of Commons, that the native Catholic converts in all Asia may be estimated at one million two hundred thousand; and of these he supposes one-half, or 600,000, to be in the peninsula of India;* and I may mention incidentally, that this part of the Catholic Church is governed in two different ways. There are four bishoprics, and an equal number of vicars-apostolic,—that is, bishops having a titular see in some other part of the Church.

The distribution of Catholics, according to his estimate, is, along the coast from Goa to Cape Comorin, including Travancore, 330,000; in the provinces of Mysore, the Deccan, Madura, and the Carnatic, 120,000; and he places the other 160,000 in the island of Ceylon, of which I will give you some more details presently.

Now, to show, from the reports sent by Catholic missionaries, and from private letters, that the work of conversion really goes on, I will read you one or two extracts. In 1825, M. Bonnand, a missionary from France, arrived at Pondicherry, and was immediately situated at Bandanaidoopale. In the course of six or seven months, he had acquired a sufficient knowledge of the

---

* See the "Colonial Intelligencer," *ubi sup.*, or the East India Magazine for June 1832, p. 564. This journal contrasts the readiness of the Abbé with the caution of the London Missionary Society's agents, exhibited in its secretary's note of 21st August, 1832: "None of the Society's agents now in this country from India appear to be willing to be examined, unless they be required by the select committee." The Abbé observes, that the number of Catholics has declined for some years past. The causes already assigned, and the great decline in the Portuguese power, by which many missions then in their territory were supported, will sufficiently account for this change. Thus, the two bishoprics of Cochin and Cranganore have been vacant for the last forty years, from want of revenues, which that government used to supply before the sees fell into the hands of England.

difficult Telinga language to preach in it; and in the course of a year and a half after his arrival, he had baptized sixty-three heathens."*

"The missions in the interior," writes another, "are interesting, not only on account of the fervor of the Christians, but also from the success which apostolic men obtain among the heathens. Every missionary has the consolation of seeing, every year, a certain number of them abandon the worship of idols, to embrace our holy religion. One of them has written, that, within these few days, eighteen numerous families have been regenerated by baptism."† A third tell us, that at Darmaboory he had baptized two hundred adults in the course of ten months' missionary labor.‡ M. Bonnand assures us, that most of the native Catholics "belong to the most distinguished castes."§ And, on another occasion, he thus expresses himself: "October 12, 1828. I celebrated my Easter at Piramguipooran. The Lord has vouchsafed to add an increase of sweet and pleasing troubles to the usual labors of this season. These proceeded from the baptism of twenty-two adult Sudras. In my journey towards the south, I baptized fifteen, almost all belonging to the best castes."‖

These statements bring me to the assertions of Heber regarding the Catholic converts in India, that they are of an inferior caste, and that it is their bad conduct and character which has given rise to the law which I will now explain, so that Protestant converts who are affected by it have been hurt by them. The law is, that a person embracing the Christian religion cannot, or could not, two or three years ago, hold any office under the government of India. Now, this law did not exist during the reign of the native princes; consequently, they who were themselves Hindoos, and the enemies of the Christian religion, were yet so satisfied with the conduct of the Catholics, that they allowed them to hold any office. And the native Catholics did so; for the Abbé Dubois tells us, that they held distinguished posts about the courts of Hindoo or Mohammedan princes, and were subject to no restrictions in the exercise of their religion. Now, if it were true, as Heber asserts, that all the Catholics were of the lowest caste, they would have been incapable of holding any office of trust under the government: and there is a contradiction in telling us that the Catholics are of a lower caste, and yet that

---

* Annales de l'Association, No. xx. April, 1830, p. 147.
† Page 170. ‡ Page 154.
§ No. xiii. March, 1828, p. 83. ‖ No. xx. p. 158.

a law was made to prevent their holding office. The fact is, that this is a law made since the English took possession of the country, and consequently it was only directed against the converts after that time.

This is the enactment of the Madras government in 1816:— "The Zillah judges shall recommend to the provincial courts the persons whom they may deem fit for the office of district moonsif; but no person shall be authorized to officiate as a district moonsif, without the previous sanction of the provincial court, nor unless he be of the Hindoo or Mohammedan persuasion." So that the British government requires persons to be of the Hindoo or Mohammedan religion, to entitle them to hold office in the country. But the bishop himself acknowledges this fact. For in his last letter to his wife, he asks whether it would have been believed, that, in the time of the Raja, the native Christians (who certainly were all Catholics) were eligible to any office in the state, while now there is an order of the government which excludes them from any employment?*

Again, "about twenty persons were present, one the Naick, or corporal, whom, in consequence of his embracing Christianity, government very absurdly, not to say wickedly, disgraced, by removing him from his regiment, though they still allow him his pay."† Now, the very fact of allowing him his pay shows that this principle was not adopted from fear of offending the natives; for government was more likely to excite their jealousy, by allowing him a pension, and exempting him from service, than by keeping him in his post. In another place he says: "I had an interesting visit from a fine gray-headed old man, who said he had been converted by Mr. Corrie to Christianity, when at Agra, and that his name was 'Noor Musseih' (light of the Messiah.) He came, among other things, to beg me to speak to the collector and Mr. Halhed, that he might not be thrust out of a small office which he held, and which he said he was in danger of losing on account of his Christianity."‡

From all these facts, it is evident, that the law in question

---

* Tom. ii. p. 280. † Tom. iii. p. 463.

‡ It is a well-known fact, that the new Christians in India are called *Rice-Christians*, or *Company's-Christians*, from the idea that their object in conversion is to gain support or patronage. I have the following anecdote from a Protestant gentleman, many years a resident in India. A missionary being in want of a servant, he recommended one to him, and was so warm in his praises, that the clergyman decided upon engaging him. In an unlucky moment, he summed up his panegyric by adding, "He is one of your own converts." "If that be the case," replied the other, "I cannot trust him. I cannot take a native Christian into my house."

could not have been made for the Catholics; and, in fact, th*t* it was enacted by the English in later times.

Then, as to the charge that the Catholics are worse in conduct, or less respectable than other persons in India, Dr. Heber, it is true, only uses the phrases, "it is said," "it is alleged." But this is a form of expression hardly becoming; because, to speak in such broad and sweeping condemnation of several hundred thousand persons—to say that they bear no good character, and consequently have injured the cause of religion, on merely hearsay evidence, and on the ground that "it is so alleged," and that others say so, is not reconcilable with a high feeling of Christian charity; and surely such statements, without better ground or proof, ought not to be sent forth.

Martyn, of whom I have so often spoken, gives a very different account of them, and at once declares his opinion of them. "Certainly," he writes, "there is infinitely better discipline in the Romish Church than in ours; and if ever I be the pastor of native Christians, I shall endeavor to govern with equal strictness."* He acknowledges that, until then, he had no congregation; and he proposes the Catholic pastors and people as an example to follow, should he ever possess one. Does this show that they are of a lower character, or of inferior morals? Persons do not propose as their models those who fall under their standard of the character of Christians. On another occasion, he speaks of a very interesting visit which he paid to a Catholic missionary, Father Antonio, at his little Church in Magliapore; and thus he expresses himself: "He read some passages from the Hindoostanee Gospels, which I was surprised to find so well done. I begged him to go on with the Epistles. He last translated the Missal, equally well done. He showed me the four Gospels in Persian, (very poorly done.) I rejoiced unfeignedly at seeing so much done, though he followeth not with us. The Lord bless his labors."† In this manner does Martyn speak of men whom Heber seems to consider hardly worthy of the name of Christians!

I will give another authority regarding the character of the Catholics of India; and it is that of Doctor Buchanan: "The Romish Church in India," he writes, "is coeval with the Spanish and Portuguese empires in the east; and though both empires are now in ruins, the Church remains. Sacred property has been respected in the different revolutions; for it is agreeable to

---

* P. 287. † P. 321.

LECTURE VII. 197

Asiatic principle to reverence religious institutions. The revenues are in general small, as is the case in Roman Catholic countries at home; but the priests live everywhere in respectable or decent circumstances. Divine service is regularly performed, and the churches generally are well attended; ecclesiastical discipline is preserved; the canonical European ceremonies are retained, and the benefactions of the people are liberal. It has been observed, that the Roman Catholics in India yield less to the luxury of the country, and suffer less from the climate, than the English; owing, it may be supposed, to their youth being surrounded by the same religious establishments they had at home, and to their being subject to the observation and counsel of religious characters, whom they are taught to reverence. Besides the regular churches, there are numerous Romish missions established throughout Asia. But the zeal of conversion has not been much known during the last century: the missionaries are now generally stationary; respected by the natives for their learning and medical knowledge, and in general for their pure manners, they ensure to themselves a comfortable subsistence, and are enabled to show hospitality to strangers. On a general view of the Roman Catholic Church, we must certainly acknowledge, that besides its principal design, in preserving the faith of its own members, it possesses a civilizing influence in Asia; and that, notwithstanding its constitutional asperity, intolerant and repulsive compared with the general principles of the Protestant religion, it has dispelled much of the darkness of paganism."*

Here we have a twofold acknowledgment:—in the first place, of the high character of the Catholic religion in India; its regularity, its morality, and the respect which it obtains; and, at the same time, of its having been effectual in dispelling the errors of paganism. And this much may, I think, suffice, regarding the character of the Catholics in India.

It appears, then, by comparing the acknowledgments which we have drawn from Protestant missionaries, with the official returns made to the British Parliament, and with the accounts of Catholic missionaries, whose statements no one has ever called in question, that we have at present native churches in India consisting of about 600,000 individuals, or considerably over half a million; and this taking it at the estimate of persons rather inclined to depreciate than to exaggerate their numbers.

---

* Memoirs, p. 12.

LECTURE VII.

Perhaps it may be a matter of interest only to mention, that a large portion of the Catholics on the coast of Malabar consist of Syrian Christians. When the Portuguese arrived there, they found a Church of Christians, who knew nothing of any other civilized community, but were in communion with, and under the authority of, the Nestorian Patriarch at Mosul; and we have the letter which they wrote to him, giving a description of the ships which arrived, and the strangers who had landed on their coast; and expressing their satisfaction at finding that they agreed with them in every point of doctrine. In course of time, conferences were held, and the differences peculiar to their sect discussed; and the consequence was, that one-half of these Churches, who may now be about 30 or 50,000, became Catholics, and have remained so ever since; having their own bishops and priests; using the Syriac, which is now a dead language, in their liturgy; and thus forming a body united with us in communion, like the united Greek and Syriac Churches in western Asia.

There is a singular mistake, for I wish to call it such, in one of the missionary reports, where this passage occurs:—"The number of these Protestant Christians (on the Malabar coast) is 60,000, and their churches amount to fifty-five."* Now, would you have believed that these 60,000 are those Nestorian Christians who have not joined the Catholics; men who believe in transubstantiation, practise confession, hold seven sacraments, pray to saints and angels, venerate images, and who, in short, believe every Catholic doctrine, except the supremacy of the Holy See, and the existence of only one Person in Christ; and who differ from the Protestant confession of faith on all these points? And are they to be considered as Protestants, and be returned in the reports as such, to the amount of 60,000, although no attempt has yet succeeded in gaining over one of them from their original belief.

But a remark has been sometimes made in missionary reports, that it is not at all wonderful that the Catholic Church should have succeeded so well in India, for this reason, that it had an establishment settled and provided for it by the Spanish and Portuguese government; so that when their dominions passed away, the Church continued to stand upon the foundation which they had given it. Hence the permanency of a native Church in India. I could read you a passage from Bishop Heber, in

---

* Christian Remembrancer, vol. vii. p. 643.

which he contrasts what the Catholics did with what the English have done since they possessed the country, and observes with what liberality the former built places of worship; while, if the English lost the dominion of India to-morrow, what very poor monuments they would leave to show that a Christian nation had therein held rule.*

But, first, the object of my comparison between the missionary success of the two Churches, is to discover which system is blessed by God's promise being fulfilled in it. The acknowledgment that the Catholic Church has been maintained in India, is a confession that we have been able to make converts and to found a Church. This is the point at issue; and the confession, that we have had the prudence to preserve it, is no disparagement of our prowess in making the spiritual conquest.

Secondly, I will enter into some details, respecting a portion of the Indian Church,—that in the island of Ceylon,—to show you how far this reasoning is correct; and I think it presents a case which will put the two groundworks of faith on a fair comparison. This island was first converted to Christianity in the following way. The natives, having heard of what was doing by St. Francis Xavier on the continent, sent a messenger, or rather an embassy, to him, requesting him to come among them. He replied that he could not go in person at that moment, as he could not abandon the mission at Travancore, but sent another missionary, who baptized many natives:—after two years, St. Francis landed there in person, and finished the work of conversion. Persecution soon arose; the king of Jaffnapatam put six hundred Christians to death in one year, and, among them, his own eldest son; so that this Church may be said to have been watered by the blood of martyrs.

In 1650, the Dutch became masters of the island; and instantly took two very important steps. The first was, as Dr. Davies tells us in his travels, to allow Wimaladarme, son of Raja Singhe, to send messengers to Siam for twelve Buddhist idolatrous priests of the highest order. These came to Candy, and ordained twelve natives to the same order, and many to the lower order; and thus they restored the religion of Buddha, for the purpose of extirpating Catholicity from the island.† In the second place, they excluded Catholic Bishops and Priests from the country, and forbade the natives to meet for religious purposes; they built Protestant Churches in every parish throughout

---

*Tom. iii. p. 91.   † Travels in Ceylon, p. 308.

the island, and compelled every one to attend that worship; and they allowed no one to hold any post or office, unless he subscribed the Protestant profession of faith.

Here, then, we have a Church established for less than a century, which yet had obtained a strong footing in the island. After this we have another religion introduced, and every thing done to counteract and destroy what had been effected in favor of the other, by a double method; first by giving those who were so inclined permission to return to their old superstitions, and affording these protection and means of propagation; and secondly, by proscription, and by endeavoring to substitute in its stead the Protestant religion. For 150 years, till it came into the possession of the English, the island of Ceylon remained in this state. During all this time, the native Catholics had no spiritual succour but what they received from the Portuguese priests, of the order of St. Philip Neri, who landed there from time to time at the risk of their lives, and administered the sacraments privately, going from house to house. We have an interesting account, given by the missionary D. Pedro Cubero Sebastian, how, during the time of this persecution, he landed there, and, disguising his character, applied to the governor Pavellon for leave to remain some time in the town of Colombo. Leave was given him, on condition that a guard of soldiers should constantly accompany him; as he was suspected. He contrived, however, to elude their vigilance; and, having lulled the attention of his guards, in the middle of the night, assembled the whole Christian community of the place, and administered to them the comforts of religion. The transaction was discovered; he was immediately sent for by the governor, and ordered instantly to quit the island. He did so, and landed on the other side; but found that, in the mean time, a courier had arrived over land, to put the governor of that district, Hoblaut, on his guard. A still more severe guardianship was the result; but, in the middle of the night, he again assembled the Christians, and administered the sacraments.*

These attempts, however, were not always so successful; for we learn that while Father Joseph Vaz, a zealous Portuguese missionary, of the order of Oratorians, was celebrating mass on Christmas night, for a congregation of 200 persons, they were suddenly surprised by guards, who broke in the door, and car-

---

* Peregrinacion del mundo del doctor D. Pedro Cubero Sebastian, predicador apos tolico. En Naples, 1682, p. 277.

LECTURE VII.

ried the entire congregation, men, women, and children, to prison. They were very cruelly treated, and next morning brought before the Dutch judge, Van Rheede; who dismissed the women, and imposed fines on the men. Eight of these, however, were reserved a severer doom; of whom one, a recent convert from Protestantism, was put to death with studied cruelty; the other seven were condemned, after a severe scourging, to irons and hard labor for life.*

Such were the means resorted to to put down the Church which had been established by St. Francis in that island; and this course was continued for 150 years, until the British took possession of it in 1795. Indeed, the laws which proscribed the Catholic religion were not repealed till 1806, when Sir Alexander Johnston, to whom the Catholics of that part of the world owe more than they can repay, obtained equality for all religions, and, consequently, the free exercise of ours.

And what do you think has been the consequence of this step? Hear how Dr. Buchanan speaks on the subject. "In the island of Ceylon, in which, by calculation made in 1801, there were 342,000 Protestants,—it is a well-known fact that more than 50,000 have gone over to the Catholic religion, from want of teachers in their own religion." So that, within a few years after liberty was restored, more than 50,000 have returned to the faith originally planted there, and afterwards crushed by persecution.† "The ancient Protestant Churches," he further observes, "some of which are spacious buildings, and which, in the province of Jaffnapatam alone, amount to thirty-two, are now occupied at will by the Catholic priests of the order of St. Philip Neri, who have taken quiet possession of the island. If a remedy be not speedily applied, we may calculate that, in a few years, the island of Ceylon will be in the same situation as Ireland, as to the proportion between Catholics and Protestants. I must further add, however painful the reflection may be, that the defection to idolatry, in many districts, is very rapid."‡

Such are the results of an attempt to establish the Protestant religion, by building and endowing Churches, and by doing precisely all that the Catholics did in the Peninsula of India. See

---

* See the life of Father Vaz, by F. Sebastian Dorego.

† The British Critic, Jan. 1828, p. 215, observes, that "the Dutch effected a *nominal* conversion in Ceylon." As to Dr. B.'s complaint of want of sufficient teachers in the Protestant religion, there are many more than kept up the Catholic faith through 150 years of persecution, and even as many as there are Catholic clergy there at present.

‡ Memoir, Dedication to the 4th ed. p. 3.

what has been the event; that whereas there were 340,000 Protestants in this neighboring island, the moment the pressure of the law was taken off, 50,000 returned to the Catholic faith, and a great many of the rest went back to their old idolatry! But you shall hear some other authorities on this subject. Bishop Heber visited also this part of his diocese, and while there, he says, "those who are still heathen are professedly worshippers of Buddha, but by far the greater part reverence nothing except the devil, to whom they offer sacrifices at night, that he may do them no harm.* Many of the nominal Christians are infected with the same superstition, and are therefore not acknowledged by our missionaries; otherwise, instead of 300 to be confirmed, I might have had several thousand candidates."† Mrs. Heber, by whom this narrative is continued, says, "the number of Christians on the coast, and in our settlements, do not fall short of half a million; very many of these undoubtedly are only nominally such, who have no objection to attend our church, and even would, if they were allowed, partake without scruple in her rites; and then, perhaps, the same evening offer a propitiatory sacrifice to the devil! Still the number of real Christians is very considerable; the congregations in the native churches are good, and the numbers who came for confirmation (none were, of course, admitted of whose fitness their ministers were not well convinced) was extremely gratifying; I think the bishop confirmed above 300." She then says, "after service, his lordship took a view of the Mission Church, and expressed his regret at the decayed state it was in, and the distress of the mission."‡

The Missionary Register observes, that "We cannot question that the Protestant congregations were as numerous as Baldeus has described them; for the ruins of a large edifice in every parish show how much was done to root up idolatry and introduce a new religion. "There are here," it adds, "many poor Protestant natives, but for the most part they have relapsed into heathenism." And another letter says that "the pagans, Mohammedans, *and Catholics are bigoted in their respective systems*, but that the Protestants, in general, are perfectly indifferent to the religion of Christ."§

---

* This is literally true; as, besides Buddhism, there exists in Ceylon a real demonology, or worship of evil beings, known by the name of *Capuism* from *Capua*, enchantment. This is described by Upham, in his history of Buddhism. See also the translation of the Yakkun Nattannawa, by Mr. Callaway, published by the Oriental Translation Committee. Lond. 1829.

† Tom. iii. p. 400.   ‡ Ib. p. 194.   § Twentieth Rep. pp. 353, 354.

Here are the results of precisely similar foundations: when laid by the Catholic Church in India, the people remained attached to that religion after the empire and dominion of the Catholics had passed away. In another case, where the same provision had been made for the Protestant Church, the moment their dominion was ended, a large portion of the people became Catholics, and a great many relapsed into their ancient idolatry.

Pursuing this matter a little farther, the returns which we have regarding the increase of Catholicity there have continued to be of the most consoling character. By official returns presented to the government, we learn that, in 1806, the number of Catholics was 66,830; by 1809, there had been an increase from 66,000 to 83,595. In 1820, the return was 130,000; and on the 16th August, 1826, the vicar-general stated the number to be 150,060; so that from 1806 to 1826, a period of twenty years, we have an increase from 66,000 to 150,000. This, assuredly, shows that religion gains ground, and makes its way without the protection of government, or any provision being made in its favor. For, although there are 250 churches in the island, there were only twenty-six priests in 1826; and it is most delightful to read the accounts of the manner in which their system is conducted. In each parish there is a catechist, who instructs the people, and reads prayers and religious discourses to them on the Sunday; and the clergy, who have all particular districts allotted to them, come at stated periods, and find all prepared to receive those consolations which the Catholic religion affords to its members.

I have had the satisfaction of seeing a later return, which gives a very full and detailed account of the state of religion in that island, drawn up by order of the present governor, Sir Wilmot Horton. In it every chapel and school is exactly laid down, with the number of attendants at each. It proves a continued and progressive increase; while, still, the same zeal and good order are observable throughout. Since I came to this country I have learnt, with sincere pleasure, that a Bishop has been appointed to that island, which has been made an apostolic vicariate; so that now provision is made for keeping up the succession of pastors there. Had I been aware that I should have been called on to treat of these subjects, I would have procured far more interesting documents than are now within my reach: at present, I can only make use of such as most easily come to hand. But to show that the conversions in this island are not merely nominal, I will read you the testimony borne to the character of the Catholics by Sir Alex. Johnston, when Chief Justice of the island. In 1807, he thus addressed the Archbishop of Goa. "The propriety of their (the Catholics') conduct reflects great honor upon the priests of the order of St. Philip Neri, who have the charge of their instruction. In a circuit which I lately made round the island, I was much pleased to find, that there was not a single Catholic brought before me for trial." Again, on another occasion, he repeats the same observation:— "The records of the circuit which the supreme court made round the island in 1806, show that not a single individual of your religion was even accused of the smallest misdemeanor during that circuit." There is another passage, in which he speaks of the example given to the whole of the East, by the zeal with which the clergy had made arrangements for the education of their flocks, and the liberality with which they had provided for it; so as to prove how they considered that a Christian ought to be distinguished beyond others, by his intelligence and superior education. I think, indeed, that it would be difficult to find a history of any Church more consoling, or more truly proving the blessing of God to be on it, and on the labours of those who watch over its care, than the history of this island.*

So far, I have been engaged on those countries in which other religions have also missionaries; and I have been able, consequently, to take these, in some respects, if not as guides, at least as guarantees for my assertions; and this circumstance affords a fair ground of comparison between what we have effected, and what they have been able to do. We must now proceed into countries where the Protestant religion has not been able to penetrate, or where, if it has attempted any thing, its labors have been perfectly without fruit. Let us begin with China, in which the mission was begun in 1583, or rather even later, when the Jesuits were admitted into court, and were allowed to preach the Catholic religion and build churches.

Before proceeding, however, I will give you the character of these missionaries, as drawn by one most intimately acquainted with China and its history. "They all happened to belong to different religious societies of the Roman Catholic persuasion, founded in different parts of the Continent of Europe; and were men who, being inspired with zeal for the propagation of the principles of their faith among distant nations, had been sent

---

* The details here given of the progress of religion in this island are chiefly taken from an interesting article in the Catholic Miscellany, vol. vii. p. 273.

abroad for that purpose by their respective superiors. Several of those who arrived in China acquired considerable wealth and influence, as well by their talents and knowledge, as by uncommon strictness of morals, disinterestedness, and humility. By means like these, they not only gained proselytes to their religion, but gave a favorable impression of the countries whence they came."*

Again, the same writer says:—"It must have appeared a singular spectacle to every class of beholders, to see men actuated by motives different from those of most human actions; quitting for ever their country and their connections to devote themselves for life to the purpose of changing the tenets of a people they had never seen, and, in pursuing that object, to run every risk, suffer every persecution, and sacrifice every comfort; insinuating themselves by address, by talent, by perseverance, by humility, into notice and protection; overcoming the prejudice of being strangers in a country where most strangers were prohibited; and gaining, at length, establishments for the propagation of their faith, without turning their influence to any personal advantage."†

But to return: within a few years after the Church was established, a partial persecution arose, which ended in the martyrdom of several missionaries, both foreign and native. Notwithstanding this, the Church there continued extremely prosperous, until the beginning of the last century, when persecution came in its fiercest form, and has continued unremittingly until the present day. Hence, every bishop and priest engaged on that mission is working with the axe suspended over his head, and in constant danger, not merely of banishment into Tartary, but even, under many circumstances, of certain death.

This is the state of the Chinese mission at present, and I have Protestant authority for what I have stated; for a missionary observes that "the Catholic missions, which have existed for a long time in China, are in a very critical state; because every now and then decrees are issued against the European religion, and both Chinese and Europeans suffer martyrdom: and that, notwithstanding all this, the Catholic religion is said to spread in the midst of these persecutions."‡

Is not this the history of the ancient Church? is it not what

---

* Authentic Account of an Embassy from the King of Great Britain to the Emperor of China, by Sir G. Staunton, Lond., 1797, vol. i. p. 3.
† Vcl. ii. p. 160.   ‡ Mission. Reg. ut sup. p. 43.

we have always read of former times, that persecution arose against the infant Church, and that Christians were called to lay down their lives for the faith? but that, instead of religion being thereby extinguished, it rather increased and flourished the more?

Such is the state of the Christian Church in China, which, notwithstanding, is acknowledged to be comparatively flourishing. One of the most important and interesting missions of this empire is the province of Su-Chuen, which is under the direction of a French Bishop, assisted by a large body of clergy, European and native. It is interesting from the frightful state of persecution under which it has labored within this century, and from the firmness with which religion has withstood and overcome its fierce assaults. In 1814, the persecution commenced, and was soon distinguished by the glorious martyrdom of Dr. Dufresne, Bishop of Tabraca and Vicar Apostolic of the province. He behaved in a manner worthy of the ancient confessors of the faith, and bowed his head to the executioner's axe with a meek fortitude which drew cries of sympathy from the heathen beholders. The striking of the shepherd produced not the dispersion of the flock, but they followed him cheerfully on his thorny path. Many of the clergy were strangled, and many sent to banishment in Tartary, where they still remain. The tortures inflicted on some of the catechists vie in cruelty with those of Dioclesian's persecution.* Of two, it is recorded that they were first scourged with thongs, then beaten with sticks; after that were kept kneeling three days and nights on chains, being prevented from even varying their position; then were hung up by the thumbs and again whipped; and after being laid all night in the stocks, had their legs crushed between rollers. The mother of one native priest allowed herself to be scourged to death, rather than betray where her son was concealed.† The seminary

---

* From the want of a sufficient number of priests, lay catechists are employed, as in Ceylon, to instruct the people, and are of two classes. The resident are married men or widowers, chosen from the best instructed, to preside at Church in the absence of a priest, and baptize infants in danger of death. The itinerants are bound to celibacy so long as they continue in the office, and accompany the clergy.

† I cannot refrain from quoting an extract of a letter, from M. Magdinier to a friend at Lyons. It is written from the Chinese College, in Pulo Pinang, an island in the straits of Malacca.

"I am quite delighted with being at this dear Seminary. All the students seem to burn with the love of God, and will doubtless hereafter become good and zealous missionaries, as well as confessors and martyrs. Although naturally timid, they have no dread of martyrdom. The relations of several of them have confessed and died for the faith. The father of one is now carrying the cangs, and the son, I assure you, is a little saint worthy of such a father."

for ecclesiastical education was laid in ashes, and the inmates had barely time to escape with their lives.

In September, 1820, the Emperor Kia-King died, and though his son was not more favorable to the Christians, circumstances led to a relaxation in the execution of the penal laws; the Church, ever unchecked in her errand of grace by the opposition of the world, had already provided for the vacant see, by the appointment of Mgr. Fontana, to be Vicar Apostolic, and Mgr. Perocheau to be his coadjutor; and in 1822 the ravages of the persecution began to be repaired. In two months of that year 254 adults received baptism, and 259 were admitted to instruction. In the following year, a change in the viceroyalty produced a return of the persecution, which only gave occasion for fresh displays of primitive fortitude.*

Mgr. Fontana, in a letter, dated 22d September, 1824, gives the following returns:—From the preceding September there had been 335 adults baptized, and 1547 were under preparation. The total number of Catholics was 46,487.† In another, dated 18th Sept., 1826, he gives the number of baptized adults as 339, and of those under instruction, as 285. He farther informs us, that in his district or diocese he had twenty-seven schools for boys, and sixty-two for girls.‡ And it has been calculated, that,

---

"One day, that I was walking with my dear seminarists, I began to question them concerning the persecutions, when I learnt that a youth, whose angelic appearance had often attracted my particular notice, had lately had ten near relations suffering for the faith. Two of these have since died in prison; six have been banished to Tartary, and his father and another are actually wearing the canga. These particulars he related in the presence of his companions with inconceivable simplicity, and he has since told me in private, that he was quite overjoyed when the above intelligence was sent to him."

This island belongs to the English, and consequently has been visited by missionaries from different societies. A free orphan school has been established by some Anglican society, and another, with a church, has been opened by the Baptists. They have distributed Bibles in abundance, but we learn that not a single convert have they made, while the native Catholics amounted some years ago to 500; the faith having been preached there by some Chinese who fled from the persecution in their own country. M. Boucho assures us that the Protestant clergyman was obliged to send for him to baptize a dying slave of his, who refused to receive that sacrament from her master, because he was not a Catholic, but an *Orang-pote*, or Englishman.—Annales, No. xv. p. 241. He also informs us, how, when a Methodist missionary had collected, with some pains and cost, an audience of seven persons, a catechist went among them, and, after a little reasoning, brought them to the Catholic College, where they were admitted as catechumens.—No. xx. April, 1830, p. 213.

* This narrative has been, in a great measure, taken from a condensed view of the reports in the Annales, published in the Catholic Magazine for 1833.

† Annales, No. xi. Aug. 1827, p. 257. In 1767, the number of Catholics was under 7000.

‡ Ibid. p. 269.

between 1800 and 1817, the number of adults admitted to baptism was 22,000.*

Besides this mission of Su-Chuen, there are French missions in two other provinces, Yunnam and Kouei-Tcheou; the Italian Franciscans have the provinces of Chensi, Kansiu, and Kaukouan; the Spanish Dominicans, those of Fokien and Kiansi; and the Portuguese, Canton and Kouansi. According to returns, published by the Dominician order, at Rome, in 1824, it appears that in their province alone there were 40,000 native Catholics.

Besides China, there is another empire in the farthest east, in which the preachers and professors of Christianity are called upon to give testimony to their faith through bonds, and even unto death, and which, consequently, is exclusively in the hands of Catholics. I allude to the united empire of Tonkin and Cochin-China. And first, I must premise that the mission of Tonkin is divided into two portions, the eastern, which is under the direction of the Spanish Dominicans, with an Apostolic Vicar or Bishop of that order, and the western, which is governed by a French Bishop, aided by a few priests of his own nation and upwards of eighty native clergy.

Now, in the first, or Spanish district of the mission, there were, in 1827, not fewer than 780 churches, eighty-seven monasteries or nunneries, and 170,000 native Catholics.† In the French district, we have up to that period, returns no less satisfactory, as will appear from the following comparative table for the years

	1824.‡	1826.§	1827.∥
Public Baptism of children of Christians	2434	8236	2050
Private ditto	No return	5375	6439
Total Baptism		8611	8489
Faithful confessed	165,064	177,456	165,943
Communicants	75,467	78,692	81,070

The entire number of Christians was estimated at 200,000, for the persecution, of which I will say something presently, prevented many parts from being visited. This district possesses also an ecclesiastical seminary, in which are, or rather were, 200 students, two colleges, and several monastic establishments, in which 700 religious lived.¶

---

* Annales, No. xiii. p. 5.
† "Piano che rappresenta il numero delle anime che la provincia del SSm. Rosario del' ordine de' Predicatori tiene a carico suo."
‡ Annales, No. x. April, 1817, p. 195.   § No. xvii. May, 1829, p. 443.
∥ No. xxi. July, 1830, p. 319.   ¶ No. x. p. 194.

The province of Cochin-China presents a no less flourishing appearance; though I cannot give you such a minute account of its condition. Suffice it to say, that in 1826, in spite of the cruel persecution, 106 converts were received, and baptism was administered to 2,955 infants, which, according to the ordinary method of calculation, would give about 88,650 native Christians.

I will now proceed to give you a few slight details of the persecution in that country. The emperor Minh-Menh has always been hostile to the Christians, but for many years had abstained from shedding their blood, in consequence, it is said, of a promise which he had made to his dying father, Gia-long, whose throne and life had been saved by Mgr. Pigneau, the vicar apostolic Still he has for many years persecuted the Catholics, by every means short of taking away their lives. As early as 1825, the clergy were dispersed, for there was an order that all the foreign missionaries should be sent to the capital, under excuse that the emperor wanted their services, and that all native priests and catechists should be pressed into the army. An interesting account of this first stage of the persecution, in a letter from the bishop, appeared at Madrid in 1826.* A still fuller account was sent by the same venerable prelate to the congregation of the Propaganda at Rome, which I had the happiness of seeing. From this it appeared that he had been living for upwards of a year,

---

* "Cartas; la una del Illmo y Rmo Señor D. Fr. Ign. Delgado, vic. ap. en al Tunkin, y la otra del coadjutor de dicho Señor Obispo, ambas relativas a la persecucion que contra la religion Cristiana acaba de estallar en los Reinos de Cochinchina y Tunkin." Nothing can be more beautiful than the truly heroic spirit displayed in these letters. [In the year 1838, this venerable bishop, 76 years of age, after 40 years of an arduous episcopacy, as well as bishop Dominick. Henares, for 38 years his coadjutor, and then in his 73d year, was arrested and imprisoned. The coadjutor was beheaded; but the venerable vicar apostolic died in his cage, of hardship and cruel infliction, the night before the day fixed for his execution. His dead body was beheaded, and the head cast into the river. Both heads were recovered by the same Christian fisherman, entire, after long immersion in the river in a tropical climate; the bishop's after four months. On the 19th of June, 1840, the Pope derogated from the length of time regularly appointed to elapse before a process of beatification and canonization can be introduced, and gave permission for the introduction of the cause of these two bishops, and the other martyrs mentioned in this Lecture, and of many more omitted in it, and bestowed upon them the preliminary title of venerable servants of God. By the death of Bishop Delgado, the title which he occupied *in partibus infidelium* as bishop of Melipotamus became vacant; and the writer having, a few days before the cited decree, been named coadjutor bishop in England, petitioned for, and obtained, the reversion of the title, not that he deemed himself worthy to succeed to so glorious a martyr, but that he hoped to have thus, in the last martyr bishop who had glorified the Church, a patron and a model, one in whose intercession and example he might humbly hope to possess a personal interest.]

LECTURE VII.

if I remember right, in a cavern, with no light but what was admitted through a natural opening, and with no food except what could be supplied by the few who knew his place of concealment. Here he continued to govern his diocese, chiefly through the agency of his native clergy, who, full of holy zeal, were ready to encounter any danger in the cause of religion. On Holy Thursday, at midnight, he had crept out of his lurking-place to his residence, which he found plundered and dismantled; and having there met by appointment a sufficient number of his native clergy, blessed the holy oils which are used in the administration of several sacraments. Throughout these letters, it is at once consoling and edifying to see the spirit of resignation and cheerfulness with which every hardship is endured, and every suffering deemed honorable, because undergone for the name of Christ.

But things have not remained in this situation. Minh-Menh at length broke through all reserve, and, on the 6th of January, 1833, issued a decree of extermination against our holy religion. It begins thus: "I Minh-Menh, the king, speak as follows. It is many years since men come from the east, to preach the religion of Jesus, and deceive the vulgar by preaching to them that there is a place of supreme happiness and a dungeon of frightful misery; they have no respect for the god Phat, and worship not their ancestors, which are truly great crimes against religion.[*] We therefore enact, that all who follow this religion, from the mandarin to the lowest of the people, sincerely abandon it. We enjoin that all mandarins diligently make inquiry whether the Christians in their respective districts prepare to obey our orders, and that they oblige them to trample on the cross in their presence, upon doing which they shall dismiss them. The houses of worship and the priests' dwellings the mandarins shall take care utterly to destroy; for, from henceforth, whoever is convicted or accused of these abominable practices, shall be punished with extreme rigor, so that this religion may be destroyed to its very last roots. And these our commands we wish to be strictly observed."

Upon the publication of this edict, the Christians prepared themselves for the combat, and quietly took down their wooden churches and other sacred buildings, which disappeared as if by

---

[*] Here follow several abominable accusations against the Christian religion, similar to those formerly invented by the pagans against the early Christians. One is that the priests pluck out the eye-balls of the dying, alluding to the anointing of the eyes in administering extreme unction.

LECTURE VII.   211

magic. The priests were obliged to conceal themselves in the meanest huts, to afford the consolations of religion to their timid and scattered flocks; and yet their letters breathe a sweet spirit of joy and self-devotion worthy of the early ages. The country is traversed by bands of soldiers, searching for new victims, the false brother and the apostate betray their friends, and the poor Christians have been wandering among rocks and forests, or have emigrated from their country, not knowing whither they were flying. Four hundred churches have been destroyed, innumerable believers of every age and every sex have confessed the name of Christ in prison and tortures, and not a few have sealed their faith with their blood.

In Tonkin, the most distinguished of these martyrs, in 1833, was a native priest, Peter Tuy, venerable for his age and virtues. When brought before the judges, a lie would have saved him, but he persisted in acknowledging himself a priest. On being condemned, he only declared that he never could have believed himself worthy of such a grace; and, after supping cheerfully, and spending the night in prayer, he walked with an alacrity which astonished the beholders to the place of execution, where he prayed for a few moments prostrate on the ground, and then presented his neck to the sword. His execution was the signal for new vigor, and many who had been set at liberty were arrested again, and shut up in prison, with the canga, or frightful Chinese collar, on their necks. Among them were women, and even children. I must pass over the afflicting yet consoling details of particular cases, as well as the beautiful letters written by the sufferers themselves, and mention one or two particulars of the persecution in Cochin-China.

This province, being the residence of the cruel emperor, has been the scene of more atrocious barbarities. Two martyrs have here more particularly distinguished themselves; the one, a European, the other a native. The former was the Abbé Gagelin, a priest of the diocese of Besançon. He was in prison, when, on the 12th of October, 1833, his friend and brother martyr, M. Jaccard, informed him of his impending death by the following note:—"I think it my duty to inform you, my happy brother, that you have been condemned to death, for having preached in different provinces. I am sure, that, if God grant you the grace of martyrdom, which you have come so far to seek, you will not forget those whom you leave behind." The blessed confessor could not believe the tidings, as being too good for his deserts; and replied, that he believed he was only condemned to exile.

Upon M. Jaccard's assuring him that his death was irrevocably decided on, he thus replied: "The news which you communicate penetrates with gladness the very centre of my heart. Never did I before experience such joy. 'I have rejoiced in the things which have been said to me, we will go into the house of the Lord.' The grace of martyrdom, of which I am every way unworthy, has been the object of my most ardent desires since my infancy; I have especially prayed for it every time that I have elevated the precious blood of Christ in the holy sacrifice of the mass. I quit a world in which I have nothing to regret; the sight of my dear Jesus crucified consoles me, and robs death of all its bitterness. All my ambition is to go out speedily from this body of sin, to be united to Christ Jesus in a happy eternity."

On the 17th of the same month, this holy priest was conducted from his prison to the place of execution, surrounded with a terrible array of troops, with their swords drawn, while before him went a herald bearing a board, on which it was recorded that he was condemned to be strangled, for having preached the religion of Jesus. This sentence was soon executed upon him, and his body was ransomed by the Christians from the guard. The king's vengeance, however, pursued him to the grave, and he ordered his place of burial to be discovered, and the body kept for some time uninterred.

The representative of the natives, and of the lay order, in this glorious conflict, was Paul Doi-Buong, captain of the royal guards. He had been already a year in prison, with six soldiers of his troop, who bore with equal fortitude with himself the horrors of imprisonment as suffered in that country, as well as many supernumerary tortures inflicted on them. Soon after the martyrdom of M. Gagelin, the king ordered him to be beheaded on the site of a ruined church, and left unburied for three days. He walked cheerfully to execution, though it was a difficult and long journey, and only asked permission to suffer on the ruins of the altar; where, having prostrated himself for a few moments in prayer, he meekly raised his head and received the glorious stroke.*

Allow me, my Catholic brethren, to ask you, if you feel not a just pride in these new testimonies to the evidences of your faith? Is it not a consolation to you to feel how, even in this eleventh hour, its radiancy and power are as strong as ever, and can

---

* I am indebted for this account of the persecution to the "Annales," or rather to an extract of them, published at Lyons in a separate form, as I cannot find access to the original work in this country.

instil into the souls of the timid and weak the heroism of an apostolic age? For, while I was recounting this touching history of a distant land, were you not inclined to imagine that time, rather than space, separated you from these glorious sufferers, and that I was but repeating the well-known history of Diocletian's cruelties? But let me also ask, if, in this, there be no sting of self-reproach? if our lukewarmness, while our fellow-members were thus suffering every extremity, nay, if our very ignorance of what was befalling them, is not a subject of just reproof? For, if the sympathy of a common body require that the most separated members should mutually feel each other's griefs, if, in former ages, when communication between country and country was more difficult, the rumor of a distant persecution, wherein the Church was glorified by new proofs of constancy, thrilled throughout its body with a holy emotion, and touching the harmonious cords which bind it together, raised a universal note of encouraging sympathy, which seemed to re-echo from the Church to heaven; is it not cruel to think how little we have partaken in spirit, in these great things, how little we have known of the contemporary yet painful triumphs of our religion?

How seldom do we speak of the natives of those distant countries, except as of barbarous tribes, with whom we have no common feeling! and yet are there among them not only many dear brethren in Christ Jesus, but venerable martyrs, the latchet of whose shoes we are not worthy to untie, the true inheritors of God's brightest promises, the surest pride and glory of our religion! How often have we chid the cold and faint-hearted spirit of our age's faith, while it was burning clear and potent in the breast of the Eastern missionary, and of the Chinese maiden; while angels, turning, perhaps, aside from our indifference, were looking down, as on a spectacle worthy of their gaze, upon the deserts of Tartary, or the noisome dungeons of Tonkin!*

But I trust that this reproach will not last longer, and that our sympathies and prayers, and, if needful, our more substantial aid, will be cheerfully impended upon our afflicted brethren.

And, to return from this painful digression, we may fairly challenge other religions to produce a parallel to what I have laid before you. Let them show us, among their missionaries,

---

* Still more splendid martyrdoms have occurred, since these lectures were delivered, for the account of which the reader is referred to the *Annals* now published in English, a work which will fully repay a regular perusal.

men who, instead of going with their wives in litters round countries where their persons are secure, and distributing Bibles,* fearlessly penetrate where they know that bonds and torments await them, and water with their blood the harvest which they sow. Let them show us thousands of Christians, converted by them, who lose all rather than renounce their faith; and who are ready to endure stripes, and imprisonment, and even death, for the name of Christ.† Nor are these the only instances which we can produce. About four years ago, the vicar-apostolic ot Siam, Mgr. Florens, sent MM. Vallon and Bérard on a mission to Pulo-Nias, an island to the west of Sumatra. The first soon died, but after having made many converts; the second was stabbed to the heart, by a heathen, while in the act of administering baptism to some converts, and was, I believe, followed in his martyrdom by all or most of his new Christians.

Some years ago, a publication in this country stated that the Catholic religion depended for its stability upon its outward establishment, while the conversions made by the Bible were necessarily lasting and indelible.‡ But surely the examples which I have given of our conversions standing the trial of blood must amply confute this bold assertion. And, if it be thought that this is not so severe an ordeal as neglect and abandonment, it would be easy to prove by example that they can stand the test of even this. Ceylon is one strong instance; and I may mention the Corea, which had been for years without a missionary, and yet continued steadfast, and annually entreated for assistance, until one was supplied. In addition, a letter was received here

---

* Such is the account given us of the Methodist missionary at Pulo-Pinang, in a letter dated 5th March, 1829. Annals, No. xx. p. 213.

† It seems, however, that an attempt is about to be made to preach the Protestant religion in China. Drs. Reid and Matheson give us an account of the resolution carried by the Episcopal Church of New York, "that something should be done for China." Shortly after, they write that the ordination of Mr. Parker, as missionary to China, had taken place.—The Catholic missions, with their glorious martyrdoms are, of course, counted as nothing.—"A narrative of the visit to the American Churches." *Lond.* 1836, vol. i. p. 56.

‡ Quarterly Review, No. lxiii. p. 3. The illustrations which the critic adduces are an admirable specimen of controversial logic. To demonstrate the permanency of Biblical conversion, he gives the example of *one* old woman, who, having received a Bible when young, at the Cape of Good Hope, was found to have retained and read it all her life, and sought out the missionaries after many years! The instability of Catholic conversion is proved by the state of Paraguay, since the suppression of the Jesuits. Now, Paraguay is Catholic still, although the beautiful organization of its community ceased with the body which ruled it. The writer confounds the religion with the peculiar form of government to which, in this happy ins*ce*, 't gave rise.

out a short time ago from Macao, in which one is quoted from that very missionary, Yu, wherein he states the extraordinary fact that the Catholic religion still survives in Japan! And yet the last missionaries who were able to land on that island were five Jesuits, who, in 1642, arrived there only to suffer martyrdom; and the Catholic religion was supposed to have been rooted up by the sword. For that Church, too, has had its martyrs.*

Not far from these countries are the Philippine islands, in which M. Dubois estimates the number of Catholics under the direction of the Spanish Dominicans at two millions. Perhaps this may be considered by some too large a return; I will, therefore, read a passage from a learned work, by Dr. Prichard, which has, indeed, no connection with our subject, but wherein he incidentally mentions our missions in those islands as follows: —"A great number of missionaries have been sent out to the Philippine islands. The first attempt was made by the Augustines in 1565, and an emigration of ecclesiastics of various orders continued during the succeeding years. The several orders divided their spiritual provinces among them, and exerted themselves with the greatest assiduity, in spreading among the pagans and savages of these islands, the population of which has been stated at three millions of persons, the blessings of the Catholic faith. They soon rendered themselves familiar with the several languages of the people among whom they were to labor, and their labors appear to have been crowned with ample success. If we are to believe the narratives of these zealous and honest missionaries, miracles have been wrought by Heaven in their favor."† Thus does he acknowledge that our labors there have been successful; and an official report gives the number of native Christians in one province alone at 150,000.‡

There is another country, beyond the Ganges, where we have seen the efforts of Protestant missionaries fail, while those of ours have been, and still are, crowned with success. I allude to the Burmese empire, consisting of the kingdoms of Ava and Pegu. The mission of the Judsons, I showed you, on their own confession, proved a complete failure. But it is, perhaps, little known, that in the mean time a considerable community of native Catholics existed in that country. Its history is briefly this.

---

* See account of them in Butler's Saints' Lives. Feb. 5.
† "Researches into the Physical History of Mankind." 2d. ed. *Lond.* 1826, vol. l p. 455.
‡ See "Piano," etc. *ut sup.*

In 1719, Pope Clement XI. sent Mgr. Mezzabarba as his ambassador to the Emperor of China, Kan-ghi.* His mission not having ended favorably, he returned to Europe, but left the clergy of his suite in different parts of the East. Two were sent into Ava and Pegu, the Rev. Joseph Vittoni, and F. Calchi, a member of the Barnabite congregation. After some difficulties, they obtained leave to preach and erect churches. The king sent Vittoni with presents to the Pope, and F. Calchi built a church at Siriam, the capital of Ava; but, worn out by fatigue, he died in 1728, in the forty-third year of his age. The mission was now so prosperous, that soon after, Benedict XIV. appointed F. Gallizia first vicar-apostolic, or bishop, in that country; F. Nerini was, however, the great apostle of this Church. The Catholic worship was publicly exercised, processions and funerals went through the streets, with all the pomp of a European Catholic country, without giving the slightest offence. In 1745, persecution overtook the Church, the bishop and two missionaries were massacred while on an errand of peace and charity; the Christians were dispersed, and F. Nerini saved his life by flying into India. He was recalled with honor in 1749, and erected the first brick building ever seen in that country; a church eighty feet long and thirty-one wide, with a house adjoining for the clergy. One Armenian alone contributed 7000 dollars to the pious work. Many other churches and schools were erected about that time.†

The mission continued to flourish, particularly under the direction of the two Cortenovis and F. Sangermano, author of an interesting work on the history and literature of that country.‡ He returned to Europe in 1808, to implore succor for his poor flock, but his zealous and learned order, which had till now supplied them with pastors, had been suppressed, with every other

---

* A partial account of this embassy is given by Auber, in his "China." *Lond.* 1834, p. 48.

† The following is a list of the principal Catholic establishments. At Ava was a large church, destroyed when the capital was removed. By a letter from F. Amato, 'n 1822, it appears that there was still a church and house there. At Siriam, now nearly in ruins, were two churches, with houses annexed, a college containing forty boys, and an establishment for orphan girls. In the city of Pegu, a church and house. At Monlà, a church, presbytery, and college, erected in 1770. The ground on which the college was built having been claimed, another was built by Cortenovi, who had 50 boys in it. In the environs of this city, six other churches. In Subaroa, two. At Chiam-sua-rocca six, which F. Amato served in 1822. In Banjoon, a church and house, with a convent and orphan school.

‡ Description of the Burmese empire, translated from his MSS. by the Rev. Dr. Tandy, and published by the Oriental Translation Committee. *Rome*, 1833, 4to.

similar institution of charity. The entire burthen was, therefore, borne by F. Amato, whose life was just prolonged till the arrival of a new supply of zealous missionaries sent from Rome in 1830. They were barely in time to afford the venerable priest the comforts of his religion. A farther supply was sent about a year ago.*

Another very interesting mission, successfully conducted by Catholics, is that among the savages of North America. These may be divided into two districts, Canada and the United States. As to the former, the French had no sooner had possession of Lower Canada, than they turned their attention to the conversion of the natives, and their success was such as completely to effect it. A letter from the Protestant Bishop of Quebec, dated 22d April, 1829, observes of them: "In Lower Canada they *all* profess the Roman Catholic religion. In Upper Canada, those within the province and the confines of it, *who are not heathens*, are Protestants, except a few near Sandwich."† The different missionary reports confirm the existence of large Catholic communities among the native tribes.

The report of the Society for the Propagation of the Gospel, for 1824, has the following passage:—"I cannot avoid mentioning a very interesting object, which presented itself about two leagues from St. Peter's, (in Duke of Kent's Island:) the Indian chapel, so called from its being exclusively the work of Indians. It is situated upon a delightful little island, with a house for the priest; this is served with tolerable regularity. St. Peter's is altogether a Roman Catholic settlement."‡ The report for 1825 gives the following notice of another congregation. "With difficulty, owing to the badness of the roads, I got to the village of St. Regis, inhabited almost entirely by Indians. They profess the Romish faith, *in common with all the Indians of the Lower Province.*"§ Again, in the year following:—"There are eighteen thousand Roman Catholics here, (Cape Breton Island,) chiefly from the Highlands of Scotland, with many French, and *five hundred Indians.*"‖

It would be tedious to enumerate the missions existing in dif-

---

* This sketch is in a great measure drawn up from inedited materials in the archives of the Barnabite Fathers at Rome. I gave the substance of it in a note appended to Dr. Tandy's book, p. 222.
† Parliamentary Papers on the Aboriginal Tribes, Aug. 1834, p. 51.
‡ Report, &c. 1825, p. 85.
§ Report, &c. 1826, p. 117.
‖ Idem, 1827, p. 75.

ferent parts of Canada, such as the one among the Iroquois at St. Regis, which is particularly flourishing; those of Montagne to the Algonquins of Habenaqui, the Three Rivers, and Saint-Louis. But, perhaps, the most beautiful of all the Canadian missions is that of the Lake of the Two Mountains, which was founded in 1717, and continues under the direction of the order of Sulpicians. It consists of two villages, with a common church, and contains about 1200 Indians. During the winter they proceed to the north, to their hunting and fishing; and, being furnished with calendars by their pastors, observe every day appointed by the Church for fasting, and keep, with scrupulous exactness, all its festivals. Their manners are pure and simple; they all learn to read and write, and well understand the principles of their religion.

The missions of the United States suffered, perhaps, beyond any others, by the suppression of the Society of Jesus, as very considerable communities existed among the native tribes under its guidance. Much, also, they have suffered by the changes which the encroachments of the white men upon their territories have obliged them, repeatedly, to make in their abodes. Still, the recollection of their religion has never been lost; they have carefully preserved all the emblems and implements of the Catholic worship, and they have always endeavored to have their children baptized. Hence, whenever a missionary has gone among them, they have been easily regained. Indeed, I should rather say that they have themselves sought for aid, and that with such discrimination, as to show that they perfectly understood the difference between the Catholic and other teachers. A few examples will suffice.

A petition, dated August 12, 1823, was presented to the President of the United States, from the Uttawa Indians, from which the following is an extract:—" Confiding in your paternal kindness, we claim liberty of conscience, and beg of you to grant us a master or minister of the gospel belonging to the society of which were the Catholic company of St. Ignatius, formerly established at Michillimakinac, at Arbre-courbé, by F. Magnet, and by other Jesuit missionaries. Since that time, we have always desired similar ministers. If you grant us them, we will invite them to occupy the lands formerly held by F. Dujaunay, on the banks of the lake of Michigan."—Four months later, another petition was presented to Congress, by another chief of the same tribe, named Magati Pinsingo, or the Black Bird, in which he says:—" We desire to be instructed in the same principles of religion as our ancestors were, when the mission of St. Ignatius yet existed. (1765.) We shall deem ourselves happy, if it shall please you to send us a man of God of the Catholic religion."*

In 1827, a chief of the Kansas came to St. Louis, in Missouri, and, in a public assembly, requested that some one might be sent to instruct his tribe in the manner of serving the Great Spirit. A Protestant clergyman rose and tendered his services. The Indian examined him from head to foot, and then replied, smiling, that he was not the sort of man whom he wanted. He added, that every time he came to Saint Louis, he was accustomed to go to the French church, where he had seen priests without families; these were the masters whom he desired to have. On his return home, he wrote to General Clarke, entreating him not to forget sending him a Catholic priest. Some delay took place; the chief renewed his request; and, upon the pressing instances of the agent, the bishop, Dr. Rosati, appointed the Abbé Lutz, a young German clergyman, to open a mission among the Kansas.†

Thanks be to God, the latest accounts from these interesting missions are such as to fulfil our desires. From the visitation made by Bishop Rézé to the mission of Arbre-Croché in 1835, it appears that the congregation of Uttawas consisted of about twelve hundred. Six or seven churches have been lately built among them; we are assured, that so far from these good Indians being addicted, like their neighbors, to the vice of drunkenness, they do not allow a drop of any fermented liquor to come near their settlement.

At Saut-Ste-Marie the Bishop was received by the Indians with a discharge of musquetry; and during his stay there, the whole time was dedicated to exercises of devotion. More than a hundred were confirmed. At Meckinack, a hundred and twenty received confirmation; and at Green-Bay, where a splendid church has been built, and where a seminary and convent will shortly be opened, one hundred and thirty, mostly Indians, were admitted to the same sacrament. The same reports‡ give a lamentable picture of the state of the Protestant missions in the neighborhood, from the frightful prevalence of intoxication among their Indians.

---

* "Annales de l'Association pour la Propagation de la Foi." No. ix. *Paris*, 1826, pp. 102–104.
† Idem, No. xviii. 1829, pp. 550–561.
‡ Idem. No. xliv. Jan. 1836, p. 293–298.

LECTURE VII.

Fourteen years ago, the Pootewatamis, who had been left without any spiritual assistance since the removal of the Jesuits from among them, and who, consequently, preserved little more than a traditional remembrance of Christianity, applied to the governor of Michigan to send them a priest, or *robe noire*, as they describe them. A Baptist minister was sent; but they soon discovered the difference, and said that they wanted some of the priests of whom their fathers had told them so many good things. They were told that the government had nothing to do with Catholics, and that they must try the preacher who had been sent them. Violent dissensions soon rose among them; presents and strong liquors were distributed in vain, and, in a few years, thirty-three Indians had been assassinated in their feuds. In 1830, a Catholic priest was promised them by the Vicar-General of Cincinnati. Every opposition was made by the government, who refused to give up the Baptist mission; but at length the Catholics prevailed; and there is now there an edifying congregation of seven hundred natives, under the care of a Belgian priest.

M. Boraga, an Illyrian, obtained permission of the Bishop to open a new mission among the Indians on the Grand River; and, in two years, he has formed a congregation of two hundred souls.*

I must cut short these details; but I cannot omit just mentioning the Spanish missions among the natives of California, which have been no less successful.

As I have wished, throughout this lengthened discourse, to contrast, as much as possible the fruits obtained by the missionaries of different communions on the same spot; and as I, perhaps, may have appeared to speak with more than usual severity of the conduct of the American missionaries in the South Sea Islands, I will conclude my narrative with a brief account of the progress made by the Catholic religion there. I have had occasion to speak of the persecutions endured by our brethren in China, and other countries, from the hands of pagans; but here we have bonds and sufferings inflicted by Protestant missionary rulers of those unfortunate countries.

A recent traveller mentions an interview which he had with a native princess of one of those islands, wherein he asked her upon what grounds she had become a Christian. Her reply was, "Because Mr. Bingham, who can read and write so well, tells me that it is the best religion; and because I see the English and Americans, who are Christians, are superior to us;" but, she

---

* Ibid. p. 303.

added, that it was only an experiment; and if it did not answer, they would return to their old worship.*

To these countries, in the year 1826, three Catholic missionaries were sent, and commenced their work by opening an oratory, in which there was a representation of our blessed Saviour crucified. The natives naturally came and asked what this signified, and the missionaries took occasion to explain the mystery of redemption; for it was impossible, without such a representation, to convey to the untutored and simple savages the history of our Saviour's passion. The consequence was, that they soon began to have persons under instruction. But, after two or three years, they were banished from the island by the power of the American missionaries, and took refuge in California. In 1833, the Catholics were summoned before these authorities, and ordered to attend the Protestant worship. On their refusal, they were condemned to hard labor on the public roads. A task was apportioned to them, and after that had been executed, they were again summoned, and asked if they would frequent the Protestant service. On their once more declining, they were allotted another task. This was repeated until the fourth time; when some of them demurred on this account, that hitherto they had been allowed to work in bodies, entirely composed of Catholics, whereas now they were ordered to be mixed with convicts, and men of the worst character, condemned for every sort of crime, the lowest and worst refuse of society. The Catholics refused to obey on this ground, and begged to be allowed to work alone. The order, however, was peremptorily urged; and not only so, but further command was given, to separate the wives from their husbands, and make them work in different parts of the island. They consulted their catechist, the only person whom they had to advise them, if they should obey. He assured them that there could be no sin in working in such company, if commanded by their ruler, on account of religion, whereas it would be sinful to disobey his orders. They took his words literally, and, as the sentence had only been pronounced by a commissary, insisted upon hearing it from the chief. Force was resorted to, the men and women were separated, and attempts were made to put them in irons. They, however, prevailed in their demand to be taken before the chief; but, on their way, the English consul rescued them, and secured them in his house from the persecution of the

---

* Kotzebue, "Narrative of a Second Voyage round the Globe," vol. ii.

Protestants. A letter of thanks was written to him by the missionaries from their exile.

Here, then, is a persecution of Catholic converts by the ministers of a Protestant religion, and a system of penal infliction pursued against those who would not abandon our religion; a system carried to such an extent, that a female of royal blood was for a time terrified from embracing it, by the threat of being sentenced to public hard labor. Here, as everywhere else, the Catholics persevered in their faith; but, what shall we say of the oft repeated boast, that Protestantism ever abhors religious persecution, and only Catholicity is of an intolerant and cruel spirit?

In April, 1833, the king published a degree, whereby all were left at liberty to neglect or attend the Protestant Churches.* The moment the decree was passed, the churches became deserted and empty; and the islanders rushed madly to their wonted sports, which had been forbidden, while the Catholics did not lose a single convert, nor did any of them frequent the games without permission of their catechists. The return of the missionaries was expected, and a bishop, Mgr. Rouchoux, has been appointed to the mission.†

Now, let any person contrast the conduct of the two Churches; the one endured persecution, and yet remained faithful; the other was supported by the law, and the moment compulsory attendance was taken off, was abandoned by its proselytes. Such a comparison, joined to the many similar examples which I have given this evening, furnishes us with matter of serious reflection, and must, I am sure, be a subject of great consolation and encouragement to those who profess the true faith of Christ.

I cannot conceive a more delightful study, than the peculiar manner in which Christianity can adapt itself to every possible state and condition of mankind. Every other religious system has been adapted for one peculiar climate or character. No ingenuity, no talent, could ever have induced the wild Huron to embrace the amphibious and abstemious religion of the Ganges, to spend half his day, and hope for his sanctification, in long and frequent ablutions in his freezing lakes, or to abstain from animal food, and subsist on vegetables, in a climate where stern nature would have forbidden such a course. The soft and luxurious inhabitants of Thibet could never have transplanted into

---

* Kotzebue tells us that he himself saw the poor natives driven into the church by blows with a stick.
† "Ami de la religion," 17th July, 1834.

LECTURE VII. 223

their perfumed groves the gloomy incantations and sanguinary divinities of the Scandinivian forests, or listened with delight to the sagas, and tales of blood and glory which nerved the heart of the Sea-king, amidst the storms of the North. Nor could he have ever learnt and practised, in his rude climate, the religions of the East, with their light pagodas, their gaudy paintings, their varied perfumes, and their effeminating morals. The worship of Egypt sprang from the soil, and must have perished, if transplanted beyond the reach of the Nile's inundation; that of Greece, with its poetical mythology, its Muses, its Dryads, and its entire Olympus, could only be the creed of a nation, which could produce Anacreon and Homer, Phidias and Apelles. Nay, even the Jewish dispensation bears manifest signs that its Divine Author did not intend it for a permanent and universal establishment. But Christianity alone is the religion of every clime and of every race. From pole to pole, from China to Peru, we find it practised and cherished by innumerable varieties of the great human family, varieties whether we consider their constitutions, their mental capacities, their civil habits, their political institutions, their very physiognomy and complexion.

But let us be just to ourselves; it is only the Catholic religion which possesses this beautiful faculty of suiting every character, national and individual, by becoming all to all, of uniting by a common link the most discordant elements, and fashioning the most dissimilar dispositions after the same model of virtue, without effacing the lines of national peculiarity. Lutheranism was for years forced upon the docile natives of Ceylon, and engendered the most horrible of religious chimeras—the worship of Christ united to the service of devils! The Independents have labored long and zealously for the conversion of the teachable and uncorrupted natives of the Sandwich and Society Islands, and they have perfectly succeeded in ruining their industrious habits, exposing the country to external aggression and internal dissension, and disgusting all who originally supported them.

But, on the other hand, the Catholic religion seems to have a grace and an efficacy peculiar to itself, which allows it to take hold on every variety of disposition and situation. It seems to work like that latent virtue of some springs, which slowly removes every frail and fading particle of the flower or bough that is immersed in them, converts them into a solid and durable material, and yet preserves every vein and every line which gave them individuality in their perishable condition. Its action is independent of civilization: it may precede it, and then it is its harbinger; it may follow it, and then it becomes its corrective. You have seen it alone raise the savage, even in his wilds, to the admiration and acceptance of the most sublime and most incomprehensible mysteries; you have beheld it in India, nerving its followers alone against the demoralizing influence of the country.

And if he who planteth, and he who watereth, is nothing, but the Lord alone giveth the increase, and if this constant and enduring success can be but the result of a divine blessing, shall not we conclude, that the kingdom of God hath been hereby brought unto so many nations, and that the system here pursued is that whereon His blessing and promise of eternal assistance was pronounced? Let us then rejoice that He has given us so consoling an evidence of His assistance to His Church; and as it has been evinced in one part of her commission, that of successfully teaching all nations, so has it been no less secured upon the other, that of teaching all things which He hath commanded, until the end of time.

LECTURE THE EIGHTH.

ON THE SUPREMACY OF THE POPE.

MATTHEW xvi. 17, 18, 19.

"*Blessed art thou, Simon Barjona; because flesh and blood hath not revealed it to thee, but my Father who is in heaven. And I say to thee that thou art Peter; and upon this rock I will build my Church; and the gates of hell shall not prevail against it. And to thee I will give the keys of the kingdom of heaven: and whatsoever thou shalt bind on earth, it shall be bound also in heaven, and whatsoever thou shalt loose on earth, it shall be loosed also in heaven.*"

THE line of demonstration, which has perhaps been somewhat interrupted by the two last discourses, has, I trust, my brethren, led you to form a conception of the Church of Christ conformable to the imagery employed and the institutions described in God's written word. It has been presented to you in both, under the form of a sacred kingdom, wherein all the parts are cemented and bound firmly together, in unity of belief and practice, resulting from a common principle of faith, under an authority constituted by God. But the application of this discovery has been necessarily postponed; for we have but vaguely determined the existence of this authority in the Church of Christ, without defining where, how, or by whom, it has to be exercised.

The tendency, so far as we have examined, of every institution in the Church, to produce and cherish this religious unity, will lead us naturally to suppose, that the authority which principally secures it, must likewise be convergent, in its exercise, towards the same attribute. We saw how, in the old law, the authority constituted to teach, narrowed in successive steps, till it was concentrated in one man and his line;* we saw how all the figures of the prophets led us to expect a form of government justly symbolized as a monarchy;† and although God is to be its Ruler, and the Son of David its eternal Head, yet as their action upon man is invisible and indiscernible, while the objects

---

* Lect. iv. p. 86.
† P. 89. See also, for the fuller development of this idea, a Sermon on the Kingdom of Christ, in "Two Sermons," &c., London, 1832.

LECTURE VIII.

and ends held in view, such as unity of faith, are sensible, and dependent on outward circumstances, we might naturally hope to find some such vicarious or representative authority, as would, and alone could, secure their advantage to the Church.

Indeed, it would appear quite unnatural, that every other institution therein should be outward and visible, and the one, of all others most necessary to give them efficacy, be of a contrary nature, and such as could have no power over the elements which it was intended to control.

It is to the examination of this important point that I wish to turn your attention this evening; and in the results of our inquiry, I trust that you will find the perfect completion of that plan which I have hitherto unfolded. For as, beginning with the foundation, laid in the simplest principles, and based on the word of God and the institutions of both covenants, we have seen gradually built up before us this sacred dwelling-place of God with men, so may this portion which I will now add be considered the cope-stone to the entire edifice, whereby it is fastened and held together, and close united, and at the same time crowned,—that which at once secures and adorns, strengthens and completes it.

But, on entering, as you will naturally have surmised that it is my intention to do, on the Supremacy of the Holy See, I feel myself met by so many popular prejudices, so many repeated misrepresentations, as to make some preliminary observations necessary. What then do Catholics mean by the Supremacy of the Pope, which for so many years we were required to abjure, if we would be partakers of the benefits of our country's laws? Why, it signifies nothing more than that the Pope or Bishop of Rome, as the successor of St. Peter, possesses authority and jurisdiction, in things spiritual, over the entire Church, so as to constitute its visible head, and the vicegerent of Christ upon earth. The idea of this Supremacy involves two distinct, but closely allied, prerogatives: the first is, that the Holy See is the centre of unity; the second, that it is the fountain of authority. By the first is signified that all the faithful must be in communion with it, through their respective pastors, who form an unbroken chain of connection from the lowliest member of the flock, to him who has been constituted its universal shepherd. To violate this union and communion constitutes the grievous crime of schism, and destroys an essential constitutive principle of Christ's religion.

We likewise hold the Pope to be the source of authority; as

all the subordinate rulers in the Church are subject to him, and receive directly, or indirectly, their jurisdiction from and by him. Thus the executive power is vested in his hands for all spiritual purposes within her; to him is given the charge of confirming his brethren in the faith; his office it is to watch over the correction of abuses, and the maintenance of discipline throughout the Church; in case of error springing up in any part, he must make the necessary investigations to discover it and condemn it; and either bring the refractory to submission, or separate them, as withered branches, from the vine. In cases of great and influential disorder in faith or practice, he convenes a general council of the pastors of the Church; presides over it in person, or by his legates; and sanctions, by his approbation, its canons or decrees.

That, with such a belief concerning the high prerogatives of the sovereign Pontiff, the greatest veneration should be felt towards him by every Catholic, cannot be matter of surprise. It would, on the contrary, be unnatural to suppose that a respect commensurate with his high office could be refused. When St. Paul had severely reproved Ananias, for ordering him to be most unjustly smitten on the mouth, and when they that stood by said, "Dost thou revile the high-priest of God?" St. Paul replied: "I knew not, brethren, that he was the high-priest: for it is written, thou shalt not speak evil of the prince of thy people."* From which words it is plain, that a respect and honor is due to any one constituted in such a dignity, independent of his personal virtues or qualifications. It follows no less, that such high dignity may be awarded without reference to the exemption of its holder from sin and crime. In fact, it is a misrepresentation often repeated, that Catholics imagine the supreme Pontiff to be free from all liability to moral transgression, as though they believed that no action performed by him could be sinful. It can hardly be necessary for me to deny so gross and so absurd an imputation. Not only do we know him, however exalted, to be as much under the curse of Adam as the meanest of his subjects, but we hold him to be exposed to even greater dangers from his very elevation; we believe him to be subject to every usual cause of offence, and obliged to have recourse to the same precautions, and the same remedies, as other frail men.

The supremacy which I have described is of a character purely spiritual, and has no connection with the possession of

---

* Acts xxiii. 4, 5.

any temporal jurisdiction. The sovereignty of the Pope over his own dominions is no essential portion of his dignity: his supremacy was not the less before it was acquired, and should the unsearchable decrees of Providence, in the lapse of ages, deprive the Holy See of its temporal sovereignty, as happened to the seventh Pius, through the usurpation of a conqueror, its dominion over the Church, and over the consciences of the faithful, would not be thereby impaired.

Nor has this spiritual supremacy any relation to the wider sway once held by the pontiffs over the destinies of Europe. That the headship of the Church won naturally the highest weight and authority, in a social and political state grounded on Catholic principles, we cannot wonder. That power arose and disappeared with the institutions which produced or supported it, and forms no part of the doctrine held by the Church regarding the papal supremacy. But on this, and other similar subjects of too ordinary prejudice, I may add some farther remarks, should time permit, at the conclusion of this evening's discourse.

As the pre-eminence claimed by the Catholic Church for the Bishop of Rome is based upon the circumstance of his being the successor of St. Peter, it follows that the right whereby that claim is supported must naturally depend upon the demonstration that the apostle was possessed of such superior authority and jurisdiction. The subject of this evening's disquisition thus becomes twofold; for, first, we must examine whether St. Peter was invested by our Saviour with a superiority, not merely of dignity, but of jurisdiction also, over the rest of the apostles; and if so, we must farther determine, whether this was merely a personal prerogative, or such as was necessarily transmitted to his successors, until the end of time.

I. It was a usual practice among the Jewish teachers to bestow a new name upon their disciples, on occasion of some distinguished display of excellence; it had been the means occasionally used by the Almighty of denoting an important event in the lives of his servants, when he rewarded them for past fidelity, by bestowing upon them some signal pre-eminence. It was thus that he altered the names of Abraham and Sara, when he made with the former the covenant of circumcision; promised to the latter a son in her old age; and blessed both, that from them might spring "nations and kings of people."* It was thus that

---

* Gen. xvii. 5, 15.

LECTURE VIII.

Jacob received from him the name of Israel, when, after wrestling with an angel, assurance was given him that he should ever be able to prevail against men.* It is singular, that the moment Simon was introduced to our blessed Redeemer, he received a promise that a similar distinction should be given to him. "Thou art Simon, the son of Jona, thou shalt be called Cephas, which is interpreted Peter."†

It was on the occasion of his confessing the divine mission of the Son of God, that the promise was fulfilled. At the commencement of our Saviour's reply, he still calls him by his former appellation. "Blessed art thou, Simon Bar-jona, because flesh and blood hath not revealed it to thee, but my Father, who is in heaven." He then proceeds to the inauguration of his new name. "And I say to thee that thou art Peter." According to the analogy of the instances above given, we must expect some allusion in the name to the reward and distinction with which it was accompanied. And such is really the case. The name Peter signifies a *rock;* for in the language spoken upon this occasion by our Saviour not the slightest difference exists, even at this day, between the name whereby this apostle, or any one bearing his name, is known, and the most ordinary word which indicates a rock or stone.‡ Thus the phrase of our Redeemer would sound as follows to the ears of his audience: "And I say to thee that thou art *a rock.*" Now see how the remaining part of the sentence would run in connection with the preamble: "and upon *this* rock I will build my Church, and the gates of hell shall not prevail against it." Such is the *first* prerogative bestowed upon Peter: he is declared to be the rock whereon the impregnable Church is to be founded.

2. Our Saviour goes on to say, "And I will give thee the keys of the Kingdom of Heaven; and whatsoever thou shalt bind upon earth shall be bound also in Heaven; and whatsoever thou shalt loose upon earth, shall be loosed also in Heaven." The second prerogative is the holding of the keys, and the power of making decrees, which shall be necessarily ratified in Heaven.

3. To the two ample powers given here we must add a third distinguished commission, conferred upon him after the resurrection, when Jesus three times asked him for a pledge of a love superior to that of the other apostles, and three times gave him a charge to feed his entire flock,—his lambs and his sheep. "When, therefore, they had dined, Jesus saith to Simon Peter;

---

* Ib. xxxii. 28.   † John I. 42.   ‡ In Syriac *Kipho.*

Simon, son of John, lovest thou me more than these? He saith to him, Yea, Lord, thou knowest that I love thee. He saith to him: Feed my lambs. He saith to him again, Simon, son of John, lovest thou me? He saith to him: Yea, Lord, thou knowest that I love thee. He saith to him: Feed my lambs. He said to him the third time: Simon, son of John, lovest thou me? Peter was grieved, because he had said to him the third time, Lovest thou me? And he said to him: Lord, thou knowest all things: thou knowest that I love thee. He said to him: Feed my sheep."*

On the strength of these passages, principally, the Catholic Church has ever maintained, that St. Peter received a spiritual pre-eminence and supremacy. And, indeed, if in these various commissions a power and jurisdiction was given to Peter, which was proper to him alone, and superior to that conferred upon all the other apostles, it will be readily acknowledged, that such supremacy, as we believe, was really bestowed upon him by God.

Now, his being constituted the foundation of the Church, implies such jurisdiction. For, what is the first idea which this figure suggests, except that the whole edifice grows up in unity, and receives solidity, from its having been mortised and riveted into this common base? But, what can be simply effected, in a material edifice, by the weight or tenacity of its component parts, can only be permanently secured in a moral body by a compressive influence, or by the exercise of authority and power. We style the laws the *basis* of social order, because it is their office to secure, by their administration, the just rights of all, to punish transgressors, to arbitrate differences, to insure uniformity of conduct, in all their subjects. We call our triple legislative authority the *foundation* of the British Constitution; because from it emanate all the powers which regulate the subordinate parts of the body politic, and on it repose the government, the modification, the reformation of the whole.

And observe, I pray you, that this reasoning excludes the possibility, not only of a superior, but even of an equal and co-ordinate authority. For, if the laws be not supreme, but there exists a rule of equal force, and not subject to their control, yet moving in the same sphere, and acting upon the same objects, you will own that they are no longer the basis of an order which they cannot guaranty and preserve. If a new authority were to arise in the state, equally empowered to legislate, to govern

---

* John xxi. 15-17.

LECTURE VIII. 231

and direct, with the present supreme authorities, without their being able to interfere, and setting them at defiance, I ask you if the whole political fabric would not be necessarily dissolved, and if a general disorganization would not ensue? Is it not plain that these authorities would lose their present denomination, and no longer form the foundation of our constitution? Apply this reasoning to the case of Peter. *He* is constituted the foundation of a moral edifice; for such is the Church. The appointment itself implies a power to hold together the materials of the building in one united whole; and this we have clearly seen to consist in the supreme authority to control and to govern its constituent parts.

It has been argued—and it is the only interpretation of the text whereby our opponents can make even a specious opposition—that this character of Peter was fulfilled in his being the first sent to convert both Jews and Gentiles, so that the Church might be said to rise and spring from him; and that, in this sense, he was the foundation of the Church. But, my brethren, was he thereby made the *rock* whereon this Church was founded? Had our Blessed Saviour said, "Thou shalt *lay* the foundation of my Church," this sense might have been given to his words. But is there no difference between such a phrase, and "thou shalt be the rock on which *I* will build it?" In other words, can this figure imply nothing more than that he should give a beginning to the edifice; that he should lay the first stone? Would any one give to another the name of a *rock*, to signify *this* relationship between him and a building? Is there no idea of stability, of durability, of firmness, conveyed by the name, but only one of simple commencement?

But let us reason a little closer. Would any one presume to apply to it a parallel instance? The Gospel was first preached to the Irish by St. Patrick, and to the Anglo-Saxons by St. Augustine; would you dare to say that Patrick or Augustine were the foundation of those two Churches, or the rock whereon they were built? When Jesus Christ is said to be the foundation upon which alone any one can build,* would you allow the Arian to maintain, that from this text nothing more could be concluded, than that Christianity sprung from him, and not that he is "the finisher, as well as the author of our faith,"† that he is the object as well as the institutor of our belief? When we are said to be "built upon the foundation of the apostles," would

---

* 1 Cor. iii. 11. † Ephes. ii. 20.

you allow the freethinker to assert that this gave them no other distinction than that of having first *preached* the faith, and that it is not meant that their authority gives evidence of Christianity, or of its truth? And yet these would have a right to argue thus, if, from Peter's being called the rock whereon the Church is founded, no other consequence could be drawn than that he was the person who had to commence its formation.

Secondly, our Saviour does not merely say, that Peter is the rock whereon the Church is to be founded; but, moreover, that, *in consequence* of this foundation, this Church is to be impregnable and immovable. "Upon this rock I will build my Church, and the gates of hell shall not prevail against it." I say, that this sentence evidently implies that the Church is to be imperishable, *in consequence* of this foundation upon Peter; because the connection between the two ideas, of a firm foundation and a durable building, is so close and natural, that the usages of language oblige us to consider them as brought together only in consequence of that connection. To prove this by a familiar instance: when our Saviour says, that the foolish man "built his house upon sand, and the floods came, and the wind blew and beat upon that house, and it fell,"* we instantly conclude, though it be not expressly said, that the easy fall of that house is meant to be attributed to the instability of its foundation. In like manner, we should have attributed the firmness of that of the wise builder to the circumstance mentioned, that it was founded upon a rock, even though our Saviour had not himself expressly given the same reason.† In our instance, therefore, as the Church of God is said to be founded upon Peter, as on a rock, and, at the same time, is declared to be proof against the powers of destruction, so we may conclude that this security from ruin is the natural consequence of its being so founded. Peter, then, is not merely the commencer of the Church, but its real support; and this, as we have already seen, requires power and authority.

The second prerogative of Peter, the commission of holding the keys, and of binding and loosing, no less implies jurisdiction and power. This has also been explained in the same manner, as though it only implied that Peter should *open* the gates of the Church to Jews and Gentiles. But can any one bring himself to believe in so cold, and, I might almost say, so paltry a signification as this? Where, on any occasion, among profane or sacred writers, was the image used in such a sense? The de-

---

* Matt. vii. 27. † Verse 25.

livery of keys has always been a symbol of the intrusting with supreme authority to command. It is so used in Scripture. God "will lay upon the shoulder" of the Messiah, "the key of the house of David: and he shall open, and no man shall shut; and shall shut, and no man shall open:"*—that is, God will give him supreme command in the house of David. In like manner, he is said to have received "the keys of death and of hell,"† to signify his supreme dominion over both.

Among oriental nations, this connection of real power with these, its emblems, is very strongly marked. We are told by the most accurate of Eastern annalists, how the keys of the temple of Mecca were in the hands of a certain tribe, and with it the command in that place; and so necessarily were the two conjoined, that, when the material keys were extorted by fraud from their possessor, he irrevocably lost his dominion over the sanctuary. And, on another occasion, he shows that the possession of the emblem really conferred the power which it represented.‡ Among European nations, the same analogy exists, though, perhaps, not so strongly. For, when the keys of a town are said to have been intrusted to any one by his sovereign, who ever thought of thereby understanding that power was given to him to unlock its gates, or shut them, to strangers and new-comers? And when the keys of a fort are said to have been delivered to a conqueror, who does not understand that possession of the strong place and dominion over it are no less transferred? And is not the same feeling implied by the practice, which now has become a mere ceremony, in this city, of its gate being closed when the monarch visits it, and the keys being presented to him by its

---

* Is. xxii. 22. Apoc. iii. 7. Comp. Job xii. 14, and Is. ix. 6, "the *government* is upon his *shoulder*."

† Apoc. l. 18.

‡ "Abu'l Feda. Specimen Histor. Arab." *Oxon*. 1806. The narrative alluded to occurs p. 474, of the text, and 533 of the version. We are there told that the care of the temple of Mecca was with the tribe of the Khozaites, till its representative, Abu-Gashan, in a state of intoxication, sold its keys to Kosay, in the presence of witnesses. Whereupon Kosay sent his son with them in triumph to Mecca, and restored them to the citizens. Abu-Gashan, on recovering his senses, repented, "when repentance was useless, and gave rise to the proverb, 'a more unfortunate loss than Abu-Gashan's.'" Pp. 482, 561, we have another illustration of the same idea. "The superintendence of the temple, *and its keys*, were with the children of Ismael, without doubt, till this authority came into the hands of Nabeth. After him, it fell into the possession of the Jorhamites, as is proved by a verse in a poem by Amer, son of Hareth, a Jorhamite.

"We possessed *the rule* of the holy house after Nabeth."

Thus, the two ideas of simply possessing the keys of a temple, and ruling over it, are manifestly identified.

chief magistrate; thereby implying that the supreme authority prevails over that which was merely delegated? When, therefore, Peter receives the keys of the Kingdom of Heaven, or of the Church, we can only consider him as invested with its supreme command.

The same must be said of the power to bind and to loose. Whether we understand by it authority to decree and prohibit, or to punish and forgive, the only two interpretations which have any plausibility; or whether, with greater probability, we unite the two, it equally implies a prerogative of jurisdiction.

Finally, the unrestricted commission to feed the entire flock of Christ implies a primacy and jurisdiction over the whole. For the commission to feed is a commission to govern and direct. In the oldest classics, such as Homer, whose imagery approaches the nearest to that of Scripture, kings and chieftains are distinguished by the title of "shepherds of the people." In the Old Testament, the same idea perpetually occurs, especially when speaking of David, and contrasting his early occupation of watching his father's flocks, with his subsequent appointment to rule over God's people.* It is a favorite image with the prophets to describe the rule of the Messiah, and of God, over his chosen inheritance, after it should be restored to favor.† And our Blessed Redeemer himself adopts it, when speaking of the connection between him and his disciples,—his sheep that hear his voice and follow him.‡ In the writings of the apostles we find, at every step, the same idea. St. Peter calls Christ "the Prince of Shepherds,"§ and tells the clergy to *feed* the flock which is among them;‖ and St. Paul warns the bishops whom he had assembled at Ephesus, that they had been put over their *flocks* by the Holy Ghost, to "*rule* the Church of God."¶

But, in fact, my brethren, to sum up the arguments drawn from these various commissions, if in them St. Peter did not receive jurisdiction and authority, neither did the apostles anywhere receive them. Take all the appointments ever given to them, and you will not discover any more decisive in favor of their authority, than their being called the foundations of the Church,—their being invested with the power of binding and loosing, with a certainty of ratification in Heaven,—and their being constituted rulers and pastors of Christ's flock.

---

* 2 Kings (Sam.) v. 2; Ps. lxxvii. 71, 72; Ezech. xxxii. 1-10; Jer. iii. 15; xxiii. 1, 2, 4; Nah. iii. 18, &c.

† Is. xl. 11; Mich. vii. 14; Ezech. xxxii. 10-23, &c.

‡ Jo. x.   § 1 Pet. v 4.   ‖ Ib. 2.   ¶ Acts xx 28.

LECTURE VIII.

St. Peter, then, my brethren, first in the vicinity of Cæsarea Philippi, and afterwards at the sea of Galilee, was solemnly invested with an authority and jurisdiction, distinctly conferred on him alone, as a reward for professions of belief and of love, which proceeded from him individually, and prefaced by a change of names, and a personal address, which showed them to be exclusively bestowed upon him. He was, therefore, invested with an authority of a distinct and superior order to that of his fellow apostles, which extended to the whole Church, by the commission to feed all the flock; which excluded the idea of co-ordinate authority, as the rock on which all are to be secured in unity; which supposed supreme command by the holding of the keys. And all this is more than sufficient to establish his supremacy.

There are but two means of escaping from this conclusion. The one denies the fact whereon our proofs are founded, and it is a weak objection; the second only denies the conclusions, and will require more attention.

In the first of these, I allude to the attempt made many years ago, and lately renewed, to prove that the rock upon which Christ promises that he will build the Church, was not Peter, but Himself. It is supposed that, having addressed this disciple in the first part of his sentence, and said to him, "thou art Peter," that is a rock, our Saviour suddenly changed the subject of the discourse, and pointing to himself, said, "And upon *this* rock I will build my Church." This interpretation you will perceive, my brethren, can boast more of its ingenuity than of its plausibility; it seems rather calculated to betray the shifts to which our opponents feel themselves obliged to resort, in order to elude our arguments, than to make any effectual resistance to their force. If the conjunctive particle, and the demonstrative pronoun *this*, be not sufficient to connect two parts of the same sentence, it is no longer in the power of grammatical forms to do so. If we may depart from the obvious signification of a phrase, by merely supposing that it was illustrated, when spoken, by signs or gestures suppressed in the narration, then the imagination must be allowed to be as useful as reason in the explanation of Scripture. Not only so, but all who are conversant with the corruptions of modern biblical science among the Protestants of Germany, are aware that by this expedient of imagining and supplying looks, gestures, and words, which they suppose to have been omitted, the most wanton attempts have been made to undermine the truth of the most important miracles of the New Testament. With just equal reason might the speech of God to

Abraham, when he changed his name, be divided; and after he addressed him in the words, "neither shall thy name be called any more Abram, but thou shalt be called Abraham, because I have made thee a father of many nations;" we might interpret the next words, "and I will make thee increase exceedingly,"* as addressed, not to the patriarch, but to his son Ismael; only by supposing, with equal right as in our Saviour's words, that the angel pointed towards the latter.

But there is another objection to our reasoning, of more plausibility and weight; because, without pretending to elude the obvious meaning of the words, it seeks to disarm them of all their force; because it admits the facts which are palpable, and only combats our conclusions. It is true, such is the argument to which I allude, that Peter received a power and jurisdiction, and that these were bestowed upon him individually and distinctively, as a reward due to his superior merits; but it is no less true that nothing was here given to Peter, but what was afterwards given to the twelve. In the Apocalypse, the twelve foundations of the heavenly Jerusalem have inscribed upon them "the names of the twelve apostles of the Lamb."† St. Paul tells the faithful, that the apostles are the foundation whereon they are built.‡ These, then, are no less the foundation of the Church than Peter. Again, in the 18th chapter of St. Matthew, precisely the same power is given to all the twelve to bind and loose on earth, with a corresponding effect in heaven, as is conferred on Peter in the 16th. Thus, the faculties here lavished on him are afterwards extended to all his companions, and whatever was given to him individually, is merged in the common and general commission, in which the rest were placed on a level with himself.

I will acknowledge, my brethren, that this argument at first sight has some appearance of strength; and I am not surprised when I see many Protestant commentators ground their rejection of the Supremacy of Peter almost exclusively upon this reasoning.§ It would be easy indeed to elude its force; but I wish to convert it into an argument in my favor. Listen, therefore, I pray you, with attention.—Peter, it is said, had no preeminence of jurisdiction bestowed upon him, because he received no power or commission individually, which was not, on another occasion, collectively bestowed upon the twelve. Now, is this the way in which you reason upon any other similar case in

---

* Gen. xvii. 5, 6.   † Apoc. xxi. 14.   ‡ Ephes. ii. 20.
§ The "Protestant Journal" for this month, June, 1836, repeats it as quite satisfactory, p. 347.

Scripture, or is it not diametrically opposite? Let us try a few instances. Our B. Saviour constantly inculcated to all his disciples, and indeed to all his hearers, the necessity of *following* him. Only "he who *followeth*, walketh not in darkness;"* all must "take up their cross and *follow* him;"† all his sheep must know his voice and *follow* the shepherd.‡ When, therefore, he addressed individually to Peter and Andrew, to Matthew and the sons of Zebedee, the very same invitation, "Follow me," did it ever occur to you to reason, that, because the very same invitation was repeated, on other occasions, to all the Jews in common with themselves, therefore, they were not meant to follow Jesus in a distinct and more peculiar manner? Again, our B. Redeemer is repeatedly said to have tenderly loved all his apostles; he called them not servants, but friends—yea, no one could have greater love for another than he manifested to them, by laying down his life for them.§ When, therefore, John is by himself simply called the *beloved* disciple, as all the other disciples are also said to have been beloved, did you ever think of arguing that, as no more is predicated of him singly in one instance than is of all the twelve in others, therefore the love of Jesus for John was nothing distinctive and pre-eminent? Once more. To all the apostles was given a commission to teach all nations, to preach the gospel to every creature, beginning with Jerusalem and Samaria, unto the uttermost bounds of the earth.‖ When, therefore, the spirit of God told them to separate Saul and Barnabas for the ministry of the Gentiles,¶ or when Paul individually calls himself their apostle, did you ever think of concluding that, as this individual commission was included and comprehended in the general one given to all, therefore Paul was never invested with any personal mission, received no more here than the other apostles, and only groundlessly arrogated to himself the apostleship of the Gentiles as his peculiar office? If in all these instances you would not allow such conclusions, how can they be admitted in the case of Peter? Why are his special powers alone to be invalidated by those which he received in common with the rest?

But I said I should not be content with answering the objection, but wished to gain an argument for my cause, and it is briefly this. From the instances I have given, it is evident that I may draw this canon or rule of interpretation in Scripture:

---

* Jo. viii. 12. † Mark viii. 38.
‡ Jo. x. 4. § Jo. xiii. 1; xv. 12, 15.
Matt. xxviii. 19, 20; Acts i. 8. ¶ Acts xiii. 2.

that when a call, a prerogative, a commission, is bestowed upon one person singly, though the very same may have been bestowed upon others collectively, and himself together with them, he must thereby be supposed to have received a distinct and superior degree of it from the rest. Thus, therefore, it must be with Peter. If the apostles were invested with authority in the commissions given to them, when even nothing but the same had been given to him individually, he must have thereby acquired a higher degree of that authority than they. But you will not be displeased to hear this objection answered by a Father of the third century, and of the Greek Church. Thus writes the acute and learned Origen. "What before was granted to Peter, seems to have been granted to all,—but as something peculiarly excellent was to be granted to Peter, it was given singly to him: 'I will give thee the keys of the kingdom of heaven.' This was done before the words 'whatsoever thou shalt bind upon earth' were uttered (in the 18th chapter.) And truly, if the words of the Gospel be considered, we shall there find that the last words were common to Peter and the others, but that the former, spoken to Peter, imported a great distinction and superiority."* I might add, that the commission to feed the flock of Christ is nowhere given to the others; and if it were, I would ask, was it necessary that our Saviour should thrice require from Peter an assurance that he loved him *more* than the rest, in order to be qualified to receive an *equal* reward?"

There is still another passage, which I have not included in those before rehearsed; because there is no express bestowal of authority conveyed in it; although it clearly draws a distinction between the prerogatives of Peter and those of the other apostles, and shows how he was to be the object of a special care and protection. "And the Lord said, Simon, Simon, behold Satan hath desired to have *you*, that he may sift *you* as wheat. But I have prayed for *thee*, that thy faith may not fail; and *thou*, being once converted, confirm *thy* brethren."† In this passage, Christ seems to draw a marked distinction between the designs of Satan against *all* the apostles, and his own interest in regard of Peter. The prayer of our Saviour is offered for him specifically, that *his* faith may not fail, and that, when he shall have risen from his fault, he may be the strengthener of that virtue among his fellow-apostles. In him, then, there was to be a larger measure of this virtue; and wherefore, if he was not to be in any respect

---

* Com. in Mat. T. III. p. 612. † Luke xxii. 31, 32.

superior to the other members of that body? Or, rather, does not the very commission to strengthen their faith imply his being placed in a more elevated and commanding station?

But I have been sufficiently diffuse upon these proofs that Peter received a supreme jurisdiction and primacy over the whole Church beyond the other apostles; and, in conformity with this view, we find him ever named the first among them,* ever taking the lead in all their common actions, always† speaking as the organ of the Church.‡

II. But, if Peter really enjoyed this distinction, as we have seen, was it not a personal privilege, which ended with him to whom it was granted? It is time to examine this point, and prove to you that he transmitted it to his successors in his see.

I presume it will not be necessary to enter into any argument, to show that St. Peter was the first Bishop of Rome. The monuments which yet exist in every part of it, and the testimony of ecclesiastical writers from the oldest times, put the fact above all doubt; and it is only sufficient to say, that authors of the highest literary eminence, and remarkable for their opposition to the supremacy of the Roman See, such as Cave, Pearson, Usher, Young, and Blondel,§ have both acknowledged and supported it. Among the moderns, it may be sufficient to observe, that no ecclesiastical writer of any note pretends to deny this fact. "To Peter," as St. Irenæus observes, "succeeded Linus, to Linus, Anacletus, then, in the third place, Clement."|| And from that moment the series of Popes is uninterrupted and certain to the present day. Thus much premised, I will proceed to state cursorily some of the arguments which prove the perpetuation of St. Peter's primacy in those who occupy his see.

1. In the first place, it has always been understood from the beginning, that whatever prerogatives, though personal, of jurisdiction, were brought to a see by its first Bishop, were continued to his successors. Thus the chair of Alexandria was first held by St. Mark, who, as a disciple of Peter, enjoyed patriarchal jurisdiction over Egypt, Lybia, and Pentapolis, and this jurisdiction remains to this day attached to his see. James first

---

* Mat. iv. 18; x. 2; Luke ix. 28, 32, &c.; Gal. i. 18; ii. 8.
† Mat. xiv. 28; xv. 15; xvi. 23; Acts iv. 19; xii. 13.
‡ Mat. xviii. 21; xxx. 27; xxvi. 23; Acts i. 15; ii. 14 seq.; iv. 8; v. 8; viii. 19; xv. 7. *et al. passim.*
§ See "Butler's Lives of Saints," June 29; or consult Baronius Natalis Alexander, or any Church historian.
|| Adv. Hær. l. iii. c. 3.

governed Jerusalem, and exercised authority over the Churches of Palestine, and the Bishop of Jerusalem remains a patriarch as yet. Peter first sat in the chair of Antioch, and that chai has ever retained its dominion over a large portion of the east. In like manner, therefore, if to the see of Rome he brought, not merely the patriarchate of the west, but the primacy over the whole world, this accidental jurisdiction became inherent in the see, and heritable by entail to his successors.

2. But this may appear to place the supremacy of the Holy See upon the same authority as that of the patriarchates, that is, on an ecclesiastical or disciplinary authority; whereas we maintain it to be held by a divine imprescriptible right. In the second place, therefore, I say it is transmitted as a divine institution in the Church of God, forming an integral and essential part thereof. Jesus Christ, my brethren, is the same yesterday and to-day. As he established his kingdom at the beginning, so was it to be perpetuated to the end; that form of government which he instituted at its foundation cannot be altered, but must continue to rule it till the end of time. Why else was not episcopal authority merely the prerogative of the apostles and disciples? Why did their successors, in their respective sees, grasp their crosier, and teach, and command, and correct, and punish, even as they had done, but that the very nature of the Church required that time should not alter its hierarchical constitution? Now, if Peter was made the foundation of the Church, it could not be intended that after his demise the foundation should be broken in pieces, and the stones of the sanctuary dispersed abroad.

Two objects are evidently included under the figure of such a foundation, unity and durability. For, unity in the building results from all its parts being connected by one united ground-plan or basement: and the early fathers understood that the supremacy was conferred on Peter, principally to secure this blessing to the Church. "One of the twelve is chosen," says St. Jerome, "that by the appointment of a head, the occasion of schism might be removed."* "To manifest unity," says St Cyprian, "he authoritatively ordained the unity to spring from one."† "You cannot deny," writes St. Optatus, "that St. Peter the chief of the apostles, established an episcopal chair at Rome: this chair was *one*, that all others might preserve unity by the unity they had with *it*, so that whoever set up a chair against it,

---

* Adv. Jovin. Lib. i. Tom. i. Ps. ii. p. 168.   † De Unit. p. 194.

should be a schismatic and a transgressor. It is in this one chair, which is the first mark of the Church, that St. Peter sat."*

Now, my brethren, if, to preserve unity in the Church, our blessed Saviour deemed the institution of a primacy necessary, while as yet the fervor of Christianity was glowing and unimpaired, while the apostles yet lived, dispersed over the world, each under the special guidance of Heaven, while the number of Christians was comparatively but small, while almost all the members of the Church belonged to one state, spoke one tongue, and were undivided by political or national prepossession; I will ask, was there less need of such a safeguard when the coldness of heavenly charity, the inferior lights of pastors, the wider dispersion of the faithful, and the division of states and kingdoms rendered the human means and the moral chances of preserving unity in belief and practice infinitely smaller? If, then, unity is an essential characteristic of the true faith, and if the appointment of a supremacy was made the means of insuring it, as the very idea of its foundation and the testimonies of the ancient Church demonstrate, then does that supremacy necessarily become equally essential to the true religion of Christ, as the unity which it supports; and consequently must be perpetual.

The second quality included under the figure of foundation upon this rock, is durability. I have already shown that the words of our Saviour clearly imply that the durability of the Church was a consequence of its foundation. But to be imperishable in consequence of its foundation, implies that the foundation itself will not fail, but shall remain for ever. We have seen that this foundation consisted in a supreme jurisdiction given to Peter; and the necessary conclusion is, that this supreme jurisdiction must last in the Church unto the end of time.

3. Thirdly, the authority of Peter must have been intended to be perpetual in Christianity, because we find that, from the earliest ages, all acknowledged it to exist in his successors, as their inherent right. Pope Clement examined and corrected the abuses of the Church of Corinth; Victor, those of Ephesus; Stephen, those of Africa. St. Dionysius, in the third century, summoned his namesake, patriarch of Alexandria, to appear before him to give an account of his faith, as he had been accused by his flock at Rome; and the holy patriarch obeyed without murmur. When St. Athanasius was dispossessed of the

* De Schism. Donat. Lib. ii. p. 28.

same see by the Arians, Pope Julius summoned all the parties before him, and was submitted to by all. Besides restoring this great patriarch to his see, he took cognisance of the cause of Paul, patriarch of Constantinople, and restored him in like manner. The great St. John Chrysostom, patriarch of the same Church, when unjustly deposed, wrote to Pope Innocent, entreating that he might be allowed a trial. I have selected these few instances of supreme authority, exercised by the Bishops of Rome over the prelates and even the patriarchs of the east, during the four first centuries, merely as specimens chosen from many more which time will not allow me to adduce.

Were I to attempt to give you, in full, the authority of the Fathers upon this subject, I should indeed prolong my discourse even beyond my usual measure. I will, therefore, content myself with a very limited selection. St. Irenæus, one of the oldest, writes as follows:—" As it would be tedious to enumerate the whole list of successors, I shall confine myself to that of Rome, the greatest, and most ancient, and most illustrious Church, founded by the glorious apostles Peter and Paul, receiving from them her doctrine, which was announced to all men, and which, through the succession of her bishops, is come down to us. To this Church, *on account of its superior headship*, every other must have recourse, that is, the faithful of all countries. They, therefore, having founded and instructed this Church, committed the administration thereof to Linus. To him succeeded Anacletus; then, in the third place, Clement. To Clement succeeded Evaristus, to him Alexander; and then Sixtus, who was followed by Telesphorus, Hyginus, Pius, and Anicetus. But Soter having succeeded Anicetus, Eleutherius, the twelfth from the apostles, now governs the Church."*

In the same manner, Tertullian gives a brief way of settling differences and controversies—by telling the contending parties to apply to the nearest apostolic Church—"if in Africa," he says, "Rome is not far, to which we can readily apply;" and then he adds:—"Happy Church! which the great apostles impregnated *with all their doctrines*, and with their blood."†

Coming down a little later, we find St. Cyprian using the very same language; for he writes in these terms:—"After these attempts, having chosen a bishop for themselves, they dare to sail, and to carry letters from schismatics and profane men to the chair of Peter, and to the principal Church, *whence the sacerdotal*

---

* Adv. Hær. l iii c. iii. p. 175.   † De Præscript, c. xxxvi. p 338.

LECTURE VIII. 243

unity took its rise; not reflecting, that the members of that Church are *Romans*, (whose faith was praised by Paul,) *to whom perfidy can have no access.*"* So that not only does he call it the See of Peter, and the principal Church, but that from which unity alone can spring, and which is secured from all error by an especial care of Divine Providence.

Another remarkable and still stronger testimony we find in the decrees of the council held at Sardica, in Thrace, at the request of St. Athanasius, at which 300 bishops were present. In its decrees we have this expression:—"It shall seem most proper, if from all the provinces the priests of the Lord refer themselves *to the head—that is, to the See of Peter.*"† So that here we have a council acknowledging that there was a final appeal to the head of the Church; and this is specified to be the See of Peter, where his successors resided.

St. Basil the Great has recourse to Pope Damasus, on the distresses of his Church; and to move him the more, gives instances of earlier interpositions by the Roman Pontiffs in the affairs of his See. These are his words:—"From documents preserved among us, we know that the blessed Dionysius—who with you was eminent for his faith and other virtues—visited by his letters our Church of Cæsarea; gave comfort to our forefathers, and rescued our brethren from slavery. But our condition is now much more lamentable.—Wherefore, if you are not at this time induced to aid us, soon all being subjected to the heretics, none will be found to whom you may stretch out your hand."‡ In another passage he says, that Eustathius, Bishop of Sebaste, being deposed, proceeded to Rome; what was transacted between him and the Bishop of that city he knew not; but on his return, Eustathius showed a letter from the Pope to the Council of Thyana, on which he was instantly restored to his See. So that here, an oriental Bishop appeals to the Pope, returns with a letter from him to a provincial synod; and, although it is evident, that in this case St. Basil thinks there was some cause for his deposition, yet, on the exhibition of the letter from the holy Pontiff, he is restored to his rights.

St. Jerome, writing to the same Pope, addresses him in such a strain as any Catholic of the present day might use, and perhaps goes even farther:—" I am following no other than Christ, united to the communion of your Holiness, that is, to the chair

---
* Ep. lv. p. 86. † Ep. Synod. ad Julium Rom. Conc. Gen. T. ii. p. 661.
‡ Ep. lxx. ad Damasum, T. iii. p. 164.

of Peter. I know that the Church is founded upon that Rock. Whoever eateth the Lamb out of that House, is a profane man. Whoever is not in the ark, shall perish by the flood. But forasmuch as, being retired into the desert of Syria, I cannot receive the sacrament at your hands, I follow your colleagues, the bishops of Egypt. I do not know Vitalis; I do not communicate with Meletius; Paulinus is a stranger to me, (men of suspected faith:) he that gathereth not with you, scattereth."*

There is one passage, to which I alluded before, as containing the sentiments of St. John Chrysostom, which I will read, because it is particularly clear and energetic. He writes to Pope Innocent, Bishop of Rome, in consequence of having been deprived of his See, and treated with the greatest injustice:—"I beseech you to direct, that what has wickedly been done against me, while I was absent, and did not decline a trial, should have no effect; and they who have thus proceeded may be subjected to ecclesiastical punishment. And allow me, who have been convicted of no offence, to enjoy the comfort of your letters, and the society of my former friends."† Does not this suppose belief that the Bishop of Rome had jurisdiction, and power to punish, over the bishops of Asia? and is not this appeal to him, from a patriarch of Constantinople, a strong attestation of his supreme dominion in the universal Church? And again, we have these still stronger expressions:—"For what reason did Christ shed his blood? Certainly, to gain those sheep, *the care of which he committed to Peter and his successors.*"‡

These quotations are not in the proportion of one in twenty to those which I omit. But there is one class of passages which I must not pass over; I mean the repeated acknowledgments of general councils, that is, councils of the whole Church, of the supreme papal authority, in decisions on all ecclesiastical matters. This, on the one hand, is claimed on its behalf by the apostolic legates, who always presided, and was ever allowed by the fathers or bishops who composed the synod. For instance, in the council of Ephesus, Philip, one of the delegates from Pope Celestine, thus addressed the venerable assembly:—"No one doubts; indeed, it has been known to all ages, that the most holy Peter, the prince of the apostles, the pillar of the faith, and the foundation of the Church, received from our Lord the keys of the kingdom, and the power of binding and of loosing

---

* Ep. xiv. ad Damasum, T. iv. p. 19.   † Ep. ad Innoc. T. III. p. 520.
‡ De Sacerd. L. ii. c. 1. T. 1. p. 372.

LECTURE VIII. 245

sins. He lives unto this day in his successors, and always exercises that judgment in them. Our holy father, Celestine, the regular successor of Peter, *who now holds his place*, has sent us in his name to this sacred council,—a council convened by our most Christian emperors, for the conservation of the faith received from their fathers."*

In like manner, the Fathers of the Council of Chalcedon, upon hearing the epistle of Pope Leo read to them, unanimously exclaimed,—"This is the faith of our fathers; Peter has thus spoken through Leo; the Apostles so taught."† And when, at the close of the synod, they addressed that holy Pontiff, their expressions are so exceedingly remarkable, that I cannot refrain from quoting them: "In the person of Peter," they write, "appointed our interpreter, you preserved the chain of Faith, by the command of our Master, descending to us. Wherefore, using you as a guide, we have signified the truth to the faithful, not by private interpretation, but by one unanimous confession. If, where two or three are gathered together in the name of Christ, he is there in the midst of them, how must he have been with 520 Ministers? Over these, *as the head over the members*, you presided by those who held your rank; we entreat you, therefore, to honor our decision by your decrees; and as we agreed with the Head, so let your Eminence complete what is proper for your children. Besides this, Dioscorus carries his rage against him, *to whom Christ entrusted the care of his vineyard, that is, against your apostolic Holiness.*"‡

Thus you see, my brethren, that this is no new doctrine, but that all antiquity supports us in the belief, that our Blessed Saviour gave to Peter a headship and primacy over his Church, and that it was continued, through the following ages, in the persons of his successors, the Bishops of Rome. We find these exercising acts of decided authority over the highest dignitaries of the Eastern Church; we see them acknowledged as supreme by the most learned fathers; we have recorded, in strong terms, the deference and submission even of general Councils to their decisions and decrees. And if all this suffice not to prove the belief of those ages in the Papal Supremacy, I know not how we can ever arrive at a knowledge of what they held on any subject.

4. But, in the fourth place, the best interpretation of a prophecy

---

*Conc Gen. Tom. iii. Act. iii. p. 626.   †Ib. Tom. iv. p. 368.
‡ Ib. p. 834, 835, 883.
21*

is the history of its fulfilment. The prophecies which foretell the dispersion and abandonment of Israel were doubtless obscure till the days of their accomplishment had arrived. Were the Jews to be merely deprived of their temple, or of every other form of collective worship? Were they to be simply destitute of a domestic government; or were they to be deprived of citizenship and community with the rest of the world? Read the prophecy by the light of history, and all is clear, consistent, and convincing. Then let us apply this rule to the promise made to Peter. A power, claiming to descend from him, is seen existing, from age to age, in the midst of Christianity, subject to none of the variations, vicissitudes, and interruptions of every temporal dominion. It forms the only clue which, unravelled and unbroken, winds through every century, and holds together the elements of sacred and profane history. For, while petty dynasties rise and dissolve around it, the chronicler can only fix the epochs of their commencement, their events, and termination, by referring them to the unfailing succession of *its* rulers. Nor does this perpetuity result from a blind homage paid to their authority. Again and again their patrimony is usurped by the foreigner, their capital is sacked by the invader, their See is laid in ashes by the barbarian; they are kept for generations in exile by their own turbulent subjects; they are cast into bonds, they are bereft of life,—all, in short, befalls them, which puts an end to mortal dynasties and human principalities. But an unknown vigor seems to animate this race of sacred princes; and though other bishoprics may be swept from the face of the earth, here Pontiff succeeds to Pontiff, in spite of every obstacle; the chapter for their election is now held in a distant province of Italy, then in France, or in Germany; still a successor is duly elected, and received by all; and every attempt to break their descent is rendered vain and abortive.

In the mean time, this establishment exercises an important influence over the civilization, the culture, and the happiness of men. With the virtues of its successive members, those of the entire earth seem to expand into bloom; with the rare but influential immorality of some among them, the whole Christian world seems to sympathize and to languish; the whole tide of human virtue rises and falls, flows and ebbs, only by their increase or wane. But its influence goes farther still. The fate of all religion seems interlaced with its destiny; for centuries this may be said nowhere to exist, except in its connection and dependence; no pastors but what receive their jurisdiction from it·

LECTURE VIII.

preachers but profess to have there learnt their doctrines; no faithful, but hope for salvation from being joined to its communion. Whatever is brilliant in religion, seems only to be a reflection of its light; forms and ceremonies, canons and laws, symbols of faith, and terms of communion—all are derived thence with implicit obedience.

My brethren, a system for so many centuries thus closely interwoven with Christianity, and regulating its very existence, cannot be a mere accidental modification; it must be either an integrant part of its scheme, or it must have existed thus long in its despite. It is either an important organ, necessary to its vital functions, and vigorously acting to the farthest extremities of the frame, yea, its very core and heart; or it is a monstrous concretion, which hath become deeply seated, and, as it were, inrooted, and it exerts an unnatural and morbid influence through the body. Do you wish to consider it in the latter sense? Then see what difficulties you incur.

First, you break in pieces, yea, utterly crush to dust all the most beautiful wonders of Christianity. The submission of the heart and of the will to the teaching of faith, the anchorage which hope giveth in another world, the bonds of religious charity and affection between persons of the most various dispositions; the attachment under every extremity to the great maxims of religion, all the learning of doctors, all the constancy of martyrs, all the self-devotion of pastors, all that makes Christianity something holier, nobler, diviner, than what earth or man had before produced; all these existed nowhere for ages, save in communion with this usurped authority, as you suppose it, and gloried in paying it deference and supporting it, and bearing testimony to it. You then proclaim that they may be testimonies to monstrous falsehood and deceit; you deprive them, consequently, of all efficacy in proof; and you must therefore seek elsewhere for the most touching and most beautiful evidences of Christianity.

Secondly, you must account for the regular unbroken support which it received from the providence of God. For the fate of human institutions is to grow, to flourish, and to wither: to be raised with labor, to stand for a while, then crumble for ever. Never was dynasty, never was kingdom prolonged for half its duration, never was the most favored design of God carried triumphantly through such varied vicissitudes. Nay, its lot seemed that of the just—tribulation appeared sent to try and chasten, and not to overthrow. Yet are we to suppose that this extraordinary exertion of Providence was all in favor of an antichristian usurpation, which was misleading men and ruining the cause of God?

Lastly, you must account how the Almighty uniformly made use of this dreadful apostasy as the only means in his hand to preserve and disseminate his religion. As the only means to preserve it: for, during the lapse of so many centuries, not a single heresy—I speak of such as Protestants themselves must call by that name—was condemned, crushed, and eradicated, except by its means, and through its decrees: Arians, Macedonians, Eutychians, Nestorians, Pelagians, and a thousand more, were anathematized by the Popes; and thus alone the doctrine of the Church was kept pure, and its faith unimpaired by their errors. Councils were called, canons framed only under their names and authority; and thus the morals of the faithful were improved and preserved. As the only means to disseminate it: for all portions of the earth, which have been converted to Christianity since the days of the apostles, owe the benefit to the Holy See. Scotland, Ireland, England, Germany, Denmark, Hungary, Poland, and Livonia were converted, from the fifth to the tenth centuries, by missionaries sent from Rome. The East and West Indies are under the same obligation: they may be said to know nothing of Christianity, except as the faith of the Roman Church, to which they bow with submission. And I will say, without fear of contradiction, that while there is hardly a country under the globe where the sovereign pontiff has not *many* subjects, no other Church, as I have before shown, can boast of the power of conversion to any extent, or with any durability. Now, at the very time that you must suppose this antichristian system to have been employed by God, as his only instrument in preserving and disseminating Christianity, observe that it publicly boasted and referred to those very circumstances as a proof that it was the rock whereon Christianity was founded,—the representative of the only authority whereon it was to be received as coming from God. And would he not have been countenancing to the utmost so horrible an untruth and deceit, if you admit this hypothesis?

You will not tell me that God knows how to bring good out of evil, and can make use of the worst agents; and that it matters not if the gospel is preached even out of contention, so that it be preached.* Such means are his extraordinary resources, they

---

* Phil. i. 17.

LECTURE VIII. 249

cannot be the ordinary course of his providence. I can conceive him sending a Sennacherib or a Nabuchodonosor, to convert his people, and purify them by chastisement; but I cannot, without blaspheming his goodness, imagine him giving such for their ordinary rulers, and intrusting to them, habitually and for ages, the protection of his inheritance and of his worship. I can imagine a Balaam, who came to curse, forced against his will to bring blessings upon the people of God, and prophesy the rising of the star from Jacob; but I cannot admit, without outraging his sanctity, that the prophets, from Samuel to Malachi, might have been a series of so many Balaams, dragged against their will to instruct a nation, whom they should have surpassed in wickedness. Nor could St. Paul have imagined all the apostles and teachers of the gospel for ages, publishing its doctrines only through a spirit of contention. Yet this is the parallel case, and such are the difficulties you incur, by supposing that the supremacy of the Holy See has existed in Christianity, in despite of the ordinances of God.

But admit it to have been given in Peter, and all is consistent; all is marvellous; all is beautiful. We trace through every age the fulfilment of the promise; we account for how it has stood the shock of so many convulsions; how it has risen unsubdued from under so many billows; how it has shaken off the mortality which gathers upon every sublunary establishment, and been the rock to which the parts of the vast edifice have been cemented, so as to have grown up into one holy building, and which has preserved them unshaken from age to age.

And it is, indeed, my brethren, an institution whose sublimity is worthy of God. To see religion thus become an object over which earth and its changes have no control; that scorns the boundaries which man's ingenuity or nature's bolder hand has traced, to intercept all communication between man and man; which can make its decrees respected and obeyed by nations who never heard the Roman name and conquests, save in connection with its truths; which can give a common interest, a bond of love, to people of the most different speech, and hue, and feature,—this is, indeed, the idea which we should naturally have formed of a religion coming from Him whose are the ends of the earth. What a thought, that when, on the coming festival of Easter, the sovereign Pontiff shall stretch forth his hand and bless his entire flock, that blessing will fly over seas and oceans, and reach climes to which the sun will not yet have risen, and fall as a dew on Churches which will not receive tidings of that day till long after the buds which are now swelling on the trees shall have seared and fallen into their autumnal grave!

It is painful to turn from these consoling thoughts, to meet the objections which prejudice or ignorance may make to this view of the papal power. But I know that some may here wish to step in, and remind me of the volumes that have been written on the crimes and iniquities of Popes. I shall be told that for ages they were but a worldly-minded race of men, only grasping at earthly power, and trying to tear crowns from the heads of sovereigns;—eager to grapple with all temporal dominion, and become at once the civil rulers and the spiritual masters of the world. In reply, I would first observe, that whatever may be the impressions of any individual regarding the character of some, or many, of the Roman Pontiffs, he has no right to apply them as a test for explaining the words of Christ, or for judging of the existence of an institution. Many holders of the Jewish high-priesthood disgraced their station, from Heli to Caiaphas, and yet was not the holiness of that state thereby lessened, nor its divine constitution; nor did our Saviour or St. Paul teach that worship and reverence were not to be shown it. We know that even among the apostles there was one capable of betraying his master,—of thus committing the foulest deed which the sun ever beheld: and yet does not that impair the character of the apostleship. And, in like manner, might we say, that if those Pontiffs who have disgraced their station were summed up, they would not bear the same proportion to those whose virtues have been an honor to Christianity, as the traitor Judas does to the apostolic body. If, therefore, the apostles' dignity was not impaired, or their jurisdiction lessened, by that circumstance, I ask whether this institution should be judged by the crimes of some among its possessors?

But on this subject there is a mass of deception or delusion constantly repeated, such as, if laid open, would astonish men, seeing how they had been led into such gross misapprehension. In the first place, it is customary to bind together the private, individual character of Pontiffs, and their public conduct; and yet there is a distinction necessary to be kept between them, as I observed at the commencement of this discourse. Our Saviour, in giving them such power, gave them a means of great evil as well as of the greatest good; yet did not, at the same time, deprive them of individual responsibility—he left them in possession of their own free will, in a position the most dangerous to which humanity could be exposed.

This supposes the possibility of a certain number being unworthy of their station; and that such has been the case, no one will deny; but, at the same time, in a number of instances, there is more misrepresentation than could be found in any other part of history. With regard to the Pontiffs of the first ages, no man will gainsay that they were all worthy of what they have received,—a place in the calendar of saints. Of the Pontiffs of the later ages, in like manner, it has been acknowledged, not only by Catholic but by Protestant writers,* not in former times, but very lately, that since the change of religion in some parts of Europe, by the Reformation, nothing could be more exemplary, or more worthy of their station, than the conduct of all those who have filled the chair of St. Peter.

The only part, then, of history, from which such objections can be drawn, is in those centuries which are commonly called the middle ages. Now, persons who profess to pass judgment on this period of history are, in general, totally unacquainted with its spirit; and without being competent to judge, by their true standard, of measures then pursued, but judging only from the no less peculiar and narrower views of their own time, many condemn the conduct of the Popes, as being directed by nothing but a desire of temporal aggrandizement and worldly imperial sway. But into this chaos and confusion, in which prejudice had plunged the history of those times, a bright light is beginning to penetrate, and it comes from such a quarter as will not easily give rise to suspicion. Within the last ten years, a succession of works has been appearing on the Continent, in which the characters of the Popes of the middle ages have been not only vindicated, but placed in the most beautiful and magnificent point of view. And I thank God, that they are, as I just said, from a quarter which cannot be suspected—every one of the works to which I allude being the production of a Protestant. We have had within these few years several lives, or vindications of the Pontiff, who has been considered the imbodying type of that thirst for aggrandizement which is attributed to the Popes of the middle ages. I speak of Gregory VII., commonly known by the name of Hildebrand. In a large voluminous work, published a few years ago by Voigt, and approved of by the most eminent historians of modern Germany, we have the life of that Pontiff, drawn up from contemporaneous documents, from his own correspondence, and the evidence of both his friends and

---

* As by Ranke, in his History of the Popes.

enemies. The result is—and I wish I could give you the words of the author—that if the historian abstract himself from mere petty prejudices and national feelings, and look on the character of that Pontiff from a higher ground, he must pronounce him a man of most upright mind, of a most perfect disinterestedness, and of the purest zeal; one who acted in every instance just as his position called upon him to act, and made use of no means, save what he was authorized to use. In this he is followed by others, who speak of him with an enthusiasm which a Catholic could not have exceeded; and of one, it has been observed, that he cannot speak of that Pontiff without rapture.*

We have had, too, within the last two years, another most interesting work, a life of Innocent III., one of the most abused in the whole line of Papal succession, written by Hurter, a clergyman of the Protestant Church of Germany. He again has coolly examined all the allegations which have been brought against him; he has based his studies entirely on the monuments of the age; and the conclusion to which he comes is, that not only is his character beyond reproach, but that it is an object of unqualified admiration. And to give you some idea of the feeling of this work, I will read you two extracts, applicable to my subject in general. Thus writes our author:—"Such an immediate instrument in the hands of God, for the securing the highest weal of the community, must the Christian of these times, the ecclesiastic, and still more, he who stood nearest to the centre of the Church, have considered him who was its head. Every worldly dignity works only for the good of an earthly life, for a passing object; the Church alone for the salvation of all men, for an object of endless duration. If worldly power is from God, it is not so in the sense, and in the measure, and in the definitiveness in which the highest spiritual power of those ages was; whose origin, development, extent, and influence, (independently of all dogmatical formulas,) form the most remarkable appearance in the world's history."†

In another passage he thus speaks:—"Let us look forward and backward *from any period*, upon the times, and see how the institution of the papacy has outlasted all the other institutions

---

* Eichhorn, Luden, Leo, Müller, and many other Protestant writers; whose attestations I hope to find a better opportunity to give at length. The English reader has, since this discourse was delivered, been enabled to study the character of this great Pope, by the interesting life of him lately published by Mr. Bowden.

† Hurter Geschichte Pabst Innocens III. und seiner Zeitgenossen, *Hamb.* 1834, vol. i. p. 56.

LECTURE VIII. 253

of Europe; how it has seen all other states rise and perish; how, in the endless changes of human power, it alone invariable has preserved and maintained the same spirit; can we be surprised, if many look upon it as the rock which raises itself unshaken above the stormy waves of time?"*

But to conclude this subject, I trust that, by degrees, what is doing abroad may be better known among us; and when we begin to contemplate those ages in the same true spirit as our continental neighbors, we shall discover many misstatements relative to persons who are most deserving of our respect and admiration, even independent of religion. And consequently the objections brought against the divine authority of the papal supremacy from individual examples will be very much diminished. I have thus endeavored to give you a summary view of the arguments whereon we rest the supremacy of the successors of St. Peter. You have seen what is the ground on which we base it; clear texts of Scripture, interpreted, I am sure without violence, but simply by their own construction, and by reference to other passages in God's holy word. You have seen how this institution has been transmitted and maintained through a succession of ages and of pontiffs, until we reach the one who at present occupies the chair of St. Peter.

The sympathies of his immediate predecessors have been particularly alive to this portion of their flock, and the very Church in which we stand† bears testimony to what the Holy See has felt and thought in your regard. I allude particularly to that venerable High Priest of God, who, of all others, exemplified in himself the indestructible tenure of his dignity; inasmuch as the mighty Emperor, who endeavored to destroy it in his person, yielded to the fate of worldly things, while he again rose, and sat in peaceful possession of the throne of his ancestors. He, Pius VII., testified his affection for this very flock, by presenting to this church, when first erected, the splendid service of church-plate, which is yet here preserved. I was in Rome at the time; and I remember well an expression which he used, when some remonstrated with him for parting with the most valuable sacred vessels in his possession: his answer was, "The Catholics of England deserve the best thing that I can give them." And from this feeling of paternal affection, he who now sits in that

---

* Hurter Geschichte Pabst Innocenz III. und seiner Zeitgenossen, *Hamb.* 1834, vol. i. p. 79.
† St. Mary's, Moorfields.

chair has not degenerated. Of him it may be said, that never did any man pass through the ordeal of prosperity more unharmed. Raised, successively and rapidly, from the humble and mortified retirement of the cloister, to be first a prince, and then the ruler, of the Church, he has changed nought of the simple habits, the cheerful piety, and the unaffected cordiality, which characterized him there. To the triple coronet which surrounds his brow has been indeed added a thorny crown, in the political turbulence of his own dominions, and the spoliating and disobedient acts of some of his spiritual provinces. But from these painful topics he can turn with consolation, to view the daily advances of our holy religion in this and other distant countries, and the constant increase of his children, where not many years ago his title could scarce have been whispered without danger. And the name which he bears is one of bright omen for us. Twice has it been the source of grateful recollection to Catholic England. It was the first Gregory who sent Augustine and his companions to convert our ancestors to the faith; and when a giddy spirit of error threatened to overthrow and destroy the work, the 13th of the name stood in the breach, supplied the means of education to our clergy, and cherished in his bosom the little spark, which is now once more breaking into a beautiful flame. It is from the very house of the great Gregory, and of his disciples, Augustine and Justus,* that the present Pontiff came forth to rule the Church, animated with the same zeal, and attached to the same cause. Oh! may the same results attend his desires; may he live to see all the sheep, which are not of his flock, joined unto it, that there may be only one flock and one shepherd; that when Jesus Christ, "the prince of pastors," whose vicar he is, shall appear, we may all "receive a never-fading crown of glory."†

---

* The Church and Monastery of St. Gregory, on the Coelian Hill, possessed by the Camaldolese Monks, were the house of that Pontiff; and on the portico of the church is an inscription, recording, that thence went forth the first apostles of the Anglo-Saxons. In this house, the present Pope lived many years, till created a cardinal.
† 1 Pet. v. 4.

LECTURE THE NINTH.

RECAPITULATION OF THE LECTURES ON THE CHURCH.

JOHN iv. 20.

" Our fathers adored on this mountain, but you say that Jerusalem is the place where men should adore."

SUCH, my brethren, was the question which divided men, and men who believed in only one God, at the time of our Saviour's mission; and precisely similar is the question which may be said to divide us now. There are some of us who say, that only we tread the true path of salvation—that only where we adore, is true sacrifice offered to the living God; and, on the other hand, there are who reply, "This is the place where our fathers have worshipped—this is the religion which we have been taught by our ancestors: why, therefore, should we be expected to abandon it on account of the claims of another, and a more exclusive system?" Happy would it be for us, if, like the Samaritan woman in this day's gospel, we had near us One to whom we could refer all our disputes—to whose judgment we should all submissively bow! Happy should we be, could we, in the presence of our blessed Redeemer, visible amongst us, examine our respective claims to be considered the true Church of Christ; and that we could be sure, through His personal decision, that the conclusions we come to are such as God hath sanctioned!

But, unfortunately I may say for us, although no doubt in the decrees of eternal Providence, most righteously, it is not given us to have such an absolute and final award pronounced in our differences; and hence it is our duty, with all regard to charity, to bring forward our respective claims—and more especially is this *our* duty, who feel sure that we rest them on the most solemn, on the most dignified, and the most highly sanctioned ground—if so, haply, we may bring to some conclusion the endless disputes touching religion, which have too long divided us, and those who have gone before us in the land. I have, so far as my small abilities allowed me, endeavored to present you with a simple, unvarnished exposition of the Catholic doctrine regarding the rule of faith. I have stated to you the grounds on which we base it—the authority, that is, of God's unerring word; so that we find ourselves bound to submit to the decisions, and to obey the authority, of a power which we are convinced has been established by Him. But, having extended my subject through so many lectures, and having, consequently, some reason to fear that, by being thus diluted, the arguments may have lost somewhat of their force, I propose, before entering, on Sunday next, upon a new and more important topic,* this evening to recapitulate the arguments which I have spread over so many successive discourses, that so their strength may be more condensedly and compactly pressed upon your consideration.

I need not state to you again the great and important difference between us and more modern creeds; that difference of which an eminent English divine, the one who, perhaps, has written most strongly in favor of the Protestant rule, observes, that "the whole of modern religion may be said to differ essentially on this one point—what is the groundwork whereon faith is to be built?† I rehearsed to you, in my preliminary dicourses, the respective opinions of the two religions; and I fully developed the principle of the Catholic rule of faith, consisting in the belief that there was constituted by God a compact body, or society of teachers, whom He promised always to assist, so as to instruct, through them, till the end of time. The conclusion was, that the Church, or organized society which He had made the depositary of His truth, should not be liable to the smallest error.

This Catholic doctrine I propounded to you, and placed in opposition to that principle of faith which constitutes each individual the judge for himself of what he must believe; which, putting the sacred volume of God's inspired word into his hand, tells him, that it is his duty to discover, and, when discovered, to believe, that which may seem there to have been taught. Now, it may be observed, that the truest and best proof of any hypothesis, simply considered as such, is to ascertain that it answers every part of the difficulty which it is intended to meet. For it is with it, as with the solution of a problem, where, if the result answer to all the data or suppositions it contains, and answer so, that on trying one portion by another, all are found to agree together, we are satisfied that the solution is correct. It is only on this principle that the best grounded and most universally

---

* The Blessed Eucharist. † Leslie.

LECTURE IX.

adopted theories of philosophy are based; it is on such reasoning as this, that the whole system of the heavens, according to the Newtonian philosophy, can be said to depend. We can have no means of arriving at an intuitive or direct knowledge of the constitution or construction of things; but where we find that laws hypothetically laid, uniformly correspond with all phenomena, and leave nothing vague, but, on the contrary, satisfactorily account for all their parts, such a result is the strongest proof that the system devised accords exactly with the truth of things.

It is on this form of argumentation that I have endeavored to proceed. First of all, I considered the outward form and inward constitution of the Church of Christ to which he confided his religion, as a state foreshown, constituted, and actually existing. As a state foreshown; inasmuch as I explained to you, how God had ever worked in a certain course or order of providence for the preservation of truth among mankind; how a certain provision was made of old, whereby doctrines and hopes revealed to mankind, but lost to most of the world in the corruption which ensued, were preserved; in the constitution of a certain establishment dedicated to that purpose. I showed you that this system was merely figurative of that which was to come; that all the figures, all the imagery and reasoning, and the very phrases which applied to it, were also applied to that which has succeeded it, as though this were to be nothing more than the perfecting and fulfilling thereof. I endeavored, at the same time, to explain how it was the natural order of God's providence, that the course once commenced should go on in a persevering ordinance, until the end; and how, although we might expect a more perfect development, and brighter manifestations, it would be expecting a violation of His plan of action among men, if we anticipated any sudden change, or complete interruption, in that course which He had once commenced.

I then showed you how, of old, there was a clear indication of some future means for the preservation of truth, and that a really efficacious provision; its necessary tendency being to perfect that of the former state, and therefore not merely to remove, but to exclude and prevent error. This forms one portion of the data given for constructing our system; and necessarily, whatever is built up as the Church of God, must be such as to fit exactly this basement presented in the old law.

We come, then, to the New Testament: all that can be required to frame this superstructure is there again and again described. We find, precisely, forms of expressions used through these descriptions which lead us to construct in our minds a perfectly corresponding system, so as to prove, that what is there established is really the fulfilment of former expectations. The same imagery is preserved, the very promises are made which seem necessary to fulfil what had been foreshown in the figurative dispensation. The harmony which reigned between the two counterparts upon the Catholic system was manifest, for the Catholic interpretation of the passages in the New Testament alone brought them into accordance with those which had before alluded to the provisions therein to be made, and thus formed the only interpretative link between the prophecy and its fulfilment. And this harmony between the two systems gives us a second element towards the resolution of the problem in hand.

Examining, then, more minutely the constitution of this new religion or Church, no longer simply with reference to that which we might expect to find it, but in its own internal and essential constitution as appointed by our blessed Saviour, we analyzed a series of texts; not, I believe, contenting ourselves with vague assertions, but decomposing them, when necessary, into words and phrases, and testing these by other passages on which there could be no doubt. The result was, that Christ did institute a governed society, or body, compactly and completely formed, which has within itself unity, and, composed of all the constitutive elements of a social body, possesses within itself authority and power, and recognises persons appointed for the exercise thereof. We found it, too, empowered and commissioned to collect under its sway the entire human race; and, what is far more worth, in it our blessed Redeemer promised so unfailingly to teach, until the end of time, and so efficaciously to assist, that whatsoever doctrines He had delivered to the apostles and their successors, should endure and be preserved in it until the final dissolution of created things. Here, then, we have several new conditions, or requisites, that must be found in the constitution of Christ's kingdom, or in the form of his Church.

In the next place, we found that there was a promise of a power to diffuse the Gospel; that a charge was given of preaching the truths of Christ to all nations and kingdoms that knew not His name, to all who sit in darkness and in the shadow of death. And, therefore, to the Church was given the power or faculty of carrying that commission into execution,—it was to be the chosen instrument of God in spreading the Gospel of Christ over the earth.

LECTURE IX.

In fine, descending into some particulars of its constitution, we examined, last evening, the provision which Christ, in the plenitude of His power, made for the preservation of unity;—by instituting the only means whereby this quality in any social body could be preserved—a centre of unity, a single point towards which all this system might turn ; by giving to the whole a firm basis, or foundation, whereon to rest; by appointing an authoritative government to control all its parts.

Such was the constitution of that Church which we had to discover,—such were the data to be verified; and no system can be the true religion of Christ which does not exactly fill up all that I have sketched out, and answer all these conditions;—which does not present a perfect correspondence with every one of these elements of demonstration. Now, I can hardly think it necessary to go into proof to show how every one of these conditions, required in the Church of Christ, we have a right to believe, exist among us. I say, I can hardly think it necessary; because I am sure that any one inclined to be on his guard against the form of argument which I have pursued, and, more particularly, any one who may have been cautioning his mind against being led away by this outline which I have drawn, of what we discovered in the Old Testament and in the Gospels, regarding the constitution of Christ's Church, if he was not at my former discourses, will suspect, that, instead of giving now the picture which we there discovered, I have been only propounding the system of Church government and authority which we maintain. For, it is impossible for any one acquainted with the Catholic doctrines on this head, not to see the exact uniformity and correspondence of parts between it and what I have here thrown together.

If it was foreshown of old, that the Church of Christ was in the form of a kingdom or government—that in the priesthood there was to be authority—that the Church should have such a saving power, such a certainty of decision, as that all its members were to be necessarily taught of God, and that all within its pale were to be peculiarly under his protection; most assuredly it is only the Catholic Church which holds such a system, which professes such a plan of Church government, as can exactly imbody all and every one of these images and types. In like manner, if it be said, that in the New Testament we shall find the fulfilment of this figure, by the institution of this authoritative system, it is certain that no Church pretends even to the possession of these rights, or professes to be so constituted, except the Catholic

Church. Again, you can want no farther details, to show that there is a power in this Church to promulgate Christianity; for, I flatter myself, I have sufficiently demonstrated, that, comparatively, or, if I may so speak, absolutely, every attempt made by other religions has proved a failure; that however bright their hopes at first, in every instance, where time has been given for full trial to be made, they have ultimately failed; while, on the other hand, not only in ancient times were Churches founded, which now have an existence requiring no foreign aid, but, since the great secession from the Church, the Gospel has been effectually preached in the east and the west, and religious communities have been established, which have stood the test of long, unwearied persecution, and of abandonment, neglect, and want.

In this manner I endeavored, step by step, to follow the different classes of proofs, and show, by a certain simple and inductive system, how aptly and completely that form of Church government—that groundwork of faith which we hold—combines and comprehends them all. I thus showed you this correspondence of parts from the first announcement to the last institution, from prophecy to its latest fulfilment, as laid down in God's infallible word.

But then, my brethren, we have examined also, although not in the same detail, that antagonist system, if I may so call it, which bases faith on a totally different principle. In my second discourse, I entered fully into the natural and internal difficulties which seemed to embarrass it. I endeavored to show you, that, instead of its proof starting essentially and logically from an admitted principle, and then going gradually forward through propositions successively demonstrated, till it closed in the full development of its principle, or rule of faith, there are breaks and chasms to be leaped over, in order to arrive at the conclusion which had been previously laid down; that there were such innumerable contradictions, difficulties, and impracticable conditions, inherent in its very scheme, as are sufficient to prove it not to be the rule of faith intended by Christ to guide the multitude of mankind unto His truths. But I did not submit it to the same process of reasoning, or the same minute inquiry, as the other. We do not ground our religion, as I have before remarked, on the exclusion of other systems, but on its own essential proofs and arguments; and, therefore, I conceived the true way of proceeding to consist in simply establishing our own faith—demonstrating that it was the only one established by Christ—and thereby leaving you to conclude the impossibility

LECTURE IX. 261

of any other's standing in competition. But it may have appeared to some, that I have shrunk from discussing, in the same form of argument, the rule of faith proposed by those who think not with us. I therefore propose to try, this evening, how far it will stand the same tests; recapitulating, first, for that purpose, some of the points on which I before touched in its regard.

I remarked that, whereas in the old law we had an express provision made for a written code, yet some of the most important doctrines known to the Jews, and by our Saviour found among them, were not contained in that volume, but handed down by oral tradition. I showed this to be the case with respect to the doctrines of the Trinity, the Word of God incarnate and suffering for the redemption of mankind, and the doctrine of a future state, and of regeneration. These observations tended to show, how strong must be the evidence which alone could establish a teaching by a written code, to the exclusion of divine traditions.

But allow me to ask, where are any of those characteristics which I have already described as exactly preserved in the Catholic system? Where is the constitution of a kingdom to be continued in a visible society of men—visible even as the former was, through external characteristics? Where is the slightest shadow of an institution corresponding to prophecy? of something which may be considered its perfection, by preserving men from error? Where is the security, in the Protestant rule, for the perpetuity of Christ's kingdom, so often clearly foretold in the prophets? For its system supposes, or rather assumes, the possibility of the entire fabric which our Saviour had raised, being reduced to ruins. Thus, if we apply the test of past dispensations, we cannot find their prophecies and symbols fulfilled and realized in the supposed Church of Christ.

But let us see what was the precise appointment made by our Saviour; and here it becomes my duty to examine those passages of the New Testament, on the authority of which it is asserted that the Scripture was to be the rule of faith in the new law—not only so, but its exclusive rule, such as at once necessarily renders not merely useless, but absolutely false, any system that supposes an infallible authority. It must be observed, that the line of argument pursued in supporting the Catholic doctrine on the subject of the rule of faith, is necessarily such as to exclude every other; in other words, that the Catholic interpretation of those texts which establish Church authority and promise the effectual and eternal assistance of the Holy Ghost, and of our blessed Saviour, therein teaching, necessarily supposes that men are implicitly to learn from that Church, in which alone is a security, on earth, against the possibility of error. You must overthrow all those express declarations and promises, at least, before you can establish the all-sufficiency of Scripture as the rule of faith.

On the other hand, the Catholic system does not in the least exclude the Scriptures; it admits them in their fullest authority; it allows that whatever is therein revealed is necessarily true; it holds that the foundation, or root, of all doctrines is to be virtually discovered in them. Thus, therefore, the Catholic rule cannot be impugned by any text that falls short of a denial of our system: so long as nothing can be alleged to the extent, that Scripture *alone* is the rule to be followed, our arguments in favor of Church authority are not impugned; because, that it is a rule of faith we admit to its fullest extent. But they who hold it as *the only* rule, exclude Church authority; consequently their texts must be so strong in favor of that only rule, as to overthrow all those that have been urged in favor of Church authority, and to compel us in spite of the minute reasoning employed to discover their meaning, to reject them, or render them compatible with the exclusive sufficiency of Scripture.

Now, in order to satisfy myself that I am not overlooking any thing on this head, I have carefully perused treatises by learned Protestant divines on this subject, so the better to see on what grounds they base the doctrine that the written word of God is the only rule of faith. I have been astonished, on opening one, and reading that portion which relates to the all-sufficiency of Scripture as the rule of faith and morals, to find the author, after simply summing up the proofs for its inspiration, proceed to say, that it contains a full knowledge of all that is necessary for man, because it teaches the unity of God in Trinity, and that Christ came on earth and died for mankind, and likewise instructs us on the way of repentance, a future state, and the resurrection of the dead: and conclude, that, therefore, Scripture was the sufficient and only rule of faith and morals.* Now, I would ask, what is the connection between the consequence and its proof? The Scripture teaches all these doctrines, therefore there is no other doctrine necessary to be learnt. This is the very question under discussion, and is assumed without proof— a form of argument which I have often had occasion to deprecate.

---

* Horne's Introduction, vol. l. p. 490, sixth edition.

LECTURE IX. 263

For, this reasoning takes for granted that those given doctrines which are laid down explicitly in Scripture are all that need be known, and this forms precisely the great difference between us.* There is in it, too, a savor of strong presumption; because it first of all pretends to settle what measure of faith God might exact, and so decide that the chosen measure, that is, what is clearly found in Scripture, must be sufficient. Now, God is master of his own institutions, and may have deemed it fitting to put the humility and faith of his people to the trial of submission, and may have chosen points of apparently minor importance for the subject of his trial; nor can we lay down, from any reasoning of our own, what are sufficient truths for salvation. We must be content to take the system as it has been framed by God, not as it might appear to suit our ideas of propriety.

The question, then, being in its nature one of arbitrary institution, is one exclusively of positive proof: and I would ask any sober and serious Protestant, if he can possibly consider such argumentation as this a sufficient ground to satisfy himself that God appointed the Scripture, the New Testament, in the first place, to be written, and, secondly, to be read by all men; and thirdly, that he pledged himself that, in spite of the errors and frailties of the human mind, all men should be able to arrive at truth by its means. Unless he can be satisfied that, in reasoning such as I have stated, all these propositions are included and demonstrated,—unless he is satisfied that they are so included and demonstrated, as at once to overthrow the conclusion naturally and obviously drawn from other parts of Scripture, wherein our Saviour appoints a Church to teach to the end of time, with a supernatural assistance, assuredly he must allow that this reasoning is not only superficial, but highly deceitful. The Catholic

---

* The reduction of this argument to logical forms will at once show its weakness and insufficiency. Mr. Horne's *thesis* or proposition, is that Scripture alone contains all that is necessary for faith, and his argument reduced to syllogism is this. "The Scripture contains the doctrines of the Trinity, repentance, &c.; now these are all the doctrines necessary for faith; therefore, the Scripture contains all such doctrines." Who does not see that the second, or *minor* proposition, contains the entire question between us, yet of this no proof is brought, but it is assumed. And, doubtless, if any one asked the propounder of such an argument on what grounds he proved these doctrines sufficient for salvation, his answer *must* be, "because they alone are clearly laid down in Scripture." I say *must* be, because his principle prevents his allowing any doctrines on any other ground. But then such an answer at once shows that the entire argument moves in a vicious circle. 1. "The Scripture is all-sufficient because it contains all doctrines necessary to be believed." 2 "The doctrines so assumed are all that are necessary to be believed, because they alone are to be found in Scripture."

LECTURE IX.

Church, on the contrary, places the ground of faith, and the rule which is to guide men to truth, manifestly on a firm, fair, and logical basis.

But there are texts of Scripture, often quoted for the purpose of demonstrating that the New Testament is the rule of faith. Our Saviour, for instance, says to the Jews,—"Search the Scriptures, and the same are they that give testimony of me."*

1. Surely, my brethren, these words, when compared with their use upon another occasion, must tend to show, upon how many accidental circumstances the use of this rule depends, and how uncertain it must be in its application. "Search the Scriptures," exclaims our Saviour to the Jews, "and the same are they that give testimony of me."—"Search the Scriptures," triumphantly cry the priests and Pharisees to Nicodemus, "and see that out of Galilee a prophet riseth not."† The one justly calls upon the impartial and docile to look into the sacred volume for evidence of his being the true Messiah; the other appeals to the very same book, for a demonstration that his claims are ungrounded. Is not this a case of daily occurrence? Do not the impugners of our Lord's divinity maintain that it is rejected in the same Scripture, wherein others see it so clearly defined? And must not the vagueness of a rule, the right use whereof so much depends on the mind of him who applies it, make it little qualified to form the sole guidance of a darkened and bewildered understanding?

2. But farther, my brethren, I cannot avoid being struck with a portion of the sentence not often quoted. Christ says: "Search the Scriptures, for in them *ye think* that ye have eternal life." These words sound to me like any thing but approbation of the principle. I would almost venture to assert, that, throughout the gospels, the verb here used, when applied out of a question,‡ is only expressive of an ungrounded opinion; in other words, that wherever any doctrine or proposition is referred to the *opinions* or *thinkings* of any one, the expression implies disapprobation. For instance:—"And when you are praying, speak not much as the heathens. For *they think* that in their much speaking they may be heard."§ "Whosoever hath not, that also which *he thinketh* he hath shall be taken away from him."‖

---

* Jo. v. 39.
† Jo. vii. 25. Such is the reading of the Vulgate and of many MSS.
‡ As "who *think ye* will this child be?" Luke i. 66, &c. In such passages no particular opinion is referred to.
§ Matt. vi. 7. ‖ Luke viii. 18.

'But Jesus spoke of his death; and *they thought* that he spoke of the repose of sleep."* But, on the other hand, when our Saviour, or the evangelists, wish to mark the correctness of the opinion, they use the verb *to know*. Thus:—"*Ye know* that the princes of the Gentiles lord it over them."† "When the branch is tender, and the leaves come forth, *ye know* that the summer is nigh."‡ "*Ye know*, that after two days shall be the pasch."§ "Rebuking them, he suffered them not to speak, for *they knew* that he was Christ."‖ "*Ye know* whence I am."¶ This invariable consistency of expression, when the opinion is approved or disapproved, seems to me to leave not the slightest doubt that our Redeemer did not approve of that almost superstitious feeling of the Jews, renewed in our times, that the possession of the word of God alone is sufficient to save. "In them *ye think* that ye have everlasting life!" Our Lord thus appeals to the Scriptures, simply as to an admitted ground, by an argument *ad hominem*, as the schools term it; that is, he even takes advantage of the excessive confidence which the Jews placed in their possession of an inspired work, and appeals to that very feeling to form the groundwork of his evidences.

3. But, after all, I would ask, what were the Scriptures, which the Jews are told to search? Were they the Old or the New Testament? Assuredly not the New, for it was not then written. Can you from such a command conclude, that because the Jews, who, as I have allowed from the beginning, had a written code, and for whom measures were taken originally and fundamentally, that they should have a written code, were referred to it, another Scripture, which did not then exist, was constituted the infallible and sole rule of faith? We cannot suppose that our Saviour would do any thing so strange, if I may so term it, as to refer them to a work then not even written; neither could they understand by his words any thing but the Old law. So that the command which he gave to the Jews, to search their own Scripture to find a testimony of him, is stretched so as to include other Scriptures thereafter to be written; or else it is maintained, on a ground of parallelism for which no proof is brought, that, in the same manner as these Jews were referred to some Scripture, so each and every Christian is obliged to search others, and therein find the truth!

4. Not only so, but the argument, to have any weight, must

---

* Jo. xii. 13, compare Luke xii. 51, xiii. 2, 4, &c.
† Matt. xx. 25, comp. Mar. x. 42.   ‡ Ib. xxiv. 32.
§ Ib. xxvi. 2.   ‖ Lu. iv. 41.   ¶ Jo. vii. 28.

be still more strongly distorted. For, because the Jews were told to search the *Old* Testament for the discovery of *one* specific truth, it is concluded that Christians must search the *New*, and will in it find *all* truth. Suppose, now, that we were speaking on any particular point of law, such as the treatment of the poor, and I were to say, "Search the statute-book, it will give you testimony or information regarding it:" would any reasonable man conclude, that I thereby meant to assert, that the entire law on every other subject, as on real property, was equally to be found specifically laid down in that volume? So here, when Jesus tells the Jews, that the Old Testament gives witness of his divine mission, who will not deem it unreasonable to infer, that another part of Scripture, not then existing, should contain the full development of his religion and law. For mind, he does not say that the Scriptures are *sufficient* to salvation,—that they contain the whole truth,—but only that they bear testimony of him; and on this one point the Scripture will truly give satisfactory demonstration.

The second, and the strongest text, is precisely of the same character. It is from the second epistle of Paul to Timothy.* "But continue thou in those things which thou hast learned, and which have been committed to thee, knowing of whom thou hast learned them; and because, from thy infancy thou hast known the Holy Scriptures, which can instruct thee unto salvation by the faith which is in Christ Jesus. All scripture inspired by God is profitable to teach, to reprove, to correct, to instruct in justice, that the man of God may be perfect, furnished unto every good work." From this text, again, it is inferred, that Scripture, or the written word of God in the New Testament, contains within it all that is necessary unto salvation through faith; and that men are required consequently to adopt it as their only rule.

1. Here, again, the same question presents itself,—what are the Scriptures of which St. Paul speaks? Of those Scriptures which Timothy has known from his infancy; consequently not the Books of the New Testament; for even here not a word is uttered about a written code for the new law—not a word about books to be compiled for the instruction of men in the doctrines of Christianity.

2. In the second place, what was to be learned from these books, that is, those of the old law?—and for what purpose was Timo-

---

* 2 Timothy iii. 14.

LECTURE IX. 267

thy to use them? The object is evidently the same as in the former case of the Jews. These Scriptures are able to instruct or make men "wise unto salvation, through faith in Christ Jesus;" that is to say, through the evidences they gave, Timothy had been brought to the faith of Christ: so that the knowledge of the Scriptures here spoken of seems only preparatory to coming into Christianity.

3. In the next place, what is the utmost said concerning them? Is it asserted that they are *sufficient* to make men perfect in faith? Are we even assured that they are *sufficient* for teaching, for reproof, and for instruction, or not rather that they are *profitable* and useful? And does not the Catholic say precisely the same? Do not we teach, that the Scripture is most profitable, most useful, and most conducive to everything good? that it should be studied and practised as the guide and rule of our lives? But is there not a wide difference between asserting a book to be *profitable* for these purposes, and considering it exclusively sufficient? Even if that sufficiency had been stated, it would not have embraced the faith of Christ, seeing it only referred to the Old Testament.

4. Again, it is manifest that St. Paul, when here speaking of the Scriptures, does not teach that they should be individually read and used by all the faithful, but speaks only of their use for the pastors of the Church. For observe, that the purposes for which he pronounces Scripture profitable, are exclusively the functions of the ministry, and not those of the hearers, and learners, and subjects of the Church of Christ. He says, "it is profitable for teaching, for reproof, for correction, for instruction in righteousness." Timothy is warned to hold fast the doctrines which St. Paul had taught him, first knowing of whom he had learnt them, that is, on the authority of the apostles. The second ground suggested is, that of the Old Testament bearing testimony to the faith of Christ. Then he is told to remember, besides, that this Scripture is profitable for the work of the ministry, for correcting, reproving, and instructing. These are manifestly all heads, not of individual conviction, but essentially appertaining to the ministry, or priesthood; and if any thing can thence be deduced regarding the use of the Scripture, it can only be that pastors should be familiar with them, and know how to use them for the edification of their flocks.

5. But, for what end is Scripture to be so used? Is it for the building up of a complete system of faith even in the minister of God? Most certainly not; the profitableness of God's word

is simply that by the teaching, the reproving, and correcting, thence drawn, "the man of God may be perfect, *furnished to every good work.*" Whether, therefore, by the man of God you understand each Christian, or, with greater probability, the minister of God,* it is the fulfilment by him of the moral law, not the construction of systematic faith, which has to be attained by the profitable use of the Bible. Surely these multiplied considerations are sufficient to disprove the application made of this passage, to show that Scripture exclusively is a rule of faith, and that for every individual. Then, too, contrast with it the proofs which I drew from the very epistles of St. Paul to Timothy, in favor of traditional teaching;† throw them into balance with the considerations which I have proposed, and then see what weight will be found in the naked words of this text, and the unproved consequences which are from it drawn.

An argument is sometimes drawn from another passage. In the Acts of the Apostles, where we read: "These (*the Berœans*) were more noble than those of Thessalonica, *in that* they received the word with all readiness of mind, and searched the Scripture daily, whether those things were so."‡ Such is the authorized Anglican version of the text; and we are triumphantly asked, is not this a clear approbation of the Protestant method, of personally investigating, through Scripture, the doctrines taught.

1. But, first, I must protest against the accuracy of the translation. In the original text, as well as in the most ancient versions, it is simply written, "they were nobler (or better disposed) *who* received the word," &c.§ Their being more noble is not proved, as the English version intimates, by their searching the Scriptures.

2. The Scriptures here alluded to are, once more, only those of the Old Testament.

3. These Berœans are supposed to be commended for search-

---

* This term "man of God" is only used in one other place in the New Testament, and then it is addressed by St. Paul to Timothy himself: "but thou, O man of God, fly these things." 1 Tim. vi. 11. This consideration makes it probable, that "the man of God" of the second epistle is Timothy individually, and then the passage will still less bear the extended interpretation given to it by Protestants. But should it be deemed necessary to extend the meaning of the phrase, we must go to the Old Testament for its explanation, where "a man of God" is invariably one sent by God as his special minister, prophet, or commissioner. Consult Deut. xxxiii. 1; Jos. xiv. 6; 1 Kings (Sam.) ix. 7, 8; 4 (1) Kings i. 9–13; iv. 7–27; 2 Chron. viii. 14; xi. 2, &c.

† See Lecture v. pp. 112–114. ‡ Acts xvii. 11.

§ Οἵτινες is the word translated by "in that." In the Vulgate, *qui*, "who;" in the venerable Syrian version it is, "*and they* heard the word."

ing in the Scriptures—to verify *whose* doctrines? Why, the very apostles! the very writers of the New Testament! Will any one push the principle of Bible investigation to this point—to say that not even the word of an inspired apostle was to be received, but was to be subjected to the private scrutiny of every ordinary Christian layman? Surely not: what then are we to understand by this passage? Clearly that persons *not yet* Christians, like the Jews of Berœa, and not convinced of the divine mission of those who preach to them, have a right, nay a duty, of investigating the evidence which they bring. The apostles, speaking to Jews, naturally appealed to the prophecies of the Old Testament, as the simplest and strongest evidence of the truth which they proclaimed. Their hearers naturally and most justly verified their quotations, and satisfied themselves of their correct application. But surely, when once convinced by these means, that those who addressed them were sent by God, this task was at an end; and nothing more remained, but that they should with docility attend to their teaching.

These are literally the only texts of Scripture brought forward, with any plausibility whatever, in favor of the word of God's being, in the new covenant, the exclusive ground of faith; and I will put it to any impartial mind, if these texts, after the reflections I have made on them, contrasted with the power given to the Church to teach, and the divine sanction permanently promised to her, are of sufficient strength to overthrow the authority on which the Catholic religion bases its rule of faith, as demonstrated by so many and such concurrent testimonies? So far, then, we have conducted our inquiry to this point—to the establishment of a system of faith, such as the Catholic Church supposes, and to the exclusion of that which expects from each one the formation of a particular code of religion, extracted from the written word of God. We have, in other words, come to the conclusion that Christ appointed a Church, with full authority to teach, and with a full guarantee from himself, that it should not fall into error.

But a question immediately presents itself. Upon what grounds does the Catholic Church arrogate to itself to be this one Church? Why should not these prerogatives reside in the Church of England? Has not it also a claim to this authority? Why not in the Greek Church, or in various other oriental Churches? Why not in the collection of all Churches together? This is the subject to which I now proceed, and I must be content to discuss it in a very compendious manner. Last Wednes-

LECTURE IX.

day, I spoke at length on what is considered by us the supreme authority of God's Church, and I necessarily went into some remarks on the constant and uninterrupted succession of pastors in our Church. On a former occasion, I showed you, likewise, (and I quoted the authority of a learned divine of the Church of England to prove it acknowledged,) that, even up to a late period, the Catholic Church was, as we believe it now, essentially the true Church of Christ,—that it was impossible to fix the period when it lost that title, other than about the time of the Reformation,—that is, at the celebration of the Council of Trent. Others, however, put the period of its supposed defection much farther back. But, at present, this matters not: for both parties concede the important fact, that we have prior existence; for both consider us as essentially connected with the foregoing and well-entitled state of the Church of Christ; and the only question is, *when* we lost our right to that title. They grant, what nobody can deny, that, so far as external connection goes, the series of bishops is uninterrupted in the Catholic Church. We can name, without a doubt of any moment, the exact order of succession, and the term of reign enjoyed by each Pontiff, in the Roman See. And in many churches of Italy, France, Spain, and Germany, we can show a succession of bishops, from him who first held the See, to the present day. Now, therefore, it requires authoritative argument to drive any one from the possession of that which he has preserved by uninterrupted links. It requires very strong proofs on the other side, to show how we have forfeited the title which we had in the beginning, to be considered the only legitimate and undisputed possessors of these Sees; or, in other words, the representatives of the Church of Christ: for it is admitted, that, when these Sees were founded, they formed the Church of Christ. Their bishops have remained in them to this moment, and they must be proved to have fallen away, and to have lost their right as the successors of that Church, which is acknowledged by all to have been originally perfect in its doctrines. If we seek a counterpart in the Greeks and their Church, we find a manifest connection and communion with us up to a certain time; they then, by a formal act, throw off their allegiance and erect themselves into an independent communion; and, while all this happens, we move not, we remain in the same position in which we were before they left us. By that act did they acquire new claims, or did we forfeit those which we had before? Coming down to a later period, it is acknowledged that the Church of England separated from that of Rome; various reasons have been brought to prove that the separation was lawful, and to justify the grounds on which it took place. There is, consequently, an acknowledgment that a change of state occurred in her, while we remain still in possession of whatever rights we previously held; and strong positive arguments must be brought to prove that we are not still what we are previously acknowledged to have been—the Church of Christ. We cannot be called upon to prove that we are to be reckoned still the same. We stand upon our rights, as the successor to a dynasty claims the crowns of his ancestors, or as any nobleman in this country holds the lands legally given to his forefathers, from whom he inherits. Whatever branches of the family may have separated from it, or may have accepted other titles or properties, that cannot affect the right line of succession which he represents.

But, without entering farther into the development of this argument, which would lead us into many secondary considerations, I am content to take the question upon common grounds. We are all agreed—at least the great majority of Christians in this country—in the acceptance of a common symbol of faith or creed; and profess in it their belief in One Holy, Catholic, and Apostolic Church.* I willingly stand upon this admitted principle. It would be exceedingly long, and in some respects invidious, to enter into a comparison of the respective claims of the Catholic, and of other Churches, to these qualifications; but there is one simple way of demonstrating which has the right to them; by showing, that is, which alone claims them. For, if we find that all others give up their right and title to these distinctives, it follows that they can have no pretensions to them; and if only one assumes them as its characteristics, assuredly we have enough to prove that it alone possesses them.

1. With regard to *unity*, all say that they believe in one Church, and profess that the true Church can be only one. But the Catholic Church is the only one that requires absolute unity of faith among all its members; not only so, but—as by principles alone I wish to try the question—the Catholic Church is the only one that holds a principle of faith essentially supposing unity as the most necessary quality of the Church. The Catholic Church lays down, as its principle and ground of faith, that all mankind must believe whatever she decides, and sanctions, with the assistance of the Holy Ghost; and this is a principle necessarily di-

---

* The Nicene Creed.

rected to bring all men's minds into oneness of thought. Its essence, therefore, its very soul, that which gives it individuality, is the principle of unity. The principle of the others is, that each individual must judge for himself, and make out his own system of faith; now dispersion, dissension, and variety, are necessarily the very essence of a Church which adopts that principle. And this, in fact, is practically demonstrated. For Leslie acknowledges, that the character, nature, and principle of private judgment is to produce variety, and difference of opinion, and even civil and general war. Thus, clearly, in the Catholic Church alone does the principle of *unity* exist.

But what shall I say of the character of *holiness?* Shall I enter into a comparison of the doctrines of the two religions, to show which is the most conducive to that attribute; or shall I compare the lives of most eminent men in our respective Churches? This is a contrast which has been often made, and may be easily repeated; and I have no hesitation in saying, that, avoiding reference to the present day, and selecting the leading characters, who in former ages have been distinguished as the public representatives of the two systems of belief, it has been made not certainly to our disadvantage, but, on the contrary, with a complete triumph in our favor. But I do not wish to enter upon this topic, as it would lead us into great details, and some, perhaps, of an unpleasant nature. Once more, therefore, I stand upon the principle. Our principle is, that the Church, as a Church, can never be immersed in vice, in wickedness, or idolatry, that she never can be but what St. Paul describes, when he speaks of her as the spouse of the Lamb, as a chaste virgin, without spot or wrinkle.* The Catholic Church maintains that, by the teaching of Christ, and the promised protection of the Holy Ghost, she is preserved essentially and necessarily from falling into a state of error, corruption, or vice. The principle of Protestantism not only supposes the contrary, but cannot be justified without it. It is only on the ground that the Church has not been always holy, that she has been, and, consequently, can be, plunged into the most disgraceful idolatry and wickedness,—it is only on this ground that Protestants can pretend to justify their separation, and the formation of a new religious system. Therefore, the Catholic principle supposes a provision for the maintenance of unfailing holiness in the Church, as one

---

* 2 Cor. xi. 2. Ephes. v. 27.

of its essential qualities; the Protestant assumes the destruction of that holiness as the ground of its justification.

The third characteristic is *Catholicity*. And here, indeed, we have the advantage of the name itself. It may be said that a name or designation is nothing—that we only arrogate it to ourselves, and have no right to it; and, consequently, that we are only grounding our claims on usurpation, when we consider ourselves the Catholic Church, because we have that name. Now, it is very remarkable, how, in the Church of old, this title was prized and valued; and how the Fathers, when proving that the Catholic is the true Church, observe that her adversaries wished to deprive her of that title, but never could succeed. They disputed her right to it, and yet were obliged to give it her. In like manner, whoever considers the present state of things, must acknowledge, that it would be as impossible to root out any established form of speech, as to make men cease calling us Catholics. They have added the word "Roman" to our title; but still, the "Catholic" cannot be separated from our name. At the same time, no other Church has succeeded in getting that title for itself. In several late works, we may notice the attempt to speak of the English Church as "the Catholic Church;" but such a phrase can only lead readers into error, or leave them in perplexity. To show the strength of this position, I will read you a few extracts from the Fathers of the Church; and you will hear how clearly they speak.

In the first century, it is said of St. Polycarp, that he used constantly to offer up prayers for the members "of the whole Catholic Church diffused throughout the world."* I mention this, merely to show, how early the name was assumed in the Church of Christ, although it was not then so extended as in later times. Three centuries after, St. Cyril, one of the most learned Doctors of the Greek Church, and Patriarch of Jerusalem, telling a person who had been converted to the Catholic Church, to persevere and keep out of the conventicles of other religions, says:— "Should you come into a city, do not inquire merely for the house of God, for so heretics call their places of meeting: nor yet ask merely for the church; but say, the *Catholic* church—for this is the proper name."†

St. Pacianus, a Father of the Latin Church, uses precisely the same argument:—"In the time of the apostles, you will say, no one was called *Catholic*. Be it so: but when heresies afterwards

---

* Euseb. H. E. Lib. iv. c. xv.   † Catech. xviii. n. xxvi. p. 729.

began, and, under different names, attempts were made to disfigure and divide our holy religion, did not the apostolic people require a name, whereby to mark their unity; a proper appellation to distinguish the head? Accidentally entering a populous city, where are Marcionites, Novatians, and others who call themselves Christians, how shall I discover where my own people meet, unless they be called *Catholics?* I may not know the origin of the name; but what has not failed through so long a time, came not surely from any individual man. It has nothing to say to Marcion, nor Appelles, nor Montanus. No heretic is its author. Is the authority of apostolic men, of the blessed Cyprian, of so many aged bishops, so many martyrs and confessors, of little weight? Were not they of sufficient consequence to establish an appellation which they always used? Be not angry, my brother: *Christian is my name, Catholic is my surname."*

In the same century, St. Epiphanius, a writer of the Greek Church, tells us that, at Alexandria, those schismatics who adhered to Meletius, called their Church "the Church of the Martyrs," while the rest retained for theirs the name of "the Catholic Church."† But another, and still more striking passage, is in St. Augustine. He says,—"It is our duty to hold to the Christian religion, and *the communion of that Church which is Catholic, and is so called, not by us only, but by all its adversaries.* For, whether they be so disposed or not, in conversing with others, they must use the word Catholic, or they will not be understood."‡ Again: "Among the many considerations that bind me to the Church, is the name of *Catholic*, which, not without reason, in the midst of so many heresies, *this Church alone has so retained*, that although all heretics wish to acquire the name, should a stranger ask where the Catholics assemble, the heretics themselves will not dare to point out any of their own places of meeting."§

These examples suffice to show the force of that name; they prove how preciously the ancient Christians guarded it, as we do; how others endeavored to wrest it from them; and how they contrasted it with those names which the others took. They remark how some were called Marcionites, others Donatists, or Nestorians; but none ever dared to take the appellation of Catholic; so that if one asked, even then, which was the Catholic chapel or church, they did not presume to direct him to any but

---

* Ep. I. ad Sympronian. Bib. PP. Max. T. iv. p. 306.
† Hæres. Tom. i. p. 719. ‡ De vera Religione, c. vii. T. i. p. 752.
§ Contra Ep. Fundam c. iv. tom. viii. p. 153.

LECTURE IX. 275

that of the true Catholics. Thus, as I have observed, the very title itself seems to give us claims to this characteristic; yet, not merely have we the title, but the thing itself. For our idea of the Church is that of its being a society or government constituted by Christ, with full dominion over the whole of the earth; so that men, whatever country they inhabit, may be brought into connection with, and attach themselves to it; and its endeavors to verify its name, by the extension of Christianity and Catholicity over the world, have been successful. But every other Church confined within its own state, every Church constituted according to a peculiar confession of faith, which its members have voluntarily defined, every such Church excludes necessarily that extension of dominion, that universality of communion, which is designated by the name of Catholic.

Once more, who are *Apostolical?* Is it meant by this term, that the doctrines taught in the Church are those of the apostles? Most certainly not. That the apostolic doctrines will be taught in the Church of Christ is certain; but that the teaching of true doctrines is the definition of apostolicity, is manifestly erroneous. For apostolicity of doctrine is identical with truth in doctrine; and the discovery of one is the discovery of the other. One cannot be a means for finding out the other. It, consequently, must consist in some outward mark, which may lead to the discovery of where the apostolical doctrines are. It is in the apostolic succession that this principle resides—in having the line of descent distinctly traced from the present holder of the apostolical See, through those who preceded him, to the blessed Peter, who first sat therein. This is what was meant of old by the apostolic Church; and this is the sense in which the Fathers applied the mark. I satisfied you, in my last discourse, how Eusebius, St. Optatus, St. Irenæus, and others, proved their faith to be the true one, by showing that they were in communion with the Church of Rome, and could trace their pedigree, through it, from the apostles. Thus did they understand apostolicity to be given as an outward mark, in the continued and unaltered succession from the time of the apostles. Here, again, although the matter is manifest, I do not wish to take it as one of fact, but to establish it on principle. We are the only Church which claims this succession; others do not; at least, the only way they can, is by tracing their episcopal line back to the time when they separated from us, and then claim as their's that succession which forms the chain of our uninterrupted hierarchy. Such a course is at once oblique, and goes not directly to the root. They wish to be engrafted on us, rather than pretend to any root in the earth itself. Yet the Catholic Church considers them as separatists from it, and, consequently, they have no right to the succession which rests on her line.

In this manner, adopting those lights which creeds or symbols of faith can give us, we come to this important conclusion—that, on principle, the Catholic Church alone maintains possession of these characteristics, usually considered as the *marks* or *notes* of the Church; that the rule of faith of other Churches, so far from supposing these to be in their possession, entirely excludes them, and allows them not to be held as ground of adhesion to themselves. And, putting the question upon an obvious, practical ground, I much doubt whether a preacher or clergyman of any Church but ours ever thought of exhorting his congregation to hold and prize their religion, or consider it exclusively true, on the grounds of its being manifestly one, *Catholic,* or *apostolical.**

A word, my brethren, which I have just used, brings me to another very important topic, connected with our present subject: I mean that doctrine which is known by the almost odious appellation of *exclusive salvation.* This is considered the harshest, the most intolerable point of the Catholic creed, touching its rule of faith; that we hold ourselves so exclusively in possession of God's truth, as to consider all others essentially in error, and not to allow that, through their belief, salvation is to be obtained.

Upon this matter allow me to observe, in the first place, that

---

* There is a striking contrast between the religion of the first ages and those sects which have sprung up in modern times, in the names wherein they respectively gloried. The former boasted of the name of *Catholics,* the latter have chosen a name expressive of *uncatholicity;* for to be called *Protestants,* or *protestors* against any other religion, is at least an admission of a rival, and, I may say, of a stronger, power. It is a name of separation, of antagonism, of dissent: it supposes struggle and warfare, so long as the name shall last—a creed built on rejection, and formed of negations, rather than a consistent and well-ordered system of belief. Again, they of old loved to be called *Apostolic;* the moderns prefer being named *Evangelical.* The former term seizes at once the great and visible demonstration of the faith, it carries the mind to the fundamental evidences of Christianity, it guides the thought along an unbroken succession of links from the latest time to the original reservoirs of incorruptible truth; the latter shows that the dead letter of the word, variously divined and understood, is the text of religious code; in other words, that the little light of individual capacity, as it is poured over its pages or successive lines, forms the guidance of each precious soul on the perilous and mysterious path of salvation! Which name seems most in accordance with the merciful ways of Providence on behalf of man? which places the evidences of his truth on the firmer basis? And does not the contrast of names, as indicative of a contrast of principles, stand well as now, if, for the *ancient* Church, we substitute the *Catholic?*

LECTURE IX. 277

you will find it difficult to analyze, to its extreme consequences, the principle of any Church professing to have a code or rule of faith, without finding yourselves led to the implicit maintenance of some such doctrine as this. When a Church draws up a confession of faith, and commands all to sign and submit to it, and proclaims that eternal punishment will reach all who refuse, assuredly it supposes that the teaching of such doctrines is essentially necessary to salvation. If not, what constitutes the necessity of doctrine in reference to the revelation from God? Our Saviour comes down from heaven, on purpose to teach mankind; does he propose his doctrines under a penalty or not? Does he say, you may receive or reject these, as you please? If not, is there not something incurred by refusing to accept them? Is there not the displeasure and indignation of God? Consequently, a penalty is necessarily affixed to the refusal of those obligations which Christ considered essential to faith. And the Church proceeds upon the principle, that these doctrines are so essential, that a violation of God's precepts and laws is involved in the rejection of them, and makes every one who culpably—mind, *culpably*—rejects, and does not believe them, guilty of refusing what Christ died to accomplish and propose. "He that believeth not shall be condemned."* This is the necessary consequence to which every formulary of faith leads; it is essential to the existence of every confession, unless a different view be expressly and definitively given.

Looking, for instance, at the formulary of the Church of England, contained in the Athanasian creed, and appointed to be read in Churches, I would ask if it be possible, for any man of common understanding, to read its commencement and conclusion, and not be satisfied that its meaning is, that whoever does not believe the dogmas contained in it, is out of the way of salvation? If that Church still compels its ministers publicly to read it, does it not thereby imply the necessity of teaching their flocks that the rejection of certain doctrines will exclude men from eternal life? and what is this but exclusive salvation? It matters not whether the distinction be wide or narrow; it matters not whether the exacted dogma be, the belief in a Trinity, in undivided Unity, or in justification in one form or the other; the principle is the same, whether it act in one degree or two. It is, therefore, most unjust to condemn the Catholic Church for holding only the same doctrine as is taught by others. And yet we

---
* Mark xvi. 16.

are perpetually taunted by this very Church, which puts so prominently forward, in one of the 39 Articles, the doctrine, that "they also are to be had accursed, that presume to say, that every man shall be saved by the law or sect which he professeth, so that he be diligent to frame his life according to that law," &c.* I have, so lately as yesterday, had a published letter put into my hands, addressed by a zealous clergyman of the Church of England, and one who has been exceedingly conspicuous in deprecating the doctrines of our religion, to a Catholic priest. He writes that he feels an anxious interest in his salvation, because he believes the doctrines of Catholicity to be fatal to his eternal welfare. He tells him that a continuance in them will involve the loss of his soul.† And what is this, but the doctrine of exclusive salvation?

Think not that we presume to pass sentence upon any individual, or pretend to pry into the secrets of the heart. God knows, my brethren, that, instead of brooding with gloomy delight over the dark and fearful statutes of His justice, we bow down in humiliation and sorrow before the awful cloud which envelops His mysterious judgment-seat. God knows, that, instead of seeking to straiten the resources of His mercy and compassion, and assuming the right of judging another's servant, we rejoice to dwell upon their varied and ingenious workings, and to trust that, while with Elias we pray for the enlargement of His inheritance, He may reprove us as he did the prophet, by assuring us, that even in the separated tribes he has reserved a host of sincere inquirers and conscientious observers, who have not knowingly bent the knee to error. He, in fine, knows that, if we have to reproach ourselves with any departure from his word on this point, it is, that we soften the severity of expressions, and too frequently cloak under soothing phrases, and often delusive hopes, the clear and uncompromising denunciations of punishment which it utters against those who do not hold all its doctrines. Surely we shall not be judged of uncharitableness, if the conduct of the meek and compassionate Jesus is to be the standard of fraternal love, and the model of his ministers. For the very gospel of this day affords us an important lesson on this subject.

Never, my brethren, were men more slightly separated from the acknowledged truth, than were the Samaritans in His time.

---

* Art. xviii.
† Letter by the Rev. Mr. Dalton to the Hon. and Rev. G. Spencer. I could give sufficient examples from other modern Protestants.

LECTURE IX.

Besides the Jews, they were, perhaps, the only nation upon the earth that believed and adored one God as a spiritual and perfect Being; and, as appears from St. John, they alone, like the Jews, expected a Redeemer and Messiah.* Not one grossly erroneous tenet of faith or morals can be substantiated against them; they, perhaps, only erred in not admitting *all* the sacred books of the Jews as canonical; a difference which modern liberality would not dare to condemn as wounding the essentials of religion. In fact, their only crime was schism in its most mitigated form: they had a rival temple, yet even in this, their priesthood was derived in unbroken succession from Aaron, and their worship was in strict conformity to the Mosaic institutions. In addition to these extenuating circumstances, there was much in their character to plead strongly in their favor. Their hospitality was so remarkable, that a Roman emperor erected a statue in their city to the hospitable Jupiter, in conformity, says an ancient historian, with the genius of the nation. Their charity was so superior, that our Saviour chose it as the model proposed in the most beautiful of His parables. Their docility was such, that, though in a state of rivalry and jealousy with the Jews, He made, in two short days, a considerable number of disciples among them. In a word, so prepared were they for the sublime truths of the Gospel, that, with a docility not equalled among their neighbors, they instantly yielded to it on the preaching of Philip, and with such unanimity, that it could be said, that, in consequence, "there was much joy in that city."†

It was with a woman of this nation that Jesus held a most interesting conference, at the well of Jacob: and, though her life had evidently been far from regular, He accosted her with that winning affability which ever distinguished His deportment. He concealed His real character, but she soon discovered Him to be a prophet; and accordingly appealed to Him, in the words of my text, on the great question of the religious differences between the two nations. My friends, what was his answer? Her very appeal to a *Jewish* prophet showed that she was sincere and confident in her persuasion; did Jesus fear to unsettle her belief, and therefore, by evasion, soothe her in her false reliance? She argues upon the most specious and most common palliative of error. "Our fathers," says she, "adored upon this mountain:"‡ does He dread to wound her feelings, or to shock the prejudices of her education? No, my brethren. Slight as were the dissenting

---

* Chap. iv. 25.   † Acts viii. 9.   ‡ John iv. 20.

LECTURE IX.

principles of these sectarians, amiable and charitable as may have been their characters, ripe as they were for Christianity, affable and conciliating as the interview had hitherto been, no sooner is this important question put, than He makes no allowance, no compromise, but answers clearly and solemnly, "*Salvation is of the Jews!*"* The woman flies to the usual subterfuge of delay; she hints at the difficulty of decision, and puts off the inquiry till a more favorable opportunity, when she may have the advantage of the Messiah's determination. But, that she might have no farther plea for her errors, and, above all, that the principle which He had just formally laid down might want no sanction, He instantly throws off his disguise, and stands revealed: "I am He who am speaking with thee."† Thus did this benign and charitable Saviour, who came to seek and save what was lost, and whose first principle it was, "I will have mercy and not sacrifice," thus did He hesitate not a moment to pronounce, in the clearest terms, that no deviation from the true religion, however trivial, can be justified or excused in His sight.

But, on this subject, I trust, I have said enough; it only remains that I draw some conclusions from the short course which I have finished this evening; and they will be addressed to you in the form of simple exhortation and unaffected counsel.

In the first place, I would beg of all, who have the true interests of religion at heart, to put themselves exceedingly on their guard against the various methods constantly pursued, to prejudice their minds against our doctrines. For many years, the Catholic religion in this country was an object of persecution, by slowly, but effectually, acting laws, tending to paralyze its energies, rather than completely deprive it of life. That period is now past, and I trust, that the remembrance of it, as far as any feeling of resentment is concerned, (indeed, it should be remembered in no way but to thank God for His mercies,) is as completely blotted out from the hearts of Catholics, as those statutes themselves are from the code of England. But unfortunately, since, another method of attack has been pursued, more open, more clamorous, more directed to wound our feelings; and not only so, but much more calculated to ruin the cause of all religion. I allude to that system of violent declamation and invective against us, in which so many, who call themselves ministers of peace, indulge throughout this country. It has been even the custom to send round men from town to town; and were

---

* John iv. 22.　　　　† Ibid. 26.

it for no other purpose than merely to preach their own doctrines in their own places of worship, we could not complain; not even if they went so far as to warn their hearers against what they conceived to be erroneous in us. But to make religion a matter of public declamation—to collect crowds of men in places usually appropriated to profane purposes, and to think it a most important duty to break, if possible, in sunder, the bonds of social community, of affection and kindness, which exist among members of different religions, must be blighting to the holiest virtues, and consequently to the interests of all Christianity. It is by the general feeling of society being declared against such a system, that it can best be checked and prevented. Whoever feels an interest in the welfare of religion, and considers it a sacred, and heavenly, and divine thing, a subject not to be approached with minds agitated by party spirit, or party violence, but rather to be meditated on in silence and in solitude, and to be argued with greater sobriety and solemnity than Plato used when demonstrating the doctrines of his moral philosophy; whoever so feels, will, I am sure, agree that this tumultuous, this unseemly, and unchristian way of appealing to the grossest passions, and exposing the doctrines of religion to an approbation or disapprobation expressed by the cheers and shouts of multitudes, is essentially degrading to its character, and tends to make men rather mix it up in their minds with the worst and most unworthy of passions and feelings, than to associate it with those sentiments of awful respect, and deep veneration, and pure affection, which it should inspire in the breasts of men.

It is only by such feelings being, as far as possible, diffused, that so odious, unjust, and cruel a system can possibly be crushed. But this is only a secondary consideration; what I wish principally to inculcate is,—that you insist always on proof, and be not satisfied with declamation. Never take the word of those who profess to give our doctrines, and who allege merely their assertions for it. Ask where those articles are recorded, where such a dogma is laid down, in what books or on what authority it is assumed that this creed, or article of faith, or practice, is taught by the Catholic Church. Insist that every point urged against us be demonstrated; and I am confident that such a system, if pursued, must lead essentially to the narrowing of differences at present existing between us, and bring many, who now wander, once more within the true Church. This anticipation may appear a dream, or an object far beyond our reach; but we have been too long divided, too long separated; and it is impossible not to suppose that divine Providence has appointed some method whereby all well-meaning and right-thinking men may be brought into one way of faith.

Another, and a still more important admonition, I wish to give, directed primarily to those who are not already members of the Church and religion which I have endeavored to uphold; that they proceed to the inquiry boldly, and without reserve; that they imagine not there is a single point whereon we shrink from individual and close investigation. They must not fancy, if they have hitherto done so, that we require so blind a submission to Church authority, as to refuse to satisfy sincere inquirers of the grounds of our faith, on every point—that we say even to the faithful, "Be silent and believe;" subject your understanding and reason to our teaching, and investigate no more. On the contrary, there is no point on which we do not court inquiry. Nothing would give us greater delight, than that any, who have been moved by what they have heard, should apply their minds to study, and seek whatever assistance we can give them in their endeavors to discover the whole truth of Christ. And again, another and still more important exhortation is this; if the inquiry, once made, shall prove satisfactory to their minds, if conviction shall follow, that the system which has been till then believed is not correct, and that the truth of Christ is to be found with us, let them not hesitate one moment between that discovery and the next step. It is fortunate that, in this country, nothing can any longer make a return to our religion odious or discreditable in any man. He does not thereby abandon the religion of his country, but only returns to that of his ancestors; to that religion to which we owe whatever is splendid in our monuments, glorious in our history, or beautiful and sacred in our institutions. When a learned and high-minded individual, after mature deliberation, and after having filled all Germany with the reputation of his writings, had become a member of the Catholic Church, that being a time when such changes were rarer among learned men than they are at present, it naturally excited considerable interest. The first time he appeared at court, he was thus addressed by his sovereign—"I cannot respect the man who has abandoned the religion of his fathers." "Nor I, Sire," he replied, "for if my ancestors had not abandoned the religion of *their* fathers, they would not have now put me to the trouble of returning to it. Such was the feeling that animated him, and made him brave the bitter taunt. Whatever apparent difficulties may seem to accompany the change, how-

LECTURE IX.

ever earth may rise against it, however connections and friends may tell you that you are making a shipwreck of all your happiness, depend upon it those difficulties will quickly disappear, and with them all that anxious care and racking uneasiness which must exist while the mind is in a state of doubt. For the moment the resolution is once taken, the hand of Providence will be instantly stretched forth to make that easy which before was difficult, and, linked in yours, will lead you forward over every rugged path, and every rising obstacle, to a secure and happy goal.

The course of lectures which I have till now delivered has been directed to point out the short and obvious way whereby this pilgrimage after God's dwelling-place with men may be best discovered. I have endeavored to show you the demonstration of Christ's rule of faith, upon broad and well-constructed principles, and tried to draw your attention from partial and detailed investigations, to the examination of the groundworks of faith.

For, my brethren, if God exacts correctness of belief in every point, He must have provided ample and easy means to attain it: and the advantage which men have taken of these means must be an important consideration in the judgment which He will make. His religion must be a path palpable and pervious, equally to the poor as to the rich; practicable to the feeble as well as to the strong: it must be a system which, while it satisfies, by its rigid demonstration, the scruples of the learned, explains itself, by the simplicity of its proofs, to the untutored inquirer. Its discovery cannot be meant to occupy the whole of life in search,—its acquisition cannot be intended to absorb all our mind by difficulties. It must be a system of belief, not of doubt; a state of peace, and not of uneasiness. It cannot, therefore, consist in the discussion of every separate point, which requires time, labor, and talent, and often ends in perplexity and agitation; it must be some visible and comprehensive whole, which unites and combines in itself the entire of God's revelation and law. In other words, it cannot consist in a mere gleaning of detached articles of faith from the most discordant communities, but it must be one of the numerous divisions of Christians which is the depositary, and holds the archives of the entire doctrine of Christ Jesus.

My brethren, if the stranger, who wished to worship the true God at Jerusalem, had been told that, though the synagogues and places of prayer might be numerous, there was only one temple in which sacrifice was acceptable to Him, in what way would he have sought this favored spot? Attracted by one superior building, would he have taken the description of the sacred edifice in the inspired pages, and endeavored to ascertain, by minute comparison with its separate parts, that this was really the fabric to which such glorious privileges were reserved? Would he have counted the exact number of its chambers, or discussed the architectural details of its vestibules and its windows, its columns and its roof? And if he thought he discovered some discrepancies in any one of these, would he have turned from it, satisfied that *its* claims were false, and determined to explore the obscurer quarters of the city, for a more exact type? Instead of this, the moment the stately, the superb, and finished edifice caught his eye, towering over every other pigmy building, exact in proportion and unity of design, resting with untottering foundations upon the very spot where its inspired builder laid its first stone; above all, when he entered the vast court, and beheld the great High Priest still wearing on his forehead the golden plate which declared him "Holy to the Lord," in uninterrupted succession to the first Pontiff of his religion, and saw the Levites sacrificing on the same altar, and performing the same liturgy, as were consecrated on the first solemn establishment of God's worship,—surely, upon seeing all this, he would yield to the overpowering conviction of his feelings, and, despising the slow process of measurement by the compass and rule, pronounce himself assured that he had found the true house of God, and be satisfied that the subsequent examination of details could not result at variance with the great and general evidences of its identity.

Reason, then, in like manner now. Think not to discover the only true Church of Christ by the painful task of minute examination; but seek out some great and striking system which may verify prophecy, and answer to the attributes of its founder. Let it be as the mountain raised upon the top of hills, a landmark, drawing towards it the gaze of nations, and a rallying point, attracting the tribes of the earth to ascend. Let it be a kingdom worthy of the son of David, refusing every name but that which designates its universal dominion, truly extending in unity of government from sea to sea, and holding in willing submission the uttermost bounds of the earth. Let it be the abode of unity, harmony, and peace, where all believe and act by the same rule; for our God is not a God of dissension, but of peace. Let it be perpetual in history, unchangeable and un-

LECTURE IX.

moved in principle; for, as the truth of God changes not, so must the depositary of it be unchanged no less. In fine, let it be one from which all others profess to have separated, but which has never departed from any; one from which others make it their boast that they have received priesthood, authority, and the word of God, but which itself scorns to derive them from any but the Eternal Founder of Christianity. If you find but one system which possesses all these qualities, and yet more, if you find only *one* which pretends to possess them, oh! by what principle of reason, or even of self-love, will you justify your refusal to embrace it? By what plea, before God, will you excuse any delay in studying and examining its claims?

Such has been our course till now: we have surveyed the building; it remains, that we boldly enter on the second task, of verifying the separate parts of that system, which, in the aggregate, so marvellously harmonizes with all that is revealed, and all that is worthy of God. This examination of particular dogmas will commence, at our next meeting, my second course.

"The grace of our Lord Jesus Christ, and the love of God, and the fellowship of the Holy Ghost, be with you all, brethren. Amen."*

---

* 2 Cor. xiii. 13.

END OF VOL. I

CARDINAL WISEMAN'S

LECTURES

ON THE

PRINCIPAL DOCTRINES AND PRACTICES

OF THE

CATHOLIC CHURCH.

VOL. II.

CONTENTS OF VOLUME II.

LECTURE X.
On the Sacrament of Penance................................... PAGE 7

LECTURE XI.
On Satisfaction and Purgatory................................... 32

LECTURE XII.
On Indulgences.. 59

LECTURE XIII.
Invocation of Saints: their Relics and Images.................... 77

LECTURE XIV.
On Transubstantiation—Part I.................................. 112

LECTURE XV.
Same Subject—Part II... 143

LECTURE XVI.
Same Subject—Part III.. 165

LECTURE THE TENTH.

ON THE SACRAMENT OF PENANCE.

JOHN xx. 23.

" Receive ye the Holy Ghost; whose sins ye shall forgive, they are forgiven them, and whose sins ye shall retain, they are retained."

I SHALL this day endeavor to explain to you, in the simplest manner, the doctrine of the Catholic Church regarding the forgiveness of sins ;. and the grounds whereupon she maintains the practice of confession to be an institution of our Lord. It would, however, be necessarily unjust to the subject to enter into it alone, and detached from those other important institutions, which we consider an essential part of the remedy appointed by Christ for the forgiveness of sins. It will, therefore, be necessary for me to enter, perhaps at some length, into other considerations connected with this subject, and endeavor rather to lay before you the entire form and substance of that sacrament, which the Catholic Church maintains to be one of the most valuable institutions left by our Saviour to the ministration of his Church—that is to say, the sacrament of penance, of which, indeed, confession is to be considered but a part.

Nothing is more common than to separate our belief and our practice; and then, placing the latter before public notice, as though standing on independent grounds, and having no connection with the former, to represent it as a mere human invention, devoid of authority in the word of God. In order to remove any impression of this nature, it will be proper to show you this institution, prescribed in the Church of Christ, as in close connection with other and still more important doctrines. I shall, therefore, endeavor to go through all the parts of this sacrament, comparing the institution believed by us to have been left by our Saviour, and preserved in the Church of God, with the method supposed by other religions to have been instituted, and to be in operation there, for the attainment of the same objects.

I have again and again inculcated, that in the works of God, or in all those institutions left by Him to mankind, there will always be found a certain consistency or harmony of parts,—so that whatever has been demonstrated regarding one portion of the system which He left on earth, must be allowed to be of considerable weight towards influencing our belief, at least as to the probability of other similar institutions having been provided. For example, with regard to the present case, all are agreed, that among the most important objects of our Saviour's coming among mankind,—I may say, indeed, the most important of all,—was that of rescuing fallen man from sin. We must, consequently, suppose that He did not leave his work imperfect; and, while we all concur in common belief, that the work of redemption was quite perfect and complete, as to his giving of a full equivalent to the divine justice, we must all likewise agree, that a means was provided by Him whereby this full and general redemption was to be applied to each individual case. No one can, for a moment, suppose, that because Christ died for our sins, we are rescued from all co-operation on our parts; that, without a single act, I do not say external, but at least of our minds, we shall have the full benefit of that redemption; that nothing was demanded from us, whereby that general redemption, which would have cancelled the sins of ten thousand worlds, was to be accepted by God in our particular case. Consequently, so far we may all be said to admit: first, that redemption was perfected by Christ's death; and, secondly, that some means or other, whether an outward act or an inward movement, is requisite to make that redemption applicable to ourselves.

But, if we look into the institutions of Christ, we shall see, that, in every other case at least, He was pleased to make use of external agency. Is not the blood of Christ applied to the sanctification of man in the waters of regeneration? Is not baptism a sacrament instituted by our Lord, for the purpose of cleansing the soul from original sin? Is not the sin there forgiven, through the only forgiving power, that is, through the cancelling blood of our Redeemer?—and yet, is not this applied by means of the outward act and ministration of man?

Was not the redemption of Christ complete in itself, so far as it was intended also for our greater sanctification? Were not His sufferings in themselves all-abundant, as directed to the end of uniting us in love and affection with Him, by making us feel what He suffered for our sakes?—and do not all agree, even those who differ from us in the real and essential character of the sacrament of the Eucharist—do they not all agree, that it is

LECTURE X.

instituted for the purpose of applying to ourselves those feelings at least which He intended to excite by His sufferings and death? And is not this again a visible institution? Is it not applied through the agency of man, and is it not done by outward acts and rites, both on the part of the minister, and of him who receives it?

Did not our Saviour come on earth to teach all mankind? Did He not establish a code of doctrines and morals, a system of laws for our edification both in faith and conduct? And has He not left an outward instrument of this in His written word? And has he not appointed ministers, and constituted a hierarchy, to whom was committed the care of His flock, with power and authority to instruct? And here, again, is not one of the most signal and important benefits which our Saviour intended to communicate to man, communicated through outward means, by an institution founded by Himself for that purpose?

Now, if the great end for which He came on earth was the abolition of sin; and that not merely considered as the cancelling of a general debt, but as a specific provision for each individual who requires the benefit of His redemption; if, at the same time, every other benefit conferred on mankind was attached to the outward observance of some given forms, committed to a ministry destined for that purpose: can we conceive the system so broken and unequal, that for this momentous object, no visible or outward means should have been instituted? On the contrary, if in the less important case—viewed with reference to the character of the guilt—of original sin, in which we have no personal participation, He was not contented that the child or adult should attain his end by any inward act of belief, or of any other virtue, formed by himself or another, but exacted that he should appear as an offender, and one seeking forgiveness and justification, that he should be interrogated and give promise of his fidelity in the face of the Church, and make confession of his faith before mankind, and so come to that visible rite whereby he is cleansed; can we believe that in the more important case, where the greater end for which He came on earth is to be fulfilled, in the wiping away of deeper and more enormous offences, actually committed by us, whereby His majesty and goodness have been more cruelly outraged, He should have left no outward visible means for the attaining of this mercy, that He should not, as in the other case, have required by outward manifestations of sorrow, some compensation in the sight of man! Now, on these grounds, even while approaching the subject from a distance, I am sure no one can consider it inconsistent with what we know of God's merciful dealings with us, of the natural line of His providential conduct towards fallen man, in the establishment of Christianity, to suppose that Christ left in His Church an express institution for the cancelling of sins, through the application of His all-redeeming and all-sufficient blood.

We now come to examine what is the Catholic doctrine regarding the existence of such an institution. The Catholic Church teaches, that Christ did establish on earth a means whereby forgiveness should be imparted to wretched sinners—whereby, on the performance of certain acts, all who have offended God may obtain authoritative forgiveness. It is generally said,—I mean by those who preach and write against our doctrines,—that the institution maintained by the Catholic Church to have been so established by Christ, is *Confession*. This, at the outset, is an error,—the Catholic Church believes that the institution left by our Saviour was the sacrament of penance, consisting of three parts, whereof confession is only one, and that one not the most essential. Here, then, is a manifest misstatement or misrepresentation, however unintentional, of our belief. For I will proceed to show you, that the Catholic Church teaches and urges the necessity of every thing that any other Church requires; and that even in more complete perfection than any. We believe, therefore, that the sacrament of penance is composed of three parts,—contrition, or sorrow—confession, or its outward manifestation—and satisfaction, which, in some respects, is also a guarantee of perseverance in that which we promise.

I. With regard to the first, the Catholic Church teaches that sorrow or contrition, which involves all that any other religion means by repentance, of which it is only a part, has always been necessary to obtain the forgiveness of God. It maintains, that, without that sorrow, no forgiveness can possibly be obtained in the new law any more than in the old; that, without a deep and earnest grief, and a determination not to sin again, no absolution of the priest has the slightest worth or avail in the sight of God; that, on the contrary, any one who asks or obtains absolution, without that sorrow, instead of thereby obtaining forgiveness of his sins, commits an enormous sacrilege, and adds to the weight of his guilt, and goes away from the feet of his confessor, still more heavily laden than when he approached him. Such is the Catholic doctrine with respect to this portion of the Sacrament.

LECTURE X.

But what is the contrition or sorrow which the Catholic Church requires? I believe that, if any one will take the trouble to analyze the doctrine of any reformed Church, on the exact meaning of the word repentance, distinguishing its different steps from the very act of forgiveness,—that is, examining closely the means by which we arrive at that last act, which purges us from sin, he will find it exceedingly difficult to resolve it into any tangible system, or any clear series of feelings or acts which will bear a strict examination. In the Articles, for instance, of the Church of England, every thing is laid down in the vaguest manner. We have it simply said, that "we are accounted righteous before God, only for the merits of Christ, by faith, and not for our own works; wherefore, that we are justified by faith only, is a most wholesome doctrine, and very full of comfort," and we are referred to the homily on justification for farther explanation.* Again, we are told that there is a place of forgiveness to such as truly repent.† If any one will read over that homily, he will find it repeated, again and again, that men are to be justified by faith alone, without works. We find, indeed, that love is spoken of as an ingredient in this faith. But we are never told how the sinner is conducted to it. We are never informed how his return, like that of the prodigal son, is to be accomplished, when he becomes sensible of his guilt; in what way he is to be gradually conducted to that faith which justifies the sinner. We are not even told in what that faith consists. Are we simply to be satisfied with the firm persuasion or conviction, that the merits of Christ are sufficient to purge us from all sin? Or, are we to believe that His Blood has been applied to us all, and that we are forgiven? Or is there a more individual application to each one, whenever sin is regretted? What are the criterions of that faith, its tests, whereby the true may be discerned from the imaginary or false? What is its process?—is it one of simple conviction? What is to authorize you to feel that conviction? What are the previous steps which make you worthy of it, which can make you suppose that you have obtained it? On all this we are left completely in the dark. Each one gives us the opinions or devices of his own mind; and hence we find as many different ideas, when we come to investigate the subject, as there are persons who have written on it.

But if we look into the works of the foreign reformers,—if we

---

* Art. xi. † Art. xvi.

examine the writings of those who may be considered the fathers and founders of the Reformation, although there is considerable contradiction and inconsistency, we yet have an attempt made to show the steps whereby the justification of the sinner is attained. We are told constantly, both in the works of Luther, and in the articles of faith of several Churches, that the first step is the terror of conscience; that the soul, contemplating the dreadful abyss of misery whereby it is surrounded, seeing itself necessarily on the brink of eternal destruction, is excited to a deep sorrow for its sins, and returning, through the merits of Christ and faith in Him, its sins are covered, and taken away in the sight of God. The preliminary step is simply terror, or dread of God's judgment,—the next and final step, is an act of faith in the power of Christ, to redeem and save by the efficacy of His Blood.* Now, not only does the Catholic Church require all these dispositions, but it considers them as mere inchoative acts, mere embryos, which must be farther matured before confession can be valid. The Council of Trent lays down a most beautiful and philosophical doctrine on the nature of this introductory act; it traces the steps whereby the soul is brought to turn away from sin by the desire of reconciliation with God. It does, indeed, represent the soul as terrified and struck with horror at the awful state to which guilt has reduced it; but this is far from immediately preceding justification,—it is but the imperfect germ which appears, before the full Christian virtue can come into bloom. For the sinner, awe-struck by the sense of God's judgment, is for a moment lost in fear and apprehension, till, turning naturally to look round him for relief, he sees, on the other hand, the immense mercy and goodness of God, and, balancing that with His more awful attributes, is buoyed up with the hope of mercy,—that he yet may rise and return, like the prodigal, to his father's house, with the prospect of being, at least, one of the last and lowest of his servants. Yet, is even this only another step towards the feelings of affection naturally excited, at thinking that God is so good,—that His kindness to us extends so far as to receive such wretched beings into His arms; and then love becomes mingled with our fear, which thus becomes the fear of the child, not of the slave; till, at last, the soul, inflamed with an ardent love of God, and determined never more to offend Him, is brought into that state which we find described in the New Testament, as the immediate precursor and

---

* See the admirable chapter on this subject, in Möhler's Symbolik.

LECTURE X.

cause of forgiveness. "Many sins are forgiven her, because she hath loved much."*

Thus, while faith is the principal root of all justification, there are yet other acts and other feelings of virtue, more conformable to the attributes of God, and more consistent with the order of His institutions in the New Law, through which the soul passes, up to that last act which seals its justification. St. Paul tells us, again and again, that, except through faith, no man can be justified, and that all justification is through Christ and through faith in Him; and so this progress of justification begins in that faith, and ends in the application of the Blood of our Redeemer, as the only means of salvation.

Thus far, therefore, we have every thing included in the order, progress, or purport of the acts of forgiveness required by any other religion for the justification of the sinner. And I will simply ask, before I come to treat of the other parts of the Sacrament, can it be said that this is a system favorable to crime? Can it be said, that the Catholic holds forgiveness or absolution to be so completely attached to an outward act, that he is reckless of the commission of offences, because he believes that his soul can be as easily cleansed from sin, as his body from outward defilement? that his penance is a bath or laver, wherein, by a plain and easy application, offences are washed away, and the soul restored to its original purity?

But we are not yet arrived at the close of this important subject: for it must be observed, that these are only the ingredients, or, rather, the preparatory steps for that act of sorrow or contrition, which is the essential concomitant of confession; and not only its concomitant, but so much superior and more important, that the Catholic Church believes and teaches,—and, in her daily practice manifests that belief,—that, if from circumstances a person have no means of practising confession, if illness surprise the sinner before the minister of repentance can approach him,— if accident place him out of the reach of such a comforter, and there be no one to apply the consolations of that institution,—an act of contrition, including a willingness, if in his power, to practise confession, because it is an institution established by Christ for the forgiveness of sins, will of itself procure their pardon, and reconcile him as completely with his God, as if he had confessed all his crimes, and received absolution. This, I say, is the practice and feeling of every Catholic, not only of the

---

* Luke vii. 47. Conc. Trid. Sess. vi. c. vi. Catech. Rom. Pa. ii. c. v.

instructed, but also of the most illiterate and least educated, that, in cases of sudden illness, or danger of being surprised by death, a fervent act of sorrow is equivalent to all that Christ instituted for the forgiveness of sins.

And what is that sorrow?—I will read you its definition in the words of the Council of Trent, of that council which has most clearly defined the Catholic doctrine on this subject. "Contrition," that is, sorrow—such being the technical term used in the Church for it, "which holds the first place among the acts of penance (or repentance,) is sorrow and detestation of sin committed, with a determination not to sin again. The holy synod declares, that this contrition contains, not only the abandoning of sin and a purpose of new life, but also a hatred of the old."* Thus you see what is expected of every penitent, before absolution can be considered of any avail, or confession worth any thing to his salvation.

II. And now we come to the second part of this Sacrament. The Catholic Church teaches that the sinner, being thus sorry for having offended God, and sorry upon the motive which I have stated,—that is, on account, not of evil thence resulting to himself, but of the graciousness and infinite goodness of the God whom he has injured,—must next perform an outward act, which would seem of itself the natural and spontaneous consequence of this feeling. Catholic divines have again and again described this sorrow for sin, when they say that it must be supernatural, that is, that its motives must be exclusively drawn from the attributes of God, from the consideration, not of what sin has brought on us, but of the manifestations of love which we receive from Him, and still more of His own essential goodness—that it must be supreme—that is, detesting, abhorring, and hating sin beyond every other evil on earth; and it must be universal—embracing, without a single exception, every fault or transgression whereby we have offended so good a God. Now, these dispositions naturally dispose the soul to make any compensation or atonement that may be required, for the offences it has committed. Not only so, but it is the very nature of love itself to make that manifestation—love, which was the last step in the work of conversion. We find it thus in the case of Magdalen, who did not rest satisfied with merely being sorry for having offended God, or with only regretting the evil done, and retiring from it, and, by a new life, proving her sorrow; but must brave

---

* Sess. xiv. cap. iv.

contumely and insult, and every other humiliation, to give public evidence of her feelings. She breaks through the crowd of attendants, penetrates into the house of the rich Pharisee, of one belonging to the proudest and most conceited class of men—she rushes forward and intrudes upon his solemn banquet, casts herself at the feet of her spiritual Physician, weeps bitter tears, and, lavishing all her precious things on his feet, shows by outward deeds, that she really loved God, that she was overwhelmed with grief from having offended Him, and was ready to make any reparation to His outraged majesty. Thus, the natural tendency of repentant love is to make some outward manifestation, to testify itself in some way by an act of sorrow, and even of humiliation before others, and so to seek that forgiveness which it so much desires. And therefore, even thus, we have a most perfect consistency in this institution, linking it harmoniously with the feelings that precede it; although, of course, this natural and spontaneous origin in no way forms the ground on which the Catholic Church believes and enjoins it.

She maintains, then, that the sinner is bound to manifest his offences to the pastors of his Church, or, rather, to one deputed and authorized by the Church for that purpose; to lay open to him all the secret offences of his soul, to expose all its wounds, and, in virtue of the authority vested by our Blessed Saviour in him, to receive through his hands, on earth, the sentence which is ratified in heaven, of God's forgiveness. But, as the primary object of this institution is the salvation of the soul, and as there may be cases where, by too easily receiving pardon, sufficient impression would not be made on the sinner to lead him to amendment of life; as it may happen that the dispositions wherewith it is approached are not sufficiently manifest, or that the sorrow is not sufficiently supreme; as also from constant relapse into sin, after forgiveness, it may appear that there was not a solid resolution of amendment, and consequently a sincere and efficient sorrow for the crimes and offences committed, so it may be prudent to deny that absolution. We believe that this case also has been provided for by Christ, inasmuch as He gave to the Church a power of retaining sins, that is, of withholding forgiveness, or delaying it to a more seasonable time.

Before entering into proofs of this doctrine, allow me to examine how far it is the sort of institution which we should expect our Saviour to have made. I have shown you already, that, consistently with the plan followed by Him, in the establishment of His religion, and according to the method of action which He has uniformly chosen, we should have expected some outward institution wherein the forgiveness of sins should be committed to his Church, and His sacred Blood be applied to the soul, for the cleansing of it from guilt. I did not, however, then enter upon the nature of the institution.

Allow me now to premise a few remarks on the aptness of such an institution as Confession, for the ends for which we believe it appointed.

1. In the first place, it seems the institution most conformable to the wants of human nature, whether we consider it in its native constitution, or in its fallen state. As to the first, it seems natural to the mind to seek relief from guilt, by manifestation: we are not surprised when we hear of culprits, who have been guilty of some great crime, and have escaped the vengeance of the law, leading a restless and unhappy life, until, of their own accord, they confess their guilt, and meet the punishment which the law awards. We are not astonished when we hear of those condemned to death, being most anxious to find some person to whom they may disclose their guilt, and when we hear it declared again and again, that they could not have died in peace, unless they had manifested their transgressions. All this shows that human nature finds herein the most natural and obvious relief, that even in that confession some balm is applied to the soul's inward suffering; because it is the only method left of making compensation to that society against which such men have transgressed. Nay, this feeling goes much farther; for the culprit, who at once humbly acknowledges his guilt, gains our compassion, and we cannot in our minds consider him any longer as the black and hardened villain, which before we were inclined to suppose him. We immediately trust that such a one is truly sorry for what he has done; and consequently his iniquity, although the crime may be equal, is not so great as his who daringly denies it. If the declaration of our Blessed Saviour had not been made to the penitent thief, or if it had not been recorded, we should in our minds have distinguished between the two companions of His sufferings, between him who humbly confessed that he died according to his deserts, and him who persisted in hardened effrontery to the end. If, therefore, God did establish any outward form, whereby the conscience might be saved from sin, we cannot conceive one more adapted to that purpose than the manifestation of sin.

It is, however, congenial to our nature, not merely in its general constitution, but still farther in its present fallen state. For

LECTURE X.

what, my brethren, is sin? It is a rising up of the pride of man against the majesty of God. The sinner, fully aware of the consequences of his iniquity, instructed in the end to which sin must lead him, seems to stand up before God's judgment-seat, and, looking his future judge in the face, insults Him by the commission of what he knows He will one day fully avenge. Now, what would be the natural corrective of this? the humiliation before others of that proud spirit that hath raised itself up against God, by its kneeling at the feet of man, and asking forgiveness, and owning itself guilty of having insulted God on his eternal throne. Pride is the very principle and root of all evil; and as the third portion of this sacrament, Satisfaction, which I shall reserve for another occasion, tends to correct that concupiscence and those passions which are the stimulants of sin, this seems to be the most completely opposed to that pride which is its principle.

So true is this connection between the confession of our guilt and the reparation made to the majesty of God, that His holy word considers the two as almost identical. For thus Josue spake to Achan: "My son, give glory to the Lord God of Israel, and confess, and tell me what thou hast done; hide it not."*

There are some beautiful reflections of Pascal's on this subject. He expresses himself astonished that any man could treat the confession of sin to one individual, under such circumstances as the Catholic Church prescribes, as any thing but the most lenient mitigation of what ought naturally to be expected. You have sinned before mankind, and outraged God by your offences; and you might naturally expect full compensation to be required, you might reasonably suppose, that He would demand a reparation as public and as open as the crime,—a humiliation as complete as was the pride in which you sinned. To consider as a hardship the manifestation of humility to one person deputed and chosen to receive it—to one bound by every possible law not to reveal, or in any way betray aught that has passed between you—to one who feels it his duty to receive you with compassion, with sympathy, and affection, and to direct, counsel, and assist you,—to consider this any thing but the most merciful mitigation of what is due from you, is an idea that fills the mind with pain and regret.†

2. But, in the second place, my brethren, not only is such an institution conformable to the wants of man; it is precisely in

---

* Jo. vii. 19.   † Ap. Möhler, *ubi sup.*

accordance with the method always pursued by God, for the forgiveness of sins. We find, in the old law, that there was an institution for this purpose, and that it was such as to make the manifestation of transgression preliminary to its application. God divided the sacrifices into different classes: there were some for sins committed through ignorance, and others for deliberate violations of the law. Now, in the 5th chapter of Leviticus, where the rules concerning such sacrifices are laid down, we find it prescribed, that if any one transgressed, he should confess his sin, and the priest should pray for him, and a particular sacrifice should be offered, and so forgiveness be obtained. Hence it appears that the manifestation of sins to the Priests of the Temple was a preliminary condition for their forgiveness, so far as legal sacrifice could be considered a means of pardon; that is to say, as a means of exciting faith in that great sacrifice, through which alone the forgiveness of sins could be obtained. I might go farther, and, as I have done again and again, point out more analogies between the systems established by God in the old law, and that by our Saviour in the new. But it is not necessary to dwell longer upon this point.

3. But, finally, such an institution is exactly consistent with the entire system of religion established through the new law. For we find, as I have taken some pains to show you, that our Saviour established a kingdom, or species of dominion, in His Church, consisting of an organized body, intended to minister to the wants of the faithful, with authority coming directly from Him, with a rule and command on the one side, and the obligation of learning and obeying on the other. Now, this system of authoritative government, which I also showed you pervaded even the minor department of the Church, as established by Christ, seems to require for its completeness and perfection, that there should be also tribunals within it, to take cognisance of transgressions committed against its laws, that is to say, the laws of God, to administer which, it was appointed. We should naturally expect, for the complete organization of such a Church, an appointment of authority within it for the punishment of offences against its fundamental laws and moral precepts; so as to be charged, not only to teach, but likewise to enforce, the practice of what is taught. Such an order, therefore, is consistent in every way, with the attributes of such a religious constitution.

Now, after these remarks, which I trust will have prepared the way, I proceed to the grounds of our doctrine, that there is a power of forgiving sins in the Church, such as necessarily requires the manifestation even of hidden transgressions, and that it was so established by Christ himself.

The words of my text are the primary and principal foundation on which we rest. I need hardly observe, that as, in the old law, a confession or manifestation of sins was appointed among the means of obtaining forgiveness, so there are allusions, in the new, to a similar practice, sufficient to continue its recollection with the early Christians, and make them conclude that Providence had not completely broken up the system it had till then pursued. They were told to confess their sins to one another.* It is very true that this text is vague,—it does not say, Confess your sins to the priest, nor to any private individual; although the mention of the priests of the Church, in the preceding verses, might naturally suggest the idea of their being a special party to the act. Further, the words, "Confess your sins one to another," seem to command more than a general declaration of guilt, or the saying what even the most hardened sinner, when all around him are joining in it, will not refuse to repeat, "I have sinned before God." They seem to imply a more peculiar communication between one member of the Church and another. At any rate, they serve to prove, that the manifestation of sin is not of modern date; and to refute the objection that there is nothing in the New Testament to show this natural, obvious, method of obtaining relief, to exist in the law of Christ.

But in the text, which I have prefixed to this discourse, have we not something far more specific? Christ was not addressing his flock in general, but was giving a special charge to the apostles; in other words, to the pastors of the Church; because I have before shown you, that when a command was given to the apostles, not of especial privilege, such as that of working miracles, but one connected with the welfare and salvation of the flock, it became a perpetual institution, to be continued in the Church. What does he tell them?—"Whose sins ye shall forgive, they are forgiven them; and whose sins ye retain, they are retained." Here is a power, in the first place, truly to forgive sins. For this expression, "to forgive sins," in the New Testament, always signifies truly and really to clear the sinner of guilt against God. "Many sins are forgiven her," says our Saviour of Magdalen. What does this mean? Surely that she was purged, cleansed from sin. Those who heard the words so understood them. For they said—"Who is this that forgiveth sins also?"† They con-

---

* James v. 16.   † Luke vii. 49.

sidered the privilege which our Saviour here claimed as superior to the power which He really possessed, though this embraced the working of miracles. Such an idea could only have been entertained of the right actually to remit or pardon an offence against God. That it was so, and moreover that they attributed a correct meaning to His words, appears not only from the parable of a debtor, which he applied to her case, but by the words which He actually addressed to her. For, first He said, "thy sins are forgiven thee;" and then, "go in peace,"—words of comfortable assurance, which must have led her to believe that she was fully pardoned. Again: Our Lord speaks to the paralytic as follows: "Be of good heart, son, thy sins are forgiven thee."[*] Those who heard Him in this case went farther than in the other, and "said within themselves, He blasphemeth:"—they considered it an assumption of a privilege belonging to God alone; they understood His words in their primary, obvious meaning, of remitting sins committed against the Almighty; and our Saviour confirms them in this interpretation, by the words that follow: "Which is easier to say, thy sins are forgiven thee, or to say, arise and walk? but that you may know that the Son of man hath power on earth to forgive sins," &c. To "forgive sins," therefore, signifies in the Gospel to pardon, to absolve, or to cleanse the soul from sin. But all this reasoning is superfluous, if we treat with those who adhere to the Anglican Church. For, their service for the visitation of the sick, directs the clergyman to say, in the very words which we use, "By his (Christ's) authority, I absolve thee from all thy sins, in the name of the Father, and of the Son, and of the Holy Ghost. Amen."

The apostles, then, and their successors, received this authority; consequently, to them was given a power to absolve, or to cleanse the soul from its sins. There is another power also given: that of retaining sins. What is the meaning of this? Clearly the power of refusing to forgive them. Now, all this clearly implies—for the promise is annexed, that what sins Christ's lawful ministers retained on earth, are retained in Heaven—that there is no other means of obtaining forgiveness, save through them. For the forgiveness of Heaven is made to depend upon that which they give on earth; and those are not to be pardoned there, whose sins they retain. Now, were a judge sent forth with this assurance, that whomever he should acquit, that person should go free; but that any one, to whom he should

---

[*] Mat. ix. 2.

LECTURE X.

refuse pardon, should be considered as not forgiven; would not this imply that no forgiveness was to be obtained except through him? And would not the commission otherwise be a nullity, an insult, and a mockery? For, would it not be an insult and a mockery of his authority, if another commission, totally unconnected with his tribunal, was at the very same time issued with equal power to pardon or punish delinquents, if there were other means of forgiveness, over which his award had no control? Not merely, therefore, a power to forgive sins is given in our commission, but such a power as excludes every other instrument or means of forgiveness in the new law. In fact, when Christ appoints any institution, for objects solely dependent on His will, that very fact excludes all other ordinary means. When He instituted baptism as a means of washing away original sin, that very institution excluded any other way of obtaining that benefit. In still stronger manner, then, does the commission here given constitute the exclusive means of forgiveness, in the ordinary course of God's dealings; for not only does it leave this to be deduced by inference, but, as we have seen, it positively so enacts, by limiting forgiveness in Heaven to the concession of it here below, by those to whom it is intrusted.

But what must be the character of that power? Can you suppose that a judge would be sent out, with a commission to go through the country, so that all whom he sentenced should be punished accordingly, and those whom he acquitted should be pardoned; and understand that this discretionary power lodged in his hands, could be properly discharged by his going into the prisons, and saying to one man, "You are acquitted," to another, "You must be punished," to a third, "You I pronounce guilty," and to a fourth, "You I declare innocent;" without investigation into their respective cases, without having the slightest ground for passing sentence of absolution upon the one, or of condemnation upon the other? Does not this twofold authority imply the necessity of knowing the grounds of each individual case? Does it not suppose that the entire cause must be laid before the judge, and that he must examine into it, and pronounce sentence consistently with the evidence before him? And can we then believe, that our Saviour gave this twofold office as the only means of obtaining pardon, to the priests of His Church, and does not hold them bound to decide according to the respective merit of each case? Does He not necessarily mean, that, if the Church retain or forgive, it must have motives for so doing? And how can we suppose these to be obtained, but by the case being laid before the judge? and who is able to do that but the offender alone? Therefore does the commission itself imply, that whoever seeks, through this only channel, forgiveness, must manifest the guilt which he has committed. He must bring the whole cause under the notice of his judge, and only upon its complete hearing can the proper sentence be pronounced.

This is the groundwork, in Scripture, of the Catholic doctrine, that sin is to be forgiven by the pastors of the Church, in consequence of the institution of Christ, who has herein appointed them as His judges, vicegerents, and ministers; and that, to obtain this forgiveness, it is necessary to lay the case—in other words, all our transgressions—before him who is intrusted with the responsibility of the sentence pronounced.

But, my brethren, clear and simple as this reasoning may be, we perhaps might feel ourselves less secure in sanctioning it, were we not so completely supported by the conduct and authority of all antiquity. Many of you may, perhaps, have heard it repeatedly said, that auricular confession, as it is called, was not heard of in the first or second century of the Church. Let it be so; let us suppose it, or rather, allow it for a moment. But do those who tell you so, (for the assertion is incorrect,) tell you also the reason why it is not so much mentioned? The reason is, that, instead of *auricular* confession, we read a great deal more of *public* confession; for, the sinner was obliged to manifest his crimes in the presence of the whole Church, and undergo a severe penance in consequence of them. And those who are such sticklers for antiquity on this head, and dislike auricular confession, should surely take antiquity to its extent; and if they reject ours, why not adopt the other practice, as consistent with the usages of the ancient Church? This is the fact; that the extent of manifestation of sins may be a matter of secondary consideration; whether the Church may direct private or public confession, is altogether matter of discipline. It is sufficient to establish that there is no forgiveness except by the manifestation of crime; that they who alone were empowered to grant forgiveness, are the priests of the Church; and that the practice of confession is exactly the same, with this exception, that in times of fervor, when crime was more rare, the Church deemed it fit that offenders should not only declare their sins in secret, but stand before the entire congregation, and manifest them publicly. Thus, instead of any argument arising against this institution, from the supposed silence of the ancient fathers, the only conclusion to which we must come, is, that there has

LECTURE X.

been a mitigation or reduction of its rigor, but no change in its essence.

I now proceed to read you passages from these fathers, and I will not come later than four hundred years after Christ; because, after that time, the texts increase immensely. I will divide them into two classes. I will first give you one or two where confession in general, that is, public confession, is alluded to; for they will show the feeling of the Church, as to its being the only means of obtaining forgiveness.

St. Irenæus, who flourished one hundred years after Christ, mentions that some women came to the Church, and accused themselves of secret crimes unknown to others. Again, of others he thus writes: "Some, touched in conscience, publicly confessed their sins; while others, in despair, renounced their faith."* Look at this alternative; some confessed, and others renounced the faith. If there had been any other means of forgiveness, why should they have abandoned their faith? Tertullian, who is more generally known, as being the oldest Latin writer, says: "Of this penitential disposition the proof is more laborious, as the business is more pressing, in order that some public act, not the voice of conscience alone, may show it. This act, which the Greeks express by the word *exomologesis*, consists in the confession of our sin to the Lord; not as if He knew it not; but in as much as confession leads to satisfaction; whence also penitence flows, and by penitence God is mollified."† This is said with reference, more or less, to the public practice. However, still more clearly as to its necessity. "If still you draw back, let your mind turn to that eternal fire which *confession* will extinguish; and that you may not hesitate to adopt the remedy, weigh the greatness of future punishment. And as you are not ignorant, that, against that fire, after the baptismal institution, the aid of confession has been appointed, why are you an enemy to your own salvation?"‡

Proceeding to the other class of passages,—for, as I have been led to speak at greater length than I intended, I must pass over several, much to the same purpose, and still speaking of the necessity of confession,—they treat of the manifestation of secret or hidden sins in confession to the clergy, as the means of obtaining forgiveness. St. Cyprian thus writes: "God sees into the hearts and breasts of all men, and He will judge, not their

---

* Adv. Hær. c. xiii. p. 63, 65.   † De Pœnit. c. ix. p. 169.
‡ Ibid. c. xii. p. 170.

actions only, but their words and thoughts, viewing the most hidden conceptions of the mind. Hence, though some of these persons be remarked for their faith and the fear of God, and have not been guilty of the crime of sacrificing (to idols) nor of surrendering the holy Scriptures, yet, if the *thought of doing it* have ever entered their mind, this they confess, with grief and without disguise, before the priests of God, unburdening the conscience, and seeking a salutary remedy, however small and pardonable their failing may have been. God, they know, will not be mocked."* Again, speaking of smaller faults, he thus expresses himself: " The fault is less, but the conscience is not clear. Pardon may more easily be obtained; still there is guilt: and let not the sinner cease from doing penance, lest what before was small, be aggravated by neglect. I entreat you, my brethren, let all confess their faults, while he that has offended enjoys life; while his confession can be received, and while the satisfaction and pardon imparted by the priests are acceptable before God."† Here we have two important points resolved:—first, that those who were guilty of only petty or smaller offences, not of great or deadly sins, went to the priest, and confessed their sins:— and, in the second place, that the pardon which these penitents received from the hands of the priest was considered valid before God.

There are a great many other passages to the same effect in this father, which I must pass over; and I will take the next from the Greek Church. Origen, after having spoken of baptism, observes: "There is yet a more severe and arduous pardon of sins by penance, when the sinner washes his couch with tears, and when he blushes not to disclose his sin to the priest of the Lord, and seek the remedy. Thus is fulfilled what the apostle says: *Is any man sick among you, let him bring in the priests of the Church*, (James v. 14.)"‡ Again: "We have all power to pardon the faults committed against ourselves; but he, on whom Jesus breathed, as He did on the apostles—he forgives, provided God forgive; and retains those (sins) of which the sinner repents not, being His minister, who alone possesses the power of remitting. So the prophets uttered things not their own, but what it pleased God to communicate."§ Once more: "They who have sinned, if they hide and retain their sin within their breast, are grievously tormented; but if the sinner becomes his own ac-

---

* De Lapsis, p. 190. † Ibid. p. 190.
‡ Homil. ii. in Levit. T. ii. p. 191. § L. de Orat. T. i. p. 22ʃ.

LECTURE X.

cuser, while he does this, he discharges the cause of all his malady. Only let him carefully consider, to whom he should confess his sin; what is the character of the physician; if he be one who will be weak with the weak, who will weep with the sorrowful, and who understands the discipline of condolence and fellow-feeling. So that, when his skill shall be known and his pity felt, you may follow what he shall advise. Should he think your disease to be such, that it should be declared in the assembly of the faithful, whereby others may be edified, and yourself easily reformed—this must be done with much deliberation and the skilful advice of the physician."* This is an interesting passage: we see an ornament of the early Church inculcating the necessity of manifesting our sins, and speaking just as we do now; exhorting the faithful to be careful to seek out and select a prudent and charitable director, and lay before him their hidden sins, and be guided by his counsel as to the propriety of making or withholding a public confession. You see, then, that the practice of public confession in the Church, so far from excluding private confession, supposes it; and that it was only to be made through the advice of a spiritual director, consulted for that purpose. And Origen expressly says, too, that only the priests have power to forgive, and that to them must our sins be manifested. Once more: "They who are not holy, die in their sins; the holy do penance; they feel their wounds; are sensible of their failings; look for the priest; implore health; and through him seek to be purified."† "If we discover *our sins, not only to God, but to those* who may apply a remedy to our wounds and iniquities, our sins will be effaced by Him who said: *I have blotted out thy iniquities, as a cloud, and thy sins, as a mist.*" Isa. xliv. 22.‡

A little later, we have some very strong passages,—several in the writings of St. Basil, who was exceedingly zealous in keeping up the penitential canons, and whose system of public penance prevailed through a great part of the East:—" In the confession of sins," he writes, " the same method must be observed, as in laying open the infirmities of the body. For, as these are not rashly communicated to every one, but to those only who understand by what method they may be cured, so the confession of sins must be made to such persons as have the power to apply a remedy."§ He tells us who those persons are:—" Necessarily,

---

* Homil. ii. in Psal. xxxvii. T. ii. p. 688.   † Homil. x. in Numb. T. ii. p. 302.
‡ Hom. xvii. in Lucan.   § In Regul. Brev. quæst. ccxxix. T. 2. p. 492.

our sins must be confessed to those to whom has been committed the dispensation of the mysteries of God."* In his canons, he declares, that persons who had been guilty of secret crimes, and had confessed them, are not to be obliged to confess them publicly :—" That women, guilty of adultery, and who had confessed it, should not be made public, agreeable to what the Fathers had appointed."† Clearly, the same discipline as is observed now, that they who receive the confession should be careful not to betray it. This is, again, auricular confession made to an individual. St. Gregory, of Nyssa, another eminent Father of the Greek Church, thus writes :—" You whose soul is sick, why do you not run to a physician? Why do you not confess, and discover your malady to *him* by confession? Why do you suffer your disease to increase till it be inflamed and deeply rooted in you? Re-enter into your own breasts; reflect upon your own ways. You have offended God, you have provoked your Creator, who is the Lord and judge, not only of this life, but of the life to come.—Inquire into the disease wherewith you are seized; be sorry; afflict yourselves, and communicate your affliction to your brethren, that they may be afflicted with you; that so you may obtain the pardon of your sins. Show me bitter tears, that I may mingle mine with yours. *Impart your trouble to the priest*, as to your Father; he will be touched with a sense of your misery. Show to him what is concealed without blushing; open the secrets of your soul, as if you were showing to a physician a hidden disorder; he will take care of your honor and of your cure."‡ Again :—" Whoever secretly steals another man's goods, if he afterwards discover, by confession, his sin to the priest, his heart being changed, he shall cure the wound : but then he must give to the poor, and thereby clearly show that he is free from the sin of avarice."§ I pass over a great many others, and quote one passage from St. Ambrose, the great light of the Church at Milan :—" There are some who ask for penance, that they may at once be restored to communion. These do not so much desire to be loosed, as to bind the priest; for they do not unburden their own conscience, but they burden his, who is commanded not to give holy things to dogs; that is, not easily to admit impure souls to the holy communion."‖ So that the persons who pretended to expect forgiveness, except by a com-

---

* In Regul. Brev. quæst. cclxxxviii. p. 516.
† Ep. cxcix. ad Amphiloch. Can. 34. T. iii. p. 295.
‡ Serm. de Pœnit. p. 175, 176, in append. ad Op. St. Basilii, Paris, 1618.
§ Ep. Canon. ad Letoium, Can. vi. T. i. p. 954. ‖ Ib. c. ix. p. 434.

plete and clear manifestation of their consciences, only deceived themselves and their director. To this authority we may add that of St. Pacianus:—"I address myself to you," he says, "who, having committed crimes, refuse to do penance; you, who are so timid, after you have been so impudent; you, who are ashamed to confess, after you have sinned without shame.—The apostle says to the priest: *Impose not hands lightly on any one; neither be partakers of other men's sins.* (1 Tim. v. 22.) What then wilt thou do, who deceivest the minister? *Who either leavest him in ignorance, or confoundest his judgment by half communications?* I entreat you, brethren, by that Lord whom no concealments can deceive, to cease from disguising a wounded conscience. A diseased man, if possessed of sense, hides not his wounds, however secret they may be, though the knife or fire should be applied.—And shall a sinner be afraid to purchase, by present shame, eternal life? Shall he dread to discover his sins to God, which are ill-hidden from him, and at the time that he holds out assistance to him?"* The confession, therefore, was complete—it extended to all sins, and obliged the sinner to manifest the whole state of his conscience to the minister of God.

These examples might be sufficient. I will, however, read one or two more from the same century. St. Jerome, after alluding to the institution of God regarding leprosy, thus writes:—"In like manner with us, the Bishop or Priest binds or looses; not them who are merely innocent or guilty; but having heard, as his duty requires, the various qualities of sins, he understands who should be bound and who loosed."† Here is precisely the same reasoning which I drew from my text, that the priest must not be content merely to give absolution on a vague impression of the guilt or innocence of the party, but that, only on judging of the different sins, can he know how to direct his sentence. I will just step, for one moment, over the limits I prescribed myself, and give you one decisive passage from Pope Leo. Thus he writes to the Bishops of Campania:—"Having lately understood, that some of you, by an unlawful usurpation, have adopted a practice which Tradition does not allow, I am determined, by all means, to suppress it. I speak of penance, when applied for by the faithful. There shall be no declaration of all kinds of sins, given in writing, and publicly read: for it is enough, that the guilt of conscience be made known to the Priest alone, by a

---

* Parœn. ad Pœnit. ibid. p. 316.
† Comment. in C. xvi. Mat. T. iv. pars II. p. 75.

private confession. That confidence, indeed, may be thought deserving of praise, which, on account of the fear of God, hesitates not to blush before men; but there are sins, the public disclosure of which must excite fear; therefore, let this improper practice be put an end to, lest many be kept from the remedies of penance, being ashamed, or dreading to make known to their enemies such actions as may expose them to legal punishment. That confession suffices, which is first made to God, and then to the priest, who will offer up prayers for the sins of penitents. And then will more be induced to apply to this remedy, when the secrets of the confessing sinner shall not be divulged in the hearing of the people."*

I should think that these passages, although I had prepared twice as many, must satisfy any unprejudiced person, that the doctrine of confession is not modern, and was not, as is commonly stated, introduced by the Council of Lateran. If any one will peruse the canon of that Council, he will find that, so far from establishing, it supposes the practice to exist over the entire Church; for it simply says, that "all the faithful, men and women, shall confess their sins, at least once a year, to a priest approved by the Church." It sanctions a discipline already observed in the Church, that all should confess their sins, at least once a year to their pastors. It takes for granted, that all know this duty; and surely it could hardly be conceived possible to introduce a new institution of this nature into this or any other country, by any act of convocation or of any other legislative body, enacting simply, that all the members of the Established Church shall confess their sins once a year to the clergy. I ask, whether such a canon as this enacts? or whether such a doctrine could be first introduced by it? Any person who should, three or four hundred years hence, say that such a practice had been so introduced into this country, would be considered very foolish and credulous. We must, therefore, conclude that it did exist, long before this canon, and that the canon only regulated the times of its observance. If you look to the nature of this institution, which the early Reformers used to call the "butchery of the soul," as being something too severe, too torturing, and cruel, to be practised, I would ask, could any one bring himself to believe, that an institution, which could merit such a name and character, could have been introduced so silently and so easily into any Church? Could it have been so introduced as to extend

---

* Ep. cxxxvi. al. lxxx. ad. Episc. Companiæ, p. 719.

immediately to all ranks, beginning with the sovereign Pontiff himself? Could it have been possible to induce all orders and conditions of men, the most learned as well as the rude, the noble as well as the plebeian, ecclesiastics as much as laymen, to go before their fellow-men, and cast themselves at their feet, and lay open all their hidden transgressions? I ask, if any thing but a conviction from the beginning, that it was an institution necessary for obtaining of forgiveness, could have secured the complete and constant exercise of this practice throughout the Church? The more difficult it is represented, the more it is said to do violence to natural feelings, to tyrannize over the human mind, the more difficult is it to suppose that it could have been brought into the Church, in this simple way, in later times. Or even, could it have been possible to find any other period at which it could have been so introduced?

But, my brethren, it is also very common to speak of this institution as one which tends to disturb the peace of families;— as one which causes great demoralization; and which leads, by the facility of obtaining pardon, to the commission of sins, from a conviction that the remedy is so easy. I have already said sufficient regarding this latter observation—I have already shown, that we require, not only whatever is required by others for the forgiveness of sin, but also a more perfect disposition, and, besides confession, the performance of that satisfaction, or those works of penance, which will form the subject of another discourse. Now, it is rather inconsistent to charge our sacrament with two contradictory defects; one of which makes it a burden too heavy to bear, and the other an incentive to sin, by rendering forgiveness so easy. These are two irreconcilable qualities, one only can belong to it; only one, at least, should be imputed to it. But is this heavy charge of immorality grounded? You will find quite the contrary expressed in their writings who caused this institution to be rejected in many parts of Europe. Thus Luther expressly says, that, although, according to him, the practice of confession, as used in the Catholic Church, cannot be clearly proved from Scripture, yet he considers it a most excellent institution; and so far from wishing to see it abolished, he rejoices at its existence, and exhorts all to use it. So that, even as a human institution, he thinks it is to be approved. In the articles of Smalkeld, we find that the practice of confession is to be continued; especially for the guidance and preservation of youth, that they may be thus directed in the paths of virtue.* Doubtless, too, the practice of confession is enjoined in the Established Church, in the same terms as by us; for we find that among the instructions laid down in the order for the visitation of the sick, it is thus prescribed: "Here shall the sick person be moved to make a special confession of his sins, if he feel his conscience troubled with any weighty matter. After which confession, the priest shall absolve him (if he humbly and heartily desire it) after this sort." Then follows, word for word, the absolution pronounced by the Catholic priest in confession. I do not quote this, to reproach the Church of England with inconsistency, nor to show how its practice and its commands are at variance, nor to charge those with injustice who impute to us as a gross perversion and corruption of the doctrines of Christianity, that which even their own Church enjoins and accuses us of usurping a power which is assumed and meant to be exercised, in the same words, by the ministers of their own persuasion. It is not for such purposes that I mention this rite; but only to prove that those who caused its abolition were convinced of its utility; and that, so far from considering it an instrument of evil, they believed it the best method of relieving the conscience, and, at the same time, of guiding men in virtue. They believed, or affected to believe, that God had left a power to his ministers to absolve from sin, and that a special confession of sins was therefore necessary: so that the difference between us is, that we practise what the others have pronounced expedient; that the Catholic Church exacts that duty which they keep confined to their books.

But I appeal to you, who know that the number of Catholics is not small; and that, even in these islands, those who profess the Catholic religion are more numerous than the followers of any other particular creed. I appeal to you, if our practice were mischievous and led to evil, would not some circumstances connected with that mischievous operation have, ere this, come before the public? Has any one ever complained of it? Has any Catholic—and assuredly every one can consult some conscientious and upright member of our Church—has any Catholic ever found that it gave him a facility for the commission of sin? that it was easier to him than the practice of other religions in this regard? or that any advantage has been taken of it, which is not strictly within the objects of the institution? Or has any Catholic father of a family, having himself, by experience, know-

---

* See Möhler, *ubi sup.*

ledge of the tendencies and uses of confession, been ever known to restrain the most delicate or timid portion of his family from its practice, or discouraged it in his servants or his children? This is surely an obvious test, when we consider the thousands that, even in this metropolis, practise it within the year; that not one case of abuse has ever been quoted, not one instance has been brought forward, of a Catholic's being led to abandon the practice of confession, by finding it conducive to any thing but good. On the contrary, if you inquire, you will find, that the Catholic considers it the greatest corrective and preservative from evil, that in his confessor he finds the most faithful, and sincere, and useful adviser, who, with the assistance of divine grace, best preserves him in that path of virtue to which he has been trained. On the other hand, one of the first symptoms of a Catholic's declining from virtue and piety is his neglecting this salutary practice: and those who have given themselves up to vice, take care to avoid it. I have said that I reserve the subject of Satisfaction for the next evening; not only because I have already detained you so long, but because it is connected with the doctrine of Purgatory, and praying for the dead, which will form, in conjunction with it, the subject of my lecture on Wednesday evening. In conclusion, I have only to exhort those who have the happiness to believe in the efficacy of the holy sacrament which I have just endeavored to explain—and those who are conscious that in it they find relief from their burthens, and forgiveness of their sins, to reflect that the time is now approaching which the Church has especially appointed for their partaking of its benefits. It is particularly at Easter that this holy Mother exhorts you to make use of this means of salvation. Employ, therefore, diligently the short interval that still remains before that holy season, as a time of more especial recollection and more peculiar fervor; retiring within yourselves, and preparing gradually for the solemn work which you have to do, not merely by looking into your transgressions, but also by studying the causes of your falls, by stirring up in your hearts a true and lively sorrow; and thus study to make your coming confession more effectual and more serviceable to your spiritual improvement than any which have preceded it.

LECTURE THE ELEVENTH.

ON SATISFACTION AND PURGATORY.

JOHN xx. 23.

" Receive ye the Holy Ghost; whose sins ye shall forgive, they are forgiven them, and whose sins ye shall retain, they are retained."

I OBSERVED, my brethren, in my opening discourse, that nothing was less easy than to render our doctrines acceptable to those who differ from our creed; because difficulties of the most contradictory character are ever found on some point of each doctrine. I may safely say that this remark is particularly true with regard to that dogma which I considered in our interview of Friday last, and which I shall continue to treat of this evening. On the one hand, as I then observed, we are told that the practice enjoined by the Catholic Church, as necessary to obtain remission of sin, is so cruel, so much beyond the power of human endurance, that it cannot be considered a means appointed by the Almighty, as indispensable for the sinner's forgiveness. I remarked that it has been called the rack, the torture, the butchery of the soul;* and it has been thought a sufficient reason for excluding it from the institutions of Christianity, that it was apparently so opposite and contradictory to its mildness.

But then, on the other hand, we are told that the Catholic theory of the forgiveness of sins leads to the commission of crime, by the encouragement held out, in the facilities which it presents of obtaining pardon. We are told that the Catholic, who has offended God, believes that he has only to cast himself at the feet of Christ's minister, and accuse himself of his offences, and that in one moment, on the raising of the priest's hand, he is perfectly restored to grace; and returns, prepared and encouraged to recommence his career of crime. How can these two objections be reconciled? How is confession so difficult a practice, and how, at the same time, does it hold out an encouragement to that evil of which it is received as a remedy? And if this answer hold with regard to that portion of the Sacrament

---

* "Carnificina animæ."

LECTURE XI. 33

of Penance, whereof I have already treated, you will see that the contradiction becomes still stronger, when you take into consideration the third part, with its accessories, which will form the subject of this evening's entertainment; that is, the doctrine of satisfaction.

But even here we are once more assailed by the same contradictory forms of reasoning. We are told, and that by learned divines of the present day, that this very principle, that man can make satisfaction to God, is enough to reconcile Catholics, through a corrupt sentiment of pride, to our doctrine of penance; that we call in the aid of that pride which is always too near to every man, by the idea that he can expiate his sins, or in any way make satisfaction to the divine justice; which feeling insinuates itself into his heart, and becomes more congenial to his spirit, than that process or means which other religions suppose necessary for justification. Assuredly they must know but little of the human heart, who reason thus. For, take a system which not merely exacts from the sinner all the sorrow and regret for sin which others ever demand; nay, which is not satisfied with merely the same determination never again to offend, and to reform his life, but, in addition to this, imposes a course of painful humiliation, consisting, first, of a declaration of hidden sins to another fellow-creature, and then of the persuasion that he must punish himself, and crucify his flesh, that he must fast, and weep, and pray, and give alms according to his ability; and will you for a moment imagine that all these difficulties become quite palatable, only because joined to the idea that an infinitely small portion of them has some sort of connection with a power, on the sinner's part, to please and satisfy God? For you will see, that the whole merit, so called, of Catholic satisfaction reduces itself to nothing more than this. Yes, I say, that they must have taken a very superficial measure of the understanding, and of the passions and feelings of men, who fancy that any other system opposes a severer barrier to sin, and can act powerfully on the offender, which does not demand from him the slightest outward act that can be disagreeable, and which places the entire difficulty in the consideration, that, by another *exclusively*, and by the application of His merits, the sinner is to be justified. Balance the two together,—weigh the systems, one against the other,—examine the internal structure of one, as I analyzed it for you at our last meeting; view it in its outward circumstances, calculate the painful sacrifices which it demands,—and, comparing it with the other, tell me which system, supposing each to be

Vol. II.—E

equally efficacious, the sinner would prefer, as most easy for obtaining pardon of sins?

But what a pity that this Protestant doctrine did not appear much earlier in the Church—what a pity that some among her zealous pastors in ancient times, holding a similar principle, did not then come forward, and, standing in the vestibules and outward courts of churches in great cities, cry out to the penitents clothed in sackcloth and ashes, some of whom had been for twenty and thirty years doing penance there, "Ye miserable, deluded men, what are you doing? You, that from a fond idea, that by these painful acts you are satisfying divine justice, are, in sooth, setting at nought the merits of the Son of God? You are undergoing all this suffering to no purpose; you are not acquiring the slightest favor or grace from God; on the contrary, you are only outraging his mercy and power, and denying the efficacy of his Christ's saving blood! Why not raise up your souls to God, and, laying hold of the merits of your Redeemer, without all these penitential works, in one moment be justified? and the time which you are now losing might be devoted to other and more useful pursuits." Such, no doubt, had been the preaching of a Protestant, had he existed in days of old. Think you that those holy penitents would have listened to it?—think you that, with the example of David and the saints before them, who feared not to expiate their sins, in humiliation and affliction before God and his people, they would, on the preaching of these doctrines, have opened their eyes, and discovered the principle on which they acted to be erroneous? Or can you believe, that, so soon after the establishment of Christianity, its vital principle was already lost?

But, my brethren, let us examine a little more closely the two principles of justification. It is said that the Catholic destroys the efficacy of Christ's merits, because he believes that it is in his power to satisfy the divine justice, in some respect, for sin: in other words, that the intervention of any human act in the work of justification, or this introduction of human merits, is radically opposed to simple justification, through the merits of Christ. I would ask, is there not as much done by man, in any other system, as there is here? How is it that, in the other system, he lays hold of the merits of his Saviour, and, by their application to himself, obtains justification? Is not man a sinner, and is not this a much more difficult act for one immersed in sin? Does it not imply greater power and energy in the criminal, than our doctrine that God alone can indeed forgive sins,

LECTURE XI.

but that He demands humiliation and painful sacrifices, to appease, in some degree, His offended majesty? Surely this is not giving very much to man, strengthened by grace; for, as you will see, the Catholic maintains grace to be the chief instrument in the work of satisfaction. But how much more do you attribute to man, when you suppose that, in a moment, while wallowing in his iniquities, he can appropriate to himself all the sublime merits of Christ, and, by an effort of his will, so completely clothe himself in them, as to stand justified and holy in the sight of God? The latter attributes to man a valid, complete act of justification, the other imposes upon him painful conditions, subject to a sacramental action, with the consoling thought that God will accept them.

But, proceeding a little nearer still with the investigation— what is the Catholic doctrine regarding satisfaction? I have proved to you, in the first instance, that sin is forgiven by a sacrament instituted by Christ for that purpose, for which the power of pronouncing judicial sentence of remission was communicated to the pastors of the Church. Now, through the whole of this process, which I showed you the Catholic doctrine requires for the forgiveness of sin, the entire power of forgiveness is vested exclusively and entirely in God: inasmuch as the minister no more acts in his own name, than he does in the sacrament of baptism, whereby it is believed that sin is forgiven; but is simply God's representative in taking cognisance of the case, and pronouncing thereon, with the assurance that ratification of his sentence will necessarily and infallibly follow. We believe that sin is forgiven and can be forgiven by God alone,—we believe, moreover, that in the interior justification of the sinner, it is only God that has any part: for it is only through His grace as the instrument, and through the redemption of Christ as the origin of grace and forgiveness, that justification can be wrought. And, in fact, no fasting, no prayers, no alms-deeds, no work that we can conceive to be done by man, however protracted, however extensive or rigorous they may be, can, according to the Catholic doctrine, have the most infinitesimal weight for obtaining the remission of sin, or of the eternal punishment allotted to it. This constitutes the essence of forgiveness, of justification, and in it we hold that man of himself has no power.

Now, let us come to the remaining part of the sacrament. We believe that upon this forgiveness of sins, that is, after the remission of that eternal debt, which God in His justice awards to transgressions against His law, He has been pleased to reserve a certain degree of inferior or temporary punishment, appropriate to the guilt which had been incurred: and it is on this part of the punishment alone, that, according to the Catholic doctrine, satisfaction can be made to God. What the grounds of this belief are, I will state just now. At present, I wish to lay down the doctrine clearly and intelligibly; that it is only with regard to the reserved degree of temporal punishment that we believe the Christian can satisfy the justice of God. But is even this satisfaction any thing of his own? Certainly not; it is not of the slightest avail, except as united to the merits of Christ's passion, for it receives its entire efficacy from that complete and abundant purchase made by our Blessed Saviour. Such is our doctrine of satisfaction, and herein consists that self-sufficiency, that power of self-justification, which has been considered sufficient to account for the Catholic's subjecting himself to the painful work of repentance, imposed upon him by his religion.

But, after all, the whole of the question necessarily rests on this consideration. Is it God's ordinance, that when He has forgiven sin, and so justified the sinner as to place him once more in a state of grace, He still reserves the infliction of some degree of punishment for his transgressions? We say, that undoubtedly it is; and I would appeal, in the first instance, to the feelings of any individual; nor do I believe there is any one, however he may think himself in a state of grace before God—however he may flatter himself that his sins are taken away—who will not answer the appeal. Why is it that, when calamity falls upon him, he receives it as a punishment for his sins? Why do our natural feelings prompt us to consider our domestic and personal afflictions as sent by God on account of our transgressions, although, at the moment when they come, we may not be conscious of lying under actual guilt? This is a feeling which pervades every form of religion, and more naturally that of Christ; because it is impossible to be familiar with the word of God, without receiving an impression, that He does visit the sins of men on their heads, although they may have endeavored, with reasonable hope of success, to obtain their forgiveness. No doubt, when we consider the trials of the just, we know they are sent for their purification, to make them more single-hearted, and to detach them from the world; we know that thereby God wishes to purge them from those lesser offences, which might otherwise easily escape their attention; but it is impossible not, more or less, to connect the idea of suffering inflicted with that of sin committed.

This principle is to be found through the whole of the Christian religion; because the very first principles of moral conduct, whether in the Old or in the New Law, seem connected with the necessity of purifications, and of works painful or disagreeable, or with sufferings sent by Divine Providence, as inflictions justly deserved. Thus, we remark constantly in the Old Law, not only visible demonstrations of repentance and sorrow, after sin has been forgiven, but clear indications of an approval of such conduct by God himself. When, for instance, He forgives the sin of David by the prophet Nathan, the man of God does not say, "The Lord hath pardoned you; arise, you have no further cause of sorrow; you are fully justified before God." But, he tells him that he still must atone for his crime; and that, therefore, his child, the fruit of his iniquity, shall be taken from him.* In like manner did God punish his later sin, of numbering the people of Israel, with a severity which extended over the whole nation.† Indeed, in every case recorded in the Old Testament, God, after forgiving the sins of His servants, fails not to reserve some temporal and expiatory chastisement to be inflicted on them, though they were His chosen and faithful friends. We see Moses and Aaron, having slightly transgressed His commands, still more severely punished by Him after He had given assurance that their trifling sin was forgiven. For, although He continued His favor and countenance to them, He deprived them of the sight of that promised land, after which they so earnestly did sigh.‡ We see Job, after he had transgressed in words, or rather exceeded in speech, therefore humbling himself, and declaring that he did penance in dust and ashes.§ When the men of Ninive had their destruction proclaimed to them by the prophet, the most obvious and natural expiation of their sins appeared to them the observance of a general fast: and all, from the king on his throne to the very animals in their stalls, were commanded to fast for three days, saying, "Who can tell if God will turn and forgive, and will turn away from His fierce anger, and we shall not perish."‖

But, my brethren, some will perhaps say, "All this happened under the older dispensation, before the law of grace and complete freedom had been introduced." But, in the first place,

---

* 2 Kings xii. 14.   † Ib. xxiv. 11.
‡ Num. xx. 12, 24.   Deut. xxxiv. 4.   § Job xlii. 6.
‖ Jonas iii. 9.

allow me to observe, that this order, observed by God's servants, belongs essentially to the natural manifestation of His attributes. It is nowhere instituted in the Old Law, it begins in the very first instance in Paradise, when our first parents' sin was forgiven, and yet the most bitter consequences were entailed on them and their posterity on this account. We never observe this practice inculcated in the form of a covenant in the Old Law, that they who so repent and afflict themselves shall be pardoned; but we see it followed by all, whether in the patriarchal times, or under the law, from a natural feeling that God required it for the forgiveness of sin. This being the case, we have every reason to conclude, that, like other institutions, which rest upon a similar basis, this is continued in the law of grace. For, even had not God said, in the New Testament, that the sinner must repent and abandon sin, to obtain forgiveness, we never should have supposed, that because all this was prescribed in the old law, it was not to be continued in the new; for the very reason which I have stated, that it does not belong to legal institutions, but essentially springs from the knowledge of God's attributes, and from an instinctive conviction on the part of man. In like manner, therefore, if we find God, from the beginning, forgiving sin with the reservation of some smaller punishment, and, at the same time, His chosen servants, instructed by Him, acting under the conviction, that, by penitential acts, that punishment could be averted or mitigated, we have equal reason to maintain, so long as there is nothing positively defined to the contrary, that the punishment, and its expiation, are continued in the New Law.

But, in the second place, is it not really and positively continued there? Consider the economy of the two Testaments, and compare them together. Will you discover in the New such words, as that the outward practice of penance, for the satisfaction of sin, is thenceforth abolished?

The objection to human satisfaction arises from its being considered essentially derogatory to Christ's infinite merits. For St. Paul tells us, that we are *justified freely by God's grace, through the redemption which is in Christ Jesus.** And to such free redemption all work of man is pronounced vitally opposed. But permit me to ask, were not they who lived under the law, justified as freely through the same redemption? Was not Christ's passion and purchase the source of all grace, and the only root of righteousness, to them as much as it is to us? If,

---

*Rom. III. 24.

LECTURE XI.

then, no injury was done to their infinite worth, by the repentance of the sinner being followed by expiatory deeds of penance, considered available towards averting God's anger, even upon sin committed; how can a similar practice now be pronounced essentially at variance with the very same merits? It is manifest that this parallel excludes the idea of any essential inherent opposition between Christ's merits and man's co-operation, between the freedom and completeness of the purchase, and its application by human acts. We require, therefore, positive testimony to demonstrate such an opposition; and it must be such, as not merely excludes the dead works of the law, abolished by the new, but as positively declares *all* work of man destructive of our Saviour's redemption.

It is often said, that the works of penance performed by the Saints of old, as well as the punishments directly inflicted on them by God's hand, after their transgressions had been pardoned, were intended only as corrections, to prevent future falls, and not as expiatory of past transgressions. But surely, my brethren, we find no traces of such a distinction in Scripture. When Nathan addresses David, he says not to him—"That thou mayest not in future cause my name to be blasphemed among the nations, the child that is born to thee shall surely die;" but, "Because thou hast given occasion to the enemies of the Lord to blaspheme, for this thing the child that is born to thee shall surely die." Nor does the royal prophet himself hint, that when he eat ashes like bread, and mingled his drink with weeping, and watered his couch with tears, and had his sin ever before him, and held himself ready for scourges, all this was as a preventive against future failings, and not rather an expiation for his double sin. In fact, examine every instance of penitential conduct, and you will find that sin committed, and not sin possible and future, is its manifest cause and motive.

But, in the third place, so far from our discovering a single passage in the New Testament, which can prove the abolition of penitential works, we shall see, that whatever was believed on this head in the former dispensation, is confirmed in the later. Does our Saviour ever tell us, that fasting, one of the most usual methods for afflicting the soul for sin committed, shall cease under His law? Does he not, on the contrary, assure us, that the moment He, the bridegroom, should be taken away, His children should fast?* Does He reprove those who had believed that

---

* Matt. ix. 15.

penance in sackcloth and ashes was efficacious for the forgiveness of sin; and not rather propose them as an example, and say that the men of Ninive shall arise in judgment against that generation, because, at the preaching of Jonas, they did penance in that way?* And does He, on any single occasion, limit the efficacy of these practices, and tell His disciples, that, if hitherto they have been considered of value towards the remission of sin, they have, from that moment, lost that worth, and were to be employed in future upon different principles, and for different motives? And if not, when he merely corrects the Pharisaic abuses in the performance of them, and gives instructions for their better observance in privacy and humility, and yet touches not once upon their intrinsic value, but leaves all as He found it,† must not they have concluded, and must not we conclude, that He tacitly approved of the doctrine then held regarding them?

But what shall we say of the language of St. Paul, when he declares, writing to the Colossians, "I now rejoice in my sufferings for you, and fill up those things which are wanting of the sufferings of Christ, in my flesh, for His body, which is the Church."‡ What is wanting of Christ's sufferings! And this to be supplied by man, and in his flesh! What sort of doctrine call we this? Is it in favor of the completeness of Christ's sufferings, as to their application? Or rather does it not suppose that much is to be done by man, towards possessing himself of the treasures laid up in our Saviour's redemption? And that suffering is the means whereby this application is made?

The doctrine which is thus collected from the word of God is reducible to these heads:—1. That God, after the remission of sin, retains a lesser chastisement in His power, to be inflicted on the sinner. 2. That penitential works, fasting, alms-deeds, contrite weeping, and fervent prayer, have the power of averting that punishment. 3. That this scheme of God's justice was not a part of the imperfect law, but the unvarying ordinance of his dispensation, anterior to the Mosaic ritual, and amply confirmed by Christ in the gospel. 4. That it consequently becomes a part of all true repentance to try to satisfy this divine justice, by the voluntary assumption of such penitential works as His revealed truth assures us have efficacy before Him.

These propositions contain the Catholic doctrine concerning satisfaction. And I think I may safely ask you, whether, inde-

---

* Mat. xii. 41.   † Ib. vi. 16.   ‡ Coloss. i. 24.

LECTURE XI.

pendently of their clear manifestation in Scripture, they are not in themselves reasonable, and consonant to justice, such as we can best conceive it. An offence may seem to require a heavy reparation; but, if friends interpose, a reconciliation is procured, on the condition that the offender make a respectful apology. The law would inflict the severest punishment, mercy steps in and pardons, but some slight and passing chastisement is imposed, as a satisfaction to public justice. Even so, when God remits a weight of eternal punishment, it seems but fair that the outrage done to His divine Majesty should be repaired by outward acts, expressive of sorrow, and directed to appease His wrath and avert those scourges which he still reserves in His hand.

Hence, in the sacrament of penance, that third part, which we call satisfaction; and in confession, the injunction of some penitential work as a portion of this satisfaction, and an earnest on the part of the sinner, of his willingness to make full reparation to God. Besides this species of satisfaction, I must not omit another very important one, and of the greatest practical benefit in the sacrament of penance. The satisfaction which I have described may be called prospective, inasmuch as it seeks to avert that temporal punishment which God has reserved for the sinner. But there is another and still more essential retrospective satisfaction, without which we cannot receive the forgiveness of our sins in this sacrament, and without which the absolution of the priest has not the slightest power; and that is, reparation to men for any injury inflicted on them by our transgression of the law, human or divine. The theft is not remitted until what has been stolen is restored, or, where this is not possible, an equivalent reparation promised, so far as possible, or even so secured, as to make us sure of its being made. Reparation must be made to any whose character may have been injured, by unjust defamation, or by any exposure of secret faults; or by any expression leading to dishonor or discredit to them, where they had before lived with honor and been considered honest and respectable. Satisfaction must be made to the wounded feelings of those who have been injured;—wherever offences have been committed against charity, all must be done once more to build up the breach and restore harmony and good feeling between the conflicting parties.

Now, my brethren, if what I have stated be the doctrine of the gospel, we must naturally expect to find some institution in the Church, from its earliest times, for the faithful practice of so essential a part of God's dispensations. And accordingly from the beginning, we find nothing so prominently inculcated, either in the writings of the early fathers, or in the discipline of the universal Church, as this necessity of doing penance and making satisfaction to God. It is the basis of the system, known by the name of the penitential canons, in which those who had transgressed were condemned to different punishments, according to the measure of their offences,—some being obliged to lay prostrate for a certain term of months or years before the doors of the Church, after which they were admitted to different portions of the divine service; while others were often excluded through their whole lives from the liturgical exercises of the faithful, and were not admitted to absolution until they were at the point of death. This system surely must have had its root in the strong conviction of the early Church, that such practices were meritorious in the sight of God; that they brought down his mercy on the sinner and propitiated his wrath. And what is all this but the belief of the doctrine of satisfaction? The belief in the power of man to make some reparation or atonement to God, by his own voluntary sufferings? The existence of this system is so certain and beyond dispute, that no one has affected to call it in question. There may be differences of opinion regarding its exact application, or the principle under which it may have been sometimes modified; but all must agree that there was an intimate persuasion or conviction in the Church, that such practices were pleasing and meritorious in the sight of God. And accordingly, we find that some modern writers, who have treated of the practice of the Catholic Church upon this point, as learnt from the fathers, fairly gave it up, and assert, that, as a doctrine of Satisfaction is not to be found in the Scripture, and yet existed in the Church in the first, second, and third centuries, we may thence deduce how completely Christianity had been already corrupted. By this concession, however, the testimony of the early Church is freely given up to us; and I will, therefore, content myself with reading one or two, out of innumerable passages, to show how its feelings accorded with ours on this head.

St. Cyprian writes thus in one of his later works, to those who had fallen from the faith: "Do entire penance; evince the contrition of a sorrowing and grieving mind. That penance, which may satisfy, remains alone to be done; but they shut the door to satisfaction, who deny the necessity of penance." He is alluding to the discipline which allowed to the faithful that had denied the faith in the time of persecution, to be received again to pardon and the communion of the Church, without going through a full course of penance; and from his words it is plain, that he considers the doctrine of satisfaction so certain, as to condemn those who reject public penance. He continues: "Whoso shall thus have made satisfaction to God, and, by penance for his sin, have acquired more courage and confidence from the very circumstance of his fall, he, whom the Lord has heard and aided, shall give joy to the Church; he shall deserve, not pardon only, but a crown."* Whoever, then, does this penance, can merit, not only pardon, but a crown of eternal reward.

In the following and in succeeding centuries, we have innumerable passages from the fathers who wrote regarding the penitential canons; we have them laying it down as the principle of those laws, that satisfaction was necessary to expiate offences committed. I will read you one or two from St. Augustine, and we cannot have a more illustrious witness to the doctrines of the Church: "It is not enough that the sinner change his ways, and depart from his evil works, unless, by penitential sorrow, by humble tears, by the sacrifice of a contrite heart, and by almsdeeds, he make satisfaction to God for what he has committed."† In the following words we have our doctrine clearly expressed, that God, after He has pardoned sin, still punishes it in His justice. "'Wash me from my sin,' said David, (Psal. 1.)—Implore mercy, but lose not sight of justice. In his mercy God pardons sin: he punishes it in his justice. But what? dost thou seek for mercy, and shall sin remain unpunished? Let David, let other sinners answer; let them answer with David, that with him they may find mercy, and say: 'Lord, my sin shall not remain unpunished; I know His justice, whose mercy I seek. It shall not remain unpunished: but that Thou mayest not punish it, I myself will.'"‡ Is not that precisely, word for word, the Catholic doctrine at this time?—that sin is forgiven, but punishment still inflicted; that God will chastise in His justice, but that the sinner may, by punishing himself, by performing certain works propitiatory before God, avert His anger, and obtain a remission of even this lesser chastisement?

I will content myself with these two or three passages, and conclude this portion of my subject, by reading to you the decree of the Council of Trent regarding Satisfaction, to show you

---

* De Lapsis, pp. 192, 193. † Homil. I T. x. p. 208.
‡ Enarrat. in Psal. 1. T. viii. p. 197.

how far the council was from excluding the merits of Christ, or inspiring the sinner with any self-sufficiency on this head. "But the satisfaction which we make for sin is not so ours, as if it were not through Jesus Christ; for we, who can do nothing of ourselves, as of ourselves, (2 Cor. iii. 5,) can do all things in Him that strengthens us. Man then has nothing wherein to glory: but all our glory is in Christ; in whom we live—in whom we merit—in whom we make satisfaction, bringing forth fruits worthy of penance. (Luke iii. 8.) These fruits have efficacy from Him; by Him they are offered to the Father; and through Him they are accepted by the Father. It is, therefore, the duty of the ministers of the Church, as far as prudence shall suggest, weighing the character of sins and the dispositions of the sinner, to enjoin salutary and proper penitential satisfactions; lest, by conniving at sins, and, by a criminal indulgence, imposing the performance of the slightest penances for great crimes, they be made partakers of other's sins. Let them ever consider, that what they enjoin must tend, not only to the maintenance of better conduct, and the cure of past infirmity, but also to the punishment of the sins that have been confessed."*

From this subject of satisfaction, I naturally proceed to the consideration of another topic, intimately connected with it, the Catholic doctrine of Purgatory. I have often had occasion to remark how every portion of the Catholic doctrine is in accordance with the rest, and what complete harmony reigns between one dogma and another; and this position seems here well illustrated. On the other hand, no doctrine has been so often held up to public dislike—although it is difficult to say why—than the doctrine of Purgatory, which follows, as a consequence or corollary, from that of which I have just treated; so much so, that the Catholic doctrine of satisfaction would be incomplete without it. The idea that God requires satisfaction, and will punish sin, would not go to its furthest and necessary consequence, if we did not believe that the sinner may be so punished in another world, as not to be wholly and eternally cast away from God.

I have said that I know not why this doctrine is so often held up to public odium, for it is difficult to see what there is in it to make it so apt and popular a handle for abuse against the Catholic religion. I am at a loss to conceive what can be considered in it repugnant to the justice of God, or to the ordinary ways

---

* Sess. xiv. c. viii.

LECTURE XI.

of Providence; what can be found therein opposed to the moral law, in the remotest degree. The idea that God, besides condemning some to eternal punishment, and receiving others into eternal glory, should have been pleased to appoint a middle and temporary state, in which those who are not sufficiently guilty for the severer condemnation, nor sufficiently pure to enjoy the vision of his face, are for a time punished and purged, so as to be qualified for this blessing, assuredly contains nothing but what is most accordant with all we can conceive of his justice. No one will venture to assert that all sins are equal before God —that there is no difference between those cold-blooded and deliberate acts of crime which the hardened villain perpetrates, and those smaller and daily transgressions into which we habitually, and almost inadvertantly, fall. At the same time, we know that God cannot bear to look on iniquity, however small; that He requires whatever comes into His presence to be perfectly pure and worthy of Him; and we might rationally conclude that there should be some means, whereby they who are in the middle state of offence, between deep and deadly transgressions on the one hand, and a state of perfect purity and holiness on the other, may be dealt with according to the just measure of His justice. What, then, in God's name, is there in this doctrine, viewed simply in itself, that can make it so popular a theme of declamation against the Catholics? The *anti-scriptural* doctrine, of Purgatory, as it is termed, is more frequently than almost any other of our less important dogmas, the theme of obloquy and misrepresentation! It seems to be fancied, in some way or other, that it is an instrument either for benefiting the clergy, or for enabling them to work on the fears of the people; that the terror of Purgatory is somehow a means of strengthening the arm of the Church over its subjects; but in what way, it is impossible for any Catholic, who knows our practice and belief, possibly to conceive.

I have more than once commented on the incorrectness of that method of arguing, which demands that we prove every one of our doctrines individually from the Scriptures. I occupied myself, during my first course of lectures, in demonstrating the Catholic principle of faith, that the Church of Christ was constituted by Him the depositary of His truths, and that, although many were recorded in His holy word, still many were committed to traditional keeping, and that Christ himself has faithfully promised to teach in His Church, and has thus secured her from error. It is on this authority that the Catholic grounds his belief in the doctrine of purgatory; yet, not so but that its principle is laid down, indirectly at least, in the word of God. To examine fully the proofs of this doctrine, it is necessary to connect it with another Catholic practice, that of praying for the dead. For this practice, as we shall see, is essentially based on the belief in purgatory; and, consequently, the principles of both are intimately connected together. Why does the Catholic pray for his departed friend, but that he fears, lest, not having died in so pure a state as to have been immediately admitted to the sight of God, he may be enduring that punishment which God has awarded after the forgiveness of his sins; and believes that, through the intercession of his brethren, he may be released from that distressing situation? I have no hesitation in saying, that the two doctrines go so completely together, that if we succeed in demonstrating the one, the other necessarily follows. For, if we prove that it has always been the belief in the Church of Christ, that they who are departed may be benefited by our prayers, and brought to the sight of God, while at the same time it has no less been its universal belief that they who had incurred eternal punishment could not be released from it, assuredly we have the same system as ours,—that there was a middle state, wherein the face of God was not enjoyed, and yet eternal punishment was not suffered. And, in fact, we shall see how the two are spoken of in common, in those passages of the oldest writers, on praying for the departed, wherein reasons are given for the practice; for they assure us that, by such prayers, we are able to release them from a state of suffering.

But, to begin with the word of God,—there is a passage with which, probably, most who have looked into this subject are well acquainted. It is in the 2d Book of Maccabees, (chapter xii.) where we are told how Judas, the valiant commander, made a collection, and "sent 12,000 drachmas of silver to Jerusalem for sacrifice, to be offered for the sins of the dead, thinking well and religiously concerning the resurrection. For if he had not hoped that they that were slain should rise again, it would have seemed superfluous and vain to pray for the dead. It is, therefore, a holy and wholesome thought to pray for the dead. that they may be loosed from their sins." (*v.* 43–46.) Many will say that the second Book of Maccabees is not part of the Scripture; that it is not included in its canon. I will waive that question for the present, although it would not be difficult to prove that it has the same right to be in the canon as many books in the Old, and still more in the New Testament: for it is quoted by the fathers as Scripture, and enumerated in its canon by councils which have drawn up catalogues of its books. But let us abstract from this consideration, which would lead us into too long a discussion. It is allowed, at any rate, by all, to contain sound, edifying doctrine; for even the Church of England allows, and even directs it to be read for instruction; whence one may conclude that she does not suppose it to contain doctrines opposed to the religion of Christ. But, my brethren, no one will pretend to deny that this is an historical work of considerable value; that it represents faithfully what the Jews believed and practised at that time. It proves, therefore, that, at the time of the Maccabees, the conviction existed, that, when prayers were offered for the dead, they were beneficial to them, and that it was "a holy and wholesome thought to pray for them." We have, therefore, the practice and belief of the Jewish Church in testimony of our doctrine. Does our Saviour ever once reprove this custom of the Jews? Does He place it among the false traditions of the Pharisees? Does He hint that this was one of the corruptions that had crept by time into the institutions of God? But you will ask, are there any other testimonies for this practice among the Jews? Most undoubtedly, for the Jews have continued the practice up to this moment, although it will hardly be suspected that they have drawn any thing from the Christian religion. In their prayer-books a form of daily prayer is appointed for the departed; and in their synagogues there is a tablet, whereon the names of the deceased are inscribed, that they may be prayed for in succession so many Sabbaths, according to a varying formula. Nor must these practices be reputed modern; for Lightfoot acknowledges that some of their oldest writers agree with us in opinion, so far as to charge them with having borrowed from us. But surely, it would have been only fair and honest to tell how and when this doctrine was received by the Jews from the Catholic Church. On the contrary, as we have found it held by Judas Maccabæus, before the time of our Saviour, we have a right to consider its existence among the Jews as anterior to His coming; and as it was never once reproved or blamed by Him, and is a point which depends not upon merely legal institution, we may justly consider it as still unchanged. It is only on this principle that the Sabbath, or Sunday, is observed with such rigor in this country; for we might ask those who are zealous for its observance with such solemn severity, whence they derive that practice, except from that prescribed by God in the old law for its Sabbath? On what ground do they continue it? Because it is not a mere legal institution, and its discontinuance not having been commanded, they think that not only itself, but the method of observing it, must be kept as it formerly was. And so it is here; if the doctrine was held by the Jews, and by the best and holiest among them —by the writer of this book, as well as by Judas Maccabæus, who sent the 12,000 drachmas for a sacrifice for the dead,—if by such men it was believed that they could assist the dead, by supplication, and loose them from their sins, and that, consequently, these were not necessarily in a state of final or eternal condemnation,—if there be nothing in the New Law to reprobate this belief, based on the consideration of common justice, and on the ordinary providence of God, we have a right to consider it a true belief at the present time, and we must expect it to be still continued, with its practical consequences, in the Church. For, if prayers would benefit the dead of old, and sacrifices too, they must continue to benefit them as much now. Nay, why not more? Is not the communion between the members of Christ's Church infinitely stronger than it was then? Are not the merits of Christ now more powerful to assist? and are they not more at the disposal of His servants than formerly, through their prayers and intercession? And what reason have we to believe that this beautiful and consoling communion, whereby they who remain were able to relieve those who were departed, hath been weakened and broken, and not rather strengthened and drawn closer?

But let us look for a moment into the New Testament, and see whether, so far from any thing being taught that should seem calculated to have undeceived the Jews, had they been mistaken in their notions concerning the dead, there be not much likely to have confirmed them. Our blessed Saviour, on one occasion, distinguishes two kinds of sin, and calls one a sin against the Holy Ghost, saying, "whosoever shall speak a word against the Son of man, it shall be forgiven him, but he that shall speak against the Holy Ghost, it shall not be forgiven him, either in this world or in the next."[*] Here is a species of sin, the aggravated nature of which is described by its not being forgiven in the next world. Should we not thence conclude, that some other sins may be forgiven there? Why give this peculiar characteristic to one, if no sin is ever pardoned in the next world? Surely, we have a right to conclude, that there is some remission

---

[*] Mat. xli. 32.

LECTURE XI. 49

of sin there; and yet it cannot be either in Heaven, or in the place of eternal punishment. We must, therefore, admit some other state in which this may be.

Thus the Jews, so far from seeing their former opinions and belief rejected, must have thought them strongly confirmed by Christ's express words. Moreover, we are assured in the New Law, that "nothing defiled shall enter" into the heavenly Jerusalem.* Suppose, then, that a Christian dies, who had committed some slight transgression; he cannot enter Heaven in this state, and yet we cannot suppose that he is to be condemned for ever. What alternative, then, are we to admit? Why, that there is some place in which the soul will be purged of the sin, and qualified to enter into the glory of God. Will you say that God forgives all sin at the moment of death? Where is the warrant for that assertion? This is an important point of doctrine; and if you maintain that God at once forgives sins, on any occasion, you must allege strong authority for it. If you find nothing of such a doctrine in His revelation, but if, on the contrary, you are told, first, that no defilement can enter the kingdom of Heaven, and, secondly, that some sins are forgiven in the next world, you must admit some means of purgation, whereby the sinner, who has not incurred eternal punishment, is qualified for the enjoyment of God's glory.

I pass over two or three other passages, that might be brought in favor of purgatory, upon one of which I shall probably have to comment a little later. All these texts, you will say, are, after all, obscure, and do not lead to any certain results. True; but we have enough said in them to guide us to some striking probabilities; these require further elucidation, and where shall we look for it, but in the Church, especially in ancient times? Take, as a similar instance, the sacrament of baptism, as now practised in the Church. The apostles were simply told to baptize all nations; but how do you prove from this that baptism is to be administered to infants? And yet the English Church articles prescribe infant baptism. Or whence comes the warrant for departing from the literal meaning of the word, which means *immersion*, and the adoption of mere effusion or sprinkling of the water? There may have been infants in the families or houses spoken of as baptized—probably so; but this is only conjecture, and not proof; surely not enough to base an important practice on, which, without better authority, should seem to con-

---
* Apoc. xxi. 27.

Vol. II.—G   5

tradict our Saviour's command, that faith should precede or accompany baptism:—"He that believeth, and is baptized, shall be saved." For, in a positive institution, wholly depending on the will of the legislator, positive authority is requisite for any modification of the prescribed act. Where is the security for these modifications, if not in the explanation of the Church, conveyed to us by her ancient practices? And thus, in like manner, if there be not clearly mentioned in Scripture a place of purgation, but still if we find forgiveness of sins in the next world spoken of,—if we find that prayers are beneficial for those that have died,—that nothing defiled can enter the kingdom of Heaven,—and that it is incompatible with God's justice, that every sin should consign the offender to eternal punishment,—we have the germs of a doctrine which only require to be unfolded; we have the members and component parts of a complete system, which, as in baptism, require only further explanation and combination from the Church of God. Now, nothing can be more simple than to establish the belief of the universal Church on this point. The only difficulty is to select such passages as may appear the clearest.

I will begin with the very oldest Father of the Latin Church, Tertullian, who advises a widow "to pray for the soul of her departed husband, entreating repose to him, and participation in the first resurrection, and making oblations for him on the anniversary day of his death, which, if she neglect, it may be truly said that she has divorced her husband."* To make an oblation on the anniversary day of his death; to pray that he may have rest,—is not this more like our language and practice than those of any other religion in England? And does not Tertullian suppose that good is done to the faithful departed by such prayer? And, moreover, does he not prescribe it as a solemn duty, rather than recommend it as a lawful practice?

St. Cyprian thus writes:—"Our predecessors prudently advised, that no brother, departing this life, should nominate any churchman his executor; and should he do it, that no oblation should be made for him, nor sacrifice offered for his repose; of which we have had a late example, when no oblation was made, nor prayer, in his name, offered in the Church."† It was considered, therefore, a severe punishment, that prayers and sacrifices should not be offered up for those who had violated any of the ecclesiastical laws. There are many other passages in this father; but

---

* De Monogamia, c. 10.   † Ep. xlvi. p. 114.

LECTURE XI.

I proceed to Origen, who wrote in the same century, and than whom no one can be clearer regarding this doctrine:—" When we depart this life, if we take with us virtues or vices, shall we receive reward for our virtues, and shall those trespasses be forgiven to us which we knowingly committed? or shall we be punished for our faults, and not receive the reward of our virtues?" That is, if there be in our account a mixture of good and evil, shall we be rewarded for the good without any account being taken of the evil, or punished for the evil without the good being taken into consideration? This query he thus answers:—"Neither is true: because we shall suffer for our sins, and receive the rewards of our good actions. For if on the foundation of Christ you shall have built, not only gold and silver, and precious stones, but also wood, and hay, and stubble, what do you expect, when the soul shall be separated from the body? Would you enter into Heaven with your wood, and hay, and stubble, to defile the kingdom of our God? or, on account of those encumbrances, remain without, and receive no reward for your gold and silver and precious stones? Neither is this just. It remains, then, that you be committed to the fire, which shall consume the light materials; for our God, to those who can comprehend heavenly things, is called a *consuming fire*. But this fire consumes not the creature, but what the creature has himself built,—wood, and hay, and stubble. It is manifest that, in the first place, the fire destroys the wood of our transgressions, and then returns to us the reward of our good works."* Therefore, according to this most learned Father, (two hundred years after Christ,) when the soul is separated from the body, if there be smaller transgressions, it is condemned to fire, which purges away those lighter materials, and thus prepares the soul for entering into Heaven.

St. Basil, or a contemporary author, writing on the words of Isaiah, " Through the wrath of the Lord is the land burned," says, that "the things which are earthly shall be made the food of a punishing fire; to the end that the soul may receive favor and be benefited." He then proceeds:—"*And the people shall be as the fuel of the fire.* (Ibid.) This is not a threat of extermination; but it denotes expurgation, according to the expression of the apostle: *If any man's works burn, he shall suffer loss; but he himself shall be saved, yet so as by fire.* (1 Cor. iii. 15.)"†

---

* Homil. xvi. al. xii. in Jerem. T. iii. p. 231, 232.
† Com. in c. ix. Isai. T. i. p. 554.

Now, mark well the word *purgation** here used. For it proves that our very term purgatory is not modern in the Church. St. Ephrem of Edessa writes thus in his Testament:—"My brethren, come to me, and prepare me for my departure, for my strength is wholly gone. Go along with me in psalms and in your prayers: and please constantly to make oblations for me. When the thirtieth day shall be completed, then remember me: for the dead are helped by the offerings of the living:"—the very day observed by the Catholic Church with peculiar solemnity, in praying and offering mass for the dead.—"If, also, the sons of Mathathias," (he alludes to the very passage which I quoted from Maccabees, 2 Maccab. xii.) "who celebrated their feasts in figure only, could cleanse those from guilt, by their offerings, who fell in battle, how much more shall the priests of Christ aid the dead by their oblations and prayer!"†

In the same century, St. Cyril of Jerusalem thus expresses himself: "Then (in the liturgy of the Church) we pray for the holy Fathers and the Bishops that are dead; and, in short, for all those who are departed this life in our communion; believing that the souls of those, for whom the prayers are offered, receive very great relief while this holy and tremendous victim lies upon the altar."‡ St. Gregory of Nyssa thus contrasts the course of God's providence in this world with that in the next. In the present life, "God allows man to remain subject to what himself has chosen; that, having tasted of the evil which he desired, and learned by experience how bad an exchange has been made, he might again feel an ardent wish to lay down the load of those vices and inclinations, which are contrary to reason: and thus, in this life, being renovated by prayers and the pursuit of wisdom, or, in the next, being expiated by the purging fire, he might recover the state of happiness which he had lost....When he has quitted his body, and the difference between virtue and vice is known, he cannot be admitted to approach the Divinity till the purging fire shall have expiated the stains with which his soul was infected.—That same fire, in others will cancel the corruption of matter and the propensity to evil."§ St. Ambrose, throughout his works, has innumerable passages on this subject, and quotes St. Paul's First Epistle to the Corinthians, (iii. 15,) which you have heard already cited by our Fathers:—"If any

---

* Καθαρσιν.   † In Testament. T. ii. p. 234, p. 371. Edit. *Oxon.*
‡ Catech. Mystag. v. n. ix. x. p. 328.
§ Orat. de Defunctis. T. ii. p. 1066, 1067, 1068.

LECTURE XI.

man's works burn, he shall suffer loss: but he himself shall be saved, yet so as by fire." I will quote one passage out of many: *"But he shall be saved, yet so as by fire.* He will be saved, the apostle said, because his substance shall remain, while his bad doctrine shall perish. Therefore he said, *yet so as by fire;* in order that his salvation be not understood to be without pain. He shows, that he shall be saved indeed, but he shall undergo the pain of fire, and be thus purified; not like the unbelieving and wicked man, who shall be punished in everlasting fire."* And in his funeral oration on the Emperor Theodosius, he thus speaks:—"Lately we deplored together his death, and now, while Prince Honorius is present before our altars, we celebrate the fortieth day. Some observe the third and the thirtieth, others the seventh and the fortieth.—Give, O Lord, rest to thy servant Theodosius, that rest which thou hast prepared for thy saints. May his soul thither tend, whence it came, where it cannot feel the sting of death, where it will learn that death is the termination, not of nature, but of sin. I loved him, therefore will I follow him to the land of the living; I will not leave him, till, by my prayers and lamentation, he shall be admitted to the holy mount of the Lord, to which his deserts call him."†

St. Epiphanius, in the same century:—"There is nothing more opportune, nothing more to be admired, than the rite which directs the names of the dead to be mentioned. They are aided by the prayer that is offered for them; though it may not cancel all their faults.—We mention both the just and sinners, in order *that for the latter we may obtain mercy.*"‡ St. Jerome:—"As we believe the torments of the devil, and of those wicked men, who said in their hearts, *there is no God,* to be eternal; so, in regard to those sinners, who have not denied their faith, and whose works will be proved and purged by fire, we conclude, that the sentence of the judge will be tempered by mercy."§ Not to be tedious, I will quote only one Father more, the great St. Augustine:—"The prayers of the Church," he writes, "or of good persons, are heard in favor of those Christians, who departed this life, not so bad as to be deemed unworthy of mercy, nor so good as to be entitled to immediate happiness. So also, at the resurrection of the dead, there will some be found, to whom mercy will be imparted, having gone through those pains to which the

---
* Comment. in 1 Ep. ad. Cor. T. ii. In App. p. 122.
† De obitu Theodosii. Ibid. p. 1197-8, 1207-8.
‡ Hær. lv. *sive* lxxv. T. i. p. 911.
§ Comment. in c. lxv. Isai. T. ii. p. 493.

spirits of the dead are liable. Otherwise it would not have been said of some with truth, that their sin *shall not be forgiven, neither in this world, nor in the world to come,* (Matt. xii. 32,) unless some sins were remitted in the next world."* St. Augustine's reasoning is here precisely the same as I have used, and as every Catholic now uses. In another passage, he quotes the words of St. Paul, as follows:—"If they had built *gold and silver and precious stones*, they would be secure from both fires; not only from that in which the wicked shall be punished for ever, but likewise from that fire which will purify those who shall be saved by fire. But because it is said, *he shall be saved,* that fire is thought lightly of; though the suffering will be more grievous than any thing man can undergo in this life."

These passages contain precisely the same doctrine as the Catholic Church teaches; and had I introduced them into my discourse, without telling you from whom they are taken, no one would have supposed that I was swerving from the doctrine taught by our Church. It is impossible to imagine that the sentiments of these writers agreed, on this point, with that of any other religion.

I observed that there was one text which I had passed over, and on which I might be led to make a few remarks a little later; and I advert to it now, not so much for the purpose of discussing whether it applies to Purgatory or not, as to show how misstatements may be made regarding the grounds of a doctrine. I alluded to the passage of St. Paul, regarding building, upon the true foundation, a superstructure of gold, silver, and precious stones, or wood, hay, and stubble; where he says, that the fire shall try every man's works, and that whatever is frail will be necessarily destroyed, while the foundation shall remain. Several Fathers, as you have heard, apply this text to the doctrine of Purgatory. Yet, very lately, a writer, commenting upon the Catholic doctrine of Purgatory, quotes this very text as an example of how the Church of Rome, as he calls us, perverts Scripture to prove her doctrine; for, he says, we have erected our doctrine of the fire of Purgatory on this text, which has nothing to do with punishment hereafter, but only refers to the tribulations endured on earth.† This is manifestly an incorrect statement, and it places the author in this dilemma; either the Church of Rome was not the first to turn this text to prove the existence

---

* De Civit. Dei, Lib. xxi. c. xxiv. p. 642.
† Horne, vol ii. p. 473, 7th ed.

of Purgatory, and then his assertion is grossly inaccurate, or else those Fathers whom I have quoted are to be included in the "Church of Rome," and are to be considered as holding the Catholic doctrine. It is not essential to our belief, that this text should refer to the doctrine of Purgatory; it is a very important one, as showing St. Paul's doctrine regarding God's conduct in punishing sin, and in distinguishing grievous transgressions and errors from those of lesser moment; and even more directly proving, that there is a place of temporary probation, which has the power of cancelling imperfections not so completely in opposition to God's law.

In addition, I need hardly observe, that there is not a single liturgy existing, whether we consider the most ancient period of the Church, or the most distant part of the world, in which this doctrine is not laid down. In all the oriental liturgies, we find parts appointed, in which the Priest or Bishop is ordered to pray for the souls of the faithful departed; and tables were anciently kept in the churches, called the *Dyptichs*, on which the names of the deceased were enrolled, that they might be remembered in the sacrifice of the mass and the prayers of the faithful.

The name of Purgatory scarcely requires a passing comment. It has, indeed, been made a topic of abuse, on the ground that it is not to be found in Scripture. But where is the word *Trinity* to be met with? Where is the word *Incarnation* to be read in Scripture? Where are many other terms, held most sacred and important in the Christian religion? The doctrines are indeed found there; but these names were not given, until circumstances had rendered them necessary. We see that the Fathers of the Church have called it a purging fire—a place of expiation or purgation. The idea is precisely, the name almost, the same.

It has been said by divines of the English Church, that the two doctrines which I have joined together, of prayers for the dead and Purgatory, have no necessary connection, and that, in fact, they were not united in the ancient Church. The answer to this assertion I leave to your memories, after the passages which I have read you from the Fathers. They surely speak of purgation by fire after death, whereby the imperfections of this life are washed out, and satisfaction made to God for sins not sufficiently expiated; they speak, at the same time, of our prayers being beneficial to those who have departed this life in a state of sin; and these propositions contain our entire doctrine on Purgatory. It has also been urged, that the established religion, or Protestantism, does not deny or discourage prayers for the dead, so long as they are independent of a belief in Purgatory: and, in this respect, it is stated to agree with the primitive Christian Church. But, my brethren, this distinction is exceedingly fallacious. Religion is a lively, practical profession; it is to be ascertained and judged by its sanctioned practices and outward demonstration, rather than by the mere opinions of a few. I would at once fairly appeal to the judgment of any Protestant here, whether he has been taught, and has understood, that such is the doctrine of his Church? If, from the services which he has attended, or the catechism which he has learnt, or the discourses which he has heard, he has been led to suppose that praying, in terms however general, for the souls departed, was noways a peculiarity of Catholicism, but as much a permitted practice of Protestantism; if, among his many acquaintances who profess his creed, he has found men who perform such acts of devotion; and if not, nay, if on the contrary, he has always understood that this rite of praying for the dead is essentially a distinctive of the Catholic religion, what matters it that Bishop Bull, and one or two other divines, should have asserted it to be allowed in the English Church? Or, how can conformity between the English and the primitive Church be proved from this tacit permission,—if such can be admitted on considering that prayers for the dead were allowed to remain in the first Anglican liturgy, and were formally withdrawn on revision,—when the ancient Church not merely allowed, but enjoined the practice as a duty —you will remember Tertullian's words—not merely opposed not its private exercise, but made it a prominent part of its solemn liturgy?*

---

* Dr. Pusey has lately written as follows:—"Since Rome has blended the cruel invention of Purgatory with the primitive custom of praying for the dead, it is not in communion with her that any can seek comfort from this rite." *An earnest remonstrance to the author of the Pope's Pastoral Letter.* (1836, p. 25.) Dr. Pusey's opinion is, 1st, that, in the ancient Church, prayers were offered for all the departed, including apostles and martyrs, in the same manner; 2dly, that such prayers had reference, not to the alleviation of pain, but to the augmentation of happiness, or the hastening of perfect joy, not possessed by them till the end of time; 3dly, that the *cruel* invention of Purgatory is modern; 4thly, that the English Church allows prayers for the dead, in that more comprehensive and general form. As to the first, there is no doubt, that in the ancient liturgies, the saints are mentioned in the same prayer as the other departed faithful; from the simple circumstance, that they were so united before the public suffrage of the Church proclaimed them to belong to a happier order. It is also true, that the Church then, as now, prayed for the consummation of their happiness after the resurrection. But it is no less true, that the ancients drew a line of distinction between the state of the two, and that the same as we. St. Epiphanius, quoted in the text, makes the distinction, saying: "We

LECTURE XI.

As a practical doctrine in the Catholic Church, it has an influence highly consoling to humanity, and eminently worthy of a religion that came down from heaven to second all the purest feelings of the heart. Nature herself seems to revolt at the idea that the chain of attachment which binds us together in life, can be rudely snapped in sunder by the hand of death, conquered and deprived of its sting since the victory of the cross. But it is not to the spoil of mortality, cold and disfigured, that she clings with affection. It is but an earthly and almost unchristian grief, which sobs when the grave closes over the bier of a departed loved one; but the soul flies upward to a more spiritual affection, and refuses to surrender the hold which it had upon the love and interest of the spirit that hath fled. Cold and dark as the sepulchral vault is the belief that sympathy is at an end when the body is shrouded in decay; and that no further interchange of friendly offices may take place between those who have laid them down to sleep in peace, and us, who for a while strew fading

---

mention both the just and sinners, that *for the latter*, we may obtain mercy." St. Augustine also writes as follows: "When, therefore, the sacrifice of the altar, or alms, are offered for the dead, in regard to those whose lives were very good, such. offices may be deemed acts of thanksgiving; for the imperfect, acts of propitiation; and, though to the wicked they bring no aid, they may give some comfort to the living." (Enchirid. cap. cx.) Here the three classes of departed souls are mentioned, with the effects of the sacrifice of the mass on each. Dr. Pusey, too, is doubtless well acquainted with the saying of the same father, that "he does injury to a martyr who prays *for* a martyr." "Injuriam facit martyri, qui orat pro martyre."

With regard to the second and third points, I refer to the texts given in the body of this lecture: St. Augustine uses the term *purgatorial* punishment (purgatorias pœnas) in the next world. (De Civit. Dei. lib. xxi. c. 16.) The passages which I have quoted are sufficient to prove a state of actual suffering in souls less perfect. There is another important reflection. The fathers speak of their prayers granting immediate relief to those for whom they offer them, and such relief as to take them from one state into another. St. Ambrose expresses this effect of prayer, when he says of Theodosius: "I will not leave him, till by my prayers and lamentations he shall be admitted to God's holy mount." This does not surely look to a distant effect, or to a mere perfection of happiness.

On the fourth, in addition to the remarks preceding this note in the text, I can only say, I wish it were better known that the Church of England considers prayers for the dead lawful and beneficial to them; for a judicial decision has lately annulled a bequest to Catholic chapels, because of there being annexed to it a condition of saying mass for the testatrix. Ap. 16, 1835. This was in the case of West and Shuttleworth, wherein the Master of the Rolls decided that, as the testatrix could not be benefited by such practices, they were to be held superstitious and not charitable; and declared the legacy null and void. Now, if his Honor had been aware, that the English Church admits prayers to be beneficial to the dead, and approves of them, and if he had judged, that our Eucharist (the oblation spoken of by the fathers) must be admitted by that Church to contain all that its own does at least, he surely would not have based a legal judgment, which, to say the least, savors much of old religious prejudices, upon so hollow a theological basis.— *Mylne and Keen*, vol. ii. p. 697.

flowers upon their tomb. But sweet is the consolation to the dying man, who, conscious of imperfection, believes that even after his own time of merit is expired, there are others to make intercession on his behalf; soothing to the afflicted survivors the thought, that, instead of unavailing tears, they possess more powerful means of actively relieving their friend, and testifying their affectionate regret, by prayer and supplication. In the first moments of grief, this sentiment will often overpower religious prejudice, cast down the unbeliever on his knees, beside the remains of his friend, and snatch from him an unconscious prayer for rest; it is an impulse of nature, which for the moment, aided by the analogies of revealed truth, seizes at once upon this consoling belief. But it is only like the flitting and melancholy light which sometimes plays as a meteor over the corpses of the dead; while the Catholic feeling, cheering, though with solemn dimness, resembles the unfailing lamp which the piety of the ancients is said to have hung before the sepulchres of their dead. It prolongs the tenderest affections beyond the gloom of the grave, and it infuses the inspiring hope, that the assistance which we on earth can afford to our suffering brethren will be amply repaid when they have reached their place of rest, and make of them friends, who, when *we* in our turns fail, shall receive us into everlasting mansions.

LECTURE THE TWELFTH.

(SUPPLEMENTARY.)

ON INDULGENCES.

2 COR. ii. 10.

" *To whom ye have forgiven any thing, I also. For what I forgive, if I have forgiven any thing, for your sakes have I done it in the person of Christ.*"

AMONG the innumerable misrepresentations to which our religion is constantly subjected, there are some which a Catholic clergyman feels a peculiar reluctance in exposing, from the personal feelings which must be connected with their refutation. When our doctrine on the blessed Eucharist, or the Church, or the saints of God, is attacked, and we rise in its defence, we feel within ourselves a pride and a spirit resulting from the very cause; there is an inspiring ardor infused by the very theme; we hold in our hand the standard of God Himself, and fight His own battle; we gather strength from the altar which is blasphemed, and are reminded of our dignity and power, by the very robe which we wear; or we are refreshed by the consciousness that they whose cause we defend, are our brethren, who look down with sympathy upon our struggle.

But when the petty and insidious warfare begins, which professes to aim at the man, and not at the cause, when, from principles of faith, or great matters of practice, the attack is changed into crimination of our ministry, and insinuation against our character; when the Catholic priest stands before his people, to answer the charge of having turned religion into a traffic, and corrupted her doctrines to purchase influence over their conscience and their purse, he must surely recoil from meeting even as a calummy, that, against which his heart revolts, and finds his very feelings, as a member of the society wherein he lives with respect, almost too strong for that office of meekness and charity which duty imposes for the undeceiving of the beguiled, and the maintenance of truth.

These sentiments are spontaneously excited in my breast, by the recollection of the very severe attacks and bitter sarcasms which the topic of this evening's discourse has for ages excited.

LECTURE XII.

Indulgences—pardon for sins, past and future, the sale of forgiveness for the grossest crimes, at stipulated sums; these, mixed up with invectives against the rapacity of the Church, and the venality of its ministers and agents, have been fruitful themes of ridicule and reproof, of sarcasm and declamation, against us, from the days of Luther, to the irreconcilable hostility of our modern adversaries.

That abuses have existed regarding the practice of Indulgences, no one will deny; and I shall say sufficient regarding them before the close of my lecture; that they were made the ground for the dreadful separation of the sixteenth century, must be deeply regretted; for no such abuses could justify the schism that ensued. But, my brethren, here, as in almost every other instance, the misrepresentation which has been made of our doctrine chiefly proceeds from misapprehension, from the misunderstanding of our real belief. I shall, therefore, pursue in its regard the same method as I have invariably followed; that is, state in the simplest terms the Catholic doctrine, and explain its connection with other points; and after that, proceed to lay before you its proofs, and meet such few objections as their very exposition does not anticipate. In fact, my discourse this evening will be little more than a rapid sketch of the history of Indulgences.

In treating of Satisfaction, I endeavored to condense the proofs of our belief, that God reserves some temporal chastisement for sin, after its guilt and eternal punishment have been remitted; and that by the voluntary performance of expiatory works, we may disarm the anger of God, and mitigate the inflictions which his justice had prepared. This doctrine I must beg of you to bear in mind, as essential for understanding what we mean by an Indulgence.

Many of you have probably heard, that this word signifies a license to sin, given even beforehand for sins to be perpetrated: at any rate, a free pardon for past sins. This is, in fact, the most lenient form in which our doctrine is popularly represented. And yet, mitigated as it is, it is far from correct. For I fear many here present will be inclined to incredulity, when I tell them that it is no pardon for sin of any sort, past, present, or future! What, then, is an Indulgence? It is no more than a remission by the Church, in virtue of the keys, or the judicial authority committed to her, of a portion, or the entire, of the temporal punishment due to sin. The infinite merits of Christ form the fund whence this remission is derived: but, besides, the Church holds that, by the communion of saints, penitential works performed by the just, beyond what their own sins might exact, are available to other members of Christ's mystical body; that, for instance, the sufferings of the spotless Mother of God, afflictions such as probably no other human being ever felt in the soul,—the austerities and persecutions of the Baptist, the friend of the Bridegroom, who was sanctified in his mother's womb, and chosen to be an angel before the face of the Christ,—the tortures endured by numberless martyrs, whose lives had been pure from vice and sin,—the prolonged rigors of holy anchorites, who, flying from the temptations and dangers of the world, passed many years in penance and contemplation, all these made consecrated and valid through their union with the merits of Christ's passion,—were not thrown away, but formed a store of meritorious blessing, applicable to the satisfaction of other sinners.

It is evident that, if the temporal punishment reserved to sin, was anciently believed to be remitted through the penitential acts which the sinner assumed, any other substitute for them, that the authority imposing or recommending them received as an equivalent, must have been considered by it truly of equal value, and as acceptable before God. And so it must be now. If the duty of exacting such satisfaction devolves upon the Church,—and it must be the same now as it formerly was,—she necessarily possesses, at present, the same power of substitution, with the same efficacy, and, consequently, with the same effects. And such a substitution is what constitutes all that Catholics understand by the name of an *Indulgence*.

The inquiry into the grounds of this belief and practice will necessarily assume an historical form. For it is an investigation into the limitations or the extent of a power, which can only be conducted by examining precedents, on its exercise by those in whom it first was vested, and by those who received it from them. For the power itself is included in the commission given by Christ to his apostles, to forgive or to retain sins. If the authority here deputed be of a judicial form, and if part of the weight imposed by sin be the obligation to satisfy the divine justice, the extent of this obligation necessarily comes under the cognisance of the tribunal. No one will, I think, deny that this application of the power committed was made in the primitive Church. No one will contend, that satisfaction was not enacted, and that the pastors of the Church did not think themselves, I will not say allowed, but obliged, to impose a long train of penitential inflictions, in punishment of sin. Something of this matter I have already touched upon; more I shall have occasion to say to-day. For the present, I am only stating my case. Well, then, the Church having, in ancient times, considered herself competent to superintend the discharge of satisfaction due for sin, and having claimed and exercised the right of exacting, in her presence, full and severe expiation, in virtue of the commission above cited; and we having thus proved its extension to the *imposition* of penance, it remains for us to see whether she went one step further, and claimed and exercised the right and power of relaxing the rigor of those inflictions, without a diminution of their value, and ascertain on what ground this relaxation was made. For, if we discover that the substitution of a lesser punishment, or the total discharge of the weight imposed, was made in consideration of the merits and sufferings of God's holy servants, and that such commutation or remission was considered valid, we shall have sufficient proof that *Indulgences* were in use, upon the same grounds whereon we admit them now. The scholastic precision of the middle ages may have prescribed for them more definite terms, and may have classified them, the source and effects, under distincter and clearer forms. But the doctrine as to substance is the same, and has only shared the fate, or rather the advantage, of every other doctrine, of passing through the refinement of judgment, which sifted the dogma till it was cleared of all the incumbrance of indefinite opinion, and stript of the husk of an ill-defined terminology. And for this purpose does divine Providence seem to have interposed that school of searching theology, between the simplicity of faith in ancient days, and the doubting latitude of opinion in modern times.

Now, therefore, let us at once enter upon the proofs of this doctrine, which forms but the completion of that already expounded, regarding the power of the Church in the remission of sin. For, a tribunal which has the power of forgiving guilt, and substituting a smaller satisfaction to the majesty of the offended, must surely have the comparatively insignificant authority still further to modify, or even to commute, the satisfaction which it has imposed.

The New Testament seems to furnish a clear instance of such a power being exercised. In his first epistle to the Corinthians, St. Paul not only severely reproved, but manifestly punished grievously, a member of that Church, who had fallen into a scandalous sin. These are his words:—"I, indeed, absent in body,

LECTURE XII.

but present in spirit, have already judged, as though I were present, him that hath so done. In the name of our Lord Jesus Christ, you being gathered together, and my spirit with the power of our Lord Jesus; to deliver such a one to Satan, for the destruction of the flesh, that the spirit may be saved in the day of our Lord Jesus Christ."*

Several remarks present themselves naturally upon the perusal of this text. First, a punishment is here inflicted of a severe character. We do not, indeed, precisely know what is meant by the delivery of the sinner to Satan. According to some, it signifies literally his condemnation to possession, like the instance of the swine in the Gospel;† others suppose it to mean the infliction of a painful sickness; a third party understands by it excommunication from the Church. Secondly, this punishment, whatever it may have been, was remedial, intended to reclaim the sinner, and, by the injury of the body, to rescue the soul from eternal loss. Thirdly, the act here described was not within the terms, strictly so called, of remission or retention of actual guilt; inasmuch as it was performed, and the punishment inflicted, by the whole congregation, with St. Paul at their head, but only in spirit, that is, sanctioning by his authority and concurrence all their acts. But the sacramental forgiveness, or retention of sin, has never been considered a congregational act, or one to be performed by the body of the faithful, nor even by any pastor of the Church, however dignified, at a distance. Hence, we must conclude, that a penance of some sort was imposed upon the incestuous Corinthian, intended for his amendment, and for reparation of the scandal and disedification committed before the Church. For this, also, is clearly intimated by the apostle, in the verses preceeding and subsequent to the passage which I have read.

Well, the consequences of this heavy infliction were such as St. Paul probably foresaw, and certainly such as he must have desired. The unfortunate sinner was plunged into a grief so excessive as to appear dangerous to his welfare. The sentence which had been pronounced is revoked, and under circumstances somewhat varied, though on that account more interesting. It appears from the second Epistle of St. Paul to the same Church, that the Corinthians did not wait for his answer upon this subject, or, even if they did, that he remitted the whole conduct and decision of the matter to their charitable discretion. For he thus

---

* 1 Cor. v. 3–5. † Mat. viii.

writes:—"To him that is such a one, this rebuke is sufficient that is given by many. So that, contrariwise, you should rather pardon and comfort him, lest, perhaps, such a one be swallowed up with over-much sorrow. For which cause I beseech you that you would confirm your charity towards him. For to this end also did I write, that I may know the experiment of you, whether you be obedient in all things. And to whom you have pardoned any thing, I also. For what I have pardoned, if I have pardoned any thing, for your sakes have I done it in the person of Christ."*
Here, again, St. Paul alludes to the severity of the chastisement inflicted, owing to its being conveyed in a public reproof of the entire congregation. He then entrêats *them* to forgive him and comfort him; and adds, that he has already confirmed the sentence which they have passed, or were going to pass. Evidently, therefore, the entire transaction is not a ministerial one, affecting the forgiveness of the crime, for that could not be in the hands of the flock.

But no less is it evident that the term of punishment is abridged, and the sentence reversed, before the completion of the awarded retribution is arrived; and this was in consequence of the very great sorrow manifested by the penitent, which was considered an equivalent for the remaining portion. This is precisely what we should call an Indulgence; or a remission of that penance enjoined by the Church, in satisfaction of God's justice. But it is likewise manifest, that such a relaxation must have been considered perfectly valid before Heaven. For, as the punishment was inflicted that his soul might be saved, it would have been an endangering of that salvation to remove the punishment, unless the same saving effects would ensue after its relaxation.

After this striking example in the word of God, we shall not be surprised at finding the Church, in the earliest times, claiming and exercising a power similar in every respect. We must naturally expect to see it imitate the apostle, first in imposing, and then in remitting or modifying, such temporary chastisements. To understand its practice clearly, it may be necessary to premise a few words on the subject of canonical penance. From the age of the apostles, it was usual for those who had fallen into grievous offences to make a public confession of them, (whereof I gave one or two examples in treating of confession,) and then to subject themselves to a course of public penance

---

* 2 Cor. ii. 5–10.

LECTURE XII.

which received the name of canonical, from the canons or rules whereby it was regulated. Such penitents, as we learn from Tertullian and other early writers, put on a black and coarse habit, and, if men, closely shaved their heads.* They presented themselves before the assembly of the faithful on the first day of Lent, when the presiding bishop or priest placed ashes on their heads, a custom still preserved in the Catholic Church; whence the name of Ash-Wednesday given to that day. The term of this penance was various, according to the grievousness of the offence. It lasted sometimes only forty days; at others, three, seven, and ten years; for some enormous crimes, its duration was the natural life of the penitent. During this course, every amusement was forbidden, the sinner's time was occupied in prayer and good works, he practised rigorous fasting, and came only on festivals to the Church, where he remained with the penitents of his class; first lying prostrate before the door, then admitted at stated intervals within, but still for a time excluded from attendance on the liturgy, till he had accomplished his prescribed term of satisfaction.

There are the strongest reasons to believe, that, in most cases, absolution preceded the allotment of this penance, or at least that it was granted during the time of its performance; so that all or much of it followed sacramental absolution. The custom of the Roman Church, and of others, was, that the penitents should be yearly admitted to communion on Holy Thursday, a circumstance incompatible with the idea of their receiving no pardon till the conclusion of their penance. Innocent I., the Council of Agde in 506, St. Jerome, and others, mention this usage.†

But while these penitential observances were considered of the greatest value and importance, the Church reserved to itself the right of mitigation under various circumstances, which I will now explain.

1. The extraordinary sorrow and fervor manifested by the penitent, during the performance of his task, was always considered a justification of a proportionate relaxation. Thus, the Council of Nicea prescribes on this subject:—"In all cases, the disposition and character of repentance must be considered. For they who by fear, by tears, by patience, and by good works, manifest a sincere conversion, when they shall have passed over

---

* Tertull. "Lib. de Pœnit." St. Pacian, "Parœnes. ad Pœnit." lib. II. &c.
† See Bellarmine, tom. III. p. 960, Par. 1613.

a certain time, and begun to communicate in prayer with the faithful, to these the bishop may show more indulgence: but not to those who manifest indifference, and think it enough that they are allowed to enter the Church. These must complete the whole period of penance."* St. Basil says, in like manner, that "he who has the power of binding and loosing can lessen the time of penance to the truly contrite."† The Council of Lerida says, —"Let it remain in the power of the Bishop either to shorten the separation of the truly contrite, or to separate the negligent a longer time from the body of the Church." That of Ancyra, in 314, decrees as follows:—"We decree, that the Bishops, having considered the conduct of their lives, be empowered to show mercy, or to lengthen the time of penance. But chiefly let their former and subsequent life be examined, and thus lenity be shown them."‡

2. Another motive of relaxation was the approach of a persecution, when the penitents would have an opportunity of testifying their sorrow by patient endurance, and where it was thought inexpedient to leave them unfortified by the blessed Eucharist, and the participation in the prayers of the Church. This, St. Cyprian informs us, in the following words, was the practice of the Church. "He that gave the law, has promised, that what we bind on earth, shall be bound in heaven, and what we loose on earth shall be loosed also in heaven. But now, not to those that are infirm, but to the healthy the peace of reconciliation is necessary; not to the dying, but to the living it must be extended; in order that those whom we incite to battle be not left without arms, but be fortified by the body and blood of Christ. For since the design of the holy Eucharist is to give strength to those that receive it, they must not be deprived of its support whom we would guard against the enemy."§

3. A similar indulgence was granted to penitents in danger of death, as was decreed by the Council of Carthage. "When a sinner implores to be admitted to penance, let the priest, without any distinction of persons, enjoin what the canons enact. They who show negligence, must be less readily admitted. If any one, after having, by the testimony of others, implored forgiveness, be in imminent danger of death, let him be reconciled by the imposition of hands, and receive the Eucharist. If he survive, let him be informed that his petition has been complied

---

* Can. xii. Conc. Gen. T. ii. p. 85. † Ep. Can. ad Amphiloch.
‡ Conc Gen. T. i. can. v. p. 1458. § Ep. lvii. p. 116, 117.

with, and then be subject to the appointed rules of penance, so long as it shall seem good to the priest who prescribed the penance."* Whence it appears that the canonical penance was to be continued after absolution and admission to the Eucharist, consequently that it was meant for satisfaction after sin remitted; and likewise that the Church held itself competent to give a mitigation or indulgence in it. For the penance after recovery was not to be the full term, but such a modification as the priest should think proper. And Pope Innocent I., in the epistle to which I have before referred, confirms this discipline. Thus he writes: "In estimating the grievousness of sins, it is the duty of the priest to judge; attending to the confession of the penitent, and the signs of his repentance; and then to order him to be loosed, when he shall see due satisfaction made. But if there be danger of death, he must be absolved before Easter, lest he die without communion."†

4. St. Augustine gives us another ground whereon mitigation of penance was sometimes granted; that is, when intercession was made in favor of the repenting sinner by persons justly possessing influence with the pastors of the Church. In the same manner, he tells us, as the clergy sometimes interceded for mercy with the civil magistrate in favor of a condemned criminal, and were successful, so did they, in their turn, admit the interposition of good offices from the magistrates in favor of sinners undergoing penance.‡

5. But the chief ground of indulgence or mitigation, and the one which most exactly includes all the principles of a modern indulgence, was the earliest, perhaps, admitted in the Church. When the martyrs, or those who were on the point of receiving the crown, and who had already attested their love of Christ by suffering, were confined in prison, those unfortunate Christians who had fallen, and were condemned to penance, had recourse to their mediation; and, upon returning to the pastors of the Church, with a written recommendation to mercy from one of those chosen servants of God and witnesses of Christ, were received at once to reconciliation, and absolved from the remainder of their penance.

Tertullian, the oldest Latin Father, is the first to mention this practice, and that under such different circumstances as render his testimony painfully interesting. First, when in communion

---

* Conc. Gen. T. ii. can. lxxiv. lxxv. lxxvi. p. 1205.
† Ep. ad Decent. Conc. Gen. T. ii. p. 1247.
‡ "Epist. ad Maced." 54.

with the Church, he approves of the practice. For, after exhorting the confessors of Christ to preserve themselves in a state of peace and communion with His Church, he thus continues:— "Which peace some not having in the Church, are accustomed to beg from the martyrs in prison; and therefore ye should possess and cherish, and preserve it in you, that so ye may, perhaps, be able to grant it to others."* Here, then, Tertullian speaks of the custom without reprehending it; and, indeed, even builds his exhortation to the martyrs upon its propriety. But after he had, unfortunately, abandoned the faith, and professed the fanatical austerity of the Montanists, he rudely reproaches the Church with this as an abuse; at the same time that he more clearly reveals the principle whereon it was founded. For thus he now speaks: "Let it suffice for a martyr to have purged his own sin; it is the part of a proud, ungrateful man, to lavish upon others. that which he hath himself obtained at a great price." He then addresses the martyr himself, in these words: "If thou art thyself a sinner, how can the oil of thy lamp suffice for thee and me?"† From these expressions it is clear, that, according to the belief of the Church, which he blamed, the martyrs were held to communicate some efficacy of their sufferings in place of the penance to be discharged, and some communion in their good deserts was admitted to be made.

St. Cyprian, in the following century, confirms the same practice and its grounds. For he expressly says, speaking of it: "We believe that the merits of the martyrs, and the works of the just, can do much with the just Judge."‡ In an epistle to the martyrs, he writes to them as follows: "But to this you should diligently attend, that you designate by name those to whom you wish peace to be given."§ And writing to his clergy, he thus prescribes the use to be made of such recommendations: "As I have it not yet in my power to return, aid, I think, should not be withheld from our brethren; so that they who have received letters of recommendation from the martyrs, and can thereby be benefited before God, should any danger from sickness threaten, may, in our absence, having confessed their crime before the minister of the Church, receive absolution, and appear in the presence of God in that peace, which the martyrs in their letters requested should be imparted to them."‖

---

* "Ad. Martyr." cap. I.   † "De Pudicit." cap. xxii.
‡ "De lapsis."   § Epist. xv.
‖ Ep. xviii. p. 40.

LECTURE XII. 69

Hence, therefore, it appears, that in the ancient Church, relaxation from the rigor of the penitential institutions was granted in consideration of the interposition of the martyrs of Christ, who seemed to take on themselves the punishment due to the penitents according to the canonical institutions. The practice, doubtless, led to abuses; St. Cyprian complains of them repeatedly; the works from which I have quoted are expressly directed to correct its evils and check its exercise, but the principle he never for a moment calls in question; he admits, on the contrary, that it should be acted on, apparently in every instance.

There appears but one only point further, requisite to complete the resemblance between ancient and modern indulgences. The instances hitherto given, apply chiefly to a diminution of punishment, not to a commutation, which seems the specific characteristic of indulgences at the present day. But, although the abridgment of a punishment and the substitution of a lighter one, are in substance the same thing, being only different forms of mitigation, yet, even in this respect, we can illustrate our practice from antiquity. For the Council of Ancyra, already referred to, expressly sanctions the commutation of public penance in the case of deacons who have once fallen, and afterwards stood firm. Later, another allows some other good work to be substituted for fasting, one of the essential parts of the old penance, in the case of persons with whose health it is incompatible; and Ven. Bede mentions the same form of indulgence by commutation.

Coming, then, to the indulgences of modern times, they are nothing more than what we have seen were granted in the first ages, with one difference. The public penance has disappeared from the Church, not in consequence of any formal abolition, but from the relaxation of discipline, and from the change of habits, particularly in the West, caused by the invasion of the northern tribes. Theodore of Canterbury was the first who introduced the practice of secret penance, and, in the eighth century, the custom became general, of substituting prayer, alms, or other works of charity, for the rigorous course of expiation prescribed in the ancient Church. It was not till the thirteenth, that the practice of public penance completely ceased. Now, the Church has never formally given up the wish, however hopeless it may appear, that the fervor and discipline of primitive times could be restored; and consequently, instead of abolishing their injunctions, and specifically substituting other practices in their place, she has preferred ever considering these as mitigations of what she still holds herself entitled to enforce. The only difference, therefore, between

LECTURE XII.

her former and her present practice is, that the mitigation or commutation has become the ordinary form of satisfaction, which, however unwilling, she deems it prudent to exact. Indeed, so completely is this the spirit and meaning of the Church, that, as we learn from Pope Alexander III., writing to the Archbishop of Canterbury, it was the custom of the Church, in granting indulgences, to add to the word the phrase "from the penance enjoined;" to intimate that primarily the indulgence regarded the canonical penance. Several general councils and Popes, down to Leo X., confirm this formula.

From all that I have said, you will easily conclude, that our indulgence, and that of the ancient Church, rest upon the following common grounds. First, that satisfaction has to be made to God for sin remitted, under the authority and regulation of the Church. 2dly, That the Church has always considered herself possessed of the authority to mitigate, by diminution or commutation, the penance which she enjoins; and that she has always reckoned such a mitigation valid before God, who sanctions and accepts it. 3dly, That the sufferings of the saints, in union with, and by virtue of Christ's merits, are considered available towards the granting this mitigation. 4thly, That such mitigations, when prudently and justly granted, are conducive towards the spiritual weal and profit of Christians.

These considerations at once give us a key to the right understanding of much that is connected with the practice of indulgences. For instance, they explain the terms employed.

First, the periods for which indulgences are usually granted are apparently arbitrary, such as in an indulgence for forty days, of seven, thirty, or forty years, or plenary. Now, these were precisely the usual periods allotted to public penance, so that the signification of these terms is, that the indulgence granted is accepted by the Church as a substitution for a penance of that duration: a plenary indulgence being a substitute for any entire term of awarded penitential inflictions.

Secondly, the phrase, forgiveness of sin, which occurs in the ordinary forms of granting an indulgence, applies in the same manner. There was in ancient times a twofold forgiveness; one sacramental, which generally preceded or interrupted the course of public penance, as I have shown you was the case in the Roman Church: this was the absolution from the interior guilt, in the secret tribunal of penance. But absolution or forgiveness, in the face of the Church, did not take place till the completion of the public satisfaction, for it was the act whereby an end was

LECTURE XII.   71

part to its duration. Now, in indulgences, as we have all along seen, the Church has no reference to the inward guilt, or to the weight of eternal punishment incurred by sin, but only to the temporal chastisement and its necessary expiation. When, therefore, an indulgence is said to be a remission or forgiveness of sin, the phrase applies only to the outward guilt, or that portion of the evil whereof the ancient penitential canons took cognisance. This is still further evinced by the practice of the Church, which always makes, and has made, confession and communion, and consequently exemption from the guilt of sin, an indispensable condition for receiving an indulgence. So that forgiveness of sin must precede the participation of any such favor.

Thirdly, the very name Indulgence becomes clear and appropriate. More errors are committed in judging of our doctrines from a misunderstanding of our terms, than from any other cause. The word indulgence is supposed to refer to something now existing; and, as there is nothing visible of which it is a relaxation, it is assumed to mean an indulgence in reference to the commission of sin. But when considered in connection with its origin, when viewed as a mitigation of that rigor with which the Church of God, in its days of primitive fervor, visited sin, it becomes a name full of awful warning, and powerful encouragement; it brings back to our recollection, how much we fall short of that severe judgment which the saints passed on transgressions of the divine law; it acts as a protest on the part of the Church against the degeneracy of our modern virtue, and animates us to comply with the substitution conceded to us, up to the spirit of the original institution, and to supply its imperfection by private charity, mortification, and prayer.

It is argued, that the works enjoined for the acquisition of an indulgence have been sometimes even irreligious or profane: at others, have had no object save to fill the coffers of the clergy; and, in modern times, are habitually light and frivolous.

I. Such charges, my brethren, proceed from ignorance; they arise from what I have just adverted to, a misunderstanding of the name. In the middle ages, Europe saw its princes and emperors, its knights and nobles, abandon country and home, and devote themselves to the cruel task of war in a distant clime, to regain the sepulchre of Christ from the hands of infidels. And what reward did the Church propose? Nothing more than an indulgence! But the form wherein it was granted proves all that I have said, that such a commutation was considered to stand in place of canonical penance, and that, far from its being compatible with sin and vice, it required a devotedness of purpose and a purity of motive which show how completely the Church only bestowed it for the sanctification of her children, through a work deemed most honorable and glorious. "Whoever," decrees the celebrated Council of Clermont, "shall go to Jerusalem to liberate the Church of God, out of pure devotion, and not for the purpose of obtaining honor or money, let the journey be counted in lieu of all penance."* It may be said that many took the cross from sordid or profligate motives. Be it so: but they did not partake in the spiritual benefit of this indulgence. They were men like Godfrey and St. Lewis, whom the Church wished to encourage to the battle of Christ; and had none gone save those, who, with them, valued her gifts beyond their earthly diadems or the repose of home, they would indeed have been in numbers few, like Gideon's host, but, like it, they would have conquered in the strength of the Most High. And who will say that this earliest public substitution or commutation was a relaxation from former inflictions? It was true that the iron minds and frames of the Northmen could not easily be bent to the prostrations, and tears, and fasts of the canonical penance, and that their restless passions could not easily be subdued into a long unvaried course of such severe virtue; but well and wisely did the Church, conscious of this, and called upon to repress aggression that had snatched from her very bosom a treasure by her dearly loved, and exterminated religion in one of her choicest provinces,—dreading, too, with reason, the persevering determination of the foe to push his conquest to her very heart and centre,—well did she to arouse the courage of her children, and to arm them with the badge of salvation, and to send them forth unto conquest; turning that very rudeness of character, which refused humiliation, into the instrument of a penance which required energy, strength, and ardor. And who that contemplates the strength of mind and the patience with which every human evil was endured,—perils on land, and perils at sea, and perils from false brethren, war, famine, captivity, and pestilence,—from an enthusiastic devotion to a religious cause, from a chivalrous affection for the records of redemption, will venture to say that the indulgence deserved that name, or imposed but a light and pleasant task? Whether the object justified the grant, some men will, perhaps, permit themselves to doubt; for there are always

---

* "Quicunque pro sola devotione, non pro honoris vel pecuniæ adeptione ad liberandam ecclesiam Dei Jerusalem profectus fuerit, iter illud pro omni pœnitentia reputatur." Can. ii. This was A. D. 1095.

LECTURE XII.

some cold hearts that measure others' ardor by their own frozen temperament, and refer the feelings of distant ages, and of men whose minds were cast in a nobler mould, to the conventional codes of modern theories. To such, the enthusiasm of the crusader will appear a frenzy, and the soil which was watered by our Saviour's blood, no possession worth reconquering. But, for our purpose, it is sufficient to know that they who imparted spiritual blessings to the warriors that placed the cross upon their shoulders judged otherwise, and believed it an undertaking of value and glory for every Christian.

II. Such is the charge of indulgences granted for profane or evil purposes; what shall we say of the avarice which has so multiplied them? For what other object was the Jubillee instituted, save to fill the coffers of the sovereign Pontiff with the contributions of thousands of pilgrims, eager to gain its special indulgences? Ay, my brethren, I have witnessed one of these lucrative institutions; for I was in Rome when the venerable Pontiff, Leo XII., opened and closed the Jubilee, or Holy Year. I saw the myriads of pilgrims who crowded every portion of the city. I noted their tattered raiment and wearied frames; I saw the convents and hospitals filled with them at night, reposing on beds furnished by the charity of the citizens; I saw them at their meals served by princes and prelates, and by the sovereign Pontiff himself;—but wealth poured into the Roman coffers I saw not. I heard of blessings abundant, and tears of gratitude, which they poured upon our charity as they departed;—but of jewels offered by them to shrines, or gold cast into the bosoms of priests, I heard not. I learnt that the funds of charitable institutions had been exhausted, and heavy debts incurred by giving them hospitality; and if, after all this, the gain and profit was in favor of our city, it is, that she must have a large treasure of benediction to her account in Heaven; for there alone hath she wished her deeds on that occasion to be recorded. Will you say that the undertaking and the hopes of these men were fond and vain? Or, that they thought to gain forgiveness by a pleasant excursion to the Holy City, and by the neglect of their domestic duties? Then I wish you could have seen not merely the churches filled, but the public places and squares crowded, to hear the word of God—for Churches would not contain the audience: I wish you could have seen the throng at every confessional, and the multitutes that pressed round the altar of God, to partake of its heavenly gift. I wish you could know the restitution of ill-gotten property which was made, the destruction of immoral and irreligious books which took place, the amendments of hardened sinners which date from that time; and then you would understand why men and women undertook the toilsome pilgrimage, and judge whether it was indulgence in crime, and facility to commit sin, that is proffered and accepted in such an institution.

And what I have feebly sketched of the last Jubilee is the description of all. So far was the very first of these holy seasons, in 1300, from bringing crowds of wealthy people to lavish their riches in the purchase of pardon, as it is generally expressed, that I have evidence, in which I am particularly interested, to the contrary. The number of English who flocked to Rome on that occasion was very great. But such was the state of destitution in which they appeared, and so unable were they even to obtain a shelter, that their condition moved the compassion of a respectable couple who had no children;* and they resolved to settle in the Eternal City, and devote their property to the entertainment of English pilgrims. They accordingly bought a house for that purpose, and spent the remainder of their lives in the exercise of that virtue which St. Paul so much commends, "harboring strangers, and washing the feet of the saints."† To this humble beginning additions were soon made; the establishment for the reception of English pilgrims became an object of national charity; a church, dedicated to the blessed Trinity, was erected beside it: and it was in latter times considered of sufficient consequence to merit royal protection. When the unhappy separation of this country from the Church took place, the stream of pilgrims ceased to flow; but the charitable bequest was not alienated. A cruel law forbade the education of a Catholic clergy in this country; and it was wisely and piously determined by Pope Gregory XIII., that, if men came no longer from our island to renew their piety and fidelity at the tomb of the apostles, the institution intended for their comfort should be employed in sending to them that which they could no longer come in person to take, through zealous and learned priests, who should imbibe the faith, or catch new fervor, from those sacred ashes. The hospital of English pilgrims was converted into a college for the education of ecclesiastics; many therein brought up have sealed the faith with their blood, on the scaffolds of this city; and now, in peaceful times, it remains a monument of English charity, dear to many,—to none more than

---

* Their names were John and Alice Shepherd. † 1 Tim. v. 10.

LECTURE XII.

to me,—and, at the same time, a record of the poverty and destitution of those for whose reception and relief it was originally erected.

Do I then mean to say, that during the middle ages, and later, no abuse took place in the practice of indulgences? Most certainly not. Flagrant and too frequent abuses, doubtless, occurred through the avarice, and rapacity, and impiety of men; especially when indulgence was granted to the contributors towards charitable or religious foundations, in the erection of which private motives too often mingle. But this I say, that the Church felt and ever tried to remedy the evil. These abuses were most strongly condemned by Innocent III. in the Council of Lateran in 1139, by Innocent IV. in that of Lyons in 1245, and still more pointedly and energetically by Clement V. in the Council of Vienna, in 1311. The Council of Trent, by an ample decree, completely reformed the abuses which had subsequently crept in, and had been unfortunately used as a ground for Luther's separation from the Church.*

But even in those ages the real force, and the requisite conditions of indulgences, were well understood, and by none better than by that most calumniated of all Pontiffs, Gregory VII. In a letter to the Bishop of Lincoln, he amply explains what are the dispositions with which alone participation can be hoped for in the indulgence offered by the Church.

We may, indeed, be asked, why we retain a name so often misunderstood and misrepresented, and not rather substitute another that has no reference to practices now in desuetude? My brethren, to this I answer, that we are a people that love antiquity even in words. We are like the ancient Romans, who repaired and kept ever from destruction the cottage of Romulus, though it might appear useless and mean to the stranger that looked upon it. We call the offices of Holy Week *Tenebræ*, or darkness, because the word reminds us of the times when the night was spent in mournful offices before God's altar; we retain the name of Baptism, which means immersion, though the rite is no longer performed by it. We cling to names that have their rise in the fervor and glory of the past; we are not easily driven from the recollections which hang even upon syllables; still less do we allow ourselves to be driven from them by the taunts and wishes of others, who seize upon them to attack and destroy the dogma which they convey. No other word could so completely

---

* Sess. xxv. Decret. de Indulg.

LECTURE XII.

express our doctrine, as this "distinguished name," to use the words of the Council of Trent.

III. After all that I have said, I need hardly revert to the common method of throwing ridicule on indulgences, by depreciating the works of piety or devotion to which they are attached. Surely, did this accusation, even in its substance, hold good, the true inquiry would be, Do Catholics, in consequence of such indulgences, perform less for God than their accusers, or than they themselves would perform, if such indulgences were not granted? I answer, unhesitatingly—No. From what good work does an indulgence, granted at any festival, hinder us? What prayer less is said than by Protestants, or even than by Catholics at other times? On the contrary, small as the work may be, while the desire is hopeless of restoring a more rigorous discipline, is it not better to exact that, which, if in no other way, by its necessary conditions, leads to what is valuable and salutary? For you, my Catholic brethren, know, that without a penitent confession of your sins, and the worthy participation of the blessed Eucharist, no indulgence is any thing worth. You know that the return of each season, when the Church holds out to you an indulgence, is a summons to your conscience to free itself from the burthen of its transgressions, and return to God by sincere repentance. You know, that, were not this inducement presented to you, you might run on from month to month in thoughtless neglect, or unable to rouse your courage for the performance of such arduous duties. The alms which you then give, and the prayers which you recite, are thus sanctified by a purer conscience, and by the hopes of their being doubly acceptable to God, through the ordinances of his Church. And let me add, that one of these times of mercy is now approaching, and. I entreat you, allow it not to pass by unheeded. Prepare for it with fervor—enter upon it with contrite devotion, and profit by the liberality with which the Spouse of Christ unlocks the treasure of His mercies to her faithful children. And thus shall the indulgence be, as it is intended, for your greater perfection in virtue, and the advancement of your eternal salvation.

LECTURE THE THIRTEENTH.

INVOCATION OF SAINTS: THEIR RELICS AND IMAGES.

LUKE i. 28.

"*And the Angel being come in, said, Hail, full of grace, the Lord is with thee: blessed art thou amongst women.*"

THE words which I have quoted to you, my brethren, are taken from the Gospel read in the festival of this day;*—a festival which, as its very name imports, commemorates the great dignity bestowed on the mother of our blessed Redeemer, through a message communicated to her by an angel from God;—a festival which stands registered in the calendar of every religious denomination, as a record and a monument of that belief which was once held by the forefathers of all, but which now has become the exclusive property of one, and for which that division of Christians is, more than for any other reason, most frequently and most solemnly condemned. For I am minded, this evening, to treat of that honor and veneration which is paid by the Catholic Church to the Saints of God,—and, beyond all others, to her whom we call the Queen of Saints, and venerate as the mother of the God of the Saints. I intend, then, to lay before you the grounds of our doctrine and practice in regard to this matter, as also with regard to some others which naturally spring from it.

Nothing, my brethren, seems so congenial to human nature, as to look with veneration and respect on those who have gone before us, holding up to us distinguished examples of any qualities which we venerate and esteem. Every nation has its heroes and its sages, whose conduct or teaching is proposed to succeeding generations as models for imitation. The human race itself, according to Holy Writ, had, in olden times, its giants, men of renown;—those who had made greater strides than their successors in the paths of distinction, whether in things earthly, or in those of a superior order; men whose fame seems the property of entire humanity, and whose memory it has become a duty,

---

* March 25. The Annunciation of the Blessed Virgin Mary.

discharged with affection, to cherish and preserve, as a public and common good, at once honorable and cheering to our nature.

But, alas! only in religion is it otherwise the case. It would seem as though many thought that the religion of Christ may be best exalted by depreciating their glory who were its highest ornaments;—by decrying their merits who were the brightest examples of virtue to the world; yea, and even by depressing below the level or standard of ordinary goodness those great men who, preceding us here below in our belief, not only have left us the most perfect demonstration of its worth, but insured us its inheritance by their sufferings, by their conduct, or by their writings. It jars most cruelly with all our natural affections, to see how such true heroes of the Church of God are not merely stripped of the extraordinary honors which we are inclined to pay them, but are actually treated with disrespect and contumely: how some should seem to think that the cause of religion can be advanced by representing them as frailer and more liable to sin than others, and ever descant, with a certain sort of gloating pleasure, on their falls and human imperfections.

Nay, it has been even assumed, that the cause of the Son of God was to be promoted, and His mediatorship and honor exalted, by decrying the worth and dignity of her whom He chose to be His mother, and by striving to prove that sometimes He had been undutiful and unkind to her; for it has been asserted, that we ought not to show any affection or reverence for her,— on the blasphemous ground that in the exercise of even filial love towards her our Saviour Himself was wanting!* Nor yet, my brethren, is this the worst feature of the case; for a graver and most awful charge is made against us, in consequence of our belief. We are even denounced as idolators, because we pay a certain reverence, and, if you please, worship, to the Saints of God, and because we honor their outward emblems and representations. Idolators! Know ye, my brethren, the import of this name? That it is the most frightful charge that can be laid to the score of any Christian? For, throughout God's Word, the crime of idolatry is spoken of as the most henious, the most odious, and the most detestable in His eyes, even in

---

* It is the reason given by more sermons than one, against our devotion to the Blessed Virgin, that our Saviour treated her harshly, especially on two occasions: John ii. 4; Mat. xii. 48. This is not the place to enter into the argument on these passages, especially the first: for which I hope soon to find a fitting opportunity.

LECTURE XIII.

an individual; what, then, if committed in a mass, by millions of men?

Then, gracious God! what must it be, when flung as an accusation upon those who have been baptized in the name of Christ, who have tasted the sacred gift of His Body, and received the Holy Ghost; and of whom, therefore, St. Paul tells us, that it is impossible that they be renewed unto penance?* for this is what St. John calls a sin even unto death, for which men are not to pray!† Assuredly, they know not what they say, who deliberately and directly make this enormous charge; and they have to answer for misrepresentation,—yea, for calumny of the blackest dye,—who hesitate not again and again to repeat, with heartless earnestness and perseverance, this most odious of accusations, without being fully assured—which they cannot be—in their consciences, and before God, that it really can be proved.

For, my brethren, what is idolatry? It is the giving to man, or to any thing created, that homage, that adoration, and that worship, which God hath reserved unto Himself; and to substantiate such a charge against us, it must be proved that such honor and worship is alienated by us from God, and given to a creature.

Now, what is the Catholic belief on the subject of giving worship or showing veneration to the saints, or their emblems? Why, it is comprised in a definition exactly contradictory of the one I have just given of idolatry! You will not open a single Catholic work, from the folio decrees of Councils, down to the smallest catechism placed in the hands of the youngest children, in which you will not find it expressly taught, that it is sinful to pay the same homage or worship to the saints, or to the greatest of the saints, or the highest of the angels in Heaven, as we pay to God: that supreme honor and worship are reserved exclusively to Him, that from Him alone can any blessing possibly come, that He is the sole fountain of salvation, and grace, and of all spiritual, or even earthly, gifts,—and that no one created being can have any power, energy, or influence of its own, in carrying into effect our wishes or desires. No one, surely, will say, that there is no distinction between one species of homage or reverence, and another; no one will assert, that when we honor the king, or his representatives, or our parents, or others in lawful authority over us, we are thereby derogating

---

* Heb. vi. 6. † 1 John v. 16.

from the supreme honor due to God. Would not any one smile, if he did not give way to a harsher feeling, were he taxed with defrauding God of His true honor, because he paid reverence or esteem to others, or sought their intercession or assistance? It is wasting time to prove that there may be honor and worship, —for, as I will show you presently, this word is ambiguous,— that there may be reverence or esteem demonstrated, so subservient to God, as in no way to interfere with what is due to Him.

What I have cursorily stated, is precisely the Catholic belief regarding the saints: that they have no power of themselves, and that they are not to be honored and respected as though they possessed it; but, at the same time, that they are intercessors for us with God, praying for us to Him, and that it is right to address ourselves to them, and obtain the co-operation of this, their powerful intercession, in our behalf. The very distinction here made, excludes the odious charge, to which I have alluded with considerable pain. For the very idea, that you call on any being to pray to God, is surely making an abyss, a gulf, between him and God;—it is making him a suppliant, a dependant on the will of the Almighty; and surely these terms and these ideas are in exact contradiction to all we can possibly conceive of the attributes and qualities of God.

But I go further still. Instead of taking any thing from God, it is adding immensely to His glory: by thus calling on the Saints to pray for us, instead of robbing Him of a particle of the honor which belongs to Him, we believe Him to be served in a much nobler way than in any other. For we thereby raise ourselves in imagination to Heaven; we see the Saints prostrate before Him in our behalf, offering their golden crowns and palms before His footstool, pouring out before Him the odors of their golden vials, which are the prayers of their brethren on earth,* and interceding through the death and the passion of His Son. And surely, if this be so, we are paying to God the highest homage, which his apostle describes as paid in heaven; for we give occasion, by every prayer, for this prostration of His Saints, and this outpouring of the fragrance of their supplications. Such being the Catholic belief regarding the Saints, we must be further convinced that it is, and can be, no ways displeasing to God, that we should show a respect and honor to their remains on earth, or to those images and representations which recall

---

* Rev. iv. 10, v. 8.

LECTURE XIII.

them to our remembrance. Nay, we believe more than this; for we believe that God is pleased with this respect which we show them, inasmuch as it is all ultimately directed to honor Him in them. We doubt not, that He may be pleased to make use of such outward and visible instruments, to excite the faith of His people, and to bring them to a disposition of fervor, which may produce salutary effects.

This is the sum of our belief on this subject, which I intend to explain and support this evening. Before leaving this introductory portion of it, allow me to make one or two remarks, on the ambiguity of terms employed in the explanation, and still more in the rejection, of this doctrine. The words "to worship," for instance, are constantly quoted; it is said, that we speak of worshipping the Saints as we do of worshipping God, and that so we necessarily pay the same honor to both. This conclusion only arises from the poverty of language, and from the difficulty of substituting another word. We all know perfectly well, that the word "worship" is used on many occasions, when it does not mean any thing more than respect and honor; and such was its ancient and primary signification in our language. For instance, in the marriage service, no one attaches to it the signification of giving supreme or divine honor to the person said to be worshipped. "With my body I thee worship." We know that it is also a title of civil honor; and no one imagines, that when a person is called "worshipful," he is put on a level with the Almighty. Why then, if Catholics use the term in speaking of the Saints,—when they tell you again and again that they mean a different honor from what they pay to God,—why shall they be charged with paying an equal honor, merely because they make use of the same term? It would not be difficult to find many words and phrases, applied to the most dissimilar acts, and used in the most varied circumstances, where no misunderstanding is occasioned, simply for the reason that I have stated; because mankind have agreed to use them for different purposes; and no one will call his neighbor to account for so using them, and taking them in any one of their various senses. It is the same with the Latin word, "to adore," of which the primary meaning was to place the hand to the mouth; it simply signified to show a mark of respect by outward salutation. The term was later applied peculiarly to supreme worship, yet so as to be extended in the Church to other objects of respect; still, in ordinary language, we no longer use it, except when speaking of God. It would be very unjust to hold us accountable for

LECTURE XIII.

the word's being found in those formulas of devotion, which were instituted before these controversies arose, and when its meaning was so well understood, that no ambiguity could occur. And certainly they are not consistent, who quote against us those services in which we are said to adore the Cross, for they are taken from liturgies used in the very earliest ages of the Church.

There is another point, on which I shall not be able to deal at length; although, if time allow me, I may touch upon it later: I mean the abuses said to follow from the Catholic doctrine. We are made responsible for all its abuses. Why so? We have only to demonstrate our doctrines; and supposing—granting, that abuses have at times and in some places crept in, I would ask is that any reason why what is in itself lawful should be abolished? Are men to be deprived of that which is wholesome, because some make an improper use of it? Is there any thing more abused than the Bible, the word of God?—is there any thing more misapplied?—has it not been employed for purposes and in circumstances which may not be named? Is there any thing which has been more frequently called in to the aid of fanatical proceedings than this sacred word of God, or which has been more repeatedly quoted in such a way, by the thoughtless and ignorant, as to expose it even to ridicule? And are others to be charged with these abuses? Shall we say that the word of God is to be abolished? The same must be said here:—when we have laid down the Catholic doctrine, with its reasons, I leave it to any one's judgment how far the Church can be expected to abolish it, if received from Christ, on the ground that it has given rise to abuse. But, as I before observed, if I have time, I may touch upon these supposed abuses, and inquire how far they exist.

The Catholic doctrine regarding the Saints is therefore twofold;—in the first place, that the Saints of God make intercession before Him for their brethren on earth;—in the second place, that it is lawful to invoke their intercession. Knowing that they do pray for us, we say it must be lawful to turn to them, and ask and entreat of them to use that influence which they possess, in interceding on our behalf.

There is a doctrine inculcated in every creed, known by the name of the Communion of Saints. Perhaps many who have repeated the apostles' creed again and again, may not have thought it necessary to examine what is the meaning of these words, or what is the doctrine they inculcate. It is a pro-

LECTURE XIII.

fession of belief in a certain communion with the Saints. How does this communion exist between us and them? May any friendly offices pass between us? Or, if no such intercourse be permitted, in what can this communion consist? For, communion among the faithful, among the members of a family, or among the subjects of a state, implies that there is among them an interchange of mutual good offices, and that one is, in some way, ready to assist the other. If, therefore, we believe in a communion between us and the Saints, assuredly there must be acts, reciprocal acts. which form the bond of union between them and us. How, then, is this kept up? The Catholic Church has always been consistent in its doctrines. It does not fear examining to the quick any proposition which it lays down, or any dogma to which it exacts submission from all its subjects; it is not afraid of pushing to the farthest scrutiny all the consequences that flow from its doctrines. Consequently, if you ask a Catholic what he means by the communion of saints, he has no hesitation on the subject; his ideas are clear and defined—he tells you at once that he understands by it an interchange of good offices between the saints in heaven and those who are fighting here below for their crown; whereby they intercede on our behalf, look down upon us with sympathy, take an interest in all that we do and suffer, and make use of the influence which they necessarily possess with God, towards assisting their frail and tempted brethren on earth. And, to balance all this, we have our offices towards them, inasmuch as we repay them in respect, admiration, and love; with the feeling that they, who were once our brethren, having run their course, and being in possession of their reward, we may turn to them in the confidence of brethren, and ask them to use that influence with their Lord and ours, which their charity and goodness move them to exert.

This is a portion of the doctrine, and seems to enter so naturally and fitly into all our ideas of Christianity, as to recommend itself at once to any unprejudiced mind. For, what is the idea which the Gospel gives us of the Christian religion? I showed you, on another occasion, how the very expressions and terms applied to religion in the Old Law were continued in the New; whence I deduced, that the religion of Christ was the perfection, the completion, but still the continuation, of that which preceded it. Well, in like manner do we find that the very terms and expressions which are applied to the Church of Christ on earth, are constantly adopted into allusion to the Church in Heaven, the reign of the saints with God. This likewise is spoken of as the kingdom of God, the kingdom of the Father and of Christ, precisely as is the Church on earth; as though it formed with us but one Church and community of brethren—they in a glorified and happy, and we in a suffering and tempted state—still having a certain connection implied, and being considered, in the same manner, under the government of God. It is spoken of in these terms by St. Paul. Instead of representing the Blessed in Heaven as removed immeasurably from us, as Lazarus in Abraham's bosom was from the rich man in hell, he speaks as if we already enjoyed society with them—as if we had already come to the heavenly Jerusalem, and to the company of many thousands of angels,* and to the spirits of the just made perfect; thus showing that the death of Christ had actually broken down the barrier or partition wall, made all extremes one, and joined the Holy of Holies to the outward precincts of the Tabernacle.

We are told, likewise, by St. Paul, that those virtues which existed on earth are annihilated in heaven—all except one, and that is Charity or Love. Faith and Hope are there extinguished, but Charity, affection, remains unimpaired, and even is become the essence of that blessed existence. Who will for a moment imagine—who can for an instant entertain the thought, that the child which has been snatched from its parent by having been taken from a world of suffering, does not continue to love her whom it has left on earth, and sympathize with her sorrows over its grave? Who can believe that, when friend is separated from friend, and when one expires in the prayer of hope, their friendship is not continued, and that the two are not united in the same warm affection which they enjoyed here below? And if it was the privilege of love on earth—if it was one of its holiest duties, to pray to the Almighty for him who was so perfectly beloved, and if it never was surmised that injury was thereby inflicted on God, or on the honor and mediatorship of Christ, can we suppose that this holiest, most beautiful, and most perfect duty of charity hath ceased in heaven? Is it not, on the contrary, natural to suppose, that, as that charity is infinitely more vivid and glowing there than it was here, in its exercise, also, it must be infinitely more powerful? and that the same impulse that led the spirit, clogged and fettered with the body, to venture to raise its supplications to the clouded throne of God for its friend, will now, after its release, act with tenfold energy, when it sees

---

* Heb. xii. 22.

LECTURE XIII.

the innumerable pitfalls and dangers, the immense risks, and the thousands of temptations, to which he is exposed, and the infinite joy he is destined to possess? which experience now teaches it are thousands and millions of times more than earth can possibly give or take away. Seeing clearly in vision the face of God, enjoying the fulness of His glory and splendor, having the willingness and power to assist—can we believe that it will not with infinitely more effect raise its pure and faultless prayers in a tone of confident supplication, in favor of him to whom it was linked in affection here below? Can we believe that God would deprive charity of its highest prerogative, when He has given it its brightest crown? Truly then, my brethren, there is nothing repugnant to our ideas of God or of His attributes or institutions in all this,—on the contrary, it seems absolutely necessary to fill up the measure of His mercy, and to complete the picture of His Church here, as connected to that above, which He has exhibited to us in His word.

But have we not something much more positive than what I have stated, in this word of God? Yes; for we have the plainest and strongest assurances that God does receive the prayers of the saints and angels, and that they are constantly employed in supplications in our behalf; and this is the chief fundamental principle of our belief. Of this we have all the proof we can desire. For we have the belief of the universal Jewish Church, confirmed in the New Law. The belief of the Old Law is clear; for we find that, in the later books particularly, the angels are spoken of constantly, as in a state of ministration to the wants and necessities of mankind. In the book of Daniel, for instance, we read of angels sent to instruct him, and we have mention made of the princes, meaning the angels of different kingdoms.* In the book of Tobias,—which, whatever any one present may think of its canonicity, as I said on a former occasion of the book of Maccabees, must be considered, at least, as a strong testimonial of the belief of the Jews,—we find these words expressly put into the mouth of an angel:—"When thou didst pray with tears, and didst bury the dead, and didst leave thy dinner and hide the dead by day in thy house, and bury them by night, I offered thy prayers to the Lord."† In the book of Maccabees, we have the same doctrine repeated. It is there said, that Onias, who had been High Priest, appeared to Judas Maccabeus, "holding up his arms and praying for the people of the Jews. After this,

---

* Dan. viii. 16; ix. 21; x. 13; xii. 1.   † Tob. xii. 12.

there appeared also another man, admirable for age and glory and environed with great beauty and majesty. Then Onias said, 'This is a lover of his brethren, and of the people of Israel: this is he that prayeth much for the people, and for all the holy city, Jeremias the prophet of God.'"* Such, then, was the belief of the Jews, and such it is at the present day.

But is there any thing in the New Testament to contradict it, and give reason to suspect for a moment, that our blessed Saviour rejected and reprobated this conviction? Does he not, on the contrary, speak of it as a thing well understood, and in terms which, so far from reproving, must have gone so far to confirm his hearers in this belief? "Even so," says our Saviour, "there shall be joy in heaven upon one sinner that doth penance, more than upon ninety-nine just that need not penance."† What is here signified, but that communion of which I spoke, whereby a sinner's repenting here below is matter of joy and gladness to the angels? And we are elsewhere taught that the saints of God shall be like His angels.‡ We have also the angels of individuals spoken of; and we are told not to offend any of Christ's little ones, or make them fall, because their angels always see the face of their Father, who is in Heaven.§ Why, this to all appearance goes as much as the Catholic belief, and more, to affect the superintendence and guidance, and general providence of God. We are to take care to avoid sin, because it offends the angels! we are to avoid being the cause of these little ones' fall, because *their* angels see the face of God! What does this mean, but that they have an influence with God, and will use it to bring down judgment on the offender? For, in fact, wherefore is the connection between the angels and men alluded to, except to show that the former, enjoying the divine presence, have a powerful advantage over us, which they will employ in visiting with severe vengeance transgressions against those entrusted to their care? And what is that but establishing a communion and connection between them and their little charge, in the way of intercession?

But, in the Apocalypse, we have still stronger authority; for we there read of our prayers being as perfumes in the hands of angels and saints. One blessed spirit was seen by St. John to stand before a mystical altar in heaven, "having a golden censer, and there was given to him much incense, that he should offer the prayers of all saints upon the golden altar, which is before

---

* 2 Mac. xv. 12.   † Luke xv. 7, 10.   ‡ Mat. xxii. 30   § Mat. xviii. 20.

LECTURE XIII.

the throne of God. And the smoke of the incense of the prayers of the saints ascended up before God, from the hands of the angels."* And not only the angels, but the twenty-four elders, cast themselves before the throne of God, and, as I before remarked, pour out vials of sweet odors, which are the prayers of the saints. What does all this signify, but that they do present our prayers to God, and become our intercessors with Him?

From all this it is proved, that the saints and angels know what passes on earth—that they are aware of what we do and suffer; otherwise they could not rejoice in any good that we do, nor resent any misfortune that befals us. In the second place, we have it sufficiently proved, that the saints do more than barely know and interest themselves about us; for they actually present our prayers to God, and intercede in our behalf with Him. Here, then, is a basis, and a sufficient one, for the Catholic belief,—such a basis as surely should give rise to some doctrine or other in the true religion. But where is this doctrine to be found in those religious systems which reject and exclude all intercession of the saints, all intercourse between those on earth and their brethren already in bliss? Assuredly these texts prove something. For if all contained in the word of God is true, and must form a rule of faith, such clear testimony as this, regarding the connection between mankind and the blessed, must form the subject of a doctrine. Where, then, is this found? Nowhere but in the Catholic belief—that prayers are offered for us by the saints, and that, therefore, we may apply to them for their supplications.

To establish this more fully, it is necessary to look into the doctrine of the Church in the earliest ages; and I can have only one fear, one motive of hesitation, in laying before you passages on this subject. It is not that I may weary you by the number of my quotations; for that, I fear, may have been the case with regard to almost every doctrine that I have supported by tradition and the testimony of the Fathers; yet, in every case, though I have read a great number of texts, I have in reality given you only a selection from many more. But my reason for apprehension at present is, that, in the authorities from the Fathers on this subject, their expressions are so much stronger than those used by the Catholics at the present day, that there is danger, if I may so say, of proving too much. They go far beyond us; and consequently, if we are to be considered idolaters, God knows

---

* Rev. viii. 3, 4.

what terms must be found to qualify their expressions. Let us begin with the very first ages of the Church, and let us not take ambiguous words, but the simplest and most natural expressions of the feelings of the earliest Christians.

Every part of Rome is undermined with catacombs, in which the bodies of saints and martyrs were deposited after their deaths. The tombs are even some of them as yet sealed up and unbroken; some with inscriptions on them, or perhaps a palm-branch rudely sculptured, to show that there repose the martyrs of Christ. We have phials, adhering and fastened to the covers of the tombs, in the walls of the catacombs, in which are sponges, or sediment, still tinged with the color of blood; indeed, the very instruments of martyrdom are constantly found in tombs. Certainly, these were men who knew Christianity, who fully appreciated what was due to Christ, for whom they died, who were fully convinced that nothing on earth was to be preferred before Him, and that no creature could pretend to one particle of the honor reserved by Him to Himself! Surely we cannot want purer or more satisfactory witnesses to what Christ instituted, than they who shed their blood to seal its truth; we cannot want teachers better imbued with the spirit of His religion, than those who were ready to lay down their lives to defend it! Let us see what was their belief regarding their brethren, when they deposited them in these tombs, and sealed them up, and inscribed on them their regrets or their hopes. Nothing is more common than to find on them a supplication, a prayer to the saints or martyrs, to intercede for the survivors with God. In the year 1694, was discovered a remarkable tomb of the martyr Sabbatius, in the cemetery of Gordian and Epimachus. On the one side, was the palm-branch, the emblem of martyrdom, and on the other, the wreath or crown given to conquerors, with this inscription, in a rude latinity:—

SABBATI ˙ DVLCIS ˙ ANIMA ˙ PETE ˙ ET ˙ ROGA
PRO ˙ FRATRES ˙ ET ˙ SODALES ˙ TVOS

"Sabbatius, sweet soul, pray and entreat for thy brethren and comrades."

These early Christians, then, pray to the martyr to intercede for his brethren on earth.

In the cemetery of Callixtus, is another inscription of the same antiquity, which runs thus:—

ATTICE ˙ SPIRITVS ˙ TVVS
IN ˙ BONV ˙ ORA ˙ PRO ˙ PAREN
TIBVS ˙ TVIS

"Atticus, thy spirit is in bliss: pray for thy parents."

LECTURE XIII.

In that of Cyriaca, we have an inscription in much the same terms:—

IOVIANE ' VIVAS ' IN ' DEO ' ET
ROG '

"Jovianus, may you live in God and pray."

In that of Pricilla, we have another, very touching and beautiful in the original:—

ANATOLINVS ' FILIO ' BENEMERENTI ' FECIT
QVI ' VIXIT ' ANNIS ' VII
SPIRITVS ' TVVS ' BENE ' REQVIES
CAT ' IN ' DEO ' PETAS ' PRO ' SORORE ' TVA

"Anatolinus made this monument to his well-deserving son, who lived seven years. May thy spirit rest well in God, and thou pray for thy sister."

Marini gives us another old Christian inscription, to this effect:—

ROGES ' PRO ' NOBIS ' QVIA ' SCIMVS ' TE ' IN ' CHRISTO

"I ray for us, because we know that thou art in Christ."

These are most of them inscriptions on the tombs of martyrs, whose bodies were deposited therein during the very first centuries of Christianity, when men were ready to die for the faith of Christ.* They were inscribed by those who saw them suffer, and who were, perhaps, themselves to be the next to lay down their lives; and yet did they not think, that by entreating their prayers, they were derogating from the glory of God, or the mediatorship of Christ.

If from these monuments, which are of the greatest interest, because they exist as they did when first erected, and cannot have been subject to the slightest change, we descend to the recorded opinions of the Fathers, we have precisely the same sentiments. And I beg particularly to direct your attention to the following circumstances in these authorities. In the first place, they directly ask the saints to pray for them; secondly, in speaking of the saints, they mention the way in which they are to be assisted by them, through intercession; and thirdly, they make use of expressions apparently requesting from the saints themselves those blessings which were to come from God. They do not simply say, "Pray for us, intercede for us:" but "Deliver us, grant us:" not because they believed the saints could do so of themselves, but because, in common parlance, it is usual to ask

---

* See my learned friend Dr. Rock's Hierurgia, where these inscriptions have been collected. Vol. ii. [A more striking inscription than any of those given in the text has been lately found in the Cemetery of St. Agnes, and will soon be published.]

directly from an intercessor, the favor which we believe his influence can obtain. I insist on this point, because it is charged against Catholics, that they ask of the blessed Virgin "deliverance;" saying, in the introduction to her Litany, "deliver us from all danger;" that they beg of the saints to help them: although this is nothing more than the same form of speech as the Fathers use. And in the fourth place, I request you to observe how they distinguished, as Catholics do, between worship due to God, and the homage due to His saints, using the selfsame terms as we.

In the second century, we have St. Irenæus telling us, that, "as Eve was seduced to fly from God, so was the Virgin Mary induced to obey Him, that she might become the advocate of her that had fallen."* In the third century, we have the testimony of several Fathers; but I will select two, one from the Greek and one from the Latin Church. Origen says: "And of all the holy men who have quitted this life, retaining their charity towards those whom they left behind, we may be allowed to say, that they are anxious for their salvation, and that they assist them by their prayers and their mediation with God. For it is written in the books of the Maccabees: *This is Jeremiah the prophet of God, who always prays for the people.*"† Again, he thus writes, on the Lamentations: "I will fall down on my knees, and not presuming, on account of my crimes, to present my prayer to God, I will invoke all the saints to my assistance. O ye saints of heaven, I beseech you, with sorrow full of sighs and tears, fall at the feet of the Lord of mercies for me, a miserable sinner."‡ St. Cyprian, in the same century: "Let us be mindful of one another in our prayers; with one mind and with one heart, in this world and in the next, let us always pray, with mutual charity relieving our sufferings and afflictions. And may the charity of him, who, by the divine favor, shall first depart hence, still persevere before the Lord; may his prayer, for our brethren and sisters, not cease."§ Therefore, after our departure from this life, the same offices of charity are to continue, by our praying for those who remain on earth.

In the fourth century, Eusebius of Cæsarea thus writes: "May we be found worthy by the prayers and intercession of all the saints."∥ In the same century, St. Cyril of Jerusalem speaking of the Liturgy, thus expresses himself: "We next

---

* Adver. Hæres. L. v. c. xix. p. 361.
† Lib. iii. in Cant. Cantic. T. iii. p. 75.   ‡ Lib. 11. de Job.
§ Ep. lvii. p. 96.   ∥ Com. in Isai. T. 11. p. 593. Ed. *Par.* 1706.

LECTURE XIII.

commemorate those who are gone before us; the patriarchs, prophets, apostles, and martyrs; begging that, through their prayers, God would receive our supplications. We then pray for the holy fathers and bishops that are dead, and for all the faithful departed, believing that their souls receive very great relief by the prayers that are offered for them while this holy and tremendous victim lies upon the altar."* St. Basil, one of the most eloquent and learned writers of that century, expresses himself in much warmer and enthusiastic terms, in his panegyric on forty martyrs, in these words: "These are they, who, having taken possession of our country, stand as towers against the incursions of the enemy. Here is a ready aid to Christians. Often have you endeavored, often have you toiled, to gain one intercessor. You have now forty, all emitting one common prayer. Whoever is oppressed by care, has recourse to their aid, as he has that prospers: the first, to seek deliverance; the second, that his good fortune may continue. The pious mother is found praying for her children; and the wife for the return and the health of her husband. O ye common guardians of the human race, co-operators in our prayers, most powerful messengers, stars of the world, and flowers of Churches, let us join our prayers with yours."†

Another saint of this age, St. Ephrem, is remarkable as the oldest father and writer of the oriental Church. His expressions are really so exceedingly strong, that I am sure some Catholics of the present day would feel a certain difficulty in using some of them in their prayers, for fear of offending persons of another religion; they go so much beyond those which we use. "I entreat you," he says, "holy martyrs, who have suffered so much for the Lord, that you would intercede for us with Him, that He bestow His grace on us."‡ Here he simply prays to the saints, asking their intercession, just as Catholics do. But now listen to the following: "We fly to thy patronage, Holy Mother of God; protect and guard us under the wings of thy mercy and kindness. Most merciful God, through the intercession of the most blessed Virgin Mary, and of all the angels, and of all the

---

* Catech. Mystag. γ. n. viii. ix. p. 327, 328. This text affords additional proof of what I advanced in a note to Lecture xi. p. 57, that the fathers clearly distinguish between the commemoration of martyrs and saints in the Liturgy, and that of other souls departed; and that they distinguish two states, one for the perfect, and the other for the imperfect.
† Hom. xix. in 40 Martyres, T. ii pp. 155, 156.
‡ Encom. in SS. Mart. T. iii. p. 251

saints, show pity to thy creature;"*—the very form of prayer quoted again and again in the itinerant discourses made against us, from the beginning of the Litany of the blessed Virgin, as the strongest proof that we worship her. There are passages, however, innumerable in his writings, much stronger; and I will read you one or two, as specimens of the many prayers found in his works addressed to the blessed Virgin. "In thee, Patroness, and *Mediatrix* with God, who was born from thee,† the human race, O Mother of God, placeth its joy; and ever is dependent upon thy patronage: and, in thee alone, hath refuge and defence, who hast full confidence in Him. Behold, I also draw nigh to thee, with a fervent soul, not having courage to approach thy Son, but imploring, that, through thy intercession ($\mu\epsilon\sigma\iota\tau\epsilon\iota\alpha\varsigma$) I may obtain salvation. Despise not, then, thy servant, who placeth all his hopes in thee, after God; reject him not, placed in grievous danger, and oppressed with many griefs; but thou, who art compassionate, and the mother of a merciful God, have mercy upon thy servant; free me from fatal concupiscence," &c. In the course of this prayer, our Blessed Lady is called, "the precious vision of the prophet, the clearest fulfilment of all prophecy, the eloquent mouth of the apostles, the strength of kings, the boast of the priesthood, the forgiveness of sins, the propitiation of the just Judge, the rise of the fallen, the redemption from sins," &c. In another prayer, we meet the following words, addressed to the same ever-glorious Virgin: "After the Trinity (thou art) mistress of all; after the Paraclete, another paraclete; after the Mediator, mediatrix of the whole world.."‡ Surely this is more than enough, to prove, that if this glory of the Syriac Church, this friend of the great St. Basil, had lived in our times, he would not have been allowed to officiate in the English Church; but would have been obliged to retire to some humble chapel, if he wished to discharge his sacred functions.

For these are stronger expressions than are ever used by any Catholic now; yet this saint is not only considered by us the brightest ornament of the Syriac and Oriental Church, but is equally regarded as such by Nestorians, and Monophysites, and other sectaries, who have separated from us since his time. We have a glowing panegyric of him in the works of St. Gregory of

---

* Serm. de Laud. B. Mar. Virg. T. iii. p. 156.

† Μεσιτην προς τον εκ σου τεχθεντα Θεον. This prayer occurs in his Greek Works, to. iii. p. 532.

‡ Ἡ μετὰ τὴν Τριάδα πάντων δέσποινα, ἡ μετὰ τὸν παράκλητον ἄλλος παράκλητος καὶ μετὰ τὸν μεσίτην μεσίτης κόσμου παντός.—P. 528.

LECTURE XIII. 93

Nyssa; he was the bosom friend of St. Basil, and is always spoken of by him with the greatest affection and reverence, as a man of distinguished virtue, and so humble that he never advanced beyond the order of deacon in the Church of Edessa. And St. Gregory of Nyssa thus addresses him after his death: "Do thou now, being present at God's altar, and with His angels offering sacrifice to the Prince of life, and to the most holy Trinity, remember us; begging for us the pardon of our sins."* The same doctrine, therefore, manifestly prevailed in every part of the Church, and was as much held in the Greek as in the Latin or Oriental.

St. Gregory of Nazianzum, speaking of his deceased friend, St. Basil, says: "Now, indeed, he is in heaven; there, if I mistake not, offering up sacrifices for us, pouring out prayers for the people: for he has not left us, so as to have deserted us. And do thou, sacred and holy Spirit, look down, I beseech thee, on us: arrest by thy prayers that sting of the flesh which was given to us for our correction, or teach us how to bear it with fortitude: guide all our ways to that which is best; and, when we shall depart hence, receive us then into thy society; that with thee, beholding more clearly that blessed and adorable Trinity, which now we see in a dark manner, we may put a final close to all our wishes, and receive the reward of the labors which we have borne."† St. Gregory of Nyssa, the brother of St. Basil, whom I have once already quoted, uses language equally expressive, in his discourse on the martyr Theodorus. These are his words: "Invisible though thou art, come as a friend to them that honor thee; come and behold this solemn feast. We stand in need of many favors: be our envoy for thy country before our common King and Lord. The country of the martyr is the place of his suffering: his citizens, his brothers, his relations, are they who possess, who guard, who honor him. We are in fear of afflictions; we look for dangers: the Scythians approach us with dreadful war. Thou, indeed, hast overcome the world; but thou knowest the feelings and the wants of our nature. Beg for us the continuance of peace, that these our public meetings be not dissolved; that the wicked and raging barbarian overthrow not our temples and our altars; that he tread not under foot thy holy places. That hitherto we have lived in safety, we owe to thy favor: we implore thy protection for the days that are to come; and if a host of prayers be necessary, assemble the

---

* Tom. ii. p. 1048. † Orat. xx. de Laud. S. Basil. T. ii. p. 372, 373.

choirs of your brother martyrs, and supplicate all together for us. The united services of so many just will cover the sins of the people. Admonish Peter, solicit Paul, call John, the beloved disciple, and let them intercede for the Churches, which they themselves have founded."*

Here is a passage from St. Ambrose: "Peter and Andrew interceded for the widow. (Luke iv. 38.) It were well if we could obtain so speedy an Intercessor: but surely those who implored the Lord for their relation, can do the same for us. You see, that she, who was a sinner, was little fitting to pray for herself, or at least to obtain what she asked. Other intercessors to the Physician were therefore necessary.—The Angels, who are appointed to be our guardians, must be invoked; and the martyrs likewise, whose bodies seem to be a pledge for their patronage. They, who in their blood washed away every stain of sin, can implore forgiveness for us: they are our guides, and the beholders of our lives and actions: to them, therefore, we should not blush to have recourse."†

Now then, I will show you, by an example, how nicely these early writers drew the distinction which Catholics now do. St. Epiphanius thus writes of the Blessed Virgin, reproving the errors of the Collyridian heretics, who adored her, and offered sacrifice to her: "Though, therefore, she was a chosen vessel, and endowed with eminent sanctity, still she is a woman, partaking of our common nature, but deserving of the highest honors shown to the saints of God—She stands before them all, on account of the heavenly mystery accomplished in her. But we adore no saint:—and as this worship is not given to Angels, much less can it be allowed to the daughter of Ann.—Let Mary then be honored, but the Father, Son, and Holy Ghost alone be adored: let no one adore Mary."‡ St. Augustine makes the same exact distinction, where he thus writes:—"The Christian people celebrate the memories of the martyrs with a religious solemnity, in order that they may learn to imitate them, and may be associated to their merits, and be aided by their prayers: but to no martyr—to the God alone of martyrs, in memory of them, do we raise altars. For what bishop, among the repositories of holy bodies, assisting at the altar, was ever heard to say: To thee, Peter, to thee, Paul, or to thee, Cyprian, do we make this offering? To God, alone, who crowned the martyrs, is sacrifice of-

---

* Orat. in Theod. Martyr. T. ii. p. 1017. † Lib. de Viduis, T. ii. p. 200.
‡ Adv. Collyridianos Hær. lix. sive lxxix. T. i. p. 1061, 1062, 1664.

fered in the places where their relics rest; that the sight of these places may excite a warmer sentiment towards those whom we should imitate; and towards him, by whose aid it can be accomplished. We venerate, therefore, the martyrs with that veneration of regard, with which holy men are here treated upon earth, who are disposed, we know, to suffer for the truth of the Gospel. When they have suffered, and have conquered, our veneration is more devoted and more firm, as they are translated from a state of conflict to a state of permanent happiness. But with that worship, which the Greeks call λατρεια, and which in Latin cannot be expressed by one word—as it is a worship properly due only to the Divinity—*with that worship we worship God alone.* To this belongs the offering of sacrifice; whence they are idolaters who sacrifice to idols. We offer no sacrifice to any martyr, nor to any saint, nor to any angel; and should any one fall into the error, sound doctrine will so raise its voice that, he be corrected, or condemned, or avoided."* Before making a few remarks on these passages, I will quote one more from this great Father, which confirms as well the doctrine of purgatory:—"It is a proof," he writes, "of kind regard towards the dead, when their bodies are deposited near the monuments of saints. But hereby what are they aided, unless in this, that, recollecting the place where they lie, we be induced to recommend them to the patronage of those saints for their prayers with God? Calling therefore to mind the grave of a departed friend, and the near monument of the venerable martyr, we naturally commend the soul to his prayers. And that the souls of those will be thereby benefited, who so lived as to deserve it, there can be no doubt."†

The distinction drawn in the two passages just quoted, and in many others, is precisely the same as we make; that sacrifice and supreme homage are reserved to God alone, but that the saints are intercessors for us, and that we may invoke them as such. What are we to say to these testimonies? Nothing can be more manifest than that the doctrine of these fathers is precisely the same as I have laid down, and just what is declared in the Council of Trent, or in the Catechisms taught to our children. Are we to say that they were involved in the same idolatry as ourselves? For it is not with this dogma as with some others: the consequences of error here are most serious. It might have been said, in other circumstances, that some errors were allowed

---

* L. xx. c. xxi. contra Faustum. T. viii. p. 347.
† De curâ pro mortuis gerenda, c. iv. T. vi. p. 519.

to creep into the Church; but when it is maintained that the entire Church was, or is all involved in idolatry, it is a fatal charge. Will you venture to say that the whole of the Church, in the first, second, third, and fourth centuries, in Italy, in Greece, in Syria, in Mesopotamia, and in every other part of the world, was universally plunged into idolatry? Is it not a fearful venture in any man to assert that a few individuals in one country, that a small Church, or rather a collection of conflicting religious communities, in one island of the globe, and perhaps a comparatively small number of Christians in some other parts, are alone the possessors, after a lapse of eighteen hundred years, of the true faith of Christ? and that to such an extent, as to suppose that from this deep morass of frightful and fetid corruption, it did not emerge until the superior illumination of this small portion of mankind enabled them to see the light of truth: to such an extent as to imagine that they who were ready to die for Him, and who were actuated by the purest zeal for his glory, were idolaters! Who will refuse to call Basil, Augustine, Jerome, Ambrose, and Irenæus, saints? Who will refuse to give them that title? Read their works, and will you venture to say that such men, such chosen, favored spirits, were immersed in that damnable idolatry in which all men were plunged for eight hundred years and more, according to the stern declaration of the Book of Homilies? Is it not on their testimony that many dogmas most essential to Christianity now rest? Is it not on their authority, and on that of others like them, that we mainly receive the doctrine of the Trinity and of Christ's Divinity? Can they have preserved these doctrines pure and uncontaminated as they came from God? and shall it yet be said that they themselves were so grossly corrupted in faith as to be wallowing in what must be considered the lowest abyss of sinful idolatry? Here is a solemn problem to be solved, not only to those who charge us with this crime, but by all who deny ours to be the true doctrine of the true Church of Christ.

Then their difficulties increase at every step; for I further ask, what will they say of the worth and power of Christ, who came to establish His religion on the ruins of idolatry, if in less than one or two hundred years it triumphed again over His work: yea, if, even while the martyr's blood flowed, it could have been written, that in behalf of idolatry it was shed, and that they, indeed, died for refusing to give homage to the false gods of the heathens, yet at the very time were showing honor to their deceased fellow-men, and thereby perpetrating the enor-

LECTURE XIII.

mous crime which they were slaughtered for refusing to commit! Surely these are difficulties that must be overcome; for is it not mocking, deriding Christ, to believe that He came down to cast a fire upon earth, saying, "I will that it be enkindled;"* that is, the fire of charity, and faith, and the true light of God; and that, after this expression of His will and determination, it should have been extinguished so soon; that the truth should have been trodden out by that very monster whose head He came to crush; that the idolatry which he came to uproot was of so powerful a growth, and the seed of His word was so feeble, that the latter should have been choked by the former before it came to maturity? Is it not an insult to the Son of God, and to His saving power, to suppose His religion so soon sunk into this degraded state: and yet this *must* be asserted, if you allow the fathers who held our doctrine to be involved, as they must be, in the same charge which is flung upon us.

Nor could it be said that they did not understand the popular and trite objection, that, through such doctrine, the merits and mediatorship of Christ are annihilated. They must have known that the entreaty for the prayers of one man by another could not interfere with that mediatorship—on the contrary, they must have felt what we feel, that there cannot be a greater homage paid to God than to consider it necessary that His Saints, after being received into final happiness, should still appear before Him as intercessors and suppliants. So far from feeling any of that delicacy which is so common now about applying the same words to God and the Saints, we have the two joined without scruple under the same expression. I will only cite one example of this; an inscription discovered two years ago, which was erected by a person of considerable consequence, being governor of the district around Rome. The inscription is in these words:—"Anicius Auchenius Bassus, who had enjoyed the consular dignity, and his wife Honorata, with their children, *devout to God and the saints.*"† We find God and the saints here joined together; nor does it appear that any apprehension was entertained of thereby derogating from the honor of the Deity.

Thus far, then, my brethren, regarding the saints themselves; such, as you have heard, is the Catholic doctrine, such its consistency, and such its proofs. Another point, intimately con-

---

* Luke xii. 49.
† ANICIVS · AVCHENIVS · BASSVS · V · C · ET · TVRRENIA · HONORATA · C · F · EIVS · CVM · FILIIS · DEO SANCTISQVE · DEVOTI.—See Letter to J. Poynder, Esq., p. 38.

nected with it, is the respect paid by us to the relics of the Saints. The Catholic believes that any thing which has belonged to men distinguished by their love of God and by what they have done and suffered in His cause, deserves that respect and honor which is constantly shown, in ordinary life, to whatever has belonged to any great, or celebrated, or very good man. Nothing is more common than to see such objects receive marks of respect. We meet with such feelings shown even in the Established Church; for we are told that in the Church of Lutterworth there is preserved the chair of Wycliffe, his desk, and a portion of his cloak. Wherefore are they kept? They are relics; precisely what the Catholic means by relics: for they are kept by those who consider him to have been a very great and good man; intending thereby to honor him, and feeling that a sort of connection or link is kept up between him and those who come, in after times, by the possession of these remembrances of him. Catholics, however, go further; for they believe that they please God by showing respect to these objects, and that, by honoring these relics of the Saints, they are incited to imitate their example.

This, many exclaim, is rank superstition! My brethren, there is no word more common than this, and yet there are few more difficult to be defined. What is superstition? It is the believing that any virtue, energy, or supernatural power exists in any thing independent of God's voluntary and free gift of such virtue to that thing. The moment you, sincerely and from conviction, introduce God—the moment you hope or believe, because you are intimately persuaded that God has been pleased to make use of any thing as an instrument in His hands, superstition ceases. And it matters not whether you speak of the natural or of the supernatural order of things. If any man believe, that by carrying a charm about him, it will do him some good, will cure him or preserve him from danger, because of some innate virtue or power of its own, or because he chooses to imagine that God has given it such a power, without any solid reason, this is superstitious. But if I take a medicine, persuaded of its natural power, resulting from the laws by which God has been pleased to regulate His creation, there is no superstition. In the same manner, whatever is practised from a sincere and well-grounded conviction that God has appointed it or approved of it, is not superstitious. It would have been a superstition in the Jews to believe that, by looking on a brazen serpent, they could be healed from the bite of fiery serpents; but the moment God ordered

LECTURE XIII.

such a symbol to be erected, with a promise of such an effect, superstition ceased. The instant He has given the command, every glance at it becomes, as it were, a look towards God, who has given it that virtue and efficacy; and what of its own nature would have been superstitious, becomes not only lawful, but most salutary. Had man raised two images of cherubims on the ark of the covenant, and bowed down before them and worshipped them, and asked that in them God would hear his prayers, it would have been gross superstition, and there would have been even danger of falling into idolatry, as in the worship of the golden calf. But the moment God directed these to be raised, and called them his mercy-seat, and said that from it He would hear the prayers of His servants, and before it the highpriest was ordered to bring his gifts, that instant it became a means appointed by God, and there was no superstition in placing a trust in its instrumentality. Had precious stones been worn on the breast, and inscribed with certain letters for oracular purposes, without a divine assurance, it would have been a charm, or whatever you please; but so soon as God orders the Urim and Thummim to be made, or when David applies to the Ephod to learn what he should do,* knowing that God had appointed it for that purpose, there is no longer any superstition. This is a distinction to be clearly kept in view, because it goes to confute the popular imputation of superstition to Catholics.

If any ignorant man prays before any object, or goes by preference to any certain place, in consequence of an experience having produced conviction in his mind, no matter whether justly or not, that his prayers are more effectual there than elsewhere, certainly, by acting on that feeling, he commits no acts of superstition; for he attributes all that special efficacy to the appointment of God, whereof he has become convinced. In other religions, the same idea may be found. Is it not common for a person to think that he can pray with more devotion in a certain part of his house, or in one oratory or chapel, rather than in another? And yet who says that such a one is superstitious? It is from no idea that the building or walls will bring down a blessing on his prayers, but from a conviction that in that place he prays better; and that, consequently, his prayers are better heard; and surely that is not superstition. Precisely in the same manner, why do some go to hear the preaching of one clergyman rather than another's, though, in reality, he is not more

---

* 1 Reg. xxiii. 9.

eloquent? And yet, perhaps, if you ask them, they cannot tell you why; only they feel that, when he speaks, his words go more to their hearts, and they receive more satisfaction. Would it be said, that this was attaching a virtue to the man, that it supposed some individual efficacy to reside in him? Consider the matter in the simplest form, that it pleases God to make that person an instrument of His work, and it loses the character of superstition, and the glory given is referred to God alone.

Apply these considerations to the relics of the saints, to those memorials of them which we Catholics bear about our persons, or preserve with care, with the feeling that they are a sort of pledge, or symbol of the saints' protection and intercession,—that they serve to record our devotion, and to remind us of the virtues that distinguished those servants of God; so long as we believe that there is no virtue in them, independently of a bestowal from the goodness and power of God, this cannot be called superstition. The belief of the Catholic simply is, that, as it has pleased God to make use of such objects as instruments for performing great works, and imparting great benefits to His people, they are to be treated with respect, and reverenced, in the humble hope that He may again so use them in our favor; and thus, we consider them as possessing that symbolic virtue which I have described. Now, we do find that God has made use of such instruments before. In the Old Law, he raised up a dead man, by his coming in contact with the bones of one of his prophets. The moment he was cast into the tomb—the moment he touched the holy prophet's bones, he arose, restored to life.* What did God thereby show, but that the bones of His saints were sometimes gifted by Him with a supernatural power; and that, on an occasion when, apparently, there was no expectation of such an extraordinary miracle? We read, that, upon handkerchiefs, which had touched the body of St. Paul, being taken to the sick, they were instantly restored to health;† and those were relics in the Catholic sense of the word. We read, that a woman was cured who touched the hem of our Saviour's garment;‡ that the very skirts of His raiment were impregnated with that power which issued from Him, so as to restore health, without His exercising any act of His will. These examples prove that God makes use of the relics of His saints as instruments for his greatest wonders. Here is the foundation of our practice, which excludes

---

* 4 Reg. xiii. 21.   † Acts xix. 11, 12.   ‡ Mat. xix. 20.

all idea of superstition. We have the express authority of God, that He chooses to make use of these means, and, consequently, there can be no superstition in the belief that He may use them so again.

Nor can it be said that there was more authority for the expectation of such assistance in these cases, than there is at present. It was nowhere told to the faithful that handkerchiefs or aprons were to be applied to the person of Paul, to receive virtue from the contact, or that, if they were so used, they would heal the sick. It is no less evident that the woman who touched our Saviour's dress did it not in consequence of any invitation or encouragement, nor from the actual experience of others; for, manifestly, it was the first experiment. Jesus attributes her cure to the faith which accompanies the act:—"Be of good heart, daughter, thy faith hath made thee whole." Now, if these persons were not superstitious by trusting for the first time to the efficacy of such means, and if, instead of being reprehended, they were praised, on account of the faith which actuated them to try them, how much less will the accusation hold, where the same faith, the same feeling, has the encouragement of the former success and the sanction of those formal approbations!

After these examples from Scripture, after this groundwork in the word of God, I have nothing to do but show you again, that, from the beginning of the Church, ours was the universal belief and practice. We find the demonstration of this in the care and anxiety with which the Christians sought to save the bodies of the martyrs from destruction. We read throughout ecclesiastical history what eagerness the Christians displayed to snatch up their relics, and sometimes, at considerable expense, to bribe the guards to give up their mangled limbs for honorable burial. This spirit carried them still further: they gathered up all their blood, as well as they could, and preserved it in vessels placed in their tombs. St. Prudentius describes a painting, which he saw in one of the catacombs, of the martyrdom of St. Hippolytus, who was dragged to death at the heels of horses. Because bearing the same name as the person fabled to have been so treated, his judge ordered him to undergo that punishment. The body of the saint is described as torn in pieces, and a crowd of Christians followed, gathering up, not only the fragments of his body, but every particle of his blood, with sponges or linen cloths, to preserve it. And, in fact, we frequently find sponges or phials, tinged with blood, on the tombs of the martyrs. Another species of relic also found there are the instruments of torture, whereby they were put to death. There is an apartment attached to the Vatican library at Rome, called the Museum of Christian antiquities, in which all such instruments are carefully preserved, after having been accurately authenticated. The Christians, therefore, it appears, collected all such instruments, and buried them with the martyrs' bodies. Another way in which they testified their respect for the relics of the martyrs, was, by always erecting their oratories, or churches, where they had suffered, and the tombs of the martyrs were their altars. Not only is this proved by the liturgy, in which the relics of martyrs are mentioned as necessarily present in the altar, and from the fact of every old church at Rome being built over the shrine of a martyr, but it is expressly enacted in the Council of Carthage, held in 398, wherein the following decree was issued: "Let those altars be overturned by the bishop of the place, which are erected about the fields and the roads, as in memory of martyrs, in which is no body, nor any relics.—Care also must be taken to ascertain genuine facts. For altars, which are raised from dreams and the idle fancies of men, must not be supported."* We have a beautiful letter of the holy Archbishop of Milan, St. Ambrose, to his sister Marcellina, wherein he relates, how when, on a certain occasion, he announced to his flock his intention of dedicating a new church, several of them cried out, that he must consecrate it, as he had done the Roman basilica. To whom he replied, "I will, if I can discover the bodies of martyrs." Whereupon, seized with a holy ardor, he commanded a search to be made, and discovered the bodies of SS. Gervasius and Protasius, with their blood, and other evidences of authenticity. They were solemnly translated to the Ambrosian basilica, and on the way a blind man recovered his sight. He then gives his sister the substance of his sermon on the occasion.†

Nothing remains but, according to my practice, to read a few out of many passages, to show you that the ancient Christians believed all regarding relics that we do. We begin with the church of Smyrna, one of the seven mentioned in the Apocalypse, and one founded by St. John; St. Polycarp, its bishop, was one of the last who had seen that evangelist, and was his personal disciple, under whom, consequently, we cannot suppose that the doctrine taught by Christ and his apostles was completely obscured. After his death, the Christians of the Church

---

* Can. xiv. Conc. Gen. T. ii. p. 1217.
† Epistolar. Lib. vii. ep. lvi. Oper. Tom. v. p. 315, Par. 1632.

LECTURE XIII.

of Smyrna wrote a letter, preserved by Eusebius, giving an account of what took place on that occasion, in which is this passage:—"Our subtle enemy, the devil, did his utmost, that we should not take away the body, as many of us anxiously wished. It was suggested that we should desert our crucified Master, and begin to worship Polycarp. Foolish men! who know not that we can never desert Christ, who died for the salvation of all men; nor worship any other. Him we adore as the Son of God but we show deserved respect to the martyrs, as his disciples and followers. The centurion, therefore, caused the body to be burnt. We then gathered his bones, more precious than pearls, and more tried than gold, and buried them. In this place, God willing, we will meet and celebrate, with joyous gladness, the birth-day of His martyr, as well in memory of those who have been crowned before, as, by his example, to prepare and strengthen others for the combat."*

In this passage there are important statements, upon which I may be permitted to enlarge. In many respects, indeed, it is a very striking narrative : it proves the eagerness of the Christians to have the body of the saint,—it shows that his bones were considered by them "more precious than pearls, and more tried than gold,"—and that they would honor them by meeting at his tomb to celebrate his birth-day. But its most striking record is this: that their enemies, the Jews, suggested that they would adore Polycarp. How comes it that their adversaries could, for a moment, have suspected, or pretended to suspect, that the Christians would worship Polycarp, and desert Christ? Certainly, if there had never been any marks shown of outward respect, or honor, to the relics of martyrs, it could not possibly have come into these men's heads that there was any danger of the Christians worshipping the body of Polycarp: the very charge supposes that such practices existed, and were well known to the adversaries of the Christians.

St. Ignatius, who suffered martyrdom at Rome, one hundred years after Christ, was Bishop of Antioch; and we read how his body was conveyed back to his see, and carried, as an inestimable treasure, from city to city.† But on this translation we have an eloquent passage of St. Chrysostom, which I must read:—
'When, therefore, he had there (at Rome) laid down his life, or rather when he had gone to heaven, he returned again crowned.

---

* Hist. Eccl. L. iv. c. xv. p. 170, 171.
† See his acts in Ruinart.

For the goodness of God was pleased that he should return to us, and to distribute the martyr between the cities. For that city received his dropping blood, but you have honored his relics. You rejoiced in his episcopacy; they beheld him struggling, and victorious, and crowned; you possess him perpetually. God removed him from you for a little while, and with much more glory has He restored him. And as they who borrow money return with interest what they received, so also God, having borrowed of you this precious treasure for a short time, and shown him to that city, sent him back to you with increased splendor. For you sent forth a bishop, and you have received a martyr: you sent forth with prayers, and you have received with crowns. And not you alone, but all the intermediate cities. For how think you were they affected, when they beheld the relics transported? What fruits of gladness did they gather? How much did they rejoice? With what acclamations did they salute the crowned conqueror? For as the spectators, starting up from the arena, and laying hold of the noble combatant who has overthrown all his antagonists, and is going forth with splendid glory, do not permit him to touch the ground, but carry him home with innumerable encomiums; so all the cities, in order receiving this holy man from Rome, carried him on their shoulders, and accompanied the crowned martyr with acclamations even to this city, celebrating the conqueror with hymns, and deriding the devil, because his artifice turned against himself, and what he had thought to do against the martyr had proved adverse to himself."* Thus do we find the relics of the saints treated with the greatest respect by the immediate disciples of the apostles, by those who knew them, and had learnt from them. Afterwards, the texts multiply without end.

St. Basil, bishop in Cappadocia, answers St. Ambrose, archbishop of Milan, who had written all that way to request a portion of the relics of St. Dionysius: and this shows the communion between the Churches in all parts of the world, and the object to which it was applied. These are his words:—"Affection to our departed brethren is referred to the Lord whom they served: and he who honors them that died for the faith, shows that he is inspired by the same ardor;• so that one and the same action is a proof of many virtues." He then relates how, much against the will of those who possessed them, the saint's relics had been

---

* Homil. in St. Ignat. Mart. xliii. is translated by the Rev. F. C. Husenbeth, in his triumphant exposure of Faber.—"Faberism Exposed," 1836, p. 623.

LECTURE XIII.

taken up, and sent; and that of their being genuine there was not the smallest doubt.*

The following is a strong passage from the saint whom I have before quoted, with particular praise, St. Ephrem:—"See, how the relics of the martyrs still breathe! Who can doubt of these martyrs being still alive? Who can believe that they have perished?" He then extols the virtues of relics, and exhorts the faithful, in every distress, to have recourse, with confidence, to them: "For the deity dwells in the bones of the martyrs, and, by his power and presence, miracles are wrought."† St. Asterius writes: "Wherefore, decently disposing of the bodies of the martyrs, let us preserve them for ages as gifts of high value. By them we are fortified; and the Church is protected, as a city is guarded by an armed force." St. John Chrysostom:—"That which neither riches nor gold can effect, the relics of martyrs can. Gold never dispelled diseases, nor warded off death; but the bones of martyrs have done both. In the days of our forefathers, the former happened; the latter, in our own."‡

There is literally no end to such testimonies. But we have, about this time, appearing in Church history, two evidences, which fully evince what the belief of the Christians was. The first is the writings of Eunapius the Sophist, about the year 380, which were directed to show that the Christians worshipped the martyrs. He charges them, in the first place, with taking great care of their bodies, and placing them under their altars; in the second place, with paying them divine adoration, and treating them as gods: whereon he accuses them of downright idolatry. So that this is not a modern accusation: it is a very old tale, a very antiquated charge, made three hundred and eighty years after Christ; when, for precisely the same belief and practice as we now follow, the entire Church was taxed by a heathen with being idolatrous. This proves, at least, what great honor and veneration was paid to the saints and to their remains.

The second evidence is,—that a few years after, we have Vigilantius condemned as a heretic, for saying that the relics of saints ought not to be honored. An express treatise yet remains, written by St. Jerome against him; but the very fact of the practice being impugned by Vigilantius shows that it existed before. St. Jerome makes a very accurate distinction: "We worship not, we adore not the relics of the martyrs;—but we

---

* Ad Ambros. Mediol. Ep. cxcvii. T. iii. p. 287.
† T. v. p. 340, Ed. Rom.   ‡ Homil. lxxi. S. Drosidis Mart. T. v. p 882.
VOL. II.—O

honor them, that our minds may be raised to Him, whose martyrs they are. We honor them, that this honor may be referred to Him, who says: *He that receiveth you, receiveth me.**

This is just what Catholics have always said in modern times: that the respect paid by them to relics is referred ultimately to God; and that in honoring His servants, we honor God, who chose them as His champions and faithful servants. About this time, therefore, we have a multiplicity, an endless variety of writers, teaching the same doctrine; and I remember particularly being struck with one of the letters of St. Augustine, meant as a letter of recommendation to some friends who were travelling in Italy. During his time, the relics of St. Stephen, the first martyr, were discovered in the East, and a portion of them brought into Africa. St. Augustine—and no one, it will be admitted, was more remote from credulity or superstition—gives an account of what happened on the introduction of his bones. The bishop of a neighboring diocese was cured of a long and harassing disease, for which he was to undergo a painful operation in a few days, by carrying the relics into the church. But the circumstance which I wished to mention relative to the recommendatory letter is, that after he has made a long encomium of the character of the travellers, he says: "What is still more precious, they carry with them a portion of the relics of St. Stephen." Were any one now-a-days to write a letter of this sort, he would be considered superstitious. And yet, who is it that writes it?—what an age did he live in, and what a man! Surely such passages as these ought, at any rate, to make our traducers modify their language, when they speak of our doctrines, if it were only out of respect to the individuals whom they involve in the same condemnation. Thus much shall suffice on the subject of our veneration for relics. We see a strong groundwork of our belief in the word of God, and we are completely borne out by the practice of the Church.

There is still another subject in connection: that of images or pictures in our churches. The Council of Trent defines two things, as the belief of the Catholic Church on this head. First, that it is wholesome and expedient to have pictures, or images and representations of the Saints; in the second place, that honor and respect are to be paid to them.† This is, therefore, the whole of the Catholic doctrine. I suppose no one will go

---

* Ep. llll. ad Riparium, T. i. 583, 584.
† Sess. xxv. "De venerat. SSorum."

the length of saying, that it is unlawful to have pictures in churches, on the ground of its being opposed to a Jewish commandment; although we have been ignorantly charged with having corrupted the decalogue, by putting one commandment into two, to get rid of the prohibition, which applied to the making of images, as distinct from that of adoring them. The first question, therefore, appears to be, is the making of all images forbidden, or are we only forbidden to worship them? If the former be the case, then no monument can be allowed in a church, and no altar-piece, and yet it is well known that there are many such in the Established Church. In the church of St. Stephen, Walbrook, I believe there is one; in that of Greenwich, there is a painting of St. Paul; and such there are in many other places of Protestant worship. We cannot suppose, therefore, that the representation of human beings is prohibited under any circumstances; and, consequently, the first part of the first commandment is modified essentially by the second, and from it only receives its force. We agree that no image should be made for adoration or worship, because the first commandment is against idolatry, or the making of images for such purpose. But the making of images was prescribed by God: for in the Tabernacle there were two cherubim in the Holy of Holies, and the walls of the Temple were sculptured with graven images; and a brazen fountain, supported by twelve oxen, stood in its court. Indeed, there is no doubt that the temple was adorned with carved images and representations of the human countenance, as much as it was possible for any building to be. The whole question, then, turns upon this: whether the Catholics are justified in making use of them as sacred memorials, in praying before them, as inspiring faith and devotion. I may be asked, what warrant there is in Scripture for all this? I might answer, that I seek none: for rather, I might ask, what authority there is, to deprive me of such objects: because it is a natural right to use any thing towards promoting the worship of God, which is not in any way forbidden. I might as well be asked, what warrant there is in Scripture for the building of churches, for the use of the organ, for the ringing of bells, for music, or for a thousand other things that appertain to the worship of the Church. Do I want a warrant, do I require Scripture, for the use of the organ?—Certainly not: because, if the thing be innocent, and serve to raise our hearts towards God, we consider that we have a right to use it, and nothing but a positive enactment can deprive us of it. And I wish to know, would any one charge me with bad feeling, if, on coming before the representation or image of any one whom I had loved and had lost, I stood before it, fixed in veneration and affection, as though the object itself were really before me? And even if my eyes were filled with tears, and I appeared to address it with feelings of affectionate enthusiasm, I might be guilty, perhaps, of some extravagance in sentiment, of too vivid a feeling; but no one, surely, would say that I was superstitious or idolatrous in its regard.

Such is precisely all that the Catholic is taught to believe regarding the images or pictures set up in churches. They are memorials in the same way as other representations are, and we consider them calculated to excite similar feelings, only of a religious class. And if I find that the gazing on that picture or representation will bring my cold and stagnant feelings into closer communion with the person whom I have loved and cherished, undoubtedly I may lawfully indulge myself, without any one presuming to blame me. In like manner, then, if I find that any picture or representation of our Saviour, or of His Blessed Mother, or of His Saints, acts more intimately on my affections, and excites warmer feelings of devotion, I am justified, and act well, in endeavoring so to excite them. It is precisely the same motive as that for going to one place of worship rather than another, because in it I find my feelings more easily drawn to God. This is an obvious and simple ground, on which to uphold the Catholic practice: that it is nowhere forbidden; and as the prohibition formerly made was only against making images to worship them as gods, that prohibition does not apply here, because ours are only made as those were which God ordered to be erected in his very temple.

Whether pictures and images were used in the Church of old, is not a point of much importance; for their use has always been a matter of discipline. The Council of Trent does not decree that we are obliged to use them; it only says that it is wholesome to have them, and that they are to be treated with respect: with a relative respect, that is, such as is shown to the portrait of a father, or of any one whom we esteem and reverence. But the Council of Trent, in its directions to the parochial clergy, expressly enjoins them to explain this doctrine to the faithful; it commands them to warn the people, and make them understand, that these images are nothing but mere representations; that any honor paid them is to be referred to the prototype

LECTURE XIII.

or being represented; but that the image itself cannot have any virtue, nor give them the slightest help.

However, although the Christians were careful, and most anxious, while idolatry was around them, to distinguish their religion from it, we find that they used these representations in the oldest times. In the catacombs, we have exceedingly ancient ones; some of them are cut in two by the tombs of the martyrs, and consequently must have been made before these were opened. D'Agincourt has compared the paintings of the sepulchre of the Nasoni family with those found in the catacombs, and has decided that they are contemporary productions, or paintings of the second century. In the same manner, Flaxman, in his Lectures on Art, acknowledges them to be of great antiquity. So that this practice of decoration was very ancient; and this is singularly confirmed by the fact that, throughout the catacombs, the representations are uniformly the same, and precisely those described by the oldest father, Tertullian, as used in Africa, on the cups of the Christians; such as the good shepherd carrying a sheep on his shoulders;—an emblem of our Saviour's charity, used, thus early, to excite feelings of affection towards him. This uniformity, especially in such distant countries, proves that the common type was much more ancient,—for all could not accidentally have agreed on the same subjects and same methods of representation; but not an inconsiderable time must have elapsed, between some one's inventing the type, and all artists in different parts adopting it.

This very brief sketch must suffice for the present. Perhaps I might be expected to say something of abuses, had I not interspersed several observations throughout my discourse, which must be, I flatter myself, sufficient. In one word, I will only remark that the charge of abuse arises, in a great measure, from persons not taking the pains to understand or know the feeling of Catholics. If we go into other countries, we find demonstrations of outward feeling, ever of a much warmer and more enthusiastic character than here; and, consequently, nothing is more common than to condemn these exhibitions, by comparison with what occurs in colder countries, and among more phlegmatic characters, as superstitious and idolatrous. But they who are acquainted with the people, and who have been instructed concerning their belief, know that, however extravagant they may outwardly appear, inwardly their faith and conviction are perfectly safe, and in accordance with that laid down as the belief of the Church.

LECTURE XIII.

This subject closes the lectures, with the exception of those on the Eucharist, which I will enter upon at our next meeting. Before concluding, this evening, I wish to make one or two remarks, which seem connected with our subject. They regard those vague declamations which are daily heard respecting the Catholic doctrines. I have not the least doubt, that this course of lectures will give rise to others of a contrary tendency;* in which attempts will be made to show that the doctrines and practices of Catholics are superstitious, idolatrous, and deserving of every opprobrious epithet. I entreat all who may be induced to listen to such replies, to keep their minds and imaginations exceedingly cool, not to allow themselves to be carried away by eloquence, however fervent, nor by assertions, however positive, but to demand proof for every proposition which affects Catholics; and if opportunity to do so is not afforded them, to search for proofs, and try to verify the grounds on which our doctrine is impugned, before yielding up their minds to the arguments by which we are attacked. I am confident that that method will save a great deal of trouble; because I am sure, that it will be found, in almost every instance, that the doctrine assailed is not that of Catholics, and that, consequently, the argument against it is thrown away; the reasons may be very good against the imaginary doctrine attacked, but worth nothing as confuting ours.

I am satisfied that we have nothing to fear from persons carrying on the discussion in the way I have represented. I am confident that the time is gone by, when they could raise against us the war-cry of our practising superstitions injurious to God, as much as it is for raising the cry of disloyalty and disaffection to the state. Both have had their day, and the day of both is passed; and no one can serve our cause better, or more thoroughly disgust his hearers, than he who shall endeavor to found his attack upon Catholics on such declamatory and groundless imputations as these. Thank God, and thank also the generosity and uprightness of our fellow-countrymen, we can now stand fairly and openly before the public. We are anxious, not to shrink from inquiry, but to court it; we throw open our places of worship to all men, we publish our books of prayer and instruction before the world; we submit the least of our children and their catechism to examination; we invite all to inspect our schools, and present the masters and their scholars to their in-

---

* This was actually the case.

LECTURE XIII.

terrogation; all that we write and read is at the command of the learned; and, if in our power, we would open our breasts, and ask them to look even into our hearts,—for God knows that we have nothing to shade, nothing to conceal;—and there let them read our belief, as written on its tablets in the simplest and plainest terms. No attack can any longer be allowed by any sensible, reasonable, generous, or liberal-minded man, except through calm and cool investigation, based entirely on the correct statement of our doctrines, and conducted exclusively, not by vague quotations from the word of God, but by arguments clearly and strongly addressed to his understanding.

These are the concluding admonitions which I wish to impress upon you. At our next meeting, I shall commence, as I have promised, the most important of all subjects, the Eucharist. Perhaps the length to which it will lead me may not allow me time to make many concluding reflections; and I did not wish you to separate, without a few such as I have just indulged in. There are a great many other observations that offer themselves, but the time has flown too rapidly, and I have only space again to assure you, as I have done before, that if I have touched lightly upon some points, and seemed to omit others, it has been solely and exclusively through feeling sensible, that almost every evening I have detained you here longer than it became me, and that I have trespassed by a desire of communicating too much, rather than by withholding any thing that appeared useful.[*]

---

[*] Acts xx. 20.

LECTURE THE FOURTEENTH.

TRANSUBSTANTIATION.

PART I.

JOHN vi. 11.

"And Jesus took the loaves; and when he had given thanks, he distributed to them that were sat down; in like manner also the fishes, as much as they would."

ALTHOUGH, my brethren, not accustomed to attach any great importance to such accidental coincidences, I will acknowledge that I felt some pleasure on discovering, when brought, this evening, by my arrangement of the topics to be discussed in your presence, to the Catholic doctrine of the Eucharist, that it was precisely the very lesson proposed to us by the Church, in the Gospel of the day. For I cannot but hope that the blessing of God will be more abundant on our labors, when our teaching is not merely in accordance with, but even in its outward forms all regulated by that authority which He has appointed to govern and instruct us. Thus, I shall enter with confidence at once upon the task which I have assigned myself; and, as the course which we shall have to pass over this evening will be rather protracted, and as, even to do it but partial and tolerable justice, it will be necessary for me to omit many merely special and digressive questions which will present themselves in our way, I will, without further preface, enter at once on the great object now before us. It is no other than to examine the grounds on which the Catholic Church proposes to us her belief on this subject,—the most important, the most solemn, the most beautiful, the most perfect of all I have proposed to treat of,—the True and Real Presence of our Lord and Saviour Jesus Christ in the Sacrament of the Altar.

This doctrine of the Catholic Church, which, perhaps, of all other dogmas, has been most exposed to misrepresentation, or, at least, certainly to scorn and obloquy, is clearly defined in the words of the Council of Trent, where we are told, that the Catholic Church teaches, and always has taught, that in the Blessed

LECTURE XIV.

Eucharist, that which was originally bread and wine, is, by the consecration, changed into the substance of the Body and Blood of our Lord, together with His soul and divinity, in other words, his complete and entire person; which change the Catholic Church has properly called Transubstantiation.* Such, my brethren, is our belief; and I will proceed to lay before you, in this and subsequent discourses, the grounds whereupon we hold this doctrine; which, to those who have not embraced it, appears most incomprehensible and repugnant, and which forms with too many the greatest bar to their uniting themselves with our communion; but which to every Catholic is the most consoling, the most cheering, and in every way the most blessed portion of his creed.

Now, before entering on the arguments from Holy Writ, regarding this point, it is important that I should lay down clearly before you the principles which will guide me in the examination of Scriptural texts. I have had, on another occasion, opportunity to remark, how there is a vague and insufficient way of satisfying ourselves regarding the meaning of Scriptural texts;—that is to say, when, reading them over, and having in our minds a certain belief, we are sure to attach to them that meaning which seems either absolutely to support it, or is, at least, reconcilable with it. It is in this way that many most opposite opinions are, by various sects, equally held to be demonstrated in Scripture. Certainly there must be some key, or means of interpreting it more securely; and on the occasion alluded to, when I had to examine several passages of Scripture, I contented myself with laying down, as a general rule, that we should examine it by means of itself, and find the key in other and clearer passages, for the one under examination. But, on the present occasion, it is necessary to enter more fully into an exposition of a few general and simple principles, which have their foundation in the philosophy of ordinary language, and in common sense, and which will be the principles that I shall seek to follow.

The groundwork of all the science of interpretation is exceedingly simple, if we consider the object to be attained. Every one will agree, that when we read any book, or hear any discourse, our object is to understand what was passing in the author's mind when he wrote or spoke those passages—that is to say, what was the meaning he himself wished to give to the

---

* Sess. xiii. c. iv.

expressions which he then wrote or uttered. At this moment, for instance, that I am addressing you, it is obvious, from every conventional law of society, that I wish and mean you to understand me. I should be trifling with your good sense, your feelings, and your rights, if I intended otherwise; and thence it follows, that I express myself to the best of my power, in the way that I believe most conducive to convey exactly to your minds the ideas passing in mine at the moment I am relating them. In fact, the object of all human intercourse, pursuant to the established laws of social communication, is to transfuse into other minds the same feelings and ideas that exist in one; and language is nothing more than the process whereby we endeavor to establish this communication.

It is evident that we have here two terms, which are to be equalized,—the mind of the speaker and that of the hearer; and if the process of communication be properly performed, the one must thoroughly represent the other. To illustrate this by comparison,—if, from the lines which you see impressed on paper from a copper-plate, you can reason, and that infallibly, to those inscribed on the plate, so can you, in like manner, if you see only the plate, just as correctly reason to the impression which must be thereby produced, provided the process followed be correct, and calculated by its nature to communicate that impression. Just so, therefore, the object of any person who addresses others, either in writing or in speech, is to convey, as clearly as possible, his meaning to their minds. If the processes of language be correct, except in extraordinary cases of error—for it is an exception, if we misunderstand one another—if the act of imprinting be correctly performed, we receive the impressions and ideas which the writer or speaker wished to convey. And hence we can accurately reason from the meaning attached to a speech by those who heard it, to the ideas passing in the speaker's mind.

If, then, we wished to ascertain the meaning of any passage in a book written a hundred or a thousand years ago, we must not judge of it by what we might understand by such words at present: we must know what their meaning was at the time they were spoken. If we open an English author one hundred years old, we shall find some words used to convey a different signification from what they do now. We find, for instance, the word *wit* to mean great and brilliant parts, including information and learning. A few centuries before, words, which are now trivial and in common use, were then dignified. Thus, in old

LECTURE XIV.

versions of Scripture, for *canticle*, the word *ballad* is constantly used; now, were any one to argue on a passage written at those times, from the meaning which such words at present bear, it is evident that he would err. The true rule of interpretation, therefore, is to know what must have been the only meaning which the actual hearers, who were alive and present at the time the words were addressed to them, could have put on any expression; and if we find that to be a certain definite signification, and the only one which *could* have been given, it is clear that it must be the true one. If we ascertain that the Jews must have attached a certain meaning to our Saviour's words, and could have conceived no other, He must have used them in that sense, if he wished to be understood. This is called, by critics, *the usage of speech*, and is considered by the writers on the interpretation of Scripture, as the true key to understanding its language.

Such is the simple process which I intend to follow. I shall investigate the expressions used by our Saviour, on different occasions—I shall endeavor to put you in possession of the opinions of those who heard them, and to make you understand, from the language in which they were spoken, what was the only signification which they could possibly have attached to them. You will thus see how their feelings must have wrought at the time they were uttered, leading them to a proper explanation; and whatever we shall find must have been the exclusive interpretation given to phrases by these persons, we shall have a right to consider their true meaning. By the same test I will try every objection,—I will inquire how far they seize the true meaning which the expressions bore at the time they were spoken; and by that ordeal only must they be justified.

If we look into ancient phrases and words, we must bear other considerations in mind; we must weigh the peculiar character of the teacher, for every person has a method of addressing his hearers—every man has his peculiar forms of speech; and it becomes necessary to make a sort of individual investigation, to see whether the explanation given can be reconciled with the ordinary method of him who spoke. Moreover, it has been justly observed by an acute writer, that he who would lead others, must in some respects, follow; that is to say, no wise and good teacher will run counter to the habits and ordinary feelings of those whom he addresses. If he have to recommend amiable and inviting doctrines, he will not clothe them in imagery which must disgust them by their very proposition. Without sacrificing one principle or particle of his opinions, he certainly will not go out of his way to render them odious. These are the principal considerations which I have deemed it necessary to present to you, before entering on the examination of what we consider the first proof of the Catholic doctrines of the Eucharist, as contained in the sixth chapter of the gospel of St. John

The question regarding the interpretation of this chapter of the gospel, like all others of the same nature, reduces itself to a simple inquiry into a matter of fact. All are agreed, for instance, both Catholics and Protestants, that the first part of the chapter, from the beginning to the 26th verse, is simply historical, and gives us an account of the miracle wrought by our Saviour, in feeding a multitude of persons with a small quantity of bread. All are also agreed as to the next portion of the chapter; that is, from the 26th, so far as about the 50th verse, that in it our Saviour's discourse is about faith. But at this point enters the material difference of opinion among us. We say, that at that verse, or somewhere about it, a change takes place in our Saviour's discourse, and that from that moment we are not to understand Him as speaking of faith, but solely of the real eating of His Body, and drinking of His Blood sacramentally in the Eucharist. Protestants, on the other hand, maintain that the same discourse is continued, and the same topic kept up to the conclusion of the chapter. It is manifest that this is a question of simple fact. It is like any legal question regarding the meaning of a document; and we must establish by evidence, whether the latter part can continue the same subject as the preceding.

I need hardly premise that nothing was more familiar with our Saviour than to take the opportunity of any miracle which He performed, to inculcate some doctrine which seemed to have a special connection with it. For instance, in the ninth chapter of St. John, having cured a blind man, he proceeds to reprove the Pharisees for their spiritual blindness. In the fifth, after restoring a man who had been deprived of the use of his limbs, or who had been at least in a very languishing state of illness, he takes occasion, most naturally, to explain the doctrine of the Resurrection. Again, in the twelfth chapter of St. Matthew, after having cast out a devil, he proceeds to discourse upon the subject of evil spirits. These examples I bring merely to infer that, such being His custom, it will not be denied, that if ever He did wish for an opportunity to propose to His hearers the doctrine of the Real Presence in the Eucharist, He could not, in the whole course of his ministry, have found one more suited to his purpose. For, as here, by blessing the bread, He gave it a new efficacy, and made it sufficient to feed several thousands. we could not suppose any thing more parallel to that sacrament, wherein His body is in a manner multiplied, so as to form the food of all mankind in whatever part of the world. This, therefore, makes it, in the first place, not at all improbable that if such a doctrine was to be ever taught,—if such an institution was to be ever made, this was the favorable moment for preparing his hearers for it.

But we can still better illustrate the natural manner in which this discourse is introduced. The Jews asked our Saviour for a sign from heaven, and the sign they insisted on was: "What sign, therefore, dost thou show us, that we may see and believe thee,—what dost thou work? Our fathers did eat manna in the desert, as it is written,—he gave them bread from heaven to eat." To which, in the following verse, he answers: "Amen, amen, I say unto you, Moses gave you not bread from Heaven, but my Father giveth you the true bread from Heaven." Now, it is remarkable that the Jews, in one of their earliest works after the time of Christ, that is, the "Midrash Coheleth," or commentary on the Book of Ecclesiastes, assert that one of the signs which the Messiah would give, was precisely this; that in the same manner as Moses had brought down the manna from heaven, so should he bring down bread from heaven. This being the persuasion of the Jews, it was natural that they should choose this criterion of Christ's being sent from God, in the same way as Moses; and that our Saviour should give a parallel on his part to the former food from heaven, in a divine institution, whereby men should be nourished by something more excellent than manna, by the true living bread coming down from heaven.

So far is but preliminary matter; now let us enter on the question itself. I feel myself strongly led to suppose that the transition takes place in the 48th instead of the 51st verse, where it is commonly put. I need not enter upon my reasons for it, because it is immaterial; it makes no difference whether we place the transition a verse or two earlier or later. These reasons are founded on a close and minute analysis of the portion of our Saviour's discourse, between the 48th and 53d verses, as compared with other discourses of His, which shows a construction indicative of a transition. I pass them over, however, as they would be likely to detain us too long, and come at once to the point.*

---

* They are given at full in my "Lectures on the Real Presence." p. 40, *&c.*

LECTURE XIV.

In the first place, it may be said, is it probable that our Saviour, who had just been speaking of Himself as the bread of life, should in the 51st verse, going on with precisely the same expressions, make such a complete transition in the subject of His discourse?—Should we not have something to indicate this change to another subject? To show that there is no weight in this objection, I will refer you to another passage in which precisely a similar transition takes place; namely, the 24th chapter of St. Matthew. It is agreed among learned modern Protestant commentators, English and foreign,—and allow me to repeat a remark which I made on a former occasion, that when I vaguely say commentators, I mean exclusively Protestant commentators; because I think it better to quote such authorities as will not be so easily rejected by those with whom we are engaged in discussion, —it is the opinion, therefore, of several such commentators, that in the 24th and 25th chapters of St. Matthew, there is a discourse of our Saviour's on two distinct topics, the first regarding the destruction of the Temple of Jerusalem; and the second, the end of the world. Any one may naturally ask, where does the transition take place? It is manifest, when looking at the extremes, that is, on comparing the phrases used in the first part of the discourse, and those in the second, that the same subject is not continued,—where then are we to find the point of separation? Now, most accurate commentators place it at the 43d verse of the 24th chapter, and I will just read to you the preceding verse, and one or two of those that follow. "Watch ye therefore, because ye know not at what hour your Lord will come. But this know ye, that if the good man of the house knew at what hour of the night the thief would come, he would certainly watch, and would not suffer his house to be broken open." You perceive no transition between these verses, and yet these commentators place the transition exactly in the middle of them. The same imagery is still continued from verse to verse, and yet it is agreed that a transition takes place from one subject to another, as distinct as the destruction of the temple of Jerusalem, which took place 1800 years ago, is from the end of the world, which may not happen for many centuries. Thus may the preliminary objection be removed, that there must be a strong and marked transition, something like a prefatory phrase, to mark the passage from one subject to another.

Now, therefore, on what ground do we say that in the preceding part of the chapter vi. and in the latter, a different topic is treated of? As I have before observed, the question is

LECTURE XIV.

point of fact, and resolves itself into two inquiries: first, is there a transition here?—and, secondly, is it to the true eating and drinking of the body and blood of Christ? In answer to the first, I say, that I believe the first portion of our Saviour's discourse to apply to faith, for this simple reason: that every expression He uses throughout it, is such as was familiar to the Jews, as referring to the subject. For, the ideas of giving bread and of partaking of food were commonly applied to teaching and receiving instruction; consequently, there was no misunderstanding them. Thus, we have it said in the book of Isaiah: "All you that thirst, come unto the waters, and you that have no money, make haste, buy and eat. Hearken diligently to me, and eat that which is good."* "To eat" is here applied to listening unto instruction. Our Saviour quotes Deuteronomy: "Not on bread alone does man live, but on every word that cometh out of the mouth of God."† Again, God used this remarkable figure, when He said, that He should "send forth a famine into the land,—not a famine of bread nor a thirst of water, but of the hearing of the word of God."‡ In like manner, Wisdom is represented as saying: "Come, eat my bread, and drink the wine which I have mingled for you."§ Among the later Jews, Maimonides and other commentators observe, that whenever the expression is used among the Prophets or in Ecclesiastes, it is always to be understood of doctrine. Therefore, when our Saviour simply addresses the Jews, speaking to them of the food whereof they are to partake, I have no difficulty in supposing that He could be understood by all, as referring to faith in Him and His teaching. But in order to contrast these expressions more strongly with those that follow, allow me to notice a peculiarity observable at the 35th verse. Throughout the first part of this chapter, if you read it carefully over, you will not once find our Saviour allude to the idea of eating; he does not once speak of eating "the bread which came down from heaven." On the contrary, in the 35th verse, he actually violates the ordinary rhetorical proprieties of language, to avoid this harsh and unnatural figure. In the instances where the figure of food is applied to hearing or believing doctrine, the inspired writers never say, "Come and eat or receive me." But our Saviour does not even speak of eating this figurative bread of His doctrine; and at the same time cautiously escapes from applying the phrase directly to His own person. For, in the

---

* Is. lv. 1, 2.   † Mat. iv. 4.   ‡ Amos viii. 11.   § Prov. ix. 5.

35th verse, Jesus said to them: "I am the bread of life: he that *cometh to me* shall not hunger, and he that *believeth in me* shall not thirst." So that when it would appear requisite to fill up the metaphor by the ideas of eating and drinking, as opposed to hunger and thirst, He carefully avoids them, and substitutes others. And the phrases selected were such as to indicate to the Jews doctrine and belief.

But, supposing that they had not understood them to be so applied, our Saviour is most careful to explain them in that sense. For the Jews made an objection, and murmured at Him because He had said that He was the bread which came down from heaven. Their objection referred not so much to His calling Himself bread, as to His saying, that He had come from heaven. For their objection is: "Is not this Jesus the son of Joseph, whose father and mother we know? how then sayeth he, I came down from heaven?"* Now, then, see how our Saviour answers this objection. He employs no less than seven or eight verses in removing it. Observing some little difficulty about the expressions which he has been using till now, and having, in verse 35, employed the words, "coming to Him," as equivalent to "believing in Him," He from that moment, until the 47th verse, never once returns to the figure of bread or food, or any thing of that sort, to inculcate the necessity or obligation of believing in Him, but speaks simply of faith in Him, or of its equivalent, coming to Him. "Murmur not among yourselves. No man *can come to me* except the Father who hath sent me draw him, and I will raise him up at the last day. Every one that hath heard of the Father, and hath learned, *cometh to me*, not that any man hath seen the Father, but he who is of God he hath seen the Father. Amen, amen, I say to you, *he that believeth in me* hath everlasting life."† He is, you see, most careful not to return again to the ideas of "eating and drinking." This explains clearly that his conversation, up to this moment, is of faith; and seeing that the expressions were of themselves calculated to convey that meaning to those who heard them, and, finding that Jesus himself so explained them, we conclude that He must have been speaking of faith.

Now, then, let us come to the second part of the discourse. The first portion He closes thus:—"Amen, Amen, I say unto you, he that believeth in me hath everlasting life." We may consider this as a proper epilogue or conclusion. But, from this

---

* Verse 42.   † Verses 45, 47.

LECTURE XIV.

moment, He begins to use another form of phraseology, which He had carefully avoided in the first part of His discourse, and it only remains to examine, whether it could convey the idea that He was still going on with the same topic, or must have led His hearers necessarily to believe that He was speaking of the real eating of His flesh, and drinking of His blood. This inquiry must be conducted on precisely the same principles. Now, I unhesitatingly assert, that there are differences of language in the words that follow, such as must necessarily have made the impression on His hearers, that is, those who were the true interpreters of His words, that he no longer meant to teach the same, but quite another doctrine.

In the first place, you will observe that our Saviour had previously avoided with care, and even at some sacrifice of the proprieties of speech, any expression, such as "eating the bread of life," much more "eating His own person." He had even abandoned the metaphor entirely, on seeing that some misunderstanding had resulted from using these expressions; and yet now, all on a sudden, He returns to them in a much stronger manner; and he does it in such a way that His hearers could not possibly have conceived from them the same meaning as before. He says,—"I am the living bread which came down from heaven. If any man eat of this, he shall live for ever; and the bread which I will give is my flesh, for the life of the world." He goes on afterwards to say:—"Amen, Amen, I say to you, except you eat the flesh of the Son of man, and drink his blood, ye shall not have life in you. He that eateth my flesh, and drinketh my blood, hath everlasting life; and I will raise him up at the last day. For my flesh is meat indeed, and my blood is drink indeed. He that eateth my flesh and drinketh my blood, abideth in me, and I in him. As the living Father hath sent me, and I live by the Father, so he that eateth me, the same also shall live by me."* Now, here are a series of expressions, which, on a simple perusal, appear a much stronger and grosser violation of propriety of speech, if our Saviour meant to be understood figuratively. But, as I before intimated, if, up to this point, He had evidently given up the figure of eating and drinking, would he have returned to it again, without any necessity? And if, from seeing that misunderstanding had before risen from it, He had discontinued it, can we believe that He would resume it, in a still more marked, and strongly characterized

* Verses 51–58.

form without some absolute necessity? This necessity could only result from the introduction of a new topic; as, otherwise, He might have persevered in the literal exposition. Here, then, we have one evidence of a transition in the discourse to a new topic; but there are other marked differences.

2dly. In the former part of His discourse, our Saviour always speaks of this bread as given by His Father. He says: "This is the bread which His Father had sent from Heaven and given to the Jews."* In the second portion, which I have just read, He no longer speaks of His Father as giving this bread, but says that He Himself gives it. The Giver is different in the two cases, and we are consequently authorized to suppose that the gift likewise is different.

3dly. Our Saviour, in the first part of the discourse, speaks of the consequence of this partaking of the bread of life, as consisting in our being brought or drawn unto Him, or coming to Him.† These expressions, throughout the New Testament, are applied to faith.‡ In a number of passages, where persons are said to be brought to Christ, it is always meant that they are to be brought to faith in Him. This is the term always used in the first part of the discourse, and exactly corresponds to our interpretation of it concerning faith. But, in the second part, our Saviour never speaks of our being brought to Him: but always of our abiding in Him, or being incorporated with Him, which expressions are always used to denote love and charity.§ This phrase occurs in this sense, John xv. 4–9, 1 Jo. ii. 24; iv. 16, 17. If, then, we find, in the first part of the discourse, the efficacy attributed to that which Christ inculcated, to be precisely what is ever attributed to faith, we see a strong confirmation that the discourse related to that virtue. But, similarly, when we find the expression changed, and one used which no longer applies to it, but to a totally different virtue, that is, to a union by love with Christ, we are equally authorized in considering a different subject introduced, and some institution alluded to, which is to unite us to Christ, not merely through faith, but still more through love.

These are striking distinctions between the first part of our Lord's discourse and the second; but the most important yet remains to be explained, and will require one or two preliminary

---

* Verses 32, 33, 39, 40, 43, 44. † Verses 35, 36, 44, 45.
‡ This is fully proved in the "Lectures on the Real Presence," p. 59, which see. See Mat. xi. 28, Lu. vi. 47, Jo. v. 40, vii. 37.
§ Verses 57, 58.

LECTURE XIV.

remarks. One of the most delicate points in the interpretation of Scripture, is the explanation of figures, tropes, and similes. It is supposed by Protestants, that by eating the flesh of Christ and drinking His blood, nothing more was meant than a figure or image of believing in Him. If this be the case, I might observe, for instance, that if to eat the bread of life simply meant to believe in Christ, it follows that the verb to *eat* is equivalent to the verb to *believe*. When, therefore, our Saviour speaks of eating His flesh, if eating be equivalent to believing, we must suppose that he meant believing in His flesh—a doctrine quite different, and totally distinct, from the other, and which no one has imagined our Saviour to have here taught. For, if the Jews offended, it was rather by too closely attending to the exterior and material appearances of things, and neglecting their spiritual value; nor can we suppose that our blessed Saviour, standing visibly before them in the flesh, would take great pains to inculcate a belief in the truth of His corporal existence,—supposing it even to have been then possibly an object of faith.

But to return: I have just remarked, that tropes, and figures, and types, form the most delicate elements of Scriptural phraseology, as, in fact, they do of every language. Although it may appear, at first sight, that nothing is so vague and indefinite in a language as figurative speech, which may be varied without limits, yet is it, in truth, quite the reverse. For there is nothing in which we are less at liberty to vary from ordinary acceptation than in conventional tropical phraseology. So long as we are using terms in their literal sense, there may be some vagueness; but the moment society has fixed on any certain figurative adaptation of words, we are no longer free to depart from it, without risking the most complete misunderstanding of our words. Nothing is easier than to try this assertion by any proverbial expression of ordinary use; but I will content myself with one simple and obvious illustration. We know that mankind, in general, have attached the idea of certain characteristic qualities to the names of some animals. Thus, when we say that a man is like a lamb, or like a wolf, we understand precisely what is meant by the expression used, we know what characteristic it indicates. If we say that a person who is ill, or in pain, suffers like a lamb, we understand the force of the expression—that he is meek and patient under his affliction. If we used it in any different sense, we should necessarily deceive our hearers. Again, we understand by the figure of a lion, a character composed of a certain proportion of strength and prowess, mixed with a degree of generous and noble feeling. By the figure of a tiger, on the other hand, we understand great animal strength, but united with fierceness, cruelty, and brutality. These two animals have many qualities in common; but still, if we say that a man is like, or is a lion, our hearers understand from the ordinary received acceptation of the word, what is meant. But suppose you meant nothing more than that his limbs were beautifully formed, that he was exceedingly agile, and that his power of leaping, or running, was very great, though these all are properties of the lion, would any body understand you? Would you not deceive your hearers? Most undoubtedly; and more by such a wrong use of an ordinary admitted form of figurative speech, than by any other departure from usual language. And if, in like manner, you called a man of great strength of limb, or agility, a tiger, you would be doing him a positive injustice; you would be guilty of calumny, because his hearers would not depart from the ordinary acceptation of the trope, and would impute ferocity to him.

If, therefore, we can establish that any expression in any language, besides its own simple, obvious, natural, and literal acceptation, had an established and recognised metaphorical one, we have no choice—no right to establish any meaning between the literal and that figurative one; and we have even no right to create another figurative one, unless we prove that it was in equal use. Now, the term *eating a person's flesh*, besides its sensible, carnal meaning, had an established, fixed, invariable, tropical signification, among those whom our Saviour addressed; and therefore, we cannot depart from the literal meaning, or, if we do, it can only be to take, without choice, that figurative one.

On this ground do I maintain, that a change of phraseology took place at verse 48; because, after that verse, our Saviour uses expressions which allow no choice between the real partaking of His Body and Blood, and a settled figurative signification, which no one will for a moment think of adopting. For I say, that, whether we examine the phraseology of Scripture, or the language spoken at this day (which is but a dialect of that spoken at the time of our Saviour) in Palestine, where all the customs, manners, and feelings, are hardly one tittle changed since His time, or if we examine the language spoken by Himself, we find the expression, to eat the flesh of any person, with a fixed, invariable signification of doing, by thought or deed, but principally by false and calumnious accusation, a grievous injury to that individual. For instance, we have, in the 27th Psalm, this expression:—"While the wicked draw near against me, to eat my flesh;"—that is, as all commentators upon it have agreed, to oppress, to vex, to ruin me. Again, in the 19th chapter of Job,—"Why do you persecute me, and are not satisfied with my flesh;"—that is, with eating my flesh, calumniating and persecuting me by words, which, as I observed, is the most ordinary meaning of the metaphor. In the prophet Micah, again,—"Who also eat the flesh of my people;"—that is, who oppress them, and do them serious injury. In Ecclesiastes, (c. iv.)—"The fool foldeth his arms together, and eats his own flesh;"—that is, he destroys, ruins himself. These are the only passages where the phrase occurs in the Old Testament, although allusion is made to the same idea in the 14th chapter of Job:—"They have opened their jaws against me,—they have filled themselves with me." In the New Testament, it occurs once or twice. St. James, (v. 3,) speaking to the wicked, says,—"Your gold and silver is cankered, and the rust of them shall be for a testimony against you, and shall eat your flesh like fire." These are the only occasions on which the expression occurs in Scripture, except where it is spoken of the very act of really eating human flesh, and in every case it has the fixed and determinate tropical signification, of doing a serious injury or harm, particularly by calumny.

The next way to investigate the meaning of this phrase, is by seeing what force it has with those who have inherited, not only the country, but all the feelings, and most of the opinions, of those among whom our Saviour spoke; that is, the Arabs, who now occupy the Holy Land. It is acknowledged by all biblical scholars, that their writings, their manners and customs, and their feelings, form the richest mine for the illustration of Scripture, in consequence of their exact resemblance on so many points to what is there described. It is singular that among these men, the most common form of expression to designate calumny, is to say that a person *eats the flesh* of another. I have collected a number of examples from their native writers, and I will give you one or two. We have, for instance, in the code of Mohammedan law, the Koran, this expression:—"Do not speak ill one of another in his absence. Would any of you like to eat the flesh of his brother, when dead? Verily, you would abhor it."—That is, equally should you abhor calumny. One of their poets, Nawabig, writes,—"You say that you are fasting, but you are eating the flesh of your brother." In a poetical work, called the Hamasa, we read,—"I am not given to detraction, or to eating the flesh of my neighbor." We have also this idea in constant allusions in their proverbs and fables.* Thus, it is completely understood by persons conversant with the language, that among the Arabs, this phrase has no other meaning than wickedly to calumniate and detract an individual. And observe, that it is not in the words that this idea rests, but in the spirit of the language; for, in every instance which I have given, there is a variety of phrase, a different verb or substantive; so that it is not merely one term always used figuratively, but it is in every instance a varied phrase, so as to prove that the idea is in the mind of the hearer.

In the third place, we come to the language in which our Saviour Himself spoke. It is remarkable, that in Syro-Chaldaic there is no expression for to accuse or calumniate, except *to eat a morsel of the person* calumniated; so much so, that in the Syriac version of Scripture, which was made one or two centuries after the time of our Saviour, there is no name given throughout to the devil, which, in the Greek version, signifies *the accuser*, or calumniator, but the "eater of flesh." Whenever the Jews are said in the Gospel to have accused our Saviour, they are said, in this version, to have eaten a morsel or portion of Him. In the Chaldaic parts of Daniel, when he is accused, it is said that the accusers eat a portion of him before the king. It would be easy to quote the authority of the first modern writers on the Hebrew, and other oriental languages, in proof of these assertions: I need only mention the names of Michaelis, Winer, and Gesenius; all of whom expressly state, in different parts of their works, that the expression is always so used, and can mean nothing else.

Let us now come to the application of this discussion. The Jews, so far as we have any means of ascertaining the signification which they attached to the expression *eating a person's flesh*, are proved to have given it a definitive figurative meaning, in the sense of doing a grievous injury, especially by calumny. According to the natural, necessary rule of interpretation, we have no choice, if we put ourselves in the position of hearers,— if we enter into the minds of those to whom our Saviour spoke, —we have no choice, except between the literal signification and that only figurative one that prevailed among them. And if any attempt be made to adopt any other figurative meaning, the least for which we have a right to ask, is an equal demonstra-

---

* See texts and references in "Lectures," as above, p. 67, *seqq.*

tion that such figurative application was so generally used among the Jews, as that there was some chance, at least, of its being so understood.

Thus far, then, may suffice on the examination of the phraseology used in our Saviour's discourse. We have found one class of phrases in the first part of the discourse, which could be understood only of faith; we have found in the second, expressions of a totally different character, which no criterion that the Jews possessed could lead them to interpret otherwise than in the literal sense, or in that one figurative sense from which all must at once recoil.

But there is another ground of proof in our favor,—the expression now used by our Saviour, of drinking his Blood, as well as eating His Flesh. I have before observed, that no person interested in having his doctrine received by his auditors can well be supposed to use an illustration of all others most odious to them, one which appeared to command something against the most positive and sacred law of God. Now we may observe two things: first, that the simple drinking of blood, under any circumstances, or in any extremity, was considered a very great transgression of the law of God; and in the second place, that partaking of human blood was considered still worse,—the greatest curse which God could possibly inflict upon His enemies. Now, I would ask, is it credible that our Saviour, when proposing and recommending to His hearers one of the most consoling and amiable of all His doctrines, would have voluntarily chosen to conceal it under such a frightful and revolting image? For it is obvious, that, as He had before used the ordinary figure of food to signify belief in Him, and in His redemption, if they wished to be saved,—there was nothing to prevent His continuing the same phrase; or, if He chose to depart from the figurative word, can we imagine that He would have selected, of all others, one most likely to convey to His hearers' minds the most disagreeable and painful idea? Such a supposition is at once manifestly repulsive.

Now, with regard to the simple drinking of blood, under any circumstances, the prohibition belongs to the oldest law given to Noah, upon the regeneration of the human race, after the deluge.* But in the law of Moses, we read,—"If any man whosoever, of the house of Israel, or of the strangers who

---

* Gen. ix. 4.

sojourn among them, eat blood, I will set my face against his soul, and will cut him off from among his people."* We find, consequently, that partaking of blood is never mentioned except as a dreadful crime. When the army of Saul had slaughtered the cattle in the blood, it was told to him, that "the people had sinned against the Lord; and he said, ye have transgressed."† And in the book of Judith, which, whatever any one's opinion of its canonical authority may be, is at least sufficient to show what the feelings of the Jews were, it is said of the people of Bethula, that "for drought of water, they are to be counted among the dead: and they have a design even to kill the cattle and drink their blood......therefore, because they do these things, it is certain they will be given up to destruction."‡ Even in cases, then, of the last extremity, it was supposed, that, if men proceeded so far as to taste blood, they had no chance of escape, but were sure to be delivered to utter destruction.

But if we come to speak of eating human flesh, or drinking human blood, we find it is never mentioned, except as the final curse which God could inflict on His people, or on their foes. "Instead of a fountain and ever-running river, thou gavest human blood to the unjust."§ In the Apocalypse, it is written:— "Thou hast given them blood to drink, for they have deserved it."‖ And Jeremiah is commanded to prophesy, as a plague which would astonish all men, that the citizens should be obliged to "eat every man the flesh of his friend."¶ With these feelings on the part of the Jews, can you suppose that our Saviour, if He was desirous of proposing to them a doctrine, would have clothed it under such imagery as was never used by them except to describe a heinous transgression of the divine law, or the denunciation of a signal curse and judgment from God? I am, therefore, warranted in arguing from this, again, that such necessity obliged Him to use these expressions, as that he could not possibly depart from them, if He wished to propound His doctrine; and that He was driven to them, however revolting, because He could not adequately state it in other words. And this necessity could only be their forming the literal expression of the doctrine proposed.

But, my brethren, hitherto we have been in a manner feeling our way; making use of such criterions, and such means of il-

---

* Lev. vii. 10. † 1 Sam. xiv. 33. ‡ Judith xi. 10–11.
§ Wisd. xi. 7. ‖ Apoc. xvi. 6. ¶ Jer. xix. 8, 9.

LECTURE XIV.

lustration, as we could collect from other sources; but, I now come to the best and surest canon of interpretation. It is not often we have the advantage of having it recorded, in so many words, what was the meaning attached to the words spoken by those who heard them. We are generally obliged to investigate a text, as we have hitherto done, by bringing it into comparison with whatever passages resemble it in other places,—it is seldom we have the hearers' own explanation,—and still seldomer that we can arrive at the teacher's declaration of what he meant. These form the surest and most convincing sources of interpretation.

It is evident that the Jews, in the former part of the discourse, when our Saviour spoke of coming down from Heaven, had misunderstood Him, so far, at least, as to call in question His having come down from Heaven. Our Saviour removes that difficulty, and goes on, again and again, inculcating the necessity of belief in Him. The Jews make no further objection; consequently, they are satisfied; and so far as that doctrine went, there was nothing more to be said against it. If we are to understand our Saviour's discourse, in the latter part of the chapter, as only a continuation of the preceding, the Jews could have no new reason to object, because their only doubt about His coming down from Heaven had been removed. How comes it, therefore, that they did not feel satisfied with what came afterwards? It can only be, that they were convinced He had passed into a new subject. After our Saviour had removed their former objection, they had rejoined nothing; but no sooner did He come to the other section of His discourse, than they immediately complained: no sooner did he say, "and the bread which I will give is my flesh," than they instantly murmured and exclaimed, "How *can* this man give us his flesh to eat?" They did not understand it as a continuation of the topic on which He had been previously addressing them; they felt that the same discourse was not continued; for this was evidently a difficulty grounded on the supposition of a change of subject. Now, what was the difficulty? Manifestly, the difficulty or impossibility of receiving the doctrine. But, if they had thought he still spoke of faith in Him, nothing was easier than to understand it. For they had already heard Him speak at length on the subject, without complaint. But the very form of expression,—"how *can* this man give us his flesh to eat?"—proves that they believed him now to propose a thing impossible to perform—they could not conceive how it was to be carried into effect. This could only be if they understood the words in their literal sense. Not only so, but this is agreed on all hands; for we are often upbraided for resembling the men of Caphernaum, in taking the expressions addressed to them in their carnal, literal sense: so that they must be considered as agreeing with us in assuming the literal interpretation. So far, therefore, we have every reason to say, that they who, in ordinary circumstances, must be considered the best interpreters of any expression used, agreed that our Saviour's words could convey no meaning to them but the literal one. I say in ordinary circumstances, because, on any occasion, were you to read an account of what had taken place many years ago, and there were expressions so obscure that you did not understand them, and could any one who had been on the spot explain them, and tell you what they meant, you would admit his testimony, and allow that, being a man of those times, he had a right to be considered a competent authority. Therefore, so far as the Jews are concerned, and so far as hearers are the proper judges of the meaning of any expression addressed to them, we have their testimony with us, that our Saviour's expressions in the latter part of the discourse, were such as could not refer to faith, but related to a new doctrine, which appeared to them impossible.

We must not, however, be satisfied with this discovery; for a great and important question here arises. The Jews believed our Saviour's words in the literal sense, even as we do: now the main point is, were they right in doing so, or were they wrong? If they were right in taking our Saviour's words literally, we also are right,—if they were wrong in taking them literally, then we also are wrong. The entire question now hinges on this point,—the ascertaining, if possible, whether the Jews were right, or whether they were wrong, in taking Christ's words in their literal sense. A most accurate criterion by which to discover whether the Jews and ourselves be right or wrong, easily presents itself, and the process of applying it is a very simple one. Let us examine, in the first place, all those passages in the New Testament, where our Saviour's hearers *wrongly* understood His figurative expressions in a literal sense, and, in consequence of this erroneous interpretation, raised an objection to the doctrine: and we shall see how our Lord acts on such occasions. We will then examine another case; that is, where his hearers take his words literally, and are *right* in doing so; and on that literal interpretation rightly taken, ground objections to the doctrine; and then we shall see how He acts in these cases. Thus we shall draw from our Saviour's method of acting, two rules for ascer-

LECTURE XIV.

taining whether the Jews were right or wrong; we shall see to which class our objection belongs—and we cannot refuse to abide by such a judgment.

I. In the first place, therefore, we have eight or nine passages in the New Testament, where our Lord meant to be taken figuratively, and the Jews *wrongly* took His words in their crude literal sense, and objected to the doctrine. We find in every instance, without exception, that He corrects them. He explains that he does not mean to be taken literally, but in the figurative sense. The first is a well-known passage, in His interview with Nicodemus, (John iii.) Our Saviour said to him: "Amen, amen, I say to thee, unless a man be born again, he cannot see the kingdom of God." Nicodemus takes this, as the Jews do in our case, literally, and objects: "How can a man be born again when he is old?" He takes the words literally, so as really to mean a repetition of natural birth, and objects to the doctrine as impracticable and absurd. Our Redeemer replies: "Amen, amen, I say to thee, unless a man be born again of water and the Holy Ghost, he cannot enter into the kingdom of heaven." This is manifestly an explanation of the doctrine, teaching him that a person must be born again spiritually, through the agency of water. He does not allow Nicodemus to remain in his mistake, which arose from a misinterpretation of the figurative expression. In the 16th chapter of St. Matthew, 5th verse, "Jesus said to His disciples, take heed and beware of the leaven of the Pharisees and Sadducees." The disciples understood Him literally, as speaking of the bread used by the Pharisees and Sadducees, and "thought among themselves, saying, because we have taken no bread." He lets them know that He was speaking figuratively: "Why do you not understand that it was not concerning bread I said to you, beware of the leaven of the Pharisees and Sadducees?" See how careful he is to correct them, although no great harm could come from this mistaken interpretation. But mark a very special circumstance with regard to this passage. Our Saviour saw that his disciples had misunderstood him, and accordingly, in the 12th chapter of St. Luke, which Doctor Townsend and others admit to contain a later discourse than the previous one, when He wished to make use of the same image to the crowds assembled, remembering how He had been on a former occasion misunderstood by His apostles, He was careful to add the explanation. "Beware," he says, "of the leaven of the Pharisees, which is hypocrisy;" thus guarding against the recurrence of that misunderstanding which had previously taken place.

In John iv. 32, Jesus said to his disciples, "I have food to eat which you know not of;" and they asked, "Hath any man brought Him any thing to eat?" Jesus said: "My food is to do the will of Him that sent me." Here again He corrects their mistake, and shows that He is speaking figuratively. In the 11th chapter of St. John, 11th verse, Jesus said to His disciples: "Lazarus, our friend, sleepeth." They here again mistake His meaning: "Lord, if he sleepeth, he will do well:" they understood that refreshing sleep would be the means of his recovery; "but Jesus spoke of death, but they thought that He spoke of the repose of sleep. Then, therefore, Jesus said to them plainly: Lazarus is dead." No harm could have ensued from their continuing in their original belief that Lazarus was likely to recover, as our Saviour intended to raise him from the dead; but He would not allow them to take His figurative words literally, and therefore He plainly said, "Lazarus is dead," showing that He meant the expression figuratively, and not literally. Another instance: when the disciples took literally His expression, in the 19th chapter of Matthew, "that it is easier for a camel to pass through the eye of a needle than for a rich man to enter the kingdom of God," He, as usual, corrects them, by adding, "that it was a thing impossible to man, but not to God." They had taken His words literally, and consequently understood them of an absolute practical impossibility: but He did not mean the figure expressive of impossibility to be pushed so far; and accordingly he rejoins, that only humanly speaking such salvation was impossible, but that with God all things are possible.

In the eighth chapter, Jesus says: "Whither I go you cannot come;"—and they said, "Will He kill Himself?" But He replied: "You are from below, I am from above,—you are of this world, I am not of this world." That is to say: "I go to the world to which I belong, and you cannot come to it, as you do not belong to it."

In all these cases our blessed Saviour explains his expressions; and there are three or four other passages of a similar nature, in every one of which He acts in the same way. We have thus our first canon or rule, based upon the constant analogy of our Lord's conduct. Where an objection is raised against His doctrine, in consequence of His words being misunderstood, and what he meant figuratively being taken literally, He invariably corrects, and lets his hearers know that He meant them to be

LECTURE XIV.

taken figuratively. I know but of two passages which can be brought to weaken this rule: one is, where Jesus speaks of His body under the figure of the temple: "Destroy this temple, and in three days I will raise it up again." The other is, where the Samaritan woman understands Him to speak of water literally, and He seems not to explain that He spoke only in figure. Now, if I had sufficient time to enter into an analysis of these two passages, which would occupy a considerable time, I could show you that these two instances are perfectly inapplicable to our case. I ground their rejection on a minute analysis of them, which takes them out of this class, and places them apart quite by themselves.* But as the instances already cited establish the first rule quite sufficiently, I shall proceed at once to the other class of texts; that is, where objections were brought against Christ's doctrine, grounded upon His hearers taking literally what he so intended, and on that correct interpretation raising an objection.

II. In the 9th chapter of St. Matthew, our Saviour said to the man sick of the palsy, "Arise, thy sins are forgiven thee." His hearers took these words in the literal sense, when He meant them to be literal, and made an objection to the doctrine. They say—"This man blasphemeth;" that is to say, He has arrogated to Himself the power of forgiving sins, which belongs to God. He repeats the expression which has given rise to the difficulty, —He repeats the very words that have given offence: "Which is it easier, to say thy sins are forgiven thee, or, to take up thy bed and walk? But that you may know that the Son of man hath power on earth to forgive sins . . . ." We see, therefore, in the second place, that when His hearers object to His doctrine, taking it in the literal sense, and being right in so doing, He does not remove the objection, nor soften down the doctrine, but insists on being believed, and repeats the expression. In the 8th chapter of St. John:—"Abraham, your father, rejoiced to see my day. He saw it and was glad." The Jews take His words literally, as though He meant to say that he was coeval with Abraham, and existed in his time. "Thou art not yet fifty years old, and hast thou seen Abraham?" They here again take His words literally, and are correct in doing so, and object to His assertion; and how does He answer them? By repeating the very same proposition:—"Amen, amen, I say to you, before Abraham was made, I am." In the 6th chapter of St. John, in

---

* See it in "Lectures on the Eucharist," p. 104-115.

the very discourse under discussion, we have an instance where the Jews say: "Is not this Jesus, whose father and mother we know,—how is it then, that He saith I came down from heaven?" They object to His assertion, and He insists on it, and repeats it again and again, even three times, saying, that He had come down from heaven.

Thus, then, we have two rules for ascertaining, on any occasion, whether the Jews were right or wrong, in taking our Lord's words to the letter:—first, whenever they took them literally, and He meant them figuratively, He invariably explained His meaning, and told them they were wrong in taking literally what He meant to be figurative. Secondly, whenever the Jews understood Him rightly in a literal sense, and objected to the doctrine proposed, He repeated the very phrases which had given offence. Now, therefore, apply these rules to our case. The difficulty raised, is, "How can this man give us His flesh to eat?" If the words were meant figuratively, Jesus, according to His usual custom, will meet the objection, by stating that he wished to be so understood. Instead of this, He stands to His words, repeats again and again the obnoxious expressions, and requires His hearers to believe them. Hence we must conclude that this passage belongs to the second class, where the Jews were right in taking the different expressions to the letter; and consequently we too are right in so receiving them. Take the three cases together.

THE PROPOSITION.

1. "Unless a man be born again he cannot see the kingdom of God."
2. "Abraham, your father, rejoiced to see my day: he saw it and was glad."
3. "And the bread which I will give is my flesh for the life of the world."

THE OBJECTION.

1. "How can a man be born again when he is old?"
2. "Thou art not yet fifty years old, and hast thou seen Abraham?"
3. "How can this man give us His flesh to eat?"

THE ANSWER.

1. "Amen, amen, I say to thee, unless a man be born again *of water and the Holy Ghost*, he cannot enter into the kingdom of heaven."
2. "Amen, amen, I say unto you, before Abraham was made, I am."

LECTURE XIV. 135

3. "Amen, amen, I say unto you, unless you eat the flesh of the Son of man, and *drink His blood*, ye shall not have life in you."

In the propositions and objections, there is a striking resemblance; but the moment we come to the reply, there is manifest divergence. In the first text, a modification is introduced, indicative of a figurative meaning; in the second, there is a clear repetition of the hard word, which had not proved palatable. And in the third, does Jesus modify his expressions? Does he say, "Amen, amen, I say to you, unless you eat the flesh *of the Son of man in spirit and by faith*, ye shall not have life in you?" Or does he repeat the very expression that has given offence? If he does, this passage belongs to the second class, when the hearers were right in taking his words literally, and objected upon that ground; and, therefore, we must conclude that the hearers of our Saviour, the Jews, were right so in taking these words in their literal sense. If they were right, we also are right, and are warranted in adopting that literal interpretation.

After this argument, I need only proceed, in as summary a way as possible, to analyze our Saviour's answer; because I am not content with showing that He merely repeated the phrase, and thereby proving that the Jews were right in their version; but I am anxious to confirm this result, by the manner in which He made His repetition, and by the particular circumstances which give force to His answer.

1. The doctrine is now imbodied into the form of a precept; and you all know that, when a command is given, the words should be as literal as possible, that they should be couched in language clearly intelligible. Now thus, our Saviour goes on to enjoin this solemn precept, and to add a severe penalty for its neglect. "Unless you eat the flesh of the Son of man, and drink His blood, you shall not have life in you." Here is a portion of eternal life to be lost or gained by every Christian; and can we suppose that our heavenly Master clothed so important a precept under such extraordinary *figurative* language as this? Can we imagine that he laid down a doctrine, the neglect of which involved eternal punishment, in metaphorical phrases of this strange sort? What are we therefore to conclude? That these words are to be taken in the strictest and most literal sense; and this reflection gains further strength, when we consider that it was delivered in a twofold form, as a command, and as a prohibition. "If any man eat of this bread, he shall live for ever;" and, "except ye eat the flesh of the Son of man, and drink His

blood, ye shall not have life in you." We have, therefore, the compliance with its promise, the neglect with its penalties, proposed to us. This is precisely the form used by our Saviour in teaching the necessity of the sacrament of Baptism. "He that believeth and is baptized, shall be saved; and he that believeth not shall be condemned." The two cases are parallel, and, being precepts, both must be taken in their literal sense.

2. In the second place, our Saviour makes a distinction between the eating of His body and the drinking of His blood; and does so in a very marked and energetic manner; repeating the expressions over and over again. If this be a figure, there is no distinction between its two parts. If it be only descriptive of faith, if only an act of the mind and understanding be here designated, we cannot, by any stretch of fancy, divide it into two acts, characterized by the two bodily operations.

3. Again, Christ subjoins a strong asseveration: "Amen, amen," which is always used when particular weight or emphasis is to be given to words; when they are intended to be taken in their most simple and obvious signification.

4. In the fourth place, we have a qualifying, determinating phrase, because it is said, "My flesh is meat *indeed*,"—that is to say, truly and verily, "and my blood is drink indeed." These expressions should certainly go far to exclude the idea that it was only figurative meat and drink of which he spoke. When a person says that a thing is *verily* so, we must understand him, as far as it is possible for language to express it, in a literal signification.

5. It is evident that our Saviour is compelled to use that strong and harsh expression, "He that eateth me," a phrase that sounds somewhat painfully harsh when repeated, however spiritually it be understood. We can hardly conceive that He would, by preference, choose so strong and extraordinary an expression, not only so, but one so much at variance with the preceding part of His discourse, if He had any choice, and if this had not been the literal form of inculcating the precept.

I have given you a very slight and almost superficial analysis of our Saviour's answer. I might have quoted many other passages, had time served, to confirm the result at which we have arrived, and to prove that the Jews were perfectly warranted in literally determining the meaning of our Saviour's expressions. We now come to another interesting incident. The disciples exclaim: "This is a hard saying,"—the meaning of which expression is: "This is a disagreeable, an odious proposition."

LECTURE XIV.

For it is in this sense that the phrase is used by ancient authors. "This is a hard saying, and who can hear it?"—"It is impossible," in other words, "any longer to associate with a man who teaches us such revolting doctrines as these." I ask, would they have spoken thus, had they understood Him to be speaking only of believing in Him? But what is our Saviour's conduct to these disciples? What is His answer? Why, He allows all to go away, who did not give in their adhesion, and at once believe Him on His word; He says not a syllable to prevent their abandoning Him, and "they walked no more with Him." Can we possibly imagine, that, if He had been speaking all the time in figures, and they had misunderstood Him, He would permit them to be lost for ever, in consequence of their refusal to believe imaginary doctrines, which He never meant to teach them? For if they left Him, on the supposition that they heard intolerable doctrines, which, indeed, He was not delivering, the fault was not so much theirs; but might seem, in some manner, to fall on Him whose unusual and unintelligible expressions had led them into error.

In the second place, what is the conduct of the apostles? They remain faithful,—they resist the suggestions of natural feeling,—they abandon themselves to His authority without reserve. "To whom shall we go?" they exclaim, "Thou hast the words of eternal life." It is manifest that they do not understand Him, any more than the rest, but they submit their judgments to Him; and He accepts the sacrifice, and acknowledges them for His disciples on this very ground. "Have I not chosen you twelve?"—"Are you not my chosen friends, who will not abandon me, but remain faithful in spite of the difficulties opposed to your conviction?" The doctrine taught, therefore, was one which required a surrender of human reasoning, and a submission, in absolute docility, to the word of Christ. But surely the simple injunction to have faith in Him, would not have appeared so difficult to them, and needed not to be so relentlessly enforced by their divine Master.

I will now sum up the argument, by a comparative supposition, which will place the two systems in simple contrast. Every action of our Saviour's life may be doubtless considered a true model of what we should practise; and in whatever capacity He acts, He must present the most perfect example which we can try to copy. He is, on this occasion, discharging the office of a teacher, and consequently may be proposed as the purest model of that character. Suppose a bishop of the established Church, on the one hand, and a bishop of the Catholic Church on the other, wished to recommend to the pastors of their respective flocks the conduct of our Saviour here, as a guide to show them how to act when teaching the doctrines of religion. The one would have, consistently, to speak thus: "When you are teaching your children the doctrine of the Eucharist, lay it down in the strongest literal terms; say, if you please, emphatically, in the words of the Church Catechism, that 'the body and blood of Christ are verily and indeed received by the faithful in the Lord's Supper.' Teach your doctrine in these words to your children. If they say to you, as doubtless they will: 'But this is the doctrine of Popery,—this is the Catholic doctrine, we cannot believe in a Real Presence,'—follow the example of our Saviour; repeat the expression again and again; give no explanation, but insist, in the strongest terms, that Christ's flesh and blood must be truly and verily received; and let your scholars fall away and leave you, as teaching untenable opinions: for, by this course, you will imitate the example left you by your divine Master." In other words, supposing you wished to give an outline of our Lord's conduct to one who did not believe in His divine mission, you would have to state that He was in the habit of teaching with the greatest meekness and simplicity; that He laid down His doctrines in the most open and candid manner; that when on any occasion His hearers misunderstood Him, and took literally what He meant figuratively, He was always accustomed to explain His meaning, to remove the difficulty, and meet every objection; but that, on this occasion alone, He completely departed from this rule. Although His hearers took His words literally, when He was speaking figuratively, He went on repeating the same expressions that had given rise to error, and would not condescend to explain His meaning. You would add, that even with His disciples He would enter into no explanation, but allowed them to depart; and that even His chosen apostles received the same unusual treatment.

But, in the Catholic explanation of this chapter, the whole is consistent, from first to last, with the usual conduct and character of our Saviour. We find that He has to teach a doctrine: we believe it to be a promise of the Eucharist; He selects the clearest, most obvious, and literal terms. He expresses it in the most simple and intelligible words. The doctrine is disbelieved as absurd: objections are raised; our Saviour, as on all other similar occasions, goes on repeating the expressions which have given offence, and insists upon their being received without re-

LECTURE XIV.

serve, thus evincing that He cares not to form a party, or gather around him a multitude of men; but that he wishes all to believe Him, whatever His doctrines, and however grating to their feelings. He would not even deign to soften the trial of faith for His disciples, but allowed them to depart the moment they did not receive His words implictly. Such is our case, perfectly consistent with the character of Christ, while the other runs counter to every thing we read of Him in the entire history of His divine mission. Such a line of conduct we could unreservedly recommend to every Catholic teacher.

It may be said that I have had the whole argument my own way; that I have not examined the grounds on which Protestants profess to differ from our explanation of this chapter. I answer, that there can be only one true meaning in these words and phrases; and that, if our interpretation be right, it necessarily excludes theirs. And I can insist upon this, that before we are called on to give up our interpretation, they show us that the Jews could have understood our Saviour, speaking in their language, in the sense attached to His phrases by others, in direct contradiction to ours. This, I maintain, has not yet been done. I do not consider myself, therefore, bound to go into the examination of other interpretations. I did not lay down a proposition, and then attempt to prove it, but I have proceeded by simple induction. I have given you a mere analysis of the text; I have proved our interpretation, by examining minutely words and phrases; and the result of all this has been, the Catholic interpretation; and, on this ground, do I admit and accept of that interpretation, to the exclusion of all others.

But I do not wish to conceal any thing, or shrink from any arguments or objections that may be made; and I have, therefore, taken some pains to look through different divines of the Protestant communion, who have defined their opinions upon this subject of the Eucharist, and to ascertain what are the grounds, not on which they object to the Catholic doctrine, but on which they base and build their figurative interpretation. But, before touching on them, I hardly need remark, that Sherlock, Jeremy Taylor, and others, interpret this chapter of the Eucharist,— even though they dissent from us as to the nature of Christ's presence in this adorable Sacrament. In confirmation of the line of argument which I have followed, I will refer to the authority of two Protestant divines, among the most learned of modern Germany. Doctor Tittman, in examining this passage, allows that it is quite impossible to argue that our Saviour was speaking of faith, from any interpretation which the Jews could have put upon it; for no usage of speech could have led them to such an explanation. The other authority to which I beg to refer is also of a Protestant writer, better known by the biblical scholars of this country. It is Professor Tholuck of Halle, of whose extensive acquaintance with oriental languages and the philological part of biblical literature, I can speak personally. He says, "It is manifest that a transition takes place in our Saviour's discourse."* I quote these testimonies merely in confirmation of what I have advanced.

To come now to objections against our explanation. I have taken some pains, as I before observed, to discover them; and I have been often surprised to find them so few, and so exceedingly superficial. I will content myself with one divine, who has summed up, in a few pages, what he considers the Protestant ground of interpretation. I allude to the Bishop of St. Asaph, Doctor Beveridge, who has pithily condensed all the reasons why this passage is not to be interpreted of the Eucharist. His arguments, in the main, are the same as others of the same opinion have given; and I will state his objections, and then answer in the words of Dr. Sherlock. The first argument which he gives for not interpreting this chapter of the Eucharist, is, "that the Sacrament was not yet ordained."† Here is the other divine's answer:—"Suppose we should understand this eating the flesh and drinking the blood of the Son of man, of feeding on Christ by faith or believing; yet they could understand this no better than the other. It is plain that they did not, and I know not how they should. For to call bare believing in Christ, eating His flesh and drinking His Blood, is so remote from all propriety of speaking, and so unknown in all languages, that, to this day, those who understand nothing more by it but believing in Christ, are able to give no tolerable account of the reason of the expression."‡

To this we may add, that when our Lord inculcated to Nicodemus the necessity of Baptism, that sacrament was not yet instituted; and therefore, in like manner, it is no sound argument to say, that, because the Eucharist was not instituted, He could not speak of it as well. These are sufficient answers to the objection; nor do I think that, even without them, it could be set

---

* Comment. on Jo. vi.
† "Thesaurus Theolog." *Lond.* 1710, vol. ii. p. 271.
‡ "Practical Discourse of Religious Assemblies." *Lond.* 1700, p. 364–7.

against the varied line of argument, and the minute analysis of the text which I have given you this evening.

The second and third reasons why this discourse should be taken figuratively, are, that our Saviour says, that those who eat His flesh and drink His blood shall live, and they who eat and drink it not shall die. These are Doctor Beveridge's second and third arguments, also much insisted on by Doctor Waterland. The reply to this is very simple—there is always a condition annexed to God's promises. "He that believeth in me hath everlasting life;"—"Except ye eat the flesh of the Son of man, and drink His Blood, ye shall not have life in you." Does the first mean that nothing more than faith is required for salvation? Is not each one bound to keep the commandments of God? The meaning clearly is,—He who believeth with such conditions, with such a fructifying faith as shall produce good works, shall have everlasting life. Here, as everywhere else, a condition is annexed to the precept,—for we must always understand the implied condition, that the duty be well and rightly discharged; and thus, in the present case, eternal life is promised only to those who worthily partake of the blessed Eucharist.

These are, literally, the only arguments brought by this renowned theologian of the English Church in favor of her interpretation. There is one popular argument, however, which I will slightly notice; though, popular as it may be, it is of no solid weight whatever. It is taken from the 64th verse:—"The flesh profiteth nothing; the words which I have spoken to you are spirit and life." Our Lord is here supposed to explain all His former discourse, by saying that the expressions He had used were all to be taken spiritually or figuratively. Upon which supposition I will only make two remarks.. First, that the words "flesh" and "spirit," when opposed to one another in the New Testament, never signify the literal and figurative sense of an expression, but always the natural and the spiritual man, or human nature, as left to its own impulses, and as ennobled and strengthened by grace. If you will read the nine first verses of the eighth chapter of St. Paul to the Romans, you will see the distinction accurately drawn: and, if necessary, this explanation may be confirmed from innumerable other passages. But, secondly, it is unnecessary to take the trouble of quoting, or even reading them, because all modern Protestant commentators agree in this explanation, and allow that nothing can be drawn from that one verse for setting aside our interpretation. I need only mention the names of Kuinoel, Horne, Bloomfield, and Schleusner, to satisfy you that neither want of learning, nor partiality for our doctrines, has dictated that decision.*

But there is one Protestant commentator, to whom I have appealed, who seems to let out the secret, and display the real ground on which the figurative interpretation of this chapter rests. "Still more," writes Dr. Tholuck, "were it not figurative, it would prove too much, namely, the Catholic doctrine!"† Here is the whole truth; but, my brethren, can such reasoning be for a moment tolerated? The falsehood of the Catholic dogma is assumed in the first instance, and then made tho touchstone for the interpretation of texts, on which its truth or falsehood must rest! And this by men who profess to draw their belief from the simple discovery of what is taught in Scripture!

At our next meeting, we shall endeavor, with God's help, to enter on the second part of our investigation,—the discussion of the words of institution. In the mean time, I entreat you to ponder and examine carefully the arguments which I have this evening advanced, and try to discover if anywhere they be assailable. If you find, as I flatter myself you will, that they resist all attempts at confutation, you will be the better prepared for the much stronger proof, which rests upon the simple and solemn words of consecration.

---

* It having been intimated to me, that several of my audience considered this answer too general, and indicative of a desire to slur over an important difficulty, I took the opportunity, in the following lecture, to return to this subject, and quote the authorities at full; as given in the "Lectures on the Eucharist," pp. 140-144. As the subject of that lecture was thereby necessarily intruded on, the interpolation, if I may so call it, will be omitted in the publication, and the reader who desires full satisfaction may consult the work just referred to.

† Comment, p. 131.

LECTURE THE FIFTEENTH.

TRANSUBSTANTIATION.

PART II.

MATT. xxvi. 26-28.

"And while they were at supper, Jesus took bread, and blessed, and brake, and gave to his disciples, and said: Take ye and eat, THIS IS MY BODY. *And taking the chalice, He gave thanks, and gave to them, saying: Drink ye all of this, for* THIS IS MY BLOOD *of the New Testament, which shall be shed for many, for the remission of sins."*

In my last discourse, regarding the Blessed Eucharist, I entered at length into the examination of the sixth chapter of St. John, which I considered as the promise of the institution of that holy sacrament; and I proved to you, from the expressions there used, and from the whole construction of our Saviour's discourse, and from His conduct both towards those who disbelieved, and towards those who believed His words, that He truly did declare that doctrine on the subject which the Catholic Church yet holds, —that is to say, that He promised some institution to be provided in His Church, whereby men would be completely united to Him, being truly made partakers of His adorable Body and Blood, and so applying to their souls the merits of His blessed passion.

According to my engagement, therefore, I proceed this evening to examine those far more important passages that treat of the institution of this heavenly rite, and see how far we may from them draw the same doctrine as we discovered in the promise. In other words, we shall endeavor to ascertain if Jesus Christ really did institute some sacrament whereby men might partake of and participate in His blessed Body and Blood. You have just heard the words of St. Matthew, in which he describes the institution of the Eucharist. You are aware that the same circumstances are related, and very nearly the same words used, by two other evangelists, and also by St. Paul, in his first epistle to the Corinthians. It is not necessary to read over the passages in them all, because it is with reference to words common to all that I have principally to speak this evening.

LECTURE XV.

We have here two forms of consecration, "This is my Body, —this is my Blood." I own that to construct an argument on these words is more difficult than it was on the sixth chapter of St. John; simply and solely for this reason, that it is impossible to add strength or clearness to the expressions themselves. It is impossible for me, by any commentary or paraphrase that I can make, to render our Saviour's words more explicit, or reduce them to a form more completely expressing the Catholic doctrine than they do of themselves. "This is my Body—this is my Blood." The Catholic doctrine teaches that it *was* Christ's Body and that it *was* His Blood. It would consequently appear as though all we had here to do, were simply and exclusively to rest at once on these words, and leave to others to show reason why we should depart from the literal interpretation which we give them.

Before, however, completely taking up my position, I must make two or three observations on the method in which these texts are popularly handled, for the purpose of overthrowing the Catholic belief. It is evident that the words, simply considered, —if there were no question about any apparent impossibility, and if they related to some other matter,—would be at once literally believed by any one who believes at all in the words of Christ. His reasoning would naturally be, " Christ has declared this doctrine in the simplest terms, and I receive it on His word." There must be a reason, as I will fully prove to you just now, for departing in this case from the ordinary, simple interpretation of the words, and giving them a tropical meaning. It is for those who say that Christ, by the words, "This is my Body," meant no more than, "This is the figure of my Body," to give us a reason why their interpretation is correct. The words themselves express that it is the Body of Christ. Whoever tells me that it is not the Body of Christ, but only its figure, must satisfy me how one expression is equivalent to the other. I will prove, too, presently, as I just said, that this is necessarily the position in which the controversy is placed; but I cannot resist the desire of exhibiting to you the difficulties in which persons find themselves involved, who wish to establish the identity of the two phrases, and the extremely unphilosophical methods which they consequently follow. I will take, as an illustration, a passage in a sermon delivered a few years ago, in a chapel of this metropolis, forming one of a series of discourses against Catholic doctrines, by select preachers. This is on the doctrine of Transubstantiation, and is directed to prove that it

LECTURE XV. 145

is unscriptural, and ought not to be held. Now hear, I pray you, the reasoning of this preacher on our subject. "We contend that we must understand the words figuratively,"—he is speaking of Christ's words in my text,—"because there is no necessity to understand them literally." What sort of a canon of interpretation is here laid down! That no passage of Scripture is to be taken literally, unless a necessity can be shown for it! that we must on principle take every thing as figurative, till those who choose the literal interpretation demonstrate that there exists a positive necessity for taking it so! I should contend rather that the obvious rule is to take words literally, unless a necessity be proved for taking them figuratively: and I wish to know how this rule would stand before those who deny the divinity of Christ, that we are not allowed to take any passage literally, unless a necessity for it be first demonstrated. Therefore, when Christ is called God, or the Son of God, we must first prove a necessity for believing Him to be God, before we can be justified in drawing conclusions from the words of those texts themselves! He proceeds: "and because it was morally impossible for His disciples to have understood Him literally." Now this is just what requires proof, because on this point hinges the entire question—it is not a proof itself, but the proposition to be proved. Well, the preacher seems to think so too, and goes on to give a proof in the following words:—"for, let me ask, what is more common, in all languages, than to give to the sign the name of the thing signified? If you saw a portrait, would you not call it by the name of the person it represents, or if you looked on the map at a particular country, would you not describe it by the name of that country?" I ask, is this a proof? But let us see what examples he chooses:—"a portrait"—as if there were no difference between taking up a piece of bread, and saying, "This is my Body," and pointing at a picture, and saying, "This is the king!" As if language and ordinary usage do not give the picture that very name; but more than that, as if it were not the very essence of that object to represent another. What other existence has a portrait, than as a type or representative? does not its very idea suppose its being the resemblance of a person? But suppose I held up an ingot of gold without the king's effigy, and said, "This is the king's body," would my audience thereby understand that I meant to institute a symbol of his person, on the ground that, had I showed them his effigy on the coin, and said, "This is the king," they would have easily understood me to intimate that it was his portrait? The second instance he gives is "a map."—What is a map but the representation of a country? What existence has it but so far as it depicts the forms of that country? If it fail to represent it, it is no map, and the expression would be no longer intelligible. But when Christ says of bread, "This is my Body," there is no natural connection or resemblance between the two; there is nothing to tell men that he meant, "This is an emblem of my body." In all such assertions there may be declamation; but there is manifestly no proof; nothing to demonstrate that the Catholic interpretation must be rejected.

I will quote another passage from a writer better known: I mean the author of the "Introduction to the Critical Study of the Scriptures." He says, that the Catholic doctrine of Transubstantiation is "erected on a *forced* and *literal* construction of our Lord's declaration." The Catholic doctrine is based on a forced and literal interpretation of Scripture! I would ask, where on earth were these two words put in juxtaposition in any argument before?—to call the literal the forced interpretation! I do not believe that in any case, except a controversy on religion, an author would have allowed himself to fall into such a proposition. If any of you had a cause before a court, and your counsel were to open it by saying, "that the case must be adjudged in favor of his client, because the adverse party had nothing in their favor except 'a literal and forced construction' of the statute provided for the case," would you not consider this equivalent to a betrayal of your cause? For, conceding thus much is literally granting that there is nothing to be said on your side. That any writer should, upon an argument so constructed, condemn the Catholic doctrine, is really extraordinary; it is surely accustoming students in theology, if the Introduction be meant for them, as well as other readers, to very superficial and incorrect reasoning, and ought, consequently, to be reprobated in severe terms.

These may serve as specimens how far from easy it is to establish grounds, even of plausibility, for the rejection of the Catholic doctrine. But there are graver and more solid writers, who satisfactorily admit, that, so far as our Lord's expressions go, all is in our favor. I will quote one passage from Paley's "Evidences of Christianity," where he is giving proofs that the Gospel's were not books merely made up for a certain purpose, but that whatever they relate did really happen. He says: "I think, also, the difficulties arising from the conciseness of Christ's expression, 'This is my Body,' would have been avoided in a made-up story." Why so? I may ask, if nothing is more common than to call signs by the name of things signified, and this was as obvious and intelligible a figure as calling a picture of the king by his name. He continues: "I allow that the explanation given by Protestants is satisfactory; but it is deduced from a minute comparison of the words in question with forms of expression used in Scripture, and especially by Christ Himself on other occasions. No writer would have arbitrarily and unnecessarily cast in his reader's way a difficulty, which, to say the least, it required research and erudition to clear up."*

Here, then, it is granted, that to arrive at the Protestant interpretation, it requires erudition and research; consequently, that it is not the simple, obvious meaning, which these words present. When you say, that to establish a construction of a passage, it requires study and learning, I conclude that it is his duty who has chosen that construction to make use of these means; and the burden rests on him of proving his interpretation, not on those who adopt the literal and obvious sense. Therefore, when the explicit, plain, and literal construction of the words is that which we adopt, it becomes the task of those who maintain us to be wrong, and say that the words, "This is my Body," did not mean that it was the Body of Christ, but only its symbol,—I contend, it becomes their duty to prove their figurative interpretation.

Their argument necessarily takes a twofold form. Reasons must be brought by them to prove,—first, that they are authorized, and secondly that they are compelled, to depart from the literal meaning. This is usually attempted by two distinct arguments. First, an attempt is generally made to establish that our Saviour's words *may* be taken figuratively; that they may be so interpreted as to signify, "This represents my Body, this represents my Blood," by bringing together a number of passages, in which the verb "to be" is used in the sense of *to represent*, and thence concluding that here, in like manner, it *may* have the same meaning. In the second place, to justify such a departure from the literal sense, it is urged, that by it we encounter so many contradictions, so many gross violations of the law of nature, that, however unwilling, we must abandon it, and take the figurative signification. This is the clearest and completest form in which the argumentation can be presented. The author, for instance, whom I quoted just now, after giving us his reason why we are not obliged to take these words literally,

* Par. ii. c. iii.

inasmuch as there is no necessity for it,—gives us as a further motive for not understanding them so, that the literal meaning leads to direct contradictions and gross absurdities. These are the two principal heads of objection which I shall have to discuss.

First, then, it is urged that we may take our Saviour's words figuratively, because there are many other passages of Scripture, in which the verb "to be" means "to represent," and a great many texts of a miscellaneous character are generally thrown together into a confused heap, to establish this point. In order to meet them, it is necessary to classify them; for although there is one general answer which applies to all, yet there are specific replies, which meet each separate class. The person who has given the fullest list of such texts, and, indeed, who has given sufficient to establish this point, if it can be established by such a line of argument, and the person above all others most popularly quoted, is Dr. Adam Clarke, in his Discourse on the Eucharist. He is, in fact, cited or copied by the two authors to whom I have already referred. I will give you all his quotations, only distributing them into classes, so as to simplify my answers.

In the first class, I place all those passages of this form: Genesis xli. 26, 27: "And the seven good kine *are* seven years." Daniel vii. 24: "The ten horns *are* ten kingdoms." Matthew xiii. 38, 39: "The field *is* the world, the good seed *are* the children of the kingdom, the tares *are* the children of the wicked one. The enemy *is* the devil, the harvest *is* the end of the world, the reapers *are* the angels." 1 Cor. x. 4: "The rock was Christ." Gal. iv. 24: "For these *are* the two covenants." Rev. i. 20: "The seven stars *are* the angels of the seven churches." Here, it is said, are a great many passages, in which the verb "to be" means "to represent;" and this forms the first class of texts.

Secondly, John x. 7: "I am the door." John xv. 1: "I am the true vine."

Thirdly, Gen. xvii. 10: "This is my covenant between thee and me:" which is commonly supposed to mean, this is a representation or image of my covenant.

Fourthly, Exodus xii. 11: "This is the Lord's passover."

Here are four classes of passages. I wish, first of all, to show you, that, independently of the general answer which I shall give to all, or at least of the minuter examination which I shall make of the first class, and which will apply to many of the others,— the texts comprised in the three last classes have nothing at all

LECTURE XV.

to do with the subject; for the verb "to be" does not signify in them "to represent;" and we must consider only those to the purpose in which it does mean "to represent." "I am the door;" "I am the true vine." I ask any one, on reflection, to answer, does "to be" mean in these passages "to represent?" Substitute the latter verb; for if the two be equivalent, the one must fit in the other's place. Compare them with the words, "the rock was Christ." If you say "the rock represented Christ," the sense is the same, because "to be" is its equivalent. "I *am* the door;" I *represent* the door,—that is not Christ's meaning. "I am *as* the door, I resemble the door;" that was what he wished to express. These passages consequently must be at once excluded; because it is evident, that if we substitute the phrase considered equivalent, we produce a totally different sense from what our Saviour intended. Moreover, the answers which I will give to the first class of passages will apply fully to these; but I consider this as a sufficient specific answer.

Secondly, "This is my covenant between thee and me." Does this mean that circumcision, of which this text speaks, represents, or was the figure of the covenant? Granted for a moment; God clearly explains himself; for He says explicitly in the next verse, that it is the sign: "And it shall be a sign or token of the covenant." Therefore, if He meant to say that this was a figure of the covenant, He goes on to explain Himself afterwards; consequently no mistake could arise from His words. In the second place, circumcision was not only a sign, but the instrument or record of the covenant. Now, common usage warrants us in calling by the name of the covenant the document or articles whereby it is effected. If we hold in our hands a written treaty, we should say, "This is the treaty." But leaving aside these answers, it is easy to prove that the verb here noways means "represents," and that there is no allusion to the type or figure in the case. This is evident, by comparing this text with every other in which a similar expression occurs. In all, the introductory formula signifies, that what follows is truly a matter of compact or covenant; so that this would be the construction of the entire text: "What follows *is* my covenant between you and me; you shall practise circumcision." Thus, for instance, Is. lix. 21: "This is my covenant with them, saith the Lord; my spirit which is in thee and my words, shall not depart out of thy mouth." Does God there mean, this is the figure of my covenant? Do not the words signify, "What I am going to express is my covenant;" so that they are only an introductory or pre-

13*

liminary formula? Another instance, 1 Sam. xi. 2: "In this will I make my covenant with you, in boring out your right eyes." Here again the hard covenant follows the introductory phrase. And this interpretation is further confirmed by the many passages in which God premises, "This is my statute or command," after which follows the very command or statute. In like manner, then, the words, "This is my covenant" do not mean "This represents my covenant," but simply, "What follows is my covenant." The examination of other passages, were there no other consideration, would thus take this out of the class applicable to our controversy; but when we further see, that in the next verse God expressly calls that rite a sign of his covenant, it is plain that the form of expression is not parallel, as here an explanation is subsequently given, which is not the case with the words of institution.

Thirdly. The fourth class contains the text, "This is the Lord's passover." This is an interesting text, not on account of its own intrinsic worth, but on account of some particular circumstances connected with its first application to this doctrine. It was on this text, and almost exclusively on its strength, that the Catholic doctrine of Transubstantiation was rejected; it was on this that Zuinglius, when he attempted to deny it at the time of the Reformation, mainly built; for he found no other text whereon to ground his objection against the words "This is my Body" being literally taken. Now, I think we can easily prove that the verb "is" has here its literal meaning. As the circumstances of his discovery are curious, I beg leave to give his own account. Yet though the narrative tells greatly in our favor, I feel a repugnance to detail it: it is degrading to humanity and to religion, that any thing so discreditable, so debasing, should be recorded by any writer of himself; and I would willingly pass it over, were it not that stern justice to the cause I am defending, demands that I show the grounds on which the Catholic doctrine of the Real Presence was first supposed to be disproved. Zuinglius, therefore, tells us himself, that he was exceedingly anxious to get rid of the Catholic doctrine of the Real Presence, but found a great difficulty in arguing against the natural and obvious signification of these words, "This is my Body—this is my Blood"—that he could find nothing in Scripture to warrant him in departing from the literal sense, except passages manifestly relating to parables.

It was on the 13th of April, early in the morning, that the happy revelation occurred. His conscience, he says, urges him

LECTURE XV. 151

to relate the circumstances, which he would gladly conceal; for he knows they must expose him to ridicule and obloquy. He found himself, in a dream, disputing with one who pressed him close, while he seemed unable to defend his opinion, till a monitor stood at his side. "I know not," he emphatically adds, "whether he were white or black," who suggested to him this important text. He expounded it next morning, and convinced his hearers that, on the strength of it, the doctrine of the Real Presence was to be abandoned!

Such is the account given us of the first discovery of a text sufficient to reject the Catholic doctrine of Transubstantiation, and that text is the one which I have just quoted to you from the 12th chapter of Exodus, 11th verse: "This is the Lord's passover." I waive several considerations which might be drawn from the circumstances in which these words were spoken, of a natural tendency to teach the Israelites that a typical institution was made, whereas at the Last Supper there was nothing done or said which could intimate that any such intention existed; also some remarks regarding the phrase itself as intelligible to the Jews, from the custom of calling sacrifices by the name of the object for which they were offered. For, in truth, the text is of no value whatever towards establishing the point that "to be" signifies "to represent."

In fact, one of the most learned of modern Protestant commentators observes, that the construction is such as always signifies "This is *the day* or *feast* of the Passover, *sacred to* the Lord." The grounds of this translation can hardly be understood, without reference to the original language; in which, as he observes, what is translated by a genitive, "the Lord's," is dative, and in this construction signifies "sacred to the Lord;" and then the verb *is* has its own obvious signification: as much as when we say, "This is Sunday," which certainly does not mean, "This represents Sunday." To prove this point, he refers to two or three other passages, where exactly the same form of expression occurs, and shows that it always has a similar meaning. For instance, in Exodus xx. 10: "This is the sabbath of the Lord," the dative form is here used: "This is the sabbath *to* the Lord," meaning the sabbath sacred to Him. Now, the construction in the original is precisely the same in both texts; nor is it ever used in the sense of a thing being an emblem or a sign. In another text, (Exod. xxxii. 5,) "the festival of the Lord," the same construction occurs, signifying the same; and, finally, in the 27th verse of the very chapter in question, we have, "This is the sacrifice of the Lord's passover;" that is, according to the original, "the sacrifice of the passover (*sacred*) to the Lord." From these parallel expressions, where in the original exactly the same construction occurs, he concludes that the verb "to be" is here literally taken.* Hence, this text affords no aid to the argument which would consider the verb substantive to mean "represent," in the words of institution; the interpretation put upon it is incorrect; and, consequently, when Zuinglius learnt it from his monitor as a sufficient ground for rejecting the Catholic doctrine, may we not conclude that it was not a spirit of truth that appeared to him, and that he rejected our doctrine on grounds not tenable, and by attributing to words a meaning which they cannot have?

I have thus first set these passages aside, because, according to the system I have endeavored to follow, I wish my answers to be strictly and individually applicable to each part of the case; although the remarks which I shall make on the first class of passages, where I own that "to be" means "to represent," will apply to almost every one of them.

Well, then, it is argued that the words "This is my body, this is my blood" may be rendered by "This represents my body, this represents my blood," in other words, figuratively, because in certain other passages quoted, it is obvious that the two terms are equivalent. The only way in which the argument can hold, is by supposing that the texts quoted form what are called *parallel passages* to the word of institution. But, first, I will ask a simple question. In these passages, the verb "to be" means "to represent;" but there are some thousands of passages in Scripture, where the verb "to be" does *not* mean "to represent." I ask the reason, why the words of institution are to be detached from these thousand passages, and interpreted by the others? I want some good reason to authorize me in classifying it with these, and not with the others. It is no reason to say, that it is necessary or convenient to take it so; I want some reason why it must be so. Therefore, merely considering the question in this indefinite way, we have a right to ask, why these words should be detached from the multitude of places where "to be" has its proper signification, and joined to the few that are always to be considered the exception.

But let us join issue a little more closely. What are parallel passages? Are any two passages where the same word occurs

---

* Rosenmüller in loc.

LECTURE XV.

to be considered parallel? There must be something more, necessary to constitute parallelism. Well, I am willing to take Horne's rule for this source of interpretation. It is briefly this: that, when struck with any resemblance between passages, you must not be content with similarity of words; but examine, "whether the passages be sufficiently similar, that is, *not only whether the same word*, but also *the same thing*, answers together."*
The rule is translated from another writer, and is more clearly expressed in the original, which says, that we must see "whether both passages contain the *same thing*, and *not only the same word*."† And the commentator on this author makes this remark: "We must therefore hold that similitude *of things*, not of words, constitutes a parallelism."

We have a rule, then, laid down, that two passages are not parallel, or, in other words, that we may not use them to interpret one another, merely because the same word is in them, unless the same thing also occur in both. Let us, therefore, ascertain whether the same thing occurs, as well as the same words, in all the passages of this class. But first, as an illustration of the rule, let me observe that, when in my last discourse I quoted several texts, I not only pointed out the same words in them, but I was careful to prove that the same circumstances occurred, —that is, that our Saviour made use of expressions which were taken literally when He meant to be understood so, that objections were raised, and that He *acted* precisely in the same manner as in the text under examination; and from this similarity of things, I reasoned, considering the passages as parallel in consequence of it. What is *the thing* in all the passages united in this class, that we may see if it be likewise found in the words of institution? We may exemplify the rule in these passages themselves. Suppose I wish to illustrate one of them by another, I should say, this text—"The seven kine are seven years"—is parallel with "The field is the world," and both of them with the phrase, "These are the two covenants;" and I can illustrate them one by another. And why? Because in every one of them the *same thing* exists;—that is to say, in every one of these passages there is the interpretation of an allegorical teaching—a vision in the one, a parable in the second, and an allegory in the third. I do not put them into one class, because they all contain the verb "to be," but because they all contain the same thing—they speak of something mystical and typical,

---

* Vol. ii. p. 531. † Ernesti, p. 61.

the interpretation of a dream, an allegory, and a parable. Therefore, having ascertained that in one of these the verb "to be" means "to represent," I conclude that it has the same sense in the others; and I frame a general rule, that wherever such symbolical teaching occurs, these verbs are synonymous. When, therefore, you tell me that "This is my body" may mean "This represents my body," because in those passages the same verb or word occurs with this sense, I must, in like manner, ascertain, not only that the word "to be" is common to the text, but that the same thing is to be found in it as in them; in other words, that in the forms of institution there was given the *explanation of some symbol*, such as the interpretation of a vision, a parable, or a prophecy. If you show me this, as I can show it in all the others, then I will allow this to be parallel with them.

This similarity of substance will readily be discovered by looking closely into those passages quoted by Dr. Adam Clarke as parallel, which I have placed in this class.—" The seven kine are seven years," Joseph is interpreting the dream of Pharaoh; "And the ten horns are ten kings," Daniel is receiving the interpretation of his vision; "The field is the world," our Saviour is interpreting a parable; "The rock was Christ," St. Paul is professedly explaining the symbols of the old law, and tells us that he is doing so, and that he spoke of a spiritual rock; "These are the two covenants," St. Paul again is interpreting the allegory upon Hagar and Sarah; "The seven stars are the angels of the seven Churches," St. John is receiving the explanation of a vision. All these passages belong to one class, because they refer to similar things;—therefore, before I join to them the words "This is my body," you must show me that it enters into the same class by the same circumstance; you must show me that not only the verb "to be," which occurs in a thousand other instances, is there; but that it is used under the same conditions, in a case clearly similar to these by the explanation of allegories, or dreams, or parables, or of any other mystical method of teaching that you please. Until you have done this, you have no right to consider them all as parallel, or to interpret it by them.

But, before finishing this consideration, allow me to observe, that not only, in every one of the instances I have quoted, is it manifest from the context that a parable, a vision, or an allegory is explained; but the writers themselves tell us that they are going to interpret such things. For, in the examples from Genesis, Daniel, and St. Matthew, it is said, "This is the inter-

LECTURE XV.

pretation of the dream"—"This is a vision which I saw"—"This is the meaning of the parable which I spoke;"—so that we are expressly told that the speakers are going to interpret a figure. St. Paul to the Galatians is equally careful, "which things are an *allegory*, FOR, these are the two covenants." In the words of institution, our Saviour does not say this is an allegory—He does not give such a key to interpret His words as in the other cases. St. Paul to the Corinthians, "All these things were done to them in figure, and they drank from the *spiritual* rock; and the rock" (that is, the *spiritual* rock) "was Christ." In the Apocalypse, it is said to John, "Write down the things which thou hast seen; the mystery of the seven stars," which, in the language familiar to St. John, signifies the *symbol* of the seven stars. It is after this introduction that he says, "And the seven stars *are* the angels of the seven Churches." In every case, the writer is careful to let us know that he is going to deliver the interpretation of a figurative teaching; and, therefore, before you can compel me to apply these passages to the explanation of the words of institution, I require you to show me that a similar instruction is found in these words as in those other passages.

But let us try the process of our opponents on another application. In the first verse of the Gospel of John, we have this remarkable expression,—"And the Word was God." Now, this has always been considered by believers in the divinity of Christ as an exceedingly strong text, and all its force lies in that little syllable "was." So strong has it appeared, that in different ways attempts have been made to modify the text,—either by separating it into two, or by reading "The Word was of God." What is the use of all this violence, if the word "was" may mean "represents?" If we are justified in giving it that interpretation in other cases, why not do it here? Compare these three texts together, and tell me between which is there most resemblance?

"The Word was God."
"The rock was Christ."
"This is my Body."

If, in the third of these, we may change the verb, because we can do so in the second, what is to prevent our doing it in the first? And instead of the Word "was God," why not interpret, "the Word represented God?" Suppose any one to reason thus, and still further to strengthen his arguments by saying,—that in 2 Cor. iv. St. Paul tells us, that Christ is "the image of God;" and in Coloss. i. says of Him, "who is the image of the invisible

God,"—might he not as justly conclude, that Christ being only the image of God according to St. Paul, the words of St. John may be well explained, conformably, as only intimating, that He represented God? No one has ever thought of reasoning in this way; and if any person had, he would have been answered, that these words cannot be explained or interpreted by "The rock was Christ," because St. Paul is manifestly explaining an allegory, or using a figurative form of teaching, of which there is no sign in St. John. He would be told that he has no right to interpret the one by the other, merely because, in both, the sentence consists of two nouns with a verb between them; for that is a parallelism of words and not of things. He must first show that St. John, in this instance, was teaching in parables, as St. Matthew, Daniel, and the others whom I have quoted. Until he does this, he has no right to interpret the phrase, "The Word was God" as parallel with "The rock was Christ." Just, therefore in the same way, you have no grounds, no reason, to put the words "This is my Body," which still less resemble, "The rock was Christ," than the text of St. John, into the same class with it, and interpret it as a parallel.

I conclude, that we must have some better argument than the simple assertion, that our Saviour spoke the words of institution figuratively, because, in some passages of Scripture, the verb "to be" means "to represent." It is manifest, that not one of these passages can be said to be a key to them, and that the words of institution cannot be figuratively interpreted by them, unless you show more than a resemblance in phraseology:—until you prove that the same thing was done in one place as in the others; otherwise, whatever is denied to us, is thereby conceded to the impugners of Christ's divinity.

Thus far we are authorized in concluding, that the attempt fails to produce passages demonstrative of the Protestant interpretation; for these are the only passages that have been quoted as parallel to the words of institution. I have shown you that they are not parallel, and consequently that they are of no value. They are not adequate to explaining ours; and some other passages must be brought by our opponents, to justify them in interpreting, "This is my Body" by "This represents my Body."

I shall probably be obliged to delay until Sunday next the second portion of the argument—that is, the examination of the difficulties in the Catholic interpretation, which are supposed to drive us to the figurative sense; because before leaving this ex-

LECTURE XV.

planation of words, this examination of phraseology, I must meet one or two objections, which may lead me into some details. I should have kept myself within the bounds of general observations, had it not been for a particular circumstance, which makes it my duty to intrude a little more personally on your notice, than I should otherwise have been inclined to do.

The first difficulty which I have to meet has been repeated again and again, and owes its origin or revival to Dr. Adam Clarke, in his work already referred to, on the Eucharist. This gentleman enjoyed, I believe, a considerable reputation for his acquaintance with oriental languages; at least, with that dialect which our Saviour and his apostles spoke. From this language he raised an objection against the Catholic interpretation, which was copied by Mr. Horne, in the very passage I have already referred to, and which has been recopied again and again, by almost every writer on this subject. Instead of quoting his words from the book itself, I prefer doing it from a letter sent to me a few days ago, after this course of instruction had commenced. And this is the circumstance, on account of which, I think myself justified in coming more personally before you, than otherwise I should have been inclined to do. The letter is as follows:—

London, March 4th.

"REV. SIR:

"I beg most respectfully to invite your attention to the following remarks on the Eucharist by a late divine, well skilled in the oriental and other languages, (Dr. A. Clarke,) and which, I think, tend very much to weaken that which Roman Catholics advance in defence of transubstantiation.

"'In the Hebrew, Chaldee, and Chaldeo-Syriac languages, there is no term which expresses *to mean, signify,* or *denote,* though both the Greek and Latin abound with them; hence the Hebrews use a figure, and say, *it is,* for *it signifies.* 'The seven kine ARE seven years.' 'The ten horns ARE ten kings.' 'They drank of the spiritual rock which followed them, and the rock WAS Christ.' This Hebrew idiom is followed, though the work is written in Greek: 'The seven stars ARE the seven churches,' besides many other similar instances.

"'That our Lord neither spoke in Greek nor Latin on this occasion needs no proof. It was most probably in what was formerly called the *Chaldaic,* now the *Syriac,* that He conversed with his disciples. In Matt. xxvi. 26, 27, the words in the Syriac version are 'honau pagree,' *this is my body*—'henau demee,' *this is my blood*, of which forms of speech the Greek is a verbal translation; nor would any man, at the present day, speaking in the same language, use, among the people to whom it was vernacular, other terms than the above, to express 'This *represents* my body—this *represents* my blood.'—*Discourse on the Holy Eucharist, by A. Clarke, D. D., London,* 1808."

Here are three distinct assertions: First, that, in the Hebrew or Chaldeo-Syriac, there is no word for "to represent;" secondly, that with the people who spoke the same language as our Saviour did in instituting the Eucharist, it was familiar or common to say, "This is," when they meant to say, "This represents;" thirdly, that if He meant to express, "This represents my body," he could do it in no other way than by saying, "This is my body." Supposing all this true, it would not be proved that our Saviour did institute a sign or symbol. For though he would have used these expressions in establishing it, yet the same phrase would be as applicable, or rather, would be necessary, for the literal declaration of the thing itself. The words would be, at most, equivocal, and we should have to look elsewhere for their interpretation.

The writer of the letter concludes in these words:—"I cannot but feel surprised that a doctrine should be so strongly upheld and defended by one who is a professor of Oriental languages, and who has access to the various versions of the Scriptures, and I humbly hope, Sir, that you will be led to see 'the error of your way.'"

I am thankful, exceedingly thankful, to the writer of this letter; in the first place, because he shows an interest regarding myself personally, which must be always a matter of obligation; and also in regard to the doctrines which I am endeavoring to explain, I am thankful, because it gives me reason to see that this objection is still popular—still known; and that, on the other hand, its confutation is not by any means so public; and on this account, I shall venture to enter more fully into the answer than perhaps I should have otherwise done. Now, I am challenged or called on by these words to account how, having acquired some little knowledge of the languages here referred to, I can maintain a doctrine so completely at variance, as Dr. Clarke asserts, with that language, or those scriptural versions, to which I have been accustomed. And I answer,—that if any thing on earth could have attached me more to our interpretation,—if any thing could have more strongly rooted me in my belief of the Catholic doctrine, it would have been the little

LECTURE XV.

knowledge I have been able to acquire of these pursuits. For I will show you how, far from this assertion of Dr. Adam Clarke's having weakened my faith in the Catholic doctrine, it must, on the contrary, have necessarily confirmed it.

About eight years ago, when more actively employed in the study of these very matters, I saw this passage from Dr. Adam Clarke, as quoted by Mr. Hartwell Horne. According to the principle I had adopted in conducting my inquiries, and in which I hope ever to persevere, I determined to examine it fully and impartially. Here were a series of bold assertions;—that in a certain language there was not one word that signifies "to represent;" that it was common to express the idea of representation by the verb "to be;" and that, consequently, our Saviour, when He wished to say, "This represents my body," was compelled to say, "This is my body." I determined to look into them as into simple questions of philological literature; to see whether the Syriac was so poor and wretched as not to afford a single word implying representation. I looked through the dictionaries and lexicons, and I found two or three words, supported by one or two examples, enough to confute the assertion; but still not enough to satisfy my mind. I saw that the only way to ascertain the fact, was to examine the authors who have written in this language; and in a work which I now have in my hand, I published the result of my researches; entitled, "Philological Examination of the objections brought against the literal sense of the phrase in which the Eucharist was instituted, from the Syriac language, containing a specimen of a Syriac dictionary." In other words, simply considering the question as interesting to learned men, I determined to show the imperfection of our means for acquiring that language, and, by a specimen, to lay open the defects of our dictionaries. The specimen consisted of a list of such words as mean "to represent, to denote, to signify, to typify," and are either wanting in the best lexicons, or have not that meaning in them.

What do you think is the number that this list contains, which extends through upwards of thirty or forty pages? In other words, how many expressions does the Syriac language, which was said by Dr. Clarke not to possess one word for "to denote, or represent,"—how many do you think it does possess? The English language has only four or five, such as "to denote, to signify, to represent, to typify;" and I think, with these, you are arrived pretty nearly at the end of the list. The Greek and Latin have much the same number. I doubt if there be ten in either. How many then does the poor Syriac language present? *Upwards of forty!* Forty words are here collected, with examples from the most classical authors; hardly one of them without several, some with twenty, thirty, or forty,—a few with nearly a hundred: and in some cases, not one half the examples have been given.

Here, then, is the first assertion, that in the Syriac language there is not one word for an idea for which it has forty-one! More, I will venture to say, more than any language of the present day can afford.

I dwell on this matter, not merely for the sake of its confutation, but as a general specimen of how easy it is to make bold assertions, relative to subjects not much studied. Thus, any person not acquainted with the language, and knowing Dr. Clarke to have been a learned man, and of course believing him to be honest in his statements, will take it for granted that his positive assertions are accurate, and on his authority reject the Catholic doctrine. Those assertions, however, are most incorrect:* the Syriac has plenty of words,—more than any other, for the purpose required.

The second assertion is, that it is common, with persons using that language, to employ the verb "to be" for "to represent." This point, also, I have, to the best of my ability, examined; and I have no hesitation in denying that it is more common with them than with any other nation, as I can show in a very simple manner. I find, for instance, in the oldest commentator on the Scripture in that language, that these words, meaning to represent, are so crowded together, that they will not stand translation. In the writings of St. Ephrem, the oldest in the Syriac language, although he tells us that he is going to interpret, figuratively or symbolically, through all his commentaries, and consequently prepares us for corresponding language, yet the verb "to be" occurs in the sense of "to represent" only twice, or at most four times, where words which signify "to represent" occur at least sixty times. In his commentary on the Book of Deuteronomy, he uses the verb substantive six times in that sense, but words significative of figure, seventy times; so that

---

* A correspondent has requested me to give some of these words, in publishing this lecture, stating that my assertions in the pulpit had been called in question. Were I to do so, I should only give a list of unintelligible sounds. But if any one be inclined to doubt my contradiction of Dr. Clarke's fearless assertion, I beg he will consult the book referred to: "Horæ Syriacæ," *Rome*, 1828, p. 18–53, of which a copy will be found in the British Museum.

the proportion of the two is nearly as six to seventy. In the second place, I find that he avoided this use of the verb "to be" in such an extraordinary way, and crowded the other words so thickly, that it was necessary, in some cases, in the Latin translation, to substitute the verb "to be" for them; so that it was easier to use it in that sense in Latin than in Syriac. In the third place, I find that words meaning "to represent" came so close together, that in eighteen half lines (for the text occupies one half, and the translation the other half of each page,—so that there are often only three or four words in a line) he uses the words that mean "to represent" twelve times. This is in page 254 of vol. i. Page 283, he uses these verbs eleven times in seventeen lines. St. James of Sarug employs them ten times in thirteen lines; and Barhebræus, another commentator, uses them eleven times in as many lines.* So much for the frequency with which it has been asserted that these writers use the verb "to be" for "to represent."

The third and more important assertion was, that any person, wishing to institute such a rite now-a-days, must compulsorily use this form; that, if he wished to appoint a figure of his body, he would be driven to say, "This is my body." I accepted the challenge in the strictest sense, and determined to verify it, by seeing if this was the case. I found an old Syriac writer, Dionysius Barsalibæus, not a Catholic writer, who uses this expression: "They are called, and are, the body and blood of Jesus Christ in truth, and not figuratively." This passage shows there is a means of expressing the idea of figure. Another passage is from a work by an old writer in Syriac, the original of which has been lost, but which was translated into Arabic, by David, Archbishop in the ninth or tenth century; and as it is a question of language, the translation will tell sufficiently well how far the assertion be correct. It says, "He gave us His body, blessed be His name, for the remission of our sins... He said, 'This is my Body,' and He did not say, 'This is a figure of my Body.'" Now, supposing the Syriac language had no word to signify 'represent,' how could this writer have expressed in the original, that our Saviour did not tell us "This is the figure of my Body?" According to Dr. Clarke's reasoning, that they who speak the language have no alternative, the passage must have run thus, "He did not say, this is my Body, but He said, this is my Body!" There is another and a still stronger pas-

---

* Ibid. p. 56.

sage from St. Maruthas, who wrote 300 years after Christ, and is one of the most venerable fathers of the Oriental Church, and it is written in the very language in question. "Besides this, the faithful who came after His time would have been deprived of His Body and Blood;"—he is giving a reason why Christ instituted the Eucharist. "But now, as often as we approach to the Body and Blood, and receive them in our hands, we embrace His Body, and are made partakers of Him; for Christ did not call it a type or figure of His Body; but said, verily, 'This *is* my Body,—this *is* my Blood.'"*

So far, therefore, from the writers of these passages believing that our Saviour wished to institute a figure, and that He had no means of using a specific word for that purpose, they expressly tell us that we must believe our Saviour to have instituted a real presence, because, speaking their language, he said, "This is my Body," and did not say, "This is the figure of my Body."

I appeal to you, now, if any knowledge which I may possess of these languages, little though it may be, is any reason for my rejection of a doctrine supported by such rash assertions as these, which a very elementary acquaintance with their source enabled me to confute? Let this serve as a warning not easily to believe general and sweeping assertions, unless very solid proof is brought forward; not to be content with the authority of any learned man, unless he give you clear and strong reasons for his opinion. I have entered more into detail, and come forward more personally than I could have wished, and than I should have done, had it not been for the manner in which I was taunted, however privately, with maintaining doctrines which my own peculiar pursuits should have taught me to reject. "If I have been foolish, it is you who have forced me."

I must not forget to mention one circumstance, in justice to my cause, and perhaps to an individual also. I have said that Mr. Horne had adopted that passage of Dr. Adam Clarke, in which this assertion was made. This transcription was reprinted through the different editions of his work, till the seventh, published in 1834, in which he expunged the passage;† showing, consequently, that he was satisfied with the explanation and the confutation given to the assertion of Dr. Adam Clarke. This was only to be expected from any honest and upright man; but

---

* P. 57–60.   † Vol. ii. p. 449.

it proves he was satisfied that the assertion which he had until then repeated was incorrect. Dr. Lee, professor of Oriental Languages at Cambridge, in his Prolegomena to Bagster's Polyglot Bible, acknowledges that his friend, Mr. Horne, was decidedly wrong in making such an assertion. These concessions do not leave the confutation to rest on my individual assertion; they prove it to be acknowledged on the other side that the question is at an end.

The second objection to which I wish to reply, contains a similar misstatement. It has been often said, that the apostles had a very natural clue to the interpretation of our Saviour's words, by the ceremony or formula ordinarily used in the celebration of the Paschal feast. We are told by many writers, and modern ones particularly, that it was customary, at the Jewish passover, for the master of the house to take in his hand a morsel of unleavened bread, and pronounce these words: "This is the bread of affliction which our fathers eat;"—evidently meaning, "This represents the bread which our fathers eat." Consequently, the formula of institution being so similar, we may easily suppose our Saviour to have spoken in the same sense, signifying, "This bread is the figure of my Body." In the first place, I deny entirely and completely, that the expression meant, "This is the figure of the bread:"—it meant, obviously and naturally, "This is *the sort of* bread which our fathers eat." If any person held a piece of some particular bread in his hand, and said, "This is the bread which they eat in France or in Arabia," would he not be understood to say, "This is *the kind of* bread they eat there," and not "This is the figure of their bread?"—and in the case referred to, is not the natural meaning of the words, "This unleavened bread is the sort of bread which our fathers eat?"

But, in fact, it is not necessary to spend much time in illustrating this reply; for no such formula existed at our Saviour's time. We have, in the first place, among the oldest writings of the Jews, a treatise on the paschal feast—it is their authoritative book on the subject—in which is minutely laid down all that is to be done in the celebration of the pasch. Every ceremony is detailed, and a great many foolish and superstitious observances are given; but not a single word of this speech, not the least notice of it. This silence of the ritual prescribing the forms to be followed, must be considered equivalent to a denial of its being used. There is also another still later treatise on the pasch, in which there is not a word regarding such a practice. We come at length to Maimonides, eleven or twelve hundred years after Christ, and he is the first writer who gives this formula. He first describes one ceremonial of the pasch, exceedingly detailed, and then concludes, "So did they celebrate the pasch before the destruction of the temple." In this there is not a word of this practice—it is not hinted at. He proceeds to say,—"at present, the Jews celebrate the pasch in the following manner." In this second rite we have that ceremony; but even then the words used are not in the form of an address, but are only the beginning of a hymn to be sung after eating the paschal lamb. Thus, the ceremony was not introduced till after the destruction of the temple; or rather, as appears from two older treatises, was not in use seven or eight hundred years after Christ; and, consequently, could not have been any guide for the apostles towards interpreting our text.

These two objections I have selected, because their answers are not so much within the range of ordinary controversy, and because they have about them an air of learning which easily imposes upon superficial readers. The great body of objections, usually urged from Scripture against our interpretation, has been incorporated in my proofs, for it consists chiefly of the texts which I have discussed at length, and proved to be of no service towards overthrowing our belief. Of one or two detached texts, I shall have better opportunity for treating, on Sunday next, when, please God, I shall proceed to finish the Scriptural proofs, and, at the same time, give you the tradition upon this important dogma, thus bringing it, and the entire course, to its conclusion. There is much to say on the various contradictions into which the Protestant system leads its upholders, and of the extravagances into which many of them have fallen. But sufficient has been said to build up the Catholic truth, and this is the most important matter. That error will be ever inconsistent, is but the result of its very nature. Let us only hope that, in its constant shiftings, it may catch a glimpse of the truth, and, from the very impulse of its restless character, be led to study it; and, by the discontent of its perpetual agitations, be brought to embrace it—in whose profession alone is true peace, and satisfaction, and joy.

LECTURE THE SIXTEENTH.

TRANSUBSTANTIATION.

PART III.

1 COR. x. 16.

"*The cup of benediction which we bless, is it not the communion of the blood of Christ? And the bread which we break, is it not the partaking of the body of the Lord?*"

WISHING, my brethren, to bring to a conclusion, this evening, the important topic which has occupied us for two successive Sundays, it will be necessary for me to step back for a few moments, to bring you to the point at which I left my argument; as the observations which must follow are necessarily the sequel to those which preceded them, and form, indeed, but part of the train of argument which I laid down for myself at the commencement of my last discourse. In stating the position which the Catholic holds, when treating the arguments for his doctrine of the Eucharist, drawn from the words of institution, I observed that the burthen of proving necessarily lies on those who maintain that we must depart from the strict and literal meaning of our Saviour's words, and that, contrary to their natural and obvious import, these words must be taken in a symbolical and figurative sense. I, therefore, laid down the line of argument which I conceived to be strongest on the side of our opponents; and it led us into a twofold investigation: first, whether the expressions in question can possibly be interpreted in their figurative signification; and, secondly, whether any reasons exist to justify this less ordinary course, and to force us to a preference of this figurative interpretation.

With regard to the first: adhering strictly to the principle of biblical interpretation which I first laid down, I went in detail through the various passages of Scripture advanced to prove that the words of institution may be interpreted figuratively, without going contrary to ordinary forms of speech in the New Testament, and more particularly in our Saviour's discourses. I canvassed them, to show you that it was impossible to establish any such parallelism between our words and the examples quoted, as could give the right to interpret our text by them. This formed the first portion of the inquiry, and occupied your attention during our last Sunday meeting.

The second portion of my task remains; to see what the reasons or motives may be for preferring that figurative and harsh interpretation, even at the expense, if I may say so, of propriety; to investigate whether there be not reasons so strong, as to oblige us to choose any expedient rather than interpret our Saviour's words in their simple and obvious meaning. I believe I noticed, that this is the argument very generally advanced by writers on this subject, that we must interpret our Saviour's words figuratively, because, otherwise, we are driven into such an ocean of absurdities, that it is impossible to reconcile the doctrine with sound philosophy or common sense. While on this subject, I may observe, that it is not very easy, even at the outset, and before examining its difficulties, to admit this form of argument. Independently of all that I shall say a little later, regarding these supposed difficulties, the question may be placed in this point of view:—are we to take the Bible simply as it is, and allow it alone to be its own interpreter?—or are we to bring in other extraneous elements to modify that interpretation? If there are certain rules for interpreting the Bible, and if all those rules in any instance converge, to show us that certain words will not, and can not, bear any interpretation but one, I ask, if there can be any means or instrument of interpretation, of sufficient strength to overpower them all? If we admit such a case, do we not reduce to a nullity the entire system of biblical interpretation?

I find, however, that, with reflecting men, or, at least, with those who are considered able divines, on the Protestant side of the question, it has become much more usual than it used to be, to acknowledge that this is not the method in which the text should be examined. They are disposed to allow that we have no right to consider the apparent impracticability, or impossibility of the doctrine, but must let it stand or fall fairly and solely by the authority of Scripture; and, however the circumstances may be repugnant to our feelings or reason, if proved on grounds of sound interpretation, admit it as taught by God Himself. To establish this concession, I will content myself with a single authority, that of one who has been not merely the most persevering, but also (for the expression is not too harsh) one of the most virulent of our adversaries, and who, particularly on this subject of the Eucharist, has taken extraordinary pains to

LECTURE XVI.

overthrow our belief. Mr. Faber writes in these words, on the subject now under consideration:

"While arguing upon this subject, or incidentally mentioning it, some persons, I regret to say, have been too copious in the use of those unseemly words, 'absurdity and impossibility.' To such language, the least objection is its reprehensible want of good manners. A much more serious objection is the tone of presumptuous loftiness which pervades it, and is wholly unbecoming a creature of very narrow faculties. Certainly, God *will* do nothing that is absurd, and *can* do nothing impossible. But it does not, therefore, follow, that our view of things should be always perfectly correct, and free from misapprehension. Contradictions we can easily *fancy*, where, in truth, there are none. Hence, therefore, before we consider any doctrine a contradiction, we must be sure we perfectly understand the nature of the matter propounded in that doctrine: for otherwise, the contradiction may not be *in the matter itself*, but *in our mode of conceiving it*. In regard to myself,—as my consciously finite intellect claims not to be an universal measure of congruities and possibilities,—I deem it to be both more wise and more decorous to refrain from assailing the doctrine of Transubstantiation, on the ground of its alleged absurdity, or contradictoriness, or impossibility. By such a mode of attack, we, in reality, quit the field of rational and satisfactory argumentation.

"The doctrine of Transubstantiation, like the doctrine of the Trinity, is a question, not of abstract reasoning, but of pure *evidence*. We believe the revelation of God to be essential and unerring truth. Our business most plainly is, not to discuss the abstract absurdity, and the imagined contradictoriness, of Transubstantiation, but to inquire, according to the best means we possess, whether it be indeed a doctrine of Holy Scripture. If sufficient evidence shall determine such to be the case, we may be sure that the doctrine is neither absurd nor contradictory. I shall ever contend, that the doctrine of Transubstantiation, like the doctrine of the Trinity, is a question of *pure evidence*."*

These observations are extremely sensible, and the comparison which the author makes with another mystery, as I shall show you later, sufficiently demonstrates it to be correct. However, I do not, of course, mean to shelter myself behind his authority, or that of any other writer; I will not content myself with saying, that sensible and acute, yes, excessively acute reasoners

---

* "Difficulties of Romanism," *Lond.* 1826, p. 54.

against us, admit that any fancied difficulties or contradictions are not to be weighed against our interpretation; and thence conclude, that having, I trust, satisfactorily examined the allegations on the other side, and proved them insufficient, we cannot, according to the obvious rule of interpretation, depart from the literal sense. I have no such intention, my brethren. On the contrary, I mean to meet these difficulties, but without departing one step from the ground which I have chosen from the beginning. I laid it down as my method and rule of interpretation, that the true meaning of words or texts, is that meaning which the speaker must have known would be affixed to his words by those whom he addressed, and that we are to put ourselves in their situation, and know what means they had for explaining his words, and then interpret according to those means alone. For, we are not to suppose that our Saviour spoke sentences, which those who heard Him had no means of understanding, but which we alone were afterwards to understand. If, therefore, we wish to ascertain what were their means of interpreting the words in question, we must invest ourselves with the feelings of the apostles, and make our inquiry in their position.

It is said, then, that we must depart from the literal sense of our Saviour's words, because that literal sense involves an impossibility or contradiction. The simple inquiry to be made, is, therefore, could the apostles have reasoned in this manner? or could our Saviour have meant them so to reason? Could they have made the possibility or impossibility of any thing He uttered be the criterion of its true interpretation? And if He did not intend that for a criterion, which, as you will see, must, if used, have led them astray, it is evident, that by it we must not interpret the text. I beg you to observe, in the first place, that the investigation into possibility or impossibility, when spoken with reference to the Almighty, is philosophically of a much deeper character than we can suppose, not merely ordinary, but positively illiterate and uneducated men, to have been qualified to fathom. What is possible or impossible to God? What is contradictory to his power? Who shall venture to define it, further than what may be the obvious, the first, and simplest principle of contradiction,—the existence and simultaneous non-existence of a thing? But who will pretend to say, that any ordinary mind would be able to measure this perplexed subject, and to reason thus—"The Almighty may, indeed, for instance, change water into wine, but that he cannot change bread into a body." Who that looks on these two propositions, with

LECTURE XVI.

the eye of an uneducated man, could say, that, in his mind, there was such a broad distinction between them, that while he saw one effected by the power of a Being believed by him to be omnipotent, he still held the other to be of a class so widely different, as to venture to pronounce it absolutely impossible? Suppose, again, that such a person had seen our Saviour, or any one else, take into his hands a certain portion of bread, seven or five loaves, and with these very identical loaves, as the Gospel narrative tells us, feed and satisfy three or five thousand individuals, so that basketfuls should remain of the fragments; not creating more substance, but making that which existed suffice for the effects of a much larger quantity, and then were told that the same powerful Being could not make a body, or other food, be at the same time in two places. Would he, think you, at once be able directly and boldly to pronounce in his mind, that, although he had seen the one, although there could be no doubt that the agent was endowed with such superior power to effect it, yet the other belonged philosophically to such a different class of phenomena, that his power was not equal to effecting it? I will say, that not merely an uneducated man, but that the most refined reasoner, or the most profound thinker, if he admitted one of these facts as having been true and proved, could not pretend to say that the other belonged to a different sphere of philosophical laws—he could not reject the one from its contradictions, in spite of the demonstration that the other had been.

Now, such as I have described, were the minds of the apostles, those of illiterate, uncultivated men. They had been accustomed to see Christ perform the most extraordinary works—they had seen Him walking on the water, His body consequently deprived, for a time, of the usual properties of matter; of that gravity which, according to the laws of nature, should have caused it to sink. They had seen Him, by His simple word, command the elements, and even raise the dead to life; they had also witnessed those two miracles to which I have alluded, that of transmuting one substance into another, and that of multiplying a body, or extending it to an immense degree. Can we, then, believe, that with such minds as these, and with such evidences, the apostles were likely to have words addressed to them by our Saviour, which they were to interpret rightly, only by the reasoning of our opponents,—that is, on the ground of what he asserted being philosophically impossible?

Moreover, we find our Saviour impressed His followers with the idea, that nothing was impossible to Him; that He never reproved them so severely as when they doubted His power. "Oh! thou of little faith, why dost thou fear?" He had so completely inspired His followers with this feeling, that when they applied to Him for any miracle, they never said, "If thou canst,—if it be in thy power;" it was only His will which they wished to secure; the man with the leprosy accordingly exclaims,—"Lord, *if thou wilt* thou canst make me clean." "Lord," said Martha, "if thou hadst been here, my brother had not died, but even now I know that *whatever* thou askest of God He will give to thee." To this extent, therefore, had their faith in Him been strengthened, as to believe that whatever He asked of God, whatever He willed, that He could effect.

Nor is this all; but our Saviour encouraged this belief to the utmost. How did He answer the man with the leprosy? "*I will*, be thou made clean." "Your cure depends on my will; you were right in appealing to this attribute—the mere act of my volition will effect it." How did He reply to Martha? "Father, I thank thee that thou hast heard me, and I know that thou hearest me always." He confirmed, therefore, this idea in them, that nothing was impossible to Him. Moreover, we hear Him commend the faith of the centurion: "I have not found such faith in Israel!" And why? Because the centurion believed and asserted, that it was not even necessary for our Saviour to be present to perform a miracle. "Amen, amen, I say to you, that I have not found such faith in Israel,"—not such an estimate of my power as this man had formed. Now, therefore, again, if such was the conviction of the apostles, and if our Saviour had taken such pains to confirm it in them, that nothing whatever was impossible to Him, can you believe for a moment, that He meant them to decide on the meaning of His words on any occasion, by assuming that their accomplishment was impossible to Him?

Furthermore, we find Him making this the great test of His false and true disciples; that the first, as we read in the 6th chapter of John, went away from Him, remarking,—"This is a hard saying, and who can hear it?" and the second remained faithful, in spite of their not being able to comprehend His doctrine. Wherefore He formally approved of the twelve, saying: "Have I not chosen you twelve?" Although evidently in some darkness and perplexity, they persevered, and remained attached to Him; they yielded up their judgment and reason to His authority: "To whom shall we go, for thou hast the words of eternal life?" Again, then, our Saviour had accustomed His

LECTURE XVI. 171

apostles to this argument on every occasion: "Although this thing may appear impossible to us, as our divine Master says it, it must be so." Can we believe, then, that, on this one occasion of the institution of the Eucharist, He made use of expressions, the only key to whose right interpretation was to be precisely the inverse of this their usual argument, namely: "Although our divine Master says, 'This is my body and blood,' because the thing is impossible it cannot be so?" If our Saviour could not possibly have expected His apostles to reason on the true meaning of His words from any question of the possibility or impossibility of what He seemed to say, if such a consideration cannot have been the key to a right understanding, which they could possibly have thought of using, then of course it cannot be the instrument of interpretation, or the key to their meaning with us; because that only is the true meaning which the apostles attached to His words, and that only is the process of arriving at it, whereby they could reach, and must have reached it.

But, my brethren, as I before hinted, are we safe in at all admitting this principle of contradiction to the law of nature, of apparent violation of philosophical principles, as a means of interpreting Scripture? What, I will ask, becomes of all mystery? Once let go the curb, and where, or how, will you stop or check your career? If the clearest words of Scripture are thus to be forced, because, as they stand, we conceive them to contain an impossibility, how will you vindicate the Trinity or the Incarnation, each of which is no less at variance with the apparent laws of nature? And, after all, what do we know of nature, we who cannot explain the production from its seed of the blade of grass on which we tread? who cannot penetrate the qualities of an atom of air which we inhale? Perplexed in our inquiries after the most simple elements of creation, baffled in every analysis of the most obvious properties of matter, shall we, in our religious contests, make a magic wand of our stunted reason, and boldly describe with it a circle round Omnipotence, which it shall not presume to overstep? But, until we can be certain that we are perfectly acquainted with all the laws of nature, and, what is more, with all the resources of Omnipotence, we have no right to reject the clearest assurances of the Son of God, because they happen to be at variance with our established notions.

Again, I ask, what becomes of that very mystery which we observed Faber put in a parallel with that of Transubstantiation when he commented upon this argument? What becomes of the Trinity? What becomes of the incarnation of our Saviour? What of his birth from a Virgin? And, in short, what of every mystery of the Christian religion? Who will pretend to say that he can, by any stretch of his imagination, or of his reason, see how, by possibility, three persons in one God can be but one Godhead? If the contradiction, the apparent contradiction, to the laws of nature, is so easily received, without being understood by us here, is it to be a principle for rejecting another doctrine as clearly laid down in Scripture? And if the doctrine of the Eucharist, which is even more plainly expressed than it, is to be rejected on such a ground, how is it possible for one moment to retain the other? Its very idea appears at first sight repugnant to every law of number; and no philosophical, mathematical, or speculative reasoning, will ever show *how* it possibly can be. You are content, therefore, to receive this important dogma, shutting your eyes, as you should do, to its incomprehensibility; you are content to believe it, because the revelation of it from God was confirmed by the authority of antiquity; and, therefore, if you wish not to be assailed on it by the same form of reasoning and arguments as you use against us, you must renounce this method; and, simply because it comes by revelation from God, receive the Real Presence at once, in spite of the apparent contradiction to the senses; for He hath revealed it, who hath the words of eternal life.

It is repeatedly said, that such a miracle as that of the Eucharist, the existence of Christ's body in the way we suppose it to be there, is contrary to all that our senses, or that experience can teach us. Now, suppose that a heathen philosopher had reasoned in that manner, when the mystery of our Saviour's incarnation, the union of God with man, was first proposed to him by the apostles; he would have had a perfect right to disbelieve it on such grounds; for he would have had not merely theory, but the most uninterrupted experience, on his side. He could have said it is a thing that never happened, which we cannot conceive to happen, and, consequently, so far as the unanimous testimony of all mankind to the possibility or impossibility of the doctrine goes, it is perfectly decisive. When, therefore, any mystery is revealed by God, and the observation applies chiefly to those mysteries which have their beginning in time, such as the incarnation, it is evident that, up to that time, there must be against it all the weight of philosophical observation, all the code or canon of laws, called the law of nature, which can be deduced solely from experience or philosophical observation. For, as the

LECTURE XVI. 173

law of nature is composed of that code of rules by which experience shows us nature is constantly guided, it is manifest that, experience not having given examples of such a fact, the law of nature must necessarily appear to stand in contradiction to the mystery. The only question is, cannot a mystery be instituted by God? Or, cannot it be revealed by Him? And is not that a sufficient modification of the law of nature? And the more so, when it pleases God to make it dependent on a consistent, however supernatural, action.

Or, to take an illustration from the sacrament of Baptism, who would say that, were it to be tried by the laws of nature, or even by the connection between the spiritual and material world, that sacrament would not stand to all appearance in contradiction with them? Who will pretend to say that there is any known connection between those two orders of being, which could prove, or make it even appear possible, that, by the bare action of water, applied with certain words to the body, the soul could be cleansed from sin, and placed in a state of grace before God? It is manifest, on the contrary, that our experience in the physical and material world would lead us to conclude that such a thing could not be. But has not God in this case modified the law of nature? Has He not allowed a moral influence to act under certain circumstances? Has He not been pleased, that the moment the sacramental act is performed, certain consequences should flow, as necessarily as the consequence of any physical law must succeed to the act that produces it? Has He not bound Himself by a covenant, in the same way as in the material world, that when certain laws are brought into action, He will give them their supernatural effect? And does not the same rule precisely apply here? If he who enacted the law of nature chooses to make this modification of it—chooses to make certain effects dependent on certain spiritual causes—it no more stands in opposition to it, than other superhuman exceptions to philosophical laws: for both stand exactly on the same strong grounds.

In fact, my brethren, this seems so obvious, that several writers, and not of our religion, agree that on this point it is impossible to assail us; and observe that this doctrine of Transubstantiation does not, as is vulgarly supposed, contradict the senses. One of these I wish most particularly to mention; it is the celebrated Leibnitz. He left behind him a work, entitled, "A System of Theology," written in the Latin tongue, which was deposited in a public library in Germany, and was not laid before the public until a very few years back, when the manuscript was procured by the late King of France, and published by M. D'Émery, in the original, with a French translation. Leibnitz, in this work, examines the Catholic doctrine on every point, and compares it with the Protestant; and on this matter, in particular, enters into very subtle and metaphysical reasoning; and the conclusion to which he comes is, that in the Catholic doctrine there is not the smallest opening for assailing it on philosophical principles; and, that these form no reasons for departing from the literal interpretation of the words of institution.

Thus, it would appear, that the ground on which it is maintained that we must depart from the literal sense, is untenable—untenable on philosophical grounds, as well as on principles of biblical interpretation. But besides this mere rejection of the motives whereon the literal sense is abandoned, we have ourselves strong and positive confirmation of it.

1. In the first place, the very words themselves, in which the pronoun is put in a vague form, strongly uphold us. Had our Saviour said, "This bread is my body,—this wine is my blood," there would have been some contradiction,—the apostles might have said, "Wine cannot be his blood,—bread cannot be a body;" but when our Saviour uses this indefinite word, we arrive at its meaning only at the conclusion of the sentence, by that which is predicated of it. When we find that in Greek there is a discrepancy of gender between that pronoun and the word "bread," it is more evident that He wished to define the pronoun, and give it its character, as designating His body and blood; so that, by analyzing the words themselves, they give us our meaning positively and essentially.

2. But, this is still further confirmed by the explanations which He adds to it; for persons using vague symbolical language, would be careful not to define too minutely the object pointed at. Now, our Saviour says, "This is my Body which is broken or delivered for you, and this is my Blood which is shed;"—by the addition of these adjuncts to the thing, by uniting to them what could only be said of His true Body and Blood, it would appear that He wanted still more to define and identify the objects which he signified.

3. There are considerations likewise drawn from the circumstances in which our Blessed Saviour was placed. Can any of you conceive yourselves, if, with a certain prophetic assurance that in a few more hours you would be taken away from your family and friends, you had called them around you, to make to them your last bequests, and explain what you wished to be per-

formed in remembrance of you for ever, that which was more especially to bind them after your death to your memory,—can you imagine yourselves making use of words, of their very nature leading to a totally different meaning from what you had in your mind, or wished to appoint? And suppose that you were gifted with a still greater degree of foresight, and could see what would in future be the result of using these words—how by far the greater part of your children, not believing it possible that you could have any hidden meaning on such an occasion, would determine to take your words quite literally, whence you foresaw the complete defeat or perversion of your wishes; while only a very small number would divine that you had spoken figuratively; do you think that under such circumstances you would choose that phraseology, when it was possible, without the waste of another syllable, explicitly to state the true meaning which you wished them to receive?

4. Again, our Saviour himself on that night seems determined to make his words as plain and simple as He can; and it is impossible to read His last discourse to the apostles, as related by St. John, and not observe how often He was interrupted by them, and mildly, and gently, and lovingly explained Himself to them. And not so satisfied, He Himself tells them—that He is not going to speak any longer in parables to them; that the time was come when He would no longer speak to them as their master, but as their friend, as one who wished to unbosom Himself completely to them, and make them understand His words; so that even they say, "Behold, now thou speakest plainly, and speakest no proverb."* Under these circumstances, can we suppose that He would make use of those exceedingly obsure words, when instituting this last and most beautiful mystery of love, in commemoration of their last meeting here on earth? These are strong corroborations, and all lead us to prefer the literal meaning, as the only reconcilable with the particular situation in which the words were uttered.

But, my brethren, there are two other passages of Scripture which must not be passed over, although it will not be necessary to dwell very long upon them; they are in the Epistles of St. Paul to the Corinthians. One of them I have chosen as my text; but the other is still more remarkable. In the first, St. Paul asks, "The cup of blessing which we bless, is it not the communion of the Body of Christ? and the bread which we break, is it not the par-

* John xvi. 29.

LECTURE XVI.

taking of the Body of the Lord?" In these words, the apostle is contrasting the Jewish and heathenish sacrifices and rites with those of the Christians. No doubt but, when he speaks of their actions and sacrifices, it is of eating and drinking really that he treats, for, indeed, he is speaking of realities throughout. When, therefore, he contrasts these with the realities of the Christian institutions, and when he asks if these be not infinitely better and perfecter than what the Jews enjoyed, because our cup is a partaking of the Blood of Christ, and our bread was a partaking of the Body of the Lord, do not these words imply that there was a contrast, a real contrast, between the two?—that the one was partaken of as really as the other? that if their victims were truly eaten, we also have one that is no less received?

But, on the other text, I have a great deal more to remark, for it is one of the strongest passages which we could desire in favor of our doctrine. In the following chapter, St. Paul enters at length into the institution of the Last Supper, and he there describes our Saviour's conduct on that occasion exactly as St. Matthew, St. Luke, and St. Mark have done, making use of precisely the same simple words. But then he goes on to draw consequences from this doctrine. He has not left us the bare narrative, as the other sacred penmen have done, but he draws practical conclusions from it, and builds upon it solemn injunctions, accompanied with awful threats. Here, at any rate, we must expect plain and intelligible phraseology, and expressions noways likely to mislead. How, then, does he write?—"He that eateth and drinketh unworthily, eateth and drinketh judgment to himself, not discerning the Body of the Lord." Again: "Whosoever shall eat this bread, or drink the chalice of the Lord unworthily, shall be guilty of the Body and Blood of the Lord."*

Here are two denunciations, founded by St. Paul on the doctrine of the Eucharist. The first is, that whosoever receives unworthily drinks judgment or damnation to himself, because he does not discern the Body of the Lord. What is the meaning of discerning the Body of Christ? Is it to distinguish it from ordinary food, to make a difference between it and other things? But if the Body of Christ be not really there, how can the offence be considered as directed against the Body of Christ? It may be against His dignity or goodness, but surely it is not an offence against His body. But, on the second sentence, it is curious to observe, that, throughout Scripture, the form of speech

---

* 1 Cor. xi. 27, 29.

LECTURE XVI.

there used occurs only once besides, in the Epistle of St. James, ii. 10, where it is said, that whoever "transgresses one commandment is guilty of all,"—that is, of a violation or transgression of all the commandments. It is the only passage parallel in construction to this, where the unworthy communicant is said to be guilty,—not of injury, not of crime,—but guilty of the thing against which the crime is committed,—that is, guilty of the Body of Christ. This is a peculiar expression, and perhaps may be illustrated by a similar form in the Roman law, where a man guilty of treason, or an offence against majesty, is simply called "guilty of majesty," (*reus majestatis*,)—that is, of an injury or offence against it. We see here, that the unworthy receiver is guilty of the Body, that is, of an offence against the Body, of Christ; but, as in the one case, if the majesty were not there, that crime could not be committed, so, likewise, unless the Body of our Saviour was here, to be unworthily approached, the abuse of the Eucharist could not be called an offence against it. Nay, rather such a designation would diminish the guilt. For to say that a person offends against Christ Himself, or that he offends against God, is a much greater denunciation of guilt, than to say that he offends against the Body of Christ, except in cases of actual personal injury. For while the greatest outrage possible would be one against His Body, when personally ill-treated, as in the case of the Jews, who buffeted and crucified him; yet, in its absence, it is the weakest mode of describing the offence, when we are to suppose Him sitting at the right hand of God, and, consequently, not to be approached by man.

Now, looking at all the Scripture texts on the Eucharist, conjointly, there is an observation which can hardly fail to strike any considerate and reflecting mind. We bring to bear on it four distinct classes of texts. First, we have a long discourse delivered by our Saviour under particular circumstances, a considerable time before his passion. Others suppose Him to have, throughout it, treated of faith, or the necessity of believing in Him. Yet, through a certain part of that discourse, He studiously avoids any expression which could possibly lead His hearers to understand Him in that sense, but again and again uses phrases which naturally bring all who heard Him to believe that it was necessary to eat His flesh and drink His blood—to receive His body; and He allows the crowd to murmur, and His disciples to fall away, and His apostles to remain in darkness, without explaining away their difficulties.

Let us allow that, for once, our Saviour spoke and acted so;

we come, secondly, to another quite different occasion. It is no longer the obstinate Jews, or unsteady disciples, whom He addresses: He is alone with His chosen twelve. He no longer wishes to speak of faith, as all agree; he wishes, according to Protestants, to institute a symbol commemorative of His passion; and, most extraordinarily, he uses words, conveying precisely the same ideas as on the other occasion, when speaking of quite another subject, having no reference at all to that institution. And all this is related by several of the evangelists without comment, in nearly the same words; they evidently consider it a most important institution;—but still we receive not a hint from one of them that the words are to be understood figuratively.

We come, in the third place, to St. Paul, where he wishes, in the words of my text, to prove that this commemorative rite of the Christians is superior to the sacrifices eaten by the Jews and heathens. Once more, although there is not the slightest necessity for such marked expressions, but he might have used the words *symbol*, or *figure*, or *emblem*,—although writing on a totally different occasion, and addressing a different people, he falls into the same extraordinary phraseology, he makes use of precisely the same words, and speaks as if the real Body and Blood of Christ were partaken of. He goes on to reprove the bad use of this rite. At least, on this fourth occasion, there is room to illustrate in a different manner,—opportunity enough to describe its true character; but once more he returns to the same unusual phrases, of Christ's Body and Blood being received, and tells us that those who partake of this Blessed Sacrament unworthily are guilty of an outrage on that Body. Now, is it not strange, that on these four different occasions, our Saviour, and his apostles, explaining different doctrines—speaking to different assemblies, under totally different circumstances,—should all concur in using these words in a figurative meaning, and not let one syllable slip as a key or guide to the true interpretation of their doctrine? Is it even possible to suppose, that our Saviour, discoursing in the 6th chapter of St. John, and St. Paul writing to the Corinthians, though treating of different subjects, under varied circumstances,—should have adopted similar, figurative, and most unusual language? But take the simple interpretation which the Catholic does, and from the first to the last there is not the slightest difficulty; there may be some struggle against the senses or feelings—it may appear new, strange, and perhaps unnatural to you; but so far as biblical interpretation goes, so far as the fair principles for examining God's word are concerned, all is consistent from first to last. You believe the expressions to be literal throughout, and you believe the very same topic to be treated in every one of these passages; and consequently, you have harmony and analogy from the first to the last on your side. Whereas, on the other hand, you must find different explanations of the same imagery and phraseology on those various occasions; and you are driven to the miserable expedient of choosing some little word or phrase in a corner of the narrative, and persuading yourself that it overthrows all the obvious consequences of the narrative itself, and balances the clear evidence of a connected and consistent proof.

To give an instance of this process:—it is said that, in the case under consideration, we still find the names "bread and wine" applied to the elements after consecration: and that, consequently, all that long line of argument which I have gone through is worth nothing: this one fact overthrows it all. Why, we Catholics call it bread and wine after it has been consecrated; and will any man thence argue, that we do not believe a change to have taken place in the elements? These names, then, may be employed, and yet the doctrine which we hold be maintained. In the 9th chapter of St. John, our Saviour performs the cure of a man that was blind; he restores him perfectly to sight; and there is a long altercation between him and the Jews on the subject, which beautifully demonstrates the miracle. The blind man is called in, and questioned again and again, as to whether he had been blind; they bring forward his parents and friends to identify him; they all testify that the man was born blind; and that Jesus, by a miracle, had cured him. But reason in the same way here as in our case. Verse 17, we read, "They say again to the *blind man;*" —he is called blind after the miracle is said to have been wrought; therefore, the whole of the reasoning based on that chapter is worth nothing; the fact of his being still called blind proves that no change had taken place! Precisely this reasoning is used against our doctrine; all the clear, express, incontestable expressions of our Saviour to the apostles are of no value, because, after the consecration, He still calls the elements bread and wine! We have a similar instance in the case of Moses, when his rod was changed into a serpent; and yet it continued to be called a rod; and are we then to suppose that no such change had been made? But it is the usage, the common method in all language, when such a change occurs, to continue the original name. It is said, in the narration of the miracle at the marriage feast, "When, therefore, the master of the feast had tasted *the water* made wine." It could not be both water and wine it should have been called simply wine, but it is called "water made wine," so as to preserve the name which it had before. These examples are sufficient to show that such expressions as these must not be taken, by any sincere inquirer, as the ground of interpretation for the entire passage, nor made to outweigh the complicated difficulties that attend its being taken figuratively.

We naturally must desire, on a question like this, to ascertain the sentiments of antiquity. Now, in examining the opinions of the early Church on this subject, we meet with a most serious difficulty, resulting from the circumstance which I made use of on a former occasion, as a strong corroboration of the Catholic rule of faith; that is, the discipline of the secret, whereby converts were not admitted to a knowledge of the principal mysteries of Christianity until after they had been baptized. The chief practical mystery of which they were kept in ignorance, was the belief concerning the Eucharist. It was the principle, as I observed on that occasion, among the early Christians, to preserve inviolable secrecy regarding what passed in that most important portion of the service, the liturgy of the Church. For instance, there is a distinction made by old writers between the Mass of the catechumens and the Mass of the faithful. The Mass of the catechumens was that part to which they were admitted, and the Mass of the faithful was that portion from which the catechumens were excluded. Consequently they, and still less the heathens, knew nothing of what was practised in the Church during the solemnization of the mysteries. This is manifest from innumerable passages, especially where the fathers speak of the Eucharist. Nothing is more common than to find such expressions as these: "What I am now saying or writing is for the initiated,"—"the faithful know what I mean." "If," says one of them, "you ask a catechumen, does he believe in Jesus Christ, he makes the sign of the cross, as a token of his belief in Christ's incarnation and death for us; but if you ask him, have you eaten the Flesh of Christ, and drunk his Blood, he knows not what you mean." We find this extraordinary passage in St. Epiphanius, when wishing to allude to the Eucharist:—"What were the words which our Saviour used at his Last Supper? He took into his hand a certain thing, and he said, it is so and so." Thus he avoids making use of words which would expose the belief of the Christians. Origen expressly says, that any one who betrays these mysteries is worse than a murderer: St. Augustine, St. Ambrose, and others, affirm that they are traitors to their religion who do so. The consequence was, as Tertullian observes, that the heathens knew nothing whatever of what was done in the Church; and when they charged the Christians with various horrible crimes, as if there perpetrated, these contented themselves with asking, how they could pretend to know any thing about mysteries, to which they were not admitted, and of which such pains were taken that they should know nothing.

This authority sufficiently proves that this discipline was not of later introduction, as some have pretended, but had been received, as early writers tell us, from the time of the apostles. For it would have been vain later to attempt concealment, if all had been open at the beginning. We have a remarkable illustration of this discipline in St. John Chrisostom. In a letter to Pope Julius, he describes a tumult in the Church of Constantinople, in which he says, "they spilled the blood of Christ." He speaks plainly, because writing a private letter to one of the initiated. Not so Palladius, when relating the same circumstance; for he says, they spilled "the symbols known to the initiated;" he was writing the life of the saint, which was to go abroad to the world, and was careful consequently to avoid communicating the mysteries to the uninitiated. There is another instance, in the life of St. Athanasius, who was summoned before a court for breaking a chalice; and the council held at Alexandria, in 360, expressed a horror of the Arians, for having brought the mysteries of the church before the world through this accusation. The same feeling is still more strongly expressed, in a letter from the Pope to him, written in the name of a Council held at Rome. He says,—"We could not believe, when we heard that such a thing as the cup in which the Blood of Christ is administered, had been mentioned before the profane and uninitiated; and until we saw the account of the trial, we did not think such a crime possible."*

This feeling and practice, you cannot fail to observe, must necessarily throw a considerable veil over what is said in early times on the Eucharist; and it is only where accident enables us to pry under it, that we are really able to see what the doctrine of those ages was. The means by which we discover it are various. The first is, the calumnies invented by the enemies of Christianity. We find it asserted by several old writers, and, among them, by Tertullian, the oldest father of the Latin Church, that one of the most common calumnies against the Christians, was, that in their

---

* See my friend Doctor Döllinger's learned treatise, "Die Lehre von der Eucharistie."

assemblies, or sacred meetings, they murdered a child, and, dipping bread in its blood, partook of it. He alludes to this charge repeatedly. St. Justin Martyr tells us that when he was a heathen, he had constantly heard this of the Christians. Origen, likewise, mentions it, as do most writers who have refuted the accusations of Jews and heathens against the Christians. In what way could this calumny have arisen: this fiction, that they dipped bread in the blood of an infant, and eat it,—if they simply partook of bread and wine? Did it not imply that something more had transpired among the heathens, and that the Body and Blood of our Saviour were said to be partaken of on these occasions? Does not the calumny itself insinuate as much?

Secondly, we gain additional light by the manner in which these calumnies are met. Suppose that the belief of the ancient Christians had been that of Protestants; what was more practicable than to refute these accusations? "We do no such thing as you imagine," would have been the reply, "nothing that can even give rise to the charge. We do no more than partake of a little bread and wine, as a rite commemorative of our Lord's passion. Come in, if you please, and see." Would not this have been the simplest plan of confutation? Instead of it, however, they meet the charge in two ways, both very different. In the first place, by not answering it at all; by avoiding the subject, because they would have been obliged to lay open their doctrines, and expose them to the ridicule, the outrage, and the blasphemy of the heathens. Although there would have been nothing at all to fear from the disclosure, had they merely believed in a commemorative rite, their belief was manifestly such as they durst not disclose; they knew to what obloquy the confession of their doctrine would expose them; and consequently, they avoided touching on the subject. A remarkable instance we have in the case of the Martyr Blandina, commended by St. Irenæus. I have not the passage here; but he tells us, that the heathen servants of some Christians, having been put to the rack, to make them reveal their masters' belief, they affirmed, after some time, that, in their mysteries, the Christians partook of flesh and blood. Blandina was presently charged with this guilt, and was put to the torture, to make her confess. But, the historian says, she "most wisely and prudently" answered:—"How can you think we can be guilty of such a crime; we who, from a spirit of mortification, abstain from eating ordinary flesh?" Now, suppose the imputed doctrine had been not at all akin to reality, what was easier than to say,—" We believe no doctrine that bears resemblance to this frightful imputation; we partake of a little bread and wine, as a bond of union, and a commemoration of our Saviour's passion. It is simple bread and wine, and we believe it to be nothing more." She, however, is praised for her wisdom and exceeding prudence, because she did not deny the charge, at the same time that she met the odious and unnatural imputation it contained. The very silence and reserve, then, of the Christians, in answering the charges of the heathens, compared with the accusations themselves, allow us to discover, with tolerable certainty, what was their belief.

However, in the second place, occasionaly an apologist did venture to remove this veil a little for the heathens. St. Justin thought it better, from the peculiar circumstance of his addressing his apology to prudent and philosophical men, like the Antonines, to explain what the real belief of the Christians was in this regard. How does he make his explanation? Remember, that the plainer he spoke the truth, the better he would serve his cause, if the Christian Eucharist was only a commemorative rite. Listen, now, to his explanation of the Christian belief, when wishing to deprive it of all its disagreeable features,—when wishing to remove prejudices and to conciliate. He says, "Our prayers being finished, we embrace one another with the kiss of peace;" a ceremony yet observed in the Catholic mass. "Then to him who presides over the brethren, is presented bread, and wine tempered with water; having received which, he gives glory to the Father of all things, in the name of the Son and the Holy Ghost, and returns thanks, in many prayers, that he has been deemed worthy of these gifts. This food we call the Eucharist, of which they alone are allowed to partake, who believe the doctrines taught by us, and have been regenerated by water for the remission of sin, and who live as Christ ordained. *Nor do we take these gifts as common bread and common drink;* but as Jesus Christ, our Saviour, made man by the word of God, took Flesh and Blood for our salvation; in the same manner, we have been taught, that the food which has been blessed by the prayer of the words which He spoke, and by which our blood and flesh, in the change, are nourished, *is the Flesh and Blood of that Jesus incarnate.*"[*] You see here how he lays open his doctrine in the concisest and simplest manner possible; telling us, that the Eucharist is the Body and Blood of Christ.

But, besides writers placed in the circumstances I have described,

---

[*] Apol. i. Hagæ Comitum. 1742. pp. 82, 83.

there is fortunately another class who have come down to us, into whom we must be naturally most disposed to look for simple information; those who expound for the first time to the newly baptized, what they have to believe on this subject. It was natural that in explaining to them what they were to believe, they should use the simplest language, and define the dogma precisely as they wished it to be believed. Another class again is composed of those whose homilies or sermons are addressed exclusively to the initiated. These two classes afford abundant proofs, besides which there are many passages scattered casually through the writings of others.

In the first instance, I will give a few of those expressly addressed to the newly baptized. The most remarkable of these addresses are those of St. Cyril of Jerusalem, for we have a whole series of his catechetical discourses. In one of them, he warns his hearers to be careful not to communicate what he teaches them to heathens or to the unbaptized, unless they are about to be baptized. Thus he addresses them: "The bread and wine, which, before the invocation of the adorable Trinity, were nothing but bread and wine, become, after this invocation, *the Body and Blood of Christ*."* "The Eucharistic bread, after the invocation of the Holy Spirit, *is no longer common bread, but the Body of Christ*."† This is the clear doctrine, most simply expressed. In another place, he says: "The doctrine of the blessed Paul alone is sufficient to give certain proofs of the truth of the divine mysteries; and you, being deemed worthy of them, are become one body and one blood with Christ." After giving an account of the institution, in the words of St. Paul, he draws this conclusion: "As then Christ, speaking of the bread, declared and said, *This is my Body, who shall dare to doubt it?* And as, speaking of the wine, He positively assured us, and said, *This is my Blood, who shall doubt it and say, that it is not His Blood?*"‡ Again: "Jesus Christ, in Cana of Galilee, once changed water into wine by His will only; and shall we think Him less worthy of credit, when He changes wine into Blood? Invited to an earthly marriage, He wrought this miracle; and shall we hesitate to confess that He has given to His children His Body to eat, and His Blood to drink? Wherefore, with all confidence, let us take the body and blood of Christ. For, in the type of bread, His Body is given to thee, and in the type of

---

* Catech. Mystag. 1, n. vii. p. 308.   † Ibid. Catech. 111. n. iii. p. 316.
‡ Ibid. iv. n. 1, p. 319.

LECTURE XVI.

wine, His Blood is given: that so being made partakers of the Body and Blood of Christ, you may become one Body and one Blood with Him. Thus, the Body and Blood of Christ being distributed in our members, we become *Christofori*, that is, we carry Christ with us; and thus, as St. Peter says, 'We are made partakers of the divine nature.'"* In another place, he expresses himself in even stronger terms: "For as the bread is the nourishment which is proper to the body, so the Word is the nourishment which is proper to the soul. Wherefore, I conjure you, my brethren, not to consider them any more as common bread and wine, since they are the Body and Blood of Jesus Christ according to His words; and although your sense might suggest that to you, let faith confirm you. Judge not of the thing by your taste, but by faith assure yourself, without the least doubt, that you are honored with the Body and Blood of Christ. This knowing, and of this being assured, that what appears to be bread, is not bread, though it be taken for bread by the taste, but is the Body of Christ; and that which appears to be wine, is not the wine, though the taste will have it so, but is the Blood of Christ."† Could the Catholic dogma of transubstantiation be laid down, by any possibility, in terms more marked and explicit than these?

Such, then, were the terms in which the new Christians were initiated and instructed; such is the dogma laid down in elementary catechetical discourses on the subject of the Eucharist.

St. Gregory of Nyssa, is another of these catechetical instructors. Hear him teaching the Christians regarding their new belief. "When this salutary medicine is within us, it repels, by its contrary quality, the poison we had received. But what is this medicine? No other than that Body, which was shown to be more powerful than death, and was the beginning of our life; and which could not otherwise enter into our bodies, than by eating and drinking. Now, we must consider, how it can be, that one body, which so constantly, through the whole world, is distributed to so many thousands of the faithful, can be whole in each receiver, and itself remain whole." The very difficulty made to the Catholic doctrine now-a-days. Hear his answer: "The body of Christ, by the inhabitation of *the Word* of God, was transmuted into a divine dignity: and so I now believe, that the bread, sanctified by *the Word* of God, is transmuted into the body of *the Word* of God. This bread, as the apostle says, *is sanctified by the Word of God, and prayer*, not that, as food, it

---

*Ibid. n. ii. iii. p. 320. †Catech. Myst. n. iv. v. vi. ix. p. 321, 322, 329.

passes into his body, but that it is instantly changed into the Body of Christ, agreeably to what he said, *This is my body*. And therefore does the divine Word commix itself with the weak nature of man, that, by partaking of the divinity, our humanity may be exalted. By the dispensation of His grace, He enters, by His flesh, into the breasts of the faithful, commixed and contempered with their bodies, that, by being united to that which is immortal, man may partake of incorruption."* In this passage we have a word equivalent to transubstantiation, transmuting or changing one substance into another.† On another occasion he says: "It is by virtue of the benediction that *the nature of the visible species is changed into His Body*."—" The bread also is, at first, common bread; but when it has been sanctified, it is called and made the Body of Christ."‡

A distinguished writer of the second class, that is, one who exclusively addresses the initiated, is St. John Chrysostom. Than his homilies to the people of Antioch, nothing possibly can be desired stronger, in demonstration of the Catholic belief. In fact, I hardly know where to begin, or where I shall close my extracts from him. I will take them, therefore, without choice. "Let us, then," he says, " touch the hem of His garment; rather let us, if we be so disposed, possess Him entire. For His Body now lies before us, not to be touched only, but to *be eaten and to satiate us*. And if they who touched His garment, drew so much virtue from it, how much more shall we draw, who *possess Him whole?* Believe, therefore, that the supper, at which He sat, is now celebrated; for there is no difference between the two. This is not performed by a man, and that by Christ. Both are by Him. When, therefore, thou seest the priest presenting the Body to thee, think not that it is his hand, but the hand of Christ that is stretched towards thee."§ Again: " Let us believe God in every thing, and not gainsay Him, although what is said may seem contrary to our reason and our sight. Let his word overpower both. Thus let us do in mysteries, not looking only on the things that lie before us, but holding fast His words; for His word cannot deceive; but our *sense is very easily deceived*. That never failed; this, often. Since, then, His word says: *This is my Body*, let us assent, and believe, and view it with the eyes of our understanding." In another place, "Who," he asks, "will give us of his flesh that we may be filled? (Job xxxi. 31.)

---

* Orat. Catech. c. xxxvii. T. ii. p. 534–7.   † Μετάνοιεισθαι.
‡ Orat. in Bapt. Christi, T. ii. p. 802.
§ Homil. l. in cap. xiv. Matt. T. vii. p. 516, 51"

LECTURE XVI.

This, Christ has done—not only allowing Himself to be seen, but to be touched, too, and to be eaten, and teeth to pierce His flesh, and all to be filled with the love of Him. Parents often give their children to be nourished by others: not so I, says Christ: but I nourish you with my Flesh, and I place myself before you. I was willing to become your brother; for the sake of you, I took Flesh and Blood; and *again I deliver to you that Flesh and Blood*, by which I became so related."*—"What sayest thou, O blessed Paul? Willing to impress awe on the hearer, and making mention of the tremendous mysteries, thou callest them the cup of benediction, (1 Cor. x. 16,) that terrible and tremendous cup. That which is in the cup is *that which flowed from his side*, and we partake of it. It is not of the altar, but of Christ Himself that we partake; let us, therefore, approach to Him with all reverence and purity; and when thou beholdest the Body lying before thee, say to thyself: By this body, I am no longer earth and ashes,—*This is that very Body which bled, which was pierced by the lance.*"†—"He that was present at the Last Supper, is the same that is now present, and consecrates our feast. For it is not man who makes the things lying on the altar become the Body and Blood of Christ; but that Christ who was crucified for us. The Priest stands performing his office, and pronouncing these words,—but the power and grace are the power and grace of God. He says, '*This is my Body,*' and these words effect the change of the things offered."‡—"As many as partake of this Body, as many as taste of this Blood, think ye it nothing different from That which sits above, and is adored by angels."§ One more short passage from him will suffice: he says:—"Wonderful! The table is spread with mysteries; the Lamb of God is slain for thee; and the spiritual blood flows from the sacred table. The spiritual fire comes down from heaven; the blood in the chalice is drawn from the spotless side for thy purification. Thinkest thou, that thou seest bread? that thou seest wine? that these things pass off as other foods do? *Far be it from thee to think so.* But as wax brought near to the fire loses its former substance, which no longer remains; so do thou thus conclude, that the mysteries (the bread and wine) are consumed by the substance of the body. Wherefore, approaching

---

* Homil. xlvi. alias xlv. in Ioan. T. viii. p. 272, 273.
† Homil. xxiv. in 1 Ep. ad. Cor. T. x. pp. 212, 213, 214, 217.
‡ Homil. i. de Prodit. Judæ. T. ii. p. 384.
§ Homil. iii. in c. 1, ad. Ephes. T. xi. p. 21.

to them, think not that you receive the divine Body from a man, but fire from the hand of the Seraphim."*

These are a few examples out of a great many more from the fathers, expressly instructing the faithful without reserve; and see what language they hold! the fact is, that beginning from the earliest times in the Church, we have texts without end, expressing the same belief, sometimes casually mentioned, at other times, although more closely veiled, betraying what their doctrine was. For instance, St. Irenæus says: "This pure oblation the Church alone makes. The Jews make it not, for their hands are stained with blood; and they received not the Word that is offered to God. Nor do the assemblies of heretics make it; for how can these prove that the bread, over which the words of thanksgiving have been pronounced, *is the Body of their Lord*, and the cup *His Blood*, while they do not admit that He is the Son, that is, the Word, of the Creator of the world?"† This is a casual passage in a writer speaking of quite another subject,—of those who deprive themselves of the benefits of redemption, by not believing in Christ.

In the following centuries, the authorities are absolutely overpowering. I will content myself with one or two that seem particularly striking. St. Augustine again and again speaks most strongly of this doctrine, as the following extracts will show. "When, committing to us His Body, He said, *This is my Body*, Christ was held in His own hands. He bore that body in His hands."—"How was He borne in His hands?" he asks in the next sermon on the same Psalm,—"because when *He gave His own Body and Blood*, He took into His hands *what the faithful know;* and He bore Himself in a certain manner, when He said, *This is my Body*."‡ Again: "We receive with a faithful heart and mouth the mediator of God and man, the Man Christ Jesus, who has given us *His Body to eat, and His Blood to drink;* although it may appear more horrible *to eat the flesh of a man*, than to destroy it, and *to drink human blood*, than to spill it."§ I will now read you a splendid testimony of the Oriental Church. It is that of St. Isaac, priest of Antioch, in the fifth century, who writes in these glowing terms: "I saw the vessel mingled, and, for wine, *full of Blood; and the Body*, instead of bread, *placed on the table*. I saw the Blood, and shuddered: I saw the Body,

---

* Homil. ix. de Pænit. T. ii. p. 349, 350.
† Adv. Hær. Lib. iv. c. xviii. p. 251.
‡ In Psal. xiv. T. iv. p. 335.
§ Contra Adv. Legis. et Proph. L. ii. c. ix. T. viii. p. 599.

and was awed with fear. *Faith whispered to me: Eat, and be silent; drink, child, and inquire not.* She showed me the Body, slain, of which, placing a portion on my lips, she said gently: Reflect, what thou eatest. She held out to me a reed, directing me to write. I took the reed; I wrote; I pronounced: *This is the Body of my God.* Taking then the cup, I drank. And what I had said of the Body, that I now say of the cup: *This is the Blood of my Saviour.*"*

I will conclude my quotations with the sentiments of another eminent father, which have been brought to light within the last few years. The passage is remarkable in itself, from the strong confirmation it gives our belief. It is, moreover, a proof how little we have to fear from the discovery of any new writings of the fathers; how much, on the contrary, we should desire to possess them all, because there is no instance of their being recovered, in which they have not done us some good. St. Amphilochius, bishop of Iconium, was the bosom friend of St. Basil, St. Gregory Nazianzen, and St. Jerome, who speak of him as one of the most learned and holy men of their time. Of this father we possess only a few detached fragments, but the little we have is worthy of the fame which he enjoyed. These few remnants contained nothing on the Eucharist, and never even glanced at the subject. Four or five years ago were published, for the first time, the acts of a council held at Constantinople, in 1166, on the text, "The Father is greater than I." The bishops, there assembled, collected a great many passages from the fathers to illustrate these words; and among the rest, one from St. Amphilochius, of which we previously possessed a fragment. The remaining portion, thus recovered, contains a powerful testimony in favor of our doctrine. As it has not yet found its way into popular works, I beg to quote it at length. The writer is asserting the equality of the Father and Son. But, as our Saviour had said, that the Father is greater than He, while on another occasion, He tells us that they are one, St. Amphilochius endeavors to reconcile the two assertions by a series of antitheses, which show how, in some respects, the Father is equal, and in others superior. This is the entire passage: "The Father, therefore, is greater than He who goeth unto him, not greater than He who is always in Him. And that I may speak compendiously; He (the Father) is greater, and yet equal: greater than He who asked, 'How many loaves have ye?'" equal

---

* Serm. de Fide, Bibl. Orient. T. 1. p. 220. *Romæ*, 1719

to Him who satisfied the whole multitude with five loaves, greater than He who asked, 'Where have ye laid Lazarus?' equal to Him who raised Lazarus by His word: greater than He who said, 'Who toucheth me?' equal to Him who dried up the inexhaustible flux of the sick woman: greater than He who slumbered in the vessel; equal to Him who chid the sea: greater than He who was judged by Pilate; equal to Him who freeth the world from judgment: greater than He who was buffeted, and was crucified with thieves; equal to Him who justified the thief freecost: greater than He who was stripped of His raiment: equal to Him who clothes the soul: greater than He to whom vinegar was given to drink; *equal to Him who giveth us His own Blood to drink:* greater than He whose temple was dissolved; equal to Him, who, after its dissolution, raised up His own temple: greater than the former, equal to the latter."* As the proof, then, that Christ and the Father are equal, this Saint alleges that Christ gave us His own Blood to drink. Now, if he had believed Him to present us nothing more than a symbol of His blood, would that be a proof of His divinity, or that the Father and He were equal? Is it of the same character as justifying the sinner freecost, as clothing the soul with grace, freeing the world from judgment, and forgiving the penitent thief, or raising Himself to life? Can the mere institution of a symbol be ranked on an equality with these works of supreme power? And yet St. Amphilochius brings it among the last of his examples of miracles, as one of the strongest proofs of Christ's equality to the Father: and we must consequently understand it to have been, in his estimation, a miracle of the highest order. Nothing but a belief in the Real Presence can justify such an argument; and this would be completely demonstrated, did time allow me to enter into further reflection on the text.† Here we have a testimony recently discovered; see how completely it accords with the doctrine which we maintain.

I have presented you with a very limited view of the argument from tradition; because I have chiefly contented myself with selecting those few fathers who have expressly treated on the Eucharist, and have consequently spoken without reserve, for the instruction of the faithful.

That there must be passages of considerable obscurity in their writings, the circumstances before detailed will lead us to ex-

---

* "Scriptorum vet. nova Collectio." *Rome,* 1831; vol. iv. p. 9.
† See the account of this text communicated to the "Catholic Magazine," vol. iv. 1833, p. 284, *seq.*

LECTURE XIV.

pect; of such instances advantage has, of course, been taken to weaken the authority of tradition in our favor, but I hesitate not to assert that, in every case, ingenuity has been baffled, and Catholic theologians have fully vindicated our interpretation of their expressions. There are two branches of this evidence, however, which I almost fear I may be taxed with injustice to my cause, if I completely overlook.

The first consists of the liturgies or formularies of worship in the ancient Church, Latin, Greek, and Oriental; in every one of which, the Real Presence, or Transubstantiation, is most clearly recorded. They all speak of the Body and Blood of Jesus Christ being truly and really present; and, what is far more important, they pray to God that the bread and wine may be changed or transmuted into that Body and Blood.* This language is so uniform, that the learned Grotius observed, it must be allowed to have come down from the apostles, and, consequently, "ought not to have been changed."

The second class of documents, which I must not totally omit, is closely allied to the first. For, among the liturgies, are those of many sects separated from our communion for upwards of a thousand years; and yet, on this point, we perfectly agree. But, in addition to these standing monuments of their belief, I can boldly invite you to look into their Confessions of Faith, or into the writings of their respective doctors; and you will find the very same doctrine taught.

Ask the Greek, who sits, like Jeremiah, among the ruins of his former empire, to what dogma of his faith he clings with most affection, as his support in his oppression, and his comfort in his degradation? and he will reply, that from his belief in this mystery, as clearly attested in the confessions of faith subscribed by his patriarchs and archbishops, he has derived his most feeling confidence and relief. Ask the Nestorian, separated since the fifth century from the communion of our Church, and secluded for ages from the rest of the world, in the uttermost bounds of India, what made his forefathers hail with such friendly interest, and regard as brothers, the first Europeans who visited them in their unknown retirement? and he will show you the published letter of his pastors, attesting that it was their consolation to find men from Portugal, a country far off, of whose existence they had never heard, celebrating the

---

* See the testimony of these Liturgies, as given by the R. R. Dr. Poynter, in his "Christianity," or in the "Faith of Catholics," 2d ed. p. 190, *seqq.*

same sacrifice, with the same belief, as themselves. Ask the swarthy Monophysite of Abyssinia, in whose geography and history the name of Rome probably had not a place before modern times, what is the first mystery among the thin and shrivelled remains of Christianity which have continued to hold their roots in his scorched and barren land? and he replies, in the confession of faith written by the hand of one of his kings, that the first and noblest of his sacraments is that of the Body and Blood of his Lord. In a word, travel over the whole of Asia and Africa, where one remnant of Christianity yet exists, ask all the scattered tribes of the desert, all the fierce hordes of the mountains, or the more instructed inhabitants of the city, what are the points on which they agree relating to the Redeemer of the world, and His divine and human nature; and you will find them at variance, and ready to combat together on the most important dogmas concerning it; but the point round which all will rally, the principle on which all will argue, as admitted equally by all, is, that their Redeemer, both in his divine and human nature, is really present in the sacrament of the altar. To this mystery all recur, as a common neutral ground, whereon to defend their respective tenets. And can this dogma have come from any source but the fountain head of Christianity? since, even when it thus flows through such broken cisterns, it appears everywhere in the same purity, and maintains its course with the same strength. When we find this column of faith, standing almost alone amidst the ruins and fragments of Christianity, wherever we meet them, and always of the same materials and proportions, always in the same integrity, must we not conclude that it formed a substantial and most valued ornament of the holy fabric, wherever the apostles erected it, and that it is a sure emblem and representative of that pillar of truth, on which the apostle of the Gentiles orders us to lean?

In concluding this subject, I beg to make a few reflections, on the beautiful manner in which the doctrine of the Eucharist is connected with the system of truth which formed the topic of my earlier discourses. You have seen how this most adorable sacrament contains the real Body and Blood of our Lord and Saviour Jesus Christ, who is, consequently, therein present, so as to be the real food of the soul; and necessarily the source and means of conveying to it that grace whereof He is the author. Now, what were the wants of human nature which our blessed Saviour came peculiarly to supply? The fall of our first parents affected their posterity in a twofold manner. In the first place,

LECTURE XVI.

having eaten of the fruit of the tree of knowledge, they were, in punishment, blinded in their understandings, and left a prey to error, uncertainty, and diversity of opinion: and this curse was entailed on the understandings of their children. At the same time, they were driven away from the tree of life, from that tree which was intended for their nourishment and ours, to give perpetual vigor to that happy state, and nourish it in a virtuous immortality. No sooner was this lost, than the soul sank in dignity and power, all its faculties and moral feelings became corrupted; and vice and depravity ensued from the irreparable loss.

We find this twofold want, of intellectual light and moral life, so completely felt in every period of the world's history, that it is impossible to doubt, that it formed the vital injury which man had undergone. We see, on the one hand, mankind seeking on every side for knowledge, not merely in vain speculations, or more profound philosophies; not merely by consulting nature through her works, or unravelling those clues of reasoning which seemed to guide them through the labyrinths of their own minds; but in ways which show how they felt the want of a superior and supernatural enlightenment, by recourse to various kinds of superstition, to vain oracles and auguries, and other fond and foolish fancies, supposed to give them some communion with heaven, or produce some glimmering spark of internal light and mysterious knowledge.

But, besides this striving after a superior light, there was ever a longing after a principle that could regenerate the human heart, and bring it closer into communion with the Deity, as of old in the normal state, wherein it was created. From what other feeling could the custom have arisen, of partaking of sacrifices offered up to the gods of paganism? Did not the very act imply, that the victim having become the property of the god, and, as it were his food, men were thereby brought into his society or hospitality, and so associated with him as to acquire a right to his protection and friendship? But in some, there was a resemblance still more marked to the paschal feast of the New Law. In the Persian rites of Mithra, in some of the sacrifices of India, and of the North, of China, and of America, the resemblance is so great, as to have excited a suspicion that they may have arisen from a corrupted imitation of Christianity.* But the mind of the philosopher, without entering into any subtle disquisition, is content to see recorded, in all such insti-

---

* See the Abbé Gerbet's treatise, "Le dogme générateur de la piété Catholique."

tutions, the want, felt by the human soul, of some regenerating and invigorating principle, of some living and quickening food, fraught with grace from above, which could bring it into communion with the God that gave it.

If our blessed Saviour came on earth to restore poor man once more to the happy state from which he had fallen, so far as was consistent with the impaired state of his intellectual and moral faculties; if He came to satisfy all the just cravings of humanity after what is good and holy,—we may expect to find in His holy religion, and in the Church—his earthly paradise—institutions fully adequate to these great ends. And such the Catholic believes to be the case.

First, he hath planted in it a tree of knowledge, as a beacon on the top of mountains, towards which all nations may flow, from which are darted rays of bright and cheering light to the benighted nations of the earth, and under whose shadow repose, and on whose wholesome fruits are fed, they who have been brought beneath its shelter. For, we believe—and my first discourses were directed to prove it—that in the Church of God is an infallible and enduring authority to teach, appointed and guarantied by Christ Himself.

And beside it, He has placed the tree of life, in the life-giving institution of which we last have treated, a perpetual memorial of the benefits of redemption, bearing that sweetest food of salvation, which weighed down with its blessing the tree of Golgotha; lasting and immortal as the plant of knowledge beside which it stands. Here we partake of a victim, which truly unites and incorporates us with God, and gives us a pledge of His friendship and love, and supplies a never-failing source of benediction and grace.

But they who sit daily round the same table, are the children of the same house; and hence is this holy institution a bond of union between the professors of the one faith. For, see how perfectly the two institutions harmonize together, and are absolutely necessary to one another. The one preserves us in religious *unity*, whereby our understandings and minds are brought into perfect accord through *faith*, the same in all; the other keeps us in *communion*, in affectionate connection, as members of one body. The very name which the participation of this sacred banquet has received amongst us, designates this its quality. And in this manner, as the one great principle may be called the mind or intellect of God's Church, which directs and governs its entire frame, this blessed sacrament may well be designated its heart, in which lies treasured an unfailing fountain of holiest affection, that flows unceasingly to its furthest extremity, in a warm stream of invigorating and spiritualizing vitality.

This influence of our belief in the Real Presence upon every part of our practical religion, is too manifest to need any illustration. Why do we, when it is in our power, and why did our forefathers before us, erect sumptuous churches, and lavish on them all the riches of earth, but that we believe them to be the real tabernacles wherein the Emmanuel, the "God with us," really dwells? Why is our worship conducted with such pomp and solemnity, save that we perform it as a personal service on the incarnate Word of God? Why are the gates of our churches, in Catholic countries, open all day, and why do men enter at all hours to whisper a prayer, or prostrate themselves in adoration, but from the conviction that God is there more intimately present than elsewhere, through this glorious mystery? The practice of confession, and consequently of repentance, is closely connected, as Lord Fitzwilliam has observed,* with this belief. For it is the necessity of approaching to the sacred table with a clean heart, that mainly enforces its practice; and the sinner in repentance is urged to the painful purgation, by the promised refreshment of the celestial banquet.

The sacred character which the Catholic priest possesses in the estimation of his flock, the power of blessing with which he seems invested, are both the result of that familiarity with which, in the holy mysteries, he is allowed to approach his Lord. The celibacy to which the clergy bind themselves is but a practical expression of that sentiment which the Church entertains of the unvarying purity of conduct and thought, wherewith the altar should be approached. In this manner does the sacrament of the Eucharist form the very soul and essence of all practical religion among Catholics. But it has a much sublimer destiny to fulfil.

I observed, in an early portion of my discourses, that the Church of Christ holds a middle state, between one that is past, and one that is yet to come. I showed you how the former, which hath passed away, by its form and constitution threw much light upon our present dispensation, whereof it was the shadow.† But our state, too, must in its turn reflect some of the brightness of our future destiny, even as the mountains and the sky receive a glow of promise, ere the sun hath risen in the fulness of his splendor.

---

* "Letters of Atticus." † See Lect. iv. vol. 1. p. 85.

And what is the essence of that blessed state but love or charity, in which, as in a cloudless atmosphere, the spirits made perfect breathe and move, and live? Through it they are brought so near unto God as to see Him face to face, and feed upon His unsating glory; through it their affections are blended together, till each partakes of the other's happiness. And how could this universal love be so well represented here below, as by a sacrament like this, which, suited by its mysterious veils to our corporeal existence, and having the root of its efficacy in a common faith—the proper virtue of our present dispensation—brings us into the closest union with God of which we can be conceived capable here below, and knits us together in a bond of inseparable love?

But, my brethren, before concluding, there is one view of the doctrine under consideration more painful indeed, and fruitful in awful reflection. I mean the balance to be struck between the conflicting beliefs of Catholics and Protestants, and the stakes which we have respectively cast upon them.

On our side, I own that we have risked all our happiness, and all our best possession here below. We have placed beside our doctrine the strongest effort of our faith, the utmost sacrifice of individual judgment, the completest renunciation of human pride and self-sufficiency, which are ever ready to rebel against the simple words of revelation. And not so content, we have cast into the scale the fastest anchor of our hope; considering this as the surest channel of God's mercy to us, as the means of individual sanctification, as the instrument of personal and local consecration, as the brightest comfort of our dying hour, the foretaste and harbinger of eternal glory. And, if these stakes were not of sufficient weight, we have thrown in the brightest links of golden charity, feeling that in this blessed sacrament we are the most closely drawn to God, and the most intimately united in affection with our Saviour Christ Jesus.

All this we have placed on our belief: but if, to suppose an impossibility, we could be proved in error, it would at most be shown that we had believed too implicitly in the meaning of God's words; that we had flattered ourselves too easily that He possessed resources of power in manifesting His goodness towards man, beyond the reach of our small intellects and paltry speculations; that, in truth, we had measured His love more lovingly than prudently, and had formed a sublimer, though a less accurate estimate of its power, than others had done; in fine, that we had been too simple-hearted, and childlike, in abandoning our

LECTURE XVI.   197

reason into his hands, because He had "the words of eternal life."

But then, if our faith be right, ponder well what infinitely heavier stakes have been ventured on the other side. For on its supposed falsehood have been risked words of contumely and scorn, of railing and most awful blasphemy! The holy sacrament has been repeatedly profaned, and its adoration mocked at as idolatrous, and its priests reviled as seducers, and the very belief in it considered abundant ground for exclusion from political and social benefits! And if what I have advanced have been well proved, then are those, who believe not with us, living in the neglect of a sovereign command, a neglect to which is attached a fearful penalty. "Unless ye eat the Flesh of the Son of man, and drink His Blood, ye shall not have life in you."

And what conclusion can we draw from this balance of our respective dangers, but the necessity incumbent on all who are in the latter condition, to try this important dogma to its foundation, and fully ascertain the ground on which they stand?

But it is time that I should close this Lecture, and with it the entire course. We have now, my brethren, for many evenings, stood here opposed face to face, and it is probable that many of us will not thus meet again, till we stand together before the judgment-seat of Christ. Days, weeks, months, and years will pass, as heretofore, quickly away; may they be with you all many and happy!—but still the end will come, and it will not be long before we are again confronted. Let us, then, make a reckoning of what we shall mutually have to answer. And first, bear with me, for a few moments, while I speak of myself.

What will it profit me in that day, if, while I have been addressing you, I have been uttering aught but my firmest and surest convictions? What shall I have gained, if I shall be proved to have sought only to enmesh you in the toils of captious reasoning and wily sophistry, and not rather to have been desirous of captivating your souls to the truth, as it is in Christ Jesus? Nay, what satisfaction could it be to me even now, did I feel a suspicion that I have been misleading you, instead of using my efforts to guide you to what my conscience tells me is the only true path of salvation? if, all this time, besides the feeling of degradation and self-reproach which such conduct must have inspired, I had felt, as I must have done, the awful conviction, that the arm of God was stretched over my head, and challenged, by every word I uttered, to strike and crush me as a lying prophet and a deceiver in His name? Nor is ours the religion which confers wealth, and dignity, and honor upon its willing ministers, or that can hold out any nominal equivalent for our only true reward.

But if, on the one hand, I am fully satisfied, not merely that no doctrine, but that not a single argument has been advanced by me, of which I have not the most entire conviction, and if I flatter myself, as I feelingly do, that you too are satisfied in this respect, I have a right to demand from you a corresponding return, and it is simply this:—Allow not any slight impression which my words have made, to pass heedlessly away. If any one shall have felt his previous system of faith in even its smallest parts shaken, let it be but a reason with him to try the security of the entire building. If some small cloud shall appear to have cast a shadow over the serenity of his former conviction, oh! let him not scorn or neglect it; for it may be like that which the prophet commanded his servant to watch from Carmel,—rich with blessing, and fertility, and refreshment, to the soul that thirsts for truth.*

No one, I am sure, who looks at the religious divisions of this country, can, for a moment, suppose that it represents the proper state of Christ's Church on earth. It is certain, that for ages unity of belief reigned amongst us, and so should it be once more. There is no doubt but individual reflection, if sincerely and perseveringly pursued, will bring all back in steady convergence towards the point of unity; and therefore I entreat, that if any little light shall have been now shed upon any of your minds, if a view of religion have been presented to you, of which before you had no idea, I entreat that it be not cast away, but followed with diligence and gratitude, till full satisfaction shall have been received.

Far be it from me to fancy that any thing which I have said can of itself be worthy of so glorious a blessing. I have but scattered a little seed, and it is God alone that can give the increase. It is not on those effects, for which I am grateful to your indulgence, and on which till my dying hour I must dwell with delight,—it is not on the patience and kindness with which you have so often listened to me, under trying circumstances, in such numbers, and at such an hour, that I presume to rest my hopes and augury of some good effect. No, it is on the confidence which the interest exhibited gives me, that you have abstracted from me individually, and fixed your thoughts and

---

* 3 Reg. xviii. 44.

LECTURE XVI.

attention upon the cause which I represent. Had I come before you as a champion, armed to fight against the antagonists of our faith, I might have been anxious to appear personally strong and well appointed. But the course which I have chosen needed not much prowess; a burning lamp will shine as brightly in the hands of a child as if uplifted by a giant's arm. I have endeavored simply to hold before you the light of Catholic truth; and to Him that kindled it be all the glory!

To Thee, O eternal Fountain of all knowledge, I turn, to obtain grace upon these lessons and efficacy for these wishes. If "my speech and my preaching have not been in the persuasive words of human wisdom,"* it is Thy word at least which I have endeavored to declare. Remember, then, Thy promise! For Thou hast said, "As the rain and the snow come down from heaven, and return no more thither, but soak the earth, and water it, and make it to spring, and give seed to the sower and bread to the eater, so shall my word be: it shall not return to me void, but shall prosper in the things for which I sent it."† Prosper it, then, now; may it fall upon a good soil, and bring forth fruit a hundredfold. Remove prejudice, ignorance, and pride, from the hearts of all who have listened to it, and give them a meek and teachable spirit; and strength to follow, and to discover, if they know them not, the doctrines of Thy saving truth. Hear, on their behalf, the last prayers of Thy well-beloved Son Jesus, when He said: "And not only for them do I pray, but for them also who through their word shall believe in me, that they all may be one, as Thou, Father, in me and I in Thee: that they may also be one in us."‡ Yes; may they all be one by the profession of the same faith; may they be one in the same hope, by the practice of Thy holy law; that so we may hereafter all be one in perfect charity, in the possession of Thy eternal kingdom. Through Jesus Christ our Lord. Amen.

---

* 1 Cor. ii. 4. † Is. lv. 10, 11. ‡ Jo. xvii. 20, 21.

FINIS.

www.ingramcontent.com/pod-product-compliance
Lightning Source LLC
Chambersburg PA
CBHW051235300426
44114CB00011B/742